THE TWELFTH

MW01140169

READINGS IN MEDIEVAL CIVILIZATIONS AND CULTURES: XIX
series editor: Paul Edward Dutton

THE TWELFTH-CENTURY RENAISSANCE

A READER

edited by

ALEX J. NOVIKOFF

UNIVERSITY OF TORONTO PRESS

Higher Education Division

www.utppublishing.com

LIBRARY AND ARCHIVES CANADA CATALOGUING IN PUBLICATION
The twelfth century Renaissance : a reader / edited by Alex J. Novikoff.

(Readings in medieval civilizations and cultures ; XIX)
Includes bibliographical references and index.
Issued in print and electronic formats.

ISBN 978-1-4426-3424-4 (hardback).—ISBN 978-1-4426-0546-6 (paperback).—
ISBN 978-1-4426-0547-3 (pdf).—ISBN 978-1-4426-0548-0 (html).
1. Renaissance—Europe—Sources. 2. Europe—Civilization—Sources.
I. Novikoff, Alex J., editor II. Series: Readings in medieval civilizations and culture ;19

CB361.T84 2016   940.2'1   C2016-904093-3
                                                                         C2016-904094-1

We welcome comments and suggestions regarding any aspect of our publications—please feel free to contact us at news@utphighereducation.com or visit our Internet site at www.utppublishing.com.

North America
5201 Dufferin Street
North York, Ontario, Canada, M3H 5T8

2250 Military Road
Tonawanda, New York, USA, 14150

ORDERS PHONE: 1-800-565-9523
ORDERS FAX: 1-800-221-9985
ORDERS E-MAIL: utpbooks@utpress.utoronto.ca

UK, Ireland, and continental Europe
NBN International
Estover Road, Plymouth, PL6 7PY, UK
ORDERS PHONE: 44 (0) 1752 202301
ORDERS FAX: 44 (0) 1752 202333
ORDERS E-MAIL: enquiries@nbninternational.com

The University of Toronto Press acknowledges the financial support for its publishing activities of the Government of Canada through the Canada Book Fund.

Printed in the United States of America

To my students—past, present, and future—and in memory of my teacher, Jill N. Claster

CONTENTS

ACKNOWLEDGMENTS

My first debt of gratitude is to Paul Edward Dutton, who enthusiastically accepted this volume into his magnificent series and has remained steadfast in his encouragement through all of the volume's unexpected hurdles and setbacks. I am equally grateful to Natalie Fingerhut and the whole production team at the University of Toronto Press for their support and assistance in matters both large and small along the way. I especially record my debts to my wonderful colleagues in North America and abroad who have championed the idea of this volume and generously supplied new translations for inclusion in the Reader: Scott G. Bruce (Doc. 7), Charles Burnett (Doc. 82), Jeremy Cohen (Doc. 30b), John D. Cotts (Docs. 23, 45), Paul Dutton (Docs. 4a, 13, 14, 16), Constant Mews (Doc. 8), Wolfgang Mueller (Doc. 41), Nicholas Paul (Doc. 73), Irven Resnick (Doc. 34), Joseph Rudolph (Doc. 62), and Marc Wolterbeek (Doc. 59). I also thank Helen Birkett, Winston Black, Cédric Giraud, James J. Murphy, Edward Peters, C. Stephen Jaeger, Rachel Fulton, Bruce Venarde, and Jan Ziolkowski, who have at various stages offered valuable input, advice, and corrections on the structure and content of this volume. I also wish to acknowledge the student assistants who helped me in compiling the selections: Joseph Rudolph, Rachel Sferlazza, Jeffrey Sullebarger, and my graduate students from Fordham and Yeshiva Universities who took my HIST 5201 seminar on the Twelfth-Century Renaissance. Rhodes College, the Dean's Office at Fordham University, and the History Department of Fordham University generously provided financial assistance toward this project.

Finally, I dedicate this volume to all my students who have shared, and I hope will continue to share, my excitement for medieval history, and in memory of my own teacher, Jill N. Claster, who first introduced me to the dazzling world of the twelfth century. I was saddened but privileged to be able to complete the last class she ever taught, a freshman seminar at NYU in the fall of 2014. Appropriately, it was devoted to the twelfth century.

INTRODUCTION

Few centuries in the roughly 1,000-year history of medieval Europe have cap-
tivated modern scholarly attention as consistently as the twelfth. Many of the
most celebrated personalities of the Middle Ages are prime examples of this
age of institutional expansion, intellectual creativity, and cultural efflorescence.
These include the patron-monarchs King Henry II and Eleanor of Aquitaine,
the poets Marie de France and Chrétien de Troyes, the intellectuals and lovers Abelard and Heloise, and the religious thinkers Bernard of Clairvaux and
Hildegard of Bingen. But are we justified in grouping this extraordinary and
diverse cast of characters into a single volume under the designation of a cultural renaissance?

Let us begin with the title of this Reader, since it is both a historiographical
hornets' nest and a useful entry point into the modern study of the Middle Ages.
Looking back from the standpoint of our profession in the twenty-first century,
the very history of the phrase "renaissance of the twelfth century" offers a
microcosm of some of the main trajectories and debates in medieval scholarship
over the past 150 years. French literary scholars first suggested the phrase in the
early nineteenth century, with special reference to the new vernacular literature
of medieval France (the *chansons de geste* and the lyrics of the Troubadours).[1] As
universities modernized and liberalized in the nineteenth century, the phrase
was then appropriated by historians of those very institutions, who saw the
twelfth-century origins of the medieval university and its revival of the ancient
liberal arts as the epitome of an intellectual rebirth as important as the more
famous northern Italian Renaissance of the fourteenth and fifteenth centuries.[2]
Major advances in the science of dating and editing medieval texts and in the
preservation of historical monuments encouraged greater historical reflection
(both positivistic and romantic). Other disciplines soon joined the fray: by the
early twentieth century, historians of law, philosophy, and secular poetry, as
well as art historians and philologists, all recognized in one fashion or another
that the twelfth century was one of extraordinary development and innovation.
Yet these investigations remained highly specialized, accessible only to others
who worked in those fields. Moreover, they were studied largely in disciplinary
isolation from one another. To the general public, the Middle Ages remained
an intellectually stagnant period governed by the uncompromising strictures of
religious dogma—dark in outlook and distinctly un-modern.

In 1927, the American medievalist Charles Homer Haskins brought the concept of a medieval renaissance to full maturity and to a wider audience with his
book entitled *The Renaissance of the Twelfth Century*. A professor at Harvard and a
former historical advisor to president Woodrow Wilson (the two met as graduate

students in the History Department at Johns Hopkins University), he was deeply committed to the same liberal and progressive ideas that Wilson believed could remake Europe after the catastrophe of World War I. Haskins was thus both a pedagogue and a visionary. Throughout his career he labored hard to make the Middle Ages relevant to a modern (American) audience. Standing on the shoulders of those scholars and editors who came before him, Haskins's contribution lay not so much in perceiving the individual aspects of intellectual and cultural renewal in the twelfth century—and certainly not in applying the term "renaissance" to it, which he duly acknowledged had been widely employed—but rather in providing conceptual clarity and ideological coherence to the very notion (and significance) of a twelfth-century rebirth.[3] For Haskins, the recovery of ancient sources and the establishment of systematic procedures and categories of analysis were not just historical curiosities of a bygone age; rather, they provided the intellectual seedbed for scientific rationalism, secularism, and modern institutions.[4] The modern world as we know it, he implied, has emerged out of new developments that began in the twelfth century. Haskins's teleological version of a medieval renaissance established the interpretative benchmark for all future studies, and it continues to find echoes today, including among scholars who would emphasize very different developments.[5]

The titles of the 12 chapters of Haskins's book outlined the major innovations as he saw them. Following a chapter on the historical background, these were: Intellectual Centers, Books and Libraries, The Revival of the Latin Classics, The Latin Language, Latin Poetry, The Revival of Jurisprudence, Historical Writing, The Translations from Greek and Arabic, The Revival of Science, The Revival of Philosophy, and The Beginnings of Universities. In the almost 100 years that have passed since that book first appeared, each of these elements has enjoyed its own renaissance as new texts have come to light and new interpretations have been suggested. The self-conscious indebtedness to Haskins has also grown stronger.[6] It would be no exaggeration to say that Haskins's book has been one of the most influential and revisited statements in all of medieval scholarship.

The popularization of the phrase "renaissance of the twelfth century" has not been to everyone's liking, however. As early as 1914, another American medievalist, Louis Paetow, warned of its dangers: "Recent books are saying much about a 'Twelfth-Century Renaissance.' This is an unfortunate term. 'New Birth' always recalls the words of the Gospels and implies some sort of a miracle which transcends the ordinary vision of historians."[7] Some have felt that the term reflects scholarly agendas more than it does the developments of the twelfth century.[8] Indeed, in 1948 Wallace Ferguson, in the final pages of *The Renaissance in Historical Thought*, characterized Haskins and others who advocated for a medieval renaissance as belonging to "the revolt of the medievalists," a mantra that many subsequent medievalists have proudly embraced.[9] In 1948 and 1951, the journal *Speculum* published a series of short and ultimately inconclusive articles on the nature and validity of this so-called renaissance. For Richard W. Southern, writing in 1960, the label of the "twelfth-century renaissance" was "a mere term of convenience which can mean almost anything we choose it to mean. . . . It achieves . . . a sort of sublime meaninglessness which is required in words of high but uncertain import."[10] The influential art historian Erwin Panofsky offered his own intervention by distinguishing medieval renascences (the Carolingian and the twelfth-century were both "not quite renaissances") from the "permanent" revival of antique forms characteristic of the Italian Renaissance of the fourteenth and fifteenth centuries.[11] Nor has the search for a golden phrase diminished in the past two generations: *reformation, renewal,* and *revolution* have all been championed as alternatives to the word *renaissance,* especially among those who stress religious rather than secular developments. An equally alluring interpretation considers a major legacy of the twelfth century to be the "discovery of the individual."[12] The observable spike in personal and autobiographical writings would seem to reinforce this claim, although even here appearances can be deceiving. Some have countered that what the twelfth century discovered was not the "individual" or the "self," but rather a mechanism for expressing affiliation with a group, a sort of corporate identity that in fact contrasts with the notion of individualism.[13] This view lends itself well to the rise of the university, the corporate and intellectual community par excellence.

Other scholars have called attention to the more sinister aspects of this period. The rise of inquisition, the aggressive confrontation with religious non-conformists, and the bloodshed and proto-colonialism of the Crusades have all served to rein in the idea that the twelfth century was a forerunner of enlightened, progressive ideals. In 1987, R.I. Moore provoked much discussion with the bold thesis that the very same personalities and institutions that contributed to a flowering of intellectual life also contributed to the "formation of a persecuting society," a phenomenon most evident in the treatment of minority groups such as heretics, lepers, and Jews.[14] Other positions of skepticism have also been advanced. C. Stephen Jaeger has pointed out that a predominant ethos of the age was not one of confidence in progress and prosperity, but rather one of pessimism.[15] How, he rightly asks, can one speak of progress and rebirth when a significant number of authors speak of decline and moral decay? In some sense, however, Jaeger's challenge is an academic version of the "glass half-empty or half-full" quandary. The twelfth century, just like the twentieth and the twenty-first, had its fair share of heralds of a new dawn as well as its prophets of doom, as the selections in this volume will show. What is certain is that the more the authors and attitudes of the century are examined, the less homogenous and uniform the century appears and the more difficult it becomes to suggest an all-encompassing label. Here it is worth recalling that a favorite phrase of the twelfth century was *concordia discors*, or "discordant harmony": many writers, poets, and musicians played with this notion of paradox, and Gratian's *Decretum* (c. 1150; see Doc. 41b) on canon law was circulated under the title *concordia discordantium canonum* ("harmony of discordant canons"). Might the aspiration for metaphysical and world harmony, however unsuccessful or unfulfilled, be a useful paradigm for making sense of the spirit of the age?

Realizing the inevitable inadequacy of defining what a renaissance is or is not, or lacking a better alternative, other scholars would prefer to dodge the problem altogether. Many now speak more innocuously of "the long twelfth century," a trend that is reflected in studies ranging from the eleventh century all the way to the nineteenth.[16] But if we speak of a "long" twelfth century, how long should it be before it loses its meaning? Are we not back to the eternal conundrum of searching for a useful periodization? The slipperiness of chronology and the uncertainty of anachronistic terminology all but guarantee that there will never be consensus as to the precise definition and scope of this "renaissance." Perhaps it is better to let the twelfth century speak for itself, rather than for us to speak on its behalf. It is in this spirit that the present Reader has been conceived.

One of the challenges to adequately teaching the twelfth century has always been the rather limited accessibility to such a vast array of texts and ideas. Classic works by Peter Abelard, John of Salisbury, Hildegard of Bingen, Marie de France, Chrétien de Troyes, and other "stars" of the period have long been available in their entirety, often in faithful and reasonably priced translations, but it is difficult to speak meaningfully in a classroom about the variety of themes and contexts on the basis of a few prolific luminaries. Scholars have long known about other less famous and in some sense equally revealing sources, but they are frequently buried deep in specialized studies and are therefore rarely presented alongside their illustrious contemporaries. The present volume is an attempt to bridge that gap, both by including selections from those classic works and by situating them among a much wider array of other sources, a number of which are translated here for the first time. Accordingly, this Reader does not seek to resolve old questions, nor does it presume stable categories about a period still vigorously debated. The goal has been to allow for the re-examination of old themes, to provoke new questions, and to allow the content of familiar and unfamiliar works to guide the historical understandings that emerge.

The decisions about what to include (and how much) and what to exclude (and at what cost) have been difficult, a dilemma that any editor will surely recognize. To keep things manageable, therefore, a few constraints had to be imposed. No attempt has been made to represent urban and courtly growth or economic expansion, features that certainly contributed to the dynamism of the period but that are already covered in volumes dealing with those themes. Likewise, this volume does not propose to offer a full selection of strictly philosophical works, even though certain philosophical themes are represented; again, this is largely because there has been no shortage of source books of medieval philosophy and political theory. The selections have been assembled according to a broad (though by no means exhaustive) survey of intellectual and cultural life, one that builds upon but extends well beyond the themes identified by Haskins. In matters of chronology, a long*ish* twelfth century has been retained. Almost all of the sources date from 1075 to 1225, with only a few sources dating from beyond those boundaries to help illustrate important themes from the twelfth century. The volume admits to a focus on northwestern Europe, where much of the intellectual energy was located, but this has been consciously expanded to include Italy, Germany, and Spain (including Muslim Spain), and one will find intellectual connectivity extending as far as Poland, Byzantium, and the Levant.

The volume has been divided into two parts (Themes and Genres) in order to highlight variety in both the currents of thought and the range of source types. Some of the chapter headings deliberately recall those of Haskins, while others reflect paths opened up by the research of the last two generations of scholars. Most notable among the latter are the chapters devoted to spirituality and theology (Chapter 1) and to interfaith polemical encounters (Chapter 3), areas that scholars now recognize as being a source of great intellectual ferment. In contrast to Haskins's heavy focus on the language of Latin, sources included in this volume include vernacular languages as well as Hebrew and Arabic. Translation in virtually all directions, scholars now recognize, was one of the great intellectual activities of the twelfth century. The demographic representation is similarly broad: we hear the voices of men and women, itinerant scholars and cloistered monks, powerful churchmen and anonymous poets. In one way or another, these sources all illustrate an expansive variety of intellectual pursuits, new ideas, and creative innovation, even as the voices of their authors sometimes stand in disaccord with each other. Finally, if there is one theme that runs through virtually all the chapters, it is surely the invocation of classical sources, often accompanied by a pronounced self-consciousness about the present age in relation to the past. This had always been a leading justification for the term "renaissance." It is not an exclusivist criterion; how and how much the authority of ancient texts matters to twelfth-century authors obviously varies greatly. Still, if we are to search for some unity in this remarkable variety—if some concord can be found in this age of great discord—then the appeal to ancient authority is surely a good place to begin.

SUGGESTED SECONDARY READINGS

Benson, Robert L., and Giles Constable, eds. *Renaissance and Renewal in the Twelfth Century.* Cambridge, MA: Harvard University Press, 1982.

Constable, Giles. *The Reformation of the Twelfth Century.* Cambridge: Cambridge University Press, 1996.

Cotts, John. *Europe's Long Twelfth Century: Order, Anxiety and Adaptation, 1095–1229.* Houndmills, UK: Palgrave Macmillan, 2013.

Haskins, Charles Homer. *The Renaissance of the Twelfth Century.* Cambridge, MA: Harvard University Press, 1927.

Luscombe, David, and Jonathan Riley-Smith, eds. *The New Cambridge Medieval History, Vol. IV, c. 1024–1198.* 2 vols. Cambridge: Cambridge University Press, 2004.

Moore, R.I. *The First European Revolution, c. 970–1215.* Oxford: Blackwell, 2000.

Noble, Thomas F.X., and John Van Engen, eds. *European Transformations: The Long Twelfth Century.* Notre Dame, IN: Notre Dame University Press, 2012.

Southern, R.W. *Scholastic Humanism and the Unification of Europe.* 2 vols. Oxford: Blackwell, 1995, 2001.

Swanson, R.N. *The Renaissance of the Twelfth Century.* Manchester: Manchester University Press, 1999.

NOTES

1 Cf. Jean-Jacques Ampère, *Histoire littéraire de la France avant le douzième siècle* (Paris, 1839–40), vol. 3, p. 457: "The intellectual movement that can be felt in France toward the end of the eleventh century offers all the characteristics of a true renaissance. . . ."

2 Chapter 2 of the first volume of Hastings Rashdall's *The Universities of Europe in the Middle Ages* (Oxford, 1895), initially published in two volumes and later re-edited in three volumes, was entitled "Abelard and the Renaissance of the Twelfth Century."

3 Haskins's role in articulating and developing the concept of "the renaissance of the twelfth century" has often been misstated. For the historiographical background, see my "The Renaissance of the Twelfth Century before Haskins," *Haskins Society Journal* 16 (2005): 104–16.

4 Haskins's chief areas of scholarly research were in medieval institutions and science, topics covered in his earlier books: *Norman Institutions* (1916), *The Rise of Universities* (1923), and *Studies in the History of Mediaeval Science* (1924).

5 Cf. Thomas N. Bisson, *The Crisis of the Twelfth Century: Power, Lordship, and the Origins of European Government* (Princeton, NJ: Princeton University Press, 2008).

6 For one such assessment of his influence, see Marcia L. Colish, "Haskins's *Renaissance* Seventy Years Later: Beyond Anti-Burckhardtianism," *Haskins Society Journal* 11 (2003): 1–15.

7 Louis Paetow, *Memoirs of the University of California*, Vol. 4: *The Battle of the Seven Liberal Arts: A French Poem by Henri D'Andeli, Trouvère of the Thirteenth Century* (Berkeley: University of California Press, 1914), 13.

8 For an excellent survey of the debates and contexts, see R.N. Swanson, *The Twelfth-Century Renaissance* (Manchester: Manchester University Press, 1999), chap. 1.

9 Wallace Ferguson, *The Renaissance in Historical Thought* (Boston: Houghton Mifflin, 1948), chap. 11. For an overview of more recent historiography, see Leidulf Melve, "'The Revolt of the Medievalists.' Directions in Recent Research on the Twelfth-Century Renaissance," *Journal of Medieval History* 32 (2006): 231–52.

10 R.W. Southern, "The Place of England in the Twelfth-Century Renaissance," *History* 45 (1960): 201.

11 Erwin Panofsky, *Renaissance and Renascences in Western Art* (Stockholm: Almqvist and Wiksell, 1960). An early version of his statement appeared in *The Kenyon Review* 6.2 (1944): 201–36.

12 Colin Morris, *The Discovery of the Individual, 1050–1200* (New York: Harper and Row, 1972).

13 Cf. Caroline Walker Bynum, "Did the Twelfth-Century Discover the Individual?," in *Jesus as Mother: Studies in the Spirituality of the High Middle Ages* (Berkeley: University of California Press, 1982), 82–109. See the remarks by Jay Rubenstein, *Guibert of Nogent: Portrait of a Medieval Mind* (New York: Routledge, 2002), 81. See also the excellent volume on this theme, Brigitte Bedos-Rezak and Dominique Iogna-Prat, eds., *L'Individu au Moyen Âge* (Paris: Éditions Flammarion, 2005).

14 R.I. Moore, *The Formation of a Persecuting Society: Power and Deviance in Western Europe, 950–1250* (Oxford: Basil Blackwell, 1987; 2nd ed. 2007). For reappraisals of Moore's thesis, see Michael Frassetto, ed., *Heresy and the Persecuting Society in the Middle Ages: Essays on the Work of R.I. Moore* (Leiden: Brill, 2006).

15 C. Stephen Jaeger, "Pessimism in the Twelfth Century 'Renaissance,'" *Speculum* 78.4 (2003): 1151–83. Contra R.W. Southern and others, Jaeger has argued for a medieval humanism that begins as early as the tenth century but passes out of existence in the middle of the twelfth century.

16 See, for example, Thomas F.X. Noble and John Van Engen, eds., *European Transformations: The Long Twelfth Century* (Notre Dame, IN: Notre Dame University Press, 2012). It might also be noted that *The New Cambridge Medieval History* devotes parts 1 and 2 of its volume IV to the period c. 1024–1198, the only period in the thousand-year sweep of the series to be given such extensive coverage.

PART 1
THEMES

CHAPTER ONE

SPIRITUAL RENEWAL AND THE FORMATION OF THEOLOGY

Spirituality and theology were not among the main twelfth-century intellectual developments originally identified by C.H. Haskins or his predecessors. The chief preoccupations of medievalists in the late nineteenth and early twentieth centuries were the progressive and secular elements of the twelfth-century renaissance, and this by nature excluded the world of religious thought. Scholars in the second half of the twentieth century, by contrast, saw dynamism and intellectual vigor in many aspects of religious life. Some have employed the term "reformation" to describe the spiritual renewal and the founding of new monastic orders that occurred in the period, thus once again prompting comparisons with a later epoch in history.

The selections in this chapter offer a sampling of the diverse and innovative dimensions of religious thought and education, beginning with the theological issues at stake during the Eucharist controversy of the late eleventh century and ending with the two most important and influential textbooks of medieval theology: Peter Lombard's *Sentences* and the *Glossa Ordinaria*, a systematic commentary on the various books of the Bible. Also included are sources relating to spiritual and affective devotion, Anselm's highly original ontological proof for the existence of God, and some poignant articulations of the expanding diversity of monastic experiences. Collectively, these sources provide a useful point of entry into the intellectually rich world of twelfth-century thought and culture, a world that was deeply rooted in matters of faith and practice.

1. TWO TEXTS ON THE EUCHARIST CONTROVERSY

The Eucharist Controversy of the second half of the eleventh century, which turned specifically on how the sacramental consecration changed the nature of the bread and wine during communion, is important not just for the theological ideas at stake in the history of Christian doctrine, but also as a key episode in the evolution of intellectual discourse and in the emergence of "academic" communities governed by distinct schools of thought. Although the issues themselves were not entirely new, what was new was the systematic stockpiling of authoritative texts accompanied by line-by-line expositions with an emphasis on raising new questions, noting definitions, and explicating specific passages. These new intellectual currents in turn gave rise to a highly distinctive genre of writing in which the opinions of contemporaries were presented for the explicit purpose of refutation.

The intensity with which the competing sides circulated their claims thus coincided with the rise of a new professional environment for learning, one that allowed masters to move more freely from one teaching position to another. To a certain extent the controversy also witnessed an increased reliance on the tools of reason derived from the renewed study of the trivium *(grammar, rhetoric, and dialectic) as well as a critical reflection on Aristotle's* Categories, *although there still remained a heavy reliance on patristic texts and concepts.*

The central figure in the early stages of this controversy was Berengar of Tours (c. 999–1088), a "scholasticus" at the cathedral school of Tours and a former pupil of the celebrated bishop Fulbert of Chartres (d. 1028). The dispute was not, contrary to contemporary assertions, about whether the body and blood of Christ were present in the Eucharist. Instead, the issue of contention was whether the presence was real and substantial in accordance with the Aristotelian concept of substance, or real but not substantial according to that same Aristotelian concept. Berengar insisted that his notion of the real presence was in no way similar to Aristotle's definition of primary substances. Several church councils were convened in order to settle the matter, ending only with the Roman council of Lent in 1079. A number of polemical treatises, some written after the fact, were generated in order to uphold the orthodox understanding of this central Christian rite, something that was just beginning to be known as "transubstantiation" and that would only achieve the level of doctrine at the Fourth Lateran Council in Rome in 1215 (see Doc. 38). Below are extracts from two of those polemics: one by Lanfranc of Pavia (c. 1005–89), the teacher of Anselm and future archbishop of Canterbury, and the other by Alberic of Monte Cassino (1030–88).

a. Lanfranc, *On the Body and Blood of the Lord*

Source: trans. Alex J. Novikoff, *De corpore et sanguine Domini adversus Berengarium Turonensem*, in J.-P. Migne, ed., *Patrologia Latina* (Paris: Garnier, 1880), vol. 150, cols. 407–30. Latin.

Lanfranc, a Catholic by the mercy of God, to Berengarius,
an adversary of the Catholic Church.

If godly devotion had deigned to breathe into your heart the desire to address me, then you would have chosen a suitable location where the matter could have been discussed competently and with salutary deliberation, since the present topic is of deep concern to both God's honor and your soul. Such an encounter would have benefited you, but it would undoubtedly have benefited very many of those whom you deceive and dismiss, liable to death, into eternal punishment. . . .

But having digested your error, you chose to defend it in secret discussions with the unlearned while simultaneously choosing openly to confess the orthodox faith in the hearing of the holy council, not out of love of truth but out of fear of death. This you do to avoid me and other religious persons who can judge your words and mine. I would have preferred to hear you and confer with you, in the presence of such persons, about no other matter than the opinions that you pretend are compatible with your own opinions. Such audacity is punishable. Furthermore, you attribute them, either from a desire to do harm, or from an ignorance of the truth, to the holy doctors, alleging that Augustine testifies to it in this work, or Gregory, or Jerome, or whoever of those men whom the Church of Christ greatly venerates by declaring their authority supreme. . . .

But you are a sacrilegious violator of this oath, and afterwards you composed a treatise against the aforementioned synod, against Catholic truth, and against the judgment of the entire Church. Trusting in Christ's mercy, I am now disposed to respond in the following little work. And so that what you say (and my response) may each appear more clearly, I shall distinguish the alternate opinions by placing our names alternately.

I will not respond to all matters either, since you have spread roses among the thorns and have colored your phantasm in black and white. You even say certain things that do not address the proposition of the question. I will thus make the work as concise as possible. For I do not wish to waste my life with nonsense, if you permit God's people to return to their former peace.

Berengarius: The document of Humbert of Burgundy, made cardinal bishop by the Romans, was written against Catholic truth, as it will be shown below; and Berengarius was forced to assert the same error as that of the most inept Burgundian.

Lanfranc: Humbert was acknowledged to be a religious man according to all who knew him either directly or by way of reputation. He was a man adorned with Christian faith, most constant in the performance of the most holy works, whose treatises on the divine sciences and secular letters were acknowledged to be of supreme erudition. Saint [i.e., Pope] Leo [IX] brought him to Rome—not from Burgundy, but from Lotharingia—and ordained him an archbishop to preach the word of God to the Sicularians. The Holy Roman Church then appointed him cardinal to preside over her. . . .

Thus when you attack Cardinal Humbert in this manner, and assert that he has written against Catholic truth, you attack not only him, but also the Roman Pontiffs, the Roman Church, and many of the Holy Fathers besides. In these assaults, you likewise attack the formulation that was agreed upon among the blessed doctors, if not in the same words, then nevertheless by the same thoughts in many places. For example, you state that every man is a heretic who disagrees with the Roman and Universal Church in the teachings of the faith. Yet, in the judgment of God, that is exactly what has happened to you, for in striving to declare others as heretics, you yourself have fallen into heresy and you have been convicted of it. . . .

Berengarius: Not every pronouncement will stand up when part of it has been overturned. This, Saint Augustine also says in his *On Christian Doctrine*: "In the very truth of eternity which God is, it stands indissolubly."

Lanfranc: Having forsaken the sacred authors, you take refuge in dialectics. And since the matter that you will hear and respond to concerns a mystery of faith, I prefer that you hear and respond on the basis of sacred authors rather than on the basis of dialectical reasoning. Indeed, our task will also be to respond to these things lest you think that, because of my ineptness in the art, I am incapable in this matter. It might seem boastful to some, and it will be labeled ostentation rather than necessity by others, but as God is my witness and my conscience, I would rather not propose nor respond to proposed dialectical questions and their solutions when treating sacred matters. When, however, the matter itself necessitates such a disputation, only then shall I address them, to the best of my ability, by such dialectical procedures. For it is only by way of the rules of its own art that [such questions] can be explained in a clear and pristine manner. In this way, I shall defend my position by that same art with propositions equal in force [*aequipollentias*] as your own. I do not therefore wish to seem as if I confide more in the art [of dialectic] than in the truth and authority of the holy Fathers. Even Saint Augustine, in some of his writings and especially in his book *On Christian Doctrine*, fully praises this discipline [of dialectic], and many times confirms that it is of great value for understanding and solving all questions that arise in the holy writings. For when he contended with the Arian heretic Felicianus, he defeated him using that very art, leaving the heretic himself unable to address the points and syllogistic reasoning with its implied logical connections and exclaiming openly: "With Aristotelian subtlety you contend with me, and everything said by me you torrentially destroy." . . .

Berengarius: Who indeed could conceive with reason—or will concede that it could happen by a miracle—that the bread broken is the body of Christ, since after the Resurrection it enjoys total incorruptibility and remains incapable of being summoned down from heaven until the time of the restitution of all things?

Lanfranc: The just man who lives by faith does not seek to investigate by argumentation and comprehend with reason how the bread is converted into flesh, how the wine is converted into blood, and how the nature of each has essentially changed. Instead, he chooses to abide by that same faith in the heavenly mysteries, so that he may eventually arrive at the rewards of faith—for when the faith is lacking, he labors in vain to understand those things which cannot be understood. And when he does arrive at those rewards, he knows that which has been written: "You should not search for things higher than you, nor should you scrutinize those things that are greater than you, but instead, that which God has commanded you, meditate always on that, and do not be curious of his many works" [cf. Ecclesiastes 3:22]. For it is not necessary to see with your eyes those things which are concealed from your sight. However, the faithful man concedes that it can be done marvelously by the agency of divine power. Nor are those who are in doubt lacking worthy miracles—miracles by which the shroud of visible and corruptible realities is removed, and Christ can be seen as he truly is, with his flesh and blood appearing to bodily eyes. In these miracles, the weakness of the infirm is mercifully healed by God's omnipotence and the detestable depravity of all heretics is mightily damned and repudiated. For Christ perfects the praise of those who take upon themselves the simplicity of a child and a nursing infant [cf. Psalm 8:2; Matthew 21:16]. Their faith is ridiculed by those who choose to understand everything according to reason alone, in other words those who consider themselves experts by their reasoning, but, on account of their hollow arrogance, instead make themselves just like a horse or a mule in which there is no understanding. And regarding the incorruptibility of the Lord's body, and the fact that it cannot be summoned down from heaven until the day of judgment, [let it be affirmed]: we believe in our faith which also declares that he [Christ] himself is verily eaten by the faithful.

b. Alberic of Monte Cassino, *Against Berengar, On the Body and Blood of the Lord*

Source: trans. Charles M. Radding and Francis Newton, *Theology, Rhetoric, and Politics in the Eucharistic Controversy, 1078–1079: Alberic of Monte Cassino Against Berengar of Tours* (New York: Columbia University Press, 2003), 127, 129, 135, 149, 159. Latin.

1. The report recently brought to us, O most blessed Father, of the questioning that has arisen in regard to the body and blood of the Lord, has suddenly filled all this land to such an extent that not only clerics and monks, whose watchful attention should be devoted to such matters, but even the very laymen are chattering about it among themselves in the town squares. What they say is that a certain Berengar of Tours, a man of great talent and profound knowledge, has come to Rome and wishes to revive anew the interpretation which he had once renounced: asserting, as they say, that in the sacrament [i.e., sacred ritual] of our redemption neither is the bread turned into flesh nor the wine into blood. How contrary this is to the Catholic Faith is well known to those whose food consists of the reading of sacred texts. The result of this has been that my brothers and neighbors, who (so to speak) often set me above myself, have stirred up my spirit to this undertaking, that I should lay out for them my own particular views on these matters. Therefore, I have gathered together these sentences of the holy Fathers that are contained in this little tract, yet with the omission of many, so that the reading might not be burdensome to the spirit of my reader,

as it would perchance be if it were too long. Moreover, I have chosen not to pour these teachings into *their* minds until they might, such as they are, be presented to *you* and be weighed and judged on your own balance-scales.

2. Now since we are to speak of the sacrament, let us first hear what a sacrament is in itself. "A sacrament is," as Isidore says, "when a thing is done with some celebration in such a way that it is understood to signify something; and a sacrament is called after sacred or hidden forces." Now a sacrament takes place at times figuratively, as the sacrament of the well-known lamb sacrificed under the Old Law; and at times in reality, as the sacrament of him who is daily eaten in the Church. Whence the blessed Ambrose says, "That you may know that this is a sacrament, the figure of it preceded it and came before." Therefore it is called a sacrament in this way, not because it points to something, but because it has been pointed to by something; just as on the other hand that former thing was called a sacrament not because it was pointed to by something, but because it carried the prefiguring of this present one. These things have been said to this end, that no one should choose to understand the sacrament of the Church typologically. And it is just the same to say, "That you may know that this is a sacrament, the figure of it preceded it and came before," as if one said, "that you may know that this is true in reality, another thing has preceded it in seeming." For this which the blessed Gregory prayed for saying that "that which we do in outward seeming, we should take in real truth," ought to have such force with us that we should believe that it is in reality the flesh and blood of him in whose commemoration we do these things. It is done in seeming indeed, because what is, is not seen. So much, then, for these matters for the moment; now let us come to the orderly laying out of the subject itself.

3. "Verily, verily I say unto you, unless you shalt eat the flesh of the son of man, and drink his blood, you will not have life in you." These are the words of him who could not lie. He wrote these words whose testimony is true. In his exposition of them, the blessed Augustine, like an eagle following an eagle, uses divine and spiritual language. Therefore he says, "And so this food and drink he wishes to be understood as the union of his body and limbs, which is the holy church, in those who are predestined and called unjustified as his saints and his faithful." And, a little later, he said, "The sacrament of this, that is of the unity of the body and blood of Christ, is prepared on the Lord's Table in some cases every day, and in some places at a fixed interval of days, and taken from the Lord's table, by some people for life and by others for destruction; but the thing itself, of which this is the sacrament, is taken by every man who participates in it for life and by no-one for destruction." Therefore the sacrament is one thing, and the force of the sacrament is another; in as much as this [force] gives life to all, that [sacrament] is taken by some for death, by others for life. Whence Augustine himself says, "This is therefore the living bread, which descends from heaven, so

that, if anyone shall eat of it, he may not die; but what pertains to the force of the sacrament, not what pertains to the visible sacrament; he who eats it within, not without; who eats it in his heart, not who grinds it in his tooth." . . .

6. And so we must determine what the saying means: He who eats my flesh and drinks my blood, remains in me, and I in him. For some eat with lips and with heart; others with heart and not with lips; other with lips and not with heart. The apostles ate with lips and with heart, that is, with the inner and outer man, and the rest of the faithful after them, those faithful who were and are and are to be, so ate, eat, and will eat. . . .

9. Having settled these matters in this fashion, let us declare what it is to eat with the heart and not with the lips. On this subject, the statements of Augustine alone would be sufficient, for he himself takes great pains over this spiritual eating and drinking. In this manner, even before he was born of the Virgin, Christ was formally eaten by the holy Fathers; in this manner he is both drunk and eaten even now by the faithful. . . .

11. Perchance these words of Augustine would suffice; but according to Cicero it is better for "some remnants" to be left over, "than" for us "to allow anyone to go away from here unfilled" [Cicero, *Topics*, 25–26]. Come then, let others now speak; and yet let us mix in among them passages that bear witness from the same Augustine. Let then the blessed Gregory [VI], the Roman pope, speak—and let the present one pass judgment who, now endowed with the same name and the same spirit, himself a Gregory, holds the place of the same Gregory; for the present Gregory [VII], as we believe, it was reserved by divine providence that he should carry out what the former one had said; moreover, these words of the blessed Gregory, which I am about to rehearse, are so deeply implanted in the heart of the present Gregory who now gives light to the world, that he unfailingly carries out daily what the former one said should be done daily. . . .

14. Therefore it is established in the authoritative statements of so many holy Fathers, both that the bread is changed into flesh, and that the wine is changed into blood. Now then, let us say something about the change itself. For substance is changed into substance either in seeming [*species*] and in reality [*res*], or in seeming and not in reality, or in reality and not in seeming. It is changed in seeming and in reality, to be sure, as earth is [changed] into mankind and the other animate creatures; similarly also water into salt, and ice into crystal; and you will be able to find many examples of this kind.

2. PROVING GOD: ANSELM'S ONTOLOGICAL ARGUMENT

In the Proslogion *(c. 1077–78), Anselm (c. 1033–1109) presents a philosophical argument for the existence of God that is intended to have validity for both the atheist and the Christian believer. In Anselm's famous phrase, God is "that than which nothing greater can be conceived," a definition that he believes even the incredulous "fool" mentioned in the Psalms would be able to understand and accept. For Anselm, this formulation does more than merely assert that God is the greatest. Rather, the definition of God rests on the use of a semantic formula that can go beyond any such focus on the greatness of beings. The intended focus is on the notion of something that by its own definition cannot be exceeded. Anselm therefore argues that the very concept of God demonstrates his existence: if one does not have the concept of God, then one does not know what one is denying; if one has the concept of God, then to deny his existence would be self-contradictory. Anselm's proof, dubbed by Immanuel Kant (1724–1804) the "ontological argument," is widely considered to be one of the most original and provocative ideas of God in the history of philosophy, influencing such philosophers as René Descartes (1596–1650), G.W. Leibniz (1646–1716), and G.W.F. Hegel (1770–1831), among many others.*

Objections to Anselm's proof began almost immediately. A monk named Gaunilo from the neighboring monastery of Marmoutier said that if the argument was convincing one could prove by the same reasoning that the most beautiful island must exist, since otherwise one would be able to imagine one even more beautiful. Anselm responded that the scenarios were different. The most beautiful island can be conceived not to exist, since there is no contradiction in imagining it to cease to exist. But the same does not hold true for God, since anything that passed out of existence, however exalted, would not in fact be God. The opening chapters from the Proslogion *supply the essence of Anselm's ontological argument and encapsulate a more philosophically and "logically" oriented path toward understanding God.*

Source: trans. Sidney Norton Deane, *Proslogium; Monologium; an appendix, In behalf of the fool, by Gaunilon; and Cur Deus homo* (Chicago: The Open Court Publishing Company, 1903), 1–9; revised by Alex J. Novikoff. Latin.

Preface

After I had published, at the solicitous entreaties of certain brethren, a brief work (the *Monologion*) as an example of meditation on the grounds of faith, in the person of one who investigates through silent reasoning with himself matters of which he is ignorant, and considering that this book was knit together by the linking of many arguments, I began to ask myself whether there might be found a single argument which would require no other proof than itself alone; and alone would suffice to demonstrate that God truly exists, and that there is a supreme good requiring nothing else, which all other things require for their existence and well-being; and whatever we believe regarding the divine Being.

Although I often and earnestly directed my thought to this end, and at some times that which I sought seemed to be just within my reach, while again it

Figure 1: The ruins of the famous Benedictine abbey of Bec in Normandy, from a mid-nineteenth-century lithograph. The abbey reached international fame in the late eleventh century under the leadership of Lanfranc of Pavia and Anselm of Aosta, both of whom went on to become archbishops of Canterbury. The late medieval Tour Saint Nicolas is one of the few structures to survive the French Wars of Religion (1562–98).

Source: From the private collection of Alex J. Novikoff.

wholly evaded my mental vision, at last in despair I was about to cease, as if from the search for a thing which could not be found. But when I wished to exclude this thought altogether, lest, by busying my mind to no purpose, it should keep me from other thoughts in which I might be successful, then more and more, though I was unwilling and shunned it, it began to force itself upon me more and more pressingly. So, one day, when I was exceedingly wearied with resisting its importunacy, in the very conflict of my thoughts, the proof of which I had despaired offered itself, so that I eagerly embraced the thoughts which I was strenuously repelling.

Thinking, therefore, that what I rejoiced to have found, would, if put in writing, be welcome to some readers, of this very matter, and of some others, I have written the following treatise, in the person of one who strives to lift his mind to the contemplation of God, and seeks to understand what he believes. In my judgment, neither this work nor the other, which I mentioned above, deserved to be called a book, or to bear the name of an author. And yet I thought they ought not to be sent forth without some title by which they might, in some sort, invite one into whose hands they fell to their perusal. I accordingly gave each a title, so that the first might be known as *An Example of Meditation on the Grounds of Faith*, and its sequel *Faith Seeking Understanding*. But, after both had been copied by many under these titles, many urged me, and especially Hugh, the reverend archbishop of Lyons, who discharges the apostolic office in Gaul, who instructed me to this effect on his apostolic authority, to prefix my name to these writings. And that this might be done more fittingly, I named the first *Monologion*, that is, a soliloquy; and the second *Proslogion*, that is, a discourse.

Chapter 1

Come now, slight man, flee for a little while from your occupations; hide yourself, for a time, from your disturbing thoughts. Cast aside, now, your burdensome cares, and put away your toilsome business. Yield room for some little time to God, and rest for a little time in him. Enter the inner chamber of your mind, shut out all thoughts save that of God, and such as can aid you in seeking him; close your door and seek him. Speak now, my whole heart! Speak now to God, saying, I seek your face; your face, Lord, will I seek [Psalm 26:8]. And come you now, O Lord my God, teach my heart where and how it may seek you, where and how it may find you.

Lord, if you are not here, where shall I seek you, being absent? But if you are everywhere, why do I not see you present? Truly you dwell in unapproachable light. But where is unapproachable light, or how shall I come to it? Or who shall lead me to that light and into it, that I may see you in it? Again, by what marks, under what form, shall I seek you? I have never seen you, O Lord, my God; I do not know your form. What, oh most high Lord, shall this man do, an exile far from you? What shall your servant do, anxious in his love of you, and cast out afar from your face? He wants to see you, and your face is too far from him. He longs to come to you, and your dwelling-place is inaccessible. He is eager to find you, and knows not your place. He desires to seek you, and does not know your face. . . .

Why did he not keep for us, when he could so easily, that whose lack we should feel so heavily? Why did he shut us away from the light, and cover us over with darkness? With what purpose did he rob us of life, and inflict death upon us? Wretches that we are, whence have we been driven out; whither are we driven on? Whence hurled? Whither consigned to ruin? From a native country into exile, from the vision of God into our present blindness, from the joy of immortality into the bitterness and horror of death. Miserable exchange of how great a good, for how great an evil! Heavy loss, heavy grief, heavy all our fate!

But alas, wretched that I am, one of the sons of Eve, far removed from God! What have I undertaken? What have I accomplished? Whither was I striving? How far have I come? To what did I aspire? Amid what thoughts am I sighing? I sought blessings, and lo, confusion. I strove toward God, and I stumbled on myself. I sought calm in privacy, and I found tribulation and grief, in my inmost thoughts. I wished to smile in the joy of my mind, and I am compelled to frown by the sorrow of my heart. Gladness was hoped for, and lo, a source of frequent sighs!

And you too, O Lord, how long? How long, O Lord, do you forget us; how long do you turn your face from us? When will you look upon us, and hear us? When will you enlighten our eyes, and show us your face? When will you restore yourself to us? Look upon us, Lord; hear us, enlighten us, reveal yourself to us. Restore yourself to us, that it may be well with us, yourself, without whom it is so ill with us. Pity our efforts and our strivings toward you since we can do nothing without you. You do invite us; do you help us. I beseech you, O Lord, that I may not lose hope in sighs, but may breathe anew in hope. Lord, my heart is made bitter by its desolation; sweeten you it, I beseech you, with your consolation. Lord, in hunger I began to seek you; I beseech you that I may not cease to hunger for you. In hunger I have come to you; let me not go unfed. I have come in poverty to the Rich, in misery to the Compassionate; let me not return empty and despised. And if, before I eat, I sigh, grant, even after sighs, that which I may eat. Lord, I am bowed down and can only look downward; raise me up that I may look upward. My iniquities have gone over my head; they overwhelm me; and, like a heavy load, they weigh me down. Free me from them; unburden me, that the pit of iniquities may not close over me.

Be it mine to look up to your light, even from afar, even from the depths. Teach me to seek you, and reveal yourself to me, when I seek you, for I cannot seek you, except you teach me, nor find you, except you reveal yourself. Let me seek you in longing, let me long for you in seeking; let me find you in love, and love you in finding. Lord, I acknowledge and I thank you that you have created me in this your image, in order that I may be mindful of you, may conceive of you, and love you; but that image has been so consumed and wasted away by vices, and obscured by the smoke of wrong-doing, that it cannot achieve that for which it was made, except you renew it, and create it anew. I do not endeavor, O Lord, to penetrate your sublimity, for in no wise do I compare my understanding with that; but I long to understand in some degree your truth, which my heart believes and loves. For I do not seek to understand that I may believe, but I believe in order to understand. For this also I believe, that unless I believed, I should not understand.

Chapter 2

Truly there is a God, although the fool has said in his heart, There is no God.

And so, Lord, do you, who do give understanding to faith, give me, so far as you know it to be profitable, to understand that you are as we believe; and that you are that which we believe? And indeed, we believe that you are a being than which nothing greater can be conceived. Or is there no such nature, since the fool has said in his heart, there is no God [Psalm 14:1]? But, at any rate, this very fool, when he hears of this being of which I speak—a being than which nothing greater can be conceived—understands what he hears, and what he understands is in his understanding; although he does not understand it to exist.

For, it is one thing for an object to be in one's understanding, and another to understand that the object exists. When a painter first conceives of what he will afterwards perform, he has it in his understanding, but he does not yet understand it to be, because he has not yet performed it. But after he has made the painting, he both has it in his understanding, and he understands that it exists, because he has made it.

Hence, even the fool is convinced that something exists in the understanding, at least, than which nothing greater can be conceived. For, when he hears of this, he understands it. And whatever is understood, exists in the understanding. And assuredly, that than which nothing greater can be conceived cannot exist in one's understanding alone. For, suppose it exists in the understanding alone: then it can be conceived to exist in reality; which is greater.

Therefore, if that than which nothing greater can be conceived exists in the understanding alone, then the very being than which nothing greater can be conceived is one than which a greater can be conceived. But obviously this is impossible. Hence, there is doubt that there exists a being than which nothing greater can be conceived, and it exists both in one's understanding and in reality.

3. BERNARD OF CLAIRVAUX ON LOVING GOD

Bernard of Clairvaux (1090–1153) was one of the most important and influential figures of the first half of the twelfth century. He entered the recently founded Cistercian monastery of Cîteaux in 1112, and three years later he founded the monastery of Clairvaux some 90 miles north. From this remote corner in northeastern France, he intervened in matters both political and ecclesiastical while overseeing an enormous international expansion that saw the young Cistercian order take root in virtually all the lands of Western Europe. In 1128 he obtained recognition for the Rule *of the new military order of the Knights Templar. He led the charge in the condemnation of Peter Abelard at the Council of Sens (1141), and he spoke out against the teachings of Gilbert of Poitiers (c. 1080–1154) at the Council of Rheims. He was instrumental in preaching the Second Crusade and called on Christians to repent for their sins following its dismal failure in 1148.*

Bernard's oeuvre *consists of treatises, numerous sermons, and an epistolary correspondence with many of the important religious leaders of the day, including Hildegard of Bingen (Doc. 6a) and Pope Innocent II (Doc. 19a). His treatise on love, explicitly written "for both the learned and the unlearned," describes the long journey toward God, who is to be loved with a love that is "without measure." Bernard combines the unrelenting desire for God characteristic of monastic spirituality with the stability of its final goal, all while probing the depths of that love and how it is to be achieved. Bernard's writings on spiritual love would exert a tremendous impact on the religious attitudes of the twelfth century, and in particular on the concept of moral reform through individual piety.*

Source: trans. Marianne Caroline and Coventry Patmore, *Saint Bernard on the Love of God*, 2nd ed. (London: Burns and Oates, 1884), 3–5, 23–26, 37–40; revised by Alex J. Novikoff. Latin.

Chapter 1: Why We Ought to Love God, and How
We Ought to Love Him

You wish to explain for what reason and in what measure we should love God.

I should say that God himself is the motive of our love to him, and that the measure of true love is to be without measure. Is this clear enough? Perhaps it may be for a person of intelligence, but I desire to answer for both the learned and unlearned; and, though I may have said enough for the former, I must remember others also. For them I will unfold my meaning, and perhaps add something to it.

There are two things that move us to love God for himself: nothing is more reasonable, nothing is more profitable.

The question of what binds us to love God may either mean, What is his title to our love? Or, how will it profit us to love God? To both these questions there is but one answer: the motive for loving God is God. No title can be stronger than this: God gave himself to us in spite of our unworthiness, and, being God, what could he give us of greater worth than himself? If, then, by asking, why we are bound to love God, we mean, what is his claim, the answer is: especially this, that he first loved us. This gives him a right to our love in return; above all, considering who he is that loves, what his loved ones are, and in what way he loves them. For who is he that loves us, but he of whom every spirit bears witness: "You are my God, you have no need of my goods," and his love is it not that charity that seeks not its own interests? But on whom is fastened this unselfish love? The Apostle [Paul] answers, "When we were yet enemies, we were reconciled to God" [Romans 5:10]. God has loved us disinterestedly, and while we were yet his enemies. But how has he loved us? Saint John says to this extreme: "God so loved the world as to give his only begotten son" [John 3:16]. Saint Paul adds, "He has not spared his only begotten son, but has delivered him up for us" [Romans 8:32], and the son says of himself, "Greater love has no man than this, that a man lay down his life for his friends" [John 15:13]. These are the claims which God, the holy, the sovereignly great and almighty, has upon the love of the infinitely little, weak, and sinful man. It may be said: yes, this is true of mankind, but it is not so of angels. I know it; for angels the same was not needful. Moreover, he who has helped man in his misery, preserved the angels from falling into the like; and if God's love for men has found them a way of escape, it is by the self-same that he kept the angels from a fall like ours.

Chapter 5: Of the Obligation to Love God, Especially for Christians

All that has been said proves most clearly the duty of loving God, and his claim upon our love. How is it with the infidel? As he knows not God the Son, so is he also ignorant of the Father and the Holy Spirit; and as he gives no glory to the son, neither does he glorify the Father who sent him, nor the Holy Spirit, the gift of both. He knows less of God than we do, therefore it is no wonder he should love him less. One thing, however, he does know: that to him, who created him, he owes himself entirely. But how will it be with me? For I can plead no ignorance. I know that God made me without any entitlement of mine, that he satisfies all my wants, comforts me with pity, and governs me with anxious care; and not only so, but I know that he is my redeemer, the author of my eternal salvation, my treasure and my glory. As it is written, "With him is plentiful redemption," and "by his own blood, he once entered into the Holy of Holies, having obtained eternal redemption" [cf. Psalm 130:7; Hebrews 9:12]. He keeps us safe, as it is written, "The Lord knows the days of the undefiled, and their inheritance shall be forever" [Psalm 37:18]. He enriches us, as he has said, "Good measure, pressed down and shaken together and running over, shall they give into your bosom" [Luke 6:38]; and elsewhere, "The eye has not seen, oh God, the things you have prepared for them that wait for you" [1 Corinthians 2:9]. He fulfills us with glory, as the Apostle says, "We wait for the savior, our Lord Jesus Christ, who will transform our body, now vile and abject, and make it like unto his own, which is full of glory" [cf. Philippians 3:21]. And again, "The sufferings of this present time are not to be compared to the glory which shall be revealed in us" [Romans 8:18], and this present time of this world's affliction (so short, so fugitive) produces to us (if only despising the visible we fix our eyes on things invisible) "an eternal and incomparable weight of glory" [2 Corinthians 4:17].

For all of this, what shall I render to the Lord? Both reason and the law of nature bind me fast to give myself undividedly to him from whom I hold all I have, and to devote my entire being to the love of him. And faith reveals to me that I am constrained to love him more than myself, the more I understand that I owe to his munificence not only all I am, but moreover the gift of himself. But let us consider that, before the day of Christian faith had come, before God had put on our flesh and died upon a cross, gone down into hell and ascended to the Father, that is, before the fullness of his love for us had shone forth, long before, man had been commanded to love the Lord his God with all his heart, with all his soul, with all his strength, that is, with his whole being, with all the love of which he is capable, as a creature endowed with intelligence and will. Could it be unjust of God to claim for himself his own work and his gifts? Why should not the work love God, who made it, having also received the power to love; and why not love him with all its powers, if it is only by God that it possesses any? Consider, too, that man has not only been called into being out of nothing, without any anterior claim, but also that he has been so called to be raised to high dignity. We shall thus see more clearly our obligation to love him wholly, and his right to our love. Moreover, when man had sunk to the level of beasts that perish, did God not intervene to reinstate and save him? Is this not the marvel of his goodness and his mercy? For by sin we had fallen from the dignity of our creation, to become imbruted like the ox that eats the grass and has not the light of reason. If I owe my whole self to my Creator, what do I not owe to my Redeemer, and to such a redeemer! It was a far lesser work to create, than to redeem; for God had but to speak the word, and all things were made; but to repair the fall of that, which one word had created, what wonders had he not to perform, what cruelties, nay, what humiliations, had he not to suffer!. . .

Chapter 8: We Begin by the Love of Self, This Being for Us the First Degree of Love

Love is one of the four natural affections that all the world knows, and which need not be enumerated. Now, it is but natural and right first of all to love the author of nature; and the first commandment, which is the greatest is, "You shall love the Lord your God." But nature is too soft and weak for such a precept; she must begin by loving herself; this is the love which is called carnal, with which man loves himself first and above all; as it is written, "That is not first which is spiritual, but that which is natural" [cf. 1 Corinthians 15:46]. We love first by nature, not by precept—"No man ever hated his own flesh" [Ephesians 5:29]. But if this love should increase too much, if like a river between banks it overflows and floods the lands about, it then becomes voluptuousness, and this dyke is opposed to it, "You shall love your neighbor as yourself" [Leviticus 19:9; Mark 12:31]. Justly may he that shares our nature share our love. Wherefore, if anyone cannot so love his brethren as to think of their wants, or let us even say of their pleasures, let him deny himself in those very things, in order that he may learn. Let a man think of himself as much as ever he will, if only he takes care to think equally of his neighbor. Such, o man, is the curb and just limit imposed upon you by the law of your being and by your conscience, that you are not carried away by your selfishness to your destruction, leaving your nature at the mercy of the enemies of your soul; that is, of your passions. It is far better that you go shares with your neighbors than with your enemies; and if, as the wise man advises, man renounces his passions, contents himself with food and raiment, and is willing to moderate his love for those things of the flesh which war against the spirit, he will, I think, find small difficulty in giving to his neighbor what he refuses to the enemy of his soul. His love will be contained within the bounds of justice and moderation, from the moment that he consecrates to his brethren that which he refuses to himself. Selfishness becomes benevolence by taking a wider range.

But if through imparting to our neighbor we bring ourselves to want? What is our remedy? Prayer. We have only to pray with confidence to him who gives all things liberally and does not upbraid; who "opens his hand and fills with blessing every living creature" [Psalm 145:16]; for we cannot doubt that he who gives to most men more than they need, will willingly give to him who prays for what is indispensable; for it is written, "Seek first the kingdom of God and his justice, and all these things shall be added unto you" [Matthew 6:33]. God hereby binds himself to provide what is essential for him who denies himself and loves his neighbor; for to put on the yoke of purity and sobriety rather than to be the slave of our passions, this is to seek first the kingdom of God and to implore his help against the tyranny of sin; and it is justice to share our natural blessings with those that share our nature.

But in order that love for our neighbor be entirely right, God must have his part in it; it is not possible to love our neighbor as we ought to do, except in God. Now he that does not love God can love nothing in him. We must therefore begin by loving God, and so love our neighbor in him. God is the author, as of all other things, of our love for him—and more—as he created nature, so he sustains it; for nature could neither exist nor subsist without him. . . .

4. THE PREMONSTRATENSIAN CHALLENGE TO TRADITIONAL MONASTICISM

Having tried and failed to implement religious reform in his native town of Xanten in Germany, Norbert (c. 1080–1134) founded a community in Prémontré, France. This marked the beginning of an ultimately very successful order, the Canons Regular of Prémontré, also known as the Premonstratensians or the Norbertines. Norbert was appointed archbishop of Magdeburg in 1126. Although he left no writings, his follow-ers wrote and circulated various works aimed at improving the status of the clergy. In their advocacy of preaching and poverty for a reformed clergy, and their high level of affective spirituality especially in relation to the Virgin Mary, the Premonstratensians stood at the forefront of twelfth-century religious change. Eschewing the more popular Rule *established by Saint Benedict (480–547), they instead embraced the older* Rule *of Saint Augustine (c. 400).*

The first selection is from a letter written in 1138 by Anselm of Havelberg (c. 1100–58), an early follower of Norbert. The incitement for this Apologetic Letter *was a regular canon and provost of Hamersleben near Magdeburg who had renounced his committment to public ministry and entered a Benedictine monastery in Huysburg. The canons of Hamersleben sought the return of this apostate, Peter, who was welcomed back into the cenobitic community by the Benedictine abbot of Huysburg, Egbert (1135–55). Anselm's* Apologetic Letter *is thus a defense of the Premonstratensian mixed life of action and contemplation provoked by the transfer of a regular religious from one house and rule to another. In fact, the situation Anselm describes is very much like the situ-ation later encountered by another follower of Norbert, Philip of Harvengt (d. 1183), the prior and later abbot of Bonne Espérance in Brabant, who in the 1140s witnessed a renegade canon of his own house flee to the neighboring Cistercians, a dispute that was eventually appealed (unsuccessfully) to the papacy. Philip's short work* On the Educa-tion of Clerics, *from which the second selection is taken, helps to illustrate the variety of disputes in which he and his brethren found themselves in the middle decades of the twelfth century. Philip puts up a vigorous defense of the relationship between action and contemplation among religious orders while also addressing the relationship of education within the cloister to the mixed apostolate.*

Source: trans. Paul Edward Dutton, from *Epistola venerabilis Anselmi Havelbergensis episcopi ad Ecbertum abbatem Huysborgensem*, in J.-P. Migne, ed., *Patrologia Latina* (Paris: Imprimerie Royale, 1855), vol. 188, cols. 1122B–1123B, 1128C–1129B, 1135D–1136C. Latin.

a. Anselm of Havelberg, *Apologetic Letter*

. . . You say that the dignity of the monastic order has been thrown into disor-der because Peter, the prior of the clerical canons of Hamersleben, who live the common life according to the profession established by the apostles, has become a monk, and is being searched for. Clearly he abandoned [the canons] without apparent cause, which is not permitted, as I can confirm, and he should be recalled to his original order. O Christian unworthy of all dignity, O contentious [one, worthy now] of only perverse indignity! But perhaps you spoke more of heavenly dignity. For there is a heavenly dignity [i.e., rank] and an earthly one. But if your contention is about earthly dignity, you are one of this earth, and reveal that you are certainly unworthy of that higher dignity, but instead merit the complete contempt of good men. But if, however, you meant to speak of heavenly dignity, why would you lament that it is thrown into disorder? For that dignity is alien to all disorder and is entirely free [from confusion and insult]. For that reason it is clear that no earthly dignity should be desired by a good Christian, nor that that heavenly dignity should be believed or said by any Christian to be cast into disorder in any way.

Further you dispute the term *regular canon* and say that it is new and, therefore, contemptible, as if it necessarily follows that "if new, then contemptible." That this contemptible argument is itself contemptible is obvious to all who are capable of speaking in syllogisms. For everything, indeed, that has become ancient or old was surely new at one time and, therefore, something is neither more nor less contemptible because it is new or was new. Nor is something more or less acceptable because it is or will be old, but should rightly be acceptable to all good men if it is good and useful whether or not it is old or new. For there are ancient goods and new goods and there are ancient evils and new evils. Surely just as the antiquity or newness of evils does not afford them any support, neither should the antiquity or newness of good things obtain dignity for them. You seem in this matter to argue not simply but cleverly, as if by insinuation, when you praise the common term cleric and attract them [the clerics] to your side when you praise [them] for their antiquity. What I fear you have actually done is not so much to praise them [clerics] as to demean those [regular canons] wantonly, as I might say, with your [false] peace. I confess, however, that I do not know how to respond to you about this phrase, because "regular" [and] "canon" seem to signify the same thing. It is as if one were to say "regular regular" or "canon canon," unless perhaps one and the same word in modern usage served the same end as in Latin and Greek, so that by doubling the old signifier there should now be a firm assertion of restored religion or a clear identification of those who do not live regular lives. . . .

It has been reported to us that you do not fear to assault the ears of some people and are not even embarrassed to tell others that regular canons do not hold parishes and ought not to direct the cure of souls of people. If that is true, then I am amazed by your judgment, since whoever would claim such a thing (which no wise man I know of believes) does it more in order to spite the canonical order than out of love of the truth. For he who reasons rightly should encourage all priests to live a regular life rather than to remove those living according to a rule from their care of the Lord's flock. The malice of others should displease them to the extent that they are known to have set aside their own interests, and they should welcome the outsider's correction of them to the extent that the outsider is prepared to correct his own life. Undeserved harm, therefore, should not much harm a fruitful olive tree, nor the order of canons within the church. The common practice of the whole church is manifest, that no monk be elevated to the archidiaconate or archpriesthood or taken into any parish. Thus, no regular canon should be removed by ecclesiastical judgment or synodal decision from the cure of souls or from any other ecclesiastical office or dignity [rank]. Instead, he is sought out, elected, elevated by the common people, and like a light shining in obscure places is loved and honored, teaching by word and example. Let all know that whoever wishes to fulfill his own ill will and so is inclined to detract from the canonical order by what he says, why he says it, and against whom he says is, is wholly ignorant and lacks any knowledge of scripture. Such a one burns maliciously with envy of the good. . . .

My plan in this part of the letter has not been to discuss the order, life, and habit of canons or to describe how that life used to be, but rather I wanted to show the order, life, and habit of monks. Provoked by the appearance of your letter, I wished to show that the contemplative life was not only or always—or it could ever wholly be—the life of all monks so far as they claim. Monks usurp to themselves before all others the special name and label of contemplation, but even this does not impede the profession of canons from on occasion, with grace leading them, being lifted up most devotedly to the highest peak of contemplation. This happens best when they tend to the care of others and serve much and many. Therefore, that we might now see the matter clearly and so that it be crystal-clear to all, even to those with little sense, let us consider whether or not the canonical order and monastic order, although both are good, present different life plans for their members. As for whether this one or that one is more useful or necessary in the church of God, let us stipulate that every kind of monk was deprived of ecclesiastical orders, as happened in antiquity, which no knowledgeable person can deny. As well, let us subtract every kind of cleric. Tell me then, brother, how can the church stand? Without archbishops, bishops, and priests, without deacons and the lower ranks of clergy, could it be called a church? Again, take away every kind of monk and let us have in the church of God, according to the establishment of Christ and to the apostles, other prophets, other apostles, other evangelists, other pastors and teachers, and other orders of clerics. Would these be enough "for the perfecting of the saints, for the work of the ministry, for the edifying of the body of Christ" [cf. Ephesians 4:12], which is the church? Yet even if a church without monks could stand well ordered, it is in fact more fittingly and beautifully adorned and enveloped with diverse orders of the elect.

b. Philip of Harvengt, *On the Knowledge of Clerics*

Source: trans. Alex J. Novikoff, from *De institutione clericorum*, in J.-P. Migne, ed., *Patrologia Latina* (Paris: Imprimerie Royale, 1855), vol. 203, cols. 706A–706C. Latin.

These and many other [biblical] testimonies are more than sufficient to show that knowledge of Scriptures is appropriate to clerics and should be sought by them with utmost diligence, but not because their involvement in other needful [activities] should be condemned, since that other need is indeed appropriate to the clerical order. Clerics may rightly obtain ecclesiastical positions, and on occassion undertake manual labor, if they have been compelled to do so by charity or necessity rather than by the vice of frivolity. The apostle himself [Christ] showed great concern for churches because charity constrained him, and he labored with his hands when necessity demanded it. Finally, when he instructed Timothy, he did not forbid him from labor but rather relegated it to its rightful place, so that he could show that from time to time it was appropriate for a cleric to do manual work provided that he understood its role. A cleric should place the diligent study of Scriptures first. He should undertake manual labor with patience, not enjoyment, so that spiritual delight draws him to the former but only unwelcome temporal necessity obliges him to the latter. As he [Christ] says: "Exercise yourself unto godliness, for bodily exercise is profitable to little, but godliness is profitable to all things" [cf. 1 Timothy 4:7–8]. By godliness he means diligence in the study of Scriptures. Through such study, with the assistance of grace, the cleric ought to know God better, love him thus known even more devotedly, and worship him more perfectly with that love. Progressing in these things he may become, in a spiritual sense, a temple of God and simultaneously a holy example to others in his knowledge and life.

5. CISTERCIAN SPIRITUALITY: AELRED OF RIEVAULX'S *DIALOGUE ON THE SOUL*

Aelred of Rievaulx was the abbot of the Cistercian abbey of Rievaulx in Yorkshire, England, from 1147 until his death in 1167. Like his Cistercian brothers, he believed that we humans are created in the image and likeness of God. Since God is ineffable, any knowledge of the divine nature can only be accessed indirectly through the imprints we perceive of it in creation. By analyzing inwardly our own human nature it may be possible to perceive some faint glimmering of God's true essence. Aelred therefore searched the human soul in order to understand by analogy some reflection of the true being of God. On account of its three faculties—reason, memory, and will—the one, indivisible soul may be seen to resemble the triune Godhead.

Book Two opens with the question of memory. It is quickly apparent that the word signifies much more than the modern psychological meaning of the term. Following Augustine, Aelred understands memory to mean not merely the remembrance of the past but everything that the soul encompasses. The teacher–student dialogue form of the work suggests that it was intended for the instruction of young brothers. Through ascetic discipline and by training their innate spiritual faculties, the early Cistercians sought to restore their followers to the original perfection in which God had created them: to remember without forgetting, to know without error, and to love without satiety.

Source: trans. C.H. Talbot, Aelred of Rievaulx, *Dialogue on the Soul* (Kalamazoo, MI: Cistercian Publications, 1981), 71–78. Latin.

Book Two

John: It is now time to discuss today those points which we deferred dealing with yesterday.

Aelred: I wish my aptitude for the task was on a par with my desire. The question to be asked is this: what can the soul, without the assistance of the senses, accomplish in itself and by itself through the memory, reason and will?

John: That is so.

Aelred: First of all, recall to mind what we said about these three faculties, memory, reason and will, namely, that they are substance of the soul and that even though certain of their activities appear to belong exclusively to one, they are inseparable.

John: I remember that very well. So return to those matters which we have put forward as the subject of our discussion.

Aelred: I think the first point to be discussed should concern the faculty of memory.

John: As you wish.

Aelred: On this power or faculty Saint Augustine has a great deal to say [*Confessions*, 10], and in his explanation he expresses astonishment both at its immensity and at its mystery. For the memory is like a vast hall containing almost countless treasures, namely, the images of different bodily objects which have been carried into it by the senses. In the memory are stored and separately labeled all those things that have been borne through its doors by the eyes, such as colors and the shapes of things; by the ears, such as every kind of sound; by the mouth, such as various tastes; by the nostrils, such as scents; and by the sense of touch, such as things hard and soft, cold or hot, smooth or rough. All these things the memory receives, and to the mind [*animus*] seeking out now one, now another, the memory presents each one in turn by means of its own particular image. Certain things come so readily to hand that they present themselves to the thinker immediately, but some, even when other things are being sought for, thrust themselves forward and are brushed aside only with difficulty. Some things are hidden beneath such a deep layer of objects that they can be retrieved from their dark recesses only with great mental effort. Others make their appearance, whenever they are required, in perfect order. In the memory the heavens, the earth, the sea, and all the creatures that can be perceived in them are present to the reflective mind. Only those things that forgetfulness has buried in its tomb are removed from its sight.

John: If the soul is incorporeal, how can it embrace within itself bodily images?

Aelred: Is it your opinion that images of bodily things are themselves bodies?

John: Not at all. At the same time, I am surprised that the soul is not a body, when its extent is such that it contains all those objects.

Aelred: Certainly it is impossible for a body of any kind to contain within itself so many things. But tell me, have you ever looked at your reflection in a mirror?

John: Very often.

Aelred: Was the size of your reflection bigger than the measurement of the mirror?

John: Not at all. The reflection was greater or smaller according to the size of the mirror.

Aelred: You see, then, that no image can be greater than the thing on which it is impressed.

John: Yes, I see that. Nothing can be more certain.

Aelred: Do you remember London and how vast it is? Do you call to mind how the river Thames flows past it, how Westminster Abbey beautifies its western side, how the enormous Tower stands guard over the east and how Saint Paul's Cathedral rises majestically in the middle?

John: I remember it all and I have forgotten nothing.

Aelred: And how do you remember these things? Is it not because you have seen images of them all in your memory?

John: That is quite true.

Aelred: Now pay attention. Does London appear smaller in your memory than it did to your eyes?

John: Neither larger nor smaller.

Aelred: Very true. You are forced to admit then that your memory, and consequently your soul, is greater than London.

John: Yes, I am bound to admit it, since the image of London is impressed on my memory, and no image can exceed the size of the thing on which it is impressed.

Aelred: If, therefore, you could see at a glance the whole world and all that is contained in it, would not anyone who wished to think of the world see its image in exactly the same size?

John: Yes, clearly.

Aelred: Is there any body or any bodily thing in which the image of the whole world can be depicted without some diminution of its size?

John: Not at all.

Aelred: So your memory is greater than the world, not in material size but in spiritual nature.

John: If the soul is so great, how is it confined to so small a body?

Aelred: From this, in fact, it can be proved quite easily that the soul is not confined within the limits of a small body or contained in a place, for though it may seem to be in a body, it somehow forms and depicts within itself so many and such great images of countless objects. For if you were to see with your own eyes thousands of worlds similar to the one we know, the likeness of them all would be impressed on your soul without losing anything of their size. So, in my memory I have at hand the heavens and the earth and the sea and all the information I can gather about them, excepting the things I have forgotten. Unless I could see them all in my memory with their vast spaces, just as I see them outside me, I should be unable to speak about the heavens or the sea or the stars or the mountains or about anything else that I have actually seen or heard others describing. Now, if we have spoken enough about this power of the soul which deals in images, let us pass on to its higher power, which is concerned not with images but with real things.

John: What do you mean, may I ask, by real things?

Aelred: Do you not consider that the science [*scientia*] of measurement, the skill of disputation and the subtlety of calculating are wonderful things? And what of the theory of measurement, the countless rules and the different arts, which pertain either to the practical side of life or to the knowledge of truth? All these are present in the memory, not through any image, but just as they are. In the same way, the virtues of prudence, fortitude, and justice, if they are in the soul at all, are not there in the guise of images, but in their true selves.

John: How can these enter the mind [*mens*] if they are not introduced there by images of some kind?

Aelred: It is quite clear, leaving other things aside, that the science of division and multiplication has no image in the mind [*animus*].

John: How can my soul gain the knowledge of multiplication except by holding small objects in my hand and sharing them out into parts, or if I wish to do this solely by thinking, by turning over and counting their images?

Aelred: Let it be so. You have learned, say, the science [*scientia*] of numbers by counting or multiplying. Do you not think that there is a difference between the science you have learned and the words or small objects or images by which you have learned it?

John: I certainly do.

Aelred: You see then that there is no image of that science.

John: Yes, I see and I am delighted, because this is for me a proof that the soul is incorporeal. In no way can a corporeal object contain an incorporeal body, nor is any bodily object capable of possessing wisdom.

Aelred: You have made a good observation. But as that science has not been seen by the eye or heard by the ear or smelled by the nostrils or tasted or touched, in what manner or by what entrance did it reach the soul, so that it resides and is retained there in such a way that I am able to bring it to mind whenever I wish and to store it away again when I like?

John: I do not know how to answer that.

Aelred: When you heard a teacher explaining the number six and its individual parts and giving such clear reasons for it that you accepted the truth of what he had said, did you simply believe him or see the reason in your own mind [*animus*]?

John: Without doubt I recognized as true in my own mind what I had heard.

Aelred: So perhaps the reason was there all the time, but you had failed to notice it.

John: It seems likely, then, that what certain secular scholars have accepted is true, namely, that the natural sciences [*artes naturales*] reside in the rational soul.

But because the corruptible body weighs down the soul and the weakness of the bodily organs dulls the senses, and the images of bodily objects darken and depress the intellect, it is only with great difficulty that they are recalled to the intellect at another's bidding, hidden as they appear to be in the innermost recesses of the memory. So when the mind does notice them, it realizes that they have not been brought in, as it were, from outside, but are implanted by nature.

Aelred: This opinion appears from the book of the *Confessions* to have the approval of Saint Augustine. But because there is difficulty in providing a convincing proof for it, let us move forward to the discussion of other things. Now the memory has one supreme quality that overrides all else: it has the capacity of receiving God. From the moment that man knows God, God begins to dwell in his memory, and as often as man brings God to mind, he finds him there.

John: Is this not common to all men, both good and bad? Am I to say, then, that God dwells in the wicked just because at some time or other, like the good, they remember him?

Aelred: You are aware of what the Apostle said about the wise men of this world, namely, that they knew God, yet they did not glorify him as God. So God dwelt in their memories but not in their love. And because they did not give glory to him as God, they have perished. Let what we have said about the faculty of memory suffice, so that we can discuss briefly the faculty of reason.

John: Do as you please. Wherever you lead I am prepared to follow.

Aelred: We have shown that reason belongs to the substance of the soul. The power of reason is so great that it distinguishes us from the rest of the animals and by it we are placed above all of them. On it the memory depends so much that it would be able to retain, to distinguish, or to judge nothing except the images conveyed to it through the senses. Yet notice, in spite of the difference in names, how great a unity of nature or substance exists between them. Memory, shorn of reason, certainly does not go beyond the power of an irrational soul, while reason without memory is unable to make anything connect or hang together. In short, memory cannot be conceived without reason or reason without memory, because they are one simple substance.

John: All that pertains to memory, then, pertains to reason. Consequently, memory and reason are one. If that is so, it seems to me that memory is reason, and reason is memory.

Aelred: Certainly reason and memory are one, and they are one soul. Yet reason is not memory, and memory is not reason. For memory signifies one power of the soul and reason another. Memory, in fact, signifies that power by which the soul recalls things and by which it links up sequences of events, connecting those that follow to those that have gone before and those of the future to those of the past. But reason distinguishes between all these and passes judgment on them, approving one as true and another as false, one as just and another as unjust, one as happy and another as unfortunate. Is not this clearer to you than light itself?

6. HILDEGARD OF BINGEN'S HEAVENLY VISIONS

Hildegard of Bingen (1098–1179) was a prolific writer, composer, philosopher, mystic, healer, abbess, and noted visionary. Founder of the Benedictine women's monastery at St. Rupertsberg in Germany, she is one of the century's most outstanding exemplars of both monastic and mystical renewal. Aware of what she called a "shadow of the living light" from early childhood, Hildegard had her first clear vision in 1141 at the age of about 43. She understood her experiences as divine revelations concerning the meaning of Scripture and obeyed the command to write them down. Her fame spread quickly. She was consulted by and corresponded with popes, kings, abbots and abbesses, and many influential contemporaries including Bernard of Clairvaux (see Doc. 3), to whom she addressed a letter in 1147 (selection a, her oldest extant letter) expressing a deep concern regarding the authenticity of her visions. He encouraged her, and in 1148 Pope Eugenius III (r. 1145–53) officially recognized her visionary powers at the Synod of Trier. Between 1160 and 1170 she undertook preaching tours to German cities and monasteries, earning her the title prophetissa teutonica *(loosely translated as "Sibyl of the Rhine").*

Hildegard's most famous work is the recording of her 26 visions from God. It is divided into three parts. The Scivias *(Know the Ways) was written down over the course of the 1140s and early 1150s and constitutes the first and most well-known part of her trilogy. It contains six visions depicting God the father and creation, as well as a prologue in which she identifies her authorial intention and the inspiration for her writings. The second part, the* Book of Meritorious Life, *has seven visions recounting Christ's work of salvation and the continuation of this work through the Church. The third part, the* Book of Divine Works, *gives 13 visions, which is also the sum of the number of visions in Parts One and Two, and focuses on the power of the Holy Spirit and the end of days. Two of Hildegard's visions from this final work are given in selection b, accompanied by her rich and original spiritual interpretations. Her line-by-line explications, it should be noted, are not unlike that of a monastic commentator doing a gloss on a text from Scripture (see for example Docs. 1, 10, and 11).*

Source: trans. Matthew Fox and Ronald Miller, *Hildegard of Bingen's Book of Divine Works, with Letters and Songs* (Santa Fe: Bear and Company, 1987), 22, 24, 222, 224, 271–72. Latin.

a. Letter to Bernard of Clairvaux

Most praiseworthy Father Bernard, through God's power you stand wonderfully in highest honor. You are formidable against the indecent foolishness of this world. Full of lofty zeal and in ardent love for God's Son, you capture men with the banner of the holy cross so that they will wage war in the Christian army against the wrath of the pagans. I beseech you, father, by the living God, hear me in what I ask you.

I am very concerned about this vision which opens before me in spirit as a mystery. I have never seen it with the outer eyes of the flesh. I am wretched and more than wretched in my existence as a woman. And yet, already as a child, I saw great things of wonder which my tongue could never have given expression to, if God's spirit had not taught me to believe.

Gentle father, you are so secure, answer me in your goodness, me, your unworthy servant girl, whom from childhood has never, not even for one single hour, lived in security. In your fatherly love and wisdom search your soul, since you are taught by the Holy Spirit, and from your heart give some comfort to your servant girl.

I know in Latin text the meaning of the interpretation of the psalms, the gospels, and the other books which are shown to me through this vision. It stirs my heart and soul like a burning flame and teaches me the depth of interpretation. And yet this vision does not teach me writings in the German language; these I do not know. I can simply read them but have no ability to analyze them. Please answer me: what do you make of all this? I am a person who received no schooling about external matters. It is only within, in my soul, that I have been trained. And that is why I speak in such doubt. But I take consolation from all that I have heard of your wisdom and fatherly love. I have not talked about this to anyone else, because, as I hear it said, there is so much divisiveness among people. There is just one person with whom I have shared this, a monk [Volmar] whom I have tested and whom I have found reliable in his cloistered way of life. I have revealed all of my secrets to him and he has consoled me with the assurance that they are sublime and awe-inspiring.

I beg you, father, for God's sake, that you comfort me. Then I will be secure. More than two years ago, I saw you in my vision as a person who can look at the sun and not be afraid, a very bold man. And I cried because I blushed at my faintheartedness.

Gentle father, mildest of men, I rest in your soul so that through your word you can show me, if you wish, whether I should say these things openly or guard them in silence. For this vision causes me a lot of concern about the extent to which I should talk about what I have seen and heard. For a time, when I was silent about these things, I was confined to my bed with serious illnesses, so intense that I was unable to sit up. This is why I complain to you in such sadness: I will be so easily crushed by the falling wood growing from the root which sprang up in Adam through Satan's influence and cast him out into a world where there was no fatherland.

But now I lift myself up and hasten to you. I say to you: you will not be crushed. On the contrary, you constantly straighten the wooden beam and hold it upright; in your soul you are conqueror. But it is not only yourself that you hold upright; you raise the world up towards salvation. You are the eagle who gazes at the sun. . . .

b. *Book of Divine Works*

Second Vision: On the Construction of the World

Then a wheel of marvelous appearance became visible right in the center of the breast of the above-mentioned figure which I had seen in the midst of the southern air. On the wheel there were symbols that made it look like the image I had seen twenty-eight years ago—then it took the form of an egg, as described in the third vision of my book the *Scivias*. At the top of the wheel, along the curve of the egg, there appeared a circle of *luminous fire*, and under it there was another circle of *black fire*. The luminous circle was twice as large as the black one. And these two circles were so joined as to form but a single circle. Under the black circle appeared another circle as of *pure ether*, which was as large as the two other circles put together. Under this ether circle was seen a circle of *watery air*, which in size was the same as the circle of luminous fire. Beneath this circle of watery air appeared another circle of *sheer white clear air*, which looked to be as tough as a sinew of the human body. The circle was the same size as the circle of black fire. Both circles, too, were so joined as to appear to be but a single circle. Under this sheer white clear air, finally, there appeared still another *thin stratum of air*, which at times seemed to raise up high, light clouds and then again deep-hanging dark clouds. At times the stratum of air seemed to extend over the entire circle. All six circles were joined together without a wide space between them. While the topmost circle exceeded the other spheres in light, the circle of watery air moistened all the other circles with dampness.

From the edge of the wheel's eastern side a line separating the northern zone from the other areas extended in a northerly direction as far as the edge of the western side. In addition, in the middle of the sphere of thin air was seen a sphere, which was equally distant all around from the sheer white and luminous air. The radius of the sphere had the same depth as the space extending from the top of the first circle to the outermost clouds, or we might say that this space extended from the distant clouds as far as the top of this sphere.

In the middle of the giant wheel appeared a human figure. The crown of its head projected upward, while the soles of its feet extended downward as far as the sphere of sheer white and luminous air. The fingertips of the right hand were stretched to the right, and those of the left hand were stretched to the left, forming a cross extending to the circumference of the circle. This is the way in which the figure had extended its arms.

At the four sides appeared four heads: those of a leopard, a wolf, a lion, and a bear. Above the crown of the figure's head, in the sphere of pure ether, I saw from the leopard's head that the animal was exhaling through its mouth. Its breath curved somewhat backward to the right of the mouth, became extended, and assumed the shape of a crab's head with a pair of pincers that formed its two feet. At the left side of the mouth the leopard's breath assumed the shape of a stag's head. Out of the crab's mouth there emerged another breath that extended to the middle of the space between the heads of the leopard and the lion. The breath from the stag's head extended as far as the middle of the space remaining between the leopard and the bear. All of these exhalations had the same length: the breath extending from the right side of the leopard's head to the crab's head; the breath stretching from the left side of the same mouth as far as the stag's head; the breath reaching from the stag's head to the middle of the space between the heads of the leopard and lion; and finally, the breath emerging from the mouth of the stag's head to the midst of the space between the heads of the leopard and lion.

All these heads breathed toward the above-mentioned wheel and the human figure.

Tenth Vision: On the End of Time

Then I saw, near the mountain and in the midst of the eastern region, a wheel of wonderful size that resembled a dazzling white cloud. To the east I saw a dark line on the left that extended obliquely to the right, looking like human breath. On the middle of the wheel and above this line another line appeared, as bright as the dawn. From the top of the wheel this line descended to the middle of the first line. The upper part of this half-wheel emitted a green glow from its left side to its midpoint while from its right side to its midpoint there was a reddish sheen. And this took place in such a way that both colors shared the same space. But the half of the wheel that lay obliquely under the line displayed a whitish color mixed with black.

And behold! In the midst of this wheel I saw again on top of the aforementioned line the figure that at the outset was named to me as "Love." But now I saw her adorned differently from the way in which she had earlier appeared to me. Her countenance shone like the sun, her clothing was a flaming kind of scarlet, and about her neck she had a golden ribbon adorned with costly gems. She wore shoes as radiant as the lightning.

Before the figure's face appeared a tablet that gleamed like crystal. And on it was the following inscription: "I shall display myself in beauty, shining like silver. For the Divinity, who is without any beginning, shines forth in great splendor." But everything that has a beginning is contradictory in its fearful existence; it cannot completely grasp God's mysteries.

The figure gazed at the tablet. And at once the line on which she was sitting sprang into motion. And at the point where the left side of this wheel was attached, the outer side of the wheel at once became somewhat watery for a narrow space and then—above the half of the divided wheel that lay obliquely under the line—it became reddish and finally pure and luminous. But the outer side of the wheel turned again cloudy and stormy near the end of that half of the wheel where the line was fastened.

And I heard a voice from heaven say unto me:

O human being, listen to and understand the words of the One who was and is here, and who is not subject to the inconstancy of the ages. Enclosed in God was that most ancient plan—the will to carry out each and every one of the divine works. Before even the days had their origin, God gazed upon these works like a sun ray because they were things that were to come. For God is One alone, and nothing can be added to the divine unity. Yet God foresaw that a certain future work would seek to usurp a resemblance to this unity. Therefore, God reacted negatively to that creature. For God is the unity that knows nothing similar to it. If this were not so, then God could scarcely be called "the One." On this account God thrust down the creature who improperly sought this unity. And thus every human soul endowed with reason exists as a soul that emerges from the true God. That soul should choose what is pleasing to it and reject whatever is displeasing. For the soul knows what is good and what is harmful.

Although God is One, God foresaw within the might of the divine heart a particular work that would be multiplied in a wondrous manner. This same God is that living fire by which souls live and breathe. God was before anything had its beginning and is both the origin and the age of ages. The present vision seeks to represent all these ideas. . . .

7. THE *LIFE* OF ANASTASIUS OF CLUNY, MONK AND HERMIT

In response to the religious currents that inspired the papal reform of the Church in the eleventh century, laymen and women of all backgrounds sought new ways to express their devotion to God. Some went on pilgrimage to the Holy Land in the decades before the First Crusade. Others abandoned promising secular careers to pursue new religious vocations. As a young man, Anselm of Bec (c. 1033–1109) weighed the virtue of entering a monastic community, founding a house for the poor on his family estate or retreating to live as a hermit in the wilderness of northern Europe. Even the vow of stability did not deter the spiritual impulses that made pious individuals restless in their search for the perfect life. The career of Anastasius of Cluny (c. 1020–85) embodies many of the religious tensions of the age. Born in Venice to a noble family, Anastasius abandoned the glories of the world to pursue a cloistered life at the abbey of Mont Saint-Michel in Normandy. Once he learned, however, that his abbot had purchased his office and was thus stained with the sin of simony, Anastasius abandoned the community to live in solitude on a remote island. His virtuous life soon attracted the attention of Abbot Hugh the Great of Cluny (r. 1049–1109), who in 1067 invited the hermit to his great abbey in Burgundy as a model of virtuous conduct for the hundreds of brethren who lived there. Anastasius lived at Cluny for many years, though he made periodic retreats into the Alps to celebrate the solemnity of Lent by himself. After a failed mission to preach among the Muslims of Spain sponsored by Pope Gregory VII (r. 1073–85), Anastasius returned to Cluny, but he could not resist the impulse to worship God in the remote wilderness, this time in the Pyrenees. Several years later, Abbot Hugh sent the hermit a letter inviting him back to Cluny. Anastasius complied but became sick and died en route. His body was buried in the church of Saint Martin in a small town called Doydes (modern Saint-Martin-d'Oydes, near Toulouse), where his tomb was the site of many miracles. The Life of Anastasius *written by Walter of Doydes in the twelfth century was a local product that apparently did not circulate beyond the small community that venerated the saint's relics.*

Source: trans. Scott G. Bruce, *Vita sancti Anastasii auctore Galtero*, in J.-P. Migne, ed., *Patrologia Latina* (Paris: Imprimerie Royale, 1882), vol. 149, cols. 423–32. Latin.

Walter of Doydes's Life of Saint Anastasius

Here begins the prologue.

1. Walter to Peter, subdeacon of the church of Doydes, and to his brother Bernard, may the Lord bring about complete devotion and prosperity in all things. You have urged me to entrust to the reed of memory for the religious edification of generations to come the life of holy Anastasius the confessor, and all the while you have pleaded ever more forcefully for immediate results. But I do not see how I can endure the task without difficulty for I lack the necessary skills. The life of a holy man should not seem to be impaired due to defects in the quality of its author, but rather celebrated in its greatness. I do not, however, want to seem to go against your request, which I ought to obey in its entirety. So although I am not really capable and the dryness of my style dissuades me, I will attempt it, safe in the protection of your bidding. For truly if I am anything, if I can accomplish anything, I should attribute it to the Lord. Since, moreover,

I claim to be your friend, it is not fitting that, if I am able to be of service to you in any way, I should omit to do so. As a wise man once said: friendship should consist only of willingness in asking and constant desire in obeying. Genuine loyalty approaches this and has the power to compel, even if all of the aforesaid qualities are absent. To that, another factor can be added, namely simple devotion, which, even if all the other aforesaid qualities are absent, has the power to compel that I apply myself boldly to your request. For while you impose on me a responsibility for such a labor, you are also showing consideration for the moral edification of generations to come in as much as you desire that to the praise and honor of God, the life of Anastasius, the holy confessor, so full of glory, be laid open so that it may be an example to future generations and also a testament to the holiness of this man. Therefore I ask and implore with all my strength that if I have investigated anything insufficiently through neglect, or left out anything through a deficiency of my intelligence, or if I have added anything worthy of being pruned back, the reader should not hesitate to add what he perceives to be more suitable or to cross out with a sideways stroke of the pen what he judges to be in need of correction. In the end, the loyalty of my petitioners will excuse my faults. As I have often said already, they urged me to undertake a work that my distrust of my own skill had advised me against.

Here begins the life of the glorious Anastasius.

2. The most glorious Anastasius, confessor of God, was born in Venice to a noble mother and father. Renowned with respect to his lineage, he shined forth according to the values of this world. From his cradle he was reborn by the water of baptism. At an early age he was drawn by his parents to the study of letters. He applied himself with such industry that he seemed to be fully steeped in knowledge as much in Greek literature as in Latin. For this reason, he was outstanding in talent, learned in speech, adorned with good conduct, and amiable in all respects, so much so that they who had given birth to such a son would be called fortunate. But because the man of God had read in the Bible that the wisdom of the world is foolishness before God and had heard Truth himself saying in the Gospel: "Unless one renounces all that he possesses, he cannot be my disciple" [Luke 14:33], not without divine grace, he began to recall these words to mind and at the same time to dwell on them, for he knew that he would receive a severe punishment if he forsook heavenly concerns for worldly ones. After considering these things for a long time, he decided at last that he would consign himself to a monastic way of life so that he might do penance for his sins. But since it is shameful to look back once your hand is on the plow and to make a twisted and useless furrow, the holy man Anastasius wanted first to mortify himself with fasts, vigils and prayers, so that in this way he could find out whether, once he had adopted the custom of monks, he would be able to persist at the proposed vocation without faltering. Therefore he first separated

himself from wine, from which comes lust, and he began to fast on Wednesdays and Fridays but in such a way that he nevertheless ate meat from time to time. He busied himself frequently with prayer and vigils.

3. After he had subdued his flesh in this manner for a considerable amount of time and was already beginning to master it according to his good plan, he rejected meat altogether. Then he began to apply himself all the more to vigils and prayers with the result that he was fasting all week long. But after he subjected himself to this degree of mortification for a time, he was so emboldened, that he seemed to himself steadfast and equal to his plan. Therefore he decided to fulfill his plan and bring it to completion. He abandoned his parents, his home and his family and sought out a suitable place to adopt the custom of monks. He came to the English Channel to a place called Port of Hercules that is also known by the name "Mont Saint-Michel in Danger of the Sea" [modern Mont Saint-Michel in Normandy]. There he found a large group of monks who were devout in all ways, except that their abbot had obtained his office through simony, and there Anastasius received his desired habit. But the man of God was unaware of the simony of the abbot. It happened, however, that a year later, as he was sitting with a certain brother after a sermon concerning the confirmation of the soul, a question was referred to them concerning the life of the holy fathers and after they had argued for a long time the discussion was finally directed to the abbot. The man of God, Anastasius, then learned that the abbot was a simoniac and had assumed his office because of all of the money that he had given. He [Anastasius] was exceedingly sad and maintained that he had been misled by a diabolical deception, in as much as he had sought out a fitting place for his plan and had nearly fallen into the snare of the evil enemy! He abandoned the monastery and went to a certain island in the mouth of the aforesaid channel, to a church of Mary, the mother of God. There he began a solitary existence and withdrew to fast, and to perform vigils and prayers in solitude.

4. He was only there for a short time before his life of exceptional conduct made him renowned and talk of it spread far and wide. A venerable abbot by the name of Hugh presided over the monastery of Cluny at this time. He was accustomed to traveling with many of his monks for the purpose of visiting monastic houses and exhorting the brethren who were serving God in many remote places. It happened that he came to the English Channel where he heard word of the life and conduct of the man of God, Anastasius. The abbot sent two of his brethren to the island and to the aforesaid church and sent word to the man of God that he should come out for the sake of conversation, for Hugh had heard about his good way of life and desired to see him. When he heard of the arrival of the venerable abbot, Anastasius went forth to greet him with great joy. The abbot received him with honor and questioned him eagerly concerning his life and conduct. And when he heard everything from him, including how,

because of simony, Anastasius had left the monastery in which he had received the habit, and had comprehended the hermit's intention, the abbot was utterly delighted about his perfect way of life and encouraged him by whatever means he could in his service to God. Over the next few days, the abbot made reference frequently to the life and conduct of the brethren of Cluny. He instructed the man of God and asked him many times to come with him to Cluny where he would be able to fulfill his vow and provide an example of excellent conduct to the rest of the monks. The man of God, Anastasius, agreed to his request and accompanied him back to Cluny where he fostered great affection and a sense of shared humility among all of the brethren. He loved them all equally and guided them all in the service of God by the example of his own life. For a long time he led an extraordinary life among them and offered himself as a model of virtuous conduct. Indeed, when the rest of the brethren hastened off to the refectory once the signal was given for a meal, the man of God remained at prayer. While the others slept, he rose and prayed on his knees for most of the night. He was content to live on bread and water and partook of them sparingly. Once a year, he left the monastery to celebrate Lent in lonely wastelands or on precipitous mountainsides and mortified himself severely by prayers, fasts, vigils and genuflections.

5. At about this time, Anastasius went to Spain at the request of our holy father, Pope Gregory VII, and the insistence of venerable Hugh, his abbot, to preach to the Muslims. After the celebration of the liturgy of the mass, he wanted to walk through a burning pyre to prove the certainty of the Christian faith and to destroy the harsh cruelty of the Muslims there. But the Muslims were not eager to agree to his proposition, for it was clear that if he emerged unharmed, then they might flee to the grace of baptism. But since they did not want to be brought back from the blindness and harshness of their hearts by any measure, Anastasius shook off the dust from his feet onto them and returned to his own monastery. It happened, however, that nearly seven years after his return, the venerable abbot wanted to go to Aquitaine to encourage certain brothers, lay-men and nobles, who wished to renounce the world and enter the monastic way of life. He wanted the man of God, Anastasius, to accompany him, for indeed he was learned in the divine scriptures and effective in his encouragement and edification of the brethren. After they had traveled through a great part of Aqui-taine and exhorted the brethren there, at last they came to the region of Toulouse, where they were about to receive a count from the town of Appamia with his wife and sons in the monastic order. Then the time approached when the man of God, Anastasius, was accustomed to celebrate Lent in lonely places or on steep heights. He became increasingly anxious and meditated on it day and night until at last he chose the nearby Pyrenees mountains as the most fitting place for him to celebrate Lent and to embrace for a time the life of a hermit. The abbot gave

consent to his prayers reluctantly because he was a support and like a pillar to the other brethren. But because the abbot recognized his steadfastness in the service of God, he did not wish to delay his good vow. Therefore, compelled and saddened, he granted Anastasius's petition. And when they reached their agreement, the venerable abbot, weeping and raining tears and sobs onto his neck, asked Anastasius to remember him and to intercede for him and the rest of the brethren before God. Bidding him farewell for the last time, the abbot returned with his brethren to the monastery.

6. Therefore, the man of God, Anastasius, who desired only to fulfill his vow, made his way to the mountains with great joy. As he approached and was finally able to have an unobstructed view of particular sites, he chose to live on the highest mountain, which is called Abriscola, because in the range in which it is located, it towered over all of the other peaks. Therefore, he left the one monk who had accompanied him at the foot of the mountain and climbed up alone. There he constructed a small hut out of branches and also an altar, where he would perform mass. Then amidst never-ending snowstorms and cold, he was serving God and busying himself constantly with fasts, vigils, and prayers. He needed nothing to eat except for bread baked in ashes and water, which he received in rations from the monk whom he had left down the mountain. But after he had persisted in these activities for some time and reports of his way of life were heard in the surrounding region, many people came and gathered around him to hear the word of life from him and to learn about his astonishing way of life. They supported him with worldly goods, while he refreshed them with divine nourishment. But the man of God received absolutely nothing from them for the needs of his body for he who refused to earn a living from the Gospel likewise did not seek to be entertained by the people. Therefore he distributed everything that was offered [to him] to the poor through the agency of certain brothers whom he knew to be outstanding and whom he considered to be suitable for the task.

7. But meanwhile, while he was striving to please God alone and was enflamed with passion for this with all of the eagerness of his mind, the devil—that ancient enemy, author of harm and adversary of the human race—began to begrudge his virtuous activities and sought day and night for a place to steal in and harm him. But since the devil discovered nothing at all that he could filch from the record of Anastasius's deeds and since he had no power over him, he plotted a way to drive him from his cell. Therefore it happened that on a certain day when his prayers were done, when the man of God, Anastasius, left his cell and was sitting outside with two brothers who had come to visit him, the devil appeared and set fire to his cell and to the altar, which he had built for the celebration of the mass. But the man of God was watching and when he saw the fire he recognized the snares of the unspeakable enemy. Rising from there and making a stand at the

very threshold of the cell, he ordered the devil to withdraw and made the sign of the cross before the fire. The devil withdrew at his command and the fire was extinguished at the sign of the cross. After news of this event circulated, almost all of the local people began to come to him and to commend themselves to his prayers and even to seek penance for their sins from him. Indeed, for the three or more years that he stayed in that inhospitable place so many people hastened to him that all of the mountains around seemed to shine with light from the candles that were burned before his cell by his visitors. Indeed, he told them often that he was not worthy of their attention, that it was a monk from whom they were seeking penance, and that he did not have permission to preach or to receive penitents. But what use was this when they arrived so rapidly and invited him to preach with tears and prayers?

8. But when God wanted to reward his labor and summon him back from the workhouse of the flesh to receive a greater crown, he desired Anastasius's mortal life to come to an end in monastic obedience. Therefore it happened that the venerable Hugh, the aforesaid abbot of the church of Cluny, burned with the desire to see his brother, for his presence benefited the other monks and his conduct fortified them. Moreover, the abbot felt his absence. So he sent a letter to him through the hands of certain brothers, summoning him back to the monastery of his brethren:

> To my most beloved brother Anastasius, your brother Hugh, a sinner, sends greetings and unto the resurrection the glorious society of the elect. I am amazed, dearest brother, that I have heard nothing from you for so long and have received no word concerning your life. I send word to your desire that, if it seems good to you, you should come down from the mountains to visit the brethren, so that, as I said, your missed presence may strengthen and exhort them. . . . Farewell, and pray for your brothers.

When he received the letter from his blessed father abbot, the man of God, Anastasius, was overjoyed and returned thanks to God that he would deem him worthy to call back to his brothers.

9. And then he came down from that wild place and arrived at a town called "At the True Body of Antoninus, the Martyr" and also known by the name Fredelas [modern Pamiers, south of Toulouse]. There the people asked him to help them move the body of the blessed martyr to a new place. As he was readying himself at their request, a sick man who had suffered from fevers for a long time presented himself to him. And once the man of God had sprinkled him with holy water that he had blessed and made the sign of the cross on his forehead, he was healed and it was as if he had never been sick. He sprinkled many people who were suffering from illness with this holy water and restored them all to health.

10. Therefore, when rumor of his departure spread, a crowd of people gathered from all around. They grieved and lamented aloud that they were going to be abandoned by such a great man, who comforted them in distress and protected them in adversity. They pleaded him with tears and wailing not to leave behind those whom he had been accustomed to assisting and whom he had not neglected to refresh with the nourishment of the divine word. But the reward for his labor was approaching and the man of God wanted to obey the summons of his father abbot so that he might earn his crown through monastic obedience. Not even bouts of fever, which seriously afflicted him, could call him back from this goal. Therefore, after addressing them with words of divine admonition and exhortation, he departed and went as far as a place called Doydes [modern Saint-Martin-d'Oydes, near Toulouse]. There his fevers grew stronger and he became gravely ill, so much so that he was certain that this illness would bring about the death of his body. As a result, when he was asked to lie still to soothe his pain awhile or to bathe to cool himself down, he denied himself both comforts, adding the explanation that from the time that he adopted the monastic life, he had never used a bath nor, indeed, had he ever furnished water for the washing of his feet and head. When the course of his race had been run and in anticipation of seizing the crown of justice in the company of the saints, the monk, hermit and confessor traveled to the Lord on 16 October. His holy body, moreover, was buried with solemnity in the church of Saint Martin, where as evidence of his sanctity, at his tomb many miracles took place very shortly thereafter with the help of God. But, lest we court displeasure if we relate at length every single story, we will now strive to relate a few anecdotes in succession, even at the expense of leaving many untold.

11. A certain young woman was possessed by three demons, who tormented her so much that they had now rendered her mute. She was led to many shrines of the saints so that she might recover her health and the demons responded at length that they would not abandon the body that they occupied unless they were led to the body of the aforesaid blessed confessor Anastasius. Therefore, those who were leading the woman from place to place discussed among themselves where they might discover it and they sought out the tomb in which the body of the saint was at rest. Indeed up to this time it was not known to many people because he had only recently departed from the world. Therefore, when they had heard that it was hidden away in the church of Saint Martin in Doydes, they bound the woman with ropes and led her there. As they approached the tomb, the demons screamed and called out: "Why do you burn us, Anastasius? Stop this torment and we will depart! Stop this scourging and we will take leave of this body that we have occupied. We have been led to many bodies of the saints and we have departed from none of them having been scourged like this! You alone burn us! You alone torment us! You are the only one who can do

us harm!" Therefore, dragging her with their hands, they pulled her into the church and laid her upon the tomb of the blessed confessor. Moreover, everyone who was present prayed on bent knee with tears, so that God might deign to show the power of his mercy to everyone there and to free this woman as a warrant to the sanctity of his confessor. They had hardly completed the prayer and behold the demons went forth from this young woman. Rising, she was truly able to speak unhindered and bore witness to the fact that she had been freed and nothing of the evil that she had endured remained.

12. Indeed, there was a woman who had been blind for seven years. After she had been led there and stood before the tomb of the holy confessor during the celebration of the night office, she regained her sight once the Gospel was read during this ceremony. Moreover, a certain priest who was struggling with madness was led to the same place bound in chains and ropes in order to restore his health. Whenever a brain-fit would befall him, if he was able to grab somebody, he would tear at that person with his teeth and nails. Once he had spent three vigils before the tomb of the blessed confessor, he was restored to health and departed free from every trace of madness and never again did he endure any recurrence of his old illness.

8. PETER ABELARD'S *THEOLOGY*

Peter Abelard (1079–1142) provoked a storm of criticism in 1120 when readers first came across his On the Divine Unity and Trinity, *a treatise that he subsequently expanded, renaming it his* Christian Theology. *As he explains in his* Story of My Misfortunes (Doc. 17), *Abelard was accused by rival teachers, in particular Alberic of Rheims and Lotulf of Novara, of expounding heretical interpretations of Christian belief at a church council held at Soissons, in March or April 1121. In this initial version of his treatise, known to scholars as the* Theologia 'Summi boni,' *Abelard sought to offer a rationally acceptable explanation of the Christian doctrine of there being three divine persons in one God, namely the Father, the Son, and the Holy Spirit. His argument that these three divine persons each signified one of three divine attributes was not controversial in itself. At about the same time, Hugh of St-Victor (d. 1141) composed a treatise* On the Three Days, *which also spoke about the power, wisdom, and benignity of God as manifest through the works of creation. Abelard's approach was to focus, not on the natural world as the medium for experiencing the divine, but on language as the medium through which we frame all our conceptions of God. In the excerpts from the* Theologia 'Summi boni' *below, we read both the opening statement of Abelard's argument about God, based on the importance of balancing power with both wisdom and benignity, as well as a sample of his argument about how we can describe the relationship between God the Son, as the eternal Word of God, and God the Father. Abelard uses the example of how language is so often shaped by social convention, by quoting examples of polite ways of describing sex and defecation as a way of saying that words about God have to be appropriate. He dropped these examples when he rewrote this account in his* Christian Theology *of how we might explain the relationship between the eternal Word of God and God the Father. Abelard, however, retained the argument that divine wisdom was related to divine power in the same way as wisdom, "a kind of power, namely that of discernment," was related to omnipotence. William of St-Thierry (whom we know was present at the Council of Soissons in 1121) renewed his criticism of Abelard's* Theologia *in a letter and treatise that he sent to Bernard of Clairvaux during Lent 1140, provoking Bernard to compose his own critique of Abelard's teaching in a letter addressed to Pope Innocent II (r. 1130–43). Abelard initially sought to defend himself against these accusations at the Council of Sens, held on 25 May 1141, after which he sought leave to appeal to Rome. In the meantime, Bernard secured a hostile papal edict, issued on 16 July 1141, excommunicating both Abelard and his disciple, Arnold of Brescia, on grounds of heresy.*

Source: trans. Constant J. Mews, from Peter Abelard, *Theologia 'Summi boni,'* ed. Eligius-Marie Buytaert and Constant J. Mews, Corpus Christianorum Continuatio Mediaevalis 13 (Turnhout: Brepols, 1987), 1.1–4 and 3.79, pp. 86–88 and 191–92. Latin.

1. What the Distinction of Persons Is About

The perfection of the supreme good, which is God, Christ the Lord, the incarnate wisdom of God, has carefully distinguished with three names when he called the unique and singular, completely undivided and simple divine substance by three names, Father, Son and Holy Spirit, for three reasons.

2. What the Names of the Persons Signify

The Father is so called according to that particular potency of his majesty which is omnipotence, by which he can carry out whatever he wishes, since nothing is able to resist him. He has said that the Son is the same divine substance according to the distinction of his wisdom by which he can judge and discern all things truly, so that nothing can be hidden, through which he might be deceived. He has called it the Holy Spirit according to the grace of his benignity, by which God does not scheme any evil but is ready to save all; not considering the merits of our weakness, he distributes the gifts of his grace to us, and those whom justice cannot save, mercy redeems. This is what it is for God to be three persons, that is Father, Son, and Holy Spirit, as if we should say that the divine substance is powerful, wise, benign, or rather to be that power, that wisdom, that benignity. In these three things, namely power, wisdom and benignity, the complete perfection of good consists, and whatever of these is considered to be minimized without the others. For someone who is powerful, if he does not know how to behave according to the measure of reason, his power is destructive and harmful. Someone wise and careful in action, but not able to act at all, lacks efficacy. If someone is powerful and wise, but not at all benign, he is much more prone to do harm, in as much as he is able to act from power and cunning to do what he wants; yet he who is not moved by the spirit of benignity does not offer hope to others for any of his benefits. It is clear that one in whom these three things occur together, who can carry out what he wishes, and wishes well as one who is benign, and does not exceed the measure of reason through foolishness, is clearly truly good and perfect in all things. This distinction of the trinity is not only suited to describe the perfection of supreme good, but benefits many in persuading humanity of the religion of divine worship. So the very incarnate wisdom of God has articulated this most fully in his preaching. Indeed there are two things that make us completely subject to God, namely fear and love. Power and wisdom generate fear in particular, since we know that he can punish mistakes and from him nothing can be concealed. But his benignity belongs to love, so that one we consider most benign, we love most fully. From this, it is certain that he wishes to avenge impiety, because the more equity pleases him, the more iniquity displeases him, just as it is written: *You have loved justice and have hated iniquity* [Psalm 44:8]. . . .

3. On the Generation of the Divine Word

If anyone should say that the Father can clearly be understood to be the beginning of the Son according to nature, not according to the sequence of existence, in that the Son is born from the Father, we cannot fault the sense of this. We think, however, that these words should be completely abandoned, because whatever way we might understand the Son of God to have beginning, that is to begin or have begun, we seem to remove eternity from him. And whatever sound meaning there is to these words for someone who says this, he can easily beget scandal in them, since in normal usage something is not said to have a beginning or to have begun other than being brought from non-being to being. But neither is it appropriate to say all things that are true, since reverence for being upright that avoids not just obscenity in actions but also of words, may often lead to using metaphors for the correct words, keeping the same sense. This may be when in common speech there is something shameful that might offend listeners, so that something shameful is not spoken of too explicitly, as when for "to have sex with," we say "to know," as in that passage of the prophet, "Adam knew his wife" [Genesis 4:1], or if we say "release" for "shit," namely to purge the bowel. If then we change correct words in creation when they give offence for something, how much more should it be abhorred in God, when words seem to do damage in something to his ineffable dignity. So, when we believe and proclaim that God is everywhere, no-one presumes to say that he is in an impure place, so that we might either call that place a latrine or assign a place by some other name of a specific impurity. But, as Boethius says [in the *Consolation of Philosophy*], "by the authority of Plato, words should be cognate to the things about which they speak," so that suitable words are thought of to match the dignity of something, particularly in relation to God, derogating in nothing of his majesty. So neither is it appropriate for a beginning to be assigned to him, nor can anything be said to exist before him, because he alone is before all things and the supreme beginning.

9. HUGH OF ST-VICTOR ON SACRED LEARNING: THE *DIDASCALICON*

Hugh of St-Victor (d. 1141) was a leading theologian, biblical exegete, and mystic of the early twelfth century. A contemporary of Peter Abelard, Hugh was a leading figure of the important school of the abbey of St-Victor in Paris, and his writings were instrumental in calling for the need to understand the literal, historical sense of scripture before undertaking its allegorical and moral interpretation. He was especially committed to the idea that an understanding of God's revelations to Jews and Christians entails an understanding of historical time, both ancient and contemporary. Hugh therefore sought the aid of contemporary Jews in order to understand the literal sense of the Hebrew Scriptures, and he inspired others, most notably Andrew of St-Victor (d. 1175) and Herbert of Bosham (fl. 1162–89), to study the Hebrew language for this exegetical purpose.

Hugh wrote many works that have survived, but the most widely read was the Didascalicon, *a neologism of a title that reflects contemporary fascination with Greek learning. The first part of the work (Books 1–3) provides a guide for the student of philosophy (see also Doc. 20), while the second part of the work (Books 4–6) provides a guide to sacred learning. The extract below is from Book 5. The section on reading Scripture specifies a sequence of disciplines of study (history, allegory, and tropology) and gives for each discipline the proper order in which to read the biblical books.*

Source: trans. Franklin T. Harkins, in *Interpretation of Scripture: Theory*, ed. Franklin T. Harkins and Frans van Liere (Hyde Park, NY: New City Press, 2013), 150–51, 161–63. Latin.

Book 5, Chapter 1: On Certain Properties of Sacred Scripture and the Manner of Reading It

That we have discussed in the preceding book the number, arrangement, and names of the divine writings in so many different ways should not be onerous for the eager student, for it is often the case that when these smallest things are unknown or overlooked, one's knowledge of great and useful things is obscured. The student, therefore, should prepare himself once and for all so that—with the first principles always ready at hand in such a way that certain conclusions become easily accessible—he will subsequently be able to run the road before him with an unencumbered stride and will not need to search for the fundamentals anew in each and every book he reads. Having set forth these basics [in Book 4], we will here provide an orderly treatment of other matters that seem useful for the task of reading Scripture.

Chapter 2: On the Threefold Understanding

First of all, it must be known that Sacred Scripture has a threefold mode of signifying and of being understood: namely, according to history, allegory, and tropology. Everything in the divine writings should not, however, be twisted in such a way that every passage is thought to contain history, allegory, and tropology simultaneously. Even if this threefold mode can aptly be found in many passages, it is nevertheless difficult—if not impossible—to see it everywhere. "With the zither and other such musical instruments certainly not all the parts that are touched or struck ring out with some melodious sound; rather, only the strings do so. Nevertheless, the other constituent parts of the zither have been made in order to hold together and stretch tightly those strings that the musician plays for the production of mellifluous refrains" [Isidore of Seville, *Quaestiones in Vetus Testamentum*, preface]. Likewise, in the divine writings certain things have been set forth that should be understood in a strictly spiritual sense, others that are devoted to the dignity of morals, and still others that have been said according to the simple sense of history. There are some things in Scripture, moreover, that can suitably be interpreted historically, allegorically, and tropologically. Thus, in an extraordinary way all of Sacred Scripture has been so suitably prepared and arranged in all its parts through the wisdom of God that everything is contained in it either, in the manner of strings, resounds with the sweetness of spiritual understanding, or—containing signs of sacred mysteries scattered throughout historical narratives and passages that seem entirely literal, and joining them together as one, in the same way that the hollowed-out wooden soundbox of the zither unites the strings that are stretched over it—receives the sound of the strings into itself and returns it sweeter still to the ears of its hearers. The strings alone, then, do not produce the final sound; it is also determined by the shape and size of the wooden soundbox. So too honey that is in the honeycomb is more pleasing, and whatever is sought with greater exertion is found with greater satisfaction. It is necessary, therefore, to interpret Sacred Scripture in such a way that we seek neither history everywhere, nor allegory everywhere, nor tropology everywhere, but rather suitably assign each of these modes in its proper place exactly as reason requires. Frequently, however, in one and the same scriptural passage all three modes can be found at the same time, as when the truth of the historical narrative [*historiae ueritas*] introduces by means of allegory something pertaining to one of the sacred mysteries and simultaneously reveals by means of tropology what the reader should do. . . .

Chapter 9: On the Four Stages

The life of the just person is trained in four things, which serve as certain stages through which he is raised to future perfection: namely, reading or learning, meditation, prayer, and action. Then follows a fifth, contemplation, in which—as if by a certain fruit of the preceding stages—the just person enjoys even in this life a foretaste of the future rewards of good work. Hence, the Psalmist, when describing and commending the decrees of God, immediately adds: "In obeying them the reward is great."

The first of these five stages, that is, reading, is for beginners; the last, that is, contemplation, is for the perfect. And the more one ascends through the stages in between, the more perfect he will be. For example, the first, reading, imparts understanding; the second, meditation, offers guidance; the third, prayer, directs one's course; the fourth, action, strives toward the goal; the fifth, contemplation, arrives at it. If, therefore, you read and gain understanding and know what you should do, this marks the beginning of the good, but it is still insufficient for you because you are not yet perfect. Climb, then, into the ark of counsel and meditate on how you might effectively carry out what you have learned you should do. For many people have knowledge, but there are few who know how they should understand. Furthermore, because the advice of humans is powerless and unavailing without divine assistance, incite yourself to prayer and seek the help of him without whom you can do nothing good, so that his grace—which has illuminated your path by going before you—might also, by following you, direct your steps along the road of peace and bring what still only exists in your will to completion as a good work. It remains, then, for you to prepare yourself for good work, so that you might merit to undertake in your actions what you have asked for in your prayers. God wishes to act or work with you; He does not compel you, but rather helps you. If you act alone, you accomplish nothing; if God acts alone, you merit nothing. Therefore, God should act so that you might be able to act; and you should act so that you might merit something. Good action or work is the road along which one advances toward life. He who runs down this road seeks to obtain life. "Be strong and act courageously" [Joshua 1:18]. The road has its reward. As often as we become exhausted from exertion along this road, we are illuminated by the grace of divine care in such a way that we "taste and see that the Lord is sweet" [Psalm 33:9]. And thus what we said above comes about, namely, that contemplation arrives at what prayer strives toward.

You see, then, how perfection runs to meet those who advance upward through these stages, so that the person who remains below cannot be perfect. Our objective, therefore, should always be to ascend; but because the instability of our present life is so great that we cannot remain in one place, we are often compelled to look back at stages through which we have already advanced. . . . Our principal concern, then, ought to be ascent, not descent.

Chapter 10: On the Three Kinds of Students

It has clearly been shown, I think, that the objective of those who are advanced and have pledged themselves to something more is not the same as that of beginners. But just as something has been rightly permitted to the advanced that beginners cannot do at all without blame, so too something is required of beginners to which the advanced are no longer obliged. Now, therefore, I return to fulfill my promise, namely, to make clear how Sacred Scripture ought to be read by those who still search for knowledge alone in it.

There are some people who seek knowledge of Sacred Scripture in order to accumulate wealth, obtain honors, or acquire fame. Their intention should be pitied to the degree that it is perverse. There are still others who take pleasure in hearing the words of God and gaining knowledge of his works not because they are salvific, but simply because they are miraculous. They wish to scrutinize hidden realities and to learn novel things; they want to know much but to do nothing. They marvel at God's power in vain since they do not love his mercy. How else can I describe what these people do than that they transform divine revelation into idle tales? This is why we usually attend plays in the theater and music concerts, namely, so that we might feed our eyes, not our minds or souls. I think that people of this sort should not be refuted as much as they should be helped. Their wills are certainly not malicious, merely shortsighted.

But there are other people who read Sacred Scripture so that, according to the teaching of the apostle [Peter], they might be prepared to give everyone who asks a reason for the faith in which they have been established, so that they might boldly refute enemies of the truth, teach the less learned, discern the way of truth more perfectly themselves, and understand more profoundly and love more dearly the hidden things of God. The zeal of these people should be praised and deserves imitation.

There are, then, three kinds of people who study Sacred Scripture: the first should be pitied, the second should be helped, and the third should be praised. But because we aim to advise all three classes of students, we want what is good to be increased in all and what is perverse to be transformed. We want all to understand what we say and all to do what we encourage.

10. A TWELFTH-CENTURY TEXTBOOK: PETER LOMBARD'S *SENTENCES*

Peter Lombard (c. 1100–60) taught theology at Paris in the middle of the twelfth century. His four books of Sentences *were written as a compendium to his teachings and quickly assumed the status of a textbook in the schools. They were commented upon and glossed by virtually every major theologian of note from the late twelfth century onwards. In the first three books, Peter sets out to explain for his readers the mysteries of God's nature, the creation and fall of angels and humankind, the mystery of Christ's incarnation, and the virtues and precepts that good Christians ought to follow in their attempt to imitate Christ. Book 4, which was the most widely commented upon of the books, opens with a reference to the distinction of things and signs, before proceeding to offer a definition of sacrament. A defining feature of Peter's method, characteristic of the schools of the twelfth century, is to amass under a particular heading (capitalized below) a series of biblical passages and writings by the Church Fathers that address the problem posed by the heading. But unlike Peter Abelard, who did not explicitly resolve apparent contradictions among authorities (see Doc. 18), Peter Lombard does conclude the discussion with a final resolution.*

Distinction 17 deals with a question that had provoked much discussion in the schools, and which has never ceased to be of abiding relevance in Christianity—namely whether confession is necessary for the remission of sins. After a careful evaluation of the seemingly contradictory authorities, Peter proposes a simple solution to the controversy by positing a distinction and interdependence between the outward satisfaction and confession of the mouth and the inward confession that results from inner contrition. The issue would continue to be a locus of discussion, and it was only at the Fourth Lateran Council convened by Pope Innocent III (r. 1198–1216) in 1215 (Doc. 38) that annual auricular confession was mandated for the faithful.

Distinction 27 forms a crucial part of an extended consideration of the sacrament of marriage, which like penance attracted the attention of twelfth-century schoolmasters. Marriage is a union constituted by two people who are not prohibited by law from establishing it; its indivisibility consists in the inability of one partner to promise sexual continence or even to abstain from conjugal sex without the other's permission.

Source: trans. Giulio Silano, from Peter Lombard, *The Sentences: Book 4: On the Doctrine of Signs* (Toronto: Pontifical Institute of Mediaeval Studies, 2010), 94–97, 161–62. Latin.

Figure 2: Peter Lombard in the historiated initial "Q" for *Que* in a late twelfth-century manuscript of his *Sentences*. While the practice of decorating an initial letter began in the early Middle Ages, the sophistication of the artistry developed significantly over the course of the twelfth century, not least because of the vast number of works that were being written and copied. The representation of Peter Lombard at the beginning of his work could be compared to modern book jackets that feature an author on the back cover.

Source: British Library, MS Yates Thompson 17 fol. 42v. In accordance with the British Library's Catalogue of Illuminated Manuscripts in the Universal Public Domain.

Distinction XVII

CHAPTER 1 (92)

1. THREE QUESTIONS ARE PUT FORTH; FIRST, WHETHER SIN IS REMITTED WITHOUT CONFESSION.

Here arises a manifold question. And first it is asked whether a sin may be remitted to someone without satisfaction and confession by the mouth, but only by contrition of the heart. Second, whether at times it suffices to confess to God, without a priest. Third, whether a confession is effective which is made to a faithful lay person.

2. For in these matters even the learned are found to answer differently, because the doctors appear to have transmitted views regarding them which are various and almost contradictory. For some say that no one is cleansed from sin without confession by the mouth and satisfaction in deed, if he had time to do these things; others say that, before confession by the mouth and satisfaction, the sin is remitted by God at the heart's contrition, if the person has the intention to confess.

3. HE PROVES BY TESTIMONIES THAT SIN IS REMITTED IN CONTRITION ALONE.

Hence the Prophet: I said: I will confess against myself my injustice to the Lord, and you have remitted, etc. [Psalm 31:5]—Cassiodorus. In expounding this, Cassiodorus says: "I said," that is, "I deliberated within myself that I will confess, and you have remitted." So great is God's pity, that it remitted the sin at the mere promise [of confession]. For the intention is adjudged as deed."—Augustine, on the same text. Also Augustine: "He has not yet spoken, and only promises to speak, but the Lord remits [the sin], because to do this is to speak something in the heart. The voice is not yet issuing from the mouth for a man to hear the confession, but God already hears it."

4. Also: "A sacrifice to God is an afflicted spirit," etc. [Psalm 50:19]. And we read elsewhere: "At whatever hour the sinner shall turn and groan, he shall surely live, and not die"; it does not say "shall have confessed by the mouth, but shall turn and groan." From this, it is given to be understood that even if the mouth is silent, we are sometimes granted forgiveness. So it was that those lepers, whom the Lord had commanded to show themselves to the priests, were cleansed on the way, before they had come to the priests [cf. Luke 17:14–15]. By this, it is indicated that before we open our mouths to the priests, that is, confess our sins, we are cleansed from the leprosy of sin. Lazarus too is not first brought out of the tomb and then raised by the Lord, but comes outside alive after being raised within, so as to show that the raising of the soul precedes confession. For no one can confess who has not been raised, because "from the dead, as from one who is

not, confession perishes" [cf. Ecclesiastes 17:26]. And so no one confesses, unless he has been raised; but no one is raised, unless he is freed from sin, because sin is the death of the soul and, as the soul is the life of the body, so God is the life of the soul.—By these and many other authorities, it is proven that sin is remitted by compulsion alone, before confession or satisfaction.

5. BUT HE ALSO PROVES BY AUTHORITIES THAT, ON THE CONTRARY, SIN IS NOT REMITTED WITHOUT CONFESSION.

But those who deny it struggle with a determination of the authorities and, to undermine the view and support their own, they adduce the testimonies of authors.

6. For the Lord says through Isaiah: "Speak your iniquities, that you may be justified" [Isaiah 43:26].—Ambrose, in the book *On Paradise*. Also, Ambrose: "No one can be justified from sin, unless he has first confessed his sins."—the same, in a lenten sermon. The same: "Confession frees the soul from death; confession opens paradise; confession gives hope of salvation: because he who is not willing to confess his sin during his life does not merit justification. That confession which is done with repentance frees us. True penance is sorrow of the heart and bitterness of the spirit for the evils which one has committed."

7. JOHN THE GOLDEN-MOUTHED. Also John: "No one can receive God's grace, unless purged from all sin by the confession of penance, or by baptism" [quoting a fragment by Bishop Chromatius of Aquileia, a contemporary of Ambrose and Jerome].

8. Augustine, *On Penance*. Also Augustine: "Do penance as it is done in the Church. Let no one say to himself: I do it secretly and before God; God knows it and forgives me, because I do it in my heart. Was it then for no cause that it was said: "Whatever you shall loose on earth, shall also be loosed in heaven" [cf. Matthew 18:18]? Job says: "If I was ashamed to confess my sins before the people" [Job 31:33–34].—Ambrose. Also, Ambrose: "That fault can be forgiven which is followed by an admission of sins."

9. AUGUSTINE. Also Augustine, on that text: "Let not the deep swallow me, nor the pit close its mouth upon me" [Psalm 68:16]: "The pit is the depth of iniquity; if you have fallen into it, it will not close its mouth upon you, if you do not close your mouth." And so confess, and say: "From the depths I have cried out to you, O Lord" [Psalm 129:1], etc., and you will escape. It closes upon him who, in the deep, "despises," from which "dead man, as from one who is not, confession perishes" [Ecclesiastes 17:26].—The same: "No one receives forgiveness for a graver punishment, unless he has paid some penalty, even if far less than what was due. For the fullness of mercy is bestowed by God in such a way that the discipline of justice may not be abandoned."

10. JEROME, ON MALACHIAS. Also Jerome: "Let the sinner bemoan his own crimes and the people's; and let him enter the Church, out of which he had gone because of his sins; and let him sleep in sackcloth, so that he may

compensate by austerity of life for the past delights by which he had offended God."—By these and other authorities, they strive to assert that no one can be cleansed from sin, without oral confession and some payment of a penalty.

11. WITH WHICH VIEW OUGHT ONE TO AGREE. What, then, is to be felt concerning this? What to be held? Surely, that sins are blotted out by contrition and humility of heart, even without confession by the mouth and payment of outward punishment. For from the moment when one proposes, with compunction of mind, that one will confess, God remits; because there is present confession of the heart, although not of the mouth, by which the soul is cleansed inwardly from the spot and contagion of the sin committed, and the debt of eternal death is released.

12. And so those things which were said above about confession and penance either are to be referred to the confession of the heart and inward punishment, as that statement of Augustine which says that none obtains forgiveness, "unless he has paid some penalty, no matter how slight"; or are to be taken as being about outward punishment, and are to be referred to those who despise it or are negligent, as in that text: "Let no one say: I do it secretly," etc. For some are ashamed or neglect to confess their sins in this life, and so do not deserve to be justified.

13. For just as inward penance is enjoined upon us, so also are outward satisfaction and confession by the mouth, if they are possible; and so he is not truly penitent, who does not have the intention to confess. And just as the remission of sin is a gift of God, so also penance and confession through which sin is blotted out cannot be other than from God, as Augustine says: "He who confesses and repents, already has the gift of the Holy Spirit, because there cannot be confession of sin and punishment in a man from his own self. Indeed, when he is angered and displeased with himself, this cannot be without a gift of the Holy Spirit." And so it is necessary for a penitent to confess, if he has the time; and yet, before there is confession by the mouth, if there is the intention in the heart, remission is granted to him.

Distinction XXVII

CHAPTER 1 (63)

WHAT THINGS OUGHT TO BE CONSIDERED IN MARRIAGE.

After these matters, it is to be considered what marriage is, what is the efficient cause of marriage and the cause for the sake of which it is to be contracted, and what are the goods of marriage, and how carnal joining is excused because of them, and which persons may lawfully contract marriage. There are also many other things which are to be considered as to marriage, which we will present in a summary way.

WHAT IS MARRIAGE.

Nuptials, or marriage, are the marital joining of husband and wife of lawful standing, maintaining an undivided manner of life.—it pertains to the 'undivided manner' that neither may profess continence, or go off to pray, without the other's consent; and that, while they both live, the conjugal bond remains between them so that it is not lawful for them to join with others; and that each treat the other as he or she would himself or herself.—In this description is included only the marriage of the faithful who are of lawful standing.

1. ON THE CONSENT WHICH MAKES MARRIAGE.

The efficient cause of marriage is consent, and not just any kind, but one expressed in words, and not of future, but of present effect.—For if they consent as to the future, saying: I shall take you as my husband, and I you as my wife, this is not a consent which effects marriage. Also, if they consent in the mind, and do not express it in words or by other certain signs, such a consent does not make a marriage. But if they express in words what they do not will in their hearts, then, if there is no coercion or fraud, that obligation of words by which they consent, saying: "I take you as my husband, and I you as my wife," makes a marriage.

2. HE PROVES BY AUTHORITIES THAT CONSENT ALONE MAKES A MARRIAGE. That consent makes a marriage is proved by the authorities below.—Isidore. For Isidore says: "Consent makes marriage."—Nicholas. Also Pope Nicholas: "In accordance with the laws, let consent alone suffice of those whose joinings are at issue; if it alone should perhaps be lacking in their nuptials, all other things, even if celebrated together with coitus itself, are vain."—John Chrysostom, On Matthew. Also John Chrysostom: "It is not coitus that makes marriage, but the will; and so the separation of bodies does not dissolve it."—Ambrose, in the book *On Virgins*. Also Ambrose: "It is not the deflowering of virginity that makes marriage, but the conjugal pact."—From these words, it is clear that it is consent, that is, the conjugal pact, that makes marriage; and from that time on there is a marriage, even if carnal joining has not preceded or does not follow.

1. WHEN DOES A MARRIAGE BEGIN TO BE. The testimonies of the Saints prove that they are spouses from the very moment of espousals, in which the conjugal pact is expressed.—Ambrose, in the book *On Virgins*. For Ambrose says:

"When the conjugal union begins, the name of marriage is decreed. There is marriage when she is joined to her husband, not when she is known carnally by him."—Isidore, in the book *Etymologies*. Also Isidore: "Conjugal partners are more truly so called from the first faith of espousal, even though the sharing of the marital bed has not yet occurred between them."

2. AUGUSTINE, IN THE BOOK *ON THE CONJUGAL GOOD*. Also Augustine: "She [Mary] is called his [Joseph's] spouse because of her first faith of espousal, although he had not known her in the marriage bed, nor was ever to do so. But the term of spouse was not lost or false, where there never had been, nor was to be, any intermingling of the flesh. Because of this joining, both deserved to be called 'parents of Christ' (not only she as his mother, but also he as his father, as his mother's spouse), both such in mind, not in the flesh."—From these words, it is clearly shown that, from the time of the occurrence of a willing and marital consent, which alone makes marriage, the bride and groom are true marriage partners.

11. READING THE BIBLE: THE *GLOSSA ORDINARIA*

The Gloss (Glossa) or Ordinary Gloss (Glossa Ordinaria) on the Bible was the ubiquitous text of the central Middle Ages. First appearing in Laon in northern France in the first decades of the twelfth century, it consists of exegetical comments relating to individual words, phrases, or short passages of the biblical text. It differs from the continuous commentary in that it is designed to accompany the books of the Bible rather than to be written separately. The format and page layout of the Glossa Ordinaria are, therefore, distinctive: the manuscript page is divided into three columns, with the biblical text written in large letters in the central column, with lines left empty between the lines of the text, and glosses written in smaller letters in the left- and right-hand columns in close proximity to the words of Scripture they are glossing. Scholars agree that the innovator of this new type of commentary was Master Anselm of Laon (d. 1117), who taught at the cathedral school, where his brother Ralph may have assisted him. Peter Abelard, in a famous passage in his autobiography, recalls how he was first attracted to Laon on account of its reputation for learning, but left utterly unimpressed by Anselm's undeserved reputation (see Doc. 17). Following Anselm's pioneering method, the Gloss text seems to have stabilized in the 1130s. Between 1140 and 1220, a series of virtually identical manuscripts of the text were produced, chiefly in Paris, the intellectual hub of theological study.

The portion of the Glossa Ordinaria that is reproduced below concerns the Song of Songs, which was one of the most studied and allegorized books of the Bible, no doubt because of its highly evocative language. Among the most frequently referred to sources in the glosses are Origen of Alexandria (c. 185–254), Gregory the Great (c. 550–604), Apponius (sixth century), the Venerable Bede (c. 673–735), Alcuin (c. 735–804),

Hrabanus Maurus (c. 780–856), Haimo of Auxerre (mid-ninth century), Robert of Tomberlaine (c. 1010–c. 1090), and Anselm of Laon. A notable theme of the gloss on the Song of Songs is the allegorical reading of the song as concerning the relation between Old and New covenants—that is, between Judaism and Christianity.

Source: trans. Mary Dove, *The* Glossa Ordinaria *on the Song of Songs* (Kalamazoo, MI: Medieval Institute Publications, 2004), 1–2, 7–9, 134–35; slightly revised.

Prefaces

1. It should be noted that the bride is always at home, either in bed or some inner place, since she desires to remain with the bridegroom, as befits women. The bridegroom, as is customary for males, calls the beloved outside, to the vineyards or to other works of this kind, because it is no wonder if the church wishes, if at all possible, to bring up offspring for the Lord in peaceful tranquility. But the bridegroom in this temporal world afflicts the bride with frequent tribulations, by means of which she may attain to the everlasting realm in a state of greater purity, lest, if she meet with prosperity, delighted with dwelling in this present exile, she may sigh less sorely for her heavenly fatherland. [Bede]

2. In this work I seem to have found four personages: the bridegroom and his companions, the bride and young girls with her. Some things are said by the bridegroom, others are said by the bride, some by the young women, certain things by the bridegroom's companions. It is appropriate enough that at the celebration of a marriage there should be a number of young girls with the bride, and a crowd of young men with the bridegroom. Understand the bridegroom to be Christ, the bride the church, "without stain or wrinkle" [cf. Ephesians 5:27]. Understand the bridegroom's friends to be angels and those who "attain to the perfect man" [Ephesians 4:13]. The young girls are the throng of potential brides, to some degree having obtained salvation. From this book, moreover, the Gentiles have appropriated to themselves the epithalamium, and this song is classified as belonging to this genre, that is, "concerning the marriage-bed," in other words a song for a wedding. Poets write comedies based on epithalamia. [Origen]

1:1 Let him kiss me with the kisses of his mouth because
your breasts are better than wine

[marginal glosses]
"Let him kiss me with the kisses of his mouth" [glosses 1–9 all gloss these words]

1. Synagogue, "assembling together," as of [inanimate] stones; church, "congregation," as of rational creatures. Both, however, are part of the inheritance of

the just, having the same faith in and love for Christ in different ages, the former awaiting his presence still to come, the latter, receiving it, made his bride. [Bede; Hrabanus Maurus]

2. The voice of those heralding the coming of Christ, who pray to the father of the bridegroom. [Bede]

3. [The bride says:] "Let him touch me with the sweetness of his presence [Bede; Gregory], which I have often heard promised by the prophets, and as if bringing a kiss let him also receive the touch of my mouth, that is, questioning me concerning the way of salvation let him hear and instruct and bring the kiss of peace, making two people one. [Bede]

4. I desire a kiss, which was my redemption, because your teachings, the milk and nourishment of your children, are better than other forms of instruction, which kill rather than foster the simple, just as wine kills children."

5. The number of precepts she knows from his preaching are as it were the number of kisses she receives from his mouth. [Gregory]

6. [Gloss only found in the 1480 printed edition, not in manuscripts.] For just as two different bodies are joined in a kiss, so in the incarnation the two substances of divinity and humanity, utterly different, are united in an inseparable conjunction.

7. "To Kiss" is to put in place of "to reconcile," in the likeness of those who have withdrawn from their lords because of conflict but return, kiss and are kissed, and are perfectly reconciled, like the synagogue.

8. This race, distanced from its God through sin, wishes to be reconciled with him through the incarnation of the Son. [Apponius; Augustine]

9. She speaks in the fashion of a lover who for the very fervor of her love cannot avail herself of the accustomed order of speech.

"because your breasts are better than wine" [glosses 10 and 11 gloss these words]

10. As she prays, her prayer is answered, and seeing the bridegroom she speaks to him ["because your breasts," etc]. [Origen]

11. He speaks of the "breasts" of the bridegroom, a female term, so that from the very beginning of this song he may reveal himself to be speaking figuratively. [Bede]

[interlinear glosses, following the syntactical structure of the Latin text:]

12. "let him kiss" let him delight and assure [Anselm of Laon]

13. "me" human nature

14. "with the kisses of his mouth" with the incarnation of his son, which is as it were a foretaste of our union with God

15. "because your breasts are better than wine" because here [there is] assisting grace and the end is [eternal] life

16. [the bride says:] "your breasts: the teaching and refreshment of your presence, which is sweet" [Anselm]

17. "than wine" than the fervor of the Old Law [Bede], or any other code of instruction

6:9 *Who is this one who comes up like the dawn rising beautiful as the moon, excellent as the sun terrible as a line of battle assembled in the camps*

"Who is this one"

56. [Now that] the Gentile church [is] thus firmly established and on every occasion spread abroad through her many branches and led on through her stages and successions right up to the end of time, at the end of time the synagogue now gazing at the church, so very effective in the past and in the present and so widely spread, [and gazing at] so many wise men following one faith without schism, besides miracles performed by the living and the dead and many other arguments for the Christian faith, now convinced, penitent, and remorseful, says wonderingly "who is this one," etc.

"like the dawn rising"

57. The church becomes full dawn when she completely dispels the darkness of mortality and ignorance. Therefore at the judgment [it will be] still dawn, but in the kingdom [of heaven] there will be day, when [the Church] will have full sight of the true sun [Christ]. [Gregory the Great]

"beautiful as the moon, excellent as the sun"

58. In the night of this present life, in which the conditions of times are varied, [the Church] is compared to the moon, because now [the moon is] clear to the earth, now despised, now [the Church is] full of the brightness of virtues, now dishonored by the vices of the wicked men. In the future blessedness [of eternity], when there is no change in the state [of things], the righteousness will "shine like the sun" [Matthew 13:43]. [Bede]

"terrible as a line of battle assembled in the camps"

59. There are certain prelates ordained by the church who lay waste our faith with plausible speeches, striking terror into us.

60. The more perfectly the church arranges the order or virtues within herself, the more terrible she is to the powers of the air [the demons], or [the same applies to] any faithful soul. [Bede]

61. the voice of the synagogue wondering at the rising church ["who is this one," etc.] [Bede]

62. "comes up" extends through all parts of the world, limited neither in space nor time [Bede]

63. "like the dawn rising" because the rising of the true light in her after the darkness of ignorance is revealed to the world [Bede]

64. "beautiful as the moon" because illuminated by the sun of righteousness [the Church] floods the night of the world with the light of the Gospel [Bede]

65. "excellent as the sun" because [the Church] bears the image of the true sun within her, walking in all justice and holiness and truth [Bede]

66. "terrible" because no adversity has been able to prevent [the Church] from manifesting in herself both the beauty of the moon, in laborious travail, and of the sun, in the hope of recompense [Bede].

CHAPTER TWO

SCHOOLS, SCHOLARS, AND
THE LIBERAL ARTS

By the turn of the twelfth century, an increasing number of schools and masters in northern Europe were attracting students to the study of the liberal arts and sacred learning. Three types of schools flourished by the early decades of the twelfth century. The first and most common of these were monastic schools, such as the Benedictine monastery of Bec, made famous by the teachings of Lanfranc and Anselm, and the Augustinian abbey of St-Victor in Paris, which maintained a distinguished line of scholars from its founder William of Champeaux to Walter of St-Victor. Second, there were the cathedral schools such as Laon, Notre Dame, Rheims, and Chartres, which likewise flourished when they could boast powerful and charismatic teachers. A third kind of school, less frequent and more ephemeral than the first two, was a private school individually established by a successful master. Peter Abelard did this more than once. While most of these schools were in northern Europe, mention should also be made of Toledo, where a distinguished group of scholars (Christian, Jewish, and Muslim) copied, translated, and studied the philosophical and mathematical works from Greek and Arabic texts; their translations later traveled north and deeply influenced the schools and scholars in France and England (see Chapter 9). The sources in this chapter illustrate the teachers, students, and attitudes toward learning that helped establish the "academic" culture out of which emerged the first universities and an agreed-upon curriculum of studies.

12. THE LETTER OF GOSWIN OF MAINZ TO
HIS STUDENT WALCHER

The renewed study of the liberal arts that crystallized in the twelfth century has long been known to reflect developments in the cathedral schools that had their beginnings in the tenth and eleventh centuries. However, the curricula of those schools has been harder to establish, in large part because of the absence of greater documentary culture for that earlier period. Certainly there are few personalities from that period to rival the luminaries of the late eleventh and early twelfth centuries, such as Anselm of Canterbury, Peter Abelard, or Hugh of St-Victor. Nevertheless, there is evidence enough to suggest that an evolution from an older form of oral learning to a newer and ultimately more textual learning was already well underway by the middle decades of the eleventh century. C. Stephen Jaeger has characterized this transition as one of "charismatic versus intellectual culture" and identifies the civic-minded cathedral schools of the Ottonian Empire as the location where that older charismatic form of pedagogy flourished.

The letter of Goswin to his student Walcher offers a glimpse of this intellectual changing of the guard. Goswin decided to retire around 1065 after a full life of teaching and public administration. He had become master of the school at Liege in 1044 and chancellor in 1050, only then to accept the invitation of Archbishop Liutpold of Mainz to teach at the school of Mainz. At first he judged his new German environment a vast improvement, going so far as to call his former abode a "vile heap of slag" in comparison. When he decided to retire and return to his old school, he wrote a letter to his former student, now a master himself, and recalled rather more fondly the student–teacher relations of the old days. He makes note of the new allure of France (likening Paris to Athens), and speaks scornfully of a new class of students and masters who have abandoned moral discipline and instead seek profit and advancement as the ends of their studies.

Source: trans. C. Stephen Jaeger, *The Envy of Angels: Cathedral Schools and Social Ideals in Medieval Europe, 900–1200* (Philadelphia: University of Pennsylvania Press, 1994), 349–50, 353, 365. Latin.

The Letter of Gozechinus [Goswin] the school master to his former pupil, Valcherus, likewise school master

To his brother and son, united with him in soul brother Goswin sends his wish that the better part of existence may be a happy coexistence. Since you have renewed the many tokens of goodwill you used to show me so often, in turn I both cherish and pay out a wealth of favor to you, dearest friend; not only for the sweet, pleasant, and delectable memory of times past, but also for the joyous receipt of this new gift. For you have sent me the book I sought, transcribed in your own hand, in which you plainly show that you hold me in a high regard and consider my wishes not among the least important things. That book has recalled so vividly to mind all those gifts of charity for which I am in your debt that the present moment seems to restore to me in one gift the sum total of all previous ones.

Hence when I first saw your gift, when I first took it into my hands and recognized your writing, or rather you yourself in it, at the same moment my deep affection for you was rekindled as if for the first time. Truly my soul rejoiced that I had once guided you with my own hand in forming those crude characters and made you atone with strokes on your back for those ill-turned lines and other sins of tender youth, since now I can rejoice in the rich harvest of fruit from our little tree having [once] thought its luxuriant growth of sheaves and leaves excessive. For who would plant a vine and not accept its fruit? I at least have reaped again and again the sweet fruit of my labor for God has granted increase to those slips which I have planted and irrigated. But however great the harvest from others, it was you who pleased me with the greatest abundance of fruits.

Would that I had nourished all the members of both my schoolrooms in the same way! Would that I could find among them even one such as you as a crutch for my old age! As the divine oracle laments through his prophet: nourish and exalt your sons today, only to have them—very few excepted—spurn their exalter. But let such men take care lest for contempt of the father who admonishes them wisely, they should be deprived of the bequest of their eternal inheritance by the father of fathers.

But you, my dearest son, continue on the way you have begun; increase those goods you have received from me, make them greater and better, nor ever stint in your abundant goodness to me, for which he who sent you to me will reward you with eternal inheritance. Nor, if you show yourself kind to me, will you be acting in a new or unaccustomed way; but even though you have long wept beneath the teacher's rod, still you served me with the same kindness. And that goodness which fear alone sufficed to extort from others, you showed of your own free will, as is natural for a man like you. You hung on the very motion of my lips, lest any of my words should fall to the earth. I began to love you as a boy for this and for certain other eminent signs of virtue; and now as you mature, I place yet higher hopes in you with each passing day, seeing the strength of your industry in clarifying obscure readings, your wisdom and vigilance, and the sharpness of your acute mind in pursuing subtle points. While other auditors of our lessons were not equal to the words of the teacher, be they spoken or written, you seemed able to transform yourself altogether into the master. Whence I gloried, along with your brother and other friends, to see so rich a space spring up in that little garden I planted—I mean you, a wise youth among mature men. . . .

While our Liège is bountifully enriched with many such blessings, still there are far greater and more worthy ones. For that flower of tripartite Gaul and that second Athens luxuriates nobly in the study of the liberal arts, and, more excellent yet, the observance of divine worship flourishes. And, if I may say so with the indulgence of the churches, where the study of letters is concerned, Plato's academy did not offer better; and in respect to the practice of religion, Leo's Rome was not superior.

Hence spreading forth in every direction the good fragrance of Christ, it attracts and receives a great multitude that flocks to it. No one who has applied himself here has failed to advance and improve himself, except the lazy and neglectful. Since our Liège is what it is, let anyone who maligns it, anyone who does not love it having once known it, have the hate of God to put it in the rustic way. So it is, my dear friend, that I constantly strike out with oaths, for though I may dwell elsewhere, yet in my soul I reside there with you.

But perhaps you will accuse me of levity, as if I would now seek a place where life is easy, leisure abundant and where I can rest on my laurels; for that is the way of a vain mind, and your sharp reply is thus: that now from home sickness and nostalgia I praise so fervently the location, the pleasantness, the affluence, and the wisdom of our Liège whom I earlier abandoned, preferring the glory of Mainz. You will say that I vacillate with such inconstancy of mind that once located in Liège I long for Mainz; and when planted in Mainz I race back in my mind to Liège. And to strengthen your case you cite that testimony of Horace, so that the tumor you think you are cutting away can be rubbed all the sorer with the salt of satire: "Those who hurry to cross oceans change their location, not their mind." And again: "The mind that never escapes itself merits blame."

I don't mean to suggest that you would say dark things against me, nor by the same token have I set myself up against you to stir up conflict. It is just that I know well those dogs who are always ready to snap at others. . . .

You, my dearest son, have reached some of these deadlines; I have reached them all, and more—and still we groan beneath our burden, still we sweat at our toils, while no distinctions and no honors of the emeritus smile upon us, which would justly compensate us for so great a labor. If there are any at all who would now take up that task, they are very few. For liberal studies are now given over to mimes and actors, who seem to go begging through taverns, where they hold forth in philosophical discourses on money. Mammon now rules in all ways over kings and monarchs. In the end beastly avarice holds sway over all the rewards of virtue and ambition takes inventory of its merchandise in the kingdom of money. And what shall we believe is to be our part of such wretched leavings, when the stones of the sanctuary are dispersed through all the streets? But what ministry of dignities or custody of spiritual vessels could be hoped for or desired, where not the vessels of compassion shaped for glory, but the vessels of wrath leading to death, are seen everywhere, from vessels of the minor arts to every vessel of the higher arts?

From this same poisoned root of avarice and from these barren tare-seeds is sprung and is still sprouting abundantly today that fatal rejection of manners and discipline. Nowhere where the regulated life is taught is it permitted to employ the solemn censure of the seniors of the rod. But where one is willing to spare the twistings and turnings of vice and withdraw the hand from the rod and the stimulus of discipline, there the seniors will find a multitude of fellow vices springing forth as their champions, or money stepping forward as their defender. For the minors, however, either ill-mannered license or flight, the liberator, will intercede with her winged feet. But better to be silent about the seniors, for telling the truth stirs hatred.

But those who should still receive their training beneath the scholar's rod give themselves over to stupidity, laziness, and their god, the stomach. Fleeing instruction in the gravity of moral discipline, they are blown about like light chaff in every wind of doctrine. And according to that same apostle, they do not endure sound doctrine, but for their own desires accumulate masters who set their ears itching. . . .

Figure 3: The west façade or *Portail Royal* of Chartres Cathedral (mid-twelfth century), one of the few elements of the church to survive the great fire of 1194. The three portals each focus on a different aspect of Christ's role: his earthly incarnation on the right, his second coming on the left, and his eternal aspect in the center. The right portal has most often been connected with the so-called school of Chartres. For a recent assessment of the school, see Édouard Jeauneau, *Rethinking the School of Chartres*, trans. Claude Paul Desmarais (Toronto: University of Toronto Press, 2009). The archivolts (sculptures) surrounding the tympanum display personifications of the Seven Liberal Arts as well as the classical authors and philosophers most associated with them (see also Figures 4A–C).

Source: Photograph by Alex J. Novikoff.

13. BERNARD OF CHARTRES: THE SOCRATES OF THE TWELFTH CENTURY

Bernard of Chartres (c. 1060–c. 1124) was the master of the cathedral school and chancellor of Chartres in the early twelfth century. He made a powerful impression upon his students and is chiefly remembered for a series of striking remarks. John of Salisbury (c. 1120–80), the student of several of Bernard's disciples, had heard much about Bernard but never knew him personally. Nonetheless, he repeated many of his poems and sayings. For John, Bernard was the archetypal master of the "good old days" at the start of the twelfth century, when a careful and deliberate study of the liberal arts provided students with a solid educational foundation. Bernard can also be thought of, in a limited sense, as a twelfth-century Socrates because of his formative influence on one stream of twelfth-century thought, his intense engagement with and influence upon his students, their vivid memory of what he said, his moral emphasis and Platonic philosophy, and the fact that we have little written work from Bernard upon which to assess his career and thought. Bernard was charismatic like Socrates, but he lacked the latter's unique mission to question everyone and everything.

Source: trans. Paul Edward Dutton from *The Glosae super Platonem of Bernard of Chartres*, ed. Paul Edward Dutton (Toronto: Pontifical Institute of Mediaeval Studies, 1991), 148, 213, 240–48. Latin.

As an Exemplary Teacher

From John of Salisbury, *Metalogicon* 1.24

Bernard of Chartres, the greatest source of letters in Gaul in modern times, taught in this way. In reading authors, he showed what was simple and done in conformity with the rule[s of grammar]. Next, he would point out literary figures, rhetorical stylings, and learned debates, and where the passage of a reading referred to other disciplines. He did this in such a way that he did not try to teach everything at once, but according to the capacity of the students and gradually according to the amount to be learned.

Speech shines either from its appropriateness, as when an adjective and a verb are elegantly joined to a noun, or from its use of metaphor, as when language is transported for good reason to another level of meaning. When the time was right, [Bernard] impressed these things upon the minds of his students. Since memory is reinforced by exercising it and natural ability is sharpened by imitating those things that students have heard, he would urge some of them on by admonition and others by beatings and punishments. The students were required each day to explain some part of what they had learned the previous day; some more, some less. The following day was, thus, the disciple of the former.

The evening lecture, which was called the Conclusion [*Declinatio*], was so full of literary instruction that if anyone participated in it for a full year, that is, if he were not particularly dull, he would have in his possession the basis for [correct] speaking and writing, and would not be ignorant of the meaning of speech in common use. But, because it is not proper for any school or day to lack religion, [Bernard] presented materials to strengthen faith and morals, and hence those who met there as if in a certain religious gathering [*collatio*] were moved to do good. The closing portion of the Conclusion or, rather, learned religious gathering manifested evidence of the faith, and it commended the souls of the dead to their redeemer with the devout reading of the Sixth Penitential Psalm [129] and the Lord's Prayer.

For the guidance of the boys on which prose and poetry to imitate, [Bernard] would specify which poets and orators to follow. Demonstrating the way diction was put together and the elegant endings of speech, he would command them to imitate their example. If anyone, however, sewed a piece of external cloth for the sake of luster onto his own work, Bernard would reject the detected theft, but most often would not impose a punishment. With the stolen bit rejected, Bernard would react with moderate indulgence, [that is] if [he determined that] an inappropriate attempt to capture the likeness of the authors had led the student [to borrow the material], and he would strive to insure that the student who was imitating the great ones of the past would be deserving of being imitated by others in the future. He would also teach among the first rudiments [of learning] and impress upon the minds [of his students] what virtue there is in an economy of words, what virtue there is in the beauty of things, and what things should be praised with words, where brevity and almost meagerness of words are an advantage, where an abundance of words is laudable, where it is excessive, and where the appropriate measure of all things lies. Indeed, [Bernard] used constantly to advise his students that stories and poems must be read entirely and he urged them not to rush as if they were spurred into flight. With constant diligence, he demanded from each student, as a daily obligation, something memorized. All the same, he used to say that the extraneous and unnecessary should be avoided; what was written by the best authors should be enough. . . .

Since nothing is of greater use in the training of those learning than to practice the discipline they are learning, [Bernard's students] wrote prose and poems daily, and he had them participate in conversations with each other, for in fact no practice is more useful in acquiring eloquence, no method is more efficient in acquiring knowledge, than that, for [learned conversation] confers much to life so long as Christian love rules commitment and humility remains while one is seeking to advance in letters. For the same man cannot be devoted to both letters and carnal vices. My grammar teachers, William of Conches and Richard, who is known as "the Bishop," a good man in his life and conversation, and now the deacon of Coutances, formerly shaped their students [according to Bernard's method]. But afterwards, when [common] opinion prejudged the truth, when people wanted to seem rather than to be philosophers, and when professors of the arts were promising students that they could impart all philosophy in less than two or three years, [William and Richard] were overcome by the demands of the unlearned rabble, and ceased teaching. From that point on, less time and care have been spent on the study of grammar.

Bernard's Six Keys to Learning

From John of Salisbury, *Policraticus* 7.3

The Old Man of Chartres [Bernard] captured in a few words the keys to learning that expedite the way for those pursuing philosophy to contemplate the nature of truth. Though I am not moved by the charm of his poem, I approve of its meaning and believe that it should be impressed firmly upon the minds of those pursuing philosophy. Thus he said:

A humble mind, a desire to learn, a quiet life,
A silent searching, an absence of riches, a foreign land,
These are the keys that unlock hidden things when we read.

Bernard on the Lover of Intelligence and Knowledge

From Bernard of Chartres, *Glosae super Platonem* 7, at *Timaeus* 46d

The lover of intelligence and knowledge, that is he who loves to teach so that he might be fully understood.

Three Kinds of Intellects

From John of Salisbury, *Metalogicon* 1.17

There are three kinds [of intellectual abilities] as Bernard, the Old Man of Chartres, used to point out to the students in constant discussion with him. For one flies high, another [crawls] on low, and another [walks] the middle way between them. The one flying high learns quickly but just as quickly forgets what he has learned, and finds no place to rest. The [crawling one] being low down cannot rise up and so knows no improvement. The one in the middle, because he has both a place to rest and can rise, does not despair of making progress, and so is best suited to the demands of pursuing philosophy.

Modern Dwarfs on the Shoulders of Ancient Giants

From John of Salisbury, *Metalogicon* 3.4

Bernard of Chartres said that we are like dwarfs sitting on the shoulders of giants. We can see more and farther than the giants could, assuredly not because we have superior sight or stand taller than they did, but because we are lifted on high and raised up by their immense height.

Bernard Wrestles with Plato's Idea of Holding Women in Common

From Bernard of Chartres, *Glosae super Platonem* 3, at *Timaeus* 18c

[Socrates] speaks then of common marriages, namely that each man may approach freely any woman he wishes just as he would the woman he has at home and that he should regard her child as his own, and that he should believe that all elders are his grandfathers or fathers or joined to him in some way, and so all are joined to each other by common affection.

But, according to this, Socrates would seem not to have presented either a just or honest arrangement of the state. Let us, therefore, say that this was said under a veil of meaning [*per inuolucrum*], which he acknowledged when he said that this [arrangement] ran counter to custom. For when Socrates treats "of marriages in common and common offspring" he said one thing, [but] he meant another. And if he said that, I do not take that as meaning "carnally," but "in affection" only, with all baseness [*turpitudo*] put aside. [It was as if he said] I wish that in the whole state each should love another as his own son, brother, or father, and the wife of another as his own, [thus] following the teaching of the prelates in this. Concerning this idea, Augustine says that Socrates instils affection, not baseness. Or it can be understood that marriages in common [meant] that they take wives not for pleasure, but for common utility, namely for the defence of the state. Whence they say of Cato that "he was father to the city and married to her."

Bernard the Complete Platonist

From John of Salisbury, *Metalogicon* 4.35

As well, Bernard of Chartres, the most complete Platonist of our age, enclosed this same opinion in verse:

> I say that being is not that, which, confined in double part,
> > Contains form joined with matter;
> But I say that being is that which consists of these together:
> > This [Plato] calls the *Idea*, That the Greek calls *hyle*.

Bernard on the Eternal Ideas in the Divine Mind

From John of Salisbury, *Metalogicon* 4.35

. . . though [Bernard] dared to call [the Idea] eternal, he refused to say that it was co-eternal. As he said in his treatment of Porphyry, the work of the divine mind is two-fold: the first which it creates out of subjected matter or which is created together with it, and the second which it makes out of and contains within itself without the assistance of any external support. As such, the divine mind from the beginning made the heavens in its mind, but to form them there it required no external matter or form. Elsewhere Bernard says:

> Time does not ruin nor old age destroy that
> First Principle [Idea] for which there was only the divine will.
> Time undoes whatever it brought into being,
> If not now, whenever it has the need.
> Thus he who moans over such a condition,
> Evidently has little or no reason to do so.

The Example of the White Virgin

From John of Salisbury, *Metalogicon* 3.2

Bernard of Chartres used to say that "whiteness" [*albedo*] signifies an uncorrupted virgin, "is white" [*albet*] the same virgin entering the bedroom or reclining in bed, but "white" [*album*] the same woman but now no longer a virgin. He put things this way since "whiteness" signifies that quality itself simply and without any participation by a subject, namely the idea of color separable from sight. "Is white" fundamentally signifies the same thing, even if it allows for the participation of a subject. For if you should examine what this verb signifies with respect to substance, the quality of "whiteness" suggests itself, but in the accidents of the verb you will discover a subject. "White" signifies the same quality, but infused and mixed together with a substance, and hence more corrupted. Indeed, the name ["white"] signifies the subject of "whiteness" when used as a substantive and the color of "whiteness" of a subject when used for a quality. It seemed to Bernard that he was supported [in this reading] by Aristotle and the authority of many others. For [Aristotle] said: "White" signifies nothing other than quality. Bernard brought forth as well many other proofs, by which he attempted to argue that a thing is predicated purely, other times approximately, and he asserted that knowledge of derivative words is extremely useful for this.

14. THE PEDAGOGICAL PROLOGUES OF THIERRY OF CHARTRES

There are many contemporary testimonies to the learned reputation and influence of Thierry of Chartres (c. 1095–1156), although much remains uncertain about his career and thought. He was chancellor of Chartres Cathedral from 1142/43, and in the following decade he retired to a Cistercian monastery, where he died. He was known both as a consummate and charismatic teacher of the language arts (the trivium*) and for* *his philosophical and scientific investigations, although he did not produce a substantial original treatise on any of these subjects. Instead, the innovative and systematic quality of his thought is revealed through his commentaries on Boethius and Cicero, his unfinished commentary on the six days of creation in Genesis, and his encyclopedic anthology on the seven liberal arts, the* Heptateuchon *(c. 1140s).*

The term Heptateuchon *is a clever play on words in Greek: it reworks the Greek term for the five books of Moses, "Pentateuch," into the Greek word for "seven" (*hepta*), thus producing a new word to signify the foundational texts of the "seven liberal arts." The encyclopedia was intended to gather all of the curricular texts that would constitute the education of the ideal clerical intellectual. It is a vast compilation of over 50 textbooks of the liberal arts: the major works of Donatus and Priscian, Ciceronian rhetoric, nearly all of Aristotle's* Organon, *the Porphyrian and Boethian sources on dialectic, and important texts for each of the sciences of the* quadrivium, *including some texts on arithmetic, geometry, and astronomy newly translated from Arabic (see Chapter 9). The prologues to the* Heptateuchon *and to the works of Donatus (an important Roman grammarian of late antiquity) supply precious insight into both the curriculum of the mid-twelfth-century schools and the pedagogical practices of a revered teacher.*

Source: trans. Paul Edward Dutton, Chartres, manuscript 497, fols. 2ra–rb, 8va, ed. Edouard Jeauneau, *Lectio Philosophorum: Recherches sur l'Ecole de Chartres* (Amsterdam: Adolf M. Hakkert, 1973), 38–39, 90–91. Latin.

[Prologue to the Heptateuchon*]*

Here begins the Prologue of Thierry on the *Heptateuchon.* Among the Latins, a certain Marcus Varro was the first to set down a volume on the seven liberal arts, which the Greeks call the "Heptateuchon." After him Pliny and then Martianus Capella [did the same], but those men [composed] their own [volumes]. We, however, have put together in fitting harmony in one volume, not our own composition, but the findings of the most learned authors on these arts. We have joined together the trivium and the quadrivium, as though by a marriage contract, for the propagation of a noble breed of philosophers. The poets, both Greek and Roman, maintain that Philology was bound to Mercury in a solemn wedding feast by the full powers of the presiding Hymen and the universal consent of Apollo and the Muses; [and so,] not unworthily, these seven [liberal] arts arose, as if nothing could be done without them. For these are the two principal tools for philosophizing: understanding and its exposition. The quadrivium enlightens understanding; the trivium allows for its elegant, rational, and decorous expression. It is obvious that the Heptateuchon is the one and only tool for all philosophy. Philosophy is the love of wisdom, and wisdom is the complete comprehension of the truth of those things that exist, which no one can gain even a little of unless he will have loved [wisdom]. No one, therefore, is wise unless he is a philosopher.

But, in this gathering of the seven liberal arts, brought together for the improvement of humanity, Grammar comes first among them [as] a mature woman with a severe countenance and manner. She summons the boys together, sets out the laws of correct writing and correct speaking, appropriately uses the peculiarities of languages, and claims as her responsibility the exposition of all the authors. Whatever is said belongs to her charge. Students should venerate, for the sake of making [good] arguments, the gray hairs of this mature woman.

> For they claim that she was born from the sacred union of old gods,
> Her father born on the banks of the Nile and her mother an Egyptian,
> At a time when Osiris was reigning in the city of Memphis.
> For a long time she was hidden [but] then was found,
> Raised by Atlantiades [Mercury], and exalted by Greek cities;
> Finally as an aged woman she reached the descendants of Romulus.

[Prologue to Donatus's Ars Minor*]*

[Donatus prospered during the times of Constantine, and Constans and] Constantius, the sons of Constantine the Great. He taught this art [grammar] with remarkable brevity, compendious aptness, and a very sophisticated style of instruction. In fact, he issued a first publication [on grammar, the *Ars Minor*] to instruct boys how to ask questions in a disciplined way and how to answer them learnedly, so that by comprehending the principal parts of the art, and with a sparsity of examples supplied, he might gather together [for them] the summary and [yet] essential wholeness [of grammar]. What others dragged out with every kind of teaching to the point of exhausting the reader, and what they burdened with endless error and difficulty, he deposited like milk in the mouths of babes. Here ends the prologue.

[Prologue to Donatus's Ars Maior*]*

This is the second publication [on grammar, the *Ars maior*] of Donatus, the grammarian of Rome, in which he is speaking to more advanced students and, accordingly, though he begins with the basics of the art, he draws out its teaching [from start] to finish. He lays out the basis of that teaching on voice and letters, on syllables and feet, on tones or accents, and on punctuation; then on that foundation he erects a theory of the parts of speech, before finally finishing his work on grammar with a sophisticated conclusion that he calls the "Barbarism." Thus, by this conclusion, advanced students can most readily see the overall composition of particulars, which they could not normally understand from the accidents belonging to the letter, syllable, word, or sentence, namely barbarisms, solecisms, and deviations or tropes, and other things of that sort. There are thus two main ways of instruction—one through learned discussion, which trains raw recruits to question their teachers, which the Greeks call the dialectical method, the other through positive affirmation, by which after long study are set out things that should be held [as true], which those same Greeks call the analytical method. Accordingly, the distinguished teacher, Donatus, employed the first method in his first publication [on grammar], the second in the second.

15. GUIBERT OF NOGENT REFLECTS ON HIS EARLY EDUCATION

The Benedictine monk Guibert of the abbey of Nogent (c. 1055–1124) was one of the most gifted and prolific writers of his day. He wrote an account of the First Crusade as well as various exegetical works of spirituality. His Memoirs *(or* Solitary Songs *to give the more literal translation of the work), were completed around 1115. It is a remarkably detailed and personal account of his life and times and offers reflections on his passage from child oblate through adulthood, including the years he spent in his eventual position as abbot of the monastery of Nogent. The passage below recounts his early education, his relations with his parents, and his relationship with his tutor. He astutely notes the counterproductive effects of physical punishment and stresses the need for the mind to engage in a variety of pursuits in order for it to remain focused and sharp. Echoing other monastic authors of the early twelfth century, Guibert describes his turn away from letters to the study of Scripture, which he ultimately found a more pleasing activity for his soul and for his mind. Far from being the musings of an erratic or psychologically disturbed personality, Guibert's autobiography reveals the reflections of an intelligent and sophisticated mind.*

Source: trans. C.C. Swinton Bland, *The Autobiography of Guibert, Abbot of Nogent-sous-Coucy* (New York: E.P. Dutton, 1925), 16–24, 67–73; revised by Alex J. Novikoff. Latin.

[Chapter 4: My Early Education]

Now after birth I had hardly learned to cherish my rattle when you, Gracious God, henceforth my Father, did make me an orphan. For when almost eight months had passed, the father of my flesh died: for that I give great thanks to you, who did cause that man to depart in a Christian state, who would undoubtedly have endangered, had he lived, the provision you had made for me. For because my person, and a certain natural quickness for one of such tender age, seemed to fit me for worldly pursuits, no one doubted that when the proper time came for beginning my education he would break the vow which he had made for me. O Gracious Provider, for the well-being of both of us did you determine that I should not miss the beginning of instruction in your discipline and that he should not break his solemn promise to me.

And so with great care did the widow, truly yours, bring me up, and at last choose the day of the festival of the Blessed Gregory for putting me in school. She had heard that your servants, O Lord, had been eminent for his wonderful understanding and had abounded in extraordinary wisdom. Therefore she strove with bountiful almsgiving to win the good word of your Confessor, that he to whom you had granted understanding might procure for me a zeal for the pursuit of knowledge. Put to my book, I had learned the alphabet, but hardly yet to join the letters into syllables, when my good mother, eager for my instruction, arranged to place me under a tutor.

There was still in my youth such a scarcity of teachers that in the towns hardly any, and in the cities very few, could be found, and those who by good chance could be discovered had but slight knowledge and could not be compared to the wandering scholars of today. Now the man in whose charge my mother decided to put me had begun to learn grammar late in life, and he was the more unskilled in the art on account of having imbibed little of it when young. Yet of such sobriety was he, that what he lacked in letters he made up for in honesty.

My mother, therefore, through chaplains conducting divine services in her house, approached this teacher, who was in charge of the education of a young cousin of mine and was very close to this cousin's parents, who boarded him at their court. He took into consideration the woman's earnest request and was favorably impressed by her honorable and virtuous character, although he was afraid to give offense to those relatives of mine and was in doubt whether to come into her house. While thus undecided, he was persuaded by the following vision.

At night when he was sleeping in his room, where I remember he conducted all the liberal studies [*studium generale*] of our town, the figure of a white-headed old man of very dignified appearance seemed to lead me in by the hand through the door of the room. Halting within hearing while the other looked on, he pointed out his bed to me and said, "Go to him, for he will love you very much." And when he let me go, loosing my hand, I ran to the man. And as I kissed him again and again on the face, he awoke and conceived such an affection for me that he put aside all hesitation and shook off all fear of my kinsfolk, on whom not only he, but also everything that belonged to him, was dependent, and he agreed to go to my mother and live in her house.

Now that same boy whom he had been educating until then was handsome and of good birth but had such a dislike for virtuous conduct, was so unsteady under all instruction, and was such a liar and a thief (as far as his age would allow) that even under guardianship he was hardly ever in school and could be found playing truant almost every day in the vineyards. My mother's friendly advances were made to him at the moment when the man was tired of the boy's childish folly, and the meaning of the vision fixed still deeper in his heart what he already desired, and so he gave up his companionship of the boy and left the noble family with whom he was living. This, however, he could not have done with impunity, had he not had the respect for my mother, as well as her power to protect him.

[Chapter 5: Reflections on the Education of Children]

Placed under him, I was taught with such purity and checked with such honesty from the excesses which are wont to spring up in youth, that I was kept well-guarded from the common games and never allowed to leave his company, to eat anywhere other than at home, or to accept gifts from anyone without his leave; in everything I had to show such self-control—in word, look and act—so that he seemed to require of me the conduct of a monk rather than a cleric. For whereas others of my age wandered everywhere at will and were unchecked in the indulgence of such inclinations as were natural for their age, I, hedged in with constant restraints, would sit and look on in my clerical garb at the squad of players like a beast awaiting sacrifice. Even on Sundays and Saints' Days I had to submit to the severity of school exercises, and on no day and hardly at any time was I allowed to take a holiday. In fact, in every way and at all times I was driven to study. And he, being allowed to have no other pupil, devoted himself solely to my education.

He worked me hard, and anyone looking on might suppose that my fledgling mind was exceedingly sharpened by such perseverance, but the hopes of all were let down. For he was utterly unskilled in prose and verse composition. Meanwhile I was pelted almost every day with a hail of blows and harsh words, all while he was forcing me to learn what he could not teach.

I passed nearly six years with him in this fruitless struggle, but got no reward worth the expenditure of time. Still, in all that is supposed to count for good training in the behavior of a gentleman, he spared no effort for my improvement. Most faithfully and lovingly did he steep me in all that was temperate and pure and outwardly refined. But I clearly perceived, at my own expense, that he had no consideration and restraint in urging me on without intermission and at great pains, all under the pretense of teaching me. For, by the strain of undue application, the natural powers of grown men, as well as of boys, are blunted and the hotter the fire of their mental activity in unremitting study, the sooner is the strength of their understanding weakened and chilled by excess and its energy turned to apathy.

It is necessary, therefore, to treat the mind with greater moderation while it is still burdened with its bodily covering; for if there is stillness in heaven for half an hour, so that even the gift of contemplation cannot be unremitting while it goes on, so too the intellect, when wrestling with some problem, will not without rest maintain what I may call its obstinacy. Hence we believe that, when the mind has been fixed exclusively on one subject, we ought to give it relaxation from its intensity, so that, after dealing by alternation with different subjects, we may return with renewed energy, as after a holiday, to that one with which our minds are most engaged. In short, let wearied nature at times be refreshed by varying its work. Let us remember that God has not made the world without variety, but in day and night, spring and summer, winter and autumn, he has delighted us by changes in the seasons. Let everyone, therefore, who holds the name of master see in what manner he may regulate the teaching of boys and young men, since such men think their students should be treated like old men who are completely serious.

Now, the love that this man had for me was of a savage sort, and excessive severity was shown by him in his unjust floggings, yet the great care with which he guarded me was evident in his acts. Clearly I did not deserve to be beaten, for if he had had the skill in teaching that he professed, it is certain that I was, for a boy, well able to grasp anything that he taught correctly. But because his elocution was poor and what he strove to express was not at all clear to him, his talk rolled ineffectively on and on in a banal but by no means obvious circle, which could not be brought to any conclusion, much less understood. For so uninstructed was he that he retained incorrectly what he had, as I have said before, once badly learned late in life, and if he let anything slip out (incautiously, as it were), he maintained and defended it with blows, regarding all his own opinions as certainly true. I think he should have avoided such folly, for as a learned teacher once said, "before one's nature has absorbed knowledge, it is less praiseworthy to say what you know than to keep silent about what you do not know."

While he took cruel vengeance on me for not knowing what he knew not himself, he ought certainly to have considered that it was very wrong to demand from a weak little mind what he had not put into it. For, just as the words of madmen can only with difficulty (or not at all) be understood by the sane, so the talk of those who are ignorant (but say that they are knowledgeable) and pass it on to others, will be darkened the more by their own explanation. You will find nothing more difficult than trying to discourse on what you do not understand, which is bewildering to the teacher and even more so to the pupil, making both look like blockheads. This I say, O God, not to put a stigma on such a friend, but for every reader to understand that we should not attempt to teach as a certainty every assertion we make and that we should not involve others also in the mists of our own conjectures. For it has been my purpose, in consideration of the poorness of my subject, to give it some flavor by reasoning about things, so that if the one deserves to be reckoned of little value, the other may be sometimes regarded as worthwhile.

[Chapter 6: Of the Difficult Relations with My Tutor]

Although he crushed me by such severity, in other ways he made it quite plain that he loved me as well as he did himself. With such watchful care did he devote himself to me, with such foresight did he secure my welfare against the spite of others and teach me on what authority I should be aware of the dissolute manners of some who paid court to me, and so long did he argue with my mother about the elaborate richness of my dress, that he was regarded as exercising the guardianship not of a master, but of a parent, and not over my body only, but my soul too. As for me, considering the dull sensibility of my age and my littleness, great was the love I conceived for him in response. In spite of the many lashes with which he marked my tender skin, it was not through fear, as is common in those of my age, but through a sort of love deeply implanted in my heart, that I obeyed him in utter forgetfulness of his severity. Indeed, when my master and my mother saw me paying due respect to both alike, they tried by frequent tests to see whether I should dare to prefer one or the other on a definite issue.

At last, without any intention on the part of either, an opportunity occurred for a test which left no room for doubt. Once I had been beaten in school, which was nothing other than the dining hall of our house since he had given up the charge of others to take me on alone after my mother wisely required him to do this for a higher wage and a better position. When, therefore, at a certain hour in the evening, my studies had come to an end, I went to my mother's knees after a more severe beating than I had deserved. And when she, as she would do, began to ask me repeatedly whether I had been whipped that day, I, not to appear a telltale, entirely denied it. Then she, whether I liked it or not, threw off the inner garment which they call a vest or shirt and saw my little arms blackened and the skin of my back everywhere swollen up with the cuts from the twigs. And being grieved to the heart by the very savage punishment inflicted on my tender body, troubled, agitated and weeping with sorrow, she said: "You shall never become a cleric, nor suffer so much anymore to get learning." Looking at her with what reproach I could, I replied: "If I had to die on the spot, I would not give up learning my book and becoming a cleric." I should add that she had already promised that if I wished to become a knight, when I reached the age for it, she would give me the arms and equipment.

But when I had, with a good deal of scorn, declined all these offers, she, your servant, O Lord, accepted this rebuff so gladly and was made so cheerful by my scorn of her proposal that she repeated to my master the reply with which I had opposed her. Then both rejoiced that I had such an eager longing to fulfill my father's vow, while I, to acquire learning more quickly, badly as I was taught, did not shirk the church offices. Indeed, when the hour sounded or there was need, I did not prefer even my meals to such place and occasion. Then indeed it was so: but you, O God, know how much I afterwards fell away from that zeal, how reluctantly I went to divine services, hardly consenting even when driven to them with blows. Clearly, O Lord, the impulses that animated me then were not religious feelings begotten by thoughtfulness, but only a child's eagerness. But after adolescence had exhausted itself in bringing out the wickedness within, I hastened toward the loss of all shame and that former zeal entirely faded away. Although for a brief space, my God, good resolve, nay, the semblance of good resolve, seemed to shine forth, it was snuffed out and overshadowed by the storm clouds of my evil imagination.

[Chapter 17: My Flirtation with Poetry. I am Saved by Scripture]

Meanwhile, after having steeped my mind unduly in the study of verse making, so as to put aside for such worthless vanities the serious things of sacred Scripture, under guidance of my folly I went so far as read the poems of Ovid and the pastoral poets and to aim at the airs and graces of a love poem in a critical treatise and in a series of letters. My mind, therefore, forgetting a proper severity and abandoning the modesty of a monk's calling, was led away by these enticements of a poisonous license, and gave weight only to whether some courtly phrase could be referred to some poet, with no thought how much the toil which I loved might hurt the aims of our holy profession. By love of it I was doubly taken captive, being snared by the wantonness of the sweet words I found in the poets and those which I poured forth myself and caught by immodest fleshly stirrings through thinking on these things and the like. For since my unstable mind, unaccustomed now to hard thinking, spent itself on these trifles, no sound could come from my lips except that which was prompted by my thoughts.

Hence it came to pass that, from the boiling over of the madness within me, I fell into certain obscene words and composed brief writings, worthless and immodest, in fact bereft of all decency. When this came to the knowledge of that master of mine he was very much grieved by it, but it happened that he fell asleep in the bitterness of his annoyance. And as he slept, there appeared to him the following vision. An old man with shining white hair, in fact that very one, I dare to say, who brought me to him at the beginning and had promised his love for me in the future, appeared to him and said with severity, "I wish you to give account to me for the writings that have been composed; but the hand which wrote them, is not his who wrote." When this had been related by my master, he and I gave much the same interpretation of the dream. And we mourned with joy in your hope, O Lord, both seeing your displeasure in that fatherly rebuke and also from the meaning of that vision taking some ground for trust that my frivolity would undergo a change to greater piety. For, when it is said that the hand that wrote the letters is said not to be his who wrote them, it is without doubt meant that it would not continue in such shameful doing. For it was mine and now is not; as it is written, "Change the wicked and they shall not be," and that which was mine in the practice of vice, when applied to the pursuit of virtue, became of no effect in that unworthy use of it. And yet you know, O Lord, and I confess, that at that time neither by fear of Thee, by shame, nor by respect for that holy vision was my life chastened. I put no check on that irreverence I had within me, and I did not refrain from the vain jests of frivolous writers. I hammered out these verses in secret and dared to show them to no one, or at least only to a few like myself. I read them out when I could, often inventing an author for them, and I was delighted when those which I thought it inconvenient to acknowledge as mine, were praised by those who shared such studies. Their author gained no praise by them; he had to be content with the enjoyment, or rather the shame, of making them. But these acts, O Father, in your own good time, you did punish, and misfortune came upon me for such work. You fenced in my wandering soul with much affliction and held me down by bodily infirmity. And so a sword pierced through even to my soul, while trouble touched my understanding.

And so, when the punishment of sin had brought understanding to my hearing, then at last the folly of useless study withered away. Yet since I could not endure to be idle, and was compelled, as it were, to cast aside vain imaginings, with renewal of my spiritual being I turned to more profitable exercises. I began, therefore, all too late to pant for that knowledge that so often had been instilled in me by many good teachers, to busy myself, that is, with commentaries on the Scriptures, to study the works of Gregory (in which are best to be found the keys to that art), and according to the rules of ancient writers to treat the words of the prophets and the Gospels in their allegorical, their moral and even their mystical meaning. In this work I had Anselm, the abbot of Bec, afterwards archbishop of Canterbury, to encourage me. He was an Italian from across the Alps, the country of Augustus [Aosta], a man of sublime example and holiness of life. While still holding office as prior in the aforesaid convent, he admitted me to his acquaintance and, utter child as I was in knowledge as well as age, he readily offered to teach me to manage the inner self, how to consult the laws of reason in the government of the body. He both before and during his abbacy, being a familiar visitor to the monastery welcomed for his piety and his teaching, bestowed on me so assiduously the benefits of his learning and with such ardor labored at this, that it seemed as if I alone was the reason for his frequent visits.

He taught us then to divide the mind into three or four parts, to treat the whole of the operations of this inner mystery under sensation, will, reason, and perception, showing that the first two, regarded by most and by myself as one and free from definite divisions, were not identical, even though it is established by evident assertions that in the presence of reason or intellect they are practically the same. After he had discussed certain chapters of the Gospels on this principle and most clearly explained the difference between will and sensation, it was plain that he did not originate this but got it from the books at hand, which did not so explicitly deal with these matters. I then began to imitate his methods in similar commentaries, so far as I could, and everywhere in the Scriptures to examine carefully with all the energy of my mind anything that was morally in agreement with those ideas. . . .

16. HERMAN OF TOURNAI DESCRIBES HIS TEACHER ODO

Herman (c. 1090–1147) was born in the Flemish city of Tournai. His father Ralph owned the brewing monopoly in Tournai and was also a member of a rich and influential group that controlled the government of the city. In 1095, the same year that Pope Urban II (r. 1088–99) preached the First Crusade, both of Herman's parents abandoned the secular world and entered the recently re-established and nearby abbey of St-Martin. Herman entered the monastery as soon as he had passed out of infancy, and was educated there under Odo of Orléans, its abbot and the former master of the cathedral school of St-Mary's of Tournai. In time Herman became prior in charge of the monastery's external affairs and eventually rose to become the third abbot in 1127. In 1142, the canons of Tournai sent Herman to Rome to petition Pope Innocent II for a resolution to an ecclesiastical peculiarity wherby the towns of Tournai and Noyon, over 100 miles to the south, were governed by a single bishop. His sojourn in Rome, which coincided with the fiftieth anniversary of the re-establishment of St-Martin's, provided the occasion for his account of the restoration of the monastery, which includes an intimate description of his teacher Odo as well as vignettes of many other events and personalities of early-twelfth-century Flanders. The passage below highlights the fame and rigor of Odo's teaching and, from Herman's perspective, the interdependence between scholarship and the religious vocation. Not to be ignored are Herman's emphasis on the new wave of dialectics current in early twelfth-century schools and his sarcastic humor in describing Odo's reputation.

Source: trans. Paul Edward Dutton, from *Herimannus Abbas, Liber de restauratione ecclesie Sancti Martini Tornacensis*, ed. R.B.C. Huygens, Corpus Christianorum: Continuatio Mediaevalis, 236 (Turnhout: Brepols, 2010), 35–38. Latin.

[Odo of Orléans: His Teaching and Scholarship]

In the time of Philip, son of Henry, son of Robert, son of that Hugh Capet who had expelled the kings of the line of Charlemagne from the kingdom and gained control, there was a native of Orléans, a cleric by the name of Odo, the son of Gerard and Cecilia. From boyhood he applied himself assiduously to the study of letters [that is, the liberal arts] so that when he was a young man he had attained such great knowledge that he was esteemed second to none among the French of his time in learning. For that reason, he was more worthily called a master than student. He first taught students in the city of Toul, but was then summoned by the canons of St-Mary of Tournai and made the master of their school. Directing that school for nearly five years, his fame spread so greatly that throngs of clerics from near (France, Flanders, and Normandy) and far (Italy, Saxony, and Burgundy) poured in daily to listen to him. If you had seen the vast numbers of men deep in debate who filled those city streets, you would have concluded that all in that town had abandoned their occupations and devoted themselves entirely to philosophy. Then, if you had approached the school, you would have seen Master Odo here strolling with his students, teaching them like one of the Peripatetics, there sitting and solving problems like one of the Stoics. During the evening hours, you would have seen him in front of the church lecturing late into the night, pointing out to his students with an extended finger the movement of the stars and showing them the difference between the Zodiac and Milky Way. Among the many gifts his students gave him was a gold ring on which was engraved this short line: "A golden ring suits Odo of Orléans."

But, although he was learned in all seven liberal arts, he especially excelled in dialectics, and the largest gathering of clerics assembled to hear him on that topic in particular. On it he wrote two books, the first entitled *Sophistem*, which helps in the recognition and avoidance of logical fallacies; the second called the *Book of Complexions*. He also composed a third book, *De re et ente*, in which he solved the problem of whether one and the same thing could be both a substance and essence. In these three books, as well as in his other works, when the opportunity arose to name himself he did not employ "Odo," but "Odoard," as he was known at the time.

You nevertheless need to understand that this master did not teach his students about words [*de voce*] as do modern teachers, but rather, like Boethius and other ancient teachers, he lectured about things according to dialectics. For this reason, Master Rainbert, who also lecturing on dialectics to his students at that time in the town of Lille, was extremely jealous and critical, as were many other masters. They said that their own lectures were better than his. Hence, some clerics were confused by this, uncertain whom to believe, especially since they saw that Master Odoard did not veer from the doctrines of the ancients, while some of them, out of that human curiosity that always desires to hear and learn something new as did the [ancient] Athenians, praised other masters more, especially since, they said, the lectures of other masters were of more help in the practice of disputation and eloquence (or, rather, of chattiness and long-windedness).

One of the canons of that cathedral, Galbert, who afterwards became a monk here and then served as an abbot in the diocese of Châlons-sur-Marne, was perturbed by the [great] range of opinions and vagaries of the clerics. And so he secretly approached a deformed, deaf-mute diviner, who was famous in the city for divination. With signs made with his fingers and nods of his head, Galbert began to ask him which of the masters should be believed. Remarkably that man at once understood Galbert's question. Pulling his right hand over the palm of his left hand as if splitting the earth apart with a plow, and pointing his finger toward the school of Master Odo, he signified that Odo's teaching was absolutely correct. But, pointing a finger toward the city of Lille, in contrast, and with his hand near his mouth he blew, indicating that the teaching of Master Rainbert was nothing but windy chatter.

I have related this not because I think diviners should be consulted or to suggest that, contrary to holy precept, they should be believed, but to reject the excessive presumption of some arrogant individuals who want nothing more than to be called wise and who would rather have their newfangled novelties read out to them from the books of Porphyry and Aristotle than to listen to a commentary on Boethius and the other ancient authors. Anselm, the archbishop of Canterbury, in his book on the Incarnation of the Word, did not call clerics of this kind dialecticians, but dialectically called them heretics, who, he said, "only through windy arrogance consider universals to be substances." They ought rightly, he said, to be blown out of the company of the wise.

While Master Odo was praised everywhere for his knowledge, his religious dignity was so great that he was held by all to be no less celebrated and universally famous for it. When there was a cohort of almost two hundred clerics moving in procession to the church, it was Odo's way to follow behind as the very last one. You could hardly have found a greater [expression of] religious practice in the strictest of monastic communities. No one presumed to speak to his companion, no one laughed, no one muttered, no one turned his eyes to the left or to the right even the slightest. When someone farted in the choir, you could not have found greater strictness [of religious observation] from a Cluniac monk. It is not necessary to speak about abuses, throngs of women or irregularities of hair, dress, and the like, which today we see being practiced here and there. Odo would either have driven such plagues from his school or he would have resigned his mastership of the school.

The discipline there was so great that no layman was permitted for any reason to enter the cloister during the reading hour. Before Odo's arrival, the knights and citizens were customarily used to employing the canons' cloister to hear and adjudicate legal cases. Odo now drove them all out, even Everard, the most powerful castellan of the city. Everard had captured the castle of Mortain, previously unconquerable, by a violent armed assault and had it added to the domain of Tournai. Even for such occasions, Odo would not permit the castellan to occupy the cloister for even an hour, although he knew that afterwards Everard was greatly offended. There was nothing that Odo feared less than the unjust anger of the rich and powerful; he used to say that it was a great dishonor for a wise man to sway even a little from the path of rectitude in pursuit of the favor or gratitude of a prince.

17. PETER ABELARD, *THE STORY OF MY MISFORTUNES*

Peter Abelard (1079–1142) is both the most famous and the most notorious personality of his age. Revered and envied by his contemporaries for his compelling lectures, and abused by his detractors for his unorthodox style as well as his illicit love affair with his student Heloise, no figure more epitomizes the charisma of twelfth-century academic life than the "Peripatetic from Pallet," as he was often called. He is the author of important works of ethics, logic, and "theology" (Doc. 8), a word he helped popularize, as well as a justly famous exchange of letters between Heloise and himself written after she had entered the monastic life (Doc. 47). His most personal and revealing work, however, remains his Historia Calamitatum *(The Story of My Misfortunes), an autobiographical letter to an unnamed (and probably non-existent) friend. In it he describes his rise to fame in and around Paris, his "conflicts of disputation" with his academic rivals, the wrath of jealousy ostensibly created by his reputation as a brilliant expositor of philosophy and Scripture, and his persecution at the hands of his enemies.*

Source: trans. Henry Adams Bellows, *Historia Calamitatum: The Story of My Misfortunes. An Auto-biography by Peter Abelard* (New York: William Edward Rudge, 1922), 11–17, 27–28; revised by Alex J. Novikoff. Latin.

[Foreword]

Often the hearts of men and women are stirred, as likewise they are soothed in their sorrows, more by example than by mere words. And, therefore, after offering you some consolation in speech when we were together, I am now of the mind to write you a letter, now that we are apart, about the suffering that has sprung out of my misfortunes. This I do so that, in comparing your sorrows with mine, you may discover that yours are in truth nothing, or at the most but very little, and so shall you come to bear them more easily.

[Of the Birthplace of Peter Abelard, and of His Parents]

Know, then, that I come from a certain town that was built on the way into lesser Brittany, distant some eight miles I think, eastward from the city of Nantes, and in its own tongue is called Le Pallet. Such is the nature of that country, or, it may be, of the quick-witted people who dwell there, that my mind bent itself easily to the study of letters. Yet more, I had a father who had some initiation in letters before he strapped on the soldier's belt. And so it came about that long afterwards his love thereof was so strong that he saw to it that each son of his should be taught in letters even earlier than in the management of arms. This indeed was done. And because I was his first-born son and for that reason the more dear to him, he sought with double diligence to have me wisely taught. For my part, the more I went forward in the study of letters, and ever more easily, the greater became the ardor of my devotion to them, until in truth I was so enthralled by my passion for learning that, gladly leaving to my brothers the pomp of glory in arms, the right of heritage, and all the honors that should have been mine as the eldest born, I fled utterly from the court of Mars so that I might win learning in the bosom of Minerva. And preferring the arms of dialectical reasoning to other forms of philosophy, I traded in all other weapons and valued the conflicts of disputation over the prizes of victory in war. Thenceforth, journeying through many provinces, and debating as I went, going wherever I heard that the study of my chosen art most flourished, I became like one of the Peripatetics.

[His Persecution at the Hands of Master William]

I came at length to Paris, where above all in those days the art of dialectics was most flourishing, and there did I meet William of Champeaux, my teacher, a man most distinguished in his science both by his renown and by his true merit. With him I remained for some time, at first indeed well liked of him; but later I brought him great grief, because I undertook to refute certain of his opinions, not infrequently attacking him in disputation, and now and then in these debates I was adjudged victor. Now this, to those among my fellow students, who were ranked foremost, seemed all the more insufferable because of my youth and the brief duration of my studies.

Out of this sprang the beginning of my misfortunes, which have followed me even to the present day; the more widely my fame was spread abroad, the more bitter was the envy that was aroused against me. Then, with confidence in my gifts beyond what my age warranted, I aspired despite my tender years to the leadership of a school and hurried to the very place where I could undertake this task, the place being none other than the town of Melun, at that time a royal seat. My teacher himself had some foreknowledge of this and tried to remove my school as far as possible from his own. Working in secret before I left his classes, he sought in every way he could to bring down the school I had planned and deprive me of the place I had chosen for it. Since, however, in that very place he had many rivals, and some of them were men of influence in the land, I instead relied on their aid and won the fulfillment of my wish. Indeed, the support of many was secured by reason of his own unconcealed envy for me. From this small inception of my school, my fame in the art of dialectics began to spread abroad, so that little by little the renown not only of my fellow students but even of our very teacher himself grew dim until it was finally eclipsed altogether. Thus it came about that, still more confident in myself, I moved my school as soon as possible to Corbeil, which is by the city of Paris, for there I knew I would be given more frequent chance for my assaults in our battles of disputation.

Not long afterwards I was smitten with a grievous illness, brought upon me by my immoderate zeal for study. This illness forced me to turn homeward to my native province, and thus for some years I was as if cut off from France. And yet, for that very reason, I was sought out all the more eagerly by those whose hearts were eager for instruction in dialectics. But after a few years had passed, and I had recovered from my sickness, I learned that my teacher, William, then archdeacon of Paris, had changed his garb and joined an order of the regular clergy. It was said that he did this in order that he might be seen to be more deeply religious, and so might be elevated to a loftier rank in the Church, something which verily came to pass, for he was made bishop of Châlons-sur-Marne. Nevertheless, the garb he had donned by reason of his religious conversion did nothing to keep him away either from the city of Paris or from his study of philosophy, and in the very monastery [St-Victor] where he had shut himself up for the sake of religion he straightway set about teaching in the same fashion as before.

I returned to him for I was eager to hear more of his lectures on rhetoric, and in the course of our many arguments on various matters, I compelled him by the most potent reasoning first to alter his former opinion on the subject of the universals, and finally to abandon it altogether. Now, the basis of this old concept of his regarding the reality of universal ideas was that the same quality formed the essence alike of the abstract whole and of the individuals, which were its parts: in other words, that there could be no essential differences among these individuals, all being alike save for such variety as might grow out of the many accidents of existence. Thereafter, however, he corrected this opinion, no longer maintaining that the same quality was the essence of all things, but that, rather, it manifested itself in them through diverse ways. This problem of universals is ever the most vexed one among logicians, to such a degree that even Porphyry, writing in his *Isagoge* regarding universals, dared not attempt a final pronouncement, saying rather: "This is the deepest of all problems of its kind." Wherefore it followed that when William had first revised and then finally abandoned altogether his views on this one subject, his lecturing sank into such a state of careless reasoning that it could scarce be called lecturing on the science of dialectics at all. It was as if all his science had been bound up in this one question of the nature of universals.

Thus it came about that my teaching won such strength and authority that even those who before had clung most vehemently to my former master and most bitterly attacked my doctrines now flocked to my school. The very man who had succeeded to my master's chair in the Paris school offered me his post, in order that he might put himself under my tutelage along with all the rest, and this in the very place where his old master and mine had previously reigned. It is not easy to find words to express with what envy he was consumed and with what pain he was tormented when my master saw me, in so short a time, directing the study of dialectics. He could not long, in truth, bear the anguish of what he felt to be his wrongs, and shrewdly he attacked me that he might drive me forth. And because there was nothing in my conduct whereby he could come at me openly, he tried to steal away the school by launching the vilest calumnies against the one who had yielded his post to me, and by putting in his place a certain rival of mine. So then I returned to Melun, and set up my school there as before, and the more openly his envy pursued me, the greater was the authority it conferred upon me. Even so held the poet: "Jealousy aims at the peaks; the winds storm the loftiest summits" [Ovid, *Remedy for Love* 1].

Not long thereafter, when William became aware of the fact that almost all his students were holding grave doubts as to his religion and were whispering earnestly among themselves about his conversion, believing that he had by no means abandoned this world, he withdrew himself and his brotherhood of students to a certain estate far distant from the city. I returned from Melun to Paris, hoping for peace from him in the future. But since, as I have said, he had caused my place to be occupied by a rival of mine, I pitched the camp of my school outside the city on Mount St-Geneviève. Thus I was as one laying siege to him who had taken possession of my post. No sooner had my master heard of this than he brazenly returned to the city, bringing back with him such students as he could and reinstating his brotherhood in their former monastery, as if to block my siege of the soldier he had formerly deserted. If it was his purpose to bring them succor, than in truth he did nothing but hurt them. Before that time my rival had indeed had a certain number of students, of one sort and another, chiefly by reason of his lectures on Priscian, on whom he was considered a great authority. After our master had returned, however, he lost nearly all of these followers, and he was thus compelled to give up the direction of the school. Not long thereafter, apparently despairing of gaining further worldly fame, he was converted to the monastic life.

Following the return of our master to the city, the combats in disputation which my scholars waged both with him himself and with his pupils, and the successes which fortune gave to us, and above all to me, in these wars, you have long since learned of through your own experience. The boast of Ajax, though I speak it more temperately, I still am bold enough to make:

> "if you would learn now
> how victory crowned the battle, by him was
> I never vanquished." [Ovid, *Metamorphoses* 13]

But even were I to be silent, the facts proclaims themselves and the outcome reveals their truth.

While these things were happening, it became necessary for me to return to my old home, because of my dear mother Lucia, who, after my father Berengar's conversion to the monastic life, was preparing to do likewise. When all this had been completed, I returned to France, above all in order that I might study theology, since now my oft-mentioned teacher, William, was active in the episcopate of Châlons. In this field of learning Anselm of Laon, who was his teacher, had for long years enjoyed the greatest renown.

[How He Came to Laon to Seek Anselm as Teacher]

I sought out this same venerable man, whose fame, in truth, was more the result of long established custom than of the potency of his own talent or intellect. If anyone came to him impelled by doubt on any subject, he went away more doubtful still. He was wonderful in the eyes of those who only listened to him, but worthless to those who asked him questions. He had a miraculous flow of words, but they were meaningless and quite devoid of reason. When he kindled a fire, he filled his house with smoke and illumined it not at all. He was a tree that seemed noble to those who gazed upon its leaves from afar, but those who came nearer and examined it more closely saw its barrenness. When, therefore, I had come to this tree so that I might pluck its fruit, I discovered that it was indeed the fig tree which our Lord cursed [Matthew 21:19; Mark 11:13], or that ancient oak to which Lucan likened Pompey, saying: "There he stood, the mere shadow of a great man, like the lofty oak in a wood" [Lucan, *Pharsalia* 1].

It was not long before I made this discovery, and stretched myself lazily in the shade of that same tree. I went to his lectures less and less often, a thing which some among his eminent followers took sorely to heart, because they interpreted it as a mark of contempt for so illustrious a teacher. Thenceforth, they secretly sought to influence him against me, and by their vile insinuations made me hated by him. It happened, moreover, that one day, after the exposition of certain texts, we scholars were jesting among ourselves, and one of them, seeking to draw me out, asked me what I thought of the lectures on the Books of Scripture. I, who had as yet studied only the philosophical sciences, replied that following such lectures seemed to me most useful in so far as the salvation of the soul was concerned, but that it appeared quite extraordinary to me that educated persons should not be able to understand the sacred books simply by studying their writings and glosses alone without the aid of any teacher. Most of those who were present mocked me, and asked whether I myself could do as I had said, or whether I would dare to undertake it. I answered that if they wished, I was ready to try it. Immediately they cried out and jeered all the more. "Well and good," said they, "we agree to the test. Pick out and give us an exposition of some doubtful passage in the Scriptures, so that we can put this boast of yours to the test." And they all chose that most obscure prophecy of Ezekiel.

I accepted the challenge, and invited them to attend a lecture on the very next day. Whereupon they undertook to give me good advice, saying that I should by no means make undue haste in so important a matter, but that I ought to devote a much longer space to working out my exposition and offsetting my inexperience by diligent toil. To this I replied indignantly that it was my custom to win success not by routine but by ability. I added that I would abandon the test altogether unless they would agree not to put off their attendance at my lecture. In truth only a few were present at this first lecture of mine, for it seemed quite absurd to all of them that someone as inexperienced in discussing the Scriptures as I should attempt such a thing so hastily. Nevertheless, this lecture gave such satisfaction to all those who heard it that they spread its praises abroad with enthusiasm, and thus compelled me to continue my interpretation of the sacred text. When word of this was passed on, those who had stayed away from the first lecture came eagerly, some to the second and more still to the third, and all of them were eager to write down the glosses which I had begun on the first day, so as to have them from the very beginning.

[Of the Persecution He Received from His Teacher Anselm]

Now this venerable man of whom I have spoken was acutely smitten with envy, and since he was already incited, as I have already mentioned, by the insinuations of sundry persons, he began to persecute me for my lecturing on the Scriptures no less bitterly than my former master William had done for my lecturing in philosophy. At that time there were in this old man's school two who were considered far to excel all the others: Alberic of Reims and Lotulf the Lombard. The better opinion these two held of themselves, the more they were incensed against me. Chiefly at their suggestion, as it afterwards transpired, the old master had the impudence to forbid me to carry on any further in his school the work of preparing glosses which I had thus begun. The pretext he alleged was that if by chance in the course of this work I should write anything containing blunders, as was thought likely enough in view of my lack of training, the error might be imputed to him. When this came to the ears of his scholars, they were filled with indignation at so undisguised a manifestation of spite, the like of which had never been directed against any one before. The more obvious this rancor became, the more it redounded to my honor, and his persecution did nothing except to make me more famous.

[How He Returned to Paris]

And so, after a few days, I returned to Paris, and there for several years I peacefully directed the school that formerly had been destined for me, nay, even offered to me, but from which I had been driven out. At the very outset of my work there, I set about completing the glosses on Ezekiel that I had begun at Laon. These proved so satisfactory to all who read them that they came to believe me no less adept in lecturing on theology than I had proved myself to be in the field of philosophy. Thus my school was notably increased in size on account of my lectures on both subjects, and the amount of financial profit as well as glory it brought me cannot be concealed from you. But prosperity always puffs up the foolish and worldly comfort enervates the soul, rendering it an easy prey to carnal temptations. Thus I who by this time had come to regard myself as the only philosopher remaining in the whole world, and had ceased to fear any further disturbance of my peace, began to loosen the rein on my desires, although hitherto I had always lived in the utmost continence. And the greater progress I made in my lecturing on philosophy or theology, the more I departed alike from the practice of the philosophers and the spirit of the divines in the uncleanness of my life. For it is well known that philosophers, and still more those who have devoted their lives to arousing the love of sacred study, have been strong above all else in the beauty of chastity. . . .

[Of His Book of Theology and His Persecution by His Fellow-Students]

It so happened that at the outset I devoted myself to analyzing the basis of our faith through illustrations based on human understanding, and I wrote for my students a certain *Treatise on the Unity and Trinity of God.* This I did because they were always seeking for rational and philosophical explanations, asking rather for reasons they could understand than for mere words, saying that it was futile to utter words which the intellect could not possibly follow, that nothing could be believed unless it could first be understood, and that it was absurd for any one to preach to others a thing which neither he himself nor those whom he sought to teach could comprehend. Our Lord himself maintained this same thing when He said: "They are blind leaders of the blind" [Matthew 15:14].

Now, a great many people saw and read this tract, and it became exceedingly popular, its clearness appealing particularly to all who sought information on this subject. And since the questions involved are generally considered the most difficult of all, their complexity is taken as the measure of the subtlety of him who succeeds in answering them. As a result, my rivals became furiously angry, and summoned a council to take action against me, the chief instigators therein being my two intriguing enemies of former days, Alberic and Lotulf. These two, now that both William and Anselm, our erstwhile teachers, were dead, were greedy to reign in their stead, and, so to speak, to succeed them as heirs. While they were directing the school at Rheims, they managed by repeated hints to stir up their archbishop, Ralph, against me, for the purpose of holding a meeting, or rather an ecclesiastical council, at Soissons, provided they could secure the approval of Conon, bishop of Palestrina, at that time papal legate in France. Their plan was to summon me to be present at this council in the city of Soissons, bringing with me the famous book I had written regarding the Trinity. In all this, indeed, they were successful, and the thing happened according to their wishes.

Before I reached Soissons, however, these two rivals of mine so foully slandered me with both the clergy and the public that on the day of my arrival the people came near to stoning me and the few students of mine who had accompanied me there. The cause of their anger was that they had been led to believe that I had preached and written to prove the existence of three gods. No sooner had I reached the city, therefore, than I approached the legate; to him I submitted my book for examination and judgment, declaring that if I had written anything repugnant to the Catholic faith, I was quite ready to correct it or otherwise to make satisfactory amends. The legate directed me to refer my book to the archbishop and to those same two rivals of mine, to the end that my accusers might also be my judges. So in my case was fulfilled the saying: "our enemies are judges" [Deuteronomy 32:31].

These three, then, took my book and looked it over and examined it minutely, but could find nothing therein which they dared to use as the basis for a public accusation against me. Accordingly they put off the condemnation of the book until the close of the council, despite their eagerness to bring it about. For my part, every day before the council convened I publicly discussed the Catholic faith in the light of what I had written, and all who heard me were enthusiastic in their approval alike of the frankness and the logic of my words. When the public and the clergy had thus learned something of the real character of my teaching, they began to say to one another: "Behold, now he speaks openly, and no one brings any charge against him. And this council, summoned, as we have heard, chiefly to take action upon his case is drawing toward its end. Did the judges realize that the error might be theirs rather than his?" As a result of all this, my rivals grew more angry day by day.

18. THE PROLOGUE TO ABELARD'S *SIC ET NON*

Peter Abelard provoked controversy in virtually all the arenas he entered. In addition to his forbidden and highly publicized affair with Heloise (Doc. 47) and his controversial and ultimately condemned work of theology (Doc. 8), he was also roundly criticized by ecclesiastical officials for a work that he boldly called Sic et Non *(Yes and No). The work consists of 158 questions that present a theological assertion and allows for its negation. The first five questions are: Must human faith be completed by reason, or not? Does faith deal only with unseen things, or not? Is there any knowledge of things unseen, or not? May one believe only in God alone, or not? Is God a single unitary being, or not? In addressing these questions Abelard juxtaposes seemingly contradictory quotations from the Church Fathers (and, in several cases, Scripture) without offering a resolution. Men like Bernard of Clairvaux (see Doc. 3) interpreted this as an assault on the harmonious truth of Christian doctrine and denounced him for it. But this is almost surely not what Abelard intended. In the prologue, which draws on classical and biblical sources, he outlines rules for reconciling contradictions, including noting that a single word may have multiple meanings, and he even highlights the advantage of starting from a position of doubt. What he seems to have intended by placing these texts side by side was to stimulate his students and readers into asking questions and seeking inner resolution through their own rational inquiry. For this reason the prologue has often been hailed as a milestone in the critical analysis of texts and ideas.*

Source: trans. Alex J. Novikoff, from *Peter Abailard: Sic et Non*, ed. Blanche Boyer and Richard McKeon (Chicago: University of Chicago Press, 1976), fasc. 1, pp. 89–90, 96–97, 104. Latin.

When, in the vast multiplicity of words that exist, some statements of the Church Fathers not only differ from each other but also appear to be contradictory, one should not pass judgment rashly upon those by whom the world itself is to be judged. For as it is written: "the saints shall judge nations" [Wisdom 3:8], and again: "You shall sit judging" [Matthew 19:28]. Let us not presume to accuse of lying or to condemn as mistaken those to whom our Lord said: "He who hears you, hears me, and he who rejects you, rejects me" [Luke 10:16]. So let us keep our inadequacy in mind, and believe that it is we who lack God's grace to understand, rather than they who were deficient in their writings. As Truth himself said: "For it is not you who are speaking, but the spirit of your Father who speaks through you" [Matthew 10:20]. And since the Spirit through which these matters were written and spoken and revealed to the writers is itself absent from us, let us not be surprised if we should also lack an understanding of these same matters.

An impediment to our understanding is the unusual style [of ancient authors] and the fact that the same words very often have different meanings, for example when a particular word has been used to express first one meaning but then another. For each writer has an abundant supply of words, just as he has of thoughts. According to Cicero [*De Inventione* I.41, 76]: "In all things uniformity is the mother of satiety," which is to say that sameness provokes distaste. The writer should therefore vary the words used in describing one and the same subject, and should not reveal all his thoughts in words which are ordinary and in common usage. For, as blessed Augustine says, these thoughts are concealed lest they become commonplace; the greater the effort spent in searching them out and the greater the difficulty in mastering them, the more attractive they become. In addition, we often must vary our language according to the differences among those to whom we are speaking, since it often happens that the correct meaning of words is unknown or less familiar to some of them. If, as is fitting, we wish to speak with a view to teaching them, we must strive to imitate their usage rather than to achieve a proper style, as indeed that prince of grammar and instructor in the various styles, Priscian, teaches. Even that most ardent teacher of the Church, Saint Augustine, realized this when, in book four of *On Christian Doctrine*, he instructs the teacher in the Church by warning him to leave out everything which prevents his hearers from understanding and to avoid literary ornament and exactness of style, if their omission produces greater success in making his audience understand. "For," he remarks, "the teacher does not care how eloquently he teaches, but rather how clearly. Sometimes passionate enthusiasm for the subject is indifferent to the elegant choice of words. Hence a certain writer, when treating of this kind of style, asserted that there was inherent in it a studied carelessness." Again he says: "Good teachers should give teaching such a high priority that a word which cannot be good Latin without being obscure or ambiguous, but is used in its colloquial form to avoid ambiguity and obscurity, should not be spoken in the form used by the educated, but rather [in that form] habitually used by the unlearned. . . . So the teacher will avoid words that do not teach." . . .

Is it any wonder, then, that judgments based on opinion rather than on truth have sometimes been expressed or even written by the holy Fathers? When conflicting views are expressed about the same topic, one should also carefully distinguish between that which the author is aiming at in the way of enforcing [God's] command and that which is offered with the lenience of pardon or in order to exhort his reader to perfection. Then may we seek a solution for that incompatibility in the difference among authorial intentions. If the statement is indeed a command, we must distinguish whether it is general or specific, in other words whether it is directed to everyone in general or to certain individuals in particular. One should also make a distinction between times and reasons for dispensations [i.e., for relaxations of rules], since what is allowed at one time is often found to be forbidden at another, and what is commanded to be rigorously enforced is often tempered as a result of dispensation. It is particularly essential that these distinctions should be made in drafting the decrees or laws of the Church. An easy solution to controversies can often be found as long as we are able to admit that the same words are given different meanings by different authors.

The careful reader who desires to resolve the conflicts in the writings of the holy Fathers will bear in mind the methods I have just mentioned. But if the conflict is so obvious that it cannot be resolved by logical reasoning, then the authorities must be compared, and the authority that holds greater weight and evidence should be retained above all. Hence the words of Isidore, writing to Bishop Massius: "I thought that this ought to be added at the end of the letter, so that whenever a discordant opinion is found in the acts of the councils, one should retain the opinion which is based on the older or better authority." . . .

These prefatory words having been said, it is my purpose according to my original intention to gather together the diverse sayings of the holy Fathers that have occurred to me as being surrounded by some degree of uncertainty because of their apparent disagreement. These may encourage inexperienced readers to engage in that most important exercise: the search for truth. The result of that search is that it sharpens their critical faculty. For consistent or frequent questioning is the first key to wisdom. Aristotle, the most clear-sighted philosopher of them all, advised his students in his preface *Ad Aliquid* to embrace this questioning wholeheartedly, saying: "Perhaps it is difficult to make a confident pronouncement on matters of this sort unless they have been thoroughly gone over many times. However, it would not be useless to have doubts about individual points." For doubting brings us to inquiry, and it is through inquiry that we perceive the truth. As Truth says: "Seek and you shall find, knock and it shall be opened to you" [Matthew 7:7]. Christ gave us spiritual instruction by his own example. When, at the age of about twelve [cf. Luke 2:41–52], he willingly sat among his teachers and asked questions, he was showing us the example of a pupil who asks questions before then showing us the example of a teacher who preaches, even though his knowledge of God was full and perfect.

When writings are quoted they arouse the reader and incite him to inquire into truth all the more, in proportion to the level of regard in which a given piece of writing is held. For this reason I decided to prefix the well-known decree of Pope Gelasius on the subject of authentic books to my work, which I have compiled from the statements of the holy Fathers gathered into one volume. Thus may it be clearly understood that I have not introduced anything from the apocryphal writings. I have also added excerpts from the *Retractions* of Saint Augustine, from which it may clearly be seen that none of the views that he later retracted has been inserted here.

19. THREE CONTEMPORARY VIEWS OF ABELARD'S TEACHINGS

Abelard was perhaps the only medieval master whose fame his contemporaries recorded so universally and with such enthusiasm and horror. Bernard of Clairvaux (see Doc. 3) was a slightly younger contemporary of Abelard, a member of the young Cistercian order, and a leader in the movement to bring Abelard to heel at the council of Sens in 1141. His letter to Pope Innocent II (r. 1130–43) illustrates both the degree of his antagonism toward Abelard and the rich biblical imagery of his epistolary style. The Vita *of Saint Goswin of Anchin tells the story of how the Flemish-born Goswin went and studied in Paris c.1112, confronted Abelard during one of his classes, but then turned away from the belligerent world of academia and retired to the monastic life in Douai. It is one of the few accounts of Abelard's classroom teachings not written by Abelard himself. The* Deeds of Frederick Barbarossa *is a lengthy historical account of the reign of the emperor, Frederick I (r. 1155–90), begun by Otto of Freising (c. 1114–58) in about 1156 but completed by his chaplain and secretary Rahewin. While the work is nominally about the deeds of the emperor, Otto also includes many vivid digressions concerning contemporary events in Italy and France, including a description of the struggle between Abelard and Bernard, as well as another of Bernard's letter and the pope's response. One should note the range of biblical and classical references, all of which suggests that both Abelard and his detractors were equally committed to marshalling authorities in defense of their positions, a method that builds upon the controversies of the eleventh century (see Doc. 1).*

Source: trans. Samuel J. Eales, *The Life and Works of Saint Bernard* (London: John Hodges, 1889), vol. 2, pp. 543–48; revised by Alex J. Novikoff. Latin.

a. Bernard of Clairvaux's Letter to Pope Innocent II (1141)

It is necessary that offenses come. It is necessary but not pleasant. And therefore the prophet says, "O that I had wings like a dove, for then would I flee away and be at rest" [Psalm 55:6]. And the apostle wishes to be dissolved and to be with Christ. And so another of the saints: "It is enough, O Lord, take away my life, for I am not better than my fathers" [1 Kings 19:4]. I have now something in common with the saints, at least in wish if not in desert. For I could wish myself now taken from the midst of this world, overcome, I confess, by the fearfulness of my spirit and by the troubles of the time. I fear lest I be found better disposed than prepared. I am weary of life, and whether it is expedient to die I know not; and so perhaps even in my prayers I differ from the saints, because they are provoked by the desire of better things, while I am compelled to depart by scandals and anxieties. He says in fact, "To be dissolved and to be with Christ is far better" [Philippians 1:23]. Therefore, in the saint desire prevails, and in me sense; and in this unhappy life neither is he able to have the good he desires, nor I not to have the trouble which I suffer. And for this reason we both desire indeed to depart, with the same wish, but not from the same cause.

I was but just now foolishly promising myself some rest, when the schism of Leo was healed, and peace restored to the Church. But lo! that is at rest, but I am not. I knew not that I was in a vale of tears, or I had forgotten that I dwell in a land of forgetfulness. I paid no attention to the fact that the earth in which I dwell brings forth for me thorns and thistles, that when they are cut down others succeed, and when these are destroyed others grow ceaselessly, and spring up without intermission. I had heard these things indeed, but, as I now find out, vexation itself brings better understanding to the hearing. My grief has been renewed, not destroyed, my tears have overwhelmed me, because evil has strengthened, and when they have endured the frost, the snow fell upon them. Who hath power to resist this frost? By it charity freezes, that iniquity may abound. We have escaped the lion, Leo, to fall on the dragon [Peter Abelard] who perhaps may do us not less injury by lurking in ambush than the former by raging on high. Although I would that his poisonous pages were still lying hid in bookcases and not read at the crossroads. His books fly abroad; and they who hate the light because they are evil have dashed themselves against the light, thinking light darkness. Over the cities and castles is darkness cast instead of light; instead of honey, or rather in honey, his poison is on all sides eagerly drunk in. His books have passed from nation to nation, and from one kingdom to another people. A new gospel is being fashioned for peoples and nations, a new faith propounded, another foundation laid than that which is laid. Virtues and vices are discussed immorally, the sacraments of the Church unfaithfully, the mystery of the Holy Trinity craftily and extravagantly; but everything is given in a perverse spirit, in an unprecedented manner, and beyond what we have received.

Goliath advances, tall in stature, clad in his armor of war, preceded by his armor-bearer, Arnold of Brescia. Scale overlaps scale, and there is no point left unguarded. Indeed, the bee which was in France has sent murmurings to the Italian bee, and they have come together against the Lord and against his anointed. They have bent their bow, they have made ready their arrows within the quiver, that they may privately shoot at them which are true at heart. In their life and habits they have the form of godliness, but they deny its power, and they thereby deceive many, for they transform themselves into angels of light, when they are Satan's. Goliath standing with his armor-bearer between the two lines, shouts against the armies of Israel, and curses the ranks of the saints, and that the more boldly because he knows that no David is present. In short, he puts forward philosophers with great praise and so affronts the teachers of the Church, and prefers their imaginations and novelties to the doctrine and faith of the Catholic Fathers; and when all fly from his face he challenges me, the weakest of all, to single combat.

The archbishop of Sens, at his solicitation, wrote to me fixing a day for the encounter, on which he in person, and with his brother bishops, should determine, if possible, on his [Abelard's] false opinions, against which I had ventured to lift my voice. I refused, not only because I am but a youth and he a man of war from his youth, but also because I thought it unfitting that the grounds of the faith should be handed over to human reasoning for discussion, when, as is agreed, it rests on such a sure and firm foundation. I said that his writings were enough for his condemnation, and that it was not my business, but that of the bishops, whose office it is to decide on matters of faith. He nonetheless, nay, rather the more on this account, lifted his voice, called upon many, assembled his accomplices. What he wrote about me to his disciples I do not care to say. He spread everywhere the report that on a fixed day he would answer me at Sens. The report reached everyone, and I could not but hear of it. At first I held back, nor was I much moved by the popular rumor. At length I yielded to the advice of my friends (although much against my will, and with tears), who saw how all were getting ready as if for a show, and they feared lest from my absence cause of offense should be given to the people and the horn of the adversary be exalted; and, since the error was likely to be strengthened if there were no one to answer or contradict it, I betook myself to the place appointed and at the time, unprepared, indeed, and unarmed, except that I resolved in my mind those words, "Take no thought how ye shall answer, for it shall be given you in that hour what ye shall say" [Matthew 10:19]: and, again, "The Lord is my helper, I will not fear what man may do unto me" [Psalm 118:6]. There had assembled, besides bishops and abbots, very many religious men, masters of the schools from different states, and many learned clergy; and the king, too, was present. And so in the presence of all, my adversary standing opposite, I produced certain articles taken from his books. And when I began to read them he departed, unwilling to listen, and appealed from the judges that he had chosen himself, a course I do not think allowable. Further, the articles having been examined were found, in the judgment of all, opposed to the faith, contrary to the truth. I have written this on my own behalf, lest I should be thought to have shown levity, or at all events rashness, in so important a matter.

But you, O successor of Peter, will determine whether he, who assails the faith of Peter, ought to have shelter at the See of Peter. You, I say, the friend of the bridegroom, will provide measures to free his bride from lying lips and from a deceitful tongue. But that I may speak a little more boldly with my Lord, do you, most loving Father, pay close attention to yourself, and to the grace of God which is in you. Did he not, when you were small in your own eyes, place you over nations and kingdoms? For what, but that you should pull down, and destroy, and build, and plant? See what great things he, who took you from your father's house, and anointed you with the oil of his mercy, has since done for your soul: what great things for his Church, by your means, in his vineyard, heaven and earth being witness, have been, as powerfully as wholesomely, uprooted and destroyed; what great things, again, have been well built, planted, and sown. God raised up the madness of schismatics in your time, that by your efforts they might be crushed. I have seen the fool in great prosperity, and immediately his beauty was cursed; I saw, I say, the impious highly exalted and lifted up above the cedars of Lebanon, and I passed by, and lo he was gone. It is necessary, Saint Paul says, "that there be heresies and schisms, that they that are approved may be made manifest" [1 Corinthians 11:19]. And, indeed, in schism, as I have just said, the Lord has proved and known you. But that nothing be wanting to your crown, lo! heresies have sprung up. And so, for the perfection of your virtues, and that you may be found to have done nothing less than the great bishops, your predecessors, take away from us, most loving Father, the foxes which are laying waste the vineyard of the Lord while they are little ones; lest if they increase and multiply, our children despair of destroying what was not exterminated by you. Although they are not even now small or few, but imposing and numerous, and will not be exterminated save by you, and by a strong hand. Iacinctus [an ancient eunuch; that is, Abelard] has threatened me with many evils; but he has not done, nor could he do, what he wishes. But I thought that I ought to bear patiently concerning myself what he has spared neither to your person nor to the Curia; but this my friend Nicholas, as he is also yours, will better tell in person.

b. The *Life* of Saint Goswin

Source: trans. Alex J. Novikoff, *Beati Gosvini Vita. . .*, ed. Richard Gibbons (Douai: M. Wyon, 1620), 12–18. Latin.

At that time, Peter Abelard, having assembled many students around him, was leading a public school [i.e., open to other religious orders] in the cloister of Mount St-Geneviève. His knowledge was well tested and his eloquence sublime, but he was the inventor of strange and unheard of things and asserted novel claims. In order to establish his own theories he set out to disprove what others had proved. He therefore provoked the hatred of those with saner minds, and just as he turned his hand against everyone, so everyone rose up in arms against him. He made pronouncements no one before him had presumed to say, and astonished everyone. So when the absurdity of his inventions came to the attention of those who were teaching in Paris, they were first shocked, then seized with the greatest desire to confound his falsities, and began to ask who among them would undertake the task of disputing him. They felt that it was indignant that among such learned people the inventor of such fables should not be met with an opponent and that if this barking man were not beaten by the stick of truth, and if someone did not step in to refute his misguided claims, he would continue to invent and speak more freely.

Since the venerable young Goswin possessed both effective eloquence and a perspicacious mind, they [the students] persuaded him to counter those frivolities. This was not hard to achieve, for he burned and seethed with desire to do so, and it would have been difficult to prevent him were he not afraid of being labeled presumptuous.

Master Jocelin, who later directed the cathedral of Soissons, having much affection for him, opposed the idea and discouraged the meeting, saying that master Peter [Abelard] was not a debater but a sophist, that he would behave more like a jester than a doctor, and that following the example of Hercules he would not easily let go of the club once it was in his hand. In other words that he was obstinate in his error and would never acquiesce to a truth that was not his own, and that he who attempted to educate a mocker would be doing injury to himself. In short, [Jocelin warned] that it was enough to comprehend his tricks and not fall prey to his vanities. The learned doctor [Jocelin] spoke these and similar words of dissuasion to the one [Goswin] who was full of eloquence and channels of wisdom wherever he wished to direct his discourse.

But Goswin paid no attention to those warnings and arguments and did not take into account the fact that he was still a young novice, whereas this master was a bellicose man accustomed to victories. He took several companions with him and ascended the mountain of St-Geneviève, just as David did battle with Goliath [1 Samuel 17], in order to confront the man who thundered forth his astonishing and unheard-of opinions for the benefit of his audience, doing so as if to deride the army of those who thought straight.

Upon arriving at the place of combat, in other words the entryway to his school, he found [Abelard] lecturing and inculcating his novelties to his students. As soon as he was there he began to speak, and he [Abelard] looked scornfully down upon him. A warrior from his youth, and seeing that the newcomer was just starting to grow a beard, he disdained him in his heart, no less than the Philistine did David. He [Goswin] was indeed of fair and handsome appearance, though of moderate height and weight. But the egotist [Abelard] was forced to respond to his pressing assailant: "Keep quiet and do not to disturb the course of my lesson." But [Goswin] had not come there to be quiet and so he fiercely persisted. Meanwhile, his adversary, holding him in disdain, paid no attention to the words that were being uttered, judging it undignified that so great a professor should answer to such a puny youth. But he was judging him on appearance, finding him contemptible on account of his age, and he did not take notice of the perceptive intelligence of his heart. But his disciples knew this young man well, and, so that he would not fail to give an answer, told him that he [Goswin] was a sharp debater and a great credit to the science [of argumentation], and that it was not dishonorable to take on the business of disputing someone like him, whereas it was most dishonorable to continue refusing. "So let him speak up," said [Abelard], "if he has something to say." Speaking his mind, he [Goswin] asserted propositions so competently that they exuded neither levity nor garrulous verbosity, and on account of their depth they drew the attention of all who were listening: the one assumed, the other affirmed, the former unable to respond to the affirmations of the latter. As those games of sophistry were blocked by the one who knew nothing of these cunning tricks, he [Abelard] was finally forced to admit that he was not in accord with reason.

c. Otto of Freising, *The Deeds of Frederick Barbarossa*

Source: trans. C.C. Mierow, Otto of Freising, *The Deeds of Frederick Barbarossa* (Toronto: University of Toronto Press, 1994), 83–87. Latin.

This Peter was a native of that province of France which is now called by its inhabitants Brittany. This region is productive of clerics endowed with keen intellects, well adapted to the arts but almost witless for other matters, such as the two brothers Bernard and Thierry, very learned men. This Peter, I say, had from an early age been devoted to literary studies and other trifles, but was so conceited and had such confidence in his own intellectual power that he would scarcely so demean himself as to descend from the heights of his own mind to listen to his teachers. However, he first had a teacher named Roscellinus who was the first in our times to teach in logic the nominalistic doctrine. Afterward he betook himself to those very distinguished men, Anselm of Laon and William of Champeaux, bishop of Châlons-sur-Marne, but did not long endure the weight of their words, judging them to be devoid of cleverness and subtlety. Then he became a teacher and went to Paris, showing great capacity by his originality in discovering matters not only of importance for philosophy but also conducive to social amusements and pastimes. On a certain sufficiently well-known occasion he was very roughly dealt with, and became a monk in the monastery of St-Denis. There devoting himself day and night to reading and meditation, from being a keen thinker he became keener, from being a learned man he became more learned, to such a degree that after some time he was released from obedience to his abbot, came forth in public, and again assumed the office of teacher.

Accordingly, holding to the doctrine of nominalism in natural philosophy, he rashly carried it over into theology. Therefore, in teaching and in writing of the Holy Trinity he minimized too much the three persons which Holy Church has up to the present time piously believed and faithfully taught to be not merely empty names but distinct entities and differentiated by their properties. The analogies he used were not good, for he said among other things: "Just as the same utterance is the major premise, the minor premise, and the conclusion, so the same being is Father, Son, and Holy Spirit." On this account a provincial synod was assembled against him at Soissons in the presence of a legate of the Roman see [1121]. He was adjudged a Sabellian heretic by those excellent men and acknowledged masters, Alberic of Rheims and Letald of Novara, and was forced by the bishops to cast into the fire with his own hand the books that he had published. No opportunity of making a reply was granted him because his skill in disputation was mistrusted by all. These things were done under Louis the Elder, king of France [Louis VI, r. 1108–37].

Then, after he had lectured again for a long time and had attracted a very great throng of pupils to him, while Innocent was pope at Rome, and in France Louis, the son of the former Louis was king [Louis VII, r. 1137–80], he was again summoned by the bishops and the Abbot Bernard to a hearing at Sens, in the presence of King Louis and Thibaud, the count palatine, and other nobles and countless numbers of the people [1141]. While his faith was being discussed there, fearing an uprising of the people, he asked that he might appear before the Roman see. But the bishops and the abbot sent a deputation to the Roman Church along with the articles because of which he was assailed and demanded a sentence of condemnation, in a letter of which this is a copy:

> To the most reverend lord and most beloved father, by the grace of God supreme pontiff, Innocent, S[amson], archbishop of Rheims, and Bishops Joscelin of Soissons, G[eoffrey] of Châlons-sur-Marne, A[lvise] of Arras send voluntary acknowledgement of due subjection. . . .
>
> Peter Abelard strives to make vain the merit of the Christian faith, since he believes he can comprehend by human reason all that is God: he mounts up to the heaven, he goes down again to the depths [Psalm 107:26]; there is nothing that is hid from him, whether in the depth of hell or in the height above [Isaiah 7:11]. The man is great in his own eyes, disputing concerning the faith against the faith, exercising himself in great matters and in things too high for him [Psalm 131:1], a searcher of his own glory [Proverbs 25:27], a contriver of heresies. In the past he composed a book about the Holy Trinity, but by the authority of a legate of the Roman Church it was tried by fire because iniquity was found in it [cf. 1 Corinthians 3:13 and Ezekiel 28:15].

Cursed be he who rebuilds the ruins of Jericho [Joshuah 6:26]. That book of his has risen from the dead, and with it the heresies of many that were asleep have risen and have appeared to many [Matthew 27:52–53]. Finally now she sends out her boughs unto the sea and her shoots unto Rome [cf. Psalm 80:11]. This is the man's boast, that his book hath where to lay its head [Matthew 8:20] in the Roman court; by this is his error strengthened and confirmed. Hence he preaches with confidence everywhere the word of iniquity.

Therefore, when the abbot of Clairvaux, armed with zeal for justice and for the faith, accused him of these matters in the presence of the bishops, he neither confessed nor made denial [Cf. John 1:20], but that he might prolog his iniquity [Psalm 129:3], he appealed, without suffering any hurt or oppression, from the time, the place, and the judge that he had himself selected for himself, to the apostolic see.

The bishops who had assembled for this sole purpose, deferring to your Reverence, have taken no action against his person, but merely—though the necessity for remedial measures, lest the disease spread—have passed judgment upon the articles once condemned by the holy fathers. Accordingly, because that man draws the multitude after him and has a people that believes in him, it is necessary that you treat this disease with a swift-acting remedy: "For too late is medicine active, when from long delay sickness has gathered strength" [Ovid, *Cures of Love*]. . . .

Innocent's reply was as follows:

Bishop Innocent, the servant of the servants of God, to the venerable brethren, the archbishops Henry of Sens and S[amson] of Rheims and their suffragans and to his very dear son in Christ, B[ernard], abbot of Clairvaux, greeting and apostolic benediction.

From the testimony of the apostle we learn that as there is one Lord, so there is one faith [Ephesians 4:5], on which as upon an immovable foundation, other than which no man can lay [1 Corinthians 3:11], the stability of the Catholic Church rests unshaken. Hence it is that the blessed Peter, the prince of the apostles, for his notable confession of this faith was privileged to hear: 'Thou art Peter, I say, and upon this rock will I build my church' [Matthew 16:18], by rock quite evidently being meant the firmness of the faith and the solidity of Catholic unity. For this is our Savior's coat without seam for which the soldiers cast lots but could not rend it [cf. John 19:23–24]. Against it in the beginning 'the heathen raged and the people imagined vain things. The kings of the earth set themselves and the rulers took counsel together' [Acts 4:25–26, Psalm 2:1–2]. But the apostles, the leaders of the Lord's flock, and their successors, the apostolic men, aflame with the fire of love and zeal for righteousness, have not hesitated to defend the faith and to plant it in the hearts of the peoples by the shedding of their own blood. When at last the fury of the persecutors ceased, the Lord commanded the winds and there was a great calm [Matthew 8:26] in the Church. But because the adversary of the human race ever walks about, seeking whom he may devour [1 Peter 5:8], he stealthily brought in the deceitful error of the heretics to combat the purity of the faith. Against these the true leaders of the churches manfully rose up and condemned their wicked teachings together with the authors of the same. For in the great Nicene synod the heretic Arius was condemned. The synod of Constantinople condemned the heretic Manichaeus with due sentence. In the synod of Ephesus, Nestorius received the condemnation befitting his error. The synod, of Chalcedon also, by a most just sentence, confuted the Nestorian heresy and that of Eutyches with Dioscurus and his accomplices.

And besides, Marcian, who though a layman was nevertheless a most Christian emperor, inflamed with love for the Catholic faith, writing to our predecessor the most holy Pope John against those who strove to profane the sacred mysteries, speaks as follows, saying (among other things): 'Let no cleric or soldier or man of any other condition attempt hereafter to discuss the Christian faith in public. For one does an injustice to the judgment of the very reverend synod, if one seeks to agitate anew and argue again about matters once decided and properly settled. And those who transgress this law shall be punished as though they had committed sacrilege. Therefore, if there shall be any cleric who dares to discuss religion in public, he shall be removed for the company of the clergy.'

Moreover, we grieve that (as we learn from an inspection of your letters and the heretical articles sent to us by you, my brothers) in the last days when perilous times impend (2 Timothy 3:1), because of the pernicious doctrine of Master P. Abelard, the heresies of those whom we have mentioned and other perverse dogmas have begun to spring up in opposition to the Catholic faith. But in this we find particular consolation and for it we give thanks to omnipotent God, that in your country He has raised up such sons to succeed fathers, and that in the time of our apostolate in his Church He has willed that there should be such illustrious shepherds who are zealous to oppose the falsehoods of a new heretic, and to present to Christ a bride without spot, a chaste virgin, to one husband [2 Corinthians 11:2]. We, therefore, who are seen to sit, although unworthy, on the chair of Saint Peter, to whom it was said by the Lord: 'and, when thou art converted, strengthen thy brethren' [Luke 22:32], we, having conferred with the council of our brethren the cardinal bishops, have condemned the articles sent us by your discretion and all the perverse teachings of Peter himself, by the authority of the holy canons, together with their author, and we have imposed perpetual silence upon him as a heretic. We decree also that all followers and defenders of this error be sequestrated from the company of the faithful and restrained by the bond of excommunication.

Given at the Lateran on the twelfth day before the Kalends of August [21 July 1141].

When Peter learned that the condemnation of his teaching had been confirmed by the Roman church, he betook himself to the monastery of Cluny and wrote an apologetic denying the words of the aforesaid articles in part and the interpretation entirely.

20. HUGH OF ST-VICTOR ON SECULAR LEARNING: THE *DIDASCALICON*

Hugh of St-Victor (d. 1141) intended his Didascalicon *as a guide to advanced learning in a monastic context. Selections from the portion of the work that deals with sacred learning were included in Doc. 9; selections concerning the methods of approach to secular learning are given below. Hugh begins by surveying the different types of students and the purpose of knowledge before launching into an explanation of the origins and contents of the liberal arts, and in particular the Greek origins of those arts. He explains the origins of logic (the third art of the* trivium*) and its usefulness to the spiritual quest for uncorrupted truth, a point that would be taken up with greater urgency by John of Salisbury (see Doc. 21). In Book 3, Hugh also highlights the necessary order and methods of reading and gives insightful pedagogical advice on the importance of memory and discipline. In his chapter on meditation, which is placed in between the chapters on reading and memory, Hugh articulates a basic principle of scholastic anthropology that traces its roots back through Christian Neoplatonism to Scripture itself (cf. Romans 1:20), asserting that the rational human mind is uniquely endowed with the ability to ascend from the apprehension of the visible realities to knowledge of the invisible realities of God.*

Source: trans. Franklin T. Harkins, in *Interpretation of Scripture: Theory*, ed. Franklin T. Harkins and Frans van Liere, Victorine Texts in Translation, vol. 3 (Hyde Park, NY: New City Press, 2013), 81–85, 93–95, 123–27. Latin.

Preface

There are many people whose very nature has left them so devoid of ability that they can barely understand things that are actually easy, and of these people there seem to me to be two kinds. For there are some who, although they are ignorant of their own dullness, nevertheless strive toward knowledge with all the effort their strength allows; and persevering in study ceaselessly, they deserve to obtain by their desire what they do not quite have as a result of their work. Others, by contrast, because they sense that they are in no way able to comprehend the highest things, disregard even the least, and, as it were, acquiescing untroubled in their own apathy, they squander the light of truth in the greatest things the more they avoid learning the least things which they are able to understand. Hence, the Psalmist says: "They were not willing to understand so that they might act well" [Psalm 34:4]. For it is one thing not to know, but a far different thing to be unwilling to know. Indeed, not to know comes from weakness, but to loathe knowledge comes from a deformed will.

There is another kind of person whom nature has greatly enriched with ability and to whom nature has supplied an easy way of coming to the truth. Among these, although there is unequal intellectual ability, there is nevertheless not the same strength or will in all to develop their natural intelligence through exercise and learning. For there are many who, because they are entangled in the business and cares of this world more than is necessary or abandoned to the vices and desires of the body, have buried the talent of God in the ground and seek from it neither the fruit of wisdom nor the interest of good work [that should have accrued to the talent]. These people are certainly very detestable. There are others for whom the lack of property and little wealth reduce the practicality of learning. Yet we believe that these people cannot at all be fully excused on account of this since we see many laboring in hunger, thirst, and nakedness to attain the fruit of knowledge. And nevertheless it is one thing when you are unable to learn—or, to speak more correctly—when you are unable to learn easily, but it is another thing to be able but unwilling to learn. Just as it is more glorious to cling to wisdom by strength alone when no resources are at hand, so too it is certainly more disgraceful to have a vigorous natural ability and to abound in riches, but to be lazy in your spare time.

There are two main things by which everyone is instructed in knowledge, namely, reading and meditation. Of these reading occupies the first place in learning, and it is reading that this book treats by offering rules for it. There are three rules most necessary for reading. First, everyone should know what one should read; second, in what order one should read, that is, what first and what afterwards; and third, how one should read. These three rules are treated one by one in this book. Moreover, it instructs the reader of secular writings as much as the reader of Sacred Scripture. For this reason, it is divided into two parts, each of which has three distinctions. In the first part it teaches the reader of the arts, and in the second part the reader in theology. It teaches in this way: by showing first what should be read, and next in what order, and finally how it should be read.

In order to know what one should read or what one should especially read, in the first part this book lists the origin of all the arts and then describes and classifies them by explaining how each art contains another or is contained by another, thereby dividing philosophy from the top all the way down to its last constituent parts. Then it lists the originators of the arts and afterwards makes clear which of these arts should especially be read. Then it also explains in what order and how they should be read. Finally, it outlines the discipline of one's life that is necessary for readers. And there the first part ends. In the second part the book determines which writings should be called sacred; then it discusses the number and order of the sacred books and their authors as well as the meanings of the names of these books. Afterwards it treats certain characteristics of Sacred Scripture that are indispensable. Then it teaches how he who seeks it in the correction of his morals and his way of life should read Sacred Scripture. Finally, it teaches the student who reads Sacred Scripture for the sake of the love of knowledge. And there the second part comes to an end.

Book 1, Chapter 1: On the Origins of the Arts

Of all things to be eagerly desired, the first is Wisdom, in which the form of the perfect good stands fixed. Wisdom illuminates the human person so that he might know himself, who was similar to the other animals in that he did not understand that he had been created higher than them. To be sure, though, his immortal mind, illuminated by Wisdom, looks back at its own beginning and realizes how unbecoming it is for it to seek anything outside itself when what it is can be sufficient in and of itself. It is written on the tripod of Apollo: *gnoti seauton*, that is, "know yourself," because without a doubt if the human person had not forgotten his own origin he would realize to what extent every mutable thing is nothing.

An opinion approved by philosophers claims that the soul is fit together from all the parts of nature. And Plato's *Timaeus* formed the entelechy [the first perfection of a natural body] out of divisible, indivisible, and mixed substance; and likewise out of same and diverse substance, and a nature mixed together from both, by which the universe is ordered. For the entelechy itself grasps not only the elements but also the things that follow the elements since it both comprehends the invisible causes of things through its understanding and brings together the visible forms of actual objects through sense perception. And divided, it gathers movement into two spheres because, whether it moves outward to sensible things through sense perception or upward to invisible things through understanding, it circles around and draws the likenesses of things to itself. And this is why the same mind, which is able to grasp all things, is joined together from every substance and nature of which it manifests a form of its likeness. For it was a Pythagorean doctrine that similars are comprehended by similars, so that certainly the rational soul could in no way comprehend all things unless it were composed of all things, according to what a certain author says [quoting from Chalcidius, who attributes the verse to Empedocles]:

> We comprehend earth with the earthly, the sky with fire,
> Liquid with water, the breathable with our breath.

We should not suppose, however, that men who were most expert in the natures of all things thought that simple essence stretched itself out into a multitude of parts. But in order to point out more clearly the extraordinary power of the soul, they affirmed that it was constituted from all natures not according to composition but according to an analogy to composition. And it also must be believed that this likeness of all things comes to the soul from a source different from or external to it; rather, the soul grasps in itself and from itself by means of a certain innate power and proper capacity. For as Varro says in *Periphysion*: "Not every change happens to things from without in such a way that it is necessary for whatever is changed either to lose something that it had or to gain something different from without that it did not have before." We see this when a wall takes on the likeness of a random image when a form is projected on it from without. When, however, a coiner impresses a figure into metal, that very metal, already something, begins to represent something else, indeed not from without, but by its very own power and natural aptitude. Truly in this way the mind, having been marked with the likeness of all things, is said to be all things, to receive its composition from all things, and to contain all things—not wholly, but virtually and potentially. And this is that dignity of our nature, which all equally possess innately, but of which not all are equally aware. For the mind, numbed by bodily passions and seduced outside of itself by sensible forms, has forgotten what it is, and because it has not remembered that it is anything different, it thinks that it is nothing beyond what is seen. We are restored, however, through learning so that we might again know our nature, and so that we might learn not to seek outside ourselves what we can find within. The greatest solace in life, therefore, is the pursuit of Wisdom. He who finds it is happy, and he who takes hold of it is blessed.

Chapter 2: That Philosophy is the Pursuit of Wisdom

"Pythagoras was the first of all to call the pursuit of Wisdom 'philosophy'" [Boethius, *On Music* II.2; Augustine, *City of God* VIII.2; Isidore, *Etymologies* VIII.6] and to prefer to be called *philosophos*; for previously philosophers had been called *sophoi*, that is, wise men. It is indeed beautiful that he called seekers of truth not "wise men" but "lovers of Wisdom," because without a doubt the whole truth lies hidden to such a degree that, however much the mind is set afire with the love of it and however much the mind ascends to the investigation of it, nevertheless, only with difficulty can the mind comprehend the truth itself as it is. Pythagoras, however, firmly established philosophy as the discipline "of those things that truly exist and of themselves possess immutable substance."

"Now philosophy is the love and pursuit of, and in a certain way friendship with, Wisdom—truly not of the kind that is concerned with certain tools and consists in a workingman's skills and knowledge, but rather of that Wisdom which, lacking nothing, is the eternal Mind and the sole primordial Reason of things. Here the love of Wisdom is the illumination of the comprehending mind by that pure Wisdom, and in a certain way drawing and calling back to Wisdom itself so that the pursuit of Wisdom appears to be friendship with the Godhead and pure Mind. This Wisdom, therefore, endows every kind of soul with the benefit of its very own divinity and brings the soul back to the proper power and purity of its nature. From it are born the truth of speculation and meditation as well as holy and pure chastity of action" [Boethius, *In Porphyrium dialogi* I.3].

"But seeing that this most excellent good of philosophy has been established for human souls, in order that our presentation might proceed along a certain thread of argument we must begin with the efficient powers of the soul" [Boethius, *In Isagogen Porphyrii Commenta* I.1]. . . .

Chapter 11: On the Origin of Logic

Having explained the emergence of the theoretical, practical, and mechanical arts, it remains to investigate the origin of the logical arts, which we consider last because they were discovered last. The other arts had been discovered earlier, but the invention of the logical arts was also necessary since no one can suitably discuss things unless he has first learned the method of speaking correctly and truly. For, just as Boethius says [*In Isagogen* I.2], when the ancients originally devoted themselves to investigating the natures of things and the distinguishing marks of moral behavior, it was inevitable that they were often mistaken because they did not have the skill of distinguishing between different words and their meanings. "This happens in many writings of Epicurus, who thinks that the universe consists of atoms and speaks deceitfully about pleasure being honorable. It is clear, therefore, that Epicurus and others fell victim to this error because, being ignorant about the nature of argumentation [*disputandi*], they imagined that whatever they had arrived at by reasoning also happened in reality. This is certainly a great error, for things do not behave in reasoning the same way as they would in calculation. For in mathematical calculation whatever one obtains by correctly counting on the fingers is also undoubtedly and necessarily obtained in reality, so that if a calculation yields one hundred it is necessary that there also be one hundred real things underlying that number. In argumentation, however, this relationship is not operative to the same degree, nor is whatever conclusion one reaches in discussion always found to be firmly established in nature. Hence, the person who has cast aside knowledge of argumentation when he carefully inquires about the nature of things necessarily falls into error. For unless one has first arrived at the knowledge of what form of reasoning remains on the true path of argumentation and what form remains only on the seemingly true path, and unless he has discerned what form of reasoning is certain and what form is suspect, he cannot discover the uncorrupted truth of things by reasoning.

The ancients, having frequently fallen into many errors, arrived at certain false and contradictory conclusions in their discussions, and when contrary conclusions were reached concerning the very same issue, it seemed impossible either that conflicting lines of arguments had reached conclusions which were both true or that it would be unclear which line of reasoning ought to be believed. For those reasons it seemed good first to consider closely the true and complete nature of argumentation itself. After learning this, they were then also able to discern whether what was discovered through argument should be really accepted. From here originated practical knowledge of the discipline of logic, which furnishes ways of distinguishing between modes of discussion and the very forms of argumentation, so that the practitioner is able to recognize which form of argumentation is sometimes true and sometimes false, which is always false, and which is never false." Indeed, this discipline is last in time, but first in order. Truly beginners in philosophy should read in this discipline first because it teaches the nature of words and their meanings, without which no philosophical treatise can be explicated rationally.

Logic derives its name from the Greek *logos*, which has a twofold meaning. *Logos* means discourse or reason, and therefore logic can be called a discursive or rational science. Rational logic, which is called disputational, contains dialectic and rhetoric. Discursive logic is genus to grammar, dialectic, and rhetoric, and so contains disputational logic under it. Actually, then, it is discursive logic that we classify as fourth after the theoretical, practical, and mechanical arts. But it must not be thought that there was no discourse before the invention or discovery of discursive logic, as if humans did not previously speak to one another. Both verbal and written discourse existed previously, but the theory of discussion and writing had not yet been organized into an art. No rules for speech and argumentation had yet been provided. For every science was a practice before it became an art. But when people afterward considered that use could be transformed into an art and that what had earlier been constant and unbridled could be restrained by fixed principles and rules, they began, as had been said, to organize into various arts the customary practices that had arisen partly by chance and partly by nature; they corrected what was corrupt in these practices, supplied what was lacking, cut back what was excessive, and prescribed fixed principles and rules for each practice.

The origin of all the arts followed this pattern. Running through each one, we find that this is true. Before there was grammar, people were both writing and speaking. Before there was dialectic, people were distinguishing true from false by reasoning. Before there was rhetoric, people were discussing the civil laws. Before there was arithmetic, people knew how to count. Before there was music, people were singing. Before there was geometry, people were measuring their lands. Before there was astronomy, people distinguished the seasons by observing the course of the stars. But then came the arts, which, although they took their beginning from use, nevertheless are improvements on it.

This would be the place to explain who the inventors or authors of each art were, when or where they lived, and how they started the disciplines. But first I want to distinguish the arts from one another by dividing philosophy in a certain way. It is necessary, then, to briefly recapitulate what we have said above, so that we might more easily transition to what follows. We have said that there are only four branches of knowledge which contain all the others: namely, the theoretical, which concerns speculation into the truth; the practical, which investigates the training of morals; the mechanical, which manages the activities of this life; and the logical, which furnishes the knowledge for speaking correctly and arguing decisively. And so we can appropriately understand the fourfold nature of the soul that the ancients appropriated in their oaths out of reverence. Hence, it was said: "By him who gave the fourfold number to our soul" [Macrobius, *Dream of Scipio* I.6.41].

Book 3, Chapter 8: On the Order of Reading

One kind of order is established in the disciplines, as when I say that grammar is more ancient than dialectic or that arithmetic is prior to music. Another kind of order is in the books, as when I say that the Catilinarian orations are prior to the Jugurthine. Another kind is in the narrative of the story, which advances in a continuous series of events. Another kind is in the exposition of a text.

The order in the disciplines is determined according to nature, in the books according to the person of the author or the subject matter, and in the narrative according to the arrangement of events. This arrangement can be of two kinds: natural, namely, when events are recorded in the order in which they happened; and artificial, that is, when an event that happened later is narrated earlier and what happened earlier is related later. In the exposition of a text, the order is determined by the inquiry [by the questions the expositor asks of the text].

The exposition of a text takes place at three levels: the letter [*littera*], the sense [*sensus*], and the meaning [*sententia*]. The letter is the suitable arrangement of words, which we also call grammatical construction. The sense is the simple and clear signification that the letter displays on the surface. The meaning is the deeper understanding that is discovered only through exposition and interpretation. The proper order of inquiry among these is first the letter, then the sense, and finally the meaning. When this has been done, the exposition of a text is complete.

Chapter 9: On the Method of Reading

The method of reading consists of analysis [*dividendo*]. All analysis begins from finite realities and proceeds all the way to infinite realities. For every finite thing is known and able to be grasped by our intellect to a greater extent than the infinite. Teaching begins with these things that are better known and through our understanding of them reaches to the knowledge of those things that remain hidden. Besides, we investigate with our reason, whose proper operation is to divide, whenever by analyzing and discovering the nature of individual things we descend from universals to particulars. For every universal is more defined than its particulars. When we learn, therefore, we ought to begin with those realities that are better known and determined and apprehended; then by descending gradually and by distinguishing each one through analysis, we ought to investigate the nature of the particulars that instantiate the universals.

Chapter 10: On Meditation

Meditation is constant reflection with a purpose, which wisely searches out the cause and the origin, the mode [of being] and the usefulness of each thing. Meditation takes its beginning from reading, but it is bound by none of its principles or precepts. For it delights to run in open areas where it fixes its keen and unrestrained vision on the contemplation of truth, now glancing at those causes of things, now penetrating the depths, leaving nothing uncertain, nothing obscure.

The beginning of learning, therefore, is in reading, but its contemplation is in meditation. If anyone learns to love it most intimately and wishes to make time for it, meditation renders his life intensely pleasing and gives him the greatest comfort in times of tribulation. For it is especially meditation that removes the soul from the din of earthly activities and even in this life gives it a certain foretaste of the sweetness of eternal tranquility. And when, through the things that have been made, a person has learned to seek and understand him who made them all, then he simultaneously instructs his mind with knowledge and drenches it with exuberant joy. For this reason there is the greatest delight in meditation.

There are three kinds of meditation. One consists in the careful consideration of morals, the second in the examination of the commandments, and the third in the investigation of the divine works. Morals are in the virtues and vices. The divine commandments either admonish, promise, or deter by instilling fear. The work of God is what his power creates, what his wisdom governs, and what his grace accomplishes through cooperation [with humans]. The more a person recognizes how worthy of admiration all these things are, the more diligently he habituates himself to meditating on the wonders of God.

Chapter 12: On Discipline

A certain wise person [Bernard of Chartres], when he was asked about the manner and form of learning, responded: "A humble mind, an enthusiasm for inquiry, a quiet life, silent scrutiny, poverty or frugality, a foreign land: for many people, these practices open up the hidden places of learning." The one who said this had heard, I think, the dictum: "Morals adorn knowledge." And so he bound precepts for living to precepts to learning, in order that the student might know both the way of life he should undertake and the manner of studying he should pursue. Knowledge that is polluted by a shameless life is not worthy of praise. And therefore a person who seeks knowledge must be very careful not to neglect discipline.

Figure 4A: Grammar from the *Portail Royal* of the Cathedral of Chartres.

Source: Portal Project Online. Courtesy of Chris Henige.

Figure 4B: Dialectic from the *Portail Royal* of the Cathedral of Chartres.

Source: Portal Project Online. Courtesy of Chris Henige.

Figure 4C: Aristotle from the *Portail Royal* of the Cathedral of Chartres.

Source: Portal Project Online. Courtesy of Chris Henige.

21. JOHN OF SALISBURY'S DEFENSE OF THE LIBERAL ARTS

John of Salisbury (c. 1115–80) was one of the foremost humanists of the twelfth century: an erudite correspondent, legal expert, historian, poet, diplomat, political thinker, and prelate of the Church. A native of Old Sarum in England, he entered a clerical career as a young man and studied in the schools of Paris and Chartres from 1136 until the mid-1140s. There he heard lectures by Peter Abelard, Robert of Melun (c. 1100–67), William of Conches (c. 1090–1154), Thierry of Chartres, Gilbert of Poitiers, and other masters of the day, experiences that are vividly recorded in Book 2.10 of the Metalogicon *(1159), excerpted below. He then traveled to Rome and entered the service of the pope. He returned to England and served as secretary to two archbishops of Canterbury, first Theobald (1138–61) and then Thomas Becket (1162–70), whose fallout with King Henry II (r. 1154–89) he witnessed first-hand, before eventually becoming bishop of Chartres from 1176 until his death four years later.*

The exact purpose of the Metalogicon *has long perplexed scholars, but it appears to have two principal aims. The first is a defense of the* trivium, *and within that especially the study of logic and grammar as the foundation of a liberal arts education. The second is to argue for the works of Aristotle as the basis for the future study of logic, a discipline he feels is in need of reform. The treatise as a whole, and the passages below in particular, offer unique insight into the schools and curriculum of twelfth-century Paris, accompanied by vivid details of the pedagogy of John's teachers (see also Doc. 13).*

Source: trans. J.B. Hall, *John of Salisbury: Metalogicon*, Corpus Christianorum in Translation, 12 (Turnhout: Brepols, 2013), 148–50, 196–99. Latin.

Book 1.12: Why the Arts Are Called Liberal

There are many kinds of arts, but those that present themselves first of all to the intelligence of the philosophical mind are the liberal arts. All of those are confined within the systems either of the *trivium* or of the *quadrivium* and, in the times of our forefathers, who studied them diligently, possessed such efficacy, we are told, as to open up all manner of reading, lift up the intellect to all pursuits, and suffice to elucidate the difficulties in all questions which are susceptible of proof. No teacher was needed by those men as they opened books or answered questions, when the force of every locution was made plain to them by their system of the *trivium* and the secrets of nature in her every aspect were unfolded by the laws of the *quadrivium*. And so, just as the arts are so called because they confine by rules and precepts, or after that quality which in Greek is termed *ares* and which strengthens the mind to perceive the ways of freedom, or after reason, called *arso* by the Greeks, to which they give nourishment and growth, just so the liberal arts are so called either because it was in them that the ancients took pains to have their children (*liberos*) educated, or because they seek to win liberty for a man so that, liberated from cares, he may have time for wisdom; and they do indeed very often liberate him from those cares in which wisdom declines to have part; necessary cares too they often exclude, so that mental activity may pursue a less impeded path to philosophy.

Book 1.13: Why Grammar Is So Called

The first of all these arts is logic, at least that part of logic which is concerned with the first principles of speech, to give the word logic (as has already been said) its widest possible extension and not simply confine it to the science of debate. For the science of correct speech and correct writing, and the origin of all the liberal disciplines, is grammar. Grammar is also the cradle of philosophy in its entirety and, so to say, the first nurse of every study involving letters; it is she who receives from the womb of nature all tender babes at the moment of birth, nurtures them in their infancy, promotes at every step their growth in the love of wisdom, and with a mother's concern leads on and safeguards at every age the lover of wisdom. Accordingly it is after the first principles both of writing and of speech that grammar receives her name. For *gramma* is a letter or line, and literal comes from the fact that grammar teaches letters, the word letters being understood to refer both to the shapes given to single sounds and to the elements, that is, the sounds represented by the shapes. Alternatively, she may also be linear because just as the first dimension of a line is found in the increase of its magnitude, forming what one may call the matter of surface or body, so it is this discipline first which comes to the aid of those aspiring to advance in wisdom, instructing their tongue and introducing wisdom both through the ears and through the eyes, so that speech may thus proceed. For words introduced through the ear strike and arouse the intellect which, in Augustine's words, is a hand of the soul, so to say, being able to grasp things and take hold of objects. Letters on the other hand, that is to say shapes, are indicative first of sounds and then of the things which they place before the soul through the windows of the eyes; and often without sound they speak the words of those absent. This art, then, transmits the first principles of speech and instructs the judgment of eyes and ears, with the consequence that one can no more easily engage in philosophy without this art than can a man who has always been blind and deaf rise to eminence among philosophers.

Book 2.10: On Whose Authority the Preceding and the Following Observations Are Based

When first as quite a young man I went abroad to study in France—it was the year after the illustrious king of the English, Henry, the Lion of Justice, departed this life [Henry I, d. 1135]—I betook myself to the Peripatetic of Le Pallet [Peter Abelard], who at that time presided at Mount St-Geneviève, a famous teacher and admired by all. There, at his feet, I received the first rudiments of this art, and, to the limited extent of my poor intellect, with all eagerness of mind snatched up every crumb that fell from his lips. After that, when he went away, all too hastily as it seemed to me, I attached myself to Master Alberic, who stood out among the rest as a dialectician of the highest renown, and was in point of fact a bitter opponent of the nominalist school. I thus spent almost two years at Mount St-Geneviève, having as my teachers in this art Alberic and Master Robert of Melun (to give him the name he has won as a teacher in the schools, for by birth he is an Englishman). The one of them, exact in every respect, found arguments to question at every turn, no surface, however polished, being in his eyes without roughness, nor any bulrush without knots, as the saying goes. For there too he would point to a knot that needed untying. The other, however, was invariably ready with a reply, never declining a proposed subject in the interests of making an escape, but always opting for the other side of a contradiction, or, by determining that an utterance had manifold meanings, proving that there was no one response. The former therefore was subtle and expansive in his questioning, while the latter was penetrating, succinct and pertinent in his responses. Had these two sets of characteristics been united in some one individual in the measure in which they were found in those two men, it would certainly not be possible in our time to find a disputator of equal capability. For they were both men of acute intelligence and unremitting study; they would, I think, have attained to the highest eminence and distinction in the study of philosophy had they supported themselves on a broad foundation of literature, and had they followed in the footsteps of their predecessors to the same extent as they applauded their own discoveries. So much for the period during which I was attracted to them. For subsequently one of them set out for Bologna and unlearned what he had taught; and then indeed came back and untaught it. Whether for the better must be assessed by those who heard him both before and after. The other went on to advance in divine letters and won glory in an even more eminent branch of philosophy, with a name even more celebrated. Through my training for a full two years in the schools of these men I grew so accustomed to assigning topics and rules and other rudimentary elements in which the minds of boys are steeped, and in which the aforementioned teachers were most powerful and most ready, that I fancied I knew all these things as well as I did my own nails and fingers. For I had unquestionably learned, in my youthful buoyancy, to set a higher value on my knowledge than it was worth. I thought myself a regular little scholar, because I could give prompt answers in matters which I had heard. After that I came to my senses and took stock of my powers, and by the good offices of my teachers I purposely transferred to the grammarian [William] of Conches, whose teaching I heard for three years. In the meantime I read a good deal, and shall never regret that period. Subsequently I attended classes by Richard named L'Evêque, a man of well-nigh universal expertise, wise but not immodest, learned but not voluble, true without conceit, and virtuous without any parade; all that I had heard from other scholars I revised with him, adding various matters relating to the *quadrivium* which had not been heard before, though I had up to a point previously heard Hardewin the German discoursing on the *quadrivium*. I also revised rhetoric which, along with various other subjects, I had picked up rather superficially from Master Thierry [of Chartres], and had hitherto only slightly understood. At a later stage I received fuller coverage of rhetoric from Peter Helias. And because I had undertaken to instruct the sons of nobles, who, when I was without support from friends and relations, provided me with subsistence— for God came to my aid in my poverty—the requirements of my duties and the demands of my young pupils forced me regularly to recall to mind what I had heard. As a consequence I came to be on close terms of friendship with Master Adam [of Petit-Pont], a man of the most penetrating intellect and, whatever others may think, a man of wide reading, who devoted himself pre-eminently to Aristotle; I did not have him as a formal teacher, but he was kind enough to impart his knowledge to me, and to confide in me to a considerable degree, something which he did to no one else, or at most to a few pupils of other scholars; for he was thought to suffer from the affliction of envy. In the meantime William of Soissons, who later devised a siege-engine to storm the old fortress of logic, as his adherents claim, constructing unthinkable consequences and demolishing the sentiments of the ancients, learned the first elements of logic from me, and was finally transferred by me to the aforementioned teacher. It was with him perhaps that William learnt that the same thing exists after a contradiction, despite Aristotle's objection, for, when the same thing both is and is not, it is not necessary for it to be the same thing, and likewise, when something is, it is not necessary for it to be the same thing and not to be the same thing. For nothing emerges from a contradiction and it is impossible for a contradiction to emerge from something. In consequence I have not been forced by the impetus of my friend's engine to believe that from one impossible thing come all impossible things. I was extricated from all this by straightened domestic circumstances and by the earnest requests of my associates and the advice of my friends that I should get to grips with my duties as a teacher. I duly complied. So then, returning at the end of the three-year period I came into contact with Master Gilbert [of Poitiers], and heard him lecturing on logic and divinity; but all too soon he was taken away. He was succeeded by Robert Pullen, a man recommended alike by his life and his learning. After him I was taken up by Simon of Poissy, a reliable lecturer but rather dull as a disputant. These two men I had as my teachers in theology alone. In this way roughly twelve years elapsed during which I was

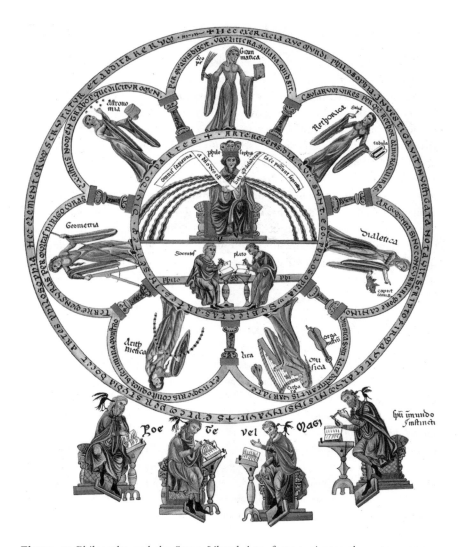

Figure 5: Philosophy and the Seven Liberal Arts, from a nineteenth-century reconstruction of the *Hortus Deliciarum* (Garden of Delights), compiled by Abbess Herrad of Hohenbourg (d. after 1196). A powerful antidote to the mostly male figures of the twelfth-century renaissance, the *Hortus* was compiled both by and explicitly for women at the Augustinian monastery at Hohenbourg in Alsace. Herrad oversaw this rich compilation of more than 1,100 textual extracts drawn from the early Christian Fathers through to the late twelfth century. In the center sits Lady Philosophy, wearing a triple crown symbolizing ethics, logic, and physics. Streams of knowledge flow forth from her breasts, and the banner in her hands asserts the divine origins of all wisdom: "All wisdom is from the Lord God"; and the freedom that comes with learning: "Only the wise are able to do what they desire." Socrates and Plato are seated below Philosophy, and the four evangelists appear at the bottom. For further discussion, see Fiona J. Griffiths, *The Garden of Delights: Reform and Renaissance for Women in the Twelfth Century* (Philadelphia: University of Pennsylvania Press, 2007).

occupied by a variety of studies. It thus seemed a pleasant idea to revisit the old comrades I had left behind, who were still detained by dialectic at Mount St-Geneviève, and to compare notes with them about our old uncertainties, that by mutual comparison we might measure our respective progress. They were found the same as they had been, and in the same position; they seemed to me not to have advanced so much as a hand's breadth. To the solution of long-standing problems they had not added even one tiny proposition. The goads with which they used to drive others now drove them. Certainly they had made progress— in just this one thing that, having unlearned moderation, they had thereby lost all modesty; so much so indeed that one might well despair of their recovery. I thus learned by experience, as may clearly be inferred, that, just as dialectic promotes other disciplines, so, if it remains on its own, it lies bloodless and barren and, if it does not conceive from some other source, it does not make pregnant the soul to bear the fruit of philosophy.

22. PHILIP OF HARVENGT ON CLERICAL AND FEMALE LITERACY

Philip of Harvengt (d. 1183) was a member of the newly founded Premonstratensian order (see Doc. 4), a religious order of canons regular whose work involved preaching and the exercise of pastoral ministry. Distinct from monks, who lived a cloistered and contemplative life and only sometimes engaged in ministry to those outside the monastery, the purpose of the Premonstratensian canons was to engage in the public ministry of the liturgy and sacraments. They followed the Rule *of Saint Augustine, but with supplementary statutes that made their life one of great austerity. In a long, multi-part work entitled* The Institution of Clerics, *Philip gives great importance to the concept of order and of knowing one's place in society. Both clerics and monks, he argues, should know the dignity and sanctity of their orders and should wish to assign everyone their due. In the following passage, which is drawn from the section on continence, he focuses especially on the question of what makes one literate, and whether it is proper to call a literate man or woman a cleric, and vice versa. The discussion reveals a nuanced understanding of the meaning of terms and of the correlation between vocabulary and figures of speech.*

Source: trans. Alex J. Novikoff, from Philip of Harvengt, *De continentia clericorum*, in J.-P. Migne, ed., *Patrologia Latina* (Paris: Imprimerie Royale, 1855), vol. 203, cols. 815–816. Latin.

Know, then, that to apply oneself to the knowledge of Scripture is the business of clerics, so that whoever wishes to become a cleric must by necessity be imbued with letters, and that without at least a minimal knowledge of them one can hardly or not at all be considered a cleric. Thus the following manner of speaking has come about: the one whom we perceive as lettered we call a cleric, and since he concerns himself with the duties of a cleric we assign that title to the office. So if one compares a literate knight to an unlettered [*idiote*] priest he will assuredly declare and swear under oath that the knight is a better cleric than the priest, since the knight can read, understand, write in prose or verse, and when he is discussing among clerics in Latin he is praised for not committing any faults. The priest, on the other hand, not only does not know how to deliver a speech in correct and irreproachable Latin, but he might not even be able to sing the divine office alone according to his rule. And yet we well know that this knight that we have called a better cleric than the priest is undoubtedly not a cleric. It is a mere figure of speech that has prevailed, so that the one who commits himself to letters, which is the business of clerics, is called a cleric even though nobody doubts that he is not [actually] a cleric. Finally, when we seek out a monk for his human qualities and his charity, without in fact knowing if he is literate or not, we ask him if he is a cleric. We are not looking to know whether he has the proper ordination to perform the service at the altar, but only to know whether he is literate. And he, responding to this question in a meaningful way, says that he is a cleric if he is literate, but that he is a lay convert if he is illiterate. Also, if among nuns and women religious who serve God in the Church through their literary work we find one who is more perfectly imbued with literary culture, we call them a good cleric in a sense that is not technically correct but merely conveys their knowledge.

One day, in my presence, a man who was religious in both his customs and his habit entered a church and found in front of the altar a nun, mature in both her age and knowledge, who was holding a small book in her hands. After a few exchanges of thoughtful words he asked about what she was holding, in other words about what she was holding in her hands. She said: "the Life of a virgin saint that I composed, which I wrote down when I was young." And she added: "for I was a good cleric." I observed in these words that nothing more was to be understood than that she was literate, for she had written this virgin's Life when she was young. And among several others that I know to be or have been particularly well versed in letters I remember having often heard the term *good cleric* when speaking about the literary culture of one of them. And I really wonder why it is that when we wish to describe a woman's clerical [i.e., literate] culture we say *good cleric* rather than a *good female cleric*, for it would seem more logical to say female cleric instead of male cleric, just as we say monk instead of nun. I find in the works of the holy Fathers that those who spend their days in a religious habit in a monastery are called holy women [*sanctimoniales*], or nuns [*nonnas*], or women monks [*monachas*], but I cannot ever recall having seen them called clerics in writing, and I do not see them called as such by any speaker of Latin. The reason for this is not clear to me, except that it confounds the opinion of our monk who thinks that the monks who are called clerics are indeed clerics, for he fails to consider that even a woman who is well versed in letters is not [actually] a cleric, even though she is judged to be a good cleric. And this same monk in his discussion clearly recognizes that clerical truth does not reside in the knowledge of letters. And so it is incontestably proved by his own testimony that it is not enough to be called a cleric to be one in reality.

23. PETER OF BLOIS ON CLERICS AND THE LIBERAL ARTS

Peter of Blois (c. 1130–c. 1212) trained from an early age at the schools of France, learning the liberal arts at Tours and Chartres before studying theology at Paris. He also spent time at the law school of Bologna before offering his services to a series of lay and ecclesiastical courts in a long career that took him to Palermo, Rouen, and Canterbury. His talents brought him moderate success, and he in turn held the archdeaconries of Bath and London. While traveling in the courts of great men, Peter compiled one of the twelfth century's greatest letter collections, which shows him trying to carve out a place for an exquisitely educated intellectual in the turbulent world of politics and administration. In the first letter below, he tells another archdeacon how young men ought to be educated, in the process offering a clear picture of the syllabus of the contemporary schools and their debt to classical antiquity. In the excerpts that conclude this section, Peter offers two views on how intellectuals should apply their learning in the world.

Source: trans. John D. Cotts, from *Petri Blesensis Opera Omnia*, in J.-P. Migne, ed., *Patrologia Latina* (Paris: Imprimerie Royale, 1855), vol. 207, cols. 311–14, 317, 346; and Lena Wahlgren, *The Letter Collections of Peter of Blois: Studies in the Manuscript Tradition* (Göteborg: Acta Universitatis Gothoburgensis, 1993), 149. Latin.

Letter 101: In Defense of the Traditional Liberal Arts

To his dearest lord and friend R., archdeacon of Nantes, Peter of Blois sends greeting and whatever might be better than a greeting.

The other day, you sent two of your nephews to me so for their education. The one is still just a boy, the other in the midst of puberty. In your letters you enthusiastically applaud and commend the talents of the elder boy, and you claim that you have never found a man of a more subtle bent. And so you urge and even beg me to give him the most zealous pedagogical attention. You think that an edifice, if begun by another's efforts, will be more easily completed. The reality, however, is quite the opposite! For I have higher hopes for the education of the boy who comes to me rough and unfinished than for that of the other, whose veins of genius have already begun to harden, and who has impressed upon himself a veritable image of another teacher. Clay and wax, and other things of that sort which can be formed and shaped, are more easily and faithfully fashioned according to the will of the fashioner if they do not already follow the traces of a pattern. Indeed, Quintilian asserts in his *Institutes of Oratory* that a certain renowned flute-player named Timothy used to charge a double fee from those who had been previously taught by another. This was because the labor became twofold in those cases: on the one hand, he had to wash away the less exemplary learning with which they had been stained. On the other hand, they had to provide the knowledge which gives rise to fortune as well as fame. For what is learned at a tender age is later unlearned only with great difficulty. As Horace says, "A jar will for a long time keep the odor of the first thing it held" [*Epistle* 1.269–70]. Moreover, civil law, based on an edict of the aediles, discouraged the purchase of older slaves who were conditioned to different customs, and sometimes it seemed that they should just be returned to their previous owners. Young slaves were regarded as preferable because they would be more likely to accept instruction, and in general would be more suited to their new jobs.

Now you consider William, the elder boy, to have a subtler mind and a sharper intellect, because he has left behind the study of grammar and the great authors, and rushed on to the trickery of the logicians. Now he learns dialectic, not from a book (as is the traditional practice), but from crib-notes and summaries. Such things are not the foundations of good literary study! Rather, the subtlety that you fawn over is in fact quite dangerous to many students. As Seneca says, "Nothing is more hateful than subtlety, when subtlety is all there is" [Letters to Lucilius 88.43]. For what does it profit them to spend their days on things that have no use at home, in the army, in the forum, in the cloister, in court, in the Church, nor really any place but the schools themselves? Seneca, again [*Epistle* 82], wrote to Lucilius: "What is sharper than a stalk of corn [wheat], and in what way is that useful?" Such is that genius which, fond only of subtlety, lacks true rigor. Icarus, lifted by youthful carelessness, was borne up to heaven only to be plunged into the waves of the sea. This is what happens to those who too hastily lift themselves up with the liberal arts, and are dashed against rocks. Certain students, before they are imbued with even the most basic studies, are taught to inquire about points and lines and surfaces, about the quantity of the soul, about fate, about the disposition of nature, about chance and free will, about matter and motion, about the principles of bodies, of the development of multiplicities, and of the division of magnitude. They ask themselves: What is time? What is a vacuum? What is meant by "place"? And still they inquire about similarity and difference, about division, about the divisible and the individual, about the substance and form of the voice, about the essence of universals, about the origin, use and goal of the virtues, about the causes of things, about ocean tides, about the source of the Nile, about various hidden secrets of nature, about the different types of cases that arise in contracts or quasi-contracts, or in crimes or quasi-crimes, about the earliest beginnings of the universe, and about many other things that require a more solid foundation of knowledge and more advanced intellectual talents.

[Someone of] tender age must first be immersed in the rules of grammatical skill, in analogies, in barbarisms, in solecisms, and in tropes and figures of speech. In all these matters Donatus, Servius, Priscian, Isidore, Bede, and Cassiodorus spent a great deal of effort, which they would not have done if the foundations of knowledge could have been laid without them. For Quintilian, who passes this learning on to us, and assures us that it must be passed on, commended it so earnestly that he publicly proclaimed that without it one could not even speak of knowledge at all. Gaius Julius Caesar wrote a book about analogy, knowing that without this knowledge he could easily gain neither prudence, in which he was most perfect, nor eloquence, in which he was most forceful. Cicero, as is clear from his frequent letters, enthusiastically encouraged his son, whom he loved dearly, to study the grammatical arts.

At any rate, what is the use in poring over notes, copying out wordy *summae*, inverting tricky sophisms, and all the while condemning the writings of the ancients and rejecting anything that is not found in the notes of one's own master? After all, Jeremiah was not pulled out of the lake until old and worn clothes were dropped down to him on ropes [Jeremiah 38:11–13]. For no one is raised from the shadows of ignorance to the light of knowledge unless he eagerly studies the writings of the ancients. Saint Jerome boasted that he had carefully mastered the writings of Origen; Horace glories in having read and re-read Homer, "who told us what is beautiful and what ugly, what is useful and what is worthless, better and more clearly than Chrysippus and Crantor" [*Epistle* 2, To Lollius].

I know that it was a great profit to me personally, that as a young boy learning poetry, I (thanks to my teacher) gathered my material not from fables but from true histories. It did me great good that I was made to copy and learn by heart the letters of Hildebert, bishop of Le Mans, which are so remarkable for their stylistic beauty and their polish. Among other books, which are renowned in the schools, I learned much by frequently exploring Trogus Pompeius, Josephus, Suetonius, Hegesippus, Quintus Curtius, Cornelius Tacitus, and Titus Livius [i.e., Livy], all of whom provide through their histories so much that can build character and provide a boy with a liberal education. I also read countless others who did not write history. In all of these, our contemporaries, if diligent, can pluck out flowers as if from a fragrant garden, and thus make a kind of honey from their polished elegance.

Therefore, do not talk to me anymore about the subtle genius of your nephew William, and do not blame me if he does not progress quickly to the end of his studies. For a patient needs to be purged before he is healed, and, according to that Timothy who demanded double pay from pupils who had had other teachers, the useless things that were learned before need to be rooted out before useful ones can be added. In the *Marriage of Mercury and Philology* [of Martianus Capella], Philology vomits out books of worthless knowledge before she is worthy to be raised to the dignified eminence she seeks. Indeed, I fear that Timothy's adage could be too true: John [the younger brother] is already ahead of William because he is learning more quickly. The head has become the tail, and if John stays on course, the younger son will supplant the first-born, just as Jacob supplanted Esau.

From Letter 6: Educated Clerics at Canterbury

In the household of my lord archbishop of Canterbury are the most erudite men, among whom you will find all the righteousness of justice, every tool of divine providence, and every model of learning. After praying and before dining they give themselves over to reading, disputing, and judging cases. All the difficult and knotty questions of the realm are referred to us, and when we approach them together in common audience, each one of us sharpens his wits and speaks his mind in his turn without quarrel or mockery, and in a subtle vein offers what seems to him the best course of action.

From Letter 14: The Trouble with Clerics at the Royal Court

Men of our calling can better service princes in churches than in their camps. I do not think it unreasonable that simpler men, who are less educated in Scripture, wish to fight in the service of the royal majesty. But for one who has taken holy orders and is instilled with sacred eloquence . . . it is altogether inexcusable to enmesh himself in secular duties.

24. GODFREY OF ST-VICTOR: *THE FOUNTAIN OF PHILOSOPHY*

Godfrey of St-Victor (c. 1130–c. 1195) was a student in the arts in Paris around 1140–50 and then seems to have studied theology in the 1150s before entering the abbey of St-Victor later in that same decade. His Fountain of Philosophy *(c. 1178) is a poetic and semi-autobiographical meditation on the liberal arts and the pursuit of wisdom and salvation. In addition to echoing the familiar themes on the importance of the liberal arts, the poem also connects in important ways with the ideas circulating within both the exegetical school of St-Victor and the more secular "humanism" of the twelfth century. Set in a dream vision, an increasingly common literary device in the twelfth century, the poem clearly builds on Hugh of St-Victor's* Didascalicon, *which had set out the order of the secular* arts as a prelude to the study of sacred Scripture (Docs. 20 and 9, respectively). The autobiographical portions of the poem, including the names of teachers and their followers, seems modeled on John of Salisbury's Metalogicon (Doc. 21). Both Godfrey and John of Salisbury were contemporaries and may have studied in Paris under the same masters. Like John, Godfrey refers to the philosophical conflict between the nominalists and the realists; he criticizes those who know only logic and pile up opinions and useless subtleties; he quotes with approval Aristotle's adage "Eloquence without wisdom is futile"; and he tells of his studies with Alberic and Robert of Melun, Gilbert of Poitiers, and Adam of Petit-Pont, all masters active in the middle decades of the twelfth century.

The 836-line poem is preceded by a dedicatory letter to abbot Stephen of St-Geneviève (1128–1203), who in 1192 became bishop of Tournai. Godfrey describes his poem as being like a mixed drink, containing a twofold mixture of subject matter and skill. In the preface, the Holy Spirit guides Godfrey on a long road in search of eloquence and wisdom. The burdens of the journey make him thirsty, and his thirst is quenched by streams of water flowing down from a high mountain (hence the fountain of the title). In another work, the Microcosmos, Godfrey devotes an entire chapter to describing the seven mechanical arts: armament, commerce, agriculture, construction, fabric making, hunting to provide food, and medicine. Here, however, those arts are muddy and tasteless waters that impede his search for true wisdom. The description of the masters of grammar and rhetoric allude to the textbooks of the schools and vividly evoke the images of the liberal arts enshrined on the west portal of the Cathedral of Chartres (See Figures 4a–c, pp. 109–110).

Source: trans. Hugh Feiss, OSB, in Interpretation of Scripture: Theory, ed. Franklin T. Harkins and Frans van Liere (Hyde Park, NY: New City Press, 2013), 390–94, 397–99. Latin.

Preface

It was the end of the night and of my sleep,
and the herald of day put to flight the darkness.
I awake, ignorant of what is to come,
led by sacred admonitions and a godly instinct.

I go out at dawn under the rising light,
signing myself with the sign of the most holy cross.
I ask for the grace of the Paraclete [Holy Spirit] as my guide,
saying, "God, direct me to the good you know."

Therefore, while I travel on a very long road,
with the guidance of the Holy Spirit that I had requested,
I become thirsty from the effort of the road
and from the heat of the sun as it rises higher.

As I am walking, suffering from thirst,
I see from afar some pleasant places,
very high up, with a serene appearance,
and as if full of the delights of Paradise.

I run more hurriedly, anxious to see,
if there have been signs holding out hope of quenching my thirst.
For soon almost a thousand rivers astound my ears
with their sweet murmuring.

On the Origin of the Mechanical [Branch of Philosophy]
and Its Arts

When I have come closer, first
I find in the fields, at the very base of the mountain,
a spring drawn from the mud that people call "mechanical,"
soiled with the dung of wrestling frogs.

From this [spring] went out abundant streams,
for they flow widely through the whole world,
to uncultivated people they are sweet,
although they are muddy, tasteless, and poisonous.

The crowd of common people, who cannot go
to the aforesaid heights, gathers to drink from these [streams],
and although dire diseases arise from these waters,
wondrously they still nurture all the sons of the earth.

Indeed, all come for the sake of healing,
but when they drink too deeply with polluted lips,
one becomes paralyzed, his limbs gone slack,
another contracts dropsy, his skin bloated.

I approached to drink because I was thirsty.
The Spirit, by whose guidance I was proceeding, said to me:
"Don't! Don't take the waters of the living spring."
And so, still thirsty, I passed them by.

As I passed by I counted seven streams,
which I noticed flow from this source.
I committed to memory only the names of these;
I did not bother to learn the rest by name.

[Part 1: The Seven Liberal Arts]

ON THE ORIGIN OF PHILOSOPHY AND ITS ARTS

From the mountain's summit an unpolluted spring was
    flowing down,
which nature had made from the earliest days;
it was gushing, living, and inexhaustible.
Coming down from the summit, it flowed to the lowest levels.

It was very sweet to the taste and savory,
but it did not taste the same to all;
indeed, to one unable to put faith in the slightest saying,
at one time it seems like vinegar, and at another time like nectar.

Its color also varied,
for the stream that came out of the deep
shone resplendent with a golden flash,
but another glistened with the sheen of silver.

The stream, divided twice in two,
stretches outward in two great branches,
which, in turn, have two natural effects:
white splendor sharpens the voice; red purges the breast.

These, both derived from the deepest spring,
go out, meandering in different areas,
and with different ways of flowing;
one flows silently, another roars in a violent flood.

ON THE PARTS OF ELOQUENCE

Both indeed are great; the lesser one
is divided into three parts, a widely expanding channel.
Latin-speakers refer to it colloquially as the "trivium,"
which provides a threefold access to eloquence.

The first of these spreads out on a wider field,
and runs down through level ground by a straighter way.
This one creates shrubbery with its moisture
and makes fruitful with another, fuller stream.

But the second, crossing hidden places,
rocks, and woods, forces its way through rugged, trackless places;
Its way is narrower and broken,
its flow stronger and more violent.

The third, frolicking through charming meadows,
makes verdant with varied flowers. The painted hollows
of this flood, wandering farther than the others,
run slowly at first, but then rapidly.

This is that widely celebrated trivium,
traveling far to all the ends of the earth.
On its banks sit many cities,
to the citizens of which it once granted pre-eminence.

Once the righteous pilgrims of the trivium
traveled to high heaven because of the fame of a great name;
they were rulers in other cities;
now they beg, miserable and thoroughly downcast.

O Socrates! O blessed times of the ancients!
How things have now changed from that pristine state;
gracious moderator of holy minds,
thus, thus, do you lie flattened, O ancient eloquence!

Learned Aristotle, although he knew these things,
would have been a nobody if he had not been a talkative decretist;
the distinguished person impersonates the physician, theologian,
magician, or lawyer; this to me is a sophist.

ON THOSE WHO STUDY THE ARTS

Many drink eagerly from these waters.
From them teenagers drink, from them adults drink.
Each does so in his own way, whether he is wise or foolish,
although the rash rush in without order.

Inexperienced in things, they run without order,
They do not have the clear eye of reason.
Therefore, they pass by without seeing the truth,
unless finally the evening light shines for them.

They believe other things are sweeter to taste,
and so they pass blindly by the first things as beneath them.
The stupid do not pay heed, because to the higher things
they rush headlong without delay and without these foundations.

They come from different lands,
seized for different reasons by a desire to study.
Impulse draws one; another, love of the waters.
The latter wants to drink, but the former has too little thirst.

Nor is it any wonder that order is confused.
If someone throws something into a sack that has a hole in it,
does he not finally deserve to be badly deluded
because he sees no use for the trivium?

Even now those who have earned this right to rule over these
    [deluded folk],
and they have drunk little by little this gracious cup,
whose parts they bring to others as well;
they also possess nothing that they have not received.

They sit in eminence among those cupbearers,
ancient men of lasting memory
whom modern crowds attend,
satisfied by the drink of heavenly grace.

These men shut or open the water gates
lest their worth be soiled by the profane;
certainly to those worthy they grant a full cup;
their record repulses the miserly possessor.

ON THE ANCIENT MASTERS OF GRAMMAR

Donatus presides on the bank of the first stream,
a line of boys presses in upon him,
whose open mouths he refreshes with a drink of milk.
His rod also corrects careless errors.

Opposite him sits Priscian;
Appollonius and Herodian instruct him

to join hands with Donatus.
Otherwise, there would be useless conflict.

Nearby sits a long line of masters,
and a much greater flock of disciples.
These thoroughly explore the depths of the streams;
others taste the surface with a touch of their lips.

ON THE MODERN PHILOSOPHERS, ESPECIALLY THE NOMINALISTS AND REALISTS

Certain nominalists [*nominales*] add themselves as associates
    [of the ancient masters],
comrades of such by name [*nomine*], not by divine will [*numine*].
Others are nearer [to the ancients], and these the thing [*res*] itself
has given the name realists [*reales*] because they truly are such.

For if on account of being guilty of various errors
These could be called "realists,"
their error is nevertheless excusable;
to contradict the mind is the custom of the insane.

For if the mind should think that a genus is just a name,
only a mentally deranged person would believe it.
Since the world is full of so many genera of things,
the one for whom genus is [merely] a name is always impoverished.

The others, realists, form many sects;
you might rightly [*recte*] call them "realists" [*reales*] from
    "accused" [*reatu*],
for they do not advance in a straight line on the road of truth
nor drink perfectly from the streams of grace.

Some of these temper the spices of Poitiers;
they believe that a genus contains a genus.
They triple the ten categories [*predicamenta*] of things,
and in so doing overturn the foundations of the ancients.

Alberic [of Rheims] errs in a different but equal way.
Like Socrates he is poor, but he does not remain sane;
because the vain person passes quickly,
even when he is dying he remains crazy.

The crowd of Robert [of Mellun's] followers cling to the top
    of a rock,
rock hard with rigor and admanatine.
Neither the rains of doctrine nor its dew waters them.
Rocky projections prevent the stream from entering.

These [Robert's followers] argue what is false,
but follow nothing truly, although they go after it.
They create nearly a thousand things from a name alone;
therefore, one may think that they are nothing.

Some have built a bridge with their own hands
And have made an easy crossing over the waters.
On this bridge each of them has built a house for himself;
Hence they have received the name "bridge-dwellers."

The material is suitable and so is the design;
cubit-square stones support it.
The solid structure stands on bronze columns.
No movements will shake it to pieces.

The work above the pavement is polished,
inscribed with golden and silver signs,
fortified all around with high walls
so the inexperienced crowd will not fear disaster.

But it also has places in which they speculate
And examine the hidden river bottom;
Others also are delighted by swimmers,
And those burned by the summer sun are refreshed.

A venerable group of elders sits here,
prominent for the grace of their teaching and moral behavior;
they teach the simple crowds of people.
Blessed are the people who have such rulers!

ON THE MASTERS OF RHETORIC

Cicero presides over the stream of rhetoric,
green and flowering with various rhetorical ornaments.

He provides easy access to his writings.
The study of speaking will connect the other [branches of philosophy].

He carries in his hands a mighty rod
divided into five segments,
reflecting here and there various colors.
With it he calls back the dead and kills the living.

Aristotle is also near these waters;
the Latin [Cicero] learned to speak from the Greek [Aristotle].
Also present is Hermagoras, but less attentively,
so he seems to Cicero like a passerby.

Many rhetors are present, and many orators;
the former are more learned, the latter more eager.
All are strong men and warriors,
with circumcised lips and mature minds.

25. GERALD OF WALES SATIRIZES THE STUDY OF DIALECTIC

Gerald of Wales (c. 1146–c. 1223) was one of the most fascinating and versatile figures of his day. Over the course of a long life, he was by turn scholar, churchman, courtier, diplomat, would-be crusader, agent of English kings, champion of the Welsh, hunted outlaw, and cathedral theologian. He was also a naturalist, gossiper, indefatigable traveler, and prolific writer. He is best known among modern readers for his travelogues through Ireland and Wales and the vivid details of their local customs that his writings uniquely record. His theological interests and background in canon law are best represented by a work entitled the Jewel of the Church, *which was written for the clergy of his archdeaconry of Brecon around 1197 and then presented to Pope Innocent III (r. 1198–1216) in 1199. The work is divided into two sections: Distinction 1 treats canon law and Distinction 2 treats moral law. Throughout the work, Gerald voices his disapproval of the vicious tendencies he finds around him and appeals to his contemporaries to reach for higher moral standards. A noteworthy critique is his mockery of the abuse of logic as it was being studied in late-twelfth-century Paris, and especially of its hairsplitting distinctions in terminology. Gerald's satire, like that of other churchmen of the day steeped in the liberal arts, carries with it the hope for reform, and he draws heavily on classical examples, in this case the Roman philosopher and dramatist Seneca (4 BCE–65 CE).*

Source: trans. J.J. Hagen, *Gerald of Wales: The Jewel of the Church* (Leiden: E.J. Brill, 1979), 271–72. Latin.

The abuser of logic has been the parasite of learning in every age, but it has never been more so than in these latter days when all things are becoming damnably worse. There was a time when men used to investigate from the arts [*ex arte*] and dispute about the arts [*circa artem*], and these discussions were useful and were applied to the successful and subtle unraveling of involved theological questions and the untying of knotty problems in other faculties. But these days this childish nonsense has proceeded so far that men never dispute *ex arte* and seldom *circa artem*. They apply themselves for appearance's sake to questions of the Quadrivium, that is, to questions of simplicity and synthesis, of shadow, motion, points and lines, acute and obtuse angles, in order that they may appear dabblers in the Quadrivium, a branch of knowledge which is much more popular in the East than in the West. And from here they have transferred themselves to false positions, to *insolubilia* [a genre of semantic and epistemic paradoxes], to fanciful relations, to long, involved circumlocutions, and to what is not Latin, as if they prognosticate by their own disputes their failure in true learning.

A very learned man once said to a "superficial" who was disputing in dialectical fashion: "Tell me, please, of what use is this kind of argumentation? I hear nothing *de arte*, nor am I to learn anything from it *ex arte*." The other replied: "But there is great subtlety in such discussion." "But of what use is this subtlety?" the learned man objected. "A spider's web is subtle enough, but in making it the wretched creature spins out its bowels. What is the use of such subtlety? It catches nothing more than gnats and flies. Just so do you eviscerate yourselves in these discussions in which there may indeed be some subtlety, but no usefulness whatever." Seneca remarks: "Why do you torment and enervate yourself in questions which it would be more subtle to spurn than to solve?" [*Epistle* 48]. These arguments are like divinations which men devise to relieve the tedium of study on a winter's night. They are engaged in today for no purpose other than to alleviate a certain lazy idleness and daintiness.

To someone who had asked the difference between the methods of ancient and modern dialectical argumentation, the pleasant comparison was made between the excellent chess players of ancient times who played with all the pieces and those [today] who play with only a partial number of pieces. In former days the dialecticians argued *de arte* and *circa artem*, like those excellent chess players who used all the pieces. But these days such long competitions are omitted as being too long and tedious, and they have turned to games with only some of the pieces because they consider them less tedious and more expeditious.

But to hear the poet decrying the decline of things even in his day:

> And so, by fate, all things fall into decay,
> > And restored again, once more fall into ruins. [Virgil, *Georgics* I]

It must, however, be admitted that the advantages of logic in itself are many, for it is a very great help [key] in solving difficulties in other faculties, provided that you do not abuse it, or let it delay you [from true learning], or let it woo you to its delights like the Sirens' songs as you grow old. Seneca tells us: "Liberal studies and praiseworthy arts and skills are useful to the extent that they equip the natural abilities and do not hold them back. As long as there is any lingering upon these things the mind is not able to move on to greater things. These studies are our elementary beginnings; they are not the so-called liberal works which are befitting a free man. There is one study above all others which is truly liberal and which makes one liberal and free—it is wisdom. All other studies are childish and effeminate" [*Epistle* 88]. And further on Seneca says: "We ought not to be learning these things now; we should have already learned them."

You will hear about and discover for yourselves among priests today not only instances such as these (and those described earlier), but other enormities far greater. How then can they instruct others when they have been so instructed themselves? Or it would be better said: how can they ruin [destroy] others when they have been so ruined [destroyed] themselves. Those who present themselves so unworthily for ordination are guilty of a great crime, but bishops who ordain such men are guilty of a far greater one. These priests place a heavy burden upon themselves; the bishops place both themselves and the priests in damnable danger. To these who thus present themselves it ought to be said: "You know what you seek," you know not the weighty burden you seek to carry, you know not the great value of the treasure you desire; finally, you do not know the things you ought, nor are you the person you should be to attain so high a state." Prelates, therefore, should not ordain anyone for the care of souls unless he is sufficiently, or at least moderately, educated. The sincere but little educated, even though they are upright and devout, should not be placed in charge where there are many souls to be cared for. They should rather be advised to enter religious orders where they may have only themselves to look after. The prophet Malachi counsels: "The lips of the priest ought to safeguard knowledge; his mouth is where instruction should be sought because he is the messenger (angel) of the Lord of Sabaoth" [Malachi 2:7]. Such are the prerogatives of priests that they are called "angels" [messengers] and even "gods"—"You shall not revile the gods," and again, "they likened Paul [and Barnabas] to gods" [Acts 14:11].

26. STEPHEN OF TOURNAI'S INVECTIVE AGAINST THE NEW LEARNING

Not all masters were excited by the new methods of employing logic and philosophy in the service of sacred learning. By the late twelfth century, an increasing number of voices, some members of the ecclesiastical ranks, others satirists, launched their own critiques against what they perceived as an excessive and abusive reliance on the tools of secular learning. Stephen, bishop of Tournai from 1191 to 1203, wrote the following letter to the Pope (either Celestine III [r. 1191–98] or his successor Innocent III [r. 1198–1216]) decrying the impudence of Parisian students who have replaced the true goal of sacred learning with the fashionable habits of contemporary scholastic discourse. His objective was clearly for the pope to step in and curb these excesses. In 1215, the papal legate Robert of Courçon (c. 1160–1219), a former chancellor of the University of Paris, was appointed to lead a commission to investigate the teaching of Aristotle's Metaphysics *that was taking place at the university. The result was the first systematic body of laws, or statutes, setting limits and privileges for the university and its members.*

Source: trans. Lynn Thorndike, *University Records and Life in the Middle Ages*, Records of Civilization—Sources and Studies, 38 (New York: Columbia University Press, 1944), 23–24. Latin.

[Letter to the Pope, 1192–1203]

Having obtained indulgence, let us speak to our lord, whose gentleness emboldens us, whose prudence sustains our inexperience, whose patience promises impunity. To this the authority of our ancestors compels us and a disease gradually insinuating whose ills, if not met at the start, will be incurable in the end. Nor do we say this, father, as if we wished to be censors of morals, or judges of doctors, or debaters of doctrines. This load requires stouter shoulders, and this battle awaits the robust frames of spiritual athletes. We merely wish to indicate the sore spot to your holy paternity, to whom God has given both the power to uproot errors and the knowledge to correct them.

The studies of sacred letters among us are fallen into the workshop of confusion, while both disciples applaud novelties alone and masters watch out for glory rather than learning. They everywhere compose new and recent *summulae* [theological summaries] and commentaries, by which they attract, detain, and deceive their hearers, as if the works of the holy fathers were not still sufficient, who, we read, expounded holy scripture in the same spirit in which we believe the apostles and prophets composed it. They prepare strange and exotic courses for their banquet, when at the nuptials of the son of the king of Taurus his own flesh and blood are killed and all prepared, and the wedding guests have only to take and eat what is set before them. Contrary to the sacred canons there is public disputation as to the incomprehensible deity; concerning the incarnation of the Word, verbose flesh and blood irreverently litigates. The indivisible Trinity is cut up and wrangled over in the trivia, so that now there are as many errors as doctors, as many scandals as classrooms, as many blasphemies as squares. Again, if a case comes up which should be settled by canon law either under your jurisdiction or within that of the ordinary judges, there is produced from the vendors an inextricable forest of decretals presumably under the name of pope Alexander of sacred memory, and older canons are cast aside, rejected, expunged. When this plunder has been unrolled before us, those things which were wholesomely instituted in councils of holy fathers neither impose form on councils nor an end to eases, since letters prevail which perchance advocates for hire invented and forged in their shops or cubicles under the name of Roman pontiffs. A new volume composed of these is solemnly read in the schools and offered for sale in the forum to the applause of a horde of notaries, who rejoice that in copying suspect opuscula both their labor is lessened and their pay increased. Two woes are the aforesaid, and lo, a third remains: faculties called liberal having lost their pristine liberty are sunk in such servitude that adolescents with long hair impudently usurp their professorships, and beardless youths sit in the seat of their seniors, and those who don't yet know how to be disciples strive to be named masters. And they write their *summulae* moistened with drool and dribble but unseasoned with the salt of philosophers. Omitting the rules of the arts and discarding the authentic books of the artificers, they seize the flies of empty words in their sophisms like the claws of spiders. Philosophy cries that her garments are torn and disordered and, modestly concealing her nudity by a few specific tatters, neither is consulted nor consoles as of old. All these things, father, call for the hand of apostolic correction, that the disorder in teaching, learning and disputing may be reduced to due form by your authority, that the divine word be not cheapened by vulgar handling, that it be not said on the street corners, "Lo Christ is here or lo He is there," lest what is holy be given to dogs and pearls be trodden under foot by swine.

27. *THE BATTLE OF THE SEVEN ARTS*: A TROUVÈRE'S SATIRE ON ACADEMIA

The Battle of the Seven Arts *is a satirical poem written most likely in the early 1230s by the French trouvère Henri d'Andeli (on trouvères, see Doc. 55). Its language is the French of the Île-de-France, the region around Paris. Very little is known about the author, except that he was probably a native of Andelys in Normandy and that he studied and later wrote in Paris. His poetic compositions include a* Battle of Wines *(c. 1225), the* Sayings of Philip the Chancellor, *a funeral eulogy for the chancellor of Notre-Dame of Paris (d. 1236), and possibly the* Lay of Aristotle *(c. 1220), a fabliau set in the context of Alexander the Great's abandonment of reason and his becoming a slave of love. All his compositions reflect a deep familiarity with the scholastic and literary culture of his time. The Battle of the Seven Arts *offers up a metaphorical but vivid battle between the forces of grammatical and rhetorical studies at Orléans, a city famous in the twelfth century for its classical commentators, and the forces of Aristotelian* *logic studied at the University of Paris. Henri revisits and distills in witty verse many of the themes that were sounded by John of Salisbury in his* Metalogicon *some 70 years earlier, only here the defense is not of the liberal arts in general but of the literary arts of grammar and rhetoric in particular. The battle, in other words, is an internal struggle among the arts of the* trivium, *with both sides summoning allies of the classical past and personalities of the scholastic present (some of them unidentifiable) to their respective causes. A particular theme of the poem is the condemnation of the narrowly specialized arts faculty at Paris, and Henri is especially critical of what he sees as the "technocracy" of logic that produces overly specialized students who have not mastered the groundwork of grammar. For some scholars, therefore, the* Battle *represents a nostalgic look back on the bygone humanism of the twelfth century. On account of its storehouse of references to authors and texts, the* Battle *is both a learned parody and a virtual encyclopedia of classical and classicizing literary culture as seen through the eyes of a cleric-trouvère at the dawn of the University of Paris.*

Source: trans. Louis John Paetow, *The Battle of the Seven Arts*, Memoirs of the University of California, vol. 4, no. 1 (Berkeley: University of California Press, 1914), 37–60; slightly revised. Old French.

> Paris and Orléans are at odds.
> It is a great loss and a great sorrow
> That the two do not agree.
> Do you know the reason for the discord?
> It is because they differ about learning; 5
> For Logic, who is always wrangling,
> Calls the authors authorlings
> And the students of Orléans mere grammar-boys.
> Each, she says, is well worth four Homers,
> For they drink huge bumpers 10
> And are so skillful at versifying
> That about a single leaf of a fig-tree
> They will compose you fifty verses.
> But they retort that verily
> They call Dialectic, 15
> In evil spite, a cock-a-doodle-doo.
> As for those of Paris, the clerks of Plato,
> They do not think them worth a button.
> However, Logic has the students,
> Whereas Grammar is reduced in numbers. 20
> Grammar is much wrought up;
> And has raised her banner
> Outside of Orléans, in the midst of the grain-fields;

There she assembled her army.
Homer and old Claudian,   25
Donatus, Persius, Priscian,
Those good author knights
And those good squires who serve them,
All set out with Grammar
When she went forth from her bookcase.   30
The knights of Orléans set out
Who were men-at-arms of the authors:
Master John of Saint Morisse,
Who knows his authors as well as one could wish,
Odo, Garnier and Balsamon,   35
Who had inscribed a salmon
On his shield, between two dace,
With a hot pepper volant,
Blacker than charcoal,
A relish for the royal fish of the Loire   40
And for drinking the wines of Orléans
Which grow without the aid of fertilizers.
Then without jest or laughter,
They marched toward Paris.
Dame Logic heard of it;   45
She cried out full of wrath:
"Alas! I lost my support
"When Raoul de Builli died."
She marshaled her forces near Tournai
Under Sir Pierre de Courtenai,   50
A very learned logician.
There was master John the rustic,
And Pointlasne, he of Gamaches,
Master Nicholas with the prominent buttocks.
These three put the trivium and quadrivium   55
In a tub on a large cart;
The bedels drew the cart.
Robert the Dwarf in great derision
Pricked them all with a goad;
He pokes old Cheron in the bag.   60
Then they all set out.
There was many a pavilion of silk
On Montlhéry near Linas;
There they gave one another cruel blows.

Civil Law rode gorgeously 65
And Canon Law rode haughtily
Ahead of all the other arts.
There was many a Lombard knight,
Marshaled by Rhetoric.
Darts they have of feathered tongues 70
To pierce the hearts of foolish people
Who come to attack their strongholds;
For they snatch up many a heritage
With the lances of their eloquence.
Augustine, Ambrose, Gregory, 75
Jerome, Bede, and Isidore,
They quoted to Divinity as authorities
That she might avoid their vanity.
Madam Exalted Science,
Who did not care a fig about their dispute, 80
Left the arts to fight it out together.
Methinks she went to Paris
To drink the wines of her cellar,
According to the advice of the chancellor,
In whom she had the greatest confidence 85
For he was the best clerk in the Isle de France;
But in one trifle he considered her foolish,
That when she holds disputations in his schools
She abandons strict theological questions
And trumpets philosophy. 90
As for the arts students, they care for naught
Except to read the books of nature;
While the grammarians perverse
Have for their part forsaken Claudian and Persius,
Two very good old books, 95
The best belonging to the grammarians;
All are in opposition
To good antiquity.
Medicine, Hippocrates, Galen,
And those bold surgeons, 100
He of the Rue Neuve, Robert,
And he of Glatigny, Hubert,
And Master Peter the Lombard
Who tricks Paris with his arts,
And Gerald, another devil, 105

And Master Henry of Venables,
And Raoul of the Charité,
Little Bridge and their vanity,
They all would turn to money making
If they saw in it no danger.   110
Villainous Surgery
Was seated near a bloody cemetery.
She loved discord much better
Than bringing about nice concord.
She carried boxes and ointments,   115
And a great plenty of instruments
To draw arrows from paunches.
It did not take her long to patch up
The bellies she saw pierced:
However, she is a science.   120
But she has such bold hands
That she spares no one
From whom she may be able to get money.
I would have had much respect for them
If they had cured my eyes;   125
But they dupe many people,
While with the copper and silver
Which they receive for their poisons
They build them fine houses in Paris.
From Toledo came and from Naples,   130
She who knew the carnage of battles,
At midnight, Necromancy,
Who clearly told them their evil destiny:
That everyone should arm his head,
Which destiny she had divined in the sword.   135
At a cross-road she made a fire,
Near a circle, at twilight.
There she had sacrificed two cats
And two stray pigeons
In the name of the malign deity   140
To search out the truth.
The daughter of Madam Astronomy,
Who was an accomplice in their evil deeds,
Told them very well that the battle
Would occur tomorrow without fail.   145
Arithmetic sat in the shade,

Where she says, where she figures,
That ten and two and one make thirteen,
And three more make sixteen;
Four and three and nine to boot   150
Again make sixteen in their way;
Thirteen and twenty-seven make forty,
And three times twenty by themselves make sixty;
Five twenties make hundred, and ten hundreds a thousand.
Does counting involve anything further? No.   155
One can easily count a thousand thousands
In the foregoing manner
From the number which increases and diminishes,
And which in counting goes from one to hundred.
The dame makes from this her tale,   160
That usurer, prince, and count
Today love the number crunching lady better
Than the chanting of high mass.
Arithmetic then mounted
Her horse and proceeded to count   165
All the knights of the army;
And she had at her side
Her companion Geometry
Who there again showed her skill.
In a spot between the combatants   170
She described a small circle,
And said that within a thousand feet of ground
This war would be brought to a close.
Madam Music, she of the little bells
And her clerks full of songs   175
Carried fiddles and viols,
Psalteries and small flutes;
From the sound of the first *fa*
They ascended to *cc sol fa*.
The sweet tones diatessaron   180
Diapente, diapason,
Are struck in various combinations.
In groups of four and three,
Through the army they went singing,
They go enchanting them with their song.   185
These do not engage in battle;
But Donatus without delay

Dealt Plato such a blow
On the chin with a feathered verse
That he frightened him thoroughly;   190
And Sir Plato in great wrath
Struck back at him so hard with a sophism
Upon his shield, in the midst of a rhyme,
That he made him tumble in the mud
And completely covered him with blood.   195
Aristotle strikes Priscian
Our noble ancient authority
That he made him drop to the ground;
He wanted to trample him under his horse,
But Priscian had two nephews   200
Who were very handsome and brave,
Sir Graecismus and the Doctrinale;
They crippled him his horse,
And rendered the animal three-legged.
Aristotle, who was unhorsed,   205
Made Grammar tumble backwards.
Then pricked forward master Persius,
Sir Juvenal and Sir Horace,
Virgil, Lucan, and Statius,
And Sedulius, Propertius, Prudentius,   210
Arator, Homer, and Terence:
All smote Aristotle,
Who stood firm as a castle on a hill.
Priscian with his two nephews
Tried to beat out his eyes,   215
When Sophistical Refutations and the two Logics,
On Interpretation and the Topics,
The books of nature, Ethics,
Madam Necromancy, Medicine,
And Sir Boethius and Sir Macrobius   220
Dressed in a caitiff garb,
And Porphyry, came on a run
To bring aid to Aristotle.
The Lorn bards of dame Rhetoric
Rode hard after Dialectic,   225
Although they did not love her.
For they were but little acquainted with her;
But they wounded many an honest man

For the booty which they won there.
The Categories and the Six Principles,   230
Two good buyers of tripe,
Pricked after Sir Barbarismus
Who rode the fiftieth of the troop.
He was liege man of Grammar
One of the best men of her bookcase;   235
But he favored this war
Because he held land from Logic
By treason he was alienated
Because he was a native of Poitou.
These bad, spiteful people   240
Attacked Grammar, their mother.
Ah! if you had seen them there throwing lances
To disembowel these good authors,
Shaking heads and beating hands,
And loosening the reins on tongues!   245
A thousand arrows flew at one time,
Worse than those made of willow or aspen,
For there is more venom in words
Than in a hundred thousand silly sticks.
The authors defended themselves   250
And struck them great wounds,
With penknives and styluses,
Long fables and lies.
Their castle would have been defensible enough
If it had not been so stocked with fables;   255
For they palm off their nonsense
As truth, by means of fine phrases.
Grammar strikes one of their disciples
In the body with a participle
Which felled him to the ground,   260
Then to him said: "Now go and learn something."
Then she stretched five more of them on the sod
At the point of her adverb;
But Sir Socrates made her hide,
For she could not answer all his questions.   265
She turned towards those of Orléans,
Who for a long time have exalted her.
From the depths of a valley
They brought forth her horse

Which was being held by Orthography, 270
The foundation of learning;
Then back with her authors
Dame Grammar retreated.
Ah! if you had seen the logicians
How they slew the authorlings 275
And caused such havoc
Among those fine constructions!
The sophists despised them
Because they did not understand each other;
For there was so much contention among them 280
That the one knew little of what the other said.
One knight, On Interpretation,
Killed my lord Architrenius,
One of the barons of Normandy;
After that he also slew Tobit. 285
Four of them he killed in one onset.
Both the *Alexandreis* of Walter of Châtillon
And the versified Bible
He then cut to pieces with a huge battle-ax.
But when against the Patronymics 290
Advanced the family of the Topics,
They failed to force their way through,
So strong are the Patronymics.
Sirs *Juste* and *Praeterea*
For this reason killed 295
The good *Ego mei vel mis*,
Who was their great enemy,
Because they did not know whence he came
Nor how he was declined.
When Logic had shown her prowess. 300
She returned with great joy
To her standard, to her banner;
Then the army withdrew.
Astronomy and Rhetoric
Advised Dialectic, 305
That, before night-fall,
They had better enter Montlhéry.
The dames, who were very wise,
Entered Montlhéry,
And they did it not from fear, 310

But rather simply from the desire
To possess the castle;
And by this they made it known
That they love lofty things,
Whereas Grammar loves the fountains.   315
The authors were much troubled
When they assembled,
So they awaited the rear guard,
Which two knights were bringing up,
Hugh Primas of Orléans and Ovid.   320
They brought to their aid,
With great impetuosity, ten thousand verses,
Inscribed on their banner.
Which Ovid wove with his hands
In the exile where he was in want: 325
Martial and Martianus Capella.
Seneca and Anticlaudian
And Sir Bernard Silvester,
Who knew all the languages
Of the sciences and the arts;   330
He did not come as a mere squire,
But he brought so large a band
That the whole place was full of them.
The Achilleis of Statius,
Strong in chest and back,   335
Bore before him the stakes.
There was the wise Cato,
Avianus and Pamphilus;
Sir Theodulus carried there
A banner bipartite;   340
In it was woven with great skill
Sir Pseustis with pierced shield
Vanquished by Alithia,
Who was pictured on the other half.
Like leopards, this whole crowd   345
Followed the banner;
So nimble they are and so quick
They almost flew,
They almost captured
Among the stakes, dame Logic,   350
Astronomy, and Rhetoric.

But they are lodged so high up
That they strike them with their whips
And with their tongues the air and the wind.
They often fatten their scholars on it,   355
Whence they themselves are altogether weak.
The dames have tiresome tongues;
Logic strikes in her hand so much
That she has torn her gown into shreds.
She makes us a knife without a blade,   360
Who wears a sleeve without the gown.
We see from the looks of her arms,
That on her body she has no substance.
Rhetoric goes to her aid,
She who earns money by pleading.   365
The Novels, Code, and Digest,
Make her hot potions for her head;
For she has so many quack lawyers,
Who of their tongues make clappers
To get the goods of the common herd,   370
That all the country is full of them.
One of the pupils of dame Logic
Was sent to Grammar;
He bore letters to make peace.
Now I simply cannot refrain from telling this,   375
That when he arrived at his destination
He did not know the sense
Of the presents nor the preterits;
And that there where he had been brought up,
He had dwelt on them but little.   380
He had not learned thoroughly
Irregular conjugations,
Which are most difficult to inflect,
Adverbs and parts of speech,
Articles and declensions,   385
Genders and nominatives,
Supines and imperatives,
Cases, figures, formations,
Singulars, plurals, a thousand terms;
For in the court of Grammar are more corners   390
Than in all of Logic's babblings.
The boy did not know how to come to the point;

143

And came back in shame.
But Logic comforted him,
Carried him to her high tower, 395
And tried to make him fly
Before he was able to walk.
Astronomy, who soars high,
Has retained neither retreat nor school,
Neither in the city nor in the country; 400
In truth, she would have been entirely lost,
Had it not been for brave master Gautier,
Who out of little makes his living,
The Englishman who holds disputations on the Little Bridge
    [Adam of Petit-Pont],
Who hides himself for poverty. 405
Grammar withdrew
Into Egypt, where she was born.
But Logic is now in vogue,
Every boy runs her course
Ere he has passed his fifteenth year; 410
Logic is now for children!
Logic is in a very bad situation
In the tower on Montlhéry;
There she practices her art;
But Grammar opposes her 415
With her authors and authorlings
Sententious and frivolous.
Echo answered in the tower
To the great blows given all around,
For there they all hurl their rhymes. 420
She defends herself with sophisms;
Often she makes them fall back
And they in turn hurl at her their verses,
So that the air is thick with them.
She defends herself with unsolvable questions, 425
With true and with false solutions.
The authorlings put in a great rage
All those assembled there
And so eager to get away,
Because, in truth, they will never raise the siege 430
Until the day that they surrender;
And if they [the besieged] fall into their hands,

They will drive them from better to worse.
All for naught they make their siege,
For Astronomy upon their tents,   435
From above, hurled her lightning;
All their pavilions she reduced to ashes;
And the authorlings fled,
And deserted Grammar.
The courtly Sir Versifier   440
Fled away between Orléans and Blois.
Henceforth he does not dare to go abroad in France
Since he has no acquaintance there;
For students of arts and of canon law
No longer care for their [the vanquished] jurisdiction.   445
The Bretons and the Germans
Still do his bidding to some extent;
But if the Lombards got hold of him,
They (in a trice) would strangle him.
Sirs, the times are given to emptiness;   450
Soon they will go entirely to naught,
For thirty years this will continue,
Until a new generation will arise,
Who will go back to Grammar,
Just as it was the fashion   455
When Henri d'Andeli was born,
Who gives it us as his opinion
That one should destroy the glib student
Who cannot construe his lesson;
For in every science that master is an apprentice   460
Who has not mastered his parts of speech.

Here ends The Battle of the Seven Arts.

CHAPTER THREE

POLEMICAL CONFRONTATIONS WITH JEWS, MUSLIMS, AND HERETICS

The twelfth century witnessed a dramatic upsurge in polemical writing, a direct product of the intellectual energies of the age and of the ecclesiastic encounter with new ideas and beliefs. Some of this polemical activity was internal to Christian society, as the proliferation of monastic orders itself engendered a certain amount of invective between members of the different orders (as witnessed in the debates among Benedictines, Cistercians, and Premonstratensians). But a special concern of twelfth-century society was with the perceived external menaces to Christian belief itself: Judaism, Islam, and heresy.

Jews had long formed a relatively integrated segment of Christian society, but the increased number of converts from Judaism to Christianity and the gradual awareness of Jewish post-biblical literature (especially the Talmud) led to increased amounts of polemical and specifically disputational writings, a good deal of which was intended to strengthen the resolve of other Christians rather than for direct missionary activity. The Christian confrontation with Muslim armies both in the Holy Land and in Spain, where the so-called Reconquest made major advances during the late eleventh century, lent urgency and necessity to combat the religion of Islam, a point well illustrated in the letters and polemics of Peter the Venerable, who commissioned the first translation of the Quran. Heresy had, of course, been a long-standing concern of the Church, but the apparent spread of heretical movements that challenged the sacred hierarchy of Rome demanded renewed attention, and it is from the efforts to correct such erroneous beliefs that the earliest inquisitorial tribunals were formed.

The selections in this chapter offer a wide sampling of the Christian polemical encounter with Judaism, Islam, and heresy. The Christian confrontation with Jews and Judaism underwent an especially critical turn in the twelfth century, since it included the first recorded accusations of ritual murder (in Norwich in 1144) and the first royal expulsion of the Jews (from France in 1182). Also included are two examples of Jewish counter-polemics to Christians. Anselm of Havelberg's description of his disputation in Constantinople has been included as a witness to the ongoing struggle between the Catholic West and the Greek Orthodox East. The chapter closes with various decrees from the Fourth Lateran Council in 1215, in which Jews, Muslims, heretics, and Orthodox Christians are all condemned. Because of its pronouncements on matters of doctrine, learning, and interfaith relations, the disciplinary decrees that resulted from this important church council provide a useful conclusion to the first three chapters of this Reader.

28. GILBERT CRISPIN'S DISPUTATION WITH A JEW IN LONDON

Gilbert Crispin (d. 1117) came from a family of noble Norman lineage. In his youth he entered the monastery of Bec, where he came to know both Lanfranc (Doc. 1a) and Anselm (Doc. 2), and there he earned an excellent education and reputation in the liberal arts. He moved to England following the Norman Conquest of 1066, and in 1085 Archbishop Lanfranc appointed Gilbert the abbot of Westminster Abbey, a position he held until the end of his life.

Gilbert wrote various theological treatises, but his most popular work was his Disputation with a Jew *(c. 1090), which he dedicated to his close friend Anselm, now the archbishop of Canterbury. There are 32 extant manuscripts of the work, 20 of which date to the twelfth century. It was used by Lambert of St-Omer in his* Liber Floridus *(1120), and it was rewritten by an imitator later in the century. Alan of Lille seems to have drawn upon it in his treatise* On the Catholic Faith against the Heretics, *toward the end of the twelfth century. Parts of the* Disputation *were translated into Hebrew by Jacob ben Reuben in his* Wars of the Lord *(1170). As a work of the anti-Jewish genre it is second in popularity during the twelfth century only to Petrus Alfonsi's* Dialogues *(Doc. 29).*

One of the often-cited reasons for the popularity of the work is the amicable tenor of the debate. The Disputation *purports to be based on a real encounter between Gilbert and a Jew from Mainz who was in London conducting business. Not only is a generous amount of space given to the Jewish interlocutor, but it also does not end with a Jewish conversion, although this by itself does not negate Gilbert or his audience's desire for Jewish conversion. For instance, approving mention is made at the end of the dedicatory letter of another Jewish convert who had become a monk at Westminster. The great attraction of the* Disputation, *it would seem, was in allowing the Jewish disputant to articulate his understanding of the Hebrew Bible at length and thereby provoke Gilbert (and by extension his reader) into thinking more allegorically and deeply about the meaning of Scripture, just as his teacher Anselm had taught. Moreover, there are a number of passages, most notably in the discussion about the Incarnation, that would seem to be indebted to Anselm, who was at the time at work on his own theological dialogue,* Why God Became Man *(c. 1092).*

Source: trans. Alex J. Novikoff, from *The Works of Gilbert Crispin*, ed. Anna Sapir Abulafia and G.R. Evans, Auctores Britannici Medii Aevi 8 (Oxford and London: The British Academy, 1986), 8–15, 39–41. Latin.

Prologue

Here begins the letter of the Lord Abbot Gilbert to the Lord Abbot Anselm about a disputation that was conducted about our faith against a certain Jew.

To Abbot Anselm, Reverend Father and Lord, his servant and son, Brother Gilbert, proctor and servant of the monastery of Westminster, [wishes you] a prosperous sojourn in this life and a beautiful eternity in the future.

I'm sending to your fatherly prudence a little book for consideration, which I recently wrote, committing to the page what a certain Jew professed about his Law while arguing [*disputans*] against our faith some time ago, and what replies I gave to his arguments in support of our faith. I do not know his origins, but he had been educated at Mainz and was well versed in both his Law and also our letters, and he possessed great expertise in Scriptures and talent in his counter arguments.

As he was familiar to me, he came to see me often, sometimes for business reasons, sometimes to visit freely, since I was necessary to him in certain affairs, and whenever we came together we soon had a conversation, in a friendly spirit, about Scriptures and our faiths. Then on a certain day, God granted us more spare time than usual, and soon, as we were accustomed, we began to question each other.

What he proposed, he proposed sufficiently and logically, and he subsequently explained what he had proposed no less sufficiently. Now, our refutation responded to his propositions at every point, and was by his own admission fully convincing by the proof of Scriptures. Those who were present therefore asked that I should memorialize [i.e., write down] our little discussion so that it might be of use to others in the future.

Thus I wrote it down, and, removing our names, I have written under the person of "a Jew" who disputes with a Christian about our faith. I transmit this work, composed and written down, for your criticism and examination. If the matter is, indeed, to be approved, it shall be acceptable after it has been approved by your judgment. If it must truly be rejected, either completely or some part of it, accept whatever must be rejected as something spoken to a friendly ear. And because it became known solely to a friend, it will be passed over, and these pages will not be read by anyone.

Either remove anything that you think should be deleted, in sound mutual love and in true, absolutely unbroken peace, or let it be rectified if you judge that what is there can in fact be corrected. I declare that I will remove with a willing heart whichever argument you point out and I will listen with an obedient ear.

However, one of the Jews who was in London at that time, with the help of God's grace, converted to the Christian faith. After professing his faith at Westminster in front of everyone, he requested baptism, received it, and, once baptized, vowed to serve God there. Once a monk, he remained with us.

After several others had been interposed, therefore, that Jewish disputant provoked me into a discussion.

Here begins the Disputation of a Jew with a Christian, edited by Gilbert, Abbot of Westminster.

[Chapter 1: Regarding the Meaning of the Laws
in the Hebrew Bible]

The Jew: Because you Christians say that you are educated in Scripture and endowed with the faculty of speaking, I would want you to address me in a tolerant spirit. By what power of reason and with what proof of authority do you blame the Jews because we observe the Law given by God and follow our lawgiver Moses? Indeed, if "the Law is good" [1 Timothy 1:8] and given by God, then it must be observed.

Whose decree will have to be observed, if God's commandment need not be observed? If, however, the Law must be observed, why do you compare its followers to dogs that need to be chased away with clubs, and why do you persecute us at every opportunity? But if on the other hand you say that it needs to be only minimially observed, then Moses must be blamed, for he handed it down to us from God, in idle vanity, in order for it to be followed.

But if you say that only that which is left after removing part of it must be observed, and that what has been removed must be observed in the least or must be abolished, then give us advice as to how we will escape the judgment given by God as a curse: "Cursed be he who will not uphold the terms of this Teaching and observe them" [Galatians 3:10; Deuteronomy 27:26].

The Lawgiver makes no exceptions, but commands that they all be universally observed. You, however, determine observance of the Law and the commandments according to your judgment. And because I want to devote more effort in these matters to reason than to sowing contention, let us pay no regard to our audience and strenuously reject any applause that our audience may bestow upon either one of us.

The Christian: All these things that you request are reasonable enough, and it is appropriate that they all be requested. But in return, I ask from you that you treat me in a patient spirit. I will be ready to deal with you in these matters and to go wherever you wish only if our discussion is kept in such a fashion that you allow whatever is attested on the pages of your Law or is adduced by a reasoning so evident that no evidence can disprove it. And I am doing this more in the name of religion and out of love for you than out of the zeal for debate. I care not for the audience's applause. May victory instead be conferred on the one for whom both reason and the authority of Scripture serve as witness.

Now then, the fact that the Law is good and was given by God is something that we declare, we hold to, and we build upon. Moreover, we stipulate that whatever is written in the Law, understood in its divinely inspired meaning and was observed in its time, must be observed. We say that the commandments of the Law must be understood in their divinely inspired meaning because, if we were to accept them all in a human and literal sense, we would find many of them to be mutually exclusive and contradictory.

If, once the creation of the world had been completed, Moses says, "God saw all that He had made, and found it very good" [Genesis 1:31], how can he later write, concerning the division of the animals, that some of the animals are pure and others impure, and allow the use of the former but command us not only not to touch the latter, but state that those who would touch them must be put to death? For if something is impure, how can it be very good? When he named them all and said that all was very good, he omitted neither this nor that animal.

For what purpose did God create all goodly animals, only later to prohibit certain animals from being eaten, and add by way of a reason that they are impure animals? He prohibited not only those that are by their very nature abhorrent for man to eat, but actually many that are pleasing in taste and wholly edible. Therefore, these commandments contain in themselves something else that may have been pronounced by God, but in a literal reading they differ widely from one another.

Likewise, we know how God said to Adam, "See, I give you every seed-bearing plant that is upon all the earth, and every tree that has seed-bearing fruit; they shall be yours for food" [Genesis 1:29]. Why did God give the first man all the trees for food, but immediately afterwards forbid him to eat from "the tree of knowledge of good and evil" [Genesis 2:17]? When he grants and bestows upon man all the trees everywhere, He implies that none are exempted. Therefore, this can only be understood in a mysterious way.

In Exodus, the Lord instructed Moses, among other precepts, to build the altar as follows: "Make an altar of earth for me and sacrifice on it your burnt offerings and fellowship offerings" [Exodus 20:24]. And thus He told him what other material could be used to make it of and how, "If you make an altar of stones for me, do not build it with dressed stones." [Exodus 20:22].

With regards to the construction of the tabernacle, its vessels and utensils, it reads, "Moses made the incense altar of acacia wood, a cubit long and a cubit wide—square—and two cubits high" [Exodus 37:25]. And then below, "They built the altar of burnt offering of acacia wood, three cubits high; it was square, five cubits long and five cubits wide" [Exodus 38:1]. Surely it was not a reckless act or out of presumption that it was built to such different measures of height and squares.

Similarly further on, "They used it to make the bases for the entrance to the tent of meeting, the bronze altar with its bronze grating and all its utensils" [Exodus 38:30], and likewise at the end: "Bring in the table and set out what belongs on it. Then bring in the lampstand and set up its lamps" [Exodus 40:4–5]. So how is it that the Lord commands that "You shall make an altar of earth and sacrifice on it your burnt offerings," while at the same time, Moses "made the incense altar of wood," and "made the altar for burnt offering of wood," and made an altar of copper, one of gold, and on this occasion he made one of stones as well?

So, it seems very contradictory that the manner in which the Lord orders something to be done through Moses should be carried out differently by Moses himself. It has a meaning, therefore, more profound than the literal one and this must be understood. . . .

This contradiction can be oberved not only in those commandments cited above, but also in many other ceremonial laws, unless we interpret them in an appropriate sense. Thus, they must be discussed and understood in a different and divinely inspired sense because it cannot happen that they all be fulfilled in a literal sense.

If we verily accept the Law in the proper sense, we will be able to observe all the commandments of the Law that must be observed by accepting that certain ones are meant literally and are not covered up by metaphors, while also understanding that others are allegorical and are concealed under a profound veil of metaphors.

Certain ones are intended to be observed at a certain time while others must be followed without any constraints in time. For where the commandments concerned the prediction and allusion to a future truth that would only become obvious by the arrival of the event and the truth of the future time, it was necessary that its prediction and allusion would remain.

Consider the alternations we use in the very usage of the spoken word, saying "it will be" provided it is in the future tense. In the present tense, we omit this very "it will be," but say "it is," and in order to indicate that something has already passed, we use "it was." Similarly, in prophetic matters relating to a sacrament, when that event is being made manifest, retaining either a metaphor or an allegorical clue would be redundant.

Those commandments, however, were not predictions of some mystery. They either openly imply a verity of faith or convey a concept of charity, but they must be observed both by you and by us, not temporarily but in perpetuity, and their transgression can never go unpunished. The true meaning of those allusions of truth that were in the Law, and which were expected for so long and over so many centuries, finally had to be revealed at some time.

Was it always to be promised, "I will open my mouth with a parable; I will utter hidden things, things from of old" [Psalm 78:2]? Was it always going to be, "until he to whom it belongs shall come and the obedience of the nations shall be his" [Genesis 49:10]? Finally there comes, in times predetermined by God, "For there is one God and one mediator between God and mankind, the man Christ Jesus" [1 Timothy 2:5], appearing to our sense, to "open [our] minds so [we] could understand the Scriptures" [Luke 24:45], and he reveals profound mysteries that had been written about him in the Law and the Prophets, and in whom you ought to believe.

[Chapter 5: Regarding the Legitimacy of Source Texts]

The Jew: If this is how Christians are supposed to read and interpret the Scriptures in regard to Christ, you will find far more that you can interpret in a similar fashion. We do not know your literature, and it is very likely that you say that many things have been written in your Scriptures that we do not believe have been written in ours. But if God were to grant you and me a lifetime, I would respond to you at greater leisure. We would bring together copies of our respective books and look up those examples. I confess that it would be the height of folly, nay madness, if you or I were to resist the obvious examples and authoritative evidence of Scripture. For that reason it is at this moment not worth the trouble to go on debating with you [about the Trinity].

For, in fact, you Christians assert many things about the Law and the Prophets that are not written in the Law and the Prophets. Concerning your quotation from Jeremiah—"[he] appeared upon earth and lived among men" [Baruch 3:37]—as well as many other claims attached to this verse, Jeremiah neither said nor wrote. If you can find that it was written in Jeremiah, then I concede that the other things were said truthfully. But if you cannot find it in Jeremiah, then let go of your animosity toward us, be ashamed of the falsehoods that you have invented against us, and acknowledge that the primary truth in the Law and the Prophets remains with us.

Or this, which you Christians always raise against us with such certainty in yourselves: "Look, the virgin is with child and about to give birth to a son" [Isaiah 7:14]; Isaiah did not say that, and he did not write it either, but rather: "Look, [the young woman]," he said, "is with child and about to give birth to a son" [Isaiah 7:14]. So even if Isaiah had said what you say—"Look, the virgin is with child and about to give birth to a son,"—he still did not add what you have added, claiming that she stayed a virgin during conception and that she remained a virgin even after giving birth. Neither Isaiah nor any other Prophet said this.

The Christian: Because Christ is the truth, faith in Christ allows no falsehood nor is there any place for falsehood in the Church of Christ. What we profess to be written in the Law and the Prophets, we accept to have been written by

Figure 6: Petrus Alfonsi (right) disputing his former self, Moses (left), from a thirteenth-century copy of his popular and influential *Dialogus contra Iudaeos*, now in Bruges. Note the Jewish conical hat worn by Moses, the staging of the debate framed by pillars in the background, and the singular strength of Petrus's reasoning embodied by his one finger versus Moses's many (possibly an allusion to the five books of Moses).

Source: Wikimedia Commons.

you [the Jewish people] in the Law and the Prophets. For the Church of Christ received the Law and the Prophets from you, and what it received from you it has kept unchanged through many centuries up to these times. In the time of King Ptolemy of Egypt, seventy interpreters, then the most erudite scholars from among your people, translated the Law and the Prophets from Hebrew into Greek. Then later our [scholars] translated it from Greek into Latin, word for word and phrase for phrase.

We received all that we have written in the Law and the Prophets from those first copies of those first translators. So read the new, read the old books of the Old Testament, read according to the Greek, read according to the Latin [manuscripts]; nowhere in the Law and the Prophets will you discover anything but the very same truth everywhere, without variation, and you will find unity of the truth in the Law and the Prophets throughout the whole world with us.

29. PETRUS ALFONSI'S *DIALOGUE AGAINST THE JEWS*

Petrus Alfonsi is the name taken by a Jew named Moses who converted to Christianity around 1106 in the northern Spanish town of Huesca, in the kingdom of Aragon. A gifted raconteur, Alfonsi was also the author of an important and influential collection of moralistic tales drawn from the Jewish and Islamic traditions. His Dialogue against the Jews, *composed in 12 books, takes the form of a spirited conversation between his former identity, Moses, and his converted self, Petrus or Peter. It was one of the most widely copied medieval treatises of the* Adversus Iudaeos *(anti-Jewish) genre, and it left an indelible imprint on polemicists of later generations, including Peter the Venerable (twelfth century), Vincent of Beauvais and Raymund Martí (thirteenth century), and Abner of Burgos (fourteenth century). It may also have been used by Pablo Christiani at the public disputation at Barcelona in 1263 and later by Jerome de Santa Fe for the disputation at Tortosa in 1413–14.*

The Dialogue *is notable because it combines arguments based on philosophical reason, the conclusions of medieval science, and a long tradition of biblical exegesis. Book Five is devoted to explaining the inadequacies of Islam as an alternative religion to Christianity, despite Islam's superiority in matters of science (see Doc. 81). More important still, Alfonsi's* Dialogue *was the first polemical work that turned systematically to Jewish post-biblical literature in general, and the Talmud in particular (although not named), in order to contrast the inferiority of Judaism to the truth of Christian teaching. The opening prologue, from which this excerpt is taken, presents Alfonsi's authorial intentions and well illustrates the new reliance on reason and argumentation as a tool of exegesis, persuasion, and polemic.*

Source: trans. Alex J. Novikoff, from *Petri Alphonsi ex Judeo Christiani Dialogi*, in J.-P. Migne, ed., *Patrologia Latina* (Paris: Garnier, 1899), vol. 157, cols. 535–40. Latin.

To the one and first eternal omnipotent creator of all things [God], who is without beginning and without end, all-knowing, and accomplishes all that he wills, who has endowed humankind with reason and wisdom above every animal, so that with these two powers [we] may desire with understanding those things that are just and escape from those that are contrary to salvation. . . . Amen.

The Omnipotent One has inspired us with his spirit and directed me to follow the correct path, first removing the white stain from my eyes and then the heavy curtain of a corrupt soul. Then the doors of the prophets were opened for us and their secret places were revealed, and we applied the mind to understanding its true meaning and we labored to interpret it. We thus considered both what ought to be understood and what ought to be believed; namely, that God is one in a trinity of persons; they are inseperable from one another by any division, and they do not precede one another in time whatsoever. Christians name these persons the Father, Son, and the Holy Spirit. And the blessed Mary, who conceived through the Holy Spirit, gave birth to Christ without mixing with a man, generating an animate body that was the dwelling place of the incomprehensible deity. Therefore, there is one Christ, complete with three substances—body, soul, and deity—and this same one is both God and man. Furthermore, the Jews crucified him by their disposition and will, and he died in the body and was buried, and on the third day was resurrected from the dead. And just as he was the Creator, he would also become the Redeemer of the entire holy Church—in other words of the faithful who both preceded and followed him. Then he ascended into heaven and he is there at the same time with the Father. He will return on judgment day, to judge both the living and the dead, just as the prophets said and predicted for the future.

When, by the impulse of divine mercy, I had therefore attained such an exalted degree of this [Christian] faith, I shed the cloak of falsehood and was stripped of the tunic of iniquity. I was baptized in the see of the city of Huesca in the name of the Father and the Son and the Holy Spirit, having been purified by the hands of Stephen, the glorious and legitimate bishop of that same city. . . . This occurred in the month of June in the year 1106, the year 1144 of the [Spanish] era from the birth of the Lord, on the feast day of the apostles Peter and Paul [June 29]. I thus chose for myself the name of the apostle Peter out of reverence for—and as a remembrance of—this very day [of my baptism]. Moreover, my spiritual father [i.e., godfather] was Alfonsus [I of Aragon, r. 1104–34], the glorious emperor of Spain, who received me at the sacred font. It is for this reason that I took for myself the name Petrus Alfonsi, appending his surname to my above-mentioned [first] name.

But when it came to the attention of the Jews—[the ones] who had known me previously and had considered me learned in the books of the prophets and the sayings of the sages, as well as having a partial, though not great, knowledge of all the liberal arts—that I had accepted the law and faith of the Christians and had become one of them, some of them thought that I only did this out of a shameless renouncement [of our traditions], and that I had gone so far as to condemn both God and the law. Others among them claimed that I had done this because I had improperly understood the words of the prophets and the law. Others still accused me of vainglory and falsely claimed that I had done this for worldly honor, because I perceived that the Christian people [*Christianorum gentem*] dominated all others.

I have therefore composed this little book so that all may know my intention and hear my reasoning. In this book I set forth the destruction of the belief of all other peoples, after which I concluded that the Christian law holds primacy over all others. Finally, I have laid down all the objections of any adversary of the Christian law and, having done so, I have destroyed them with reason and authority according to my knowledge.

I have arranged the entire book in the form of a dialogue, so that the mind of the reader may more quickly achieve an understanding. To defend the arguments of the Christians, I have used my present Christian name, whereas in the arguments of the adversary refuting them, I have used the name that I had before baptism, Moses. I have divided the book into twelve headings, so that the reader may find more quickly whatever he desires in them. . . . Here ends the prologue. The book begins.

Since tender boyhood a certain and most perfect friend named Moses stuck by my side, and he has been my companion and fellow student from the very earliest age. When word reached him that I had chosen the Christian faith after having renounced the law of my fathers, he left his place of residence and came to me in haste. Bearing an indignant expression on his face as he approached, he greeted me not as a friend but almost as a stranger, and he initiated thus: "Oh, Petrus Alfonsi, much time has passed since I have wanted, desperately, to come and see you, to speak with you, and to be with you, but my desire remained unfulfilled until just now, when, by the grace of God, I see you with an expression of happiness on your face. Now, then, I beg you to make known to me [your] intention and why you deserted the old Law, or reveal the reason that you chose a new law. For I knew well that you once excelled in the writings of the prophets and the sayings of our sages. Since boyhood you were more zealous for the law than all your contemporaries, and with a shield of defense you used to oppose any adversary. You [also] preached to the Jews in the synagogues, so that none might withdraw from the faith, and in teaching your fellow disciples, you even led the learned toward greater things. See, then, that I neither know nor see what has moved you to become estranged from the path of rectitude, for this, to my mind, I judge as having been done in error."

And I said to him: It is the custom of Jewish and uneducated people that if they observe someone who does something contrary to their own custom, even if it remains correct and most just, nevertheless in their estimation and judgment that person will be guilty of the crime of injustice. With what effrontery can you cast blame on me, you who have been nurtured in the cradle of philosophy and suckled on the breasts of philosophy, until you have been able to determine whether my deeds are just or unjust?

Moses: Two contrary arguments come to mind: either I consider that you are a man of prudence who could not have withdrawn from the law which you held unless you knew that the one you have received is truly better; or, alternatively, I consider that the law which I hold and which you renounced is better. This is why I judge what you have done to be an error, and I do not know to which side I should acquiesce. For this reason I beg you to dispel from my mind the anxiety of this doubt, and to let us both take turns running back and forth on the field of argument, until I arrive at an [adequate] consideration of this matter and may be able to learn whether your action is just or unjust.

Petrus: Human nature shows that some matters may cause the soul to become confused, since it lacks the eye for judgment in discerning truth and falsehood. And unless you remove all confusion from your heart, so that following the custom of wise men we may praise together what is just and spurn what is unjust without contention, no end for our task will be reached and we will cast our words into the void.

Moses: I willingly accept this agreement, and I ask that you accept the same.

Petrus: Certainly, I agree happily.

Moses: I further implore, if you please, that if you introduce some authority from the Scriptures, you choose to do this according to the Hebrew truth [*Hebraica veritas*]. Otherwise, you know I will not accept it. But if I also advance some [proof-text] of ours in a similar manner, I want you not to contradict it in any way but to receive it and acknowledge it as true.

Petrus: Certainly I do not refuse this, for I strongly desire to slay you with your own sword.

Moses: Furthermore, if something which seems to be irrelevant to a discussion of laws should come up, I beg you to not let it annoy you, but to strive to respond to the questioner from the other arts, when a convenient place arises. I also want you to agree that sometimes it will be appropriate to question me, sometimes to respond to me, and sometimes to oppose me, just as the discussion will permit me to do.

Petrus: I agree. Now, may it be granted that you ask about whatever you wish to know and with whatever intention you like. . . .

Moses: Is it to be understood from your words that you comprehend the law and the prophets in their correct sense, whereas the Jews, who are worshippers of the same law, in your judgment stand outside its correct intention and seem to understand it poorly? . . . Make me understand, then, how it seems to you that the Jews have erred in the explanation of the law, which you understand better.

Petrus: Since I see that they only attend to the superficial [understanding] of the letter of the law, and do not explicate it spiritually, but carnally, this is why they are especially deceived by error. . . . Do you not recall your teachers [i.e., rabbis] and the teachings that they wrote [i.e., the Talmud], on which your entire law relies? How, according to you, can they claim that God has a form and a body, and how can they attribute such things to his ineffable majesty, so wicked to believe and absurd to hear, seeing that they are not founded on reason? They have put forth opinions concerning him that appear to be nothing other than the words of little boys joking in school, or women gossiping in the streets [plateis]. Again, explaining the law according to your intellectual capacity, you hope to evade captivity in a manner that cannot happen. Furthermore, you hope that God will perform an extraordinary miracle to help you escape, and that he will raise your dead, who will begin to live on the earth as they once did before. I similarly note that while living in captivity you observe very few of all the precepts of the law, and they do not even accord with your own explanation. And those [laws] which you do [observe], you believe are pleasing and acceptable to God, but you never admit that he will hold you guilty for what you leave out, and you seem to have fulfilled for yourselves everything which clearly holds the greatest place of error.

30. PETER THE VENERABLE ON JEWS AND JUDAISM

Peter the Venerable (c. 1092–1156) was one of the most significant churchmen of the twelfth century. Elected ninth abbot of the Benedictine abbey of Cluny in 1122, he was an energetic and skillful administrator of a vast monastic organization comprising over 1,000 dependent monasteries and priories. In addition to his involvement in ecclesiastical affairs, Peter the Venerable also wrote several polemical treatises intended to refute contemporary challenges to Christianity and maintained an extensive correspondence (193 letters are extant) with some of the most important secular and religious personalities of the day (see, for example, Doc. 6a). The two selections below illustrate the abbot's concern with Judaism, a very ancient problem in the history of Christianity, and with the excessive tolerance of local Jews, a more contemporary issue aggravated by the advent of the Crusades.

Against the Inveterate Obduracy of the Jews *(c. 1144–47) has been characterized as a turning point in medieval anti-Jewish polemics. The stated intention of bringing about the conversion of the Jews would appear to rest on an assumption that Jews are rational beings who may be persuaded of Christian truths by philosophical argument, empirical evidence, and a proper exegetical understanding of the Bible. But Peter is also convinced that their enduring "blindness" stems from a persistent and blameworthy strain of bestial irrationality. Peter traces this irrationality to the Jewish commitment to the Talmud, thus building upon and in a certain sense surpassing Petrus Alfonsi, who had ridiculed Talmudic folklore in his* Dialogue against the Jews *(Doc. 29) without actually naming the Talmud as such. By stressing the irrationality of the Jews, Peter questions their essential humanity and opens the door to an increasingly harsh treatment of the Jewish minority in medieval Christendom.*

Letter 130, addressed to King Louis VII of France (r. 1137–80), clearly displays the abbot's growing aggravation at local Jewish populations that not only resided, but also prospered, in Christian lands. By connecting the king's commitment to waging war against the Muslims in what is now called the Second Crusade (1144–47), Peter draws a direct link between anti-Judaism and crusading fervor, all while clearly showing his awareness of the Augustinian injunction to "slay them not" (a gloss on Psalm 59:12 found in the City of God, *XVIII.46). The advice that Peter gives the king is thus of a more economic sort, asking that their trade and livelihood be curtailed as punishment for their continued disbelief in Christ. The letter in many ways encapsulates the profound historical and psychological connection that existed for many twelfth-century Christians between concerns for the Holy Land and hatred for local Jews, even though the more obvious military threat were Muslims, whose religion Peter targets in a separate polemic (Doc. 34).*

a. *Against the Inveterate Obduracy of the Jews*

Source: trans. Alex J. Novikoff, from *Petris Venerabilis: Adversus Iudeorum Inveteratam Duritiem*, ed. Yvonne Friedman, Corpus Christianorum Continuatio Mediaevalis, 58 (Turnhout: Brepols, 1985), 125–27. Latin.

Chapter 5: On the Ridiculous and Very Foolish Fables of the Jews

It seems to me, O Jew, that on account of such a quantity of authorities and arguments I have satisfied every human being on those matters relating to the question that has been raised. Or so I believe. But if I have satisfied every human being, then [surely] I have satisfied you too, if indeed you are human. In fact, I do not even assert that you are human, dare I lie, because I recognize that the rational faculty that distinguishes a human from other animals or beasts and gives precedence over them is extinct (or more precisely entombed) inside of you.

I find evidence of these things even in your psalm, where it deplores that a man is turned into a wild beast [brutus]. For it says, "Man when he was in honor did not understand; he has been compared to senseless beasts, and made like unto them" [Psalm 48:21]. Although, in some sense, this can be understood to have been said of all mankind (that is, of the human species), nonetheless you cannot deny that it is said of you both specifically and individually, in whom all reason has been concealed. So why should you not be called a wild animal, why not a beast, or even a beast of burden? Take for instance the cow, or, if you prefer, an ass (for among the herd animals there is none more stupid), and listen together with it to whatever they can hear. What difference, what distinction, will there be between the hearing of an ass and your own? The ass hears but does not understand; the Jew hears but does not understand. Now, am I the first to point this out? Was not the same thing said many centuries ago? Did your sublime prophet [Isaiah] not make the same claim when he said, "With the ear you shall hear, and shall not understand; and seeing you shall see, and shall not perceive" [cf. Isaiah 6:9; Acts 28:26]? And although it has been fully proven by these sacred authorities that you are a beast of burden or a wild animal, and although I have made this sufficiently clear in the preceding four chapters (even if you remained unmoved by them), nonetheless a fifth chapter shall be added. From the light it produces, it shall be made manifest not only to Christians but also to the whole world that you are truly a beast of burden and that when I affirm this I have neither over-reached nor in any way exceeded the limit of truth.

Then I lead the monstrous beast out from its lair, and push it laughing onto the stage [in theatro] in view of all peoples, for the whole world to observe. I display that book of yours to you in the presence of all, O Jew, O wild beast, that book, I say, your Talmud, that egregious teaching of yours that you prefer to the books of the prophets and to all authentic judgments. But do you wonder, since I am not a Jew, how this name was made known to me? From whence did it assault my ears? Who revealed the Jewish secrets to me? And who unrobed your intimate and most hidden secrets? It is he, he, I say, the Christ whom you deny. Is it the Truth that has stripped naked your falsehood, unveiled your ignominy, which says: "For nothing is covered that shall not be revealed: nor hid, that shall not be known" [Matthew 10:26; cf. Luke 12:2]? It will assuredly be shown from your book, and clearly revealed from it, how God's just judgment has given you over "to a reprobate sense" [Romans 1:28], since you want to achieve the clear-est truth without the labor of human studies, and so are easily satisfied with the darkest falsehood. In you and others like you are the words of our apostle [Paul] fulfilled, who said: "Therefore God shall send them the operation of error, to believe lying; that all may be judged who have not believed the truth, but have consented to iniquity" [2 Thessalonians 2:10–11]. It is a plain surprise, and an unbelievable one at that, that men do not believe a credible and fully revealed truth, but instead believe in an incredible falsehood. But on the other hand it is no wonder if the once dense darkness of the Egyptians drove [the Jews] out of Egypt, seizing Jewish hearts while every vestige of light withdrew, because according to a true Scripture "there is no concord between Christ and Belial, nor any fellowship between light and darkness" [cf. 2 Corinthians 6:15, 14]. But now this darkness must be removed, and your chosen writings, the Talmud, must be exposed. According to you and your like, it is so great and has such great dignity and loftiness that "God does nothing in heaven but read that text continually and confer over it with the wise Jews who composed it" [Midrash Gen. Rabbah 64:4; Babylonian Talmud Ber. 8a, Abodah Zarah 3b].

But what am I to do? If I begin to respond to this or any other similar insanity, I myself will also appear almost insane. Will the one who replies to a man that suffers either from madness or from a devil's furious assault not be considered insane when he says strange or incredibly absurd things? Will he not appear crazy if he strives to debate [disputare] reasonably with the kind of man in whom the whole of reason has been entombed, and who proffers nothing but vain and foolish remarks? The same might also be believed of me, were it not for the fact that the certitude of reason protects me from this stupidity. That certitude of reason is that even if I am unable to benefit all Jews with my disputation [mea disputatione], nonetheless I will perhaps be able to accomplish something with some of them. Presently they have been properly cast aside by God for their iniquity and they will not, according to the prophet, be recalled to him until the multitude of the Gentiles has gone first, at which time a remnant of Israel will be saved. Nevertheless, heavenly compassion sometimes gathers up some in the interim and separates others (if only a few) from the deceased masses. It is for them that this response or disputation of mine will perhaps have some use. Those among the Jews who have for a long time been contaminated [infecti] by the aforementioned impurities will be able to be more completely cleansed once they cross over to the Church of Christ, and once they have been treated by such an antidote, than those who are contaminated by that devastating book [the Talmud]. Hear then, O Jew, of your insanity and of the insanity of your people and, even worse, of your blasphemy.

b. Letter 130 to the King of France

Source: trans. Jeremy Cohen, from The Letters of Peter the Venerable, ed. Giles Constable (Cambridge, MA: Harvard University Press, 1967), vol. 1, pp. 327–30. Latin.

To the illustrious and magnificent prince, the lord Louis, glorious king of the Franks, brother Peter, humble abbot of Cluny [wishes] that he rule felicitously in this world and that he see the king of kings in his kingdom and splendor.

Although I am not able to accompany the army of the eternal king to distant lands—the army he has determined that you, the terrestrial king, amass against the enemies of his cross, I desire to accompany you in my prayer and devotion, in my counsel and assistance, to the extent that I can. Do not be amazed. For who—even if he is the very last to be called by the name of a Christian—will not be attracted by the wondrous movement of the army of the Lord of hosts? Who will not strive with all his strength and power to aid this expedition for the sake of God? Behold ancient times have been renewed, and those very miracles that occurred to God's people of old are now being repeated in the new age of grace. Then Moses left Egypt and devastated the Amorite kings and their subject peoples. After him rose Joshua, defeated the Canaanite kings and their innumerable pagan subjects at God's command, and, upon the elimination of the impious, divided the land among God's people by lot. Now the Christian king is departing from the farthest regions of the West—if you will, from the very place where the sun sets—and marches on the East; and, armed with the cross of Christ, he attacks the wicked Arab or Persian people, that seeks once again to subjugate the holy land. Though those princes of the Jews were great and outdid present-day princes in the sanctity of their lives, they do not seem superior—but rather, inferior—to this king of the Christians. At the divine command, they destroyed godless peoples and took their lands for God and for themselves, while he, at the order of the same God, will destroy the Saracens, enemies of the true faith, and will toil to conquer their lands for God, not for himself. The former observed the divine command- ments, but, to a certain extent, they exerted themselves in combat out of hope for an earthly reward; yet the latter endangers and even sacrifices his kingdom, his wealth, and even his life not so that the great king might reap some earthly reward but so that, after the disappearance of his mortal kingdom, he might be crowned with honor and glory by the king of kings. Sublime victory is therefore assured that king, armed with heavenly weapons more than earthly ones, since the eastern barbarians will not at all be able to resist the army of the living God. For who can resist those who elected to abandon honor, wealth, pleasure, and even homeland and parents in order to follow their redeemer—to labor, to fight, to die, and to live for his sake? Who on earth, I say, can impede the army of him who says of himself [Matthew 28:18], "All power is given to me in heaven and on earth." (Although he received this power from God, having assumed human form for the sake of humankind, nevertheless he had it, as the true God, from all eternity.)

Toward what end should we pursue and persecute the enemies of the Chris- tian faith in far and distant lands if the Jews, vile blasphemers and far worse than the Saracens, not far away from us but right in our midst, blaspheme, abuse, and trample on Christ and the Christian sacraments so freely and insolently and with impunity? How can zeal for God nourish God's children if the Jews, enemies of the supreme Christ and of the Christians, remain totally unpunished? Has the king of the Christians forgotten what once was said by a certain holy king of the Jews [Psalm 139:21]? Said he: "Have I not hated them that hated you, O Lord, and pined away because of your enemies? I have hated them with a perfect hatred." If the Saracens must be detested because, although they acknowledge (as we do) that Christ was born of a virgin and they share many beliefs about him with us, they reject God and the son of God (which is more important) and they do not believe in his death and resurrection (the most essential elements of our salvation), how much more must we curse and hate the Jews who, believing nothing concerning Christ or the Christian faith and denying the virgin birth and all the sacraments of human salvation, blaspheme and insult him! I do not say these things in order to incite the divine or royal sword to destroy those evil people. For I recall that written about them in the divine psalm, the prophet speaking thus in the spirit of God: "God," he said, "has shown me with regard to my enemies: slay them not" [Augustine, *City of God* 18.46; Psalm 59:12]. For God does not wish them to be entirely killed and altogether wiped out, but to be preserved for greater torment and reproach, like the fratricide Cain, in a life worse than death. For when Cain said to God after shedding his brother's blood [Genesis 4:14], "every one that finds me shall kill me," it was said to him: God did not say that you should expect to die, but groaning and as a fugitive shall you be on the earth, "which hath opened her mouth and received the blood of your brother at your hand" [Genesis 4:11]. Thus has the fully just severity of God dealt with the damned, damnable Jews from the very time of the passion and death of Christ—and will do so until the end of time. Those who shed the blood of Christ, their brother according to the flesh, are enslaved, wretched, fearful, mournful, and exiled on the face of the earth—until, as the prophet has taught, the remnants of this wretched people shall turn to God once the multitude of the Gentiles has already been called, and, in the words of the apostle, "all Israel will be saved" [Romans 11:26].

I urge not that they be killed but that they be punished appropriately. And what manner is more appropriate than that of condemning iniquity and advocating charity? What is more just than depriving them of those things that they have gained fraudulently and have secured wickedly—as is done to thieves, and, how much the more so, those who have thus far acted audaciously and with impunity? Everyone knows whereof I speak. Not from simple agriculture, licit warfare, or honest, productive trade have they filled their storehouses with fruit, their cellars with wine, their purses with coins, and their coffers with gold and silver, but rather, as I have said, from that which they have deceitfully taken from the servants of Christ, from that which they have stealthily procured from thieves, purchasing the most expensive items at little cost. If a nocturnal thief invades a Church of Christ, sacrilegiously daring to carry off candelabra, ewers, censers, and even sacred crosses and consecrated chalices, he flees the Christians and seeks refuge among the Jews, finding among them the most execrable security. Not only does the refuge sustain him, but those things which he stole from holy churches he sells to the synagogues of Satan. The vessels of the flesh and blood of Christ he leaves among those who slew the body and shed the blood of Christ, those who inflicted him with as much insult and injury as they could while he was alive; and now, while he basks in the majesty of his eternal divinity, do not cease from attacking him orally with as many blasphemies as they so dare. These holy vessels are held captive among them as I have explained, just as they were once held captive among the Chaldeans, although they are insensible, they are not immune to injury. Christ perceives the outrageous insults of the Jews upon these sacred vessels, which these objects do not perceive for themselves, since, as I have often heard from trustworthy people, they use those heavenly vessels for their evil uses, to the disgrace of Christ and ourselves, things too horrifying to consider and detestable to mention. Moreover, the nefarious commerce of the thieves and the Jews was rendered more secure by an ancient though satanic law, which originated among Christian princes themselves, to the effect that if ecclesiastical property or, even worse, a sacred object be found in the possession of a Jew, the Jew may be compelled neither to return the sacrilegiously stolen object nor to produce the vile thief. The Jew goes unpunished for that detestable crime, for which the Christian suffers a horrifying death by hanging. The Jew grows fat and revels in his pleasures, while the Christian hangs from a noose!

One should take from the Jew—or limit as far as possible—his riches that he acquired illicitly; and, as the Christian army which sets out against the Saracens does not spare its own lands and money out of its love for Christ, let it not spare the treasures of the Jews amassed through vile means. Let their lives be spared but their money taken away, so that through the power of the Christians, fortified by the wealth of the blasphemous Jews, the audacity of the Saracen infidels may be overcome. Let the riches of the Jews, even against their will, serve the needs of the Christians, just as once, when the ancestors of the Jews were still in God's favor, the riches of the Egyptians were given over to their possession according to divine command. I have written these things, O beneficent king, out of love for Christ, for you, and for the Christian army, since I think it would be foolish, and even offensive to God, if Christian property be impounded for the holy expedition, as is appropriate, and the wealth of the unholy not be exploited even more.

31. THE FIRST ACCUSATION OF RITUAL MURDER: NORWICH 1144

Among the more notorious episodes in the history of Jewish–Christian relations is the medieval accusation of ritual murder, which makes its first documentary appearance in the middle of the twelfth century. According to the charge, Jews were responsible for seizing a Christian child, usually a boy, whom they then killed in a sort of ritual re-enactment of the crucifixion of Jesus. The first known case occurred in England in 1144, when the mutilated body of a 12-year-old apprentice skinner was found in the woods at the time of Easter. At first no particular charges were made against the Jews, and when charges were brought against the local community there was no specific mention of a crucifixion. In fact, the sheriff of Norwich protected the Jews and refused to allow them to be prosecuted. Around 1150, however, a Benedictine monk at the Norwich cathedral priory named Thomas of Monmouth began his lengthy and largely legendary account of the "passion" and "martyrdom" of little William. It was through Thomas's writings that the accusation that the Jews had crucified the boy appeared for the first time. The cult of Saint William grew, and with it further accusations of ritual murder. Other cases that similarly involved the ritual murder of a young boy occurred at Gloucester in 1168, Bury St Edmunds in 1181, Bristol in 1183, and again in Norwich in 1235. Variants of the same accusation make their first appearance on the continent later in the twelfth century, the most famous one being at Blois in northern France in 1171, which resulted in the killing of over thirty members of the local Jewish community.

The precise relation between the charges of ritual murder and the related but possibly distinct accusations that Jews used the blood of Christian children for ritual purposes (known collectively as the Blood Libel) has never been established with certainty. On some level, both would appear to arise from a heightened suspicion and paranoia of Jews who were living in close proximity to Christians in the expanding urban centers of the twelfth century, where they were already widely and negatively associated with the practice of money lending. What is clear is that it is on the heels of both theological attacks against Jewish disbelief in Christianity and accusations of the ritual murder of innocent children that royal and municipal expulsions were enacted, leading to an increased marginalization of the Jews of Europe. The first expulsion from France in 1182 was temporary (see Doc. 32), but the expulsion from England in 1290 was more permanent. Jews would not be readmitted into the realm of England until the seventeenth century.

Source: trans. A. Jessopp and M.R. James, *The Life and Miracles of St. William of Norwich* (Cambridge: Cambridge University Press, 1896), 10, 12–23, 35–37, 41–48; slightly revised. Latin.

The Life and Passion of Saint William of Norwich, *by Thomas of Monmouth*

BOOK I

1. . . . . The mercy of the divine goodness desiring to display itself to the parts about Norwich, or rather to the whole of England, and to give it in these new times a new patron, granted that a boy should be conceived in his mother's

womb without her knowing that he was to be numbered among the illustrious martyrs and worthy to be honored among all the army of the saints, and moreover brought it about that he should grow up little by little as a fragrant rose from her thorns.

His father was a certain Wenstan by name. His mother was called Elviva, and they passed their lives as honest people in the country, being somewhat well supplied with the necessaries of life and something more. Let it not seem absurd to any that a boy of such sanctity and destined for such honor should by God's will be born from lowly parents, when it is certain that he himself [Christ] was pleased to be born from among the poor. . . .

[Concerning his birth and infancy]

Some time having elapsed and the day having arrived for his bringing forth, a son was born to the woman, and his name was called William. He was born on the day of the Purification of the Blessed Virgin Mary, that is on Candlemas [2 February]. Perhaps this indicated how great the purity and sanctity of the child would be, and that he would greatly love candles and the brightness of them. But one circumstance, which I subsequently learned from his mother and his brothers and the priest who had baptized him, I have judged ought not to be passed over, but inserted here. On the day of his weaning, when his father Wenstan was entertaining his kindred who had been invited to the feast, a man who was undergoing penance, with iron bands upon his arms, presented himself to the guests as if begging for alms; who after the dinner waxing merry, while he held the child in his hands as if admiring him, and the baby, in the innocence of childhood wondering at the iron fetters, began to handle them; suddenly the bonds broke and shivered into pieces. The guests, amazed at the sight, were greatly astonished, and attributed what had occurred to the merits of the child. Wherefore the penitent, set free by divine favor, went his way, giving thanks, and the priest, who was present among the guests, collecting the broken rings, placed them in his church at Haveringland and deposited them in a conspicuous place, as well for maintaining the memory of those living as for a record to such as should come after; and he was careful that they should be safely preserved.

The mother, as she loved her child exceedingly, so did she educate him with exceeding care, and by carefully educating she brought him up from his infancy to the years of intelligent boyhood. When he was but seven years old—as I learnt from the mother's narrative—he became so devoted to abstinence that, though his elder brothers did not fast, he himself fasted on three days of the week—to wit the second, fourth, and sixth days—and also celebrated the vigils of the apostles and of other saints that were given notice of to the people by devout fasting. And his zeal going on increasing, he used to pass many days content with nothing but bread and water; and his whole inner man overflowing with piety, whatever he could save from his own portion of food or extort from his mother by his entreaties, he used to bestow upon the poor, sometimes openly and sometimes secretly. But while acting thus he conducted himself so dutifully, kindly and prudently, that as far as possible he at once benefited the poor and did not cause his parents any annoyance. He was a most joyful attendant at church; he used to learn his letters and the psalms and prayers, and all the things of God he treated with the greatest reverence. . . .

[How he was accustomed to resort to the Jews, and having been rebuked by his own people for so doing, how he withdrew himself from them]

When therefore he was flourishing in this blessed boyhood of his, and had attained to his eighth year, he was entrusted to the skinners to be taught their craft. Gifted with a teachable disposition and bringing industry to bear upon it, in a short time he surpassed lads of his own age in the aforesaid craft, and he equaled some who had been his teachers. So leaving the country, by the drawing of a divine attraction he went to the city and lodged with a very famous master of that craft, and some time passed away. He was seldom in the country, but was occupied in the city and sedulously gave himself to the practice of his craft, and thus reached his twelfth year.

Now, while he was staying in Norwich, the Jews who were settled there and required their cloaks or their robes or other garments (whether pledged to them, or their own property) to be repaired, preferred him before all other skinners. For they esteemed him to be especially fit for their work, either because they had learnt that he was guileless and skillful, or because attracted to him by their avarice, they thought they could bargain with him for a lower price. Or, as I rather believe, because by the ordering of divine providence he had been predestined to martyrdom from the beginning of time, and gradually step by step was drawn on, and chosen to be made a mock of and to be put to death by the Jews, in scorn of the Lord's passion, as one of little foresight, and so the more fit for them. For I have learned from certain Jews, who were afterwards converted to the Christian faith, how at that time they had planned to do this very thing with some Christian, and in order to carry out their malignant purpose, at the beginning of Lent they had chosen the boy William, being twelve years of age and a boy of unusual innocence. So it came to pass that when the holy boy, ignorant of the treachery that had been planned, had frequent dealings with the Jews, he was taken to task by Godwin the priest, who had the boy's aunt as his wife, and by a certain Wulward with whom he lodged, and he was prohibited from going in and out among them any more. But the Jews, annoyed at the thwarting of their designs, tried with all their might to patch up a new scheme of wickedness, and all the more vehemently as the day for carrying out the crime they had determined upon drew near, and the victim which they had thought they had already secured had slipped out of their wicked hands. Accordingly, collecting all the cunning of their crafty plots, they found—I am not sure whether he was a Christian or a Jew—a man who was a most treacherous fellow and just the fitting person for carrying out their execrable crime, and with all haste—for their Passover was coming on in three days—they sent him to find out and bring back with him the victim, which, as I said before, had slipped out of their hands.

[How he was seduced by the Jews' messenger]

At the dawn of day, on the Monday after Palm Sunday, that detestable messenger of the Jews set out to execute the business that was committed to him, and at last the boy William, after being searched for with very great care, was found. When he was found, he [the messenger] got round him with cunning word games, and so deceived him with his lying promises. For he pretended that he was the cook of William, archdeacon of Norwich, and that he wished to have him as a helper in the kitchen, where if he should continue steadily with him he would get many advantages in his situation. The simple boy was deceived, and trusted himself to the man; but, wishing to have his mother's favorable consent—for his father had died by this time—he started with the fellow to find her. When they had come to where she was, the boy told her the cause of his errand, and the traitor according to the tenor of his previous offer cast the net of his treachery. So that son of perdition by many promises easily prevailed upon the boy's mind by his tempting offers. Yet at first he could not at all gain the mother's consent; but when the scoundrel persisted the innocent boy agreed, though his mother, moved by presentiment, resisted, and in her motherly affection [felt] some fear for her son. . . .

So the traitor took three shillings from his purse with intent to get the better of the mother's fancy and to bend the fickle stubbornness of a fickle woman, seduced by the glitter of money and the lust of gain. Thus the money was offered as the price of the innocent's service, or rather in truth as the price of his blood. But not even yet was the mother's devotion appeased, nor the presentiment of a coming evil easily removed. The wrangling still went on: on one side with prayers, and on the other with the pieces of silver, if so be that, though he could not prevail upon her stubbornness by his continual offers, the brightness of the coins that smiled at her might serve as a lure to her avarice. So the mother's mind was cruelly vanquished by these, even though the maternal affection only slowly gave way under the temptation and, seduced at last by the shining pieces of silver, she was the victim of her covetousness . . . and the boy William was given up to the betrayer.

[How on his going to the Jews he was taken, mocked, and slain]

In the morning accordingly that traitor, the imitator in almost everything of the traitor Judas, returns to Norwich with the boy, and as he was passing by the house of the boy's aunt he went in with him and said that the mother had entrusted the boy to himself, and then he went out again hastily. But the boy's aunt said quickly to her daughter, "Follow them at once, and take care you find out where that man is leading the boy to." Thus the girl ran out to explore the way they were going; and she followed them at a distance as they turned about through some private alleys, and at last she saw them entering cautiously into the house of a certain Jew, and immediately she heard the door shut. When she saw this, she went back to her mother and told her what she had seen.

Then the boy, like an innocent lamb, was led to the slaughter. He was treated kindly by the Jews at first, and, ignorant of what was being prepared for him, he was kept till the morrow. But on the next day, which in that year was the Passover for them, after the singing of the hymns appointed for the day in the synagogue, the chiefs of the Jews assembled in the house of the aforesaid Jew suddenly seized hold of the boy William as he was having his dinner and in no fear of any treachery, and ill-treated him in various horrible ways. For while some of them held him behind, others opened his mouth and introduced an instrument of torture which is called a teazle, and, fixing it by straps through both jaws to the back of his neck, they fastened it with a knot as tightly as it could be drawn. After that, taking a short piece of rope of about the thickness of one's little finger and tying three knots in it at certain distances marked out, they bound round that innocent head with it from the forehead to the back, forcing the middle knot into his forehead and the two others into his temples, the two ends of the rope being most tightly stretched at the back of his head and fastened in a very tight knot. The ends of the rope were then passed round his neck and carried round his throat under his chin, and there they finished off this dreadful engine of torture in a fifth knot.

But not even yet could the cruelty of the torturers be satisfied without adding even more severe pain. Having shaved his head, they stabbed it with countless thorn-points, and made the blood come horribly from the wounds they made. And cruel were they and so eager to inflict pain that it was difficult to say whether they were more cruel or more ingenious in their tortures. For their skill in torturing kept up the strength of their cruelty and ministered arms thereto. And thus, while these enemies of the Christian name were rioting in the spirit of malignity around the boy, some of those present adjudged him to be fixed to a cross in mockery of the Lord's passion, as though they would say, "Even as we condemned the Christ to a shameful death, so let us also condemn the Christian, so that, uniting the lord and his servant in a like punishment, we may retort upon them the pain of that reproach which they impute to us."

Conspiring, therefore, to accomplish the crime of this great and detestable malice, they next laid their blood-stained hands upon the innocent victim, and having lifted him from the ground and fastened him upon the cross, they vied with one another in their efforts to make an end of him. And we, after inquiring into the matter very diligently, did both find the house, and discovered some most certain marks in it of what had been done there. For report goes that there was instead of a cross a post set up between two other posts, and a beam stretched across the midmost post and attached to the other on either side. And as we afterwards discovered, from the marks of the wounds and of the bands, the right hand and foot had been tightly bound and fastened with cords, but the left hand and foot were pierced with two nails: so in fact the deed was done by design that, in case at any time he should be found, when the fastenings of the nails were discovered it might not be supposed that he had been killed by Jews rather than by Christians. But while in doing these things they were adding pang to pang and wound to wound, and yet were not able to satisfy their heartless cruelty and their inborn hatred of the Christian name, lo! after all these many and great tortures, they inflicted a frightful wound in his left side, reaching even to his inmost heart, as though to make an end of all, they extinguished his mortal life so far as it was in their power. And since many streams of blood were running down from all parts of his body, then, to stop the blood and to wash and close the wounds, they poured boiling water over him.

Thus, then the glorious boy and martyr of Christ, William, dying the death of time in reproach of the Lord's death, but crowned with the blood of a glorious martyrdom, entered into the kingdom of glory on high to live forever. Whose soul rejoices blissfully in heaven among the bright hosts of the saints, and whose body by the omnipotence of the divine mercy works miracles upon earth. [The murderers then dumped William's body in the woods on Good Friday and bribed the sheriff to keep their secret, but the body was found with miraculous assistance. The finders did not immediately bury it.]

[Concerning the lamentations of the mother]

Just at this time, as the report was spreading, the story of her son's murder came to the ears of his mother who, naturally overwhelmed by the sad tidings, straightway swooned away as if she were dead. After a while, however, recovering herself she without delay hastened to Norwich to enquire into the truth of the matter. But when she learnt by the relation of many people that her son was dead and was buried in the wood immediately with torn hair and clapping of hands she ran from one to another weeping and wailing through the streets like a mad woman. At last going to the house of her sister whom I mentioned before and enquiring now of the priest Godwin, now of her sister, she could learn no more about the circumstances and the truth than that he had been slain in an extraordinary way. But from many probable indications and conclusions she was convinced that they were not Christians but Jews who had dared to do the deed. With a woman's readiness of belief she easily gave credence to these conjectures. Whereupon she at once burst forth into denouncing the Jews with words of insult and indignation. Sometimes she behaved like a mother moved by all a mother's love, sometimes she bore herself like a woman with all a woman's passionate rashness. And so, assuming everything to be certain which she sus-pected and asserting it to be a fact, as though it had actually been seen—she went through the streets and open places and, carried along by her motherly distress, she kept calling upon everybody with dreadful screams, protesting that the Jews had seduced and stolen her son away from her and killed him. This conduct very greatly worked upon the minds of the populace to accept the truth, and so everybody began to cry out with one voice that all the Jews ought to be utterly destroyed as constant enemies of the Christian name and the Christian religion.

32. THE MONK RIGORD EXPLAINS THE REASONS FOR THE EXPULSION OF THE JEWS

The monk and royal chronicler Rigord (d. 1209) composed his History of Philip Augus-tus *at the abbey of St-Denis in the first decade of the thirteenth century. It is a detailed and invaluable record of the first 25 years of the French king's long reign (1179–1223). Rigord writes in the twelfth-century tradition of royal biography that flourished at St-Denis, and thus he might equally have been placed in Chapter 8 as an example of historical writing. But his account also provides important information regarding the first royal expulsion of the Jews from France (which in 1182 was a domain considerably smaller than what it is today). While Rigord's descriptions are often tinged with hyperbole, his comments on the king's decision to expel the Jews from France are a good illustration of how closely royal policy, intellectual traditions, and anti-Judaism were connected, begin-ning in the twelfth century and for many centuries to come.*

Source: trans. Alex J. Novikoff, from Rigord, *Histoire de Philippe Auguste*, ed. Élisabeth Carpentier, Georges Pon, and Yves Chauvin (Paris: CNRS Éditions, 2006), 144, 146, 148, 150, 152, 154. Latin.

The reasons for which the very Christian king Philip ever Augustus chased the Jews out of France: Explanation of the first cause

At that time a great multitude of Jews lived in France, having arrived a long time ago from diverse parts of the world owing to the lasting peace and openness of the French people. Indeed, the Jews had heard about the might shown by the kings of France against their enemies and of their great generosity toward their subjects. This is why their leaders and those most learned in the laws of Moses, whom the Jews called *didascali*, decided to come to Paris. There, over the course of their long stay, they accrued such wealth that they took over almost half of the property of the city and, contrary to God's decree and the rules of the Church, they employed Christian servants and workers in their houses who, clearly drifting away from the faith of Jesus Christ, judaized with those same Jews. And because the Lord said through the mouth of Moses in Deuteronomy [cf. 23:19–20]: "You shall not charge interest on loans to a brother, but to a foreigner," the Jews, misunderstanding Christians to be foreigners, lent their money usuriously to Christians. They so overwhelmed the citizens, knights, and peasants in the countryside, fortresses, and villages that many were forced to relinquish their possessions. Others, compelled by oath to reside in the homes of Jews, were held captive as if in a prison. Learning of this, the very Christian king Philip was moved by piety and took counsel about what to do from a hermit named Bernard, a holy and religious man who at that time lived in the forest near Vincennes. Acting on his advice, he [the king] discharged all Christians of his realm from their debts to the Jews, keeping for himself one fifth of the sum total.

Explanation of the second cause

The height of their damnability was this: the objects of the church dedicated to God—gold and silver crosses bearing the image of the crucified Lord Jesus Christ as well as chalices—which the church had out of necessity pledged on loan, were treated poorly for the sake of disparaging and disgracing the Christian religion. They drank from these chalices, where the body and the blood of our Lord Jesus Christ were consecrated, and their children ate dumplings dipped in the wine. They did not wish to recall what was written in the book of Kings [cf. 2 Kings 25]: In the eleventh year of the reign of King Zedekiah of Jerusalem, the king of Babylon, Nebuchadnezzar, had the holy city of Jerusalem taken by Nebuzaradan, the captain of the guard, on account of the sin of the Jews. He pillaged the Temple and took away with him the precious vessels dedicated to God that the wise Solomon had made. But although he was pagan and an idolater, Nebuchadnezzar feared the god of the Jews and did not want to drink from these vessels nor use them for his own purposes. In fact, he had them preserved in his own temple next to the idol, like a sacred treasure. But then Belshazzar came along, the sixth king after him, who offered a great feast to his lords and princes. He commanded that they bring the vessels that his progenitor had taken from the Temple of the Lord so that the king, his lords, their wives and concubines might drink from them [cf. Daniel 5:1–5]. At that very hour, the Lord, angered with Balthazar, showed him the sign of his destruction in the form of a hand that drew on the wall in front of him: *Mane, Techel, Phares*. These are interpreted to signify: number, weight, and division [cf. Daniel 5:25–28]. That same night, Babylon was captured by Cyrus and Darius and Belshazzar was killed in mid-feast, just as Isaiah had foretold long before: "prepare the table, look in the mirror—that is, the wall—those who eat and drink in the vessels of the Lord; princes, rise up, take up arms, for the city has been captured." And no sooner did the Medes and the Persians rise up unexpectedly and kill Belshazzar in mid-feast. Of what followed, who would dare hide what God intends to reveal?

Exposition of the third reason for the expulsion of the Jews

At this time, while the Jews were worrying that their homes would be searched by the king's men, there appeared a Jew who was then living in Paris and who held on loan certain objects of the church, namely, a gold cross encrusted in gems and an evangeliary [i.e., a Gospel book] handsomely decorated in gold and precious stones, as well as silver dishes and other vessels. He placed them in a bag and—how painful!—tossed them shamefully in a deep ditch where he had the habit of emptying his stomach. Shortly thereafter, all of these objects were, thanks to divine revelation, discovered by the Christians in the same spot. Once one fifth of the total debt was rendered to the lord king, they were returned with the greatest of joy and with much honor to their church of origin. This year truly merits being called a jubilee year [cf. Leviticus 25:8–10]: indeed, in conformity with the ancient Law, in a jubilee year all the possessions are freed from all charge and returned to their ancient owners and all debts are forgiven. Similarly, after the very Christian king granted this pardon of debt, the Christians of the kingdom of France were freed in perpetuity from their debts toward the Jews.

History of the third year of the reign of Philip Augustus, king of the French

In the year of our Lord's incarnation, 1182, in the month of April, which the Jews call Nisan, an edict went forth from the most serene king, Philip Augustus, that all Jews of his kingdom should prepare to depart by the coming Feast of Saint John the Baptist [24 June]. And the king allowed them to sell each their household goods before the appointed time, that is, the Feast of Saint John. But their houses, fields, vineyards, barns, winepresses, and the like, he reserved for himself and his successors, the kings of the French. When the faithless Jews heard this edict, some of them were born again of water and the Holy Spirit and converted to the Lord, remaining steadfast in the faith of our Lord Jesus Christ.

Out of consideration for the Christian religion, the king restored to them the entirety of all their possessions and gave them perpetual liberty.

Others were blinded by their ancient error and persisted in their perfidy. They sought to win with gifts and golden promises the princes of the kingdom, in other words the counts, barons, archbishops, bishops, that through their influence and advice and through the promise of infinite wealth, they might change the king's mind from his fixed decision. But the merciful and compassionate God, "who does not forsake those who put their hope in him" and "who humbles those who presume their own strength" [cf. Judith 13:17; 6:15], spreading his celestial grace and burning with the strength of the Holy Spirit, so fortified the mind of the illustrious king that he could not be softened by prayers nor promises of temporal things. To tell the truth, what is said of Saint Agatha might well be said of him: "One could more easily soften stones and change iron into lead than change the mind" of the very Christian king whose "intention" was inspired by God.

The rejection of the princes

The infidel Jews, perceiving that the princes of the land, through whom they had been accustomed easily to influence the king's predecessors, had suffered rejection, and amazed and stupefied by the mental determinancy of King Philip and his constancy in the Lord, exclaimed "Shema Israel," or "Hear Israel," and prepared to sell all their household goods. The time was now at hand when the king had ordered them to leave France altogether, and there could be no further delay. Then did the Jews sell all their household possessions in great haste, while their landed property reverted to the crown. Thus the Jews, having sold their goods and paying the price for the expense of the journey, departed with their wives and children and all their households in the aforesaid year of the Lord 1182, in the month of July, which is called by the Jews Tamuz, in the third year of the reign of King Philip Augustus, and in the seventeenth year of his life, which began the previous August on the feast of Saint Symphorian, the eleventh of calends of September [22 August]. So the seventeenth year of the king's life was completed in the month following the expulsion of the Jews, namely in August. For they left in the month of July, as previously stated; there they thus remained for three weeks (or twenty-one days) to the completion of his seventeenth year.

How King Philip forever Augustus converted the synagogues of the Jews into churches

Following the expulsion of the infidel Jews and their dispersal throughout the entire world, King Philip Augustus, aware of their deeds, in the year of our Lord

1183, at the beginning of the eighteenth year of his life, through the grace of God, gloriously finished the effort that he so gloriously begun. For all the synagogues, which the Jews call schools and where, in the name of a false faith, they convene daily under the pretense of prayer, he ordered cleansed. Against the will of all the princes, he caused those synagogues to be dedicated to God as churches,

Figure 7: A nineteenth-century sketch of a roundel from the *Bible moralisée* (c. 1240), showing Jews on the left (pointing to their scrolls) debating with Christians on the right in the presence of either the Virgin Mary or possibly Queen Blanche of Castile (r. 1223–26), the mother of Louis IX of France (r. 1226–70). For further discussion, see Alex J. Novikoff, *The Medieval Culture of Disputation: Pedagogy, Practice, and Performance* (Philadelphia: University of Pennsylvania Press, 2013), 196.

Source: Paul Weber, *Geistliches Schauspiel und Kirchliche Kunst* (Stuttgart: Verlag von Ebner & Seubert, 1894), 113.

and he ordered altars to be consecrated in these synagogues in honor of our Lord
Jesus Christ and of the blessed Mother of God, Virgin Mary. Indeed, he piously
and properly believed that where the name of Jesus Christ of Nazareth used to
be blasphemed daily, as indicated by Jerome in his commentary on Isaiah, the
Lord, who alone accomplishes great miracles, should be praised by the clergy and
by all Christians.

33. TWO JEWISH POLEMICS AGAINST CHRISTIANITY

*From the late eleventh century onward, many Christian anti-Jewish polemics resorted
to rational methods of argumentation, hoping thereby to better prove the validity of
Christian law over Jewish law. Beginning in the twelfth century, Jews responded to these
attacks by composing their own philosophical polemics. The aim of these works, written
in Hebrew and intended for a Jewish audience, was to present Judaism as internally
and logically consistent with its teachings. Among the earliest such works is the* Book
of the Covenant *by Joseph Kimhi (c. 1105–c. 1170), a rabbi who fled the Almohad
persecutions of 1148 in Spain and settled in the southern French city of Narbonne.
Kimhi's activities as translator, exegete, grammarian, and teacher led him to the role of
defender of the faith against Christian antagonists. The brief work takes the form of a
dialogue between a heretic or unbeliever (min) and a believer (ma'amin). The* Book of
the Covenant *presents a vigorous defense of Judaism on the basis of reason and literal
biblical exegesis, suggesting that some conversions were, indeed, taking place as a result
of increased Christian proselytizing. The biblically inspired title of the work is probably
an allusion to Kimhi's attempts to bring back those who had abandoned the covenant.*

*Many of the themes and arguments of anti-Christian Jewish polemic are represented
in the* Nizzahon Vetus, *or Old Book of Polemic, a manual of debate that antholo-
gizes a wide range of twelfth- and early-thirteenth-century works of polemic. Although
the author is unknown, the work was composed in northern Europe at some point in
the mid-thirteenth century. It consists of two sections: a commentary on the Hebrew
Bible and critiques both of the Gospels specifically and of Christianity more generally.
Interspersed with the commentary are debating tips—witticisms, anecdotes, and also
vituperative attacks on Christians (often called "heretics" or "apostates") and Christian
religious figures.*

*Hebrew polemics against Christianity contribute to our understanding of Jewish–
Christian intellectual relations on several levels. The extensive use of the Gospels, including quotations in Latin in the* Nizzahon Vetus, *is a testimony to increased literary
contact between Jews and Christians, a phenomenon that is likewise reflected in the use
of Hebrew in the Victorine school of biblical interpretation. The deepening theological
sensitivity of twelfth-century exegetical commentary, among both Jews and Christians,
is reflected in Joseph Kimhi's discussion of literal versus figurative biblical interpretation.
The simultaneous use of the New Testament both as the butt of attacks and as a source of*

Jewish defense parallels the Christian use of Hebrew and post-biblical Jewish literature in Christian polemics against Jews. The central role that Jewish martyrdom and sufferance play in the Nizzahon Vetus *in demonstrating the truth of Judaism echoes the historical reality of the increased persecution (and occasional expulsions) of Jews during this period. Arguments from the prominence of Islam found in the* Nizzahon Vetus *to counter Christian supersessionist claims reflect the expanding horizons of Jewish–Christian debate. A final note is the treatment of monasticism, one of the most central and expanding institutions in twelfth-century Christendom. It is significant that monasticism was the single area that seems to have challenged Jewish self-perceptions of chosenness and moral superiority. Jewish response consisted largely of challenging the Christian execution of the monastic ideal, rather than the ideal itself. In this area, as in the increased desire or need to provide a rationally convincing polemic, it may reasonably be said that Jews had internalized certain broader patterns of Christian culture and argumentation.*

a. Joseph Kimhi, *Book of the Covenant*

Source: trans. Frank Talmage, *The Book of the Covenant of Joseph Kimhi* (Toronto: Pontifical Institute of Mediaeval Studies, 1972), 27–28, 39–41. Hebrew.

I have observed that the children of the impudent among our people [cf. Daniel 11:14] have audaciously proclaimed all manner of falsehood and nonsense. Their foolishness and stupidity have completely misled them and their ignorance has enticed them into misinterpreting the words of the living God, the words of the prophets, and to apply them in an improper fashion to the matter of Jesus the Nazarene. They have explained them senselessly and have turned from the way of the truth.

One of my students has requested me to assemble and collect all the visions and prophecies in the Torah, Prophets, and Writings, in which there are [contained] refutations against the heretics and deniers who polemicize against our faith. I have seen fit to fulfill his request. In this there will be found much benefit, in that it will add [to the glory of] the faith of the God of Israel. The wise man will grow stronger and "those who are wise" shall understand and "shall shine as the brightness of the firmament and those who turn many to righteousness are like the stars for ever and ever" [Daniel 12:3]. I shall begin by the grace of God to search and investigate by the paths of reason and to answer with understanding and knowledge.

They profess and believe in the Trinity—Father, Son, and Spirit—and claim that the Creator is the Father of all and that he created the entire world. At the beginning of the Book of Genesis, it states, "and the Spirit of the Lord hovered over the face of the waters" [Genesis 1:2]. Hence: Father and Spirit. We reply: I believe that wisdom corroborates them and reason is on their side. He is the

Father of the world, having engendered it and brought it into being ex nihilo, and the [existence of] the Holy Spirit [may be seen in this verse also]. But who will constrain me to believe that he has a son [in the same way that] reason constrains me [to believe] in the Father and Spirit. . . .

The *min* said: I shall now reprove you and expound my teachings based on the prophecies, some of which are written in the Torah of Moses, some in the prophets, and some in the Writings, most of which originated with David, the man of God. I shall test you and ask you of these [verses] which are all prophecies of Jesus and you shall not be able to contradict or deny any one of them. The first is written in the Book of Genesis: "Let us make man in Our image, after Our likeness: then, and God made man in His image, in the image of God he created Him" [Genesis 1:26]. The plural form of the verb proves [the existence] of the Father, Son, and Spirit as do the plural possessives: *in* our *image, after* our *likeness*. In addition, the image and likeness which the Divinity adopted in Jesus. You cannot contradict this.

The *ma'amin* said: You have neither teachings nor prophecies which I cannot explain according to their plain sense and context. With reference to the plural form of "Let Us make," some explain that at the beginning of creation, He created four elements—the higher, fire and air, and the lower, earth and water. Then he gave them the faculty to produce all creatures by virtue of their natural qualities. It is thus written "The earth brought forth vegetation" (v. 12), "let the earth sprout vegetation" (v. 11); let the earth bring forth swarms (v. 20). This was so until the sixth day when he created man along with the four elements, saying "Let Us make man." It is in their nature to produce the body which is material in character, while he breathed into the supernal soul possessing intellect and rational wisdom. As for image and likeness, nothing which he created in the world resembles him except man alone. In what ways does he resemble him? In the image of dominion and the likeness of rulership, for just as the Holy One, blessed be He, rules over all, so does man rule. It is thus stated "You have given him dominion over Your handiwork. You have put all things under his feet; all sheep and oxen and the beasts of the field, the fowl of the air and the fish of the sea" [Psalm 8:7]. This is proven by the text, for after it states, "Let Us make man in Our image, after Our likeness," it says, "They shall rule the fish of the sea, the birds of the sky" (v. 26). Here image and likeness are not to be taken literally but metaphorically. Image is dominion and likeness is rulership, not a physical image. What is the matter with you? On the basis of one obscure passage, you deny his unity and expound it as [proof] of a plurality? Indeed, the philosophers said in their wisdom, "A ship is no good with too many captains," and Solomon said "When a land transgresses, it has too many rulers" [Proverbs 28:2]. Now if you say that he is more than one, can He act independently or not? If he can act independently, then any addition is superfluous. If not, you believe in an impotent creature. Do you not see that it is apparent from all of creation that there is only one governor, be he exalted and extolled! I shall explain this with a parable. When we see a book in a uniform hand, we say that one scribe wrote it. Even though it is possible that more than one scribe wrote it, we need not believe this unless there are witnesses to the effect that two or more scribes, whose hands are uniform, wrote it. If reason pointed to less than one scribe, we would believe it. It is clear that the [number of] prior causes is less than the [number of causes] posterior, as is explained in the works of logic, known as the science of *dialectica* and in Arabic as *al-mantiq*.

b. Nizzahon Vetus

Source: trans. David Berger, *The Jewish-Christian Debate in the High Middle Ages: A Critical Edition of the Nizzahon Vetus* (Philadelphia: The Jewish Publication Society of America, 1979), 41–44, 100, 103, 133, 169, 224, 229. Hebrew.

[The Pentateuch]

With good fortune I shall begin to write *The Book of Polemic*.

My help comes from the Lord, Creator of heaven and earth [Psalm 121:2].

Blessed is he who gives power to the weak and increases strength to them that have no might [Isaiah 40:29].

A Gentile defiantly asked a Jew: Why did the Holy One, blessed be he, begin his Torah with the word *Bereshit* [in the beginning]? The reason is that by doing so he referred to the son, the holy spirit, and the father. The Jew answered him: You have expounded the *bet*, *resh*, and *aleph* as you wished. Now finish the word and you will find *shin*, *yod*, *tav*; these too constitute an acrostic. Thus I knew how to uphold the truth. Furthermore, I might add that if you know a man who persists in his error by expounding Scripture in a manner contradictory to our Torah, then with God's help I have many ways of silencing his error, upholding truth by means of acrostics as well.

The Gentile continued his defiant questioning and asked: Why did the Holy One, blessed be he, begin the Torah with a *bet* and not with a different letter? Surely, he did so in order to make reference to the existence of two persons who are father and son, and it is also in reference to them that David said, "My God, my God, why have you forsaken me?" [Psalm 22:2]. Moreover, it is for this reason that you will find "the Lord God" as one name in a number of passages. And if you will ask, "Where is the trinity?" the answer is that the spirit was not included because it is intertwined in the two of them—in the father and son—and is a substance that is between them. Similarly you say of the two attributes law and mercy that the attribute of grace mediates between them.

One may respond to this: The reason he began the ten commandments with the word *anokhi*, which begins with the letter aleph, was to inform everyone that he is one and there is no second, that he cannot be separated into different bodies, that his attributes are not unequal in age as a father is older than a son, and that there is no separability in him as would be implied by the belief that the father dwelt in heaven and the son went down to earth. Moreover, according to your belief that there are two persons equal in age, greatness, and wisdom, one could make a decree which the other might annul, and one could send abundant food to the world while the other sent famine. . . .

"Let us make man" [Genesis 1:26]. Answer the apostates: The Holy One, blessed be he, told the earth, "Let us make man between the two of us; you contribute your share—dust, and I my share—spirit.". . . The heretics say that "Let us make" implies two, and they are the father and son. You can put off such a heretic by answering: Indeed, the matter is as you say. The father told the son, "My son, help me, and let you and I make man." The son, however, rebelled and did not wish to help his father, and so the father made man alone without the son's help, as it is written, "And God created man," with a singular rather than a plural verb. Consequently, the father became angry with his son and said, "If the time should come when you need my assistance, I shall not help you just as you have not helped me." So when the day came for the son to be stoned and hanged, he cried out in a bitter voice, "My Lord, my Lord, why have you forsaken me?" [Matthew 27:46]. . . .

Consequently, how could this man be God, for he entered a woman with a stomach full of feces who frequently sat him down in the privy during the nine months, and when he was born he came out dirty and filthy, wrapped in a placenta and defiled by the blood of childbirth and impure issue. The Torah, on the other hand, warns against approaching a menstruant woman, a woman who has an impure issue, and one who has just given birth. . . .

You may argue that he was not defiled in her womb since Mary had ceased to menstruate and it was the spirit that entered her; subsequently, he came out unaccompanied by pain or the defilement of blood. The answer is that you yourselves admit that she brought the sacrifice of a childbearing woman.

[Isaiah]

"Behold, a young woman [*'almah*] shall conceive and bear a son, and shall call his name Immanuel" [Isaiah 7:14]. The heretics say that this was said of Jesus, and they argue: What sort of novelty is it that a young woman should conceive in the natural way through intercourse with a man? You must say therefore, that Scripture refers to a virgin who had no such intercourse. The answer is: King Solomon said, "There are threescore queens and fourscore concubines, and young women ['alamot] without number" [Song of Songs 6:8], and in Proverbs too it is written, "The way of a man with a maid ['almah]" [Proverbs 30:19]; thus, even one who is not a virgin is called 'almah. Indeed, such a woman can even be called betulah, as it is written, "Lament like a betulah girded with sackcloth for the husband of her youth" [Joel 1:8]. Moreover, since they interpret this prophecy as a reference to Jesus, why did they not call him Immanuel? The fact is that in their entire Torah he is called only Jesus. . . .

Now if you would prefer to answer briefly, then tell him: granted that the prophet said that a virgin would give birth to a son. So what? There is, after all, no doubt that the Lord's hand is not incapable of fulfilling his will and desire, and that he is a ruler who can do whatever he wishes, but still how do you know that this virgin is Mary? Where do you find that name or that of her son so that you may know? I could say, rather, that this refers to another virgin or that it will happen in the future.

[Psalms]

On the basis of this psalm [Psalm 15], the heretics curse us and ask why we take interest from Gentiles. After all, it says in this psalm, "He who does not lend his money at interest" [Psalm 15:5] without any qualifications; neither the uncircumcised nor the circumcised are excluded. The answer is: who gave the Torah to Israel? God. Through whom? Through Moses. Now, Moses said, "You may take interest on loans to a Gentile, but do not take any on loans to your brother" [Deuteronomy 23:21]. If you then say that the descendants of Esau are also called brethren, as it is written, "You shall not abhor an Edomite, for he is your brother" [Deuteronomy 23:8], the answer is: it is true that they were once brethren and it was forbidden to take interest from them; now, however, they have disqualified themselves and are considered strangers, for when the Temple was destroyed they did not come to help. . . . Moreover they consider themselves foreigners, for they are not circumcised. . . .

[A Critique of the Gospels and Christianity]

Be diligent in the study of Torah in order to be able to answer a heretic and question him. When you speak to them, do not allow your antagonist to change the subject, for it is the usual method of the assertive and impatient Gentile to skip from one subject to another. He does not continue to stick to the point, for when he realizes his inability to verify his statements, he begins to discuss other matters. One who argues with them should be strong-willed by asking questions or giving responses that deal with the specific issue at hand and not permitting his antagonist to extricate himself from that issue until it has been completed.

Then you will find the Gentile thoroughly embarrassed; indeed, he will be found to have denied their central dogmas, while all Israel "will speak lovely words" [Genesis 49:21]. . . .

The heretics ask: Why are most Gentiles fair-skinned and handsome while most Jews are dark and ugly? Answer them that this is similar to a fruit; when it begins to grow it is white but when it ripens it becomes black; as is the case with sloes and plums. On the other hand, any fruit which is red at the beginning becomes lighter as it ripens, as is the case with apples and apricots. This, then, is testimony that Jews are pure of menstrual blood so that there is no initial redness. Gentiles, however, are not careful about menstruant women and have sexual relations during menstruation; thus, there is redness at the outset, and so the fruit that comes out, that is, the children, are light. One can respond further that Gentiles are licentious and have sexual relations during the day, at a time when they see the faces on attractive pictures; therefore they give birth to children who look like those pictures. . . .

The heretics anger us by charging that we murder their children and consume the blood. Answer by telling him that no nation was as thoroughly warned against murder as we, and this warning includes the murder of Gentiles, for in connection with "Do not covet" [Genesis 20:17], it says "your neighbor," but in connection with "Do not murder," "Do not commit adultery," and "Do not steal" [Genesis 20:13–15], it does not say "your neighbor." This shows that "Do not murder" refers to any man; thus, we were warned against murdering Gentiles as well. . . . Moreover, we were also warned against blood more than any nation, for even when dealing with meat that has been slaughtered properly and is kosher, we salt it and rinse it and bother with it extensively in order to remove the blood. The fact is that you are concocting allegations against us in order to permit our murder.

34. PETER THE VENERABLE'S *SUMMA* AGAINST THE SARACEN HERESIES

Peter the Venerable exhibited a sustained concern about the non-Christians of his day. In addition to his invective against Jews and Judaism (Doc. 30), the abbot of Cluny also wrote two polemics against Islam and one against the Petrobrusians, a contemporary Christian heretical group. In 1142, Peter traveled to Spain with a large entourage for the inspection of Cluniac monasteries and properties, and while there he seized on the opportunity to become better acquainted with Islam through the translation of original sources. His plan was to provide himself and other Christian scholars with a body of authentic Islamic texts on the basis of which they could both understand and better refute Islam's claims. The Summary of the Complete Heresy of the Saracens, *from which the following selection is taken, was probably written shortly after Peter's return to Cluny from Spain in 1143. It is the first of his two polemics against Islam.*

In the excerpt that follows, Peter makes use of his newfound knowledge of the Quran, the translation of which was completed by an Englishman named Robert of Ketton, who was part of Peter's translation team. Although deeply flawed, Robert of Ketton's translation would go on to become the most widely read Latin version of Islam's holy book, and it was printed twice in the mid-sixteenth century. Peter the Venerable's prejudice is obvious, but he also displays a deeper awareness of the teachings of Mohammad and the precepts of Islam than almost any previous Christian author of the medieval West. By identifying the "errors" of Islam through a close analysis of specific passages, he is also able to hold up the "truth" of Christianity as revealed in Scripture and in patristic authorities. Peter's repeated grouping of Judaism, Islam, and heresy as dangerous menaces to Christian society is accompanied by an unflagging commitment to employing the sources of his adversaries in order to rebuke them. In this regard, Peter's corpus of polemics may be seen as constituting a unified program to defeat what were perceived to be the most significant contemporary challenges to Christian faith and power.

Source: trans. Irven M. Resnick, from Peter the Venerable, *Summa totius haeresis Saracenorum*, ed. Reinhold Glei, in *Petrus Venerabilis Schriften zum Islam*, Corpus Islamo-Christianum, Series Latina I (Altenberge: CIS-Verlag, 1985), 2–22. Latin.

This is a summary of the entire heresy, and of the diabolical sect of the Saracens, or the Ishmaelites.

Foremost, the first and greatest of their errors that ought to be cursed is that they deny the Trinity in the unity of the deity, and in this way while shunning number in unity, they do not believe in the triune number of persons in the one essence of divinity, while I say that the beginning and end of all forms is threefold, and thus they do not receive the cause and origin and end of all things that are formed, although confessing God with their lips, they do not know him in a profound way. These foolish ones, these inconstant ones, confess that there is a principle for change and for every difference, to wit one that is binary in the unity, namely the divine essence itself, and its soul [*anima*]. For this reason the Quran—with which name they call their law, and Quran, translated from Arabic, means collection of precepts—always introduces God speaking in the plural.

Furthermore, these blind ones deny that God the creator is Father, because, according to them, no one is a father without sexual intercourse. And although they accept that Christ was conceived from a divine spirit, they do not believe that he is the Son of God, nor, moreover, that he is God, but [only] a good, most truthful prophet, free from all deceit and sin, the son of Mary, born without a father, who never died, because he did not deserve death; instead, [they] accept that] although the Jews wanted to slay him, he slipped through their hands, ascended to the stars, and lives there now in the flesh in the presence of the Creator, until the advent of the Antichrist. When he comes, this same Christ himself will slay him with the sword of his virtue, and he will convert the remaining Jews to his religion [ad legem]. Moreover, he will teach his religion perfectly to the Christians, who a long time ago lost his law and Gospel, on the one hand owing to his departure, and on the other hand owing to the death of the apostles and disciples, by which [religion] all Christians at that time will be saved, just like his first disciples. Even Christ himself will die with them and with all creatures at one and the same time, when Seraphim—whom they say is one archangel—sounds the trumpet, and afterward he will rise with the rest, and he will lead his own to judgment, and he will assist them and pray for them, but he will not himself judge them. Indeed, God alone will judge. The prophets and the individual messengers, however, will be present among them as their intercessors and to assist them. Thus, indeed, the very wretched and impious Mohammad has taught them, who, denying all the sacraments of Christian piety, by which especially men are saved, has, with tales of unheard-of foolishness, condemned already nearly a third of the human race to the devil and to eternal death—by what judgment of God, we do not know.

It seems that one must speak about who he [Mohammad] was, and what he taught, for the sake of those who will read that book, so that they might better understand what they read, and come to know how detestable both his life and teaching were. For some think that he was that Nicholas who was one of the first seven deacons [Acts 6:5], and that the sect of the Nicholaitans that is named after him, which is denounced in the Apocalypse of John [Apocalypse 2:6, 15], is this religion [lex] of the contemporary Saracens. And others dream up other individuals, and as they are careless in reading, and unacquainted with the actual events so, just as in other cases, they conjecture every manner of falsehood.

This one [Mohammed] however, as even the chronicle translated from Greek into Latin by Anastasius the librarian of the Roman church clearly relates, [who lived] during the age of the emperor Heraclius, a little after the time of the great Roman Pope, Gregory I, almost 550 years ago, one who was of the Arab nation, of low birth, at first a worshipper of the old idolatry, just like the other Arabs were at that time, unlearned, nearly illiterate, active in secular affairs, and very shrewd, he advanced from one of low birth and from poverty to riches and fame. And here, increasing little by little, and frequently attacking neighbors and espe- cially those related to him by blood, with ambushes, robberies, and incursions, killing those whom he could by stealth, and those whom he could publicly, he increased fear of him, and because he often came out on top in these encounters, he began to aspire to kingship over his race. And when, with everyone equally resisting [him] and condemning his low birth, he saw that he could not pursue this path for himself as he had hoped, because he was unable to do so by the power of the sword, he then attempted to become king under the cloak of religion and under the name of a divine prophet.

And since he lived as a barbarian among barbarians, and as an idolater among idolaters, and among those who, more than all races, were unacquainted with and ignorant of law, both human and divine, he knew that he could easily seduce them, and he began to undertake the iniquitous task he had conceived. And since he had heard that God's prophets were great men, and saying that he is his prophet, so as to pretend to be something good, he attempted to lead them partly away from idolatry, yet not to the true God, but rather to his own false heresy which he had already begun to bring forth.

And although meanwhile in the judgment of him who is said to be "terrible in his counsels over the sons of men" [Psalm 66:5] and who "has mercy on whomever he chooses, and hardens the heart of whomever he chooses" [Romans 9:18], Satan bestowed success upon error, and he sent the monk Sergius, a sectarian follower of the heretical Nestorius, who had been expelled from the church, to those parts of Arabia, and united the monk-heretic with the false prophet. Consequently Sergius, joined with Mohammad, supplied what he [Mohammad] lacked, and explicating for him the sacred scriptures—both of the Old and the New Testament—in accord with the understanding of his master, Nestorius, who denied that our savior is God, [and] partly in accord with his own conception, and at the same time completely filling him up with fables from apocryphal books, he made him into a Nestorian Christian.

And, in order that the complete fullness of iniquity should come together in Mohammad, and so that nothing should be lacking for his damnation or for that of others, Jews were joined to the heretic, and lest he become a true Christian, the Jews, shrewdly providing to the man who was eager for novelties, whispered to Mohammad not for the truth of the scriptures but their fables, which still today they have in abundance. And in this way, taught by the best Jewish and heretical teachers, Mohammad created his Quran, and having fabricated it both from Jewish fables and the foolish nonsense of heretics, he wove together that wicked scripture in his own barbarous fashion. Lying that this was conveyed to him gradually, chapter by chapter [per tomos], by Gabriel, whose name he knew already from sacred scripture, he poisoned a people that was ignorant of God with a lethal draught, and, in the manner of men such as this, coating the rim of the chalice with honey, with the deadly poison following after, he destroyed—oh woe!—the souls and bodies of that miserable race.

Clearly that impious one did so when, commending both the Christian and Jewish religion, confirming that neither one ought to be embraced, he rejected [them] while proving himself reprobate. For this reason he confirms that Moses was the best prophet, that Christ the Lord was greater than all, proclaims that he [Christ] was born of a virgin, confesses that he was the messenger of God, the word of God, [and] the spirit of God, yet he does not understand or confess [that Christ was] the messenger, Word or Spirit as we do. Actually, he mocks the [Christian teaching] that he is to be called or believed to be the Son of God. And measuring the eternal birth of the Son of God in comparison to human generation, the bovine man [*vaccinus homo*] denies and mocks with as much effort as he can that God could either beget or be begotten. With frequent repetition he affirms the resurrection of the flesh; he does not deny that there is a general judgment at the end of time, but [he affirms that] it must be carried out not by Christ but by God. He insanely affirms that Christ, as the greatest of all after God, will be present at that judgment and that he himself will be present to assist his people.

He [Mohammad] describes the torments of hell such as it pleased him to do, and such as it was fitting for the great false prophet to invent. He painted a paradise that is not of the company of angels, nor of a vision of the divine, nor of that highest good that "no eye has seen, nor ear heard, nor the human heart conceived" [Isaiah 64:4; 1 Corinthians 2:9], but painted one such as truly flesh and blood desired, or rather the filth [*faex*] of flesh and blood, and one which he desired to be prepared for himself. He promises to his followers there a meal of meats and of every kind of fruit, rivers of milk and honey, and sparkling waters, the embrace and sexual satisfaction of the most beautiful women and virgins, in which the whole of his paradise is defined. Vomiting up again among these nearly all of the dregs of the ancient heresies, which he had absorbed from the devil's instruction, he denies the Trinity with Sabellius, rejects the deity of Christ with Nestorius, [and] repudiates the death of the Lord with Manichaeus [i.e., Mani, the prophet and founder of Manichaeism, c. 215–276], although he does not deny his return to the heavens.

Instructing the people in these and similar [teachings], not for improvement but for damnation, he completely turned [them] away from God and, lest a Gospel word besides could have a place among them, just as for those who know everything that pertains to the Gospel and Christ, he blocked entry to their hearts with the iron barrier of impiety. He decreed, moreover, that circumcision ought to be observed, just as it had been adopted by Ishmael, the father of that people, and in addition to all these things, so that he could attract to himself more easily the carnal minds of men, he relaxed the reins on gluttony and libidinal pleasure, and having himself eighteen wives at one and the same time, and the wives of many others, committing adultery as if in response to divine command, he joined a larger number of the damned to himself just as if by prophetic example. And lest he appear completely disgraceful, he commends a zeal for almsgiving and certain acts of mercy, he praises prayer, and in this way, as a certain one says, he joins "to a human head a horse's neck, and the feathers" of birds [to create] something altogether monstrous [cf. Horace, *Ars Poetica* 1.1–2].

Seeing that, at the persuasion of the monk already mentioned and the aforementioned Jews, he [Mohammad] completely abandoned idolatry, and persuaded those whom he could that it ought to be abandoned, and proclaimed that there is one God that ought to be worshipped, a multiplicity of gods having been abandoned, he seemed to say things not before heard to those that are rude and unschooled. And because, in the first place, this preaching was in harmony with their reason, they believed him to be God's prophet.

From then, in the progress of time and of error, he was raised up by them to the kingship that he desired. Thus, mixing good things with evil, confusing true things with false, he sowed the seeds of error and, partly during his time and partly and especially in the time after him, he produced a nefarious harvest that should be burned up by everlasting fire. At once, as the Roman empire was declining or rather nearly ceased to exist, with the permission of him "through whom kings reign" [Proverbs 8:15], the dominion of the Arabs or the Saracens arose, infected with this plague, and, little by little occupying by force of arms the largest parts of Asia with the whole of Africa and part of Spain, just as it transferred its rule upon those subject to it, so too did it transfer [its] error.

Although I would name them heretics, because they believe some things with us, in most things they depart from us, [and] perhaps more correctly I should name them pagans or heathens, which is worse. For although they say some things about the Lord that are true, nonetheless they proclaim many others that are false, and they participate neither in baptism, nor the sacrifice [of the Mass], nor penance, nor any Christian sacrament, which everyone other than these heretics had done

The highest aspiration of this heresy is to have Christ the Lord believed to be neither God, nor the Son of God, but, although a great man and beloved by God, nonetheless a mere man, and certainly a wise man and a very great prophet. What once, indeed, were conceived by the devil's device, first disseminated by Arius and then advanced by that satan, namely Mohammad, will be fulfilled completely, according to a diabolical design, through the Antichrist. In fact, since the blessed Hilary said that the origin of the Antichrist was in Arius [*De trinitate* 6.43; cf. 2.23], then what he began by denying that Christ is the Son of God and by calling him a creature, the Antichrist will at last consummate by asserting that in no way was he God or the Son of God, but also that he was not a good man; this most impious Mohammad seems to be properly provided for and prepared by the devil as the mean between both of them, who became in a certain sense even an extension of Arius and the greatest support for the Antichrist, who will say worse things before the minds of the unbelievers.

To be sure, nothing is so contrary to the enemy of the human race as the faith of God incarnate, by whom we are particularly aroused to piety, and renewed by the heavenly sacraments with the operative grace of the Holy Spirit, we hope to return again to that place from which he took pride in having cast us out, namely to the vision of the king and of our fatherland, with the king himself and the creator God descending to our place of exile, recalling us to himself with mercy. From the beginning he endeavored to extinguish equally the faith and love of piety and of the divine dispensation in the hearts of men, and he attempted to eradicate this also at the beginning of the still nascent church, if then it were to be permitted, by the most ingenious subtlety, and almost in the same way in which, later, he was permitted to seduce that most unhappy race.

Indeed, the blessed Augustine says that the philosopher Porphyry, after he had wretchedly become an apostate from Christianity, reported this in his books that he produced against the Christians, to wit that he consulted the oracle of the gods, and asked concerning Christ, what he was. The reply to him was, actually, from the demons, that Christ was indeed a good man, but that his disciples had sinned gravely when ascribing divinity to him, they invented something which he had never said about himself. This opinion is very often found among those fables [of the Saracens], almost in the same words. How great was this subtlety of the devil that he said something good about Christ, when he knew if, completely, he spoke evil of him, in no way would one believe him, not caring what Christ was thought to be so long as divinity, which especially saves men, was not believed to be in him; if anyone wishes to understand more fully, let him read the eighteenth book by this same father Augustine, and the nineteenth book, of *The City of God*, and the first [book] of *The Harmony of the Evangelists*. In fact there, if one has a good and studious talent, he should be able to surmise with certainty both what the devil planned to do then but was not allowed to do, and what at length he did, with a hidden judgment allowing it, in this single most wretched race once he was unleashed.

In no way, in fact, could any mortal have invented such fables as the ones written that are singled out here, unless by the assistance of the devil's presence, through which [fables], after many ridiculous and insane absurdities, Satan planned particularly and in every way to bring it to pass that Christ would not be believed to be Lord, the Son of God and True God, the creator and Redeemer of the human race. And in reality this is what he wanted to introduce at that time through Porphyry, but through God's mercy he was blown away from the church which was burning still at that time with the first fruits of the Holy Spirit, [but] at length, [he] used that most wretched man Mohammad (and as it is reported by many, one who is possessed by an evil spirit and by epilepsy) as an instrument and implement, as it were, most suited to him, alas, he plunged into eternal damnation, along with himself, a very large race and one which at present can be reckoned as nearly a half part of the world. Why this was permitted to him he alone knows to whom no one can say, "Why do you do this?" and who said "even from among the many that are called, few are chosen" [Matthew 20:16; 22:14].

For this reason I, choosing to tremble all over rather than debate, have briefly noted down these things so that the one who reads [them] will understand, and if there is such a one as wishes to and can write against this entire heresy, he will know with what kind of enemy he will do battle. Perhaps there yet will be one whose spirit the Lord will awaken, in order to free the church of God from the great disgrace that it suffers therefrom, because although up until our own time, you may be sure, it [the Church] has confounded all heresies—both ancient and modern—by responding, not only has it not at all replied to this one alone which, beyond all others, has caused the unbounded destruction of the human race, both in bodies and in souls, but neither has it attempted to inquire—even a little or inadequately—how great a plague it is or whence it came.

It was for this entire reason that I, Peter, humble abbot of the holy church of Cluny, when I tarried in Spain for the visitation of our properties that exist there, had translated from Arabic into Latin, with great effort and at great expense, that entire impious doctrine, and the accursed life of its terrible inventor, and, once laid bare, had it come to our acquaintance, so that one would know how foul and frivolous a heresy it is, and so that some servant of God, with the Holy Spirit enkindling [him], would be spurred on to refute it with a written composition. O shame! that there is none who will do this, because already with nearly all ardor of this sort for the saints' efforts everywhere grown cool in the church, I waited a long time, actually, and [because] there was no one who would open [his] mouth and move the pen and growl with the zeal of holy Christianity, I myself at least, if my extensive business obligations permitted, proposed for some time to undertake this, with the Lord assisting. Nonetheless I would always prefer that this be done better by someone else, than worse by me.

35. ANSELM OF HAVELBERG'S DISPUTATION WITH THE GREEKS IN CONSTANTINOPLE

The Anticimenon *(c. 1150) of Bishop Anselm of Havelberg (c. 1100–58) is an extraordinary and unique work on ecumenical dialogue with the Orthodox Church and one of the century's most important explorations of the theology of history. Like Philip of Harvengt and Herman the Former Jew (see Docs. 4, 22, 67), Anselm was a member of the young Premonstratensian order. In 1136 the Holy Roman Emperor Lothair II (r. 1133–37) sent him as an ambassador to Constantinople. There he held theological discussions with the Patriarch of the Orthodox Church, Nicetas of Nicomedia, the contents of which were subsequently recorded in his* Anticimenon, *written ostensibly at the bequest of Pope Eugenius III (r. 1145–53).*

The veracity of the discussions as Anselm presents them has long been a matter of some uncertainty, and not simply because of the time lag between the encounter and its written rendition. The work is divided into three books, the first of which is in treatise format and addresses in didactic fashion the question of why there is division and disunity among the Christian faithful. The remainder of the work records the "controversies" that

Anselm held with Nicetas and his learned entourage while on mission in Constantinople. Not surprisingly, Anselm emerges the better debater. Throughout books 2 and 3, Anselm displays his exegetical skill as well as his commitment to the historical level of interpretation, while also making a compelling case for Latin Roman beliefs and the primacy of the Roman See. The format and apologetic tone of the work recalls the anti-Jewish dialogues, and the accusations of heresy evince contemporary concern with the spread of false beliefs. Nevertheless, Anselm shows genuine interest in the unity of the two branches of Christianity. His writings are a unique specimen of what a theological debate between a Latin and a Greek in the twelfth century may have looked like.

Source: trans. Ambrose Criste, O.P., and Carol Neel, *Anselm of Havelberg: Anticimenon, On the Unity of the Faith and the Controversies with the Greeks* (Collegeville, MN: Liturgical Press, 2010), 98–99, 177–79. Latin.

Book 2, Chapter 4: That just as the Father begot, but did not beget himself, and just as the Son was begotten, but not by himself, so too the Holy Sprit proceeds, but not from himself

Anselm, bishop of Havelberg, then said: "The Father is God, the Son is God, and the Holy Spirit is God, yet there are not three gods but one. And although we say rightly that God the Father begot God the Son, since there is one God, nevertheless we cannot rightly say about God the Father, 'God the Father begot himself,' nor can we rightly say of God the Son, 'God the Son was begotten by himself.' So too, although the Father, Son, and Holy Spirit are one God and we rightly believe that the Holy Spirit proceeds from the Father and the Son, nevertheless we cannot, therefore, correctly say that he proceeds from himself. Although the Spirit is one in substance with the Father and the Son, he is by no means the same as the Father or the Son such that he might proceed from himself as he proceeds from them. Therefore, just as the Father begot but did not beget himself, and just as the Son was begotten but not by himself, so too the Holy Spirit proceeds but not from himself. The Gospel of John reveals this in the text about the Holy Spirit: 'For he will not speak on his own, but will speak whatever he hears' [John 16:13]. This speech will not come from the Spirit because he is not of himself, and because he is not of himself neither does he—whose essence is the same as that which proceeds—proceed from himself. Therefore whence he exists, thence he proceeds, and whence he proceeds, thence he exists. His being consists in his procession. Just as the role proper to the Father is to beget the Son, and just as the role proper to the Son is for the Father to beget him, so too the role proper of the Holy Spirit is to proceed from both as if from one principle."

Nicetas, archbishop of Nicomedia, answered: "We intended to treat the procession of the Holy Spirit, but in order to prove your opinion you have adduced your thought on the Father as begetting and the Son as begotten. You have done so appropriately, for I acknowledge that your arguments are satisfying. But respond now to this question: what is the procession of the Holy Spirit of which we speak, or how does it occur? Does it seem true to you that we must say that the Holy Spirit proceeds according to the substance common to the other persons or according to his discrete and proper person?"

Chapter 5: That just as we do not understand how the Father is begotten by no other or the Son is begotten, so too we do not understand how the Holy Spirit proceeds

Anselm, bishop of Havelberg, then said: "Tell me how the Father is begotten by no other and how the Son is begotten, and I shall then tell you how the Holy Spirit proceeds! But we should both be foolish to pry so into divine mysteries, wishing to find rational explanation for these things we know to be ineffable, beyond all the comprehension of any rational creature. They surpass all human, even all angelic understanding in their profundity and sublimity. But if you press me and if you wish to be irksome over this question, then suffice it to hear what it suffices for me to believe: the Father is begotten by no other, the Son is begotten, and the Holy Spirit proceeds. This is enough for my belief. As I see it, how the Father is begotten by no other, how the Son is begotten, or how the third person proceeds should be honored in reverent silence. Our role is so to believe these great matters as not to investigate how they are so with our intellectual curiosity, for to understand how is granted not even to the angels, much less to us. But the Father who begot, the Son who was begotten, and the Holy Spirit who proceeded from both all understand the Son's divine, eternal procession in that conscious rationality only they eternally process. So they know the manner and character of the Spirit's generation and procession, but these matters are inaccessible to the dark cloud of human lowliness in which vanity sometimes works against truth. . . .

Book 3, Chapter 11: That heresies arising in Constantinople or anywhere in the East have been destroyed there

Nicetas, archbishop of Nicomedia, then spoke: "It may be as you say. But earlier you said that the Church of Constantinople, rather almost the entire east, has been polluted by various heresies. You said this and it was true in part, and since I am a servant of the truth I should not deny it. But say, I ask you, where have those heresies been condemned? Who has condemned them? If they have arisen here among perverse and evil men, they have also been condemned here by good and catholic men. After the emperor Constantine the Great was converted to the faith and wrote laws pleasing to God for the Christian people, Rome along with all the West and Constantinople along with all the East hastened to the faith as a result of the emperor's decrees. Because this new and heretofore unknown faith was suddenly proclaimed publically and because the study of the liberal arts flourished in this city, and because many skilled in logical argument and discriminating in dialectic excelled here in discursive reasoning, those learned men began to examine the Christian faith through that discourse. But they fell short in their investigation and rational consideration. Pressing their investigations too far and professing themselves to be wise, they became fools. They emptied themselves into their own thoughts as they investigated without humility what they should have piously and humbly believed. Even as they strained to the height of human knowledge in the arrogance of their reason, they fall into the pit of faithlessness. Many became heretics and created for themselves many sects. They confused and mangled the Christian faith, splitting it into many divergent heresies. But then the church of the East, seeing that men abused secular learning and that heretical leaders bubbled up at various times and places celebrated many councils after sending synodal letters everywhere and gaining the support of pious emperors. The first such council was at Nicaea in the province of Bithynia. There the Arian heresy was condemned and the creed for all Catholics was drafted, then ratified by the inviolable authority of the Holy Spirit and of 318 fathers.

"Afterward, as various other heresies followed, many other councils were celebrated for the destruction of the different heresies and for building up the catholic faith. In the church of Chalcedon and here in Constantinople as in Ephesus, Antioch, and Alexandria, general councils have been solemnly held for the condemnation of heretics and for strengthening the faith and unity of all the churches. Thus, as I have said, if heresies have arisen here, they have also been destroyed here. Clearly the church of God increased more and more in the knowledge of the scriptures through the occasion of these heresies, and the faith grew stronger with their extinction. But after the catholic faith was defined and then perfected, the holy fathers rightly forbade that anyone should dare to argue further about the faith in public, since we must add or take away nothing else. When the truth has been found and anyone wishes to seek further, what else can he find but falsehood? Of course one may question humbly in order to discern something previously unclear about the faith, providing he does not contentiously cast doubt on anything defined by the holy fathers as a secure boundary of faith. This no mortal may revise, as the gravest anathemas forbid.

"So stop reproaching us, as you have wished, about heresies. All wise men know that the truth and power of the good prevail over the lies and offenses of the wicked. Tell me, I ask you, where those heretics are now? They are not here, nor are their names heard anywhere in the East, rather Catholics throughout the

Orient offer God fitting homage with clear, sound faith. Perhaps in the city of Rome such heresies have not arisen because wise, discriminating men and scholars of scripture were not there as they are among us. The empty knowledge by which the heretics were misled is indeed blameworthy, and so too the rusticity of Roman knowledge is greatly to be praised, according to which they have said neither one thing nor the other about the faith but have listened to others in simplicity before speaking and teaching, because they themselves were untaught. But this lack of knowledge seems to have resulted from negligence in the study of the faith, from the dullness of stupidity, or perhaps from the heavy obstacle of worldly occupation. For the learned to think or speak is either entirely good or bad, but for the unwise or unlearned to think or speak is neither."

36. BARTHOLOMEW OF EXETER'S *PENITENTIAL* CONDEMNING SUPERSTITIONS

Bartholomew, bishop of Exeter from 1161 to 1186, is the author of many works, including treatises on the doctrine of free will and predestination, a collection of over 100 sermons, and an anti-Jewish work entitled Dialogue against the Jews. *His* Penitential *devotes particular attention to the sins of witchcraft and superstition and shows a genuine concern for deviant practices in contemporary society at large. A penitential is a book or set of rules concerning the Christian sacrament of penance that was first developed in Ireland in the sixth century. It consisted of a list of sins and the appropriate penances prescribed for them, and served as a type of manual for confessors. Penitentials became increasingly important in the twelfth century as the theory and practice of penance itself developed and became more fixed. The perceived menace of witchcraft, sorcery, and magic, although not unique to the twelfth century, did during this period become the basis for some of the most systematic campaigns of attacks against Christian heretics and other non-conformists.*

Source: trans. G.G. Coulton, *Life in the Middle Ages*, Vol. 1 (Cambridge: Cambridge University Press, 1910), 33–35. Latin.

(1) Whosoever shall strive to take away from another, and gain for himself, by any incantation or witchcraft, another's plenty of milk or honey or of other things; (2) Whosoever ensnared by the Devils' wiles, may believe and profess that they ride with countless multitudes of others in the train of her whom the foolish vulgar call Herodias or Diana, and that they obey her behests; (3) Whosoever has prepared a table with three knives for the service of the fairies, that they may predestinate good to such as are born in the house; (4) Whosoever shall have made a vow by a tree or water, or anything save a church; (5) Whosoever shall pollute New Year's Day by magic enquiries into the future, after the pagan fashion, or who begin their works on that day, that they may prosper better than

in any other year; (6) Whosoever makes knots or sorceries and divers enchantments by charms of witchcraft, and hide them in the grass or in a tree or in a branching road, in order to free their beasts from murrain; (7) Whosoever shall have set his child on the house-roof or in an oven to recover its health, or for the same purpose shall have used charms or characters or anything fashioned for divination, or any artifice whatsoever save godly prayers or the liberal art of medicine; (8) Whosoever, while gathering medicinal simples, shall have said any charm save such as are godly, as the Lord's Prayer or the Creed or suchlike; (9) Whosoever, laboring in wool or dyeing or other works, shall use charms or lay spells thereon that they may prosper; or who shall forbid the carrying away of fire or aught else from his house, lest the young of his beasts perish; (10) Whosoever shall work witchcraft from a dead man's funeral or corpse or garments, lest the dead folk take some vengeance, or lest some other die in the same house, or to obtain thereby some other profit or well-being; (11) Whosoever on Saint John's Day shall have wrought any witchcraft to foretell the future; (12) Whosoever shall believe that good or evil comes to him from the croak of a jackdaw or raven, or from meeting a priest or any animal whatsoever; (13) Whosoever, in visiting the sick, shall conceive any omen of good or evil from the motion of any stone on his outward or homeward way, or by any other sign whatsoever; (14) Whosoever shall believe that a man or woman may be changed into the shape of a wolf or other beast; (15) Whosoever shall spy out the footsteps of Christian folk, believing that they may be bewitched by cutting away the turf whereon they have trodden; (16) (From the Council of Agde [506 CE].) The priest must inquire whether there be any woman who professes to be able to change men's minds by sorcery or enchantments, as from hate to love or from love to hate, or to bewitch or steal men's goods: also whether there be any professing to ride on certain nights and upon certain beasts with a host of demons in women's shape, and to be enrolled in the company of such. Let any woman of this sort be chastised with birchen twigs and cast forth from the parish.

37. BERNARD OF CLAIRVAUX'S SERMON AGAINST HERESY

Bernard of Clairvaux composed 86 sermons on the Old Testament Song of Songs alone, which, like Origen before him, he interpreted as a spiritual allegory of the love between God and the soul rather than as a physical passion shared between two created beings. Sermon 65 is devoted to the topic of heresy and the need to remove it from contemporary society. Drawing on biblical citations, as he so often does, Bernard clearly views the problem of heresy as a pressing concern for the Church. He characterizes heresy as a domestic vine or weed that, if not properly rooted out, threatens destruction of the whole crop.

As with his letter denouncing Peter Abelard to Pope Innocent II (Doc. 19), he deliberately uses his eloquence as a weapon in response to what he saw as the mortal attacks being made on God's servants.

Source: trans. Samuel J. Eales, in *Life and Works of Saint Bernard, Abbot of Clairvaux*, 4 vols. (London: J. Hodges, 1889–96), vol. 4, pp. 393–98. Latin.

Sermon 65 on the Song of Songs

I have already delivered to you two sermons upon one verse; I propose to deliver a third, if it will not weary you to listen. And I think it even necessary to do so; for though, as far as relates to our domestic vine, which is no other than yourselves, my brethren, I have, I think, sufficiently forearmed you in the two preceding sermons against the crafty advances of three kinds of foxes; namely, flatterers, calumniators, and certain seducing spirits who are skilled and experienced in presenting evil under the guise of good; yet that is not the case with the dominical, that is, the Lord's vine. I speak of that vine which has filled the earth, and of which we also are a part; a vine great and spreading, planted by the hand of the Lord, redeemed by his blood, watered by his word, propagated by his grace, and rendered fruitful by his spirit. The more carefully I have dealt with that which was of private and personal concern, the less valuable were my remarks with regard to that which was common and public. But it troubles me greatly, on behalf of that vine, to behold the multitude of its assailants, the fewness of its defenders, and the difficulty of the defense. The hidden and furtive character of the attack is the cause of this difficulty. For from the beginning the Church has had foxes; but they have been soon found out and taken. A heretic combated openly (indeed, that was the principal reason why the name was given, because the desire of the heretic was to gain an open victory), and was manifestly overcome. Those foxes, therefore, were easily taken. But what if a heretic, when the truth was set clear in the light before him, remained in the shadow of his obstinacy, and, bound (as it were) hand and foot in the outer darkness, withered away in solitude? Even then the fox was deemed to be "taken" when his impiety was condemned, and the impious one cast out, thenceforth to live in a mere show of life without fruitfulness. From this to such a one, according to the prophet, comes a sterile womb and dry breasts [Hosea 9:14]: because an error, publicly confuted, does not soon shoot up again, and an evident falsehood does not take root.

What shall we do to take those foxes, the most malignant and dangerous of all, who prefer the inflicting of severe injury to the enjoyment of open victory, and who crawl to, and steal upon, their purpose in order not to be seen? With all heretics their one intention has always been to obtain praise for themselves by the remarkable extent of their knowledge. But there is a heresy which alone is more malignant and more artful than others, since it feeds upon the losses of others, and neglects its own glory. It is instructed, I believe, by the examples of those ancient heresies which, when betrayed, were by no means suffered to escape, but were forthwith captured; and so is careful to actuate secretly, by a new method of mischief, this mystery of iniquity, and that with the greater freedom the less it is suspected. Furthermore, its promoters have met together, as it is said, at places appointed in secret and concerted together their nefarious discourses. "Take oaths, if needful; take them even falsely," they said the one to the other, "rather than betray the secret." But at another time they do not consider it right by any means to swear, not even in the smallest degree, because of those words in the gospel: "Swear not at all; neither by heaven . . . nor by the earth" [Matthew 5:34–35], etc. O foolish and hard of heart, filled with the spirit of the Pharisees, ye, too, strain at a gnat and swallow a camel [Matthew 23:24]. To swear is not permitted, but to swear falsely, that is permissible, as if the allowance to do the latter did not carry with it the former also! In what passage of the gospel, of which you do not, as you falsely boast, pass over one iota, do you find that exception? It is clear that you, both by superstition, forbid the taking of an oath, and, at the same time, wickedly presume to authorize a perjury. O strange perversity! That which is given only as a counsel of perfection—namely "Swear not"—that they observe as rigidly and contentiously as if it were a positive command; while that which is laid down as an unchangeable law—namely, never to be guilty of perjury—they dispense with at their own will as a thing indifferent. No, say they; but let us not make known our secret. As if it were not to the glory of God to make known teaching [that is to edification] [Daniel 2:28–29]! Do they envy the glory of God? But I rather believe that they are ashamed to have their secret known, being conscious that it does not redound to their glory; for they are said to practice in secret things obscene and abominable, even as the hinder parts of foxes are offensive.

But I do not wish to speak of that which they deny; let them answer only to those which are known and manifest. Are they careful, according to the gospel precept, not to give that which is holy unto the dogs, or to cast pearls before swine [Matthew 7:6]? But do not they who regard all who belong to the church as dogs and swine, plainly confess that they are not of the Church themselves? For they consider that their secret, whatever it is, should be kept wholly from the knowledge of all, without exception, who are not of their sect. What their doctrine is they do not avow, and they adopt every means to avoid its becoming known; but yet they do not succeed. Reply to me, O man, who are wise above that which is meet, and yet more foolish than can be expressed in words. Is the secret which you are concealing of God, or is it not? If it is, why do you not make it known to his glory? For it is to the glory of God to reveal that which comes from him. But if it is not, why do you put faith in that which is not of God, unless because you are a heretic? Either, then, let them proclaim the secret as coming from God to the glory of God, or let them confess that the secret is not of God, and thereby allow that they are heretics; or, at least, let them allow that they are manifestly enemies of the glory of God, since they are unwilling to make manifest a thing which would be conducive to that glory. For it is stated with preciseness in the scripture: It is the glory of kings to conceal a matter, but it is the glory of God to reveal discourse. Are you not willing to reveal it? Then you do not desire to glorify God. But perhaps you do not receive this scripture. Doubtless this is the case, for [sectaries] profess that they are followers of the gospel, and the only ones. Let them, then, reply to the gospel. "What I tell you in darkness," says the Lord, "that speak in light: and what you hear in the ear, preach that upon the housetops" [Matthew 10:27]. Now it is not permitted to you to be silent. How long is that kept under the veil of secrecy which God declares is to be made known? How long is your gospel to be hidden? I suspect that your gospel is not that of Saint Paul, for he declares that his gospel is not hidden, or rather he says this: "If our gospel is hidden, it is hidden to them that are lost" [2 Corinthians 4:3]. Does not this apply to you who have among you a gospel that is hidden? What is more plain than that you are in the way of being lost? Or perhaps you do not receive even the Epistles of Saint Paul. I have heard that it is so with certain persons among you. For, although you all agree in differing from us, you do not all agree in all respects among yourselves.

Have we reached any result? I think we have; we have taken the fox, since we have discovered his deception. Those pretended Catholics who were really destroyers of the Church have been made manifest. Even while you were raking with me sweet [and heavenly] food, I mean the body and blood of Christ, while we walked in the house of God as friends, a place for persuasion, or, rather, an opportunity for perversion, was found, according to the saying of scripture: "A hypocrite with his mouth destroys his neighbor" [Proverbs 9:9]. But now I easily, according to the wise admonition of Saint Paul, avoid "a man that is a heretic after the first and second admonition, knowing that he that is such is subverted, and sins, being condemned of himself" [Titus 3:10–11], and that it behooves me to be on my guard, lest he cause my subversion also. It is, then, something gained according to the word of the wise, that transgressors should be taken in their own naughtiness [Proverbs 9:6], and especially those transgressors the weapons of whose warfare are deceit and snares. Open attack and defense they do not venture upon, for they are a despicable and rustic race, devoid of education, and wholly destitute of generous courage. In short, they are foxes, and little foxes. Even their errors are not defensible, not clever and able, not even plausible, except only to country women and ignorant persons, such as are all those of their sect who I have as yet seen. For I do not recall, among all their assertions which I have heard (and they are many), anything novel or extraordinary, but only commonplaces long since broached among the heretics of old, and by our divines confuted and crushed. Yet it ought to be shown, and I will endeavor to show, what absurdities these are, being partly such as they have fallen into through incautiously taking one side or the other in questions disputed between Catholics, partly such as they have exposed themselves to by their dissensions with each other, and partly such as some of them who have returned to the Church have discovered to us, and this I will do, not that I may reply to them all (for that is unnecessary), but in order that they may be known. But that will be a task for another sermon to the praise and glory of the name of him who is the bridegroom of the church, Jesus Christ our lord, who is above all, God blessed for ever. Amen.

38. DISCIPLINARY DECREES OF THE FOURTH LATERAN COUNCIL

The Fourth Lateran Council, convened in Rome by Pope Innocent III (r. 1198–1216) in the fall of 1215, was the largest and arguably the most important ecclesiastical gathering of the entire Middle Ages. Much had happened in matters both political and intellectual since the previous Lateran council of 1179, and these are reflected in the various canons issued at the council. The Third and Fourth Crusades had both failed to retake Jerusalem, and, as a consequence of the latter failure, the Byzantine capital of Constantinople was now under Latin rule. The final decrees of the council dealt with renewing the crusading efforts, while several others addressed the subservient status of Byzantine orthodoxy. The ecclesiastically driven war on heresy in southern France went from cold to hot with the murder of the papal legate Peter of Castelnau in Toulouse in 1208; the crusade that Pope Innocent III launched against the Cathars would become known as the Albigensian Crusade, after the Cathar stronghold of Albi in southern France. Appropriately, therefore, the first canon opens with a rather polemical profession of faith anathematizing both non-Catholic (i.e., Byzantine) Christianity and the Cathar heresy.

Christian intolerance toward local Jewish populations had likewise increased markedly in the previous decades. The first royal expulsion from France had taken place in 1182 under the orders of King Philip II Augustus (see Doc. 32), although they were recalled several years later. The advancing Christian Reconquest of Spain brought significant populations of Muslims under Christian rule. Consternation over Christian commercial and social interactions with non-Christians forms the background to the council's attempt (the first in Christian history) to enforce distinctive clothing to be worn by both Jews and Muslims (canons 67–68). Additionally, with Innocent's help, the schools of Paris merged and received official sanction as a studium generale, *which in turn prompted the first official statutes of the University of Paris. Extending an enactment of the Third Lateran Council, canon 11 decreed that each cathedral should have a master of grammar who would instruct the clergy and poor scholars free of charge, and in metropolitan churches there should also be a master of theology, who would teach priests and others "in the sacred page" and who would instruct them in matters that pertained to the care of souls. Finally, and perhaps most consequentially from a doctrinal perspective, canon 1 resolved the Eucharist debate over the issue of transubstantiation (see Doc. 1), while canon 21 further established that all Catholic Christians must provide auricular confession to their priest at least once a year.*

Source: trans. H. J. Schroeder, *Disciplinary Decrees of the General Councils* (St. Louis: B. Herder, 1937), 237–38, 242–43, 252, 290–91. Latin.

1. We firmly believe and openly confess that there is only one true God, eternal and immense, omnipotent, unchangeable, incomprehensible, and ineffable, Father, Son, and Holy Ghost; three Persons indeed but one essence, substance, or nature absolutely simple; the Father [proceeding] from no one, but the Son from the Father only, and the Holy Ghost equally from both, always without beginning and end. The Father begetting, the Son begotten, and the Holy Ghost proceeding; consubstantial and coequal, coomnipotent and coeternal, the one principle of the universe, Creator of all things invisible and visible, spiritual and corporeal, who from the beginning of time and by his omnipotent power made from nothing creatures both spiritual and corporeal; angelic, namely, and mundane, and then human, as it were, common, composed of spirit and body. The devil and the other demons were indeed created by God good by nature but they became bad through themselves; man, however, sinned at the suggestion of the devil. This Holy Trinity in its common essence undivided and in personal properties divided, through Moses, the holy prophets, and other servants gave to the human race at the most opportune intervals of time the doctrine of salvation.

And finally, Jesus Christ, the only begotten Son of God made flesh by the entire Trinity, conceived with the cooperation of the Holy Ghost of Mary ever Virgin, made true man, composed of a rational soul and human flesh, one Person in two natures, pointed out more clearly the way of life. Who according to his divinity is immortal and impassable, according to his humanity was made passable and mortal, suffered on the cross for the salvation of the human race, and being dead descended into hell, rose from the dead, and ascended into heaven. But he descended in soul, arose in flesh, and ascended equally in both; He will come at the end of the world to judge the living and the dead and will render to the reprobate and to the elect according to their works. Who all shall rise with their bodies which they have that they may receive according to their merits, whether good or bad, the latter eternal punishment with the devil, the former eternal glory with Christ.

There is one Universal Church of the faithful, outside of which there is absolutely no salvation. In which there is the same priest and sacrifice, Jesus Christ, whose body and blood are truly contained in the sacrament of the altar under the forms of bread and wine; the bread being changed [*transubstantio*] by divine power into the body, and the wine into the blood, so that to realize the mystery of unity we may receive of him what he has received of us. And this sacrament no one can effect except the priest who has been duly ordained in accordance with the keys of the Church, which Jesus Christ himself gave to the apostles and their successors.

But the sacrament of baptism, which by the invocation of each Person of the Trinity, namely, of the Father, the Son, and Holy Ghost, is effected in water, duly conferred on children and adults in the form prescribed by the Church by anyone whatsoever, leads to salvation. And should anyone after the reception of baptism have fallen into sin, by the true repentance he can always be restored. Not only virgins and those practicing chastity, but also those united in marriage, through the right faith and through works pleasing to God, can merit eternal salvation. . . .

3. We excommunicate and anathematize every heresy that raises itself against the holy, orthodox, and Catholic faith which we have explained; condemning all heretics under whatever names they may be known, for while they have different faces, they are nevertheless bound to each other by their tails, since in all of them vanity is a common element. Those condemned, being handed over to the secular rulers of the bailiffs, let them be abandoned, to be punished with due justice, clerics being degraded from their orders. As to the property of the condemned, if they are laymen, let it be confiscated; if clerics, let it be applied to the churches from which they received revenues. But those who are only suspected, due consideration being given to the nature of the suspicion and the character of the person, unless they prove their innocence by a proper defense, let them be anathematized and avoided by all until they have made suitable satisfaction; but if they have been under excommunication for one year, then let them be condemned as heretics. Secular authorities, whatever office they may hold, shall be admonished and induced and if necessary compelled by ecclesiastical censure, that as they wish to be esteemed and numbered among the faithful, so for the defense of the faith and to the best of their ability to exterminate in the territories subject to their jurisdiction all heretics pointed out by the Church; so that whenever anyone shall have assumed authority, whether spiritual or temporal, let him be bound to confirm this decree by oath. But if a temporal ruler, after having been requested and admonished by the Church, should neglect to cleanse his territory of this heretical foulness, let him be excommunicated by the metropolitan and the other bishops of the province. If he refuses to make satisfaction within a year, let the matter be made known to the supreme pontiff, that he may declare the ruler's vassals absolved from their allegiance and may offer the territory to be ruled by Catholics, who on the extermination of the heretics

may possess it without hindrance and preserve it in the purity of faith; the right, however, of the chief ruler is to be respected so long as he offers no obstacle in this matter and permits freedom of action. The same law is to be observed in regard to those who have no chief rulers (that is, are independent). Catholics who have girded themselves with the cross for the extermination of the heretics, shall enjoy the indulgences and privileges granted to those who go in defense of the Holy Land. . . .

11. Since there are some who, on account of the lack of necessary means, are unable to acquire an education or to meet opportunities for perfecting themselves, the Third Lateran Council in a salutary decree (18) provided that in every cathedral church a suitable benefice be assigned to a master who shall instruct gratis the clerics of that church and other poor students, by means of which benefice the material needs of the master might be relieved and to the students a way opened to knowledge. But, since in many churches this is not observed, we, confirming the aforesaid decree, add that, not only in every cathedral church but also in other churches where means are sufficient, a competent master be appointed by the prelate with his chapter, or elected by the greater and more discerning part of the chapter, who shall instruct gratis and to the best of his ability the clerics of those and other churches in the art of grammar and in other branches of knowledge. In addition to a master, let the metropolitan church have also a theologian, who shall instruct the priests and others in the Sacred Scriptures and in those things especially that pertain to the *cura animarum*. . . .

21. All the faithful of both sexes shall after they have reached the age of discretion faithfully confess all their sins at least once a year to their own [parish] priest and perform to the best of their ability the penance imposed, receiving reverently at least at Easter the sacrament of the Eucharist, unless perchance at the advice of their own priest they may for a good reason abstain for a time from its reception; otherwise they shall be cut off from the Church [excommunicated] during life and deprived of Christian burial in death. Wherefore, let this salutary decree be published frequently in the churches, that no one may find in the plea of ignorance a shadow of excuse. But if anyone for a good reason should wish to confess his sins to another priest, let him first seek and obtain permission from his own [parish] priest, since otherwise he [the other priest] cannot loose or bind him. . . .

67. The more the Christians are restrained from the practice of usury, the more are they oppressed in this matter by the treachery of the Jews, so that in a short time they exhaust the resources of the Christians. Wishing, therefore, in this matter, to protect the Christians against cruel oppression by the Jews, we ordain in this decree that if in the future under any pretext Jews extort from Christians oppressive and immoderate interest, the partnership of the Christians shall be denied them till they have made suitable satisfaction for their excesses.

The Christians also, every appeal being set aside, shall, if necessary, be compelled by ecclesiastical censure to abstain from all commercial intercourse with them. We command the princes not to be hostile to the Christians on this account, but rather to strive to hinder the Jews from practicing such excesses. Lastly, we decree that the Jews be compelled by the same punishment [avoidance of commercial intercourse] to make satisfaction for the tithes and offerings due to the churches, which the Christians were accustomed to supply from their houses and other possessions before these properties, under whatever title, fell into the hands of the Jews, that thus the churches may be safeguarded against loss.

68. In some provinces a difference of dress distinguishes the Jews and Saracens from the Christians, but in others confusion has developed to such a degree that no difference is discernible. Whence it happens sometimes through error that Christians mingle with the women of Jews and Saracens, and, on the other hand, Jews and Saracens mingle with those of the Christians. Therefore, that such ruinous commingling through error of this kind may not serve as a refuge for further excesses, we decree that such people of both sexes [that is, Jews and Saracens] in every Christian province and at all times be distinguished in public from other people by a difference of dress, since this was also enjoined on them by Moses. On the days of the Lamentations and on Passion Sunday they may not appear in public, because some of them, as we understand, on those days are not ashamed to show themselves more ornately attired and do not fear to amuse themselves at the expense of the Christians, who in memory of the sacred passion go about attired in robes of mourning. That we most strictly forbid, lest they should presume in some measure to burst forth suddenly in contempt of the Redeemer. And, since we ought not to be ashamed of him who blotted out our offenses, we command that the secular princes restrain presumptuous persons of this kind by condign punishment, lest they presume to blaspheme in some degree the one crucified for us.

CHAPTER FOUR

ESTABLISHING A NEW ORDER: GOVERNMENT AND LAW

Two aspects of civic society have been paired together in this chapter, both of which illustrate important developments in the growing institutionalization and systematization of law and order in the twelfth century. The expansion of government, most evident in England and France, led to new offices and new guidebooks for the holders of those offices. The delicate balance, some would say struggle, between secular and ecclesiastical rule likewise led to new currents in political thought. The roots of this struggle between church and state reach back to the Investiture Conflict of the eleventh century, but the increasing centralization of political power during the course of the twelfth century provoked some of the most original ideas in political theory since Roman times, as well as some of the most memorable conflicts between kings and churchmen. Lastly, and perhaps most importantly, a growth in legalism served as a catalyst to two significant realms of the twelfth-century renaissance. The first is the revival of ancient Roman law. The second is the growing attention to and study of canon law, or Church law, especially following the redaction of Gratian's *Concordance of Discordant Canons* (also known as the *Decretum*) around 1150.

39. THE *CONSTITUTIONS OF CLARENDON*

The Constitutions of Clarendon *were a set of legislative procedures passed by King Henry II of England in 1164. Henry (r. 1154–89) wished to assert more authority over the Church, whose system of ecclesiastical courts he believed offered excessive papal protection to clergy who broke the law. The* Constitutions *were Henry's shrewd attempt to both solve these problems while also increasing his own power at the helm) by claiming secular jurisdiction over clergymen once they had been tried and defrocked by the ecclesiastical courts. The king and his court claimed, somewhat disingenuously, that they were merely restoring the judicial customs observed during the reign of Henry I (r. 1100–35), when in fact they were part of Henry's larger expansion of royal jurisdiction into church and civil law. Archbishop Thomas Becket (1118–70) resisted the* Constitutions, *especially the clause concerning "criminous clerks," and thus began his famous feud with the king that resulted in his murder.*

Source: trans. H. Gee and W.G. Hardy, *Documents Illustrative of the History of the English Church* (London: Macmillan, 1910), 68–72; revised. Latin.

In the year 1164 from our Lord's Incarnation, the fourth of the pontificate of Alexander, the tenth of Henry II, most illustrious king of the English, in the presence of the same king, was made by this remembrance or acknowledgment of a certain part of the customs, liberties, and dignities of his ancestors, that is of King Henry his grandfather, and of others, which ought to be observed and held in the realm. And owing to strife and dissensions that had taken place between the clergy and justices of the lord king and the barons of the realm, in respect of customs and dignities of the realm, this recognition was made before the archbishops and bishops and clergy, and the earls and barons and nobles of the realm. . . .

Now of the acknowledged customs and dignities of the realm a certain part is contained in the present document, of which part these are chapters:

1. If controversy should arise between laymen, or clergy and laymen, or clergy, regarding advowson [patronage of a nominee to a vacant ecclesiastical benefice or church living] and presentation to churches, let it be treated or concluded in the court of the lord king.

2. Churches belonging to the fee of the lord king [that is, churches on the royal demesne] cannot be granted in perpetuity without his own assent and grant.

3. Clerks cited and accused of any matter shall, when summoned by the king's justice, come into his own court to answer there concerning what it shall seem to the king's court should be answered there, and in the church court for what it shall seem should be answered there; yet so that the king's justice shall send into the court of holy church to see in what way the matter is there treated. And if the clerk be convicted, or shall confess, the church must not any longer protect him.

4. Archbishops, bishops, and parish clergy of the realm are not allowed to leave the kingdom without license of the lord king; and if they do leave, they shall, if the king so please, give security that neither in going nor in staying nor in returning, they will seek the ill or damage of the lord king or realm.

5. Excommunicate persons are not to give pledge for the future, nor to take oath, but only to give security and pledge of abiding by the church's judgment that they may be absolved.

6. Laymen are not to be accused save by proper and legal accusers and witnesses in the presence of the bishop, so that the archdeacon does not lose his right nor anything due to him thence. And if the accused be such that no one wills or dares to accuse them, the sheriff, when requested

by the bishop, shall cause twelve lawful men from the neighborhood or the town to swear before the bishop that they will show the truth in the matter according to their conscience.

7. No one who holds the king in chief, and none of his demesne officers are to be excommunicated, nor the lands of any one of them to be put under an interdict unless first the lord king, if he be in the country, or his justice if he be outside the kingdom, be applied to in order that he may do right for him; and so that what shall appertain to the royal court be concluded there, and that what shall belong to the church court be sent to the same to be treated there.

8. In regard to appeals, if they shall occur, they must proceed from the archdeacon to the bishop, and from the bishop to the archbishop. And if the archbishop fail in showing justice, they must come at last to the lord king, that by his command the dispute be concluded in the archbishop's court, so that it must not go further without the assent of the lord king.

9. If a dispute shall arise between a clerk and a layman, or between a layman and a clerk, whether a given tenement is held in free alms or as a lay fee, it shall be concluded by the consideration of the king's chief justice on the award of twelve lawful men . . . before the king's justiciar himself. And if the award be that it is held in free alms, it shall be pleaded in the church court, but if to the lay fee, unless both claim under the same bishop or baron, it shall be pleaded in his own court, so that for making the award he who was first seised [that is, in possession] lose not his seisin until the matter be settled by the plea.

10. If anyone of a city, or castle, or borough, or a demesne manor of the lord king, be cited by archdeacon or bishop for any offense for which he ought to answer them, and refuse to give satisfaction at their citations, it is well lawful to place him under interdict; but he must not be excommunicated before the chief officer of the lord king of that town be applied to, in order that he may adjudge him to come for satisfaction. And if the king's officer fail in this, he shall be at the king's mercy, and thereafter the bishop shall be able to restrain the accused by ecclesiastical justice.

11. Archbishops, bishops, and all persons of the realm who hold of the king in chief, have their possessions from the lord king as a barony, and are answerable therefor to the king's justices and ministers, and follow and do all royal rights and customs, and like all other barons, have to be present at the trials of the court of the lord king with the barons until it comes to a judgment of loss of limb, or death.

12. When an archbishopric or bishopric is vacant, or any abbey or priory of the king's demesne, it must be in his own hand, and from it he shall receive all revenues and rents as demesne. And when it is time to install a clergyman in the church, the lord king must cite the chief clergy of the church, and the election must take place in the chapel of the lord king himself, with the assent of the lord king, and the advice of the persons of the realm whom he shall have summoned to do this. And the person elected shall there do homage and fealty to the lord king as to his liege lord for his life and limbs and earthly honor, saving his order, before he be consecrated.

13. If any of the nobles of the realm forcibly prevent the archbishop or bishop or archdeacon from doing justice in regard to himself or his people, the lord king must bring them to justice. And if perchance anyone should deforce [forcibly resist] the lord king, the archbishops and bishops must judge him, so that he gives satisfaction to the lord king.

14. The goods of those who are under forfeit of the king, no church or cemetery is to detain the king's justice, because they belong to the king himself, whether they be found inside churches or outside.

15. Pleas of debts due under pledge of faith or without pledge of faith are to be in the king's justice.

16. Sons of villeins ought not to be ordained without the assent of the lord on whose land they are known to have been born.

Now the record of the aforesaid royal customs and dignitaries was made by the said archbishops and bishops, and earls and barons, and the nobles and elders of the realm, at Clarendon, on the fourth day before the Purification of the Blessed Mary [29 January], ever Virgin, the lord Henry the king's son with his father the lord king being present there. There are, moreover, many other great customs and dignities of holy mother church and the lord king and the barons of the realm, which are not contained in this writing. And let them be safe for holy church and the lord king and his heirs and the barons of the realm, and be inviolably observed.

40. RICHARD FITZNEAL'S *DIALOGUE OF THE EXCHEQUER*

The Dialogue of the Exchequer *is a late-twelfth-century treatise on the practice of the English Exchequer written by Richard FitzNeal (c. 1130–98), the royal treasurer of King Henry II. Apparently written at the bequest of the king, the work is often described as the first administrative treatise of the Middle Ages. Certainly it constitutes a unique source of information on royal finances and the methods of collecting them in the twelfth century. The treatise is framed as a didactic conversation between a master and a disciple and ranges over the various offices and responsibilities of the royal treasury. The preface instructs the novice that it is not the function of the exchequer officials to decide on the merit of royal policy, but merely to execute it. In emphasizing that the office of the exchequer is the instrument of the king's will, the* Dialogue *may profitably be compared to the* Constitutions of Clarendon *(Doc. 39), as both documents are illustrative of the increasing bureaucratization of the English realm under Henry II.*

Source: trans. Ernest F. Henderson, in *Select Historical Documents of the Middle Ages* (London: G. Bell & Sons, 1907), 22–25, 35–38; revised. Latin.

First Book

In the twenty-third year of the reign of King Henry II, while I was sitting at the window of a tower next to the River Thames, a man spoke to me impetuously, saying: "master, have you not read that there is no use in a science or a treasure that is kept hidden?"

When I replied to him "I have read so," straightway he said: "why, then, do you not teach others the knowledge concerning the exchequer for which you are so well known and commit it to writing? Otherwise, it will die with you."

I answered: "My brother, you have now for a long time sat at the exchequer, and nothing is hidden from you, for you are painstakingly precise. And the same is probably the case with the others who have seats there."

But he said, "Just as those who walk in darkness and grope with their hands frequently stumble, so many sit there who seeing do not perceive, and hearing do not understand."

Then I replied, "You speak irreverently, for my knowledge is neither great nor does it concern important things, but perhaps those who are occupied with truly important matters have hearts like the claws of an eagle, which do not retain small things, but from which great ones do not escape."

Then he said, "So be it: but, although eagles fly very high, they still rest and refresh themselves in humble places, and, therefore, we beg you to explain humble things which will be of profit to the eagles themselves."

Then I said: "I have feared to put together a work concerning these things because they lie open to the bodily senses and grow common by daily use: there is not, nor can there be in them a description of subtle things or a pleasing invention of the imagination."

And he replied, "Those who rejoice in imaginings, who seek the flight of subtle things, have Aristotle and the books of Plato. Let them listen: your book is not to be theoretical but useful."

Then I said, "It is impossible to speak of those things which you demand except in common discourse and in ordinary words."

"But," he said, as if now angry, for to a mind so filled with desire nothing goes quickly enough, "writers on the liberal arts, to keep from seeming ignorant about many things and so that their work might be more difficult to understand, have compiled large volumes and have concealed them in obscure language, but you are not undertaking to write about an art, but about the customs and laws of the exchequer; and since these ought to be common, common words must necessarily be employed, so that the style may have relation to the things of which we are speaking. Moreover, although it is very often allowable to invent new words, I beg, nevertheless that you not be ashamed to use the common names of the things themselves which readily occur to the mind, so that no new difficulty from using unfamiliar words may arise to disturb us."

Then I replied, "I see that you are angry; but be calmer; I will undertake what you urge. Rise, therefore, and sit opposite to me; and ask me about those things that occur to you. But if you should bring up something unheard of, I will not blush to say, 'I do not know, but let us both consult wiser folk.' And although it may be a disgraceful and ridiculous thing for an old man, I will nevertheless begin with the most basic elements."

What the Exchequer is, and what is the reason of this name

Disciple: What is the exchequer?

Master: The exchequer is a quadrangular surface, about ten feet by five, placed before those who sit around it like a table, and all around it has a rim about the height of one's four fingers, so that anything placed on it won't fall off. There is placed over the top of the exchequer a cloth bought at the Easter term, not an ordinary one, but a black one marked with stripes, which are distant from each other the space of a foot or the breadth of a hand. In the spaces, moreover, are counters placed according to their values: about these we shall speak below. But, though such a surface is called the "exchequer," this name is transferred to the court itself which sits when the exchequer does; so that if, at any time through a decree any thing is established by common counsel, it is said to have been done at the "exchequer" of this or that year. As we say today "at the exchequer," they used to say "at the tallies."

Disciple: What is the reason of this name?

Master: No truer one occurs to me at present than that it has a shape similar to that of a chessboard.

Disciple: Would the prudence of the ancients ever have called it so for its shape alone, when it might for a similar reason be called a table [*tabularium*]?

Master: I was right in calling you painstaking! There is another, more hidden, reason: just as, in a game of chess, there are certain types of pieces, and they proceed or stand still by certain laws or limitations, some presiding and others advancing, in this, some preside, some assist by reason of their office, and no one is free to exceed his fixed laws, as will be clear from what is to follow. Moreover, as in chess, the battle is fought between kings, in this it is chiefly between two— the treasurer, and the sheriff who sits there to render account—that the conflict takes place and the war is waged. The others sit by as judges.

Disciple: Will the accounts be received then by the treasurer, although there are many there who, by reason of their power, are greater?

Master: That the treasurer ought to receive the account from the sheriff is mani- fest from this: that the same is required from him whenever it pleases the king, and that could not be required of him which he had not received. Some still say that the treasurer and the chamberlains should be accountable only for what is written in the rolls in the treasury, and that, for this, an account should be demanded of them. But it is better to think that they should be responsible for the whole writing of the roll, as will be readily understood from what is to follow.

As to the Chancellor

Master: The chancellor is first in order, and, as in the court, he is so important at the exchequer that without his consent and advice nothing great can be done. When he sits at the exchequer, his duty is as follows: he has custody of the king's seal which is in the treasury, but it does not leave there except when, by order of the Justice, it is brought by the treasurer or chamberlain from the lower to the upper exchequer, and then only for the purpose of carrying on the business of the exchequer. Once this is done, it is put in its box and the box is sealed by the chancellor and given to the treasurer to be guarded. Likewise, when it becomes necessary, it is handed (still sealed) to the chancellor before the eyes of all; it is never to be handed over, by him or by another, in any other way. Likewise, he holds custody, by his deputy, of the Chancellor's roll; and, as it has seemed appropriate to great men [barons], the chancellor is equally responsible with the treasurer for all the writing on the roll, except for what has been recorded as having been received "in the treasury," for although he may not prescribe how the treasurer writes, if the latter makes a mistake, it is allowed to him or to his clerk with modesty to reprimand the treasurer and suggest what he should do. But if the treasurer insists and is unwilling to change, being himself confident in what he has done, the chancellor can accuse him before the barons, who will then decide what ought to be done.

Disciple: It seems probable that the guardian of the third roll is bound by the same responsibility for the writing.

Master: It is not only probable but true! For its authority is equal to that of the other two rolls, since it was written with them, and the author himself [the king] agreed.

As to the Constable

Master: In the case of royal writs concerning the issue of treasure or concerning any accountings to be made, the Constable's duty is to be witness (together with the president) for those who make the account. For in all such Writs it is necessary, according to ancient custom, that two witnesses must be provided. It is also his duty, when the king's soldiers come to the exchequer for their pay (whether they reside in the castles of the king or not) to compute their payments, to take their oaths concerning overdue payments, and to cause what remains to be paid. To do this, he takes with him the clerk of the constabulary whose duty it is to know their terms of payment, and the marshal of the exchequer. For every payment of all persons, whether of hawkers, falconers, or bear-wardens, are his duty if he is present, unless the lord king has previously assigned someone else to this duty: for the constable can not easily be torn from the king, who often needs him for greater and more urgent business. It is to be noted that the marshal of the exchequer takes from the payments of native knights, but not from foreign ones, what belongs to him by virtue of his office. This the constable has in common with the Barons, that no great measure can be taken without consulting him.

As to the Chamberlains

Master: The office of the chamberlains is closely tied to the office of the treasurer, for they share together all honor and loss, and they have one will with regard to the king's honor: what has been done by one may not be declared invalid by any of them. The treasurer receives the accounts for all of them, and, according to the nature of the items, furnishes the wording for the writing of the roll. In all of these things they are bound equally together, and it is the same with regard to all other things which are done by him or by them (except for their fealty to the lord king), whether in the matter of writing, receipts, tallies, or expenses.

As to the Marshal

Master: It is the work of the marshal to put aside in his box the tallies of the debtors which the sheriff hands in (even though they are also put down on the roll) as well as the writs of the king concerning the computing, remitting, or giving of those things which are demanded of the sheriff through the summons. On that box is placed the name of the county to which these belong, and it is necessary that, for the separate counties, separate boxes should be supplied to the marshal by the sheriff.

Disciple: There is something here that troubles me.

Master: I knew this would happen. But wait a little. Everything will be plain from what follows. If any debtor, not giving satisfaction for the amount of his summons, has deserved to be arrested, he is handed over to the marshal, and when the exchequer of that day is finished, the marshal can, if he wishes, send him to the public jail. He shall not, however, be chained or thrust into the dungeon, but shall be apart by himself above the dungeon. For although he is not solvent, he has, nevertheless, not deserved to be put with the criminals, that is, unless he is a knight, for concerning knights held for debt there is a well-known decree of the king, which will be discussed below when we treat the sheriff. It is likewise the marshal's job, when the account of the sheriff, administrator, or whatever person sits to render account is finished, to take an oath from him in public to the effect that, upon his conscience, he has rendered a true account. But if the sheriff, or whoever has accounted, is bound by any debt, he shall add that he will not depart from the exchequer, that is, from the outskirts of the town in which it is, without permission of the barons, unless he is going to return on the same day. Likewise the marshal must receive the summons made out against the term fixed for the next exchequer, sealed with the royal seal, and must deliver them with his own hand to the usher of the upper exchequer to be carried throughout England.

There you have it. All the different offices of those who sit on the first bench.

41. LAW AND THE INVENTION OF CRIMINAL HOMICIDE

The following three texts illustrate fundamental social changes of the kind that would necessitate the rise of professional lawyers during the twelfth-century renaissance. From about 1000, signs started to multiply of a new vision of public order. Fundamentally, the idea of peace as the normal state of affairs started to gain ground at the expense of contrary assumptions that the warrior existence was the fullest expression of nobility and that the use of physical force, including the killing of human beings, was inseparable from the honorable conduct of noble leaders and their duty to protect the clan, or familia.

The first text, from c. 1041, illustrates the demands of the eleventh-century Peace Movement and highlights some of the chief concerns raised by those who supported the transition from a warlike and feuding society to a more pacific one. Questions of whether submission to peace had to be secured voluntarily and by oath, of how to distinguish justified from unjustified violence and homicide, private from public justice, and punishment from revenge immediately arose and found their first provisional answers in a culture that had just begun to ask them. The second text was written toward the end of the twelfth century (c. 1188–90) by an Italian church lawyer named Huguccio (d. 1210). It demonstrates the degree to which Western intellectuals had managed not only to answer these same questions, but also to systematize their responses into logically coherent statements. Huguccio's explanations progress in typically scholastic fashion by way of distinctions, which allow him to emphasize the will to kill as key to the proper assessments of liability, a truly universal standard obliging everyone alike. In addition, Huguccio hints at the difference and possible tensions between sin (known to God) and guilt (verifiable for him as a lawyer of the Church).

The final text shows how reflection on homicide and liability started to be channeled into separate disciplinary discourses, faculties, and institutions as well. Unlike Huguccio, who taught at a law school, Peter the Chanter (d. 1197) pioneered the teaching of moral theology at the cathedral school of Notre Dame in Paris. He sought to assess liability before God and not just guilt that could be verified in a judicial court, allowing him to apply far greater psychological subtlety to the subject in line with God's presumed insight into all sinners' hearts. Peter's text further allows us to look into the workshop of scholastic thinkers. His work was unfinished when he died in 1197. At the time, he was still busy with casuistry, assembling concrete examples (casus) of homicide and hoping to distill from them abstract distinctions (like Huguccio's) later on.

a. Peace and Truce of God

Source: trans. Wolfgang Mueller, from *Studien zur Rechtsgeschichte der Gottesfrieden und Landfrieden* I: *Die Friedensordnungen in Frankreich,* ed. L. Huberti (Ansbach: C. Brügel & Sohn, 1892), 272–74. Latin.

1. In the name of the almighty Father, Son, and Holy Spirit, Reginbald, archbishop of Arles, along with the Bishops Benedict of Avignon and Nitard of Nice, and the venerable Abbot Lord Odilo and all of the other bishops and abbots, and all of the clergy residing in Gaul, to the clergy residing all over Italy. Grace to you and peace from the almighty lord Father, who is, who was, and who will come. . . .

3. Receive, then, and hold the peace and this truce of God. Which we, too, inspired by divine pity, have already accepted as it was sent to us from heaven. Which we firmly hold thus constituted and imposed, that is, that from the evening hours of Wednesday, among all Christians, friends and enemies, neighbors and strangers, there be firm peace and stable truce until sunrise on Monday. To the effect that, on those four days and nights, they all will be safe at any hour and do whatever may be necessary, free of any fear of their enemies, and reassured by the tranquility of the peace and of this truce. . . .

5. Those, however, who have promised to keep the truce and want to break it knowingly be excommunicated by the lord the almighty Father and his son Jesus

Christ and the Holy Spirit, and by all of the saints of God. They be excommunicated, cursed and detested, here and forever after, and be damned like Dathan and Abiron, and like Judas, who betrayed the Lord, and be drowned in the depths of hell like Pharaoh in the middle of the sea, unless they come to make amends as is constituted.

6. Namely, if someone commits homicide during those days of the truce, he shall be exiled and ejected from his own home and shall suffer to go to Jerusalem with long exile on his way there. But if he breaks the aforesaid truce of God and the peace in any other way, he shall be forced to be examined by the decrees of secular law and pay according to his measure of guilt. And by the rules of the holy canons he will be judged to do double penance. . . .

8. Should it occur to someone to take revenge on those who have dared to break this charter and truce of God, the avengers shall not be liable to any guilt, but may leave and return as servants of the cause of God, blessed by all Christians. If, however, something is taken on the remaining days, and is found on the days of the truce, nobody is bound by it, lest an opportunity be given to the enemy. . . .

9. May the Lord free you of all sins in this life, and after this life, he who lives and rules with God the Father and the Holy Spirit as God for all eternity may lead you to the kingdom of Heaven. Amen.

b. Huguccio, *Summa* on Gratian's *Decretum*

Source: trans. Wolfgang Mueller, *Summa Decretorum*, D.50 d.p.c.36 s.v. *Casu quoque* (Munich, Bayerische Staatsbibliothek lat. 10247, fol. 55ra); text 2: ibid. c.39 s.v. *voluntate* (fol. 55rb). Latin

1. Homicide is committed either by word of mouth or in fact. By word of mouth is to say due to an order or through advice. . . . In fact means either willfully, out of necessity, or by accident.

If willfully. . . , it is indifferent in this case whether a Jew, a pagan, or a Christian is killed. . . .

If out of necessity, that is, in defense of one's body or belongings, he either could evade otherwise or he could not; if he could, he is completely liable . . . if he could not [evade] otherwise, he is still guilty and sins mortally because he should have endured death rather than inferred it . . . and this holds true in general for clerics as well as laypersons provided the killed person was not an enemy, because neither clerics nor laypersons are permitted to kill in defense someone who is not an enemy . . . if he is an enemy, however, a cleric is not permitted to kill him as has been said, but if a layperson kills an enemy to defend himself or his belongings he is immune from punishment and guilt according to Roman and canon law.

If by accident, either by previous or intervening guilt, or not.

If by previous or intervening guilt, it is imputed [in terms of liability].

If not, it is not. Or you may distinguish in another way which amounts to the same: he who commits homicide by accident is involved either in an illicit or a licit activity; if it is illicit, it is imputed to him whether he applies all diligence or not; if it is licit or if he applies the necessary diligence, it will not be imputed to him by any means.

2. *Willfully* and directed toward homicide. Because if someone hits someone else and does not want to kill him and he dies nevertheless, the hitter is not a homicide in God's judgment, although he is one in the eyes of his Church who does not know about the inner will; but if she [the Church] knew, she would impose a reduced punishment or would not consider the homicide a punishable one. . . .

And the act, while being a mortal sin cannot be called a homicide in the proper sense but rather [constitutes] a human casualty. Because homicide in the proper sense refers to the act of killing [a human being] willfully.

c. Peter the Chanter, *On Cases of Conscience*

Source: trans. Wolfgang Mueller, from Pierre le Chantre, *Summa de sacramentis et animae consi-liis: Liber casuum conscientiae*, ed. Jean-Albert Dugauquier, Analecta Mediaevalia Namurcensia 21 (Louvain and Lille, 1967), III.2, paragraph 369 (rubric: *That the Atrocity of Homicide Committed by One's Own Hand Aggravates the Sin*), 558–62, lines 14–25, 56–73. Latin.

Suppose, for example, that two tyrants inspired by the same contempt send two innocent people into a lions' cage and one is killed by the lions, the other is not. We believe that those tyrants are alike presuming that all other circumstances are alike. But suppose that they order their officials to kill two; the officials of one spare [them]; the officials of the other kill. Are [the tyrants] equally bad? It does not seem so because one is a homicide only in intent, the other in intent and by his act. But we say that the proposition "He is a homicide by act," which means: he adds the act to his ill intent, does not apply here; or: this intent is turned into effect but by someone else, and then it does apply here and we consider them to be equally bad.

Also suppose that one tyrant orders someone to kill an innocent person and he instantly kills; another (tyrant) orders someone else the same three or four times and he finally kills. Who of them sins more gravely? And likewise, one tyrant kills with one strike, another by several, so who of them sins more gravely?

In the first case we say that they sin equally if he who repeats the command does so continuously and as if it was one command so that there is only one empowerment. If there are several commands he perhaps sins more gravely, because in his first command he already sins as much as the other [tyrant].

With the second [command] he sins again so that the sin is increased. But does he sin more with the first or with the second command? That is for someone else to decide.

In the second case we say that if it is not up to the one who kills with several strikes to kill with the first if he could, then he kills as much as the other; or rather more because he sins with the first strike as much as the other and aggravates the sin with the subsequent strikes. If it is however in his might and his heart softened with the first strike so that he thought of sparing in that strike, he does not sin as much as the other. But whether he sins as much as the other in the homicide overall is doubtful.

42. ROGERIUS, *QUESTIONS ON THE INSTITUTES* OF JUSTINIAN

Rogerius was among the leading teachers of Roman law at the University of Bologna in the second half of the twelfth century. The renaissance in legal studies began sometime in the early decades of the twelfth century with the recovery and intense study of Justinian's sixth-century Corpus Juris Civilis, *which in addition to the* Codex *also included the* Digest, *an encyclopedia composed of brief extracts from the writings of Roman jurists, and the* Institutes, *a student textbook that introduced the* Codex *and provided important conceptual elements for discussing law. Earlier masters at Bologna such as Irnerius initiated a standard method of glossing or adding interlineal explanations to the texts, a practice that had parallels in the schools of theology in northern France, and especially at Laon. Rogerius's* Questions on the Institutes *differs in a number of respects from earlier and contemporary glossators. His use of certain words and metaphors reflect an affected elegance that he probably thought sounded Ciceronian, but which was a feature of neither classical nor contemporary authors.*

Source: trans. Donald T. Jacques, from Rogerius, "Questions on the Institutes," in *Medieval Europe*, ed. Julius Kirshner and Karl F. Morrison, Readings in Western Civilization, vol. 4 (Chicago: Chicago University Press, 1986), 215–16. Latin.

Justice and Law

These institutes are laws which Justinian urged us to receive and make the object of enthusiastic study. Because of the instruction they give to men in the conduct of their lives, these laws are meant to be read in advance of others which have been written down; and for this reason, they claim as peculiarly their own, by virtue of a certain pre-eminence, the title common to all such writings [*Institutes* or *Principles of Instruction*], especially since they spring from the fountainhead of justice and law. Because they do so, we should, in this introduction entitled "Justice and Law," look first of all at some of their universal qualities, fulfilling the expectations raised by our chapter heading, in order to get to know as best we can what law and justice are, and what they effect, by defining them on the one hand, and considering their precepts on the other. "Now justice is a constant and perpetual will allotting each person his right."

Rogerius: Please explain why the word "will" is used in that definition of justice, and the other terms as well. Do you mean to say that justice is the will?

Jurisprudence: No, justice is not the will; but in setting out to define justice for men, Justinian first uses the word "will" because men observe justice by, above all else, an exercise of the will. Furthermore, because justice is limitless in capacity and able to give each his right, that which men have in rather greater supply, namely, will, is central to the concept of justice. Because of their similar extent, and because will is the means by which justice is observed, just is thus rightly called "will." And indeed, those two words "constant" and "perpetual" are added in praise of justice. In fact, they can even constitute a defining quality of justice, for justice used to be considered variable and inconstant in legal cases, since in one case it shields and defends through its protection, while in another—even at the same time—it rebuffs and condemns the same man. As a result, it was judged guilty of deceit and fickleness, subject to chance at different times, and was said not to be "perpetual" but variable (at one moment it gives, at the next it takes away). But this diversity (if there is any) is a function not of justice but of human affairs; and that changeableness, a function of circumstances. Indeed by these very examples justice is rather shown to be constant and perpetual: for it is on your side when you pursue a just cause; against you, when you pursue an unjust cause; and it awards you something if you live righteously, and takes it away after you go astray. If this were not the case, then justice would be termed, with greater truth, lying or fickle. And so, to remove such suspicions and to honor justice itself—or even for the sake of a clear definition—justice is said to be "constant and perpetual." That which follows, namely, "allotting each man his right," is also included for the sake of the definition which distinguishes justice from the other virtues on the strength of its unlimited capacity.

Rogerius: Is the above-mentioned definition of justice that of its essence?

Jurisprudence: Yes.

Rogerius: Specify, then, what in the definition are general characteristics, and what the particular.

Jurisprudence: This whole phrase, "a constant and perpetual will" is put there for the general class, which is virtue. In fact, because virtue is a "quality of heart or of a well-ordered mind," that is what "a constant and perpetual will" means in

FOUR: ESTABLISHING A NEW ORDER: GOVERNMENT AND LAW

this definition. And the phrase "allotting to each man his right" is added to serve as a particular characteristic which distinguishes justice from the other virtues. Once these points are understood, that question as to why one's right, which is not justice, nonetheless is used in defining it becomes rather silly.

Rogerius: Since justice is a virtue "allotting each man his right," no one can be called just, because no one can allot each his right.

Jurisprudence: Even though no one has the power to render each his right in the actual fact, in intention of will and mind—of which, as we said, justice consists—this is possible for just about anyone you please. Hence, that man is correctly called just who is of such intent and purpose that, if he could, he would allot every man his right; for this man bestows upon each his right even if not in deed, yet at least in mind, which is the greater seat of all the virtues. With this in view, the legislator used the word "will" for the general term in his description of justice; and through this definition just as one comes to know what justice is, so, too, he comes to know who is just. No doubt, in the same way that justice is "a constant and perpetual will," that is, virtue "allotting each his right," so is that man just who has such a will, even if he does not bring it to fruition. Next we must ask, What is jurisprudence? Now, that is "the knowledge of things divine and human, the science of the just and the unjust."

Rogerius: I do not see why jurisprudence is described here.

Jurisprudence: The reason is this: just as justice has to do with law, from which it derives its name, so too does jurisprudence, although in a different way. For justice is related to the law as its source and origin, since law comes to be through it.

43. IVO OF CHARTRES'S PROLOGUE TO HIS CANONICAL COLLECTION

Educated at Bec under Lanfranc, Ivo of Chartres (c. 1040–1115) was one of the most renowned and influential legal scholars of the late eleventh and early twelfth centuries. Before becoming bishop of Chartres in 1090, he was master of the cathedral school at Beauvais. His writings show a concern with the concordance of legal theory and practice that is not often found among his reform-minded contemporaries. Ivo is credited with compiling or greatly assisting in the compilation of three canonical collections: the Excerpta ex Decretis Romanorum Pontificum, *the* Decretum, *and the* Panormia. *The following text is excerpted from a prologue that precedes the latter two texts. It has often been called the first extended treatise on ecclesiastical legal practice. Its primary concerns are the apparent contradictions often found between canons, and the mutable or immutable nature of certain precepts. On the whole, the prologue seems intended to cultivate the manner in which prospective readers of the collection would use the text, tempering strict justice with merciful charity when appropriate.*

Source: trans. Robert Somerville and Bruce C. Brasington, eds. and trans., *Prefaces to Canon Law Books in Latin Christianity: Selected Translations, 500–1245* (New Haven, CT: Yale University Press, 1998), 133–38. Latin.

Here begins the Prologue of the lord bishop, Ivo of Chartres, concerning the excerpts of the ecclesiastical canons.

Excerpts of ecclesiastical rules, partly drawn from the letters of Roman pontiffs, partly from the deeds of the councils of catholic bishops, partly from the treatises of the orthodox Fathers, partly from the institutes of catholic Kings: these I have gathered into one body—and not without labor—so that anyone who might not be able to have at hand the works from which these have been drawn may simply take here what he judges advantageous for his case. Thus, from the foundation of the Christian religion, that is, beginning with faith, we have assembled, arranged under general titles, what pertains to the ecclesiastical sacraments, to the institution or correction of morals, to the investigation and resolution of every matter, so that it should not be necessary for the investigator to turn through the whole volume, but simply to note the general title appropriate to his question, and then to run through the canons under it without pause. In this we have been led to caution the prudent reader that if perhaps he would read some things that he may not fully understand, or judge them to be contradictory, he should not immediately take offense but instead should diligently consider what pertains to rigor, to moderation, to judgment, or to mercy. For he did not perceive these things to disagree among themselves who said, "Mercy and judgment I will sing to you, O Lord," [Psalm 101:1] and elsewhere, "All the pathways of the Lord are mercy and truth" [Psalm 25:10].

Concerning the intention of the divine page

Indeed all ecclesiastical discipline chiefly has this intent: either to tear down every structure that raises itself up against the knowledge of Christ, or to build up the enduring house of God in truth of faith and honesty of character, or if that house of God be defiled, to cleanse it with the remedies of penance. The mistress of this house is charity, which sees to the welfare of our neighbors commanding that it be done for others what one wishes to be done for himself [Matthew 7:12].

That charity should be the mistress of every good thing

Every ecclesiastical doctor should thus interpret or moderate ecclesiastical rules so that he may refer to the kingdom of charity those matters that he teaches; nor does he err or sin here, because, concerned for the welfare of his neighbors, he endeavors to achieve the required goal in the holy institutes. Whence the blessed

Augustine says when considering ecclesiastical discipline: "Have charity and do whatever you will. If you correct, correct with charity. If you pardon, pardon with charity." But in these matters the highest diligence must be exercised and the eye of the heart must be cleansed as well, for sincere charity should aid the ills to be cured by punishing or pardoning. And no one should seek there something for himself, as is the case with venal doctors, lest he incur that reproach of the prophet, "Souls are perishing that were not dying, and souls are restored to life that were not alive" [Ezekiel 13:19].

The purpose of bodily medicine is either to drive out diseases or to cure wounds in order to preserve health, or to strive to improve it. Nor does it appear wrong that a doctor sometimes applies harsh medicines to a patient and sometimes gentle medicines, according to the quality or degree of the patient's sickness. Sometimes he cuts with the knife that which cannot be healed with a poultice. Sometimes, conversely, he heals with a poultice what he dared not cut with the blade. Thus spiritual physicians, namely doctors of the holy church, contradict neither themselves nor each other when they prohibit illicit things, order necessary things, exhort the highest things, permit milder things—when they impose severe laws of penance according to the hardness of heart of the delinquent for their correction or for the restraint of the rest, or when they lift these restrictions and apply the salves of indulgence according to the devotion of those repenting and desiring to change, having considered the frailty of the vessel they bear. For those who are lenient look to the removal of greater ills, those who prohibit illicit things deter from death, those who command necessary things wish to preserve health, and those who exhort the highest things strive to increase health. Considering these matters the diligent reader will understand, when he clearly determines the meaning of admonition, precept, prohibition, and remission, that there is only one form of holy eloquence, and that these categories do not oppose or stand apart from one another, but that they dispense the remedy of health to all, for their direction.

But now we must further distinguish the weight these individual things have or to whom they are appropriate, and which are remissible, which irremissible, and when or concerning which cases they may be remitted.

Concerning admonition

And the first—admonition—does not bring punishment to someone who did not pursue it, but instead promises a reward to those acquiring it. And the Lord says in the Gospel, "If you wish to be perfect, go sell all you possess and give it to the poor, and you will have treasure in heaven" [Matthew 19:21]. Behold this Gospel lesson, placing perfection in the will of man, neither compels nor intends threats, just as that lesson does not which, praising eunuchs who have castrated themselves on account of the kingdom of heaven, adds, "Whoever is able to understand, let him understand" [Matthew 19:12]. Yet, when someone binds himself by a vow to its fulfillment, or to a rank which no one without the virtue of continence is able to reach, it then becomes necessary and worthy of penalty if what was voluntary before this ascent is not maintained. Whence the Lord says, "No one who looks back after placing his hand on the plow is worthy of the kingdom of God" [Luke 9:62]. What had been able before this ascent to be inferior but not wrong is now, afterward, both inferior and wrong. So much for admonition.

Concerning indulgence

But it seems to us that indulgence, because it does not choose the better things, certainly offers a remedy not a reward, though if anyone should fall from this he should merit fatal judgment. For example, we know, just as we have learned from the Apostle [Paul], that in order to avoid fornication marriage is granted to the human race [1 Corinthians 7:2], and that someone who violates it should merit eternal punishment, as the same Apostle testifies. Indeed, he says, "God will judge fornicators and adulterers" [Hebrews 13:4]. As we have said concerning admonition, this status compels no one except him who has earlier bound himself to it. It is voluntary, not necessary. Otherwise anyone who had not taken a wife would be a transgressor. But after he has bound himself in marriage he would listen to the Apostle who says, "Are you bound to a wife? Do not seek divorce" [1 Corinthians 7:27]. When speaking about marriage, the same Apostle also did not say that a woman should deserve reward if she marries, but rather said that she would not sin if she did [1 Corinthians 7:28]. Again, if anyone should invite another to daily fasting, he urges something worthy to be gained and persisted in. Yet, whoever would not gain it would not become inferior, for although remaining inferior to one doing it, he would not become worse in himself. But he who falls from a vow becomes inferior and worse. If anyone should restrain himself under a regimen of sobriety and frugal diet, he is not seeking the rewards of the highest things; but if he should fall thence into gluttony and drunkenness, it is shown that he has done something worthy of reprehension and rebuke.

Thus there are two conditions, one superior, the other inferior, which before a vow are both voluntary, but afterward are binding and have their modes and teachings which, when observed, as already mentioned, gain a remedy for some and reward for others, but when they are not observed merit instead eternal punishment. These things ought to be pondered before a vow is undertaken, but after a vow is made must be carried out. Having considered these things, we must now discuss other matters concerning precept and prohibition.

Concerning precept and prohibition

Precepts and prohibitions: some are mutable, some immutable. Immutable precepts are those which eternal law sanctions and which, when observed, confer salvation, but remove it when not observed. These kind are: "You will love the Lord your God with all your heart and your neighbor as yourself," and "honor your father and mother," and others like them. Mutable precepts, however, are those which eternal law does not sanction, but which the diligence of tradition has discovered by reason of utility, not principally for the acquisition of salvation but rather for guarding it more securely. An example of this comes from the words of the Apostle: "Shun the person who is a heretic after the first and second warning" [Titus 3:10], not because conversation with him would by itself prevent salvation, but instead because frequency of contact might indirectly corrupt the simplicity of some. And you will find many examples of this sort in the canonical teachings. Similarly, immutable prohibitions are those which speak out against vices, such as "You shall not kill, you shall not lust, etc" [Exodus 20:13–14]. These are those minor precepts about which the Lord says, "Whosoever breaks these and teaches the same will be the least in the kingdom of heaven" [Matthew 5:19]. But whoever observes them will not immediately be worthy of the kingdom of God, since these are only basic precepts, not advanced ones.

Other things are interdicted in which neither would death be at work nor salvation endangered had they not been forbidden. But the sacred authority of the holy Fathers decreed them for this purpose, not that sincere charity should oppose things which are present, but rather it should provide for the restraint or avoidance of greater evils.

44. THE DECRETISTS: COMMENTATORS ON GRATIAN'S *DECRETUM*

Around 1140, an obscure teacher of law in Bologna known simply as Master Gratian compiled a collection of canon law known as the Concordance of Discordant Canons, *which became more commonly known as the* Decretum. *It was not the first such legal compendium, but its range far exceeded that of any previous compilation, and during the remainder of the twelfth century it gradually came to replace its predecessors. By the early thirteenth century it was virtually ubiquitous in the classrooms of the West. A second and expanded recension of the work, possibly by someone other than Gratian, seems to have been compiled around 1150. The* Decretum's *distinctions (*distinctiones*) and cases (*causae*) examined a vast array of subjects and furnished readers with a detailed review of canonical traditions. The first part of the work presented 101 distinctions with categories ranging from the sources of law to the nature of church–state relations. The*

second part of the collection contained short statements of hypothetical cases (causae).
These allowed for analysis of individual topics through a series of questions addressing
specific legal situations. In its methodological approach to resolving contradictions and
its search for systematic completeness, Gratian's Decretum *bears a strong intellectual*
resemblance to both Peter Lombard's Sentences *(Doc. 10) and Abelard's* Sic et Non
(Doc. 18).

Students of Gratian's Decretum, *known as the Decretists, extended, modified, and*
questioned Gratian as well as one another. Scattered glosses on selected texts soon became
layers of sustained analysis and commentaries, and schools of interpretation identified with
particular masters and their disciples arose. Over time, these commentaries were detached
from the margins of the Decretum *and circulated as self-standing, organized treatises*
(summae) that did far more than merely offer a summary of the original collection. The
prologues to these commentaries, one of which (from c. 1150) is given below, offer insight
into the legal mind of the twelfth century and constitute a central element of the wider
renaissance in learning that blended the ancient with the new.

Source: trans. Robert Somerville and Bruce C. Brasington, eds. and trans., *Prefaces to Canon Law Books in Latin Christianity: Selected Translations, 500–1245* (New Haven, CT: Yale University Press, 1998), 185–89. Latin.

[Preface to the Stroma *of Rolandus on Gratian's* Decretum*]*

Here begins the extraordinary and very beautiful *Stroma* of Rolandus, culled from the corpus of decrees.

The merciful Father, desiring to satisfy the tripartite genus of humans with the fourfold genus of nourishment on the table of presentation, arranged, by means of the service of Moses, to make square a ternary. For he instructed Moses, saying:

> You will make a table from acacia wood, of two cubits in length, one in width, and one and a half in height, covered with purest gold. And you will make for it four legs, and also four gold rings attached to the legs; and you will make two poles from acacia wood covered with purest gold, which will always be in the rings at the top of the table. You will make also a gold lip around it, and a polished gold crown of four fingers' height; and you will make a small gold cap which you will place on the crown. You will also place the twelve loaves of presentation, of finest wheat flour, on the table, with twelve gold covers over them, upon which the purest frankincense will be placed. These loaves will be on the table from Sabbath to Sabbath, and none may be removed unless another is freshly added [Exodus 25: 23–30].

This table signifies sacred scripture, which is well called a table, for just as a physical table holds bodily refreshment, a spiritual table serves spiritual nourishment. Likewise it is said to be made of acacia wood, because it is constructed out of the strong sayings and actions of the holy Fathers. And not undeservedly it is called gilded, that is, adorned with the wisdom of heaven. The length of two cubits signifies perseverance of action, which is appropriately designated in two cubits, because it is chiefly based in two virtues, namely, innocence and purity. This table is also one cubit in length, because sacred scripture teaches perfection in charity, and one and a half cubits in height, because it introduces the unity of the hope of heaven toward which it indoctrinates us, that is, the less perfect "halves." Further, it has a gold lip around it, because the teaching of the sacred word is furnished through the pure mouths of preachers.

Through the crown, which is appropriately enjoined to be made four fingers high, since one comes to it by the teaching of the four evangelists and by the good work of the four principal virtues, the merit of eternal reward is indicated; and in [this] quaternary we understand faith in the Trinity, with purity of works, through which we trust we are going to gain the prize of eternal reward at last. This crown is worthily said to be polished, because there will be a variety of rewards for the merits of diverse individuals, whence the Lord in the Gospel says: "In my father's house there are many mansions" [John 14:2]. Through the gold cap placed on top of the polished crown is understood the special quality of those who, it is not doubted, excel among others. Paul recognized this when he said: "It is better for me to die than that anyone should deprive me of my glory" [1 Corinthians 9:15]. To this cap pertains that song which virgins alone can sing [Revelation 14:1–5].

Through the four legs the four senses of divine scripture are understood, namely, the historical, the allegorical, the moral, and the anagogical. By these four legs the table is supported, because by the above-mentioned four modes divine scripture is expounded. Through the four rings the books of the Gospels are signified. A ring lacks beginning and end, and for this reason the books of the Gospels are signified by the term rings, because they concern principally that which utterly lacks beginning and end. Through the two poles, we understand those preaching about two peoples. They [the poles] are appropriately covered with purest gold, because they [the preachers] are adorned with the splendor of wisdom in both word and in deed. They ought always to be inserted into the rings, for it is necessary that their mind adhere closely to the lesson of the Scriptures, so that according to blessed Peter they may be always ready to render an account concerning the faith and hope which is in them [1 Peter 3:15].

The twelve loaves designate the apostles and "apostolic men," [bishops and/or popes] who are rightly said to abide at the table, that is, in the contemplation and teaching of the scriptures; [it is said] "from Sabbath to Sabbath," because from the Sabbath of hope, which happens now, until the Sabbath of splendor, which is hoped for in eternal life. No one is taken up, that is, removed, by judgment or by death unless another is immediately set in his place. Gold covers are placed on these loaves. In the gold covers are signified the hearts of preachers, lifted up through charity, in which the purest frankincense, that is, prayers, ought always to be contained. Indeed, with the word frankincense prayer is understood according to that verse: "Let my prayer be directed, etc." [Psalm 141:2].

In this table, therefore, a ternary is clearly made square by sacred scripture, that is, the faith of the holy Trinity is taught and fixed by the books of the four Gospels. Alternatively the ternary of the law, the prophets, and the psalms is made square, that is, it is expounded in four modes, namely, historically, allegorically, morally, and anagogically. Or again, through the ternary three types of people are understood: the righteous, the ordinary, and the evil, and through the quaternary we understand four ways of speaking of divine law. For all law consists in precepts, prohibitions, permissions, and counsels, and in face the ternary, that is, the triple genus of people, is made square, that is, fully instructed, by the quaternary of counsel, permission, prohibition and precept. Counsel is for the righteous, permission for the weak, and precepts and prohibitions for all, for there are precepts of things to be done, prohibitions of things to be avoided, permissions of things to be tolerated, counsels of nonobligatory or most excellent things. For this reason some, considering this fourfold character [of law], wondering especially at its dissonance and hindered by the weakness of their perceptions, believed that the statutes of the holy Fathers very often are mutually contradictory. For since certain things sometimes are tolerated which at other times are utterly prohibited, and other things are advised which are never commanded, they seem to have rational excuses for their doubt.

Master Gratian, therefore, considering the doubts of these men and desiring to advise those present and future, composed this work. In introducing it, the title, the reason for writing, for whom he wrote, the subject matter, the intention, [and] the method of composition are sought. This work received its title from the compiler, not because he was the author of the decrees, but because he collected them from diverse places into one location. The reason for writing was to demonstrate the concord of the canons, to reduce their difference to concord. We believe he wrote it, as if providing for the whole world, for all who wish to apply themselves to the reading of the sacred canons. The subject matter consists of the things which it treats. Since, therefore, a concord of canons treats the business of churches by settling questions, by establishing concord in the canons, by reducing dissonance among them to harmony, these same things comprise its subject matter. The method of composition is this. He begins with a twofold law, namely, of nature and of customs, showing what the law of nature is and in what things it is contained. He continues with the similarity and difference

of the same, adds the definition and the cause of legislation, [and] provides cat-
egorization and etymologies of terms. After this he treats the canons by setting
out their differences, and so that this can be clarified in a better way, he treats
councils. The remainder the prudent and solicitous reader should endeavor to
discover for himself.

45. PETER OF BLOIS: A QUESTION CONCERNING MARRIAGE LAW

*In the following letter, Peter of Blois (c. 1130–c. 1203) addresses several legal questions
pertaining to marriage that were raised during a scholastic debate in Paris. The first
question is whether a woman who has entered a convent after believing in good faith that
her husband had died while abroad is able to leave that convent and return to married
life if he suddenly returns. The second question, an extension of the first, is whether it
is licit for her to re-engage in conjugal relations after having taken vows of celibacy. In
formulating his answers, Peter makes recourse to the main canonical collection of the
twelfth century (Master Gratian's* Decretum; *see Doc. 44), while also employing the
so-called scholastic method of gathering and then comparing authorities to illustrate a
point of canon law.*

Source: trans. John D. Cotts, from *Petri Blesensis Opera Omnia,* in J.-P. Migne, ed., *Patrologia Latina*
(Paris: Imprimerie Royale, 1855), vol. 207, col. 69–71. Latin.

A Question Concerning Marriage Law

(from Letter 19)

Peter of Blois, archdeacon of Bath, sends greeting, and whatever might be better,
to R., his dear friend and companion.

Recently in a debate at the schools, certain questions arose, and they have
thrown your mind into doubt, or so you tell me. You now put them to me, and
plead with me for their answer. While you are in the schools, however, I am out
here working. And since you have now spent two years engaged with laws and
decretals, I suspect that you are doing this to test me, that you might slyly catch
me in all my naivety. I should tell you what that wise woman is said to have
responded to Joab when he sought the head of Seba: "A saying was used in the
old proverb: They that inquire, let them inquire in Abela" [2 Samuel 20:18].
Well, I say: "They that inquire, let them inquire at Paris, where the most intricate
knots of the most difficult questions are untied!" There you will more easily find
the answer to the questions you are putting forward. But I will not begrudge you
what I know. Would that God will make *the free offerings of my mouth acceptable*

[Psalm 108:118] to you, so that the questions you put forward can be answered, if not quite well enough with regard to reason, at least well enough for a man. For my part, I think that it will suffice if I support the answer I am giving you with the authority of so much as a single law or canon.

You ask about a woman who, based on the credible report of good men, thought that her husband had died after he went abroad. If he unexpectedly returns, can she leave the convent on her own authority and return to him if he does not demand her back? You also ask if, after she declared her intention to remain chaste, she should be returned to her husband, and if she was and he later died, if she should then be obliged to observe her vow (given that the reason for the vow's suspension was gone).

To the first question, I respond that the vow of continence is not binding, since she made it without the consent of her husband and without regard to his authority. This is manifestly clear from the Eighth Synod, from the synod of Pope Eugenius, from the letter of Gregory the Great to Urbicus, from the letter of Pope Nicholas, and from various statements of Saint Augustine. Saint Jerome emphatically affirmed the same thing in his commentary on the epistle to Titus. Ambrose, in his *Book of Questions on the New and Old Testament*, discounts the woman's vow unless the husband consented to it and he vowed in like manner. Augustine, moreover, plainly says the same thing when he considers his questions on Numbers. But though it might seem from the council held at Compiègne that, unless the man had recalled her, she could not leave, you should understand that she could not do this unless the man wished to take a vow of continence himself. Otherwise, if the husband refused to be converted or despised to take his wife back, he ought to be compelled by the church either into taking her back or to binding himself with the bond of chastity, as Augustine suggested when commenting on Psalm 149.

Now you could object that it was in her power to renounce sex, and that she could thus bind herself, but to this I respond: The Apostle Paul says that "the wife hath not power of her own body, but the husband" [1 Corinthians 7:4], and vice versa, so she cannot impose the law of chastity on her body without the leave of her husband—it was not in fact in her power. You will find this in the letter of Pope Alexander II to Landulph. What is more, since she was led by error into taking a vow of chastity, that vow (to which, I can say truly, she did not consent), does not seem to be binding. According to civil law, there is nothing that gets in the way of consent than an error that exposes ignorance. Therefore, if she wants to be a mother, let her leave the convent in the name of God, and, let her seek out the conjugal embrace of her husband if he refuses to take a vow of chastity or if he refuses to call her back. But if the husband later dies, she will be freed from the control of her husband, and she can marry whom she will in God. Nor can she be compelled to observe the vow which from the beginning did not bind her. By way of comparison, take the example [found in Gratian's *Decretum*] of a slave that a lord takes out from a monastery. If the slave later gets his freedom, he cannot be compelled to pursue the harsher [monastic] way of life, though there is nothing to stop him from doing so.

I offer you these responses to your query, just as *God* in his *sweetness has provided for the poor* [Psalm 68:11]. If anything more compelling should be given to you from on high, do not keep it from me. For I am prepared to learn from my student just as from a teacher, since it would be quite shameful for me not to accept the gift of learning from a novice as I would from an expert.

46. ROMAN LAW AND LEGAL STUDY IN ITALY

The texts included here attest to the rise of legal studies in medieval Bologna. The first, a letter written in 1124/27 by a Provençal monk to his abbot requesting permission to study law at Pisa, reveals the reputation that Italian legal studies had already achieved in the early twelfth century, and the combination of intellectual and practical interests that brought students to Italy for the study of law. The second document is an imperial decree issued in 1155/58 by the German emperor Frederick I Barbarossa (1123–90) granting protection to students, in particular those studying law. The emperor's legal advisors were themselves from Bologna and sought to establish Roman law as the appropriate mechanism for imposing imperial rule over the independent-minded civic communes of twelfth-century northern Italy. As Sean Gilsdorf points out, Frederick's decree was thus simultaneously a reward to his advisors, a mark of political patronage, and a calculated act of imperial munificence meant both to echo the deeds of the emperor Justinian (r. 527–565) and to be incorporated within the corpus of Roman law itself.

Source: trans. Sean Gilsdorf, in *Medieval Italy: Texts in Translation*, ed. Katherine L. Jansen, Joanna Drell, and Frances Andrews (Philadelphia: University of Pennsylvania Press, 2009), 168–69. Latin.

a. Letter to Abbot Bernard III of St-Victor, Marseille

. . . I began a voyage to Rome; proceeded companionless and in utter poverty to Pavia; and set out for Rome in that company of strangers. But since the divine will did not wish me to complete the voyage that I had begun, the animal in whose cart I planned to reach Rome first became ill on the way, before dying on the spot. I, thus, was unable to proceed any further, but I was deeply embarrassed to return immediately with my task still incomplete. At first I hesitated about what to do, before deciding to devote myself to literary studies, and since by God's grace I had been delayed for a time in that place, I remained there for the purpose of training my mind. This, then, most beloved lord, is the reason why I, after realizing that my heart's deepest desire had come to pass, did not hurry back to you. Instead, I determined to study even more, so that I might be able to serve you better in the future, as long as I live.

Now, when I constantly see scholars in Italy, particularly ones from Provence (some of whom are monks like myself), many of them flocking to the study of the laws, and I think about our monastery continually assaulted by the lawsuits of clerics and laymen alike, and enduring the loss of its justly held possessions, I wish to have at least some knowledge of this kind. For if, by God's grace, I could become adept in such matters, I would not pursue worldly cases, but would only advance the just interests of our monastery to the best of my ability. If it should please your honor, most exalted Father, that I might dedicate myself to the study of this subject, I ask and beseech you as a supplicant to grant me your gracious permission to do so, and to send written instructions to the prior at Pisa to offer me his assistance. If I obtain what I desire from your mercy, I will proceed to Pisa to begin my studies, God willing. In the meantime, I will wait until the feast of Saint Michael [29 September] for your consolation's instructions.

Farewell.

b. Frederick I Barbarossa's Imperial Decree: *Habita*

After carefully considering this matter together with the bishops, abbots, dukes, and all the judges and magnates of our sacred palace, we bestow this pious gift upon all those who travel for the purpose of study, students and especially teachers of divine and sacred laws: namely, that they as well as their messengers may travel safely to the place where they are engaged in the study of letters and safely dwell there. Since those who do good deserve our praise and protection, we consider it appropriate that we, with particular affection, defend from every injury all whose knowledge illuminates the world and directs our subjects to obey God and us, his minister. Who among them ought not to be pitied? Made exiles through their love of knowledge, they exhaust their wealth and impoverish themselves, expose their lives to every danger, and suffer unwarranted bodily harm at the hands of the vilest men. Truly, this is a most heavy burden. Therefore, by this general and eternally enforceable law we decree that from this time forward, no one should be so bold as to inflict any injury upon students, or impose upon them any penalty stemming from a debt incurred by someone else from their province—a thing which we have heard is done on occasion, in accordance with a perverse custom. Let those rash enough to disregard this holy law know that they shall be forced to restore to the local authorities, fourfold, the goods that they have seized, and that they, marked by the infamy which this law imposes, shall be deprived of their offices forever. Nevertheless, if anyone should wish to bring a charge against these [students] on account of some matter, let him call them into the presence of their lord, their master, or the bishop of the city, to whom we have granted jurisdiction in such cases; and let the choice among these [persons] be made by the student. Whoever attempts to hale them before another judge shall forfeit his case, even if it be thoroughly just, on account of his attempt. We command, moreover, that this law be added to the imperial constitutions under the title "Let no one for his father. . . ."

CHAPTER FIVE

LOVE AND ITS DISCONTENTS

The twelfth century has often been called the age of courtly love, owing to a wide poetic and learned discourse about courtly or "refined" love. And yet neither Haskins nor most of the historians following in his immediate footsteps sought to treat love as a major historical theme of the twelfth-century renaissance. In part this is a consequence of disciplinary divides, with historians preferring to treat more highbrow topics such as philosophy, politics, and law. The theme of secular love was nevertheless a major preoccupation for many twelfth-century authors. Partially this was due to the reception of ancient authorities on love (Ovid and others), and partially this belonged to the increased attention to the love of God. Just as religious thought and spirituality were topics that generated new ideas and forms of expression, so too did thinking about love produce new modes of discourse. The selections from this chapter address love from several angles. There are intellectual approaches to discussing love, as witnessed in the famous exchange between Abelard and Heloise or in Alan of Lille's verse satire on the negative consequences of improper love, and there are systematic attempts to define the proper stages of courtly affection, as witnessed in the treatise on the *Art of Courtly Love* by Andreas Capellanus. There are also poems that express a range of amorous emotions, some seemingly exploring the ethical and moral dimensions of love. Sexual encounters both heterosexual and homosexual were topics of extensive commentary, some of it implicit and some of it explicit. Finally, there is the question of the origins of Troubadour love poetry, a debate represented by the inclusion of selections of Hispano-Arabic love poetry from the eleventh and twelfth centuries.

47. ABELARD AND HELOISE REVISIT THEIR LOVE AFFAIR

The ill-fated love affair between Peter Abelard (1079–1142) and his pupil Heloise (d. 1164) has always loomed large in the romantic notion of twelfth-century love. Around 1115 or 1116, Fulbert, a canon of Notre Dame, employed Abelard as the tutor to his talented niece, Heloise, and the two began an affair. Eventually, Fulbert discovered the liaison, and Heloise, who was pregnant, was sent to be looked after by Abelard's family in Brittany. To appease Fulbert, Abelard agreed to marry Heloise, although on condition that it should be kept secret. Heloise was against the marriage, and when Fulbert began spreading the word, Heloise denied that it had taken place. To protect her from her uncle, Abelard sent Heloise to a nunnery in Argenteuil, where she had been brought up.

She participated in most aspects of the nun's life, but she was not veiled. Fulbert, most probably believing that Abelard's intentions were to be rid of her, arranged in 1117 for a band of men to break into Abelard's room at night and castrate him. Humiliated, Abelard decided to become a monk at the royal monastery of St-Denis, north of Paris (see Doc. 64), and insisted that Heloise become a full nun at Argenteuil.

By some accounts, the correspondence between Abelard and Heloise after their final separation constitutes the most intense personal exchanges of the entire twelfth century. Abelard provoked the correspondence with an epistle (Letter 1) dedicated to an anonymous friend recounting his rise to fame in the schools around Paris, and his initial success in winning the favors of Heloise. He presents Heloise's objections to marriage and his justification for his own actions. When the letter comes to the attention of Heloise, an exchange of views between the two then follows. In her first letter of response (Letter 2), Heloise gives her own version of the affair, why it broke down, and how she now feels about it. She is clearly learned in both classical letters and philosophy (articulating, for instance, Abelard's ethical teaching that sin depends on one's intentions rather than one's actions), and although she is very self-debasing in her words, the singularity of her own experience and the manner in which she subtly challenges Abelard's version of their relationship demonstrate that she was no passive victim.

Abelard, The Story of My Adversities *(Letter 1)*

Source: trans. Henry Adams Bellows, *The Story of My Misfortunes: The Autobiography of Peter Abelard* (Glencoe, IL: The Free Press, 1922), 16–30; revised by Alex J. Novikoff. Latin.

And now it is my desire that you should know the stories of these events, understanding them from learning the facts rather than from hearing what is spoken of them, and in the order in which they came about. I had no dealings with the foulness of prostitutes, and the demands of my scholarly life kept me from association with the women of noble birth and from the common talk of ordinary women. But perverse and fickle fortune produced an occasion for casting me down from the heights of my own exaltation. In this case not even divine goodness could redeem one who, having been so proud, was brought to such shame, were it not for the blessed gift of grace.

Now there dwelt in that same city of Paris a certain young girl named Heloise, the niece of a canon who was called Fulbert. Her uncle's love for her was equaled only by his desire that she should have the best education which he could possibly procure for her. Of no mean beauty, she stood out above all by reason of her abundant knowledge of letters. Now this virtue is rare among women, and for that very reason it doubly graced the maiden, and made her the most worthy of renown in the entire kingdom [then but a few hundred square miles in size]. It was this young girl whom I, after carefully considering all those qualities which are wont to attract lovers, determined to unite with myself in the bonds of love, and indeed this seemed to me very easily achievable. So distinguished was my name, and I possessed such advantages of youth and appearance, that no matter what woman I might favor with my love, I feared the rejection of none. Then, too, I believed that I could win the maiden's consent all the more easily by reason of her knowledge of letters and her zeal for them; so, even if we were parted, we might yet be together in thought with the aid of written messages. Perchance, too, we might be able to write more boldly than we could speak, and thus at all times could we live in joyous intimacy.

Thus, utterly aflame with my passion for this maiden, I sought to discover means whereby I might have daily and familiar speech with her, thereby the more easily to win her consent. For this purpose I persuaded the girl's uncle, with the aid of some of his friends, to take me into his household—which was near my school—in return for the payment of a small sum. My pretext for this was that the care of my own household was a serious handicap to my studies, and likewise burdened me with an expense far greater than I could afford. Now he was a man keen in avarice and likewise he was most desirous for his niece that her study of letters should ever go forward, so, for these two reasons I easily won his consent to the fulfillment of my wish, for he was in greed of my money, and at the same time believed that his niece would vastly benefit by my teaching. More even than this, by his own earnest entreaties he fell in with my desires beyond anything I had dared to hope, opening the way for my love; for he entrusted her wholly to my guidance, begging me to give her instruction whenever I might be free from the duties of my school, no matter whether by day or by night, and to punish her sternly if ever I should find her negligent of her tasks. In all this the man's simplicity was nothing short of astounding to me. I should not have been more smitten with wonder if he had entrusted a tender lamb to the care of a ravenous wolf. When he had thus given her into my charge, not alone to be taught but even to be disciplined, what had he done save to give free scope to my desires, and to offer me every opportunity, even if I had not sought it, to bend her to my will with threats and blows if I failed to do so with caresses? There were, however, two things which particularly served to allay any foul suspicion: his own love for his niece, and my former reputation for continence.

Why should I say more? We were united first in the dwelling that sheltered our love, and then in the hearts that burned with it. Under the pretext of study we spent our hours in the happiness of love, and learning held out to us the secret opportunities that our passion craved. Our speech was more of love than of the books which lay open before us; our kisses far outnumbered our reasoned words. Our hands sought less the book than each other's bosoms—love drew our eyes together far more than the lesson drew them to the pages of our text. In order that there might be no suspicion, there were, indeed, sometimes blows, but love gave them, not anger; they were the marks, not of wrath, but of a tenderness surpassing the most fragrant balm in sweetness. What followed? No degree in love's progress was left untried by our passion, and if love itself could imagine any wonder as yet unknown, we discovered it. And our inexperience of such delights made us all the more ardent in our pursuit of them, so that our thirst for one another was still unquenched.

In measure as this passionate rapture absorbed me more and more, I devoted ever less time to philosophy and to the work of the school. Indeed, it became loathsome to me to go to the school or to linger there; the labor, moreover, was very burdensome, since my nights were vigils of love and my days vigils of study. My lecturing became utterly careless and lukewarm; I did nothing because of inspiration, but everything merely as a matter of habit. I had become nothing more than a reciter of my former discoveries, and though I still wrote poems, they dealt with love, not with the secrets of philosophy. Of these songs you yourself well know how some have become widely known and have been sung in many lands, chiefly, I think, by those who delighted in the things of this world. As for the sorrow, the groans, the lamentations of my students when they perceived the preoccupation, nay, rather the chaos, of my mind, it is hard even to imagine them.

A thing so manifest could deceive only a few, no one, I think, save him whose shame it chiefly bespoke, the girl's uncle, Fulbert. The truth was often enough hinted to him, and by many persons, but he could not believe it, partly, as I have said, by reason of his boundless love for his niece, and partly because of the well-known continence of my previous life. Indeed we do not easily suspect shame in those whom we most cherish, nor can there be the blot of foul suspicion on devoted love. Of this Saint Jerome in his epistle to Sabinian says: "We are wont to be the last to know the evils of our own households, and to be ignorant of the sins of our children and our wives, though our neighbors sing them aloud." But no matter how slow a matter may be in disclosing itself, it is sure to come forth at last, nor is it easy to hide from one what is known to all. So, after the lapse of several months, did it happen with us. Oh, how great was the uncle's grief when he learned the truth, and how bitter was the sorrow of the lovers when we were forced to part! With what shame was I overwhelmed, with what contrition smitten because of the blow which had fallen on the one I loved, and what a tempest of misery burst over her by reason of my disgrace! We each grieved most, not for our own fate, but for the other. Each sought to allay, not our own sufferings, but those of the one we loved. The very sundering of our bodies served but to link our souls closer together; the plentitude of the love which was denied to us inflamed us more than ever. Once the first wildness of shame had passed, it left us more shameless than before, and as shame died within us the cause of it seemed to us ever more desirable. And so it chanced with us as, in the stories that the poets tell, it once happened with Mars and Venus when they were caught together.

It was not long after this that Heloise found that she was pregnant, and of this she wrote to me in the utmost exultation, at the same time asking me to consider what had best be done. Accordingly, on a night when her uncle was absent, we carried out the plan we had determined, and I stole her secretly away from her uncle's house, sending her without delay to my own country. She remained there with my sister until she gave birth to a son, whom she named Astrolabe. Meanwhile her uncle after his return, was almost mad with grief; only one who had then seen him could rightly guess the burning agony of his sorrow and the bitterness of his shame. What steps to take against me, or what snares to set for me, he did not know. If he should kill me or do me some bodily hurt, he feared greatly lest his dearly-loved niece should be made to suffer for it among my kinsfolk. He had no power to seize me and imprison me somewhere against my will, though I make no doubt he would have done so quickly enough had he been able or dared, for I had taken measures to guard against any such attempt.

At length, however, in pity for his boundless grief, and bitterly blaming myself for the suffering which my love had brought upon him through the baseness of the deception I had practiced, I went to him to entreat his forgiveness, promising to make any amends that he himself might decree. I pointed out that what had happened could not seem incredible to any one who had ever felt the power of love, or who remembered how, from the very beginning of the human race, women had cast down even the noblest men to utter ruin. And in order to make amends even beyond his extremist hope, I offered to marry her whom I had seduced, provided only that the thing could be kept secret, so that I might suffer no loss of reputation thereby. To this he gladly assented, pledging his own faith and that of his kindred, and sealing with kisses the pact which I had sought of him, and all this that he might the more easily betray me.

I then returned to my own country, and brought her back as my mistress, so that I might make her my wife. She, however, most violently disapproved of this, and for two chief reasons: the danger it posed, and the disgrace which it would bring upon me. She swore that her uncle would never be appeased by such satisfaction as this, as, indeed, afterwards proved only too true. She asked how she could ever glory in me if she should make me thus inglorious, and should shame herself along with me. What penalties, she said, would the world rightly demand of her if she should rob it of so shining a light! What curses would follow such a loss to the Church, what tears among the philosophers would result from such a marriage! How unfitting, how lamentable it would be for me, whom nature had made for the whole world, to devote myself to one woman solely, and to subject myself to such humiliation! She vehemently rejected this marriage, which she felt would be in every way ignominious and burdensome to me.

Besides dwelling thus on the disgrace to me, she reminded me of the hardships of married life, to the avoidance of which the Apostle Paul exhorts us, saying: "Are you free of wedlock? Then do not go about to find a wife. Not that you commit sin if you marry, nor if she marries, has the virgin committed sin. It is only that those who do so will meet with outward distress. But I leave you in freedom" [1 Corinthians 7:27]. And again: "I would have you free from concern" [1 Corinthians 7:32]. But if I would heed neither the counsel of the Apostle nor the exhortations of the saints regarding this heavy yoke of matrimony, she bade me at least to consider the advice of the philosophers, and weigh carefully what had been written on this subject either by them or concerning their lives. Even the saints themselves have often and earnestly spoken on this subject for the purpose of warning us. Thus Saint Jerome, in his first book *Against Jovinian*, makes Theophrastus set forth in great detail the intolerable annoyances and the endless disturbances of married life, demonstrating with the most convincing arguments that no wise man should ever have a wife, and concluding his reasons for this philosophic exhortation with these words: "Who among Christians would not be overwhelmed by such arguments as those advanced by Theophrastus?" Again, in the same work, Saint Jerome tells how Cicero, asked by Hircius after his divorce of Terentia whether he would marry the sister of Hircius, replied that he would do no such thing, saying that he could not devote himself to a wife and to philosophy at the same time. Cicero does not, indeed, precisely speak of "devoting himself," but he does add that he did not wish to undertake anything that might rival his study of philosophy in its demands upon him.

Then, turning from the consideration of such hindrances to the study of philosophy, Heloise bade me observe what were the conditions of honorable wedlock. What possible concord could there be between scholars and domestics, between authors and cradles, between books or tablets and distaffs, between the stylus or the pen and the spindle? What man, intent on his religious or philosophical meditations, can possibly endure the whining of children, the lullabies of the nurse seeking to quiet them, or the noisy confusion of family life? Who can endure the continual untidiness of children? The rich, you may reply, can do this, because they have palaces or houses containing many rooms, and because their wealth takes no thought of expense and protects them from daily worries. But to this the answer is that the condition of philosophers is by no means that of the wealthy, nor can those whose minds are occupied with riches and worldly cares find time for religious or philosophical study. For this reason the renowned philosophers of old utterly despised the world, fleeing from its perils rather than reluctantly giving them up, and denied themselves all its delights in order that they might repose in the embraces of philosophy alone. One of them, and the greatest of all, Seneca, in his advice to Lucilius, says "philosophy is not a thing to be studied only in hours of leisure; we must give up everything else to devote ourselves to it, for no amount of time is really sufficient hereto."

It matters little, she pointed out, whether one abandons the study of philosophy completely or merely interrupts it, for it can never remain at the point where it was thus interrupted. All other occupations must be resisted; it is vain to seek to adjust life to include them, and they must simply be eliminated. This view is maintained, for example, in the love of God by those among us who are truly called monastics, and in the love of wisdom by all those who have stood out among men as sincere philosophers. For in every race, gentiles or Jews or Christians, there have always been a few who excelled their fellows in faith or in the purity of their lives, and who were set apart from the multitude by their continence or by their abstinence from worldly pleasures.

Among the Jews of old there were the Nazarites, who consecrated themselves to the Lord, some of them the sons of the prophet Elias and others the followers of Elias, the monks of whom, on the authority of Saint Jerome, we read in the Old Testament. More recently there were the three philosophical sects which Josephus defines in his *Book of Antiquities*, calling them the Pharisees, the Sadducees and the Essenes. In our times, furthermore, there are the monks who imitate either the communal life of the apostles or the earlier and solitary life of John. Among the gentiles there are, as has been said, the philosophers. Did they not apply the name of wisdom or philosophy as much to the religion of life as to the pursuit of learning, as we find from the origin of the word itself, and likewise from the testimony of the saints?

There is a passage on this subject in the eighth book of Saint Augustine's *City of God*, wherein he distinguishes between the various schools of philosophy. "The Italian school," he says, "had as its founder Pythagoras of Samos, who, it is said, originated the very word 'philosophy.' Before his time those who were regarded as conspicuous for the praiseworthiness of their lives were called wise men, but he, on being asked of his profession, replied that he was a philosopher, that is to say a student or a lover of wisdom because it seemed to him unduly boastful to call himself a wise man." In this passage, therefore, when the phrase "conspicuous for the praiseworthiness of their lives" is used, it is evident that the wise, in other words the philosophers, were so called less because of their erudition than by reason of their virtuous lives. In what sobriety and continence these men lived it is not for me to prove by illustration, lest I should seem to instruct Minerva herself.

Now, she added, if laymen and gentiles, bound by no profession of religion, lived after this fashion, what ought you, a cleric and a canon, to do in order not to prefer base voluptuousness to your sacred duties, to prevent this Charybdis from sucking you down headlong, and to save yourself from being plunged shamelessly and irrevocably into such filth as this? If you care nothing for your privileges as a cleric, at least uphold your dignity as a philosopher. If you scorn the reverence due to God, let regard for your reputation temper your shamelessness. Remember that Socrates was chained to a wife, and by what a filthy accident he himself paid for this blot on philosophy, in order that others thereafter might be made more cautious by his example. Jerome thus mentions this affair, writing about Socrates in his first book *Against Jovinian*: "Once when he was withstanding a storm of reproaches which Xantippe was hurling at him from an upper story, he was suddenly drenched with foul slops; wiping his head, he said only, 'I knew there would be a shower after all that thunder.'"

Her final argument was that it would be dangerous for me to take her back to Paris, and that it would be far sweeter for her to be called my mistress than to be known as my wife; nay, too, that this would be more honorable for me as well. In such case, she said, love alone would hold me to her, and the strength of the marriage chain would not constrain us. Even if we should by chance be parted from time to time, the joy of our meetings would be all the sweeter by reason of its rarity. But when she found that she could not convince me or dissuade me from my folly by these and like arguments, and because she could not bear to offend me, with grievous sighs and tears she made an end of her resistance, saying: "Then there is no more left but this, that in our doom the sorrow yet to come shall be no less than the love we two have already known." Nor in this, as now the whole world knows, did she lack the spirit of prophecy.

So, after our little son was born, we left him in my sister's care, and secretly returned to Paris. A few days later, in the early morning, having kept our nocturnal vigil of prayer unknown to all in a certain church, we were united there in the benediction of wedlock, her uncle and a few friends of his and mine being present. We then departed stealthily and by separate ways, nor thereafter did we see each other save rarely and in private, thus striving our utmost to conceal what we had done. But her uncle and those of his household, seeking solace for their disgrace, began to divulge the story of our marriage, and thereby to violate the pledge they had given me on this point. Heloise, on the contrary, denounced her own kin and swore that they were speaking the most absolute lies. Her uncle, aroused to fury thereby, visited her repeatedly with punishments. No sooner had I learned this than I sent her to a convent of nuns at Argenteuil, not far from Paris, where she herself had been brought up and educated as a young girl. I had them make ready for her all the garments of a nun, suitable for the life of a convent, excepting only the veil, and these I requested that she put on.

When her uncle and his kinsmen heard of this, they were convinced that now I had completely played them false and had rid myself forever of Heloise by forcing her to become a nun. Violently incensed, they laid a plot against me, and one night while I, all unsuspecting, was asleep in a secret room in my lodgings, they broke in with the help of one of my servants whom they had bribed. There they had vengeance on me with a most cruel and most shameful punishment, such as astounded the whole world; for they cut off those parts of my body responsible for the cause of their sorrow. This done, straightway they fled, but two of them were captured and suffered the loss of their eyes and their genital organs. One of these two was the aforesaid servant, who even while he was still in my service, had been led by his avarice to betray me.

Heloise to Abelard (Letter 2)

Source: trans. Mary Martin McLaughlin with Bonnie Wheeler, *The Letters of Heloise and Abelard: A Translation of Their Collected Correspondence and Related Writings* (New York: Palgrave MacMillan, 2009), 54–55. Latin.

. . . God knows, I have never asked anything of you but only you yourself. I wanted you alone, not what was yours. You know that I did not hope for marriage or for any dowry. I did not seek to gratify my own pleasures or desires, but only yours. If the name of wife seems holier and more impressive, to my ears the name of mistress always sounded sweeter or, if you are not ashamed of it, the name of concubine or whore. For I thought that the more I humbled myself for you, the more completely I might win your love, and that in this way I might do less damage to your great fame. You had not completely forgotten this love in the letter you wrote to console your friend, since you did not consider it beneath you to report the various arguments by which I tried to dissuade you from our marriage, to keep you from an ill-starred bed. But you neglected to mention the many reasons that made me prefer love to marriage, liberty to bondage. As God is my witness, if Augustus, who ruled over the whole earth, should have thought me worthy of the honor of marriage and made me ruler of all the world forever, it would have seemed sweeter and more honorable to me to be called your mistress [*meretrix* can also mean a registered prostitute] than his empress.

The fact that a man is rich and powerful does not make him therefore better; the one depends on fortune, the other on character. The woman who marries a rich man rather than a poorer one, and desires her husband's possessions more than the man himself, should realize that she is only putting herself up for sale. Surely anyone who is led to marry by this kind of greed deserves to be paid rather than loved by her husband. It is obvious that what she is seeking is not a man but what he owns, and that if she could, she would prostitute herself to a richer man. This point is made in the argument by which, as Aeschines Socraticus tells us, the wise Aspasia tried to convince Xenephon and his wife. After she had explained the reasons why this pair should become reconciled with one another, she concluded her argument with these words: "it is only when both of you come to realize that there is not a better man or a more desirable woman in the world that you will always seek above all what seems best to each of you: one to be the husband of the best of women, and the other to be the wife of the best of men" [Cicero, *De inventione rhetorica*]. This is surely a holy saying, and more than philosophic; it may, indeed, be said to spring from wisdom rather than philosophy. For it is a pious error and a blessed fallacy in those who are married to think that a perfect love can keep the bonds of matrimony unbroken, not so much by the continence of their bodies as by the purity of their hearts.

But what other women have deceived themselves into thinking was in my case nothing less than the truth. What they believed to be true if their husbands, I, and everyone else as well, not merrily believed, but knew to be true of you, since the more truly I loved you, the less I could be in error about you. What kings or philosophers could rival you in fame? What kingdom or city or village did not yearn with eagerness to see you? Who did not rush to look at you when you appeared in public, and crane his neck and strain his eyes after you as you departed? What girl or woman did not long for you when you were gone and burn with desire in your presence? What queen or great lady did not envy me my joys and my bed?

You had, I admit, two special gifts by which you could instantly captivate the heart of every woman: the gifts of composing and singing songs, gifts that other philosophers, as we know, have rarely possessed. In these arts, as in a kind of play, you found recreation from the labor of your philosophical studies, and the many love songs you composed have been sung repeatedly because of the great sweetness of their words and melodies, and they have kept your name constantly on everyone's lips. For the charm of your tunes would not let even the unlettered forget you. It was for this reason, above all, that women sighed for love of you. Since most of these songs told the story of our love, they quickly spread my fame in many lands and made other women envious of me.

What grace of mind or body did not adorn your youth? What woman who envied me then is not now compelled by my disaster to pity one who has been robbed of such delights? What man or woman, even though at first unfriendly to me, is not now softened by the compassion I deserve? Although I am exceedingly guilty, you know that I am also most innocent. For it is not the deed itself but the intention of the doer that makes the sin. Equity weighs not what is done, but the spirit in which it is done. Only you, who have known them, can judge my intentions toward you. I submit everything to your scrutiny. I yield to your decision.

Tell me just one thing, if you can: why it is that ever since we entered the religious life, which you alone decided we should do, you have so neglected and forgotten me that I am not refreshed in spirit by words when I am with you or comforted by a letter when we are apart? Tell me if you can, I beg you, or let me say what I feel or, rather, what everyone suspects. Lust, not love, inspired the ardor of your desire for me. Then, after what you desired came to an end, whatever feelings you had shown for this reason vanished at the same time.

48. ANDREAS CAPELLANUS, *THE ART OF COURTLY LOVE*

Andreas Capellanus (or Andrew the Chaplain) wrote De amore *(conventionally translated as* The Art of Courtly Love*) at the request of Countess Marie of Troyes (1145–98), the daughter of Eleanor of Aquitaine. The book may partly have been intended to capture the spirit of Queen Eleanor's court at Poitiers, or it may have been intended to provide practical advice about how to win and retain a lover's affection, but the work covers such a wide social range of amorous situations that it would be impossible to connect the text to a single court or segment of society. Some modern scholars have suggested that the work may represent a priest's satirical take on the conditions of his time. Whatever may have been Capellanus's true intentions, there is little doubt that this work represents the most significant treatise on love since antiquity and reflects the widespread twelfth-century interest in the nature of love, and more specifically fin'amor ("refined love"), the special focus of the Troubadours in southern France (see Doc. 51). The work also reflects the contemporary penchant for blending classical and Christian sources, and there are numerous references to ancient authorities such as Ovid and Seneca, as well as to more contemporary authors such as the Parisian monk Hugh of St-Victor (see Docs. 9, 20).*

The Art of Courtly Love is composed of three books. The first covers the etymology and definition of love and takes the format of a treatise. The second consists of sample dialogues between members of different social classes and would seem to display how the romantic process between the classes should work. The third book comprises stories from actual courts of love presided over by noble women. Female patronage, it is important to recognize, was a major stimulus to learned and poetic writings in the twelfth century.

Source: trans. John Jay Parry, from Andreas Capellanus, *The Art of Courtly Love* (New York: Columbia University Press, 1941), 28–29, 32–35, 149–50, 144–46. Latin.

Chapter 1: What Love Is

Love is a certain inborn suffering derived from the sight of and excessive meditation upon the beauty of the opposite sex, which causes each one to wish above all things the embraces of the other and by common desire to carry out all love's precepts in the other's embrace.

That love is suffering is easy to see, for before love becomes equally balanced on both sides there is no torment greater, since the lover is always in fear that his love may not gain its desire and that he is wasting his efforts. He fears, too, that rumors of it may get abroad, and he fears everything that might harm it in any way, for before things are perfected a slight disturbance often spoils them. If he is a poor man, he also fears that the woman may scorn his poverty; if he is ugly, he fears that she may despise his lack of beauty or may give her love to a more handsome man; if he is rich, he fears that his parsimony in the past may stand in his way. To tell the truth, no one can number the fears of one single lover [Ovid, *Art of Love* 2.517ff.]. This kind of love, then, is a suffering which is felt by only one of the persons and may be called "single love." But even after both are in love the fears that arise are just as great, for each of the lovers fears that what he has acquired with so much effort may be lost through the effort of someone else, which is certainly worse for a man than if, having no hope, he sees that his efforts are accomplishing nothing, for it is worse to lose the things you are seeking than to be deprived of a gain you merely hope for. The lover fears, too, that he may offend his loved one in some way; indeed he fears so many things that it would be difficult to tell them.

That this suffering is inborn I shall show you clearly, because if you will look at the truth and distinguish carefully you will see that it does not arise out of any action; only from the reflection of the mind upon what it sees does this suffering come. For when a man sees some woman fit for love and shaped according to his taste, he begins at once to lust after her in his heart; then the more he thinks about her the more he burns with love, until he comes to a fuller meditation. Presently he begins to think about the fashioning of the woman and to differentiate her limbs, to think about what she does, and to pry into the secrets of her body, and he desires to put each part of it to the fullest use [cf. Ovid, *Metamorphoses* 6.490–93]. Then after he has come to this complete meditation, love cannot hold the reins, but he proceeds at once to action; straightway he strives to get a helper and to find an intermediary. He begins to plan how he may find favor with her, and he begins to seek a place and a time opportune for talking; he looks upon a brief hour as a very long year, because he cannot do anything fast enough to suit his eager mind. It is well known that many things happen to him in this manner. This inborn suffering comes, therefore, from seeing and meditating. Not every kind of meditation can be the cause of love, an excessive one is required; for a restrained thought does not, as a rule, return to the mind, and so love cannot arise from it.

Chapter 5: What Persons Are Fit for Love

We must now see what persons are fit to bear the arms of love. You should know that everyone of sound mind who is capable of doing the work of Venus may be wounded by one of Love's arrows unless prevented by age, or blindness, or excess of passion. Age is a bar, because after the sixtieth year in a man and the fiftieth in a woman, although one may have intercourse his passion cannot develop into love; because at that age the natural heat begins to lose its force, and the natural moisture is greatly increased, which leads a man into various difficulties and troubles him with various ailments, and there are no consolations in the world for him except food and drink. Similarly, a girl under the age of twelve and a boy before the fourteenth year do not serve in love's army. I say, however, and insist that before his eighteenth year a man cannot be a true lover, because up to that age he is overcome with embarrassment over any little thing, which not only interferes with the perfecting of love, but even destroys it if it is well perfected. But we find another even more powerful reason, which is that before this age a man has no constancy, but is changeable in every way, for such a tender age cannot think about the mysteries of love's realm. Why love should kindle in a woman at an earlier age than in a man I shall perhaps show you elsewhere.

Blindness is a bar to love, because a blind man cannot see anything upon which his mind can reflect immoderately, and so love cannot arise in him, as I have already fully shown. But I admit that this is true only of the acquiring of love, for I do not deny that a love which a man acquires before his blindness may last after he becomes blind.

An excess of passion is a bar to love, because there are men who are slaves to such passionate desire that they cannot be held in the bonds of love—men who, after they have thought long about some woman or even enjoyed her, when they see another woman straightway desire her embraces, and they forget about the services they have received from their first love and they feel no gratitude for them. Men of this kind lust after every woman they see; their love is like that of a shameless dog. They should rather, I believe, be compared to asses, for they are moved only by that low nature which shows that men are on the level of the animals rather than by that true nature which sets us apart from all the other animals by the difference of reason. Of such lovers I shall speak elsewhere.

Chapter 6: In What Manner Love May Be Acquired,
and in How Many Ways

It remains next to be seen in what ways love may be acquired. The teaching of some people is said to be that there are five means by which it may be acquired: a beautiful figure, excellence of character, extreme readiness of speech, great wealth, and the readiness with which one grants that which is sought. But we hold that love may be acquired only by the first three, and we think that the last two ought to be banished completely from Love's court, as I shall show you when I come to the proper place in my system.

A beautiful figure wins love with very little effort, especially when the lover who is sought is simple, for a simple lover thinks that there is nothing to look for in one's beloved besides a beautiful figure and face and a body well cared for.

I do not particularly blame the love of such people, but neither do I have much approval for it, because love between incautious and unskilled lovers cannot long be concealed, and so from the first it fails to increase. For when love is revealed, it does not help the lover's worth, but brands his reputation with evil rumors and often causes him grief. Love between such lovers seldom lasts; but if sometimes it should endure it cannot indulge in its former solaces, because when the girl's chaperone hears the rumors, she becomes suspicious and watches her more carefully and gives her no opportunities to talk, and it makes the man's relatives more careful and watchful, and so serious unfriendliness arises. In such cases, when love cannot have its solaces, it increases beyond all measure and drives the lovers to lamenting their terrible torments, because "we strive for what is forbidden and always want what is denied us" [Ovid, *Art of Love* 3.4.17].

A wise woman will therefore seek as a lover a man of praiseworthy character—not one who anoints himself all over like a woman or makes a rite of the care of the body, for it does not go with a masculine figure to adorn oneself in womanly fashion or to be devoted to the care of the body. It was people like this the admirable Ovid meant when he said,

Let young men who are decked out like women stay far away from me,
   A manly form wants to be cared for within moderate limits [*Heroides* 4.75–76].

Likewise, if you see a woman too heavily rouged you will not be taken in by her beauty unless you have already discovered that she is good company besides, since a woman who puts all her reliance on her rouge usually doesn't have any particular gifts of character. As I said about men, so with women—I believe you should not seek for her beauty so much as for excellence of character. Be careful, therefore . . . not to be taken in by the empty beauty of women, because a woman is apt to be so clever and such a ready talker that after you have begun to enjoy the gifts you get from her you will not find it easy to escape loving her. A person of good character draws the love of another person of the same kind, for a well-instructed lover, man or woman, does not reject an ugly lover if the character within is good. A man who proves to be honorable and prudent cannot easily go astray in love's path or cause distress to his beloved. If a wise woman selects as her lover a wise man, she can very easily keep her love hidden forever; she can teach a wise lover to be even wiser, and if he isn't so wise she can restrain him and make him careful. A woman, like a man, should not seek for beauty or care of the person or high birth, for "beauty never pleases if it lacks goodness," and it is excellence of character alone which blesses a man with true nobility and makes him flourish in ruddy beauty. For since all of us human beings are derived from the same stock and all naturally claim the same ancestor, it was not beauty or care of the body or even abundance of possessions, but excellence of character alone which first made a distinction of nobility among men and led to the difference of class

Chapter 11: The Love of Peasants

But lest you should consider that what we have already said about the love of the middle class applies also to farmers, we will add a little about their love. We say that it rarely happens that we find farmers serving in Love's court, but naturally, like a horse or a mule [Tobit 6:17], they give themselves up to the work of Venus, as nature's urging teaches them to do. For a farmer hard labor and the uninterrupted solaces of plough and mattock are sufficient, and even if it should happen at times, though rarely, that contrary to their nature they are stirred up by Cupid's arrows, it is not expedient that they should be instructed in the theory of love, lest while they are devoting themselves to conduct which is not natural to them the kindly farms which are usually made fruitful by their efforts may through lack of cultivation prove useless to us. And if you should, by some chance, fall in love with some of their women, be careful to puff them up with lots of praise and then, when you find a convenient place, do not hesitate to take what you seek and to embrace them by force. For you can hardly soften their outward inflexibility so far that they will grant you their embraces quietly or permit you to have the solaces you desire unless first you use a little compulsion as a convenient cure for their shyness.

Chapter 9: Love Got with Money

Real love comes only from the affection of the heart and is granted out of pure grace and genuine liberality, and this most precious gift of love cannot be paid for at any set price or be cheapened by a matter of money. If any woman is so possessed with a feeling of avarice as to give herself to a lover for the sake of pay, let no one consider her a lover, but rather a counterfeiter of love, who ought to join those shameful women in the brothel. Indeed, the wantonness of such women is more polluted than the passion of harlots who ply their trade openly, for they do what one expects them to, and they deceive no one since their intentions are perfectly obvious. But those others who pretend to be fine ladies of the very best breeding force men to languish for love of them, and under the false veil of affection they gleefully rob of all their wealth those who have been smitten by Cupid's arrow. . . . These women have all sorts of ways of asking for things, and so long as they see that a man can respond to their greedy desire for gifts, they say that he is their adored lover, and they never cease to drain away his property or ruin him by their constant demands. But when his substance is gone and his

Figure 8: This nineteenth-century lithograph was inspired by the legend of the two lovers associated with the mountain of the same name in Normandy, the very location referred to in Marie de France's *Lay of the Two Lovers*.

Source: From the private collection of Alex J. Novikoff.

patrimony is exhausted they despise and hate him and cast him aside like an unproductive bee, and then they begin to appear in true colors. . . . A woman who is really in love always rejects and hates gifts from her lover and devotes her efforts to increasing his wealth so that he may always have something he can give away and thereby increase his good name; she does not expect anything from him except the sweet solaces of the flesh and that her fame may increase among all men because he praises her. . . .

Whenever you notice a woman reminding you how generous someone else was in showering gifts upon his beloved, or hear her praise someone else's jewelry, or complain that some of her things have been pawned, or, under some pretext or other, ask for a piece of jewelry [cf. Ovid, *Art of Love* 1], you must take good care to guard yourself against her wiles, for she doesn't want to be loved, but to draw money out of you. If nothing else could convince you of the truth of this, the rule of Love which says that love and avarice cannot dwell in the same abode would prove it. For if love does not come from the pure pleasure of giving and is not given without payment, it is not love, but a lying and profane imitation of it.

49. MARIE DE FRANCE'S *LAY OF THE TWO LOVERS*

Very little is known about Marie de France (fl. c. 1160–99), but she was the creator of the finest short fiction before Boccaccio (1313–75) and Chaucer (c. 1343–1400) and one of the most celebrated female writers of the entire Middle Ages. Her name tells us that she was of French birth, and her writings inform us that she wrote for the English court, which, as a result of the Norman Conquest of 1066, was French-speaking in her days. In the prologue to her Lais *she states that she has undertaken the novel task of translating a body of love tales created by the Bretons, who were famous exponents of the art of exotic storytelling. She wrote all of her lais in Old French octosyllabic couplets, drawing on Celtic tales, probably oral, and French sources, in some cases written. She seems to have known Ovid and contemporary versions of other classical materials, such as Wace's* The Roman de Brut *(Doc. 71) as well as Arthurian tales and the Tristan story (Doc. 53).*

The Lay of The Two Lovers *takes its name from a mountain in Normandy known as the "Mont des Deux Amants," at the top of which there is, still today, the ruins of a twelfth-century priory dedicated to "the two lovers," Injuriosus and Scholastica, whom legend has it retired to a monastic life together. Marie borrowed the legend on the mountain and wove it into an elaborate tale of young love impeded both by parental obstacles and by its own exuberance. There are some indications that the lai may have been intended as a form of self-parody rather than as a serious statement of the tragic consequences of courtly love. Also of note is the reference to a female medical practitioner in Salerno, from whom the young man must obtain a secret potion for strength of courage. Salerno (see Chapter 9) was the locus of much medical knowledge in the late eleventh and early twelfth centuries, and the woman in question may well have been the reputed author of the* Trotula *(Doc. 80).*

Source: trans. Robert Hanning and Joan Ferrante, *The Lais of Marie de France* (Grand Rapids, MI: Baker Books, 1995), 126–33. Old French.

Les Deus Amanz (The Two Lovers)

There happened once in Normandy
a famous adventure
of two people who loved each other;
both died because of love.
The Bretons composed a lai about it;   5
and they gave it the title, *The Two Lovers*.

The Truth is, that in Neustria,
which we call Normandy,
there's a wondrously great, high mountain:
the two youngsters lie buried up there.   10
Near one side of that mountain,
with much deliberation and judgment,
a king who was lord of the Pistrians
had a city built;
he named the city after the Pistrians—   15
he called it Pistre.
The name has lasted ever since;
the town and its dwellings still remain.
We know the region well:
it's called the valley of Pistre.   20
         The king had a beautiful daughter,
an extremely gracious girl.
He found consolation in the maiden
after he had lost his queen.
Many reproached him for this—   25
Even his own household blamed him.
When he heard that people were talking about his conduct
he was saddened and troubled;
he began to consider
how he could avoid   30
anyone's seeking to marry his daughter.
So he sent word far and near, to this effect:
whoever wanted to win his daughter
should know one thing for certain:
it was decreed and destined that he   35

would have to carry her in his arms
to the summit of the mountain outside the city
without stopping to rest.
When the news was known
and spread throughout the region,   40
many attempted the feat,
but couldn't succeed at all.
There were some who pushed themselves so hard
that they carried her halfway up the mountain;
yet they couldn't get any farther—   45
they gave up there.
So, for a long time, he put off giving her away,
because no one wanted to ask for her.
      There was a young man in that country,
the son of a count, refined and handsome;   50
he undertook great deeds
to win renown beyond all other men.
He frequented the court of the king—
He stayed there quite often
and he came to love the king's daughter,   55
and many times he pleaded with her
to grant him her love
and become his mistress.
Because he was brave and refined,
and because the king thought highly of him,   60
she granted him her love
and he humbly thanked her for it.
They often conversed together
and they loved each other truly,
and as much as they could they hid their love   65
so that no one would discover it.
This restraint disturbed them greatly;
but the young man made up his mind
that he would rather suffer such hardships
than be too hasty in his love and thus lose everything.   70
He was hard pressed by love for her.
      So it chanced one day
that the young man—who was so wise, so brave, and so
    handsome—
came to his beloved
and made his complaint to her: 75

he earnestly begged her
to run away with him—
he couldn't stand the pain any longer;
if he asked her father for her,
he knew that the king loved her so much   80
that he'd refuse to give her up,
unless the suitor could carry her
in his arms to the summit of the mountain.
The maiden answered him: "Dearest," she said, "I know very well
that you couldn't carry me up there for anything: 85
you aren't strong enough.
If I ran away with you,
my father would be grief-stricken and angry;
he would suffer the rest of his life.
Certainly, I love and cherish him enough   90
that I would never want to upset him.
You'll have to think of another scheme,
Because I don't want to hear any more of this one.
I have a relative in Salerno,
A rich woman with lots of property;   95
She's lived there more than thirty years.
She's practiced the medical arts for so long
That she's an expert on medicines.
She knows herbs and roots so well
that if you want to go to her   100
bringing a letter from me with you,
and tell her your problem,
she'll take an interest in it;
then she'll make up such prescriptions
and give you such potions   105
that they'll fortify you,
give you lots of strength.
When you return to this region,
you'll ask my father for me;
he'll think you're just a child,   110
and he'll tell you the agreement—
that he won't give me away to any man,
whatever pains he may take,
if he can't carry me up the mountain
in his arms, without stopping to rest."   115
     The youth listened to the idea

and the advice of the maiden;
it delighted him, and he thanked her.
He took leave of his mistress,
and went off to his own country.   120
Quickly he supplied himself
with rich clothes, money,
palfreys and pack mules;
only the most trustworthy of his men
did the youth take with him.   125
He went to stay in Salerno,
to consult his beloved's aunt.
On her behalf he gave her a letter.
When she had read it from one end to the other,
She kept him with her   130
until she knew all about his situation.
She strengthened him with medicines
and gave him such a potion that,
no matter how fatigued he might be,
no matter how constrained, or how burdened,   135
the potion would still revive his entire body—
even the veins and the bones—
so that he would have all the strength he needed,
the moment he drank it.
She poured the potion into a bottle;   140
he took it back to his own land.
        The young man, joyful and happy,
wasted no time at home
on his return.
He went to the king to ask for his daughter: 145
if the king would give her to him, he would take her
and carry her to the summit of the mountain.
The king made no attempt to refuse him,
though he took him for a great fool,
because the lover was so young.   150
Many great men, hardy and wise,
had undertaken this task
and none could accomplish it at all!
The king named and set a date;
then sent for his vassals, his friends,   155
everybody he could get;
he wouldn't let anyone stay behind.

Because of his daughter, and the young man
who was taking the chance
of carrying her to the mountain's top,   160
they came from everywhere.
The damsel prepared herself:
she fasted and dieted,
cut down on her eating,
because she desired to help her lover.   165
        On the day when everyone arrived,
The youth was there first;
He didn't forget to bring his potion.
Toward the Seine, out in the meadow,
and into the great crowd assembled there   170
the king led his daughter.
She wore nothing except her chemise;
her suitor lifted her into his arms.
The small phial containing his potion
He gave her to carry in her hand: 175
he knew well she'd no desire to cheat him.
But I'm afraid the potion did him little good,
because he was entirely lacking in control.
Off he went with her at top speed,
and he climbed until he was halfway up the mountain.   180
In his joy for his beloved
he forgot his potion.
She noticed he was growing weak:
"Love," she said, "drink!"
I can tell you're getting tired—   185
Now's the time to regain your strength!"
The youth answered:
"Sweetheart, my heart is very strong;
I wouldn't stop for any price,
not even long enough to take a drink,   190
so long as I can still move an inch.
The crowd below would raise a racket,
Deafen me with their noise;
Soon they'd have me all confused.
I don't want to stop here."   195
When they had gone two thirds of the way up,
he was on the verge of collapsing.
Again and again the maiden begged,

"Dearest, take your medicine!"
But he wouldn't listen or take their advice;   200
in great anguish he staggered on.
He reached the top of the mountain in such pain
that he fell there, and didn't get up;
the life went out of his body.
The maiden looked down at her lover,   205
she thought he had fainted.
She knelt beside him,
attempting to give him his potion;
but he couldn't respond to her.
That's how he died, as I've told you.   210
She grieved for him with loud cries;
She emptied and threw away
the bottle that contained the potion.
The mountain got well doused with it,
and the entire region and countryside   215
were much improved thereby:
many a fine herb now found there
owes its start to the potion.
          Now I'll tell you about the damsel:
When she knew she had lost her lover,   220
you never saw anyone so sad;
she lay down and stretched out beside him,
took him in her arms, pressed him to her,
kissed his eyes and lips, again and again;
sorrow for him struck deep in her heart.   225
She died there too,
that maid who was so brave, so wise, so beautiful.
The king and the others who were waiting for them,
when they saw that they weren't returning,
went after them and found them.   230
The king fell down in a faint.
When he could speak again, he grieved greatly,
and so did all the strangers.
They stayed there mourning for three days.
Then they ordered a marble tomb   235
and placed the two youngsters inside it.
On the advice of everyone present
they buried them on the mountain's summit,
and at last they went away.

Because of the sad adventure of the young folk,   240
the place is now called the Mount of the Two Lovers.
It happened just the way I've told you;
The Bretons made a *lai* about it.

50. HISPANO-ARABIC LOVE POETRY: A SOURCE OF LYRIC COURTLY LOVE?

One of the most vexed questions in the history of secular love poetry is of the relation between the vernacular and amorous lyrics of the Troubadours and the love poems of Muslim Spain, which flourished in the eleventh and twelfth centuries. A philological tradition among Arabists holds that the very term trobar *derives from the Arabic* taraba, *"to sing," and more specifically to sing poetry (*tarab *meant "song"). This alleged etymology has not proved convincing to most scholars of Romance linguistics, but a growing scholarly appreciation of the interaction and intellectual exchange between Christians and Muslims in Spain has made the question of the cultural overlap all the more intriguing, particularly when one broadens the scope to include philosophical and classically inspired themes, as well as more structural elements such as meter and rhyme.*

Love poetry has deep roots in the Arabic literary tradition, but several themes and genres are known to be the unique product of poets active in Muslim Spain. One theme concerns the elaboration of passages in Aristotle's De anima *that spell out the relationship between the active intellect of God and the passive intellect of man. According to his modern translator, it was the application of this philosophical superstructure to traditional Arabic love poetry that permitted Ibn Hazm (d. 1064), one of the greatest poets of Muslim Spain, to create a veritable doctrine of courtly love. His system stresses the ennobling power of love and the supremacy of spirituality over materiality. Ibn Hazm is ultimately less interested in the corporeal form of physical beauty than the spiritual union of the lovers.*

Much scholarly attention has also focused on Andalusian strophic poetry, and especially the form known as muwashshah. *The* muwashshah *exemplifies a cultural pluralism that allowed for differences and similarities, clashes and juxtapositions, and relations between the sexes. Recent scholars have noted that it embraces non-Arabic and non-learned cultures, recognizes female voices, and exposes the sociocultural relations between various ethnic groups. It likewise gives expression to the tension and rapprochement between secular and religious sentiments, all while reflecting life in the court and on the streets. These themes are well illustrated in the poems of Ibn Ubada al-Qazzaz (eleventh century) and Ibn Quzman (d. 1160), who also composes in the* zajal, *a traditional form of oral strophic poetry declaimed in a colloquial dialect.*

Source: trans. James T. Monroe, *Hispano-Arabic Poetry* (Berkeley: University of California Press, 1974), 170, 172, 174, 176, 218, 274, 276, 278. Arabic.

Ibn Hazm

(I)

I love you with a love that knows no waning, whereas some of men's loves are midday mirages.

I bear for you a pure, sincere love, and in [my] heart there is a clear picture and an inscription [declaring] my love for you.

Moreover, if my soul were filled by anything but you, I would pluck it out, while any membrane [covering] it would be torn from it by [my] hands.

I desire from you nothing but love, and that is all I request from you.

If I should come to possess it, then all the earth will [seem like] a senile camel and mankind like motes of dust, while the land's inhabitants will [seem like] insects.

(II)

My love for you, which is eternal by reason of its very nature, has reached its maximum proportions, hence it can neither decrease at all, nor increase.

Its only cause is the will, and no one knows any cause other than that!

When we discover that a thing is its own cause, then it is an existence that is unperishing,

But when we find that [its cause] is in something other than itself, its destruction will come about when we lack that which gave it existence.

(III)

Are you from the world of angels, or are you mortal? Explain this to me, for inability [to reach the truth] has made a mockery of my understanding.

I see a human shape, yet if I use my mind, then the body is [in reality] a celestial one.

Blessed be he who arranged the manner of being his creation in such a way that you should be the [only] beautiful, natural light [in it].

I have no doubt but that you are that spirit which a resemblance joining one soul to another in close relationship has directed toward us.

We lacked any proof that would bear witness to your creation, which we could use in comparison, save only that you are visible.

Were it not that our eye contemplates [your] essence we could only declare that you are the Sublime, True Reason.

(IV)

I enjoy conversation when, in it, he is mentioned to me and exhales a [scent] of sweet ambergris for me.

If he should speak, among those who sit in my company, I listen only to the words of that marvelous charmer.

Even if the Prince of the Faithful should be with me, I would not turn aside [my love] for the former.

If I am compelled to leave him, I look back [at him] constantly and walk like [an animal] wounded in the hoof.

My eyes remain fixed firmly upon him though my body has departed, as the drowning man looks at the shore from the fathomless sea.

If I recall my distance from him, I choke as though with water, like the man who yawns in the midst of a dust storm and the sun's noonday heat.

And if you say: "It is possible to reach the sky," I reply: "Yes, and I know where the stairs may be found."

(V)

He who claims to love lyingly commits perjury, just as Mani [i.e., the founder of Manichaeism] is belied by his principles.

In the heart there is no room for two beloveds, nor is the most recent of things always the second.

Just as reason is one, not recognizing any creator other than the One, the Clement,

Likewise the heart is one and loves only one, though he should put you off or draw you to him.

[He who claims to love two] is suspect in the law of love; [he is] far from the true faith.

Likewise, religion is one and straight, while he who has two religions is a profound disbeliever.

(VI)

Men have observed that I am a youth driven desperate by love; that I am broken-hearted, profoundly disturbed. And yet, by whom?

When they look at my condition they become certain [of it], yet if they inquire into the matter they are left in doubt.

[I am] like a handwriting whose trace is clear, but which, if they seek to interpret it, cannot be explained;

[I am] like the sound of a dove over a woody corpse, cooing with its voice in very way,

Our ears delight in its melody, while its meaning remains obscure and unexplained.

They say: "By God, name the one whose love has driven sweet sleep from you!"

Yet I will never [name him]! Before they obtain what they seek, I will lose all my wits and face all misfortunes.

Thus will they ever remain prey to doubts, entertaining suspicion like certitude and certitude like suspicion.

(VII)

Having seen the hoariness on my temples and sideburns, someone asked me how old I was.

I answered him: "I consider all my life to have been but a short moment and nothing else, when I think reasonably and exactly."

He replied to me: "How was that? Explain it to me, for you have given me the most grievous news and information."

So I said: "To the [girl] possessed of my heart I once gave one single kiss by surprise.

Hence, no matter how many years I live, I will not really consider any but that brief moment to have been my life."

(VIII)

They said: "He is far away." I replied: "It is enough for me that he is with me in the same age without being able to escape.

The sun passes over me just as it does over him every day that shines anew.

Furthermore, is one between whom and me there lies only the distance of a day's journey really far away,

When the wisdom of the God of creation joined us together? This mutual proximity is enough [for me]; I want nothing further."

Ibn Ubada al-Qazzaz

I would give my father in ransom for a precious possession that clings to [my] soul!

I loved a new moon unique in its beauty borrowing from the gazelle its glances and [slender] neck.

A full moon that shone in shapely proportion was proud of its beauty, desiring no increase.

Grace had adorned him; his figure was graceful!

A full moon that conquered with evident charm, cheek down curling over a jasmine [complexion],

A lily placed in line with a well-guarded rose; when it appeared it [proudly] trailed the edges of beauty's robe.

Before me a creature appeared that was worthy of love!

My eyelids live only to find out about him; if my soul had but feathers, I would fly to him.

Beauty placed armies upon his pupils and [upon] the [arrow-like] glance feathered with licit charm.

He has a tall, graceful figure, hence [my] heart is in thrall to desire!

He has made it his aim to shun me ever since I have submitted to his love, yet have I squandered my patience despite the length of his shunning.

The water of beauty flows on his cheek's surface; his front teeth have put rows of pearls to shame;

His mouth is a receptacle for sweets worthy of being kissed!

When he donned a stylish robe as a costume, I wished to kiss his voluptuous, deep red lips,

So he said in verse, trying to act as one who refuses, and inclining coquettishly, with the sweetest of words:

"I see that you will not taste the tempting morsel, by God!"

Ibn Quzman

I am madly in love despite the angry behavior of one who finds
    fault [with me]!
I am the lover of my time:
I fear no one in matters of love!
Love has made me thin, it has turned me pale:
Look, and see how my color has changed!
Yet I can still say, "Ah" O dark-skinned one!
As for my clothes, there is no flesh inside them.
You would not see me
Were it not that I still moan!
By God, I am a man enmeshed in love's snares
And my condition proves that I speak the truth.
Moreover, I excel in composing this *zajal*;
Poetry passes through my mind whenever [its sword] is drawn;
As for the sword of my tongue,
No coat of mail can stop it!
Spare me the method of Jamil and Urwa,

Since people have a model in al-Hasan.
And say to one who does not follow the method of al-Urwa:
"O you who honor a certain person even more than Hatim,
What is the method used by a certain debauched fellow
Who is ostracized throughout the land?"
Throw off your restraint in loving the youthful,
And as for the beloved, if you see that his sash is hard to undo,
Give him to drink, and do it again, as often is needed.
Then, if he drinks from the large cup and endures,
Pour him out a second:
He will collapse though he be a lion!
When my beloved drank his cup for you,
And drunkenness made him droop among his seated companions,
I redoubled my efforts whenever he raised his head;
My beloved drank; he drank until he keeled over.
There is no safety from me
For one who gets drunk and then falls asleep!

51. THE TROUBADOURS

The Troubadours were lyric poets who wrote in Occitan (also called Provençal), the language of southern France in the twelfth and thirteenth centuries. The preserved corpus of songs includes about 2,500 compositions by about 450 poets. The Occitan word trobador *is a compound of the root "to find" with the suffix expressing agency, and thus it means "one who finds" verses (that is, one who composes), presumably a man. The feminine suffix produces* trobaritz, *of which about 20 are known.*

The Troubadours made fin'amor, *or "refined love," sometimes called "courtly love," their subject of choice. Arriving at a definition of this term has proved notoriously difficult, largely because it is impossible to account for the broad spectrum of literary creations that gave expression to love in all of its sensual, ironic, exalted, and spiritual directions. Nevertheless, a few essential themes can be discerned. According to William Paden, a leading scholar of the Troubadours,* fin'amor *is the expression of a male subjectivity confronted with the joyous exaltation and pain of erotic desire, usually accompanied by a consequent fear of isolation and potential loss. Metaphoric expressions of love's enslaving power frequently draw from the vocabulary of armed combat or imprisonment, familiar realities in this age of chivalry and crusade. A common pretext for the narrative setting of these poems is adultery, often an adulterous triangle, which allows for further exploitation of the moral and social ramifications of love. The songs represented below range from the bawdy (a) to the meditative (b), to the amorous (c), with further examples of the refined (d and e) and ennobling (f) qualities of love.*

William IX of Aquitaine (1071–1126) is the first Troubadour whose works are extant. At the age of 15 he inherited lands more vast than the king of France, his nominal lord. He was one of the leaders of the First Crusade and he successfully led a crusading army to Spain in 1120, but had an uneasy relationship with the Church. He was excommunicated twice, the second time for allegedly abducting the wife of the viscount of Châtellerault, who was one of his vassals. Jaufre Rudel, another of Duke William's vassals, was active from 1125 to 1147, when he went on crusade to the Holy Land. In his poem (c), Jaufre distances himself from his libertine lord and creates a new, more sublime love. This more sublime love is taken up in (d) by Bernart de Ventadorn (c. 1125–c. 1200), who is considered by many to be the greatest love poet of the Troubadours. His romanticized biography, or vida *(e), states that he was of humble origins but rose to sing his love for the wife of the lord of Ventadorn, before eventually retiring to the Cistercian abbey of Dalon, but in truth little about his life is known with certainty. His poetry, characterized by a melodious language, nostalgic tone, and vivid imagery, earned him admirers and imitators among medieval poets. The Comtessa de Dia is probably the best known of the* Trobaritz. *Little is known of her, although she may be the eldest daughter of the count of Dia, near Valence. Her poem (f) reverses the passive role of the lady, and places the discerning judgment of the woman at the center of the story.*

Source: trans. William D. Paden, *An Introduction to Old Occitan* (New York: Modern Language Association of America, 1998), 523–25, 534–36, 520–21. Old Occitan.

a. William IX of Aquitaine, "En Alvernhe part Limozi"

In Auvergne beyond the Limousin
I went all alone [dressed] in a pilgrim's cloak;
I found the wife of Sir Guari
    and [the wife] of Sir Bernart;
they greeted me heartily
    by Saint Leonard.

Hear what I answered them:
I never mentioned iron or wood,
But I spoke to them these words:
    "Tarrababart,
marrababelio riben
    saramahart."

Lady Agnes and Lady Ermessen said,
"We've found what we have been seeking!
Let's put him up, simply and nicely,

for he cannot speak,
and through him our secret
     will never be known."

The one took me under her cloak
And [that] was just fine with me;
They led me to their hearth,
     and I liked the fire,
and I warmed myself gladly
     by the great coals.

To eat they gave me capons,
and I dined avidly,
and the bread was hot, and the wine was good,
     strong and abundant;
and there was not even a scullion,
     just us three.

Sister, this man is deceptive
and has stopped his speaking because of us.
Bring out our red cat
     quick and snappy,
for it will make him tell the truth,
     if he's lying at all.

When I saw the awful creature coming
(his fur was long, his whiskers ferocious,
I didn't like his company at all!),
     I was thoroughly frightened;
I nearly lost my desire
     and my courage.

When we had drunk and eaten,
I undressed according to their desire;
behind me they brought the cat,
     mean and nasty;
and they flayed me from my head
     down to my heel.

Lady Ermessen took it by the tail
and yanks, and the cat scratches;

they gave me more than a hundred wounds
      that time;
he seared me, but for all that
      I didn't move at all.

Nor would I have even if someone had killed me,
Until I had fucked them both
a lot, and it happened
      just as I wished;
I preferred to suffer the pain
      And the grievous torment.

I fucked as much as you will hear:
a hundred eighty-eight times!
My belt nearly broke
      and my harness;
and very great discomfort came to me.
      it hurt so bad.

Monet, you will go for me in the morning,
and carry my song in your pack
straight to the wife of Sir Guari
      and [to the wife] of Sir Bernart,
and tell them, for love of me,
      to kill the cat!

b. William IX of Aquitaine, "Pos de chanter m'es pres talenz"

Since a desire to sing has come over me,
I shall make a song about what I am sad about;
no more shall I be obedient
in Poitou or in Limousin,

For now I shall go into exile;
in great fear and in great peril,
in war I shall leave my son,
and his neighbors will do him harm.

Departure is very difficult for me
from the lordship of Poitiers;

in protection of Foulque of Angers
I leave the land and his cousin.

If Foulque of Angers doesn't help him,
and the king from whom I hold my fief,
many men will do him harm,
treacherous Gascons and Angevins.

If he is not very wise and worthy
when I shall have left you,
soon they will have overturned him
for they will see [that he is] young and weak.

For mercy I beg my companion;
if ever I wronged him (her), let him (her) pardon me
and pray to Sir Jesus of heaven
in vernacular and in his Latin.

I have been of prowess and joy,
but now we both do part;
and I shall go away to him
in whom all sinners find peace.

I have been very pleasant and joyful,
but our Lord wants it no more.
Now I can no longer bear the burden,
so near I have come to the end.

I have given up all I used to love,
chivalry and pride,
and since it pleases God, I accept it all,
and pray him to retain me with him.

All my friends I pray at my death
to come [where I am], all [of them], and honor me well;
for I have had joy and pleasure
far and near and in my domain.

Thus I give up joy and pleasure
And vair and gray [fur] and sable.

c. Jaufre Rudel, "Lanquan li jorn son lonc en mai"

When the days are long in May
I like a sweet song of birds from afar;
and when I have gone away from there,
I remember a love from afar.
I go bent and bowed with desire,
so that neither song nor hawthorn flower
pleases me more than frozen winter.

Never shall I enjoy love
if I do not enjoy this love from afar,
for neither fairer nor better do I know
anywhere, neither near nor far.
Her merit is so true and fine
that there in the kingdom of the Saracens
[I wish] I were called, for her sake, a captive.

Saddened and rejoicing will I depart
when I see this love from afar;
but I do not know when I shall see her,
for our lands are very distant.
There are many passes and roads,
and for this reason I am not a prophet;
but let all be as it pleases God.

Joy will surely appear to me when I seek there,
for the love of God, lodging from afar;
and if it pleases her, I shall lodge
near her, though I am from afar.
Then will conversation seem noble,
when I, a distant lover, shall be so near
that with gracious words I shall enjoy solace.

I hold indeed the Lord to be true
through whom I shall see the love from afar.
But for one good thing that befalls me,
I have two harms, because it is so far from me.
Oh! [I wish] I were a pilgrim there
so that my staff and my cloak
would be reflected in her beautiful eyes!

May God, who made all that comes and goes
and formed this love from afar
give me power, for I have the intention,
to see soon the love from afar
truly in agreeable places,
so that the chamber and the garden
might forever seem a palace to me.

He speaks the truth who calls me covetous
and desirous of love from afar,
for no other joy pleases me as much
as enjoyment of love from afar.
But what I want hates me so much
that my godfather fated me
to love but not to be loved.

But what I want hates me so much. . .;
a curse on the godfather
who fated me not to be loved!

d. Bernart de Ventadorn, "Chantars no·m pot gaires valer"

Singing, for me, cannot be good
unless the song comes from the heart;
and song cannot come from the heart
unless there is true, sincere love there.
That's why my singing is best,
for I engage and devote to joy of love
my mouth and eyes and heart and mind.

May God never give me such power
that desire for love would not strike me;
even if I could never manage to get any of it
but every day sorrow would come to me,
I'll always have a good heart, at least;
and I have much more enjoyment,
for I have a good heart from it, and am attentive to it.

They criticize love out of ignorance,
foolish people, but there is no harm [to love];
for love can scarcely decline,

unless it is vulgar love.
That is not love; that
has only the name of it and the appearance,
which loves nothing unless it takes [profit].

If I wanted to tell the truth,
I know well from whom the deception comes:
from [women] who love for money,
and they are venal merchants.
[I wish] I were a liar and false!
I tell the truth in coarse language,
and I'm sorry that I'm not lying.

In pleasing and in yearning
is the love of two true lovers;
nothing can do any good
unless the desire is mutual.
And he is surely a fool since birth
who chides her for what she wants
and advises her what is not fitting.

I have placed my good hope very well,
since she shows me friendly looks
whom I most desire and want to see,
noble and sweet, true and loyal,
with whom the king would be blessed.
Pretty and graceful, with a lovely body,
she has made me a rich man from nothing.

I neither love nor fear anything else,
and nothing would be a hardship for me
if only I could please my lady,
for that day seems like Christmas to me
when she looks at me with her pretty,
spirited eyes—but she does it so slowly
that just one day lasts a hundred to me.

My verse is true and natural,
and good [is] he who understands it well;
and better he who awaits the joy.

Bernart de Ventadorn understands it,
and says it and makes it, and awaits the joy!

e. *Vida* of Bernart de Ventadorn

Bernart de Ventadorn was from the Limousin, from the castle of Ventadorn. He was of poor birth; he was the son of a servant who was a baker, who would heat the furnace to cook the bread of the castle. And he became a handsome man and clever, and learned how to sing well and to compose, and he became courtly and well educated. And the viscount of Ventadorn, his lord, was greatly pleased by him and his manner of composition and his singing, and did him great honor.

Now the viscount of Ventadorn had a wife, young and noble and joyful. And she was pleased by Sir Bernart and by his songs, and fell in love with him and he with the lady, so that he made his songs about her, about the love that he had for her and about her merit. Their love lasted a long time before the viscount became aware of it; he became aloof from him, and had his wife closed up and guarded. And he made the lady dismiss Sir Bernart, to depart and go far away from that region.

And he departed and went to the duchess of Normandy, who was young and of great merit and very keen on reputation and honor and well-expressed praise. And the songs of Sir Bernart pleased her greatly, so she received him and welcomed him very warmly. For a long time he stayed in her court, and he fell in love with her and she with him, and he made many good songs about her. And while he was with her, King Henry of England took her as his wife, and took her away from Normandy and took her to England. Sir Bernart remained over here sad and grieving, and went to the good Count Raymond of Toulouse, and stayed with him until the count died. And because of that grief, Sir Bernart entered the order of Dalon, and there he died.

And what I, Sir Uc de Saint Circ, have written about him Viscount Eble de Ventadorn told me, who was son of the viscountess whom Sir Bernart loved. And he made these songs that you will hear. . . .

f. Comtessa de Dia, "Ab joi ab joven m'apais"

I nourish myself on joy and youth
     and joy and youth nourish me,
for my lover is the most joyful,
      so that I am charming and joyful;
      and since I am true to him,

it is quite fitting for him to be true to me;
for I never have ceased loving him,
        nor have I any intention to cease.

I am very pleased, for I know he is worth most,
        the one that I most desire to have me,
and as for the one who first brought him to me,
        I pray God to bring him great joy;
        and whoever may tell him evil about him,
let him not believe it, except what I have told him;
for a man often picks the rods
        with which he himself is beaten.

So a lady who cares for good reputation
        must surely put her affection
on a worthy, noble knight,
        once she recognizes his worth.
        Let her dare to love him openly,
for once a lady loves openly,
never again will the worthy or the valiant
        say anything but praise of her.

I have chosen one [who is] worthy and noble
        by whom merit improves and is ennobled,
generous and adroit and discerning,
        in whom there is wit and wisdom.
        I pray him to believe me,
and not to let people make him believe
that I would commit a disloyalty toward him—
        provided that I not find disloyalty in him.

        Lover, the worthy and valiant
recognize your valor;
and for this reason, I ask at once,
        if you please, your support.

52. LOVE LYRICS FROM THE *CARMINA BURANA*

Carmina Burana *refers to the songs* (carmina) *contained in the Codex Buranus, a manuscript discovered in the Bavarian monastery of Benediktbeuren in 1803 and subsequently transferred to the state library in Munich, where it currently resides. The original collection of 228 poems was assembled around 1230, possibly in Austria, and preserves poems that date chiefly from the late twelfth or early thirteenth century, some of which are attributable to known poets but most of which are anonymous. The first group includes moral and satirical poems dealing with avarice and simony, the instability of fortune (lyrics famously used by Carl Orff in his 1929 eponymous musical setting), the decline and improvement of morals, conditions at Rome, the Crusades, particular events of political significance, and several exorcisms. The second and largest group of poems is a collection of about 120 "love lyrics" and laments, a few of which are represented in the selection below. The love songs represent a broad spectrum of viewpoints and range from descriptions of evocative sceneries to tales of unbridled obscenity. Two prominent features are the use of a nature introduction set in springtime and a sophisticated manipulation of scholastic subjects, particularly classical mythology and allegory. A third group of poems consists of a random assortment of drinking and gambling songs attributed to the Goliards (Doc. 61), and a fourth group includes liturgical plays and other compositions.*

Source: trans. P.G. Walsh, *Love Lyrics from the Carmina Burana* (Chapel Hill: The University of North Carolina Press, 1993), 110–17, 146–47, 151. Latin.

Phyllis and Flora

In the blooming season of the year, as the sky grew clearer and the earth's bosom was dappled with a range of colors, when Dawn's messenger routed the stars, sleep quitted the eyes of Phyllis and Flora.

The maidens decided to take a stroll, for their wounded hearts rejected sleep. So step for step they passed into a meadow, so that the setting might lend additional charm to their disputation.

Both were maidens, and both high-born. Phyllis let her hair flow free, while Flora's locks were elegantly braided. Their beauty is not that of maidens but of goddesses, and their faces shine like the morning light.

They are vulgar neither in birth, nor appearance, nor adornment; they carry the years and spirit of youth. But they are a little at odds, and rather sharp with each other, for one is taken with a cleric, but the other with a knight.

There is no contrast between their figures or features; they are identical within and without. They have the same bearing and the same disposition; their only difference is the form of their loving.

A seasonal breeze whispered softly. The place was bright with green grass, and through the grass flowed a running stream, sportive with prattling murmur.

To increase the beauty of the spot and to moderate its heat, beside the rill was a spreading pine, its charm enhanced by its foliage and spreading wide its bosom, so that no foreign heat could penetrate it.

The maidens seated themselves; the grass afforded a couch. Phyllis sat by the stream, Flora further away. As both settled themselves and recovered their breath, love stabbed at their hearts and pierced one and the other.

Love lurks hidden within them and draws from their hearts sighs most pronounced. Wanness drains their cheeks, their faces change their color, but their fierce love is buried beneath their modesty.

Phyllis detects Flora sighing, but then Flora rebukes Phyllis on the same count. Thus each catches out the other, and at last both uncover their sickness and reveal their wounds.

Their conversation is punctuated with much hesitation; it forms a sequence wholly concerned with love. Love is in their hearts and on their lips. At length Phyllis begins, directing a smile at Flora.

Says she: "Illustrious knight, my heart-throb Paris, where are you now campaigning, and where are you lodged? The life of soldiering, that life unrivaled, is the only life that deserves the joy of Venus's household!"

As the girl calls to mind the knight her love companion, Flora smiles and flashes at her a sideways look; with a laugh she utters an unfriendly word: "You might say that your lover is a beggar.

But what is my heart-throb Alcibiades doing, a creation worthier than any creature, whom Nature has endowed with every grace? Sovereign rights of clerics, you alone are blessed."

Phyllis rebukes Flora for her harsh comment and speaks in words calculated to rouse her: "Just look at this dear, clean-hearted maid whose noble breast is enslaved to an Epicurus!

Rouse yourself, rouse yourself poor girl, from this foul madness! I account a cleric as nothing but an Epicurus. I grant no elegance to the cleric, with his fat bulk bulging all around him!

He keeps his heart far removed from Cupid's camp; he feels the need for sleep and food and drink. My high-minded girl, we all know that the knight's aspiration is a far cry from this.

The knight is content with needs alone. He does not concentrate his life on sleep, food, and drink. Love prevents him from nodding off. A knight's love and exultant youth are his food and drink.

Who would harness our love partners together? Would law or nature allow them to be associated? My lover's knowledge lies in love-sport, yours in feasting; giving is mine's invariable mark, but receiving is that of yours."

Flora drains the blood from her modest face, and her second laugh makes her look more beautiful. At last with eloquent utterance she unbars the thought she had begotten in a heart fertile in rhetorical skills.

"You have spoken, Phyllis, quite without inhibition. You are swift and sharp enough in expression, but you have not effectively pursued the truth, so that through you the hemlock prevails over the lily.

You have said that the cleric is self-indulgent; you call him the slave of sleep, drink, and food. Such jibes are how true worth is usually described by a jealous person. But grant me a moment; I shall reply to you.

I claim that my friend's possessions are so numerous and great that he gives never a thought to other people's property. Store-cupboards full of honey, oil, corn, wine, gold, jewels, and goblets are at his call.

In this abundance of the cleric's life, so sweet that no words can depict its nature, Love circles round and beats applause with twofold wings—Love that is unfailing, Love that is immortal.

The cleric endures Venus's weapons and Cupid's wounds; but he is not skinny or downtrodden, for he is deprived of none of joy's blessings, and the unfeigned affection of his lady harmonizes with his.

But your chosen one is emaciated, pale, and poverty-stricken; he has barely a cloak and no fur to cover him. His limbs are frail, his chest unhealthy, for when the cause is lacking the effect too is wanting.

The poverty which looms over your lover is demeaning. What can a knight offer to one who solicits him? But the cleric bestows a great deal, and his store is copious, so great are his riches and his revenues."

Phyllis objects to Flora: "You have much experience of the pursuits and lives of both. Your lives have been quite persuasive and beguiling, but this dispute will not be settled on these terms.

When the hour of a feast day brings joy to the world, the cleric then makes his quite disreputable appearance. His hair is tonsured, and his clothes are black, and he bears the traces of his gloomy pleasure.

No one is so moronic or blind as not to witness the knight's glory. But your lover lives in idleness like a brute beast, whereas mine feels the rubbing of his helmet and sits astride a horse.

My lover scatters enemy positions by force of arms, and if he chances to enter battle alone on foot, while his Ganymede holds Bucephalas, he recounts my name in the midst of slaughter.

When he has routed the enemy and ended the fighting, he returns, and pushing back his helmet often gazes on me. So by rightful reasoning based on these and other factors, I put the life of soldiering first."

Flora notes Phyllis' anger and panting breast and in return launches many barbs at her. "Your words are vain as you raise your praise to heaven," she said. "You are trying to thrust a camel through the eye of a needle.

You are forsaking honey for gall, and truth for falsehood, when you seek to approve soldiering by rebuke of the clergy. Is it love which makes the knight vigorous and spirited? No; it is poverty and lack of possessions which move him.

Lovely Phyllis, if only you would love wisely and not contest true opinions in this matter further. Both thirst and hunger bear heavily on your knight, and because of this he seeks the path to death and hell.

The knight's disastrous condition is most wearing; his lot is hard and constrained, for his life hangs in the balance, in uncertainty that he can obtain the necessities of life.

You would not label the black clothes and shorter hair of the cleric a reproach if you knew the convention. The clerics wear these to denote the greatest distinction, to show that he is greater than all others.

Clearly all things are subject to the cleric, and the mark of his authority he bears in his tonsure. He gives commands to knights and bestows gifts upon them. The personage who issues commands is greater than the servant.

You swear that the cleric is always idle. I grant that he scorns cheap and grinding occupations, but when his mind rises high to its concerns, he distinguishes the paths of heaven and the elements of the universe.

My lover is clad in purple, yours in a breastplate. While your lover joins in battle, mine is in his litter, where he reviews the ancient achievements of princes, and writes, investigates, ponders wholly on his mistress.

My cleric is pre-eminent in knowledge and instruction on the power of Venus and of the god of love. It is through the cleric that the knight has become a follower of Venus. Through these and similar facts your arguments are indictable."

Flora abandoned the argument and contest alike, and demanded for herself Cupid's adjudication. Phyllis initially objected but then agreed, and once they had approved the judge they made their way back over the grass.

The whole contest is left to the discretion of Cupid; people say that he is a true and experienced judge because he knows the manner of life of both suitors. They now prepare themselves to go to listen to him.

The maidens are matched in beauty and modesty. Their aspirations in their warring too are matched, and so is their complexion. Phyllis' robe is white, Flora's two-toned. A mule was Phyllis' steed, a horse was Flora's.

Phyllis' mule was the one which Neptune bred, nourished, and trained. After the fury of the boar and the death of Adonis, he sent it as a consoling gift to the Cytherean goddess.

Venus finally bestowed it on the beautiful mother of Phyllis, an honest Spanish noblewoman, because she had devoted herself to the work of the goddess. See, then, how by a happy outcome Phyllis came to possess it.

The mule did a lot for the maiden's bearing; it was handsome, presentable, and well built, as befitted one which the sea god had sent to Venus from so distant a region.

Those who inquire about trappings and bit—for the mule's teeth champed on nothing but silver—should know that all these things were such as befitted a gift of Neptune.

Phyllis at that moment was not lacking in beauty, but appeared most opulent and handsome. And Flora showed both qualities no less, for with her bridle she governed the mouth of a horse exceedingly rich.

That horse, subdued by the reins of Pegasus, had much beauty and strength and was dappled with a pattern of differing colors, for mingling with black was the color of the swan.

It was of presentable beauty and of youthful years; its gaze was somewhat lordly but not savage. Its neck was high, its mane spread smoothly out, its ears short, its chest pronounced, its head small.

Along its curved back the spine, without earlier experience of any sagging weight, extended for the maiden to sit upon. Its hooves were hollow; it was straight-shinned, big-shanked. The steed reflected the whole of Nature's skill.

The saddle placed upon the horse gleamed bright, for a gold frame enclosed ivory within. As the saddle had four raised corners, a starlike jewel enhanced each of them.

On it were many engravings with marvelous markings depicting unknown events of the past—the marriage of Mercury, with the gods introduced there, the compact, the wedding, the abundant dowry.

No part of the saddle is unadorned or without relief. It contains more than the human mind can take in. Vulcan alone had engraved these scenes, and when he eyed them he scarcely believed that his hands could have achieved them.

Vulcan had neglected the shield of Achilles and had toiled at the trappings and given free scope to them. He nailed shoes on the hooves, affixed a bridle on the jaws, and reins made from his bride's hair.

Cloth of purple sewn on with cotton covered the saddle. Minerva had abandoned her other pursuits and had interwoven it with acanthus and narcissus patterns. Along the edges she had worked a tasseled fringe.

The two damsels fly along side by side on their mounts, their faces modest and their cheeks glowing with youth. They are like blossoming lilies or new-sprung roses, or like twin stars speeding side by side down from the sky.

Their planned destination is the park of Love. Sweet anger lends life to the features of both. Phyllis Flora's laughter, Flora that of Phyllis. Phyllis bears a falcon on her wrist, Flora a sparrow hawk.

After a short lapse of time they lighted on a glade. A stream whispers at the entrance to this glade, from which a breeze bears the scent of myrrh and spice. The sound of timbrels and a hundred harps is heard.

Of a sudden the maidens hear there all that can be taken in by the minds of men. In that place contrasting melodies are in evidence. Both diatessaron and diapente resound.

Timbrel, harp, lyre, and drum resound and beat in harmony. There viols play most sacred notes, and the boxwood pipe brings forth its tune from many apertures.

All the tongues of the birds sing out full-throatedly. The sweet and enchanting voice of the blackbird is heard. So too are the crested lark, the jackdaw, and the nightingale, which never stops lamenting the pains she has endured.

The musical instruments, the tuneful voices, then too the appearance of various flowers which they behold, as well as the charming scent wafted abroad, lead them to infer that this is the chamber of the young Cupid.

The maidens enter somewhat apprehensively, and as they draw nearer their feelings of love wax greater. Every bird sings out her own melody, and their spirits are fired by the diversity of the cries.

Any person remaining there would become immortal. Each and every tree rejoices in its particular fruit. The paths are fragrant with myrrh, cinnamon, and balsam. One could guess from the house who is its master.

They behold bands of young men and damsels. The persons of each and all are like so many stars. The hearts of the girls are suddenly entranced with the great wonder of these unprecedented sights.

Side by side they rein in their horses and dismount. The sound of harmonious music almost makes them forget their plan. But the song of the nightingale is heard again, and at once the maidens' hearts again wax hot.

At the center of the wood is a hidden spot where the god's worship throbs with most intense life. Fauns, nymphs, satyrs, a numerous band of escorts, beat their drums and sing in harmony before the god's presence.

In their hands they bear wine and garlands of flowers. Bacchus schools the nymphs and the bands of fauns; so they preserve the due arrangement of the dances and playing of the instruments, except that Silenus [the satyr] staggers and does not sing in harmony.

That elder, riding ahead on a donkey, nods off and diverges from his path, causing the god's heart to dissolve in floods of laughter. "Wine!" cries Silenus, but his shout remains slurred, for wine and old age block the progress of his voice.

In the midst of this the son of the Cytherean goddess is sighted, his face starbright and his shoulders winged. His left hand wields his bow, and his arrows hang at his side. One can safely guess at his power and high status.

The boy leans on a scepter wreathed with flowers. Sweet-scented nectar drips from his combed locks. The three Graces with fingers interlocked attend him and with bent knee bear Love's cup before him.

The girls draw near and with self-assurance worship the god who is invested with reverend youth. They delight in the mighty power of his divinity. The god gazes at them, and offers a greeting first.

He asks the reason for their journey; the reason is explained, and both are praised for daring to undertake so burdensome a task. He addresses each of them: "Now rest awhile till this unresolved case is clarified by the judgment."

He who spoke was divine. The maidens know that he is a god, and it was unnecessary to recount each detail. They leave their horses and wearily take their rest. Love commands his officers to deliver judgment unambiguously.

Love possesses judges and has laws. Love's judges are Experience and Nature. The entire judicial process of the court is entrusted to them, for they know both the past and the future.

They depart and give free rein to the power of justice, and bring its rigor duly aired back to the court. They pronounce the cleric more suited to love by virtue of his knowledge and by virtue of his way of life.

The court approved the pronouncement of the law and decreed that it be observed for the future. So those who court the knight and claim that he is of greater worth are taking insufficient precautions against things which will do them harm.

What a Lying, Crafty Tongue

What a lying, crafty tongue, a wanton, poisonous tongue, a tongue deserving to be cut out and consumed by fire!

For it says that I am a deceiver and not a faithful lover, that I have abandoned the girl I loved and passed on to another.

I call God, I call the gods to witness: I am not guilty of this charge! I call the gods, I call God to witness: on this charge I am not guilty!

So I swear by the nine Muses, and more important by Jupiter, who took the shape of gold for Danaë's sake, and that of a bull for Europa.

I swear by Apollo, I swear by Mars, for they know the art of love; I swear by you too, Cupid, of whose bow I stand in fear.

I swear by your bow and arrows which you keep discharging against me; I wish to preserve this compact without deceit and guile.

I wish to maintain this compact. Moreover, I shall tell you why: among all the bands of maidens I have seen none so outstanding.

Among them you appear like a pearl set in gold. Your shoulders, breast, and belly are so beautifully shaped!

Forehead, throat, lips, and chin add fuel to my passion. Her hair, too, I have come to love because of its blonde color.

So until night becomes day, till toil becomes rest, till water becomes fire, till the forest becomes woodless,

Till the sea has no sails, till the Parthian has no missiles, you will always be dear to me. If I'm not deceived, you will not be deceived either!

Death-Bearing Gossip

Death-bearing gossip repeatedly wounds me, heaping sorrows on my evil plight. Word of your sinning, now resounding throughout the boundaries of the world, punishes me sorely. Jealous Rumor deals with you harshly. Love more circumspectly, that discovery may not overtake you! Do what you do in the dark, far from the eyes of Gossip! Love with its sweet allurements and sportive whispers rejoices in hiding places.

No foul gossip besmirched as long as we two were fastened in the bonds of love. But now that our desire grows cold, you are suddenly blackened by the indictment that spells death. Rumor, which takes joy in a new marriage union, rushes irrevocably through the streets. See how your palace of chastity is exposed as a brothel for all, for the virginal lily withers in shameful transactions from the touch of tawdry men.

Now I mourn for the bloom of your innocent youth, which shone more brightly than Venus' star, that erstwhile dovelike sweetness of heart which is now the bitterness of the snake. You repel with aggressive words those who entreat you, but you caress in bed those who bring you gifts. Those from whom you get nothing you bid depart, but the blind and lame you take in, and you beguile men of fame with your poisonous honey.

Figure 9: Facsimile of a miniature of the thirteenth century, representing a scene of an old romance: the beautiful Josiane disguised as a female jongleur (minstrel), playing a Welsh air on a rebec (fiddle) to make herself known to her friend Bevis.

Source: Paul Lacroix, *The Arts in the Middle Ages and at the Period of the Renaissance* (London: Chapman and Hall, 1870), 457.

53. THE ROMANCE OF TRISTAN AND YSEUT

The romance of Tristan and Yseut is one of the most famous and widely disseminated medieval love stories. It recounts the legend of Tristan (or Tristran), nephew of King Mark of Cornwall and a knight of the Round Table, and the king's Irish wife Yseut (or Isolde), who fall passionately in love with each other after mistakenly drinking a potion. The secrecy of their affair becomes compromised by the fading effects of the magic and the harrassment of the king's barons, ultimately ending in tragedy. The tale was inspired by Celtic legend, and possibly by the eleventh-century Persian story of Vis and Ramin. It was made popular in the middle decades of the twelfth century through French poetry, forming an important branch of the Matter of Britain. There are several versions of the tale, but the verse adaption by the Norman poet Béroul (c. 1170), the earliest of the so-called vulgar versions, places great emphasis on the impulsive and often brutal behavior of the characters. The tenderness and tension of two people struggling against their destiny adds poignancy to this version of the romance. The legend inspired many works of the Arthurian tradition, and was the basis for Richard Wagner's influential opera Tristan und Isolde *(1865). In the passage below, a hermit gives advice to the two lovers. It is a poignant commentary on the theme of illicit love and its consequences.*

Source: trans. Stewart Gregory, *The Romance of Tristran by Beroul* (Amsterdam: Rodopi, 1992), 111–15. Old French.

> My lords, now hear of the queen:
> head bowed, she fell at the hermit's feet
> and lost no time in begging his help,
> begged him to reconcile them with the king:
> 'For never in my whole life   5
> shall I have any thought of illicit love.
> Not, you understand, that I am sorry for a minute about my love for
> Tristran, nor that I do not love him honorably
> as a friend, and without shame;
> it is just that intercourse between him and me   10
> is completely at an end.'
> The hermit heard her speak and wept,
> and praised God for what he had heard:
> 'Oh God, just and almighty king,
> I thank you from the bottom of my heart   15
> that you have allowed me to live long enough
> to see these people come to me
> to take advice about their sin.
> May I offer my profound thanks to you!

I swear by my faith and my religion   20
that you shall have good counsel from me.
Tristran, hear these few words of mine,
now that you have come to my dwelling,
and you, queen, do not be foolish
but heed my words.   25
       When a man and a woman sin,
if, having first come together, they then part,
and provided they first do penance,
and show true repentance,
God will forgive them their sin,   30
however horrible and ugly it might be.
Tristran, and you, queen, hear me
but a little while and take note:
to remove shame and cover up a misdeed
one sometimes has to tell a white lie.   35
Since you have asked for my advice, you shall have it forthwith.
I shall take a leaf of parchment to write a letter,
bearing greetings at the top.
This you will send to Lantyan,
containing, with your regards to the king; these words: 40
that you are living in the wood with the queen,
but that, if he wanted to take her back
and put aside his anger,
you would do this much for him:
you would go to his court.   45
And let King Mark have you hanged
if anyone there, however exceedingly wise or stupid,
dared to say that you had formed
an adulterous relationship
and you could not defend yourself against the charge.   50
       Tristran, the reason I dare to give you this advice
is that you will never find your equal at court
prepared to give a pledge to fight you.
I can give you this advice in good faith,
for this he cannot gainsay: 55
when he sought to have you put to death
by burning, because of the dwarf—
men at court and the common people were to witness it—
he would not hear your defense.
After God had shown you mercy,   60

so that you escaped from there,
as it is well known,
because, had it not been for God's power,
you would have died a shameful death—
the leap you made was such that there is no man   65
from Constantine to Rome who,
beholding that cliff, would not shudder with fright—
you fled here in terror.
You rescued the queen,
and have since been here in the wood.   70
When you brought her from her own land,
you gave her to him in marriage.
He knows full well that that was done;
she married her in Lantyan.
It would have been wrong of you to fail her,   75
so you preferred to flee with her.
If he can accept to hear your defense
in the presence of the court and the common people,
you can offer to do so at his court.
And if it were his wish,   80
following your reinstatement as his faithful vassal,
with the agreement of his vassals
let him take back his noble wife.
And, if you know he is not opposed to it,
you will be a warrior in his company   85
and give him unstinting service.
But should he not want your service,
you will cross the sea to Dumfries
to go and serve another king.
That will be the content of the letter.' 'I agree to this.   90
Except, dear Friar Ogrin, that this much
should be added to the letter, with your permission,
that I have lost all confidence:
he has issued a proclamation against me.
But I beg him, as a lord   95
I truly love,
to prepare a letter in his answer,
containing all his wishes.
He should hang his letter on the Red Cross,
out on the open heath—that is my demand.   100
I do not dare tell him where I am,

for I fear he would do me some mischief.
I will be quite prepared to trust him when I have
his letter, and I shall do whatever he wishes.
Master, let my letter be sealed!   105
At the end of it write: *Vale!*
There is no more I can think of for the moment.'
The hermit Ogrin rose to his feet,
took pen, ink, and parchment,
and wrote all the words down that Tristran had said.   110
When he had finished, he took a ring
and impressed the stone on the wax.
So, the letter was sealed, and handed to Tristran,
who took possession of it most graciously.
'Who will take it?', asked the hermit.   115
'I shall.' 'Tristran, how can you say that?'
'I shall, sir, indeed I shall,
since I know well the land of Lantyan.
Fair Ogrin, with your permission,
the queen will remain here,   120
and immediately when night falls,
when the king is sound asleep,
I shall mount my horse,
taking with me my companion.'

54. AN ANONYMOUS LOVER'S LAMENT

This anonymous lament from a twelfth-century French collection of poems displays many of the themes current in contemporary discourse about love: a grieving heart, self-pity, a sense of longing and estrangement, the subjection of passion. Also notable are the classical allusions. Some are direct—for instance to Venus, Jupiter, and Corinna, the subject of many of Ovid's love poems—while others are more indirect, with phrases that draw from Ovid, Catullus, and Seneca.

Source: trans. Jan M. Ziolkowski and Justin Lake, in *A Garland of Satire, Wisdom, and History: Latin Verse from Twelfth-Century France (Carmina Houghtoniensia)*, ed. Ziolkowski et al. (Cambridge, MA: Harvard University Press, 2007), 31–32. Latin.

A Lover's Lament

Alas, what am I to do? I bear a wound within my sad heart;
smitten within, I grieve exceedingly to the very marrow of my bones;

I am tortured and held fast, captured by the snare of Venus;
troubled through and through, I am bound by the bonds of Love.
The beauty that I follow has wounded me and has clung to my heart.
It is my snare, from it come cares that will not pass away.
I will erect a statue to Venus and will arrange to be healed of sickness.
Let the person who suffers pain hurry inside: a pleasing sacrifi-
    cial animal given by him
will fall and, not undeservedly, I will place incense devoutly in
    the fire.
I will worship her alone, if she dispels the trouble she harshly
    threatens.
Therefore bring aid, Venus, I ask, to me here because I am wounded.
I ask, be gentler to me, sad and wretched as I am.
Carry out what I ask. Indulge me, banish my sorrow;
bind my fatal wounds, goddess, return me to myself,
for I have been lovingly captured, wretchedly wrenched from myself.
Haughty Corinna, fit for Jupiter, holds me to punish me.
Of her own free will the proud girl seeks and wages war against me.
When I weep and grieve, wretched equally by night and day,
she grows keener and harsher; and she takes care that passion
    burns me more keenly.
I am tortured and blinded, because my entreaties puff up the
    heart of my mistress.
Impel you, goddess, the rebellious heart of the girl to this wish.
She spurns and refuses to be joined with like mind to me.
She laughs when she sees that I am entirely distraught;
she laughs at the frenzy and lamentation of a weeping lover.
Therefore my mind is shattered: the signs of grief can be seen
    outwardly,
and my passion is not hidden, but displayed with sure indications;
for when the flesh seldom has what it wishes, it withers and
    wastes away.
Laughter is gone, power of sight wastes away from plentiful tears.
But grief, passion, the flush of emotion, and moans are many
    times repeated.
What is her food? Her food is what is worst for me.
She is graceless and unruly in play, no different from lionesses.
You, goddess sweet as nectar, sprinkle nectar so that that
unruly and violent girl may then be gentle and mild.
When I court her with gifts and entreaties and visit her home
    constantly,

what do I achieve? I plow a shore, to which in the end I should
consign seeds?
When I follow her about and beg, she shuts her ears and hears
nothing.
Therefore I grieve more, the frenzy grows, and I am inflamed more.
Tired and overpowered, at length I suffer a great illness.
Death is close: stripped of resources, I see my demise nearby.

55. LOVE SONGS OF THE TROUVÈRES AND WOMEN TROUVÈRES

The trouvères, inspired by their Provençal counterparts, the Troubadours, were poet-composers who practiced their art in the northern French dialect, the langue d'oïl. *Well over 2,000 strophic songs for single voice have survived from this rich cultural production that spanned the late twelfth century until the end of the thirteenth century. Almost half of the texts are unique, while the rest occur in up to ten versions, and about two-thirds survive with their music. With few exceptions, the subject of trouvère lyrics was love. Inspired by the Troubadour idea of refined love or fin'amor (see Doc. 51), they sang of amorous longing and of the interplay between desire and creativity. Despite what some might see as the depersonalizing abstractness and conventional vocabulary of their lyrics, the subtle use of emotion and metaphor in fact reveals a great range of individual inventiveness and even virtuosity.*

Approximately 250 trouvères have been identified, beginning with Chrétien de Troyes (c. 1130–c. 1190), the earliest known composer of lyrics in French. Many of the lyrics are anonymous or of uncertain attribution. Grace Brulé (fl. 1180–1213) is both one of the earliest and the most prolific composers of trouvère love lyrics. He was a knight of Champagne who had several patrons among the highest nobility, including possibly Marie de France (see Doc. 49). In his style of poetry he adhered quite closely to the themes and techniques of the more southerly Troubadours.

While the existence of female trouvères has been a hotly debated issue among medievalists, there is significant evidence in literature, iconography, and historical documents to suggest that women were active poets and musicians alongside their male counterparts. And although there is only a small group of known medieval female songwriters, there is a large body of lyrics that give voice to women and explore the range of emotions typically associated with women. The songs of the women trouvères that are included below are an anonymous chanson d'amour *(Song of Love), which treats the same refined love found in the lyrics of the Troubadours, and a* chanson de croisade *(Crusade Song), which expresses the pain of separation from a woman's perspective.*

Figure 10: A twelfth-century sculpture of a trouvère and his viol (fiddle) from the Abbey of St-Denis in Paris.

Source: Paul Lacroix, *Sciences et Lettres au Moyen Age et à l'Époque de la Renaissance* (Paris: Librairie de Firmin-Didot, 1877), 465.

Songs of the Trouvères

Source: trans. Frederick Goldin, *Lyrics of the Troubadours and Trouvères: An Anthology and a History* (Gloucester, MA: Peter Smith, 1983), 383, 385, 387, 409, 411. Old French.

Anonymous, *Voulez-Vous Que Je Vous Chant*

Would you like me to sing you
A sweet song of Love?
No country bumpkin made it
But a knight
Beneath the shade of an olive tree
In the arms of his love.

She wore a skirt of fine linen,
And a white cloak of ermine,
And a tunic of silk;
Greaves of gladiolus;
And slippers of May flowers
Fitting snug.

She wore a girdle of leaves
That grows green when it rains,
The buckle was of gold;
Her purse was of love,
The pendants of flowers.
It was given for love.

She was riding a mule
With silver shoes
And a golden saddle;
Behind her on the crupper
She had planted three rose trees
To give her shade.

She comes along the meadow;
Knights have encountered her
And greeted her courteously.
"Beautiful, where were you born?"
"I am of France, the celebrated,
of a very high degree.

"My father is the nightingale
Who sings on the branch
In the highest trees.
My mother is the siren
Who sings in the salt sea
On the highest bank."

"Beautiful, may you be born for happiness:
you are of noble kin
and of very high degree.
I wish to God our Father
You were given as my
Wedded wife to me."

Grace Brulé, *Les Oiseillons De Mon Païs*

The little birds of my country
I have heard in Brittany.
When their song rises up, I think
I used to hear them, once,
In sweet Champagne,
If I am not mistaken.
They have put me in such gentle thought,
I have set myself to sing
Till I at last attain
What Love has long been promising.

I am troubled by long hope
And must not complain.
That takes away my joy and laughter,
For no one tormented by love
Is mindful of anything else.
I find my body
And face poised on the thought of her so many times,
That now I have the look of a madman.
Others have done other wrongs in love,
But my great fault is to show my suffering.

My sweet gentle lady
Kissing me stole away my heart;
It was crazy to quit me

For her who torments me.
Alas, I never felt it
Leaving me;
She took it so gently,
she drew it to her as I sighed;
she covets my mad heart
but will never have pity for me.

That one kiss, which is always on my mind,
Is over, I now realize—
It has betrayed me,
I do not feel it on my lips.
When she permitted,
God! What I am telling of,
Why didn't she furnish me against my death.
She knows I am killing myself
In this long expectation,
My face is pale and colorless.

And so she takes away my joy and laughter
And makes me die of longing;
Love makes me pay dearly
Again and again for her obligingness.
Alas, I don't dare go to her,
Because I have this crazy look
Which these false lovers get me blamed for.
I am dead when I see them talking to her there,
Because not one of them will find
Any of their treachery in her.

Grace Brulé, *Li Pluseur Ont D'amours Chanté*

Most have sung of Love
As an exercise and insincerely;
So Love should give me thanks
Because I never sang like a hypocrite.
My loyalty kept me from that,
And Love, which I have in such abundance
It is a miracle if I hate anything,
Even that crowd of pests.

The truth is, I have loved with a loyal heart
And will never love another way;
My lady could have put this to the test
Just by taking notice.
I do not say that I am irked
Because she does not do as I wish:
All my thoughts are of her,
I am much pleased by whatever she permits.

If I have been outside the land
Where I look for my pleasures and joy,
It has not made me forget
How one keeps faith in love;
If my requital has been slow in coming,
I have found much comfort in this thought:
In a little moment one has gotten
What one has wanted a long, long time.

Love has proved to me by reason
That a true lover suffers and waits;
Whoever is hers and in her power
Must beg for mercy openly,
Or it is pride: I have experienced this.
But these false summer lovers,
Who have blamed me for my love—
They never love but when the lust comes on them.
Even if these slanderers had sworn to,
They would never be fine enough to be of any use
In this affair, where they have taken such great pains
To do me harm, with all their malice.
And they must have forsworn God himself.
They have conspired so busily for my unhappiness,
I shall scarcely see this suffering
End, that makes me burn with love.

But in Brittany the Count
Has advised me, whom I have loved my whole life long,
And if he has given me good counsel
I should know it very soon.

Songs of the Women Trouvères

Source: trans. Eglal Doss-Quimby, Joan Tasker Grimbert, Wendy Pfeffer, and Elizabeth Aubrey, eds., *Songs of the Women Trouvères* (New Haven, CT: Yale University Press, 2001), 123, 146–47. Old French.

[Chanson D'amour]

Full of anger and despair
I weep: by singing I recover joy.
You may be sure that I acted very wrongly,
For I was much too bold
When I made moan with heart and mouth
Ay anything joyful,
Were it not that in this way I express
My anger and my grief and sorrow.

I thought I was another's lady,
But I am sure I acted foolishly,
For I am conquered by the one
I thought I had conquered.
Now the worst has devolved on me,
For he is his and I too am his:
Thus we are both his,
If things are as I imagine.

I made a terrible mistake
When despite him I made myself his,
For he shows no concern, it seems to me,
Either for me or for my comfort;
Since he does not love me, I hate myself,
Yet I will always be his love,
Though he be my enemy:
So do I seek and pursue my death.

[Chanson De Croisade]

Jerusalem, you cause me great harm,
Taking from me what I loved most.
Know in truth that I will no longer love you,
For that is what brings me the most doleful joy;

Often I sigh and am so short of breath
That I am on the verge of turning against God,
Who has deprived me of the great joy I had.

Dear sweet beloved, how can you endure
Such great pain for my sake on the salty sea,
When nothing in this world could ever express
The great sorrow that has entered my heart?
When I recall the sweet, radiant face
I used to kiss and caress,
It is truly a wonder I do not go mad.

So help me God, I cannot escape:
Die I must, such is my fate;
Yet I know truly that whoever dies for love
Has more than one day's journey to God.
Alas! I would rather embark on such a journey
To find my dear beloved
Than remain here forsaken.

PART 2
GENRES

CHAPTER SIX

EXPERIMENTATIONS IN LITURGICAL AND SECULAR POETRY

Poetry was one of the major forms of creative expression in the twelfth century, so it is only natural that the religious reform and classical renewal that were so central to the ethos of the age should affect poetic developments as well. The lyrics of the Troubadours and the love poems of the *Carmina Burana* have already been covered in Chapter 5; the selections in this chapter offer examples of experimentations in both devotional and secular poetry. Hildebert of Lavardin was one of the finest secular poets of his day, but in his hymn he offers up a stirring praise of the Trinity in octosyllabic verse, a poetic form that became popular (in both Latin and vernacular languages) in the twelfth century. The Augustinian abbey of St-Victor in Paris, already encountered in Chapters 1 and 2 as the seat of important religious and educational reform, is here represented by the musical form of the sequence, which developed out of a pre-existing tradition of hymns but evolved considerably over the course of the late eleventh and twelfth centuries. New experimentations in secular poetry include the classically inspired poems of Marbod of Rennes, Peter of Blois, and Hildebert of Lavardin, while a fancy for satire and bawdy humor is evident in the verses of the Goliards and the Archpoet. Two anonymous poems praising nature and patriotism likewise show the impact of a changing society on newer forms of poetic expression.

56. HILDEBERT OF LAVARDIN'S HYMN ON THE TRINITY

Hildebert of Lavardin (c. 1055–1133) was one of the finest poets and hymnologists of his age. Born in Lavardin, near Vendôme, he later became bishop of Le Mans. He is often classified with Marbod of Rennes (Doc. 59) and Baudri of Bourgeuil as part of a group of classically inspired Loire Valley poets of the early twelfth century (for Hildebert's secular poems, see Doc. 62). His extant writings consist of letters, poems, a few sermons, two saints' lives, and one or two treatises. His hymn on the Trinity, composed in octosyllabic meter, has been described as one of the greatest Latin verse compositions of the twelfth century. It was popular throughout the Middle Ages, including in more secular milieus, and offers a good illustration of the intersection of literary creativity and devotion. The translation, though slightly antiquated, preserves the meter and the rhyme.

Source: trans. Erastus C. Benedict, *The Hymn of Hildebert and Other Mediaeval Hymns* (New York: Anderson D.F. Randoph & Co., 1868), 3–17. Latin.

TO THE FATHER

Father, God, my God, all seeing!
Alpha and omega being—
Thou whose power no limit showeth
Thou whose wisdom all things knoweth,
God all good beyond comparing—   5
God of love for mortals caring—
            Over, under, all abounding,
In and out and all surrounding—
            Inside all, yet not included,
Outside all, yet not excluded,   10
Over all, yet not elated,
Under all, yet not abated—
            Thou above—thy power ordaining—
Thou beneath—thy strength sustaining—
Thou without—the whole embracing—   15
Thou within—thy fullness gracing.
            Thee within, no power constraineth—
Thou without, no freedom gaineth—
Over all, thee none sustaineth,
Under all, no burden paineth.   20
            Moving all, no change thou knowest—
Holding fast, thou freely goest.
Changing time, thou art unchanging
Thou the fickle all arranging.
Force and fate whichever showing   25
Are best footsteps of thy going,
Past and future to us, ever
Are to thee but now forever.
Thy to-day, with thee abiding
Endless is, no change dividing—   30
Thou, in it, at once foreseeing
All things, by thee perfect being,
Like the plan thy mind completed,
When creation first was meted.

TO THE SON

Son, the Father's equal ever,
From his substance changing never,

Like in brightness and in feature,
Though creator, still a creature,
Thou our human body worest   5
Our redemption too thou borest.
     Endless, still thy time declaring,
Deathless, though thy death preparing,
Man, and God, divided never,
Thou man-God, unmixed forever,   10
God is not to flesh converted,
Nor by flesh the God perverted—
God in human form appearing,
Never human weakness fearing—
With the Father equal being   15
Fleshly weakness disagreeing,
God the God begetting solely,
Virgin both conceiving wholly.
     In this union, thus created,
Both the natures there are mated,   20
Each its own existence taking,
Both a new existence making.
     He, alone our leader,
He the law and Gospel heeded,
To the cross and grave proceeded,   25
There he slept and there descended,
There he rose and then ascended.
Judged on earth—in heaven he liveth,
And the world its judgment giveth.

TO THE HOLY SPIRIT

     Comforter, denominated,
Never born and not created,
Both the Son and Father knowing—
Spirit from them both outgoing,
Thus in power their equal being   5
And in quality agreeing,
Great as they, he still remaineth,
All their goodness, he retaineth,
With them from the first existing,
All their power in him subsisting.   10
     Father he begetting showeth,

Son, from human birth he groweth,
Spirit, from them both outflowing,
They are one, the Godhead showing.
Each is God, in fullness ever,   15
All are God and three Gods never.
In this God, true God completing,
Three in one, are ever meeting,
Unity in substance showing,
Trinity in persons knowing.   20
      Of the persons none is greater,
Neither less and neither later,
Each one still itself retaining,
Fixed and constant still remaining,
In itself no variation,   25
Neither change, nor transmutation.

This is true faith, for our keeping.
Error bringeth sin and weeping—
As I teach it, I believe it,
Nor for other will I leave it.   30
Trusting Lord thy goodness ever
Though I sin, I hope forever.
Worthy death, but not despairing,
By my death, my life preparing.
When I please thee, nothing showing   35
But the faith on thee bestowing.
Hear my prayer, my faith perceiving,
From my burden, me relieving—
Here, my sickness now revealing,
Let thy med'cine be my healing.   40
      Now, without the city taken,
Dead, offensive and forsaken,
Grave clothes bind, the stone confineth—
At thy word the grave resigneth—
Speak! the stone away is rolling—   45
Speak! The shroud no more controlling—
When "Come forth" thy summons sayeth,
Then at once the dead obeyeth.
      On this sea of troubles resting
Pirates are my bark infesting—   50
Strifes, temptations, billows sweeping,

Everywhere are death and weeping,
Come, good pilot, calm proclaiming,
Hush the winds, the billows taming,
Drive these pirates to their hiding,   55
Safe to port my vessel guiding.
      My unfruitful fig tree growing,
Dry and withered branches showing,
Should'st thou Judge, the truth discerning,
Thou would'st give unto the burning—   60
But another season bless it,
Dig about it, Lord, and dress it,
If it then no fruit returneth,
I will praise thee while it burneth.
      Me the evil one possessing,   65
Flames and floods by turns oppressing,
Feeble, sick and helpless lying,
To thy grace, my soul is flying.
That my weakness all may vanish,
Thou the evil spirit banish.   70
Teach me Lord, my weakness staying,
Grace of fasting and of praying,
This alone, the Savior telleth,
Such a demon e'er expeleth.
Thou my sickened sense restoring—   75
Faith and penitence imploring—
Give me fear which, once ejected,
Leaves salvation all perfected.
Faith and hope and love conferring,
Give me piety, unerring,   80
Earthly joys forever spurning,
Heavenward still my footsteps turning.

      God, in thee, all things desiring,
From thee, every thing requiring—
Thou my praise, my good abiding,   85
All I have, thy gift providing—
In fatigue, thy solace feeling,
In my sickness, thou my feeling,
Thou, my harp, my grief assuaging,
Thou who soothest all my raging,   90
Thou who freest my enthralling,

Thou who raisest me when falling,
'Tis thy grace my footsteps guideth
Strengthening hope, when it subsideth.
None would hurt, but thou forefendest,   95
Who may threaten, thou defendest,
What is doubtful, thou revealest,
What is mystery, thou concealest.
   Never, Lord, with thy permission,
Let me enter in perdition,   100
Where is fear and where is wailing,
Shame and weeping unavailing,
Every loathsome thing displaying,
In confusion, disarraying,
Where the fierce tormentor lieth,   105
And the worm that never dieth,
Where this endless woe, infernal,
Maketh death and hell eternal.

Let me be in Sion saved,
Sion, peaceful home of David,   110
Built by him, the light who maketh,
And the cross for portals taketh—
And for keys the welcome given
By the joyful saints in Heaven—
Walls of living stone erected,   115
By the prince of joy protected—
Where the light, that God is sending,
Endless spring and peace are blending.
Perfume, every breeze is bearing,
Festive strains the joy declaring.   120
No corruption there appeareth,
None defect, or sorrow feareth,
None deformed or dwarfed remaining,
All the form of Christ retaining.
   Heavenly City! happy dwelling!   125
Built upon that stone excelling.
City safe in heavenly keeping
Hail! in distant glory sleeping!
Thee I hail, for thee am sighing—
Thee I love, for thee am dying.   130
   How thy heavenly hosts are singing—

And their festive voices ringing—
What the love their souls conforming—
What the gems the walls adorning—
Chalcedon and jacinth shining   135
Know they all, those walls confining.
     In that City's glorious meeting,
Moses and Elias greeting—
Holy prophets gone before us—
Let me sing the heavenly chorus.   140

57. THE LITURGICAL POETRY OF ADAM OF ST-VICTOR

Adam of St-Victor was a prolific composer of Latin hymns and sequences who flourished in the first half of the twelfth century. He was first affiliated with the Cathedral of Notre Dame but left around 1133 for the abbey of St-Victor, which followed the Rule of Saint Augustine. *He most likely had contact with a number of the important theologians, poets, and musicians of his day, including Peter Abelard and Hugh of St-Victor (see Chapters 1 and 2).*

*The sequence (*sequentia*) was at its beginning a liturgical addition to the Alleluia and served as an intermediary between the Mass and the reading of the Gospels. In its early phases, it became a place in the liturgy to expose not only the contrast between humans and angels, but also the mystery of the celebration. By the twelfth century, sequences emerged as poetic and musically independent pieces, even if they followed the Alleluia on most occasions. Adam's strongly rhythmic and imagery-filled poetry reflects the Augustinian-inspired commitment to reform typical of contemporary Victorine exegetes. The themes are readily perceived in the sequences devoted to the feast days of Saint Denis (patron saint of France and the first bishop of Paris), Saint Catherine of Alexandria (who reportedly defeated pagan philosophers and orators in a public debate organized by the emperor), and Saint Augustine, whose conversion from a world of pride and heresy to one of piety and learning in the liberal arts provides the impetus for some especially stirring verses.*

Source: trans. Digby S. Wrangham, *The Liturgical Poetry of Adam of St. Victor* (London: Kegan Paul, Trench, and Co., 1881), vol. 3, pp. 29–35, 77–83; vol. 2, pp. 55–59. Latin.

Saint Denis (9 October)

Greece! rejoice in thy son!
Let all France's pride be shown
     In Saint Denis, her own sire!
And let Paris too, become

Famed through his blessed martyrdom 5
    Show a joy yet more entire!

Specially with heart and voice
Both the happy Church rejoice
    Over all her martyr-bands;
Those whose patronage hath made 10
Far and wide the country glad,
    And through whom the kingdom stands.

Near this father placed, a band
Of illustrious warriors stand,
    Worthy of all memory; 15
But, O royal Church! of all
Dost thou constantly recall
    This one more especially.

By the sovereign pope to France
    Sent forth, he no fear displays 20
At the reckless violence
    Of its unbelieving race

The apostle set o'er Gaul
    To Lutetia came, a town
Which the crafty foe of all 25
    Held in thralldom, as his own.

Here 'mid errors' loathsome mass
    Lay heaped all impurity,
Here a wretched populace
    Gloried in idolatry. 30

Mercury's image they adored,
    A profane and lying god;
But Saint Denis' faith assured
    Soon the devil's work downtrod.

He, while building there God's temple, 35
Taught by word and by example,
    Bright with miracles' bright fame.
    Truth is heeded,

Errors ceded;
As faith growth,   40
Glory gloweth
Round so great a bishop's name.

When the fierce Domitian heareth,
He beside himself appeareth,
    And Sisinnius sendeth down,   45
Who to torture forthwith leadeth,
This good shepherd, who souls feedeth,
    For his faith, life, signs, well known.

Scourge, chains, incarceration,
Feels the old man in his passion;   50
O'er iron bed and fierce flames' heat
And rack his victory is complete.

Fierce wild beasts by prayer he tameth,
Bears his cross, slacks fire that flameth;
After the nails and gibbet–tree   55
Conducted to a jail is he.

As the old man celebrateth
Mass, and near a vast crowd waiteth,
Christ his presence indicateth
    With the heavenly host around.   60
In his close incarceration
Christ still gives him consolation,
And life's bread for sustentation,
    With great glory to be crowned.

Forth to fight the martyr goeth,   65
Heedless what the headsman doeth;
    Till the lictor
    Strikes, and victor
    Makes his victim, as he bled.
Soon the trunk resuscitated,   70
Bearing off its head truncated,
Hither, with that burden weighted,
    Came, by angel–cohorts led.

Let this martyrdom so bright
Fill our hearts with pure delight! Amen.   75

Saint Catharine (25 November)

Let our chorus' voice sonorous
Sound our Maker's praise, who for us
     All things doth in place maintain:
Through whom fight the'unwarlike even,
Through who 'tis to maidens given   5
     Victory over men to gain.

Through whom Alexandria cowered,
By a woman's wits o'erpowered,
     That no woman's strength reveal,
When Saint Catherine, doctors' learning   10
By her doctrines' lore o'erturning,
     In her patience quelled the steel.

She for purity of morals,
Added to ancestral laurels,
     Gained herself a brilliant name;   15
Eminent through her forefathers,
By her holy life she gathers,
     Through higher grace, yet higher fame.

All her bloom of tender beauty
Reading and the toilsome duty   20
     Of deep study wore away:
For to learning she was given,
Secular and sacred, even
     In her first youth's earliest day.

She, a vessel pure, elected,   25
Deemed as mire to be rejected
     Transitory good things here;
All the riches of her father,
All the wealth his sires did gather,
     But contemptible appear.   30

Full of oil her vessel being,
This wise virgin and foreseeing
    Forth the bridegroom goes to meet;
That at once, when he arriveth,
She may at the feast he giveth   35
    Be prepared to take her seat.

She—to die for Christ delighted!—
When before the emperor cited
    In his presence standing, then
With such maiden vigor speaketh,   40
That she mute and silent maketh
    Fifty wise and learned men.

Horrible incarceration,
Hunger-pangs and sore privation,
    That dread frame of spike-set wheels,   45
Yea, whate'er man to her doeth,
She, for God's sake, undergoeth,
    And 'neath all like nerve reveals.

Tortured, she the torturer cheateth,
And the emperor defeateth,   50
    By her woman's constancy;
That the torturer wholly faileth,
And his torture naught availeth,
    Wounds the emperor fearfully.

Then at last, to death commended,   55
She, when death by death is ended,
    Enters on life's joyful day.
Soon their care the angels make it
To remove her corpse, and take it
    For interment far away.   60

From her tomb an oil there stealeth,
Which full many a sick man healeth,
    Clearly by a grace divine.
Ointment rare to us she giveth,
If her prayer our souls relieveth,   65
    As our vices' medicine.

Present with us she may see
  With like joy our joy in her,
And throughout futurity
  All present gifts confer: 70
Here her joy, O may we be,
  And she ours in glory *there*! Amen.

The Conversion of Saint Augustine (5 May)

Let the faithful tell around
  Augustine's praises publicly;
And tongue, heart, life, together sound
  In spiritual ecstasy!

Our father's solemn festal rites,   5
  Returning to us year by year,
Invite us to those pure delights,
  Which nevermore shall disappear.

Well-learned in all those arts was he,
  Which "liberal" we account to be;   10
And in all Scriptures equally,
  From which his thoughts were never free.

At first, puffed up with earthly lore,
  Which neither end nor object knew,
He wished unseen things to explore   15
  By light his senses on them threw.

Whilst he was still a Gentile youth,
  He falls into that error's snares,
Which would believe as very truth,
  That fig-trees, stripped of leaves, she tears. 20

When there from Carthage he had come
  To lecture upon rhetoric,
Though calledst him, O Lord! at Rome
  To the true faith, the Catholic.

When, by God's will and not his own,   25
    He comes to Milan to reside,
To Ambrose there becoming known,
    He straightway takes him for his guide.

When afterwards he was baptized
    By that blest prelate, throughly he   30
The pomp of his poor world despised,
    And changed his life most wondrously.

He, whilst his studies he directs
    Towards the words of Holy Writ,
The witness for all time collects   35
    Of many a writer touching it.

He 'gainst the Manichaean sect
    Proved an insuperable wall;
And by his preaching a respect
    Most wonderful obtained from all.   40

When Monica his mother, who
    Had come from Africa, first knew
Of the conversion of her boy,
    Her heart within her leaped for joy.

For she beholds that very son,   45
    Once as a Manichean known,
Converted from his former state,
    Seeking his Lord to imitate.

Illustrious pastor! us, we pray,
    Who now thine endless praise declare,   50
From this world's ruin and decay
    Preserve thou by unceasing prayer.

Jesu! sweet refuge, where those slake
    Their griefs, who refuge with thee take!
Grant us for this our father's sake   55
    A good departure hence to make. Amen.

58. ANONYMOUS SEQUENCES FROM ST-VICTOR IN PARIS

At the Abbey of St-Victor, a school made famous by several generations of influential scriptural commentators, a new exegesis developed out of the power of musical symbolism and the ability of a single melody to accommodate and even interrelate several texts at once. Building on the poetry of Adam of St-Victor (Doc. 57), the second half of the twelfth century witnessed important expansions of the sequence repertory, even if much of it comes to us anonymously. Laudes Crucis *is a sequence for the feasts of the Finding of the Cross (3 May) and the Exaltation of the Cross (14 September). According to Margot Fassler, the influence of the renewed study of Augustine is reflected both in the language of this sequence and also in the treatment of the subject. The historical exposition of the cross is based on exegetical commentary of the sort found in the writings of the Church Fathers, particularly in the writings of Augustine and those who followed him. Written in the early twelfth century, Fassler has suggested that this sequence may have helped lead the way in the speculative biblicism that is characteristic of the century. The most widespread of all twelfth-century sequences,* Templum Cordis *is a sequence for the Purification (2 February). The feast commemorates the story recounted in Luke 2:22–38 of the Blessed Virgin submitting to the rites of purification after birth, and presenting her child in the temple. In keeping with the Western theological tradition of this rite, the sequence focuses more on the Virgin than on the coming of Christ to the temple; it both explains how Mary can serve as a model for human "Christ-bearers" and how the purity of her life can serve as an inspiration for reformed members of the ecclesiastical heirarchy.*

Source: trans. Margot E. Fassler, *Gothic Song: Victorine Sequences and Augustinian Reform in Twelfth-Century Paris*, 2nd ed. (Notre Dame, IN: University of Notre Dame Press, 2011), 70–72, 331–32. Latin.

a. *Laudes Crucis*

Let us raise praises of the cross
We who exult
By their special glory of the cross.

Let sweet melody touch heaven.
We believe the sweet wood is   5
Worthy of sweet melody.

Let not life be in discord with voice:
When the voice does not disquiet life,
The harmony is sweet.

Let the servants of the cross praise the cross,   10
Who rejoice to be given for themselves
The gifts of life through the cross.
Let all say together and singly,
"Hail salvation of the entire race,
Salvation-bearing tree."   15

O how splendid, how beautiful
Was this altar of salvation,
Red with the blood of the Lamb;
Of the Lamb without stain
Who cleansed the world   20
From the ancient crime

This is the ladder of sinners
Through which Christ, king of heaven,
Drew up all things of himself;
The form of that which   25
Encompasses the four regions of the earth
Shows these things.

These are not new signs,
Not recently was this religion
Of the cross invented: 30
It made waters sweet,
Through it the rock gave water
By Moses's office.

No salvation is in a house
Unless a man protects   35
With the cross on his threshold:
None felt the sword
Nor lost a son
Who did so.

The ark swimming on the water   40
Saves the living species
As many as Noah brought together;
The ark signifies the cross; Noah, Christ;
The waves of his baptism
Which Christ conferred.   45

Gathering sticks in Zarephath
The poor woman
Obtained the hope of salvation:
Without the sticks of faith
Neither the cruse of oil   50
Nor the little pile of meal is any good.

[Rome saw all the ships sunk in the deep,
Together with Maxentius.
Thracians fled, Persians slain,
And the leader of adverse foes   55
Conquered by Heraclius.]

In Scripture under figures
These benefits of the cross are hidden
But now lie open:
Kings believe, enemies recede   60
By the cross alone with Christ leading
One gives flight to thousands.

This ever makes its own courageous
And victorious;
Makes well the sick and languishing,   65
Restrains demons.
It gives freedom to the captives,
Confers the newness of life:
The cross restores all things
To the former worth.   70

O cross, triumphant wood,
True salvation of the world, farewell!
Among woods, none is such wood
With leaf, or flower, or seed.
Christian medicine   75
Save the well, make well the sick:
What human power cannot do
Is done in your name.

Consecrator of the cross, hear
Those standing by for praise of the cross,   80
And, after this life,

SIX: LITURGICAL AND SECULAR POETRY

Take the servants of your cross
To the palace of true light;
Those whom you are willing to subject to torments
Make them not feel the torments;   85
But when the day of wrath will come,
Confer to us and grant to us
Eternal joys. Amen.

b. *Templum Cordis*

Let us adorn the temple of the heart,
Let us renew with new heart
The new joy of the old man:
While he embraces it with his arms
Thus is fulfilled the long-standing desire   5
Of the aged man.

Standing as a sign for the peoples,
He fills the temple with light, the choir with praises,
Hearts with glory;
Now a boy presented in the temple,   10
Later a man offered on the cross,
The sacrifice for sins.

Therefore the savior, therefore Mary;
Let the holy boy, the holy mother
Begin this ceremonial dance,   15
And with prayers
Let the work of the light be carried out,
The work signified by the light of lights.

The word of the father is the true light:
The virginal flesh is the wax,   20
Christ is the shining candle;
He lights up the heart to wisdom,
By which the one straying in sins
Seizes the path of virtue.

Everyone holding Christ through love,   25
Properly, according to the custom of the feast,
Bears a lighted candle;

Just as the old man embraced with his prayers
The word of the father and with his arms
The corporeal pledge of the mother.   30

Rejoice, mother of the creator,
Guileless within, pure without,
Free from wrinkle or stain;
Chosen before by the beloved,
Loved before by the chosen,   35
Handmaiden to God.

Every beauty is clouded over,
Deformed, made hideous,
To those contemplating your beauty;
All flavor grows bitter,   40
Is rejected and grows foul,
To those foretasting your savor.

Every smell seems not to smell
But to stink
To those smelling yours;   45
Every love is wont to be put aside
Immediately, or neglected
By those fostering your love.

Beautiful light of the sea,
Beauty singular among mothers,   50
True parent of truth,
Of the way, of life, of piety,
Medicine of the ages;
Watercourse of the living fountain of life,
Rightfully thirsted for by all,   55
Draught of the strengthening cup,
Sweet to the healthy and the sick,
Health-bearing to the fainting.

Fountain sealed with sanctity,
Pour out streams, flood us;   60
Fountain of inner gardens,
Water thirsting minds
With the flood of your streams;

Abounding fountain, may you overflow,
Wash all that is corrupt in our hearts;   65
Mudless fountain, totally pure,
Purify the heart of worldly people
From the impure world. Amen.

59. MARBOD OF RENNES: POET OF THE LOIRE VALLEY

Marbod of Rennes (c. 1035–1123) was an archdeacon and schoolmaster at Angers and the bishop of Rennes, as well as a respected poet, hagiographer, and hymnologist. He is often grouped with Hildebert of Lavardin (see Doc. 56) and Baudri of Bourgueil as one of the chief examples of the so-called Loire Valley poets who were active around the turn of the twelfth century and drew inspiration from classical themes and especially the lyrics of Ovid. Marbod produced poetry on a wide variety of subjects, ranging from erotic love lyrics to classical and religious verse. Many of his shorter poems were collected in florilegia for the use of students. The poems below include allusions to antiquity, a fondness for nature, descriptions of masculine physical beauty, and a desire for moral reform—in short, they provide a fine assortment of many poetic themes of the twelfth century.

Source: trans. Marc Wolterbeek, from J.-P. Migne, ed., *Patrologia Latina* (Paris: Imprimerie Royale, 1854), vol. 171, cols. 1653, 1685, 1719, 1717, 1717–18; and from Jakob Werner, *Beiträge zur Kunde der lateinischen Literatur des Mittelalters* (Aarau: Sauerländer, 1905), 5. Latin.

[Marbod, Bishop of Rennes, to Hildebert, Bishop of Le Mans]

When I am reading my verses and then bring my eyes to yours,
I seem to see worlds emerging from the sky;
With sublime flight, they rise above the clouds,
Not clinging to the earth, creeping with humble steps.
Often reread, they please only the wise,
Touching arcane matters with few words.
Like great jewels encased in common gold,
With smooth surface they open to learned and unlearned,
No doubt a skill with little painstaking preparation,
And easily flowing from the common current.
Your muse often turns herself with antitheses
Creating recurring circles and sinuous patterns;
For us it suffices to follow a direct path
And weave Minerva's clever words with the dull
So we are not struck by Arachne's plain shuttle.

[The Broken Vase]

While walking through a Roman portico,
I was seeking new sights and came across a sapphire vase.
An ignorant hawker was selling incense within sapphire.
My friend bought three sticks of incense for three cents;
I, prodigal, bought a vase for three and a half.
While I was anxious to carry off the intact piece,
I also bought an empty wicker basket;
I thought a sound vase was placed within,
But I was saddened, most wretched, when I removed a cracked one.
This vase's value would have impressed dinner guests
If the one removed was the one placed within,
But the trickster concealed it—may he never prosper!

[To A Friend]

Returned to these fields after five summers
You want me to write a few songs for you.
Just a few songs, but you want them sweet,
You ask for a mixed plate, just for yourself.
I give you what you seek, what you seek and what I love,
So the song runs quickly on a smooth path.
I want whatever you want, I don't want what you don't want,
And what I don't want, I want you not to want.
Joy that is delayed a long time is stronger;
May the fates grant you a quick return.

[Description of Vernal Beauty]

The grace of spring keeps me from savage ways
As I take my mind's forms from the elements;
I thank Nature herself, rightfully so.
Diverse flowers set off a thousand colors,
Earth has brought forth her fertile wool.
We see groves grow fruit and turn green with leaves
As orioles, blackbirds, jackdaws, woodpeckers, nightingales
Vie in praise, each modulating its own song.
The nests of some lie in trees, not without chicks,
And new progeny without wings hide in thickets.

Green plots are beautiful with blooming roses.
Near them a field ripens with corn,
Near them vines and eggs and nuts.
You cannot count the number of young women and mothers,
The games of youths, the joyful days and feasts.
Whoever sees such beauty, if he does not turn or smile,
Is a savage with strife in his heart.
Whoever does not want to praise earth's beauty
Envies the maker, to whose honor
Frozen winter, summer, autumn, and spring's beauty serve.

[Satire of a Lover (With an Assumed Persona)]

Horace composed an ode about a boy
Whose beauty could have easily been a girl's:
His hair flowed over an ivory neck—
More golden than gold, the kind I've always loved;
His brow was white as snow, his eyes black as pitch,
His unfledged cheeks full of sweetness,
Blooming red and white in light;
His nose was straight, his lips crimson, his teeth pretty.
My mental image of his body keeps within due measure.
He desired his body that clothes should have hidden;
It befits him just as his face does.
The sight of his mouth, radiating and full of grace,
Kindles the heart of the spectator with the brand of love.
But this boy, too pretty and special,
An enticement for any onlooker,
Whom nature formed so wild and fierce
May he consent, before he dies, to be loved.
Harsh and ungrateful, as though born of a tiger,
He laughed so much at the tender words of his supplicant,
He laughed at cares that would never be fulfilled,
And he laughed at the tears of the sighing lover.
He laughed at those he caused to die;
Wicked he is, cruel and wicked,
Who in foul manner denies his beautiful body.
A beautiful face seeks a good mind and a suffering one,
Not haughty, but ready for this and that.
The little flower of youth is quick, too brief.

Afterwards it wastes away, falls, and does not reflourish,
This flesh so light, so milky, and so spotless,
So good, so beautiful, so fleeting, and so tender.
The time will come soon when it becomes vile and rough:
When the worthless flesh, the boyish flesh, weeps.
Therefore, while you flourish, take on mature manners.
While you are able and you are sought, do not be slow to yield
    to love,
Through which you will be dear, nor will you be the less
    because of this.
These words of advice, dearest one,
Are sent to you alone—do not show them to others!

[Listen, Dregs of Youth]

Listen, dregs of youth, whose words are poison,
Whose work is garbage, whose heart is full of dung,
Who you are—look upon and laugh at your own evils, not mine—
Or rather weep, and amend your ways.
You stay awake all night, you sleep during the day;
You praise the adulterous and detest the chaste.
You condemn the satisfied, you love the opulent,
You oppress the unfortunate, and you extol the wealthy.
You sadden seeing the joyful, you laugh seeing the sad.
Your present mind is shaken by a shifty wind;
It wants what it did not want; it does not want what it
    wanted before.
After dining, you swear you tasted nothing, and you don't care
Who dies of hunger, so long as you are full.
You are shattered by adversity; you are proud of prosperity;
You corrupt married women; you break vows made with whores;
You copulate like an animal, never sparing your loins;
You prefer debauchery rather than honest gain;
You prefer cheating rather than letting ships reach port;
You are devoted to usury, you rage not without crime.
Accompanied by minstrels, with interest gained from gems,
You seek dinner guests and wash half-eaten plates.
First you drink wine and later drain the dregs.
You vomit what you eat; then you bring out stored wines.
Hence your filth: with what impudence do you vex others?

60. POEMS OF NATURE AND PATRIOTISM

The following two anonymous poems correspond to a model of panegyric that became increasingly widespread in the late eleventh and early twelfth centuries in which praise of a ruler was connected to the land over which he (and occasionally she) ruled. In the first poem, the two French kings being praised are Philip I (r. 1060–1108) and his son Louis VI (r. 1108–37). In making Nature responsible for the blessing of the land with such a capable ruler, the poet interestingly does not conform to the incipient development of a French royal ideology emphasizing the sacred element of monarchy. Rather, the poem has more in common with the importance of nature found in some other classicizing works in this volume. Various passages draw on the language of classical authors such as Ovid, Statius, and probably Virgil, Lucretius, and Silius Italicus. Nevertheless, there is an unmistakable royal patriotism to the poem, and the poet shows how the Capetian kings of the twelfth century strove to appropriate some of the glory of the Carolingian past for their own dynasty. Louis is compared favorably with the illustrious Carolingians Pepin the Short (d. 768) and Charlemagne (d. 814).

The second poem, Rothoma nobilis, *was written for Geoffrey of Anjou as duke of Normandy and can be dated to the year 1148. Central to this poem is the celebration of Rouen (Rothoma) as a classical Roman foundation, whose name is in fact Rome (Roma) with the three middle letters left out. The link with Rome is not only explicit, but it is also reflected in the opening words, which echo a tenth-century poem* O Roma nobilis, orbis et domina. *It celebrates the city as the capital of the Norman people, who invited the city of Rouen to rule them, a city that now in turn is ruled by Geoffrey. Also noteworthy are the anti-English stance (although hardly surprising given Empress Matilda's failure to wrestle the throne from her cousin Stephen's grip) and the antagonism toward France, which allows a date before the Angevin reconciliation with King Louis VII in 1149. Equally significant is the poet's proposal for a political realignment with the Normans of southern Italy in his striking juxtaposition of Geoffrey of Anjou (count of Anjou 1129–51; duke of Normandy 1144–c. 1150) and Roger II of Sicily (count 1105–30; king 1130–54) as leader of the Normans.*

["Hail, Sweet France"]

Source: trans. Jan M. Ziolkowski and Justin Lake, in *A Garland of Satire, Wisdom, and History: Latin Verse from Twelfth-Century France (Carmina Houghtoniensia)*, ed. Ziolkowski et al. (Cambridge, MA: Harvard University Press, 2007), 105–8. Latin.

Hail, sweet France, fortunate region, beautiful, wholesome,
    delightful, powerful, fruitful, very spacious
renowned for distinctions in war and for a fierce people,
      who are not capable of fearing anything unvanquished.

Winter does not bind you overmuch, nor heat melt you;   5
      thus you have the joys of an almost everlasting spring.
You do not create monsters; you beget no monstrosities; nor are
      you accustomed even to produce anything frightful to see.
In this you have surpassed the countless riches of the Orient,
      that a foreign race never overcomes yours.   10
But, I admit, these are very precious things, and your
      name will therefore be always renowned,
and yet that King Louis bears your scepter lays claim
      for you to high praise in greater quantity than the other things;
both a famous physical appearance and love of prowess   15
      protect him, well enough worthy of greater honor.
It is enough that Nature blessed you in him more
      than whatever she had granted to many generations before.
He, while in tender years, undertook responsibility for ruling
      for the common good and ornament of justice,   20
a marvelous man to watch over the lives and deaths of men,
      and to examine burdens upon the scales.
Harsh and almost fierce in his zeal for justice,
      and cutting off all crimes at the root,
he knows that the medicine does not provide complete health   25
      that does not deeply penetrate wounds.
Often, nevertheless, he moderates his anger in accordance with
  the time and situation;
      he himself, quite just, refrains from doing damage to justice.
He is accessible and accommodating to the prayers and tears of
  the guilty,
      so that he himself entreats on the behalf of his suppliants.   30
He knows that a good part of the world will be laid bare at once
      if all should perish who deserved to die.
Therefore he wishes to be considered just in this way, merciful
  in this way,
      so that neither virtue destroys the other.
This man was born to love the good, hate the faults of the wicked, 35
      bring forth peace, follow the law, and keep moderation,
abundant and thrifty, lest anything be excessive, always hating leisure,
      always loving something useful,
not incautious, not deceitful or violent,
      not dealing with anything precipitately,   40
he deems a twofold heart, a written hand, a chattering tongue
      to be the causes of deadly crime.

Stiff necks and foolish hearts
      as he is brave, he subdues, as he is wise, he chides.
In his devotion he has made Aeneas live again; in his strictness,
  Cato;   45
      in his intellect, Socrates; in his wisdom, Nestor.
In deeds he imitates Ajax, in words Ulysses.
      In appearance he is Paris; in his mind he acts as Hector,
not the kind of Hector whom Achilles dragged behind the chariot,
      but the one who terrified the Danaean ships with fire.   50
Surely Philip did not show himself as such a one earlier,
      who is the father of this man in blood, but not in deserts.
That one is not your king, since, a king in name only,
      he gave you and your people into the hands of the sword.
Since this man thinks nothing cheap, nothing unworthy,   55
      he is fully your king, in both name and reality.
Truly, anyone who is a father is not always wise;
      it is something to disregard foolish fathers.
Nature has provided the example, that often a lovely flower
      is born from a badly twisted vine.   60
A precious fountain often springs up through an ugly channel
      and acquires no flaw from it,
and a savage heart, from a heart full of venom,
      many times sweet and pious speech rings out.
For this reason it is nothing marvelous if, by a similar principle,   65
      the wicked man has vanished, the noble comes forth.
He does not slip who does not imitate a wicked father,
      but rather he who scorns to follow a just one.
Instead, greater praise is won in perpetuity for him
      who by his own virtue advances himself toward reward.   70
Just as he is wretched to the end who desires to be first in perpetuity,
      ever most wicked to his forebear,
so, when there are children of value, each one is protected
      who strives to be the model of his kin.
Louis is confirmed to have done this fully,   75
      and he will do it, since in that way he pleases himself.
Understanding usually exists, usually is found in olden times;
      now our ties sing of something else.
Recently you went astray, wretched, under a gray-haired king
  [Philip I];
      now a young man [Louis VI] leads you along a better path. 80
Recently you were a desert, the empty spoil of robbers,

to the same degree as your cloisters are now green
    with waterings,
and, as if after winter, the warmth of spring returns to you,
    while after sorrows you are full of joy.
On all sides wars are silent, and throughout castles, throughout
    cities,   85
    throughout towns the holy sanction of law flourishes.
Thus this king of yours makes you powerful over yourself,
    so that now no one opposes your commands.
He has compacted a strong and steady peace for you,
    which it is safety to preserve and death to violate.   90
He looks back to the great-grandfathers of his kinsfolk, and
    their fathers and grandfathers
    who have made you the head of kingdoms.
He looks back to Charles and the father of Charles; this man's
    father was
    Pepin, a dwarf in stature, but a giant in mind.
Pepin and Charles, like two lights of the world,   95
    were a great example of goodness to all.
Both were fathers of the fatherland, both kings among kings,
    adorned by the flowers and radiance of their good morals.
Under them a thousand proofs confirm
    that the distinction of the empire grew greatly,   100
whence they procured the everlasting claims to their fame,
    which is righteous to recall, but laborious to count.
The glory of Pepin and Charles remains and will remain,
    since a fame that cannot die immortalizes them
No less is he, although young and a novice, than that man;   105
    rather, if it should be granted him to live, he will be greater.
He will be greater, since he will accomplish things greater by far,
    so that the distinction of our age will be multiplied.
He will be greater in understanding, greater in the love of what
    is right,
    greater in wisdom, greater too in intelligence.   110
In him has come to rest an exceedingly profound strength of
    understanding,
    which will soon become widely known.
Nor will resourceful Nature leave anyone in doubt
    that this man has wholly won her over.
Therefore long live King Louis and everyone   115
    who after this discourse offers kind prayers.

[Rothoma nobilis (*Noble Rome*)]

Source: trans. Elisabeth van Houts, in *Society and Culture in Medieval Rouen, 911–1300*, ed. Leonie V. Hicks and Elma Brenner (Turnhout: Brepols: 2013), 119. Latin.

Noble Rouen, ancient city, mighty and
     beautiful.
The Norman people put you in charge of them;
Imperial honor adorns you;
Like Rome you are, in reputation and in name,

Remove the middle [Ro 'tho' ma]
     and Rouen becomes Rome.
Conquered Brittany, subdued by your army,
     is a servant;
The arrogant English, the cold Scots,
     and savage French
Beg to pay you what they owe.
Under Duke Godfrey the enemy was slain,
     weapons are idle;

Duke Geoffrey, whose name is known
     by all as 'joy'
In such a ruler fortunate Rouen rejoices.
Sprung from you of famous Norman blood,
Rules Roger victorious, wise, and wealthy
You mighty Roger, you greater glory
     amongst kings;

You conquered Italy and Sicily, and Africa;
Greece and Syria are afraid of you, as is Persia
Black Ethiopia and white Germany return
To seek your command and your protection.
True faith bestows on you the large scepter;
You alone are worthy to rule the world.

61. THE GOLIARDS: POETS OF WINE, WOMEN, AND SONG

Goliard is a catch-all term that refers to a mostly anonymous subset of writers who wrote bibulous, satiric Latin poetry. Precursors to their art can be traced back to Carolingian times, but the term refers mainly to those poets who flourished in the twelfth and early thirteenth centuries, when schools and universities cultivated an increasingly educated class of students and scholars equipped with the skills (and disillusionment) to mock the scholastic and ecclesiastical environment they knew so well. Because so little is known about the identity of these poets, there is some uncertainty as to who exactly their literate audience may have been or, indeed, whether they constituted an organized class of poets at all. The word goliard itself is of uncertain derivation. Gerald of Wales tells us that it comes from the Latin gula, or gluttony, while modern scholars have suggested that it relates to the French gaillard, a gay or cheerful fellow. In his letter to Pope Innocent II (see Doc. 19), Bernard of Clairvaux refers to Abelard as Goliath, and there are some who believe that the term may refer either specifically to adherents of Peter Abelard or more generally to some mythical "Bishop Golias," a medieval Latin form of the name Goliath, who evidently inspired several poems, including the Archpoet's mock Confession (Doc. 63). A number of these so-called goliardic poems have come down to us, either individually or in collections such as the Carmina Burana codex (see Doc. 52). There is no single thread or subject matter that unites these poems, but recurring themes include irreverent mockery of the clerical classes, disillusionment with the status quo, and depictions of the physicality of love. A number of poems concern youth, drinking, and raucous debauchery—timeless themes, no doubt, in the history of student life.

Source: trans. John Addington Symonds, *Wine, Women and Song: Mediaeval Latin Students' Songs Now First Translated into English by John Addington Symonds* (London: Chatto & Windus, 1884), 59–60, 78, 162–63; and George F. Whicher, *The Goliard Poets: Medieval Latin Songs and Satires* (Westport, CT: Greenwood Press Publishers, 1979), 25, 249. Latin.

[The Invitation to Youth]

Take your pleasure, dance and play,
Each with other while ye may:
Youth is nimble, full of grace;
Age is lame, of tardy pace.

We the wars of love should wage,
Who are yet of tender age;
'Neath the tents of Venus dwell
All the joys that youth loves well.

Young men kindle heart's desire;
You may liken them to fire:
Old men frighten love away
With cold frost and dry decay.

[There's No Lust Like to Poetry]

Sweet in goodly fellowship
    Tastes red wine and rare O!
But to kiss a girl's ripe lip
    Is a gift more fair O!
Yet a gift more sweet, more fine,
    Is the lyre of Maro!
While these three good gifts were mine,
    I'd not change with Pharaoh.

Bacchus wakes within my breast
    Love and love's desire,
Venus comes and stirs the blessed
    Rage of Phoebus' fire;
Deathless honor is our due
    From the laurelled sire:
Woe should I turn traitor to
    Wine and love and lyre!

Should a tyrant rise and say,
    "Give up wine!" I'd do it
"Love no girls!" I would obey,
    Though my heart should rue it.
"Dash thy lyre!" suppose he saith,
    Naught should bring me to it;
"Yield thy lyre or die!" my breath,
    Dying, should thrill through it!

[A Wandering Student's Petition]

I, a wandering scholar lad,
    Born for toil and sadness,
Oftentimes am driven by
    Poverty to madness.

Literature and knowledge I
    Fain would still be earning
Were it not that want of pelf
    Makes me cease from learning.

These torn clothes that cover me
      Are too thin and rotten;
Oft I have to suffer cold,
      By the warmth forgotten.

Since I can attend at church,
      Sing God's praises duly;
Mass and vespers both I miss,
      Though I love them truly.

Oh, thou pride of N—,
      By thy worth I pray thee
Give the suppliant help in need,
      Heaven will sure repay thee.

Take a mind unto thee now
      Like unto Saint Martin;
Clothe the pilgrim's nakedness,
      Wish him well at parting.

So may God translate your soul
      Into peace eternal,
And the bliss of saints be yours
      In his realm supernal.

[Invitation to a Mistress, from The Cambridge Songs*]*

Nay, come and visit me, sweet friend,
Heart of my heart, this prayer I send:
Enter, I beg, my little room
So trimly decked—you know for whom.

There stand the chairs, in each a cushion,
And lovely curtains in addition;
About the house are scattered flowers
And scented herbs most sweet in bowers.

There likewise is the table set
Where dainties brought from far are met;
There clear and plenteous wines invite you,
And all things else, dear, to delight you.

And while we dine, sweet sounds shall come
From high-pitched pipe and punctual drum;
Skillful performers, girl and boy,
Will play the songs you enjoy.

His quill will twang the cither's wire,
Her hand will pluck the sweeter lyre,
While servants from full platters pass
Spiced wine in cups of colored glass.

No joys that banquets can afford
Can match our converse afterward,
For one choice intimacy brings
Delights that cause no surfeitings.

Sweet sister, come—my only goal
And choicer portion of my soul,
Dear beyond all, light of my eyes,
My hope, my joy, my life, my prize.

"I've been alone in darkling woods,
Seeking the deepest solitudes;
I've fled from voices time again
And kept aloof from sight of men."

No more delay, dearest, permit;
Love is our book—let's open it.
Without you I am scarce alive,
Only by loving can we thrive.

Why not be brave and say that you
Will do soon what you're bound to do?
What sense is there in hesitating?
Come, precious—I'm not good at waiting.

[Belly-Worship, from Carmina Burana*]*

Epicurus loudly cries:
"A well-stuffed belly satisfies."
Belly's my god, and I his slave,
Such a god our palates crave,

With a kitchen for a shrine—
Ah, that incense is divine!

Here's a proper god at last.
No time is his time to fast;
Every morning ere he sups
He is belching in his cups,
And his liquor and his food
Are his true beatitude.

Lust for guzzling he indulges,
Like a leathern flask he bulges;
Lunch prolongs itself to dinner,
Hence his cheeks are never thinner
But are laced with many a vein.
Appetite is still his chain.

Strict religious exercise
Causes Belly's gorge to rise:
Inward qualms make Belly roar,
As when wine with mead makes war;
Life is happy, life is easy,
Just so Belly be not queasy.

Belly says: "I care for nought
Save myself; my only thought
Is to vegetate in quiet
Tending to my proper diet;
Give me but meat and drink, with those
Secure I sleep, serene repose."

62. THREE MODELS OF SECULAR POETRY

Many secular poems from the twelfth century are anonymous, but a few poets are known by name, even if not much is known about them. Peter of Blois (c. 1135–1212) is one of the best-known composers of secular Latin poetry, in large part because his career as archbishop is so well documented, especially through his extensive correspondence. Peter is also known to have been very interested in poetic metaphors, as is evidenced in his treatise on the art of letter writing. Among the poems attributed to him is a corpus of love lyrics in a manuscript now in the British Library (Arundel 384), which, if they are indeed

Peter's, would constitute a good illustration of the interpenetration of the various branches of the rhetorical arts. They are equally notable for their classical allusions. Arundel 16 provides a good example of these interweaving themes: it describes the lover's experience of the beloved as he yearns to win her while fearing her loss, but it is also adorned with phrases and imagery from Martianus Capella's The Marriage of Philology and Mercury, *a text that generated much commentary in the twelfth century and inspired many writers of philosophical epic.*

Much less is known about the poet known by his Latin pseudonym, Hugh "Primas," but he won great acclaim as a wit and as an acerbic critic of churchmen. Like the poems of the Goliards, his wry verses document certain institutional problems in French society, most especially church reform and the election of bishops. Hugh Primas was also inspired by classical themes—for instance, the fall of Troy appears in several of his poems—but his most memorable lines are the ones that deploy verbal weapons such as wit, humor, irony, sarcasm, and obscenity. His poem addressed to a bishop concisely encapsulates these themes.

The third model of secular poetry in this selection is Hildebert of Lavardin, whose hymn on the Trinity opened the chapter (Doc. 56). Here his classical knowledge is clearly on display in a lengthy poem inspired by his three visits to the city of Rome, as well as in a shorter poem on the theme of Lucretia's rape and suicide.

Source: trans. Joseph Rudolph, from *The Oxford Poems of Hugh Primas and the Arundel Lyrics*, ed. C.J. McDonough, Toronto Medieval Latin Texts (Toronto: Pontifical Institute for Mediaeval Studies, 1984), 76, 78 for Peter of Blois; 178 for Hugh Primas. Latin.

[Attributed to Peter of Blois: Arundel 16]

With this fresh birth of leaf on bough
    and grasses sprouting forth,
a gentler force makes fruitful now
    the fecund womb of earth.
The sun sets equal day and night
and steers his lofty horses' flight
    beneath bright Aries' way.
The north wind has been tamed at last!
The elements, in bliss bound fast,
    hold wedding feasts today.

    Ah, Venus! She
    lays her commands on me
    so heavily!
    Aside they can't be sent.
    Love's law, racked with anxiety,

it rules lawlessly—
    an enemy
to every law's intent.

This flower the north wind had hid
    in a cold stepmother's crease;
now mother Rhea, of Saturn rid,
    with a rustle of sweet breeze
returns the bloom to life anew,
steeped in sweets of springtime dew.
    She paints and gilds the ground
while the sun with his bright rays
rebuilds what things the shorter days
    had strewn as waste around.

    Ah, Venus! She . . .

But, following the camp of love,
    the mind to phantoms strays.
Even the mighty gods above
    Love's mad liquor sways!
Happy in my hapless ill,
I used to want with all my will
    a healed-over scar,
but, with a kiss and laughing wild,
Flora all my wits beguiled—
    all reason gone afar!

    Ah Venus! she . . .

Her face, a false interpreter
    for the meaning of her mind,
now shows it to be set and sure
    that Cupid, so unkind
and cruel, can never be pressed back.
No vow she makes, yet in her look
    a different wish expressed.
By hapless hope I, drawn astray,
can only wish to hear them say:
    "grant him eternal rest"

    Ah Venus! she . . .

[Hugh Primas: To a Bishop]

To the Bishop, from Primas:
you play well, they like to stress,
And, by their rumor, you
are a man most upright too.
And the way you dress and dine,
I'd say you're doing fine.

Now to maintain the good life's arts
(with the way you use your parts!)
you'd better drink, drink, drink,
or you'll get sick, I think.

Hildebert of Lavardin

Source: trans. Joseph Rudolph, from *Hildebertus Cenomannensis Episcopus: Carmina Minora*, ed. Brian A. Scott, Bibliotheca Scriptorum Graecorum et Romanorum Teubnerinia (Munich: KG Saur, 2001), 9–10, 22–24. Latin.

De Roma

Nothing that stands can be your equal, Rome,
though you so near to total ruin lie.
Broken you teach how great you were once, whole.
A long age has destroyed your haughty might:
Caesar's strongholds, the temples of the proud,   5
they all in bogs of mouldering ruin rest.
A fierce Araxes shuddered to behold
that labor, labor laid to waste, when firm
it stood, and then he mourned to see it fall—
a city that the swords of mighty kings,   10
the wisdom of old men, and, high above,
the mighty gods all made head of the world.
Caesar wished more to have it by a crime,
than as a father and a faithful friend.
The city, swelling with a tribal zeal,   15
tamed friends and foes and felons by her strength,
and broke them with her laws, and brought them in.
As she was rising at the riverside,
the care of her forebears kept earnest watch,

and strangers' loyalty made glad the task.   20
Each region sent her workers, wealth, and stones;
she ringed herself around in mighty walls;
princes with treasures paid, with favors fate,
and craftsmen each with all their well-plied trades,
all riches of the world.
      The city fell,   25
and if I dare to undertake this task
to speak a single worthy thing of her,
I can but say, "Rome was."

But O! Not year on year, nor flame, nor sword
has brought this city's honor to decay!   30
So much yet stands, so much in ruin lies
that neither standing part may be brought down,
nor ruined part rebuilt.
      Gather riches,
fresh marble blocks, and favor of the gods;
let craftsmen's hands now labor at new works,   35
yet still no scheme can match the standing wall
nor bring a single ruin back again.
The care of men has built up mighty Rome
so great no work of gods could lay it low.
Even the gods themselves here gaze in awe   40
at shapely forms of high divinity,
and yearn to match their sculpted visages.
Nature could not make gods with such a face,
by which man here made god in wondrous forms.
These gods have faces, and are honored more   45
for artifice than for divinity.
Happy this city, were it now without
these dominating men or if to them
it were hateful to lack that ancient faith.

Lucretia

When Lucretia took the sword
and buried it in her chaste breast,
she said, as her warm blood poured forth:
"Now go, my witnesses, and tell
that I was not a tyrant's friend:

blood before men, to gods my soul.
Called forth, they shall speak well for me:
one to the shades, one to the sky."

63. THE ARCHPOET, *CONFESSION OF GOLIAS*

*Little is known about the secular verse writer known simply as the Archpoet (fl. 1159–
65). His epithet derives from the titles of his patron, Rainald of Dassel (c. 1120–67), who
was arch-chancellor to Holy Roman Emperor Frederick I Barbarossa (r. 1155–90) and
archbishop of Cologne. The Archpoet occupied the same position in Rainald's household
as minstrel in a secular court, and he used his talents to secure favors for himself and his
friends. His* Confession of Golias *is perhaps the most famous of all goliardic poems,
even though some have argued that the Archpoet was no goliard at all. Indeed, over the
years, many different interpretations of the poem's meaning and significance have been
proposed. Some have called it the greatest drinking song in the world. Others have focused
on the inherent ambiguity of the poem, suggesting that beyond its defiant, humorous,
and parody-filled lyrics lies a penetrating psychological study of a character in the grip
of vice. The translation by the nineteenth-century English poet and literary critic John
Addington Symonds takes some liberties of interpretation, but successfully preserves both
meter and rhyme.*

Source: trans. John Addington Symonds, *Wine, Women, and Song* (London: Chatto and Windus,
1884), 55–62. Latin.

Boiling in my spirit's veins
With fierce indignation,
From my bitterness of soul
    Springs self-revelation:
Framed am I of flimsy stuff,   5
    Fit for levitation,
Like a thin leaf which the wind
    Scatters from its station.

While it is the wise man's part
    With deliberation   10
On a rock to base his heart's
    Permanent foundation,
With a running river I
    Find my just equation,
Which beneath the self-same sky   15
    Hath no habitation.

Carried am I like a ship
       Left without a sailor,
Like a bird that through the air
       Flies where tempests hale her;   20
Chains and fetters hold me not,
       Naught avails a jailer;
Still I find my fellows out
       Toper, gamester, railer.

To my mind all gravity   25
       Is a grave subjection;
Sweeter far than honey are
       Jokes and free affection.
All that Venus bids me do,
       Do I with erection,   30
For she ne'er in heart of man
       Dwelt with dull dejection.

Down the broad road do I run,
       As the way of youth is;
Snare myself in sin, and ne'er   35
       Think where faith and truth is;
Eager far for pleasure more
       Than soul's health, the sooth is,
For this flesh of mine I care,
       Seek not truth where truth is.   40

Prelate, most discreet of priests,
       Grant me absolution!
Dear's the death whereof I die,
       Sweet my dissolution;
For my heart is wounded by   45
       Beauty's soft suffusion;
All the girls I come not nigh,
       Mine are in illusion.

'Tis most arduous to make
       Nature's self surrender;   50
Seeing girls, to blush and be
       Purity's defender!
We young men our longings ne'er

Shall to stern law render,
    Or preserve our fancies from   55
        Bodies smooth and tender.

Who, when into fire he falls,
        Keeps himself from burning?
Who within Pavia's walls
        Fame of chaste is earning?   60
Venus with her finger calls
        Youths at every turning,
Snares them with her eyes, and thralls
        With her amorous yearning.

If you brought Hippolitus   65
        To Pavia Sunday,
He'd not be Hippolitus
        On the following Monday;
Venus there keeps holiday
        Every day as one day;   70
'Mid these towers in no tower dwells
        Venus Verecunda [a modest Venus].

In the second place I own
        To the vice of gaming:
Cold indeed outside I seem,   75
        Yet my soul is flaming:
But when once the dice-box hath
        Stripped me to my shaming,
Make I songs and verses fit
        For the world's acclaiming.   80

In the third place, I will speak
        Of the tavern's pleasure;
For I never found nor find
        There the least displeasure;
Nor shall find it till I greet   85
        Angels without measure,
Singing requiems for the souls
        In eternal leisure.

In the public-house to die
  Is my resolution;   90
Let wine to my lips be nigh
  At life's dissolution:
That will make the angels cry,
  With glad elocution,
"Grant this toper, God on high,   95
  Grace and absolution!"

With the cup the soul lights up,
  Inspirations flicker;
Nectar lifts the soul on high
  With its heavenly ichor: 100
To my lips a sounder taste
  Hath the tavern's liquor
Than the wine a village clerk
  Waters for the vicar.

Nature gives to every man   105
  Some gift serviceable;
Write I never could nor can
  Hungry at the table;
Fasting, any stripling to
  Vanquish me is able;   110
Hunger, thirst, I liken to
  Death that ends the fable.

Nature gives to every man
  Gifts as she is willing;
I compose my verses when   115
  Good wine I am swilling,
Wine the best for jolly guest
  Jolly hosts are filling;
From such wine rare fancies fine
  Flow like dews distilling.   120
Such my verse is wont to be
  As the wine I swallow;
No ripe thoughts enliven me
  While my stomach's hollow;
Hungry wits on hungry lips   125
  Like a shadow follow,

But when once I'm in my cups,
    I can beat Apollo.

Never to my spirit yet
    Flew poetic vision   130
Until first my belly bad
    Plentiful provision;
Let but Bacchus in the brain
    Take a strong position,
Then comes Phoebus flowing in   135
    With a fine precision.
There are poets, worthy men,
    Shrink from public places,
And in lurking-hole or den
    Hide their pallid faces;   140
There they study, sweat, and woo
    Pallas and the Graces,
But bring nothing forth to view
    Worth the girls' embraces.

Fasting, thirsting, toil the bards,   145
    Swift years flying o'er them;
Shun the strife of open life,
    Tumults of the forum;
They, to sing some deathless thing,
    Lest the world ignore them,   150
Die the death, expend their breath,
    Drowned in dull decorum.

Lo! my frailties I've betrayed,
    Shown you every token,
Told you what your servitors   155
    Have against me spoken;
But of those men each and all
    Leave their sins unspoken,
Though they play, enjoy to-day,
    Scorn their pledges broken.   160

Now within the audience-room
    Of this blessed prelate,
Sent to hunt out vice, and from

Hearts of men expel it;
Let him rise, nor spare the bard,   165
    Cast at him a pellet:
He whose heart knows not crime's smart,
    Show my sin and tell it!

I have uttered openly
    All I knew that shamed me,   170
And have spewed the poison forth
    That so long defamed me;
Of my old ways I repent,
    New life hath reclaimed me;
God beholds the heart—'twas man   175
    Viewed the face and blamed me.

Goodness now hath won my love,
    I am wroth with vices;
Made a new man in my mind,
    Lo, my soul arises!   180
Like a babe new milk I drink—
    Milk for me suffices,
Lest my heart should longer be
    Filled with vain devices.

Thou Elect of fair Cologne [i.e., Rainald of Dassel],   185
    Listen to my pleading!
Spurn not thou the penitent;
    See, his heart is bleeding!
Give me penance! what is due
    For my faults exceeding   190
I will bear with willing cheer,
    All thy precepts heeding.

Lo, the lion, king of beasts,
    Spares the meek and lowly;
Toward submissive creatures he   195
    Tames his anger wholly.
Do the like, ye powers of earth,
    Temporal and holy!
Bitterness is more than's right
    When 'tis bitter solely.   200

CHAPTER SEVEN

ART AND ARCHITECTURE: THEORY AND PRACTICE

In the history of art and architecture, the notion of a "renaissance of the twelfth century" is both convenient and confusing. Between the spread of new ideas and the evolution of craftsmanship there was naturally some relation, but establishing its nature and meaning has long proved elusive, and scholars remain divided on the degrees of relation and the direction of influence. The selections in this chapter draw attention to two related developments in the history of the material arts: the meaning and symbolism behind the new styles in twelfth-century craftsmanship, and the craftsmanship itself.

The twelfth century saw the rise of the Gothic, first visible in Abbot Suger's building program of St-Denis (Doc. 64). It used to be thought that the essence of the switch from Romanesque to Gothic was the introduction of the pointed arch, and that this was due to Muslim influence. Other factors were clearly also involved, including technological advances, new elements of style, and a new relationship between geometry and proportion. The attention that Suger gave to light, size, and elaborate ornamentation influenced generations of master builders, but it also provoked reactions from influential figures such as Bernard of Clairvaux and Peter the Chanter (Docs. 66 and 68). The monk Theophilus's treatise (Doc. 65) displays a range of thought from the patron's mind and devout purposes through to the minute technical details of craftsmanship in a single book, while the debate between Rupert of Deutz and Herman-Judah of Cologne (Doc. 67) addresses questions of the representation of the crucifixion in the Jewish–Christian controversy specifically, and of the symbolism in medieval art more generally.

64. ABBOT SUGER ON THE ART TREASURES OF ST-DENIS

St-Denis was the favored royal abbey of the kings of France, both before the twelfth century and long afterwards. Suger (c. 1081–1151) was its abbot from 1122 until his death, during which time he also served as a valued counselor and biographer to two kings. Under his direction, the abbey prospered as never before. He was meticulous in documentation and oversight, and by his own account he more than tripled the revenues of the royal domain. In 1127 he undertook major moral and architectural reforms of the abbey. The building campaign was conducted in three stages, beginning with the west façade, which Suger completed in 1140 (except for the west towers). He then turned east and rebuilt

Figure 11: A nineteenth-century lithograph by Félix Benoist of the Basilica of St-Denis, the royal burial site of French kings since the early Middle Ages. The flying buttresses and spire are Gothic, but the radiating chapels that envelop the interior choir are from the twelfth-century program of expansion initiated by Abbot Suger.

Source: Wikimedia Commons.

the choir, which included a double ambulatory, pointed arches, and ribbed vaulting (see fig. 12). In the choir, which he dedicated in 1144, walls were pierced by tall windows of stained glass that let in a flood of light, embodying the Neoplatonic ideal of luminosity. As he explained, the "new light" was intended to instruct the worshipper that there was a reality beyond that perceived by the senses. Finally, he began work on the nave, which remained incomplete at the time of his death.

Suger gave great attention to the power of objects and light to function in a spiritual and pedagogical capacity. Many of his most striking innovations in architectural design were the product of a personal metaphysic derived, most likely, from a reading of Pseudo-Dionysius the Areopagite, a fifth-century Neoplatonic writer whom legend identified with Saint Denis—apostle to France, first bishop of Paris, and patron of the abbey. Some scholars therefore contend that on the basis of the Dionysian theory

Figure 12: The double ambulatory of the choir at St-Denis, enlarged by Abbot Suger according to his specifications.

Source: Photograph by seir+seir on flickr.com; https://www.flickr.com/photos/seier/6471134549. See license at https://creativecommons.org/licenses/by/2.0/.

of emanations, Suger saw art as a means to raise the mind from a focus on the material world to an examination of the power and majesty of God. In the second work excerpted below, On What Was Done under His Administration, *Suger details the various objects of his collection and the functions they served within the liturgical service of the abbey. The final section describes an ancient Egyptian porphyry vase that was mounted in a silver-gilt eagle, "for the service of the altar." A photograph of "Suger's Eagle," as the vase has come to be known, graces the cover of this book, a fitting symbol of the old made new.*

Source: trans. Erwin Panofsky, Abbot Suger, *On the Abbey Church of St. Denis and Its Art Treasures,* 2nd ed. (Princeton, NJ: Princeton University Press, 1979), 83, 87, 89, 91, 41, 47, 49, 51, 57, 59, 63, 65, 79. Latin.

The Other Little Book on the Consecration of the
Church of St-Denis

The admirable power of one unique and supreme reason equalizes by proper composition the disparity between things human and divine; and what seems mutually to conflict by inferiority of origin and contrariety of nature is conjoined by the single, delightful, concordance of one superior, well-tempered harmony. Those, indeed, who crave to be glorified by a participation in this supreme and eternal reason often devote their attention to this continual controversy of the similar and dissimilar, and to the trial and sentence of the litigant parties, sitting on the throne of the acute mind as though on a tribunal. With the aid of loving-kindness, whereby they may withstand internal strife and inner sedition, they drink wholesomely from the fountain of the reason of eternal wisdom, preferring that which is spiritual to that which is corporeal, that which is eternal to that which is perishable. They set aside the vexations and the most grievous anxieties of corporal sensuality and of the exterior senses; elevating themselves from the oppression by these, focusing the undivided vision of their mind upon the hope of eternal reward, they zealously seek only that which is eternal. They forget carnal desires to the admiration and amazement of others; thus, through communion with supreme reason and eternal bliss, they rejoice—according to the promise of the only-begotten Son of God: "In your patience possess ye your souls" [Luke 21:19]—in being deservedly united with the glorious consciousness. Yet human nature, debased and gravely impaired by the corruption of its first condition, embracing the present rather than expecting the future, would in no wise be strong enough for this, were it not for the fact that the abundant aid given to human reason and rational intelligence by supreme and divine loving-kindness mercifully enables us to carry it into effect. Hence we read: "His tender mercies are over all His works" [Psalm 144:9]. . . .

When the glorious and famous king of the Franks, Dagobert, notable for his royal magnanimity in the administration of his kingdom and yet no less devoted to the Church of God, had fled to the village of Catulliacum in order to evade the intolerable wrath of his father Clothaire the Great, and when he had learned that the venerable images of the holy martyrs who rested there—appearing to him as very beautiful men clad in snow-white garments—requested his service and unhesitatingly promised him their aid with words and deeds, he decreed with admirable affection that a basilica of the saints be built with regal magnificence. When he had constructed this [basilica] with a marvelous variety of marble columns he enriched it incalculably with treasures of purest gold and silver and hung on its walls, columns and arches tapestries woven of gold and richly adorned with a variety of pearls, so that it might seem to excel the ornaments of all other churches and, blooming with incomparable luster and adorned with every terrestrial beauty, might shine with inestimable splendor. Only one thing was wanting in him: that he did not allow for the size that was necessary. Not that anything was lacking in his devotion or good will; but perhaps there existed thus far, at that time of the Early Church, no [church] either greater or [even] equal in size; or perhaps [he thought that] a smallish one—reflecting the splendor of gleaming gold and gems to the admiring eyes more keenly and delightfully because they were nearer—would glow with greater radiance than if it were built larger.

Through a fortunate circumstance attending this singular smallness—the number of the faithful growing and frequently gathering to seek the intercession of the saints—the aforesaid basilica had come to suffer grave inconveniences. Often on feast days, completely filled, it disgorged through all its doors the excess of the crowds as they moved in opposite directions, and the outward pressure of the foremost ones not only prevented those attempting to enter from entering but also expelled those who had already entered. At times you could see, a marvel to behold, that the crowded multitude offered so much resistance to those who strove to flock in to worship and kiss the holy relics, the nail and crown of the Lord, that no one among the countless thousands of people because of their very density could move a foot; that no one, because of their very congestion, could [do] anything but stand like a marble statue, stay benumbed or, as a last resort, scream. The distress of the women, however, was so great and so intolerable that you could see with horror how they, squeezed in by the mass of strong men as in a winepress, exhibited bloodless faces as in imagined death; how they cried out horribly as though in labor; how several of them, miserably trodden underfoot [but then] lifted by the pious assistance of men above the heads of the crowd, marched forward as though upon a pavement; and how many others, gasping with their last breath, panted in the cloisters of the brethren to the despair of everyone. Moreover the brethren who were showing the tokens of the Passion of Our Lord to the visitors had to yield to their anger and rioting and many a time, having no place to turn, escaped with the relics through the windows. When I was instructed by the brethren as a schoolboy I used to hear of this; in my youth I deplored it from without; in my mature years I zealously strove to have it corrected. "But when it pleased Him who separated me from my mother's womb, and called me by His grace" [Galatians 1:15], to place insignificant me, although my merits were against it, at the head of the so important administration of this sacred church; then, impelled to a correction of the aforesaid inconvenience only by the ineffable mercy of almighty God and by the aid of the holy martyrs our patron saints, we resolved to hasten, with all our soul and all the affection of our mind, to the enlargement of the aforesaid place—we who would never have presumed to set our hand to it, nor even to think of it, had not so great, so necessary, so useful and honorable an occasion demanded it.

Since in the front part, toward the north, at the main entrance with the main doors, the narrow hall was squeezed in on either side by twin towers neither high nor very sturdy but threatening ruin, we began, with the help of God, strenuously to work on this part, having laid very strong material foundations for a straight nave and twin towers, and most strong spiritual ones of which it is said: "For other foundation can no man lay than that is laid, which is Jesus Christ" [1 Corinthians 3:11]. Leaning upon God's inestimable counsel and irrefragable aid, we proceeded with this so great and so sumptuous work to such an extent that, while at first, expending little, we lacked much, afterwards, expending much, we lacked nothing at all and even confessed in our abundance: "Our sufficiency is of God" [2 Corinthians 3:5]. Through a gift of God a new quarry, yielding very strong stone, was discovered such as in quality and quantity had never been found in these regions. There arrived a skillful crowd of masons, stonecutters, sculptors and other workmen so that—thus and otherwise—divinity relieved us of our fears and favored us with Its goodwill by comforting us and by providing us with unexpected [resources]. I used to compare the least to the greatest: Solomon's riches could not have sufficed for his temple any more than did ours for this work had not the same author of the same work abundantly supplied his attendants. The identity of the author and the work provides a sufficiency for the worker.

In carrying out such plans my first thought was for the concordance and harmony of the ancient and the new work. By reflection, by inquiry, and by investigation through different regions of remote districts, we endeavored to learn where we might obtain marble columns or columns the equivalent thereof. Since we found none, only one thing was left to us, distressed in mind and spirit: we might obtain them from Rome (for in Rome we had often seen wonderful ones in the Palace of Diocletian and other baths) by safe ships through the Mediterranean, thence through the English Sea and the tortuous windings of the River Seine, at great expense to our friends and even by paying passage money to our enemies, the nearby Saracens. For many years, for a long time, we were perplexed, thinking and making inquiries—when suddenly the generous munificence of the almighty, condescending to our labors, revealed to the astonishment of all and through the merit of the holy martyrs, what one would never have thought or imagined: very fine and excellent [columns]. Therefore, the greater acts of grace, contrary to hope and human expectation, Divine mercy had deigned to bestow by a suitable place where it could not be more agreeable to us, the greater [acts of gratitude] we thought it worth our effort to offer in return for the remedy of so great an anguish.

The Book of Suger, Abbot of St-Denis, on What Was Done under
His Administration

In the twenty-third year of our administration, when we sat on a certain day in the general chapter, conferring with our brethren about matters both common and private, these very beloved brethren and sons began strenuously to beseech me "in charity" [1 Corinthians 4:21, 16:14; Ephesians 1:4, 3:17, 4:2, 4:16; Colossians 2:2; 1 Thessalonians 5:13; 2 Thessalonians 3:5] that I might not allow the fruits of our so great labors to be passed over in silence; and rather to save for the memory of posterity, in pen and ink, those increments which the generous munificence of almighty God had bestowed upon this church, in the time of our prelacy, in the acquisition of new assets as well as in the recovery of lost ones, in the multiplication of improved possessions, in the construction of buildings, and in the accumulation of gold, silver, most precious gems, and very good textiles. For this one thing they promised us two in return: by such a record we would deserve the continual fervor of all succeeding brethren in their prayers for the salvation of our soul; and we would rouse, through this example, their zealous solicitude for the good care of the church of God. We thus devoutly complied with their devoted and reasonable requests, not with any desire for empty glory nor with any claim to the reward of human praise and transitory compensation; and lest, after our demise, the church be diminished in its revenue by any or anyone's roguery and the ample increments which the generous munificence of God has bestowed in the time of our administration be tacitly lost under bad successors, we have deemed it worthy and useful, just as we thought fitting to begin, in its proper place, our tale about the construction of the buildings and the increase of the treasures with the body of the church of the most blessed martyrs, Denis, Rusticus, and Eleutherius. . . .

Of the Cast and Gilded Doors

Bronze casters having been summoned and sculptors chosen, we set up the main doors on which are represented the Passion of the savior and his resurrection, or rather ascension, with great cost and much expenditure for their gilding as was fitting for the noble porch. Also [we set up] others, new ones on the right side and the old ones on the left beneath the mosaic which, though contrary to modern custom, we ordered to be executed there and to be affixed to the tympanum of the portal. We also committed ourselves richly to elaborate the tower[s] and the upper crenellations of the front, both for the beauty of the church and, should circumstances require it, for practical purposes. Further we ordered the year of the consecration, lest it be forgotten, to be inscribed in copper-gilt letters in the following manner:

For the splendor of the church that has fostered and exalted him,
Suger has labored for the splendor of the church.
Giving thee a share of what is thine, O martyr Denis,
He prays to thee to pray that he may obtain a share of Paradise.
The year was the one thousand, one hundred, and fortieth
Year of the Word when [this structure] was consecrated.

The verses on the door, further, are these:

Whoever thou art, if thou seekest to extol the glory of these doors,
Marvel not at the gold and the expense but at the craftsmanship
   of the work.
Bright is the noble work; but, being nobly bright, the work
Should brighten the minds, so that they may travel, through the
   true lights,
To the true light where Christ is the true door.
In what manner it be inherent in this world the golden door defines:
The dull mind rises to truth through that which is material
And, in seeing this light, is resurrected from its former submersion.

And on the lintel:

Receive, O stern judge, the prayers of thy Suger;
Grant that I be mercifully numbered among thy own sheep.

Of the Enlargement of the Upper Choir

In the same year, cheered by so holy and so auspicious a work, we hurried to
begin the chamber of divine atonement in the upper choir where the continual
and frequent Victim of our redemption should be sacrificed in secret without
disturbance by the crowds. And, as is found in [our] treatise about the consecration of this upper structure, we were mercifully deemed worthy—God help-
ing and prospering us and our concerns—to bring so holy, so glorious, and so
famous a structure to a good end, together with our brethren and fellow servants;
we felt all the more indebted to God and the holy martyrs as he, by so long a
postponement, had reserved what had to be done for our lifetime and labors.
"For who am I, or what is my father's house" [1 Kings 18:18], that I should have
presumed to begin so noble and pleasing edifice, or should have hoped to finish
it, had I not, relying upon the help of divine mercy and the holy martyrs, devoted
my whole self, both with mind and body, to this very task? But he who gave the
will also gave the power; because the good work was in the will therefore it stood

in perfection by the help of God. How much the hand divine which operates in such matters has protected this glorious work is also surely proven by the fact that It allowed that whole magnificent building [to be completed] in three years and three months, from the crypt below to the summit of the vaults above, elaborated with the variety of so many arches and columns, including even the consummation of the roof. Therefore the inscription of the earlier consecration also defines, with only one word eliminated, the year of completion of this one, thus:

> The year was the one thousand, one hundred, forty and
> fourth of the Word when [this structure] was consecrated.

To these verses of the inscription we choose the following ones to be added:

> Once the new rear part is joined to the part in front,
> The church shines with its middle part brightened.
> For bright is that which is brightly coupled with the bright,
> And bright is the noble edifice which is pervaded by the new light;
> Which stands enlarged in our time,
> I, who was Suger, being the leader while it was being accomplished.

Eager to press on my success, since I wished nothing more under heaven than to seek the honor of my mother church which with maternal affection had suckled me as a child, had held me upright as a stumbling youth, had mightily strengthened me as a mature man, and had solemnly "set me among the princes" [1 Kings 2:8] of the Church and the realm, we devoted ourselves to the completion of the work and strove to raise and to enlarge the transept wings of the church [so as to correspond] to the form of the earlier and later work that had to be joined [by them].

Of the Golden Crucifix

We should have insisted with all the devotion of our mind—had we but had the power—that the adorable, life-giving cross, the health-bringing banner of the eternal victory of our savior (of which the Apostle says: "But God forbid that I should glory, save in the cross of our Lord Jesus Christ" [Galatians 4:14]), should be adorned all the more gloriously as the "sign of the Son of Man," which "will appear in Heaven" [Matthew 24:30] at the end of the world, will be glorious not only to men but also to the very "angels"; and we should have perpetually greeted it with the apostle Andrew: "Hail Cross, which art dedicated in the body of Christ and adorned with His members even as with pearls." But since we could not do as we wished, we wished to do as best we could, and strove to bring it about by the grace of God. Therefore we searched around everywhere by ourselves and by our agents for an abundance of precious pearls and gems, preparing as precious a supply of gold and gems for so important an embellishment as we could find, and convoked the most experienced artists from diverse parts. They would with diligent and patient labor glorify the venerable cross on its reverse side by the admirable beauty of those gems; and on its front—that is to say in the sight of the scarifying priest—they would show the adorable image of our Lord the savior, suffering, as it were, even now in remembrance of his Passion. In fact the blessed Denis had rested on this very spot for five hundred years or more, that is to say, from the time of Dagobert up to our own day. One merry but notable miracle which the Lord granted us in this connection we do not wish to pass over in silence. For when I was in difficulty for want of gems and could not sufficiently provide myself with more (for their scarcity makes them very expensive); then, lo and behold, [monks] from three abbeys of two orders—that is, from Cîteaux and another abbey of the same Order, and from Fontevrault—entered our little chamber adjacent to the church and offered us for sale an abundance of gems such as we had not hoped to find in ten years, hyacinths, sapphires, rubies, emeralds, topazes. Their owners had obtained them from Count Thibaut for alms; and he in turn had received them, through the hands of his brother Stephen, King of England, from the treasures of his uncle, the late King Henry, who had amassed them throughout his life in wonderful vessels. We, however, freed from the worry of searching for gems, thanked God and gave four hundred pounds for the lot though they were worth much more.

We applied to the perfection of so sacred an ornament not only these but also a great and expensive supply of other gems and large pearls. We remember, if memory serves, to have put in about eighty marks of refined gold. And barely within two years were we able to have completed, through several goldsmiths from Lorraine—at times five, at other times seven—the pedestal adorned with the four evangelists; and the pillar upon which the sacred image stands, enameled with exquisite workmanship, and [on it] the history of the savior, with the testimonies of the allegories from the Old Testament indicated, and the capital above looking up, with its images, to the death of the Lord. . . .

Often we contemplate, out of sheer affection for the church our mother, these different ornaments both new and old; and when we behold how that wonderful cross of Saint Eloy—together with the smaller ones—and that incomparable ornament commonly called "the Crest" are placed upon the golden altar, then I say, sighing deeply in my heart: "Every precious stone was thy covering, the sardius, the topaz, and the jasper, the chrysolite, and the onyx, and the beryl, the sapphire, and the carbuncle, and the emerald" [Ezekiel 28:13]. To those who know the properties of precious stones it becomes evident, to their utter astonishment, that none is absent from the number of these (with the only exception of the carbuncle), but that they abound most copiously. Thus, when—out of my delight in the beauty of the house of God—the loveliness of the many-colored gems has called me away from external cares, and worthy meditation has induced me to reflect, transferring that which is material to that which is immaterial, on the diversity of the sacred virtues: then it seems to me that I see myself dwelling, as it were, in some strange region of the universe which neither exists entirely in the slime of the earth nor entirely in the purity of Heaven; and that, by the grace of God, I can be transported from this inferior to that higher world in an anagogical manner. I used to converse with travelers from Jerusalem and, to my great delight, to learn from those to whom the treasures of Constantinople and the ornaments of Hagia Sophia had been accessible, whether the things here could claim some value in comparison to those there. When they acknowledged that these here were the more important ones, it occurred to us that those marvels of which we had heard before might have been put away, as a matter of precaution, for fear of the Franks, lest through the rash rapacity of a stupid few the partisans of the Greeks and Latins, called upon the scene, might suddenly be moved to sedition and warlike hostilities; for wariness is preeminently characteristic of the Greeks. Thus it could happen that the treasures which are visible here, deposited in safety, amount to more than those which had been visible there, left [on view] under conditions unsafe on account of disorders. From very many truthful men, even from Bishop Hugues of Laon, we had heard wonderful and almost incredible reports about the superiority of Hagia Sophia's and other churches' ornaments for the celebration of Mass. If this is so—or rather because we believe it to be so, by their testimony—then such inestimable and incomparable treasures should be exposed to the judgment of the many. "Let every man abound in his own sense." To me, I confess, one thing has always seemed pre-eminently fitting: that every costlier or costliest thing should serve, first and foremost, for the administration of the Holy Eucharist. "If" golden pouring vessels, golden vials, golden little mortars used to serve, by the word of God or the command of the Prophet, to collect the "blood of goats or calves or the red heifer: how much more" must golden vessels, precious stones, and whatever is most valued among all created things, be laid out, with continual reverence and full devotion, for the reception of the "blood of Christ" [Hebrews 9:13, 14]!

. . . And further we adapted for the service of the altar, with the aid of gold and silver material, a porphyry vase, made admirable by the hand of the sculptor and polisher, after it had lain idly in a chest for many years, converting it from a flagon into the shape of an eagle; and we had the following verses inscribed on the vase:

> This stone deserves to be enclosed in gems and gold.
> It was marble, but in these [settings] it is more precious than marble.

65. THE MONK THEOPHILUS'S TREATISE
ON THE DIVERSE ARTS

The treatise On the Diverse Arts *is a comprehensive, detailed, and remarkably original witness to artistic production in the twelfth century. It describes art techniques, such as oil painting and painting on tin, and contains one of the first direct references to paper in the Latin West. The treatise itself is divided into three books, each with its own preface. The first book deals with the materials and art of painting, how to make the various pigments, glues, and varnishes, how to gild and how to paint in books, on walls, and on panels. The second is concerned with glass: ordinary glass, stained glass, glass windows, and glass vessels, both plain and decorated. The third and longest book discusses metalwork: the working of iron, copper, silver and gold, repoussé work, die-stamping, the making of various tools, enamels, ecclesiastical vessels such as chalices and censers, and musical instruments for the church like the bell and organ. Even beyond its content, the work is a sophisticated treatise with a didactic purpose and a theological agenda. Its attention to order and detail are grounded in twelfth-century ideas of theory and practice that are more formally expressed in the exegetical texts of Rupert of Deutz and the pedagogical texts of authors such as Hugh of St-Victor (Docs. 9, 20).*

The author of On the Diverse Arts *has long been something of a mystery. He names himself Theophilus in the prologue, and from internal evidence it has been suggested that he was a monk from German lands active during the first half of the twelfth century. One possibility is that he was a monk in the valley of the Rhine and Meuse rivers. The region was home to a number of Benedictine monasteries and to a burgeoning mercantile economy based in the urban centers of Liège, Huy, Cologne, and Maastricht, inhabited by increasing numbers of tradesmen and lay craftsmen. Much of the economic growth of the region was founded on the trading and mining of metals, in which abbeys and cities alike played a part.*

Source: trans. Robert Hendrie, *An Essay upon Various Arts in Three Books, by Theophilus, Called Also Rugerus, Priest and Monk* . . . (London: John Murray, 1847), xlv, li, 37–41, 209–11, 279–83; revised by Alex J. Novikoff. Latin.

Prologue

I, Theophilus, a humble priest, servant of the servants of God, unworthy of the name and profession of a monk, to all wishing to overcome or avoid sloth of the mind or wandering of the soul, by useful manual occupation and the delightful contemplation of novelties, send a recompense of heavenly price. . . .

Wherefore, gentle son, whom God has rendered perfectly happy in this respect, that those things are offered to you gratis which many, ploughing the seawaves with the greatest danger to life, consumed by the hardship of hunger and cold, or subjected to the weary servitude of teachers, and altogether worn out by the desire of learning, yet acquire with intolerable labor, covet with greedy looks this "Book of Diverse Arts," read it through with a tenacious memory, embrace it with an ardent love.

Should you carefully peruse this book, you will here find whatever Greece [Byzantium] possesses in kinds and mixtures of various colors; whatever Russia knows of in mosaic, or in variety of enamel; whatever Arabia shows forth in repoussé or casting or openwork; whatever Italy ornaments with gold, in diversity of vases and sculpture of gems and ivory; whatever France loves in a costly variety of windows; whatever industrious Germany approves in work of gold, silver, copper and iron, or woods and of stones. . . .

Of Grinding Gold for Books and of Casting the Mill

When you have traced out figures or letters in books, take pure gold and file it very finely in a clean cup or small basin, and wash it with pencil in the shell of a tortoise, or a shell which is taken out of the water. Have then a mill with its pestle, both cast from metal of copper and tin mixed together, so that three parts may be of pure copper, and the forth of pure tin, free from lead. With this composition the mill is cast in the form of a small mortar, and its pestle round about an iron in the form of a knot, so that the iron may protrude to the thickness of a finger, and in length a little more than half a foot, the third part of which iron is fixed in wood carefully turned, in length about one yard, and pierced very straightly; in the lower part of which, however, of the length of four fingers from the end, must be a revolving wheel, either of wood or of lead, and in the middle of the upper part is fixed a leather strap, by which it can be pulled, and, in revolving, be drawn back. Then this mill is placed in a hollow, upon a bench fitted for it, between two small wooden pillars firmly fixed into the same branch, upon which another piece of wood is to be inserted, which can be taken out and replaced, in the middle of which, at the lower part, is a hole in which the pestle of the mill will revolve. These things thus disposed, the gold, carefully cleansed, is put into the mill, a little water added, and the pestle placed, and the upper piece of wood fitted, the strap is drawn and permitted to revolve, again pulled and again it revolves, and this must so be done for two or three hours. Then the upper wood is taken off, and the pestle washed in the same water with a pencil. Afterwards the mill is taken up, and the gold, with the water, is stirred to the bottom with the pencil, and is left a little, until the grosser part subsides; the water is presently poured into a very clean basin, and whatever gold comes away with the water is ground. Replacing the water and the pestle, and wood above being placed, again it is milled in the same way as before, until it altogether comes away with the water. In the same manner are ground silver, brass, and copper. But gold is ground most carefully, and must be lightly milled; and you must often inspect it, because it is softer than the other metals, that it may not adhere to the mill or the pestle, and become heaped together. If through negligence this should happen, that which is conglomerate is scrapped together and taken out, and what is left is milled until finished. Which being done, pouring out the upper water with the impurities from the basin, wash the gold carefully in a clean shell. Then pouring the water from it, agitate it with the pencil, and when you have had it in your hand for one hour, pour it into another shell, and keep that very fine part which has come away with the water. Then again, water being placed with it, warm it, and stir it over the fire, and, as before, pour away the fine particles with the water, and you may act thus until you have purified it entirely. After this wash with water the same refined part, and in the same manner, a second and a third time, and whatever gold you gather mix with the former. In the same way you will wash silver, brass, and copper. Afterwards take the bladder of a fish which is called huso, and washing it three times in tepid water, cut it into very small pieces, and putting it into a very clean pot with water, leave it to soften a night, and on the morrow warm it on the fire, so that it does not boil up until you prove with your fingers if it adhere, and when it shall adhere strongly, the glue is good.

How [Powdered] Gold and Silver Are Laid in Books

Afterwards take some pure minimum [lead] and add to it a third part of cinnabar, grinding it upon a stone with water. Which being carefully ground, beat up the white of an egg, in summer with water, in winter without water, and when it is clear, put the minimum into a horn and pour the white upon it, and stir it a little with a piece of wood put into it, and with a paintbrush fill up all places with it upon which you wish to lay gold. Then place a little pot with glue over the fire, and when it is liquefied, pour it into the shell of gold and wash it with it. When you have poured this into another shell, in which the purifying is kept, again pour in warm glue, and holding it in the palm of the left hand, stir it carefully with the paintbrush, and lay it on thick or thin as you prefer, but so that there is not too much glue, because, should it be excessive, it blackens the gold and does not receive a shine. But after it has dried, polish it with a tooth or bloodstone carefully filed and polished, upon a smooth and shining horn tablet. But should it happen, through negligence of the glue not being well cooked, that the gold crumbles into dust with the rubbing, or rises on account of too great thickness, have near you some old egg white beaten up without water; when it is dry, again rub it with the tooth or stone. Lay in this manner the silver, brass, and copper in their place, and polish them.

The Construction of the Workshop

Build a spacious and lofty house for yourself, the length of which must stretch towards the east; in the southern wall of which make as many windows as you wish and are able, so as five feet may exist between two windows. But separate half of the house, for making molten work, and for working copper, tin and lead, by a wall reaching to the summit; and again divide that part left into two, by one wall, for working gold in one part, silver in the other. The windows must not rise higher than a foot from the ground; let their height be three feet, their width two.

The Work Furnace

Near the wall, by the window, on the left side of the person sitting, a piece of wood is fixed in the ground (three feet in length) in width two and in thickness scarcely two fingers, which, when it is firmly fixed, may have a perforation in the midst of the size of a finger, four fingers high above the ground. Let it have also in front a straight piece of wood joined to it, and fixed with wooden pegs, four fingers in breadth, and the length of which is equal to the large piece of wood. In front of this you fasten another wood of equal breadth and length, so that between these two woods there may be a space of four fingers, and fasten that outside by two or three stakes; and taking clay, not beaten, nor mixed with water, but newly dug up, put at first a little of it into this space, and compress it strongly with a rounded piece of wood, the more, and again beat it; and do thus until two parts of this space are filled, and leave the third empty. Then take away the wood in front, and with a long knife cut the clay evenly in front and on the top, then with a thin piece of wood beat it strongly. After this take clay beaten and mixed with horse dung, and make the furnace and its hearth, covering the wall that it may not be burned by the fire, and with a slender piece of wood perforate the clay through the opening which is in the wood behind. In this manner compose all smiths' furnaces. . . .

Enamel

Take a thin piece of gold and join it to the upper rim of the vase, and measure it out from one handle to the other; this piece must be of the breadth as is the size of the stones which you wish to place upon it; and, arranging them in their order, thus dispose them. First a stone must stand, four pearls being placed at its angles, then a glass gem, next this a stone with pearls, and again a glass gem; and you will so arrange them that the stones may always stand next the handles, the setting and grounds of which, and those settings in which the glass gem is to be placed, you compose and solder in the order above. And you do the same on the other side of the vase. If however you wish to place gems and pearls in the center of the body, you act in the same manner. This being done, join and solder them as the handles. After this you will adapt thin pieces of gold in all the settings in which the glass gems are to be placed, and, carefully fitted, you take them out, and with a measure and rule you cut a small band of gold, which must be somewhat thicker; and you will bend them round the rim of each in a double manner, so that a minute space may exist around between these small bands: this space is called the border of the enamel. Then, with the same measure and rule you cut small bands of exceedingly thin gold, in which you will bend and fashion whatever work you may wish to make in enamel, whether circles, or knots, or small flowers, or birds, or animals, or figures; and you will arrange the small pieces delicately and carefully, each in its place, and will fasten them with moistened flour over the coals. When you have filled one portion, you will solder it with the greatest care, that the slender and fine gold may not be disjoined nor liquefy; and do thus twice or three times, until the separate pieces adhere a little.

All the enamels being composed and soldered in this manner, take all kinds of glass which you had prepared for this work, and breaking a particle from each piece, place all the fragments together upon a piece of copper, each piece by itself, and placing it in the fire arrange the coals around and above it, and blowing carefully, you will see whether they melt equally; if so, use them all; if however a particle is harder [than the rest] place it by itself. Taking separate piece of the proved glass, place them in the fire one by one, and when each one has become glowing, throw it into the copper vessel in which there is water, and it instantly flies into small fragments, which you break with a round pestle until made quite fine, and you will thus wash it and put it into a clean vessel, and you cover it with a linen cloth. In this manner you prepare the separate colors. This being done, take a piece of the soldered gold, and you will fasten it upon a smooth table with wax in two places, and taking a goose quill cut to a point, as if for writing but with a longer beak and not split, you take out with it one of the colors of glass, whichever you please. That which remains, replace in its small cup and cover it, and do this with each color until one piece is filled: taking away the wax, to which it had adhered, place this piece upon a thin iron, which may have a short handle, and cover it with another iron which is hollow like a cup, and let it be perforated finely all over, so that the holes may be inside flat and wide, and outside finer and rough, in order to stop the cinders if by chance they should fall upon it; this iron may also have a mall ring above, in the middle, by which it may be superposed and taken off. This being done, arrange large and long coals, making them very hot, among which you make a space, and equalize with a wooden mallet, into which the iron is raised by the handle with the pincers, so that when covered you will place it carefully and arrange the coals around and above it everywhere, and taking the bellows with both hands you will blow on every side until the coals glow equally. You have also a wing of a goose, or other large bird, which is extended and tied to wood, with which you will wave and fan strongly over it, until you perceive between the coals that the holes of the iron quite glow inside, and thus you will cease to fan. Waiting then about half an hour you uncover by degrees until you remove all the coals, and you will again wait until the holes of the iron grow black inside, and so raising the iron by the handle, you place it, covered as it is, in the furnace, behind, in a corner until it has become quite cold. Then opening it you take out the enamel and will wash it, and will again fill it and melt as before, and you do this until, melted equally everywhere, it has become full. In this manner you will compose the remaining pieces.

Figure 13: The Auvergne region of France is graced with superb examples of Romanesque architecture. This nineteenth-century lithograph of the collegial abbey of Notre-Dame du Port in Clermont (today Clermont-Ferrand) displays some of the features most characteristic of twelfth-century religious architecture: thick walls, rounded arches, ornate capitals depicting biblical scenes, and a semi-circular choir surrounded by an ambulatory from which open four radiating chapels, thus forming a *chevet*.

Source: From the private collection of Alex J. Novikoff.

66. BERNARD OF CLAIRVAUX'S PROTEST AGAINST DISTRACTING ART

Bernard of Clairvaux (1090–1153) frequently protested the menaces posed by contemporary society, be they heresy (Doc. 37), scholastic teaching (Doc. 19), or distracting displays of artistic luxury. In a letter of 1125 to his close friend William of St-Thierry, the abbot of a Benedictine monastery near Rheims, Bernard reacted to the contemporary fad for increasingly sumptuous ornamentation, the very sort extolled by Suger of St-Denis (Doc. 64). Bernard was willing to tolerate architecture, monumental painting, and sculpture within the confines of monasteries, but he took issue with gold-covered relics, images of saints, decorated chandeliers, candelabra, and floor images. Bernard's objections center on excesses in material, craftsmanship, size, and quantity and should be understood within the context of the Cistercian movement for simplicity and reform to which he was so central.

Source: trans. G.G. Coulton, *A Medieval Garner* (London: Constable and Co., 1910), 70–72; slightly revised. Latin.

But these are small things; I will pass on to matters of greater importance, yet seemingly smaller because they are more usual. I say naught of the vast height of your churches, their immoderate length, their superfluous breadth, the costly polishings, the curious carvings and paintings which attract the worshipper's gaze and hinder his attention, and seem to me in some sort a revival of the ancient Jewish rites. Let this pass, however: say that this is done for God's honor. But I, as a monk, ask of my brother monks as the pagan [the poet Persius, 34–62 CE] asked of his fellow-pagans: "Tell me, O Pontiffs," he said, "what doeth this gold in the sanctuary?" [*Saturae* 2.71–72]. So say I, "Tell me, poor men," for I break the verse to keep the sense, "tell me, you poor if, indeed, you be poor, what doeth this gold in your sanctuary?" And indeed, the bishops have an excuse which monks have not; for we know that they, being debtors both to the wise and the unwise, and unable to excite the devotion of carnal folk by spiritual things, do so by bodily adornments. But we who have now come forth from the people; we who have left all the precious and beautiful things of the world for Christ's sake; who have counted but dung, that we may win Christ, all things fair to see or soothing to hear, sweet to smell, delightful to taste, or pleasant to touch—in a word, all bodily delights—whose devotion, pray, do we monks intend to excite by these things? What profit, I say, do we expect therefrom? The admiration of fools, or the oblations of the simple? Or, since we are scattered among the nations, have we perchance learnt their works and do we yet serve their graven images? . . . Thus wealth is drawn up by ropes of wealth, thus money brings money, for I know not how it is that, wheresoever more abundant wealth is seen, there do men offer more freely. Their eyes are feasted with relics cased in gold, and their purse-strings are loosened. They are shown a more comely image of some saint, whom they think all the more saintly that he is the more gaudily painted. Men run to kiss him, and are invited to give; there is more admiration for his comeliness than veneration for his sanctity. Hence the church is adorned with gemmed crowns of light—nay, with lusters like cartwheels, girt all around with lamps, but no less brilliant with the precious stones that stud them. Moreover, we see candelabra standing like trees of massive bronze, fashioned with marvelous subtlety of art, and glistening no less brightly with gems than with the lights they carry. What, think you, is the purpose of all this? The compunction of penitents, or the admiration of beholders? O vanity of vanities, yet no more vain than insane! The church is resplendent in her walls, beggarly in her poor; she clothes her stones in gold, and leaves her sons naked; the rich man's eyes is fed at the expense of the indigent. The curious find their delight here, yet the needy find no relief. Do we not revere at least the images of the saints, which swarm even in the inlaid pavement whereon we tread? Men spit oftentimes in an Angel's face; often, again, the countenance of some saint is ground under the heel of a passerby. And if he spare not these sacred images, why not even the fair colors? Why do you make that so fair that which will soon be foul? Why lavish bright hues upon that which must needs be trodden under foot? What avail these comely forms in places where they are defiled with customary dust? And, lastly, what are such things as these to you poor men, you monks, you spiritual folk? Unless perchance here also you may answer the poet's question in the words of the Psalmist: "Lord, I have loved the habitation of your house, and the place where your honor dwells" [Psalm 25:8]. I grant it, then, let us suffer even this to be done in the church, for, though it be harmful to vain and covetous folk, yet not so to the simple and devout. But in the cloister, under the eyes of the brethren who read there, what profit is there in those ridiculous monsters, in that marvelous and deformed comeliness, that comely deformity? To what purpose are those unclean apes, those fierce lions, those monstrous centaurs, those half-men, those striped tigers, those fighting knights, those hunters winding their horns? Many bodies are there seen under one head, or again, many heads to a single body. Here is a four-footed beast with a serpent's tail; there, a fish with a beast's head. Here again the forepart of a horse trails half a goat behind it, or a horned beast bears the hinder quarters of a horse. In short, so many and so marvelous are the varieties of diverse shapes on every hand, that we are more tempted to read in the marble than in our books, and to spend the whole day in wondering at these things rather than in meditating the law of God. For God's sake, if men are not ashamed of these follies, why at least do they not shrink from the expense?

67. HERMAN-JUDAH AND RUPERT OF DEUTZ DEBATE RELIGIOUS IMAGERY

Sometime around 1150, an otherwise obscure Jew born in the city of Cologne under the name Judah wrote a Latin account of his conversion to Christianity under his new name of Herman. The story of Herman-Judah (or "Herman the Former Jew" as he is also called) has long puzzled historians: is this the true story of one man's conversion from Judaism to Christianity, or is it the invented work of an imaginative Christian polemicist? Recent interpretations suggest that it may be something of each, in other words an embellished account of an original conversion story intended for internal Christian consumption rather than a text meant to inspire further conversions. Among the events that the account narrates is a debate held between Herman and the Benedictine abbot Rupert of Deutz (c. 1075–c. 1130) on the role of imagery in Christian devotion. The didactic and spiritual explanations offered by Rupert recall themes encountered in Chapters 1 and 2, as well as the detailed explanation given by Abbot Suger (Doc. 64), while as a text of interfaith encounters the debate may also profitably be compared to the more overtly disputational works in Chapter 3.

Source: trans. Alex J. Novikoff, from Jean-Claude Schmitt, *The Conversion of Herman the Jew: Autobiography, History, and Fiction in the Twelfth Century* (Philadelphia: University of Pennsylvania Press, 2010), 206–10. Latin.

. . . As time went on, the intense conversations [that I overheard among Christians] made me increasingly eager to inquire quite diligently into the sacraments of the Church. I entered the basilica that I had once denigrated as a pagan temple not so much out of devotion as out of curiosity.

Examining all things with great care, I saw among the sculptured devices and variety of paintings a monstrous idol. I discerned one and the same man humiliated and exalted, abased and lifted up, ignominious and noble. He was hanging wretchedly from high to low on a cross, and from low to high, by the deceiving effects of the painting, he was sitting enthroned and as if deified. I admit I was stupefied, suspecting that effigies of this sort were likenesses of the kind common among the pagans. The doctrines of the Pharisees had, in the past, easily persuaded me that it was truly thus. . . . In addition, I frequently entered the schools of the clergy and received books from them, with which I considered the properties of individual grammatical elements and studied the words in detail. I began at once, without a teacher and to the immense astonishment of those who listened, to join letters to syllables and syllables to expressions so that, in brief, I came to know how to read Scripture. If this seems incredible, it should be ascribed not to me but to God, for whom nothing is impossible.

At that time a man named Rupert, the abbot of the monastery of Deutz, was staying [in Cologne]. He was subtle in temperament, learned in eloquence, and most accomplished in sacred as well as human letters. I saw him and invited him to engage in disputational conflict. . . . I addressed him in the following way: "You Christians bear a great prejudice against the Jews. You spit upon them and loathe them with curses as though they were dead dogs, even though you read that in antiquity God chose them for himself, as his own people, from among all the nations in the world. . . . Laughable as it is, you correct the Law as it pleases you. You accept some things but reject others. Either you reject things as superstitious, or you accept them as mystical, though not in the way in which they were actually said, but according to whatever stupidities, old wives' tales, and depraved fictions anyone pleases. It is plain stupid temerity and folly worthy of derision for human beings to wish to correct what God established and commanded them to observe under penalty of a terrible curse.

"You Christians are especially liable to the curse, since while you presume to be judges of the Law, you are also condemned as its prevaricators. For the moment, let one thing from among the many suffice to illustrate your total damnation. Why is it that you who vaunt yourselves on the observance of the Law defy it with the impiety of manifest idolatry? Behold what I have seen with my own eyes. In your temples you have erected for yourselves as objects of adoration large images skillfully adorned with the arts of painters and sculptors. If only, to consummate your perdition, you worshipped the likeness of something besides that of a crucified man!" . . .

To these remarks Rupert answered: "In these circumstances, I am undaunted by any of the arguments that you have set up for me to oppose. For in order to defend and confirm the truth of our religion there is in your very own books an abundant supply of authorities from which to draw. Armed with these authorities, as with an invisible shield, we may be able both to dodge and to return the shots of your objections. From them I shall now demonstrate by conclusive reasoning, if you accord me your patient attention, that what you call our idolatry is full of piety and religion and radiates the light of all truth.

"We therefore abhor and execrate in every way the crime of idolatry that you are attempting to impose upon us. We faithfully embrace the cult of the one and true God. Nor do we worship as a divinity the image of a crucified man or of anything else, as your slander maintains. Rather, with pious devotion, we represent to ourselves through the adorable form of the cross the Passion of Christ, who 'redeemed us from the curse of the law by becoming a curse for us' [Galatians 3:13]. We do this so that while externally we project the image of his death through the likeness of the cross, internally we are inspired with love for him so that we may continually remember that he, entirely untainted by any sin, endured so ignominious a death for us and that we, enveloped in as many and great sins as we are, may always consider with pious reflection what a great obligation we owe to him. This is the general explanation for the images that you observe among us.

"There is also a specific explanation. Images were devised for the benefit of the simple and unlettered so that those who could not learn about the Passion of the Redeemer by reading books could see the very price of their redemption through the visual appearance of the cross. What codices represent to us, images represent to the uneducated masses.

"But to keep the ritual of our religion from appearing to be constructed by human reason alone, allow me to demonstrate its support in the authority of the Old Testament, for ancient history provides us with a very similar account. When the children of Israel were led into the promised land, 'the Reubenites and the Gadites and the half-tribe of Manasseh' [Joshua 22:9–10], they went into that land of theirs and came to the hills along the Jordan where they built an altar of immense size. But the Lord had commanded by law that all the children of Israel should have one altar in common for celebrating the rite of sacrifices and that it should stand in the place that God chose for invoking the power of his majesty. That place, as everyone knew, was located in Shiloh. . . . And so they constructed an altar, not to sacrifice victims and burnt offerings upon it, but to demonstrate by such a testimony that they and their posterity belonged to God's people. Thus we, too, and for a similar reason, hold the cross of Christ in great reverence because of who hangs on it, but in no way do we worship it as divine. Just as the altar was made for them in the form of a testimony, so also the cross is for us a witness, so that while we may consider that the price of our redemption hangs upon it, we may also rejoice that through that price we belong to the company of saints and to the eternal heritage of the Heavenly Jerusalem."

In this way Rupert met all my objections, both with the most elegant arguments and with the most valid authorities of Scripture.

68. PETER THE CHANTER'S CRITIQUE OF SUMPTUOUS ARCHITECTURE

Peter the Chanter (d. 1197) was a theologian and master in the schools of Paris in the last decades of the twelfth century. In 1183 he was named chanter (cantor) of the Cathedral of Notre Dame, a position that gave him responsibility for the daily liturgical services and put him in charge of the cathedral's choir school. This helped to place him at the center of an important and influential circle of scholars who were concerned with biblical study and moral reform. In his Verbum abbreviatum, *Peter notes many material and moral abuses that were latent in contemporary society. In a chapter entitled "Against the Superfluity and Expenses of Clothing," he identifies current excesses in materials and dyes, as well as in the form, composition, diversification, and mutation of materials. He contrasts the simplicity of how the Lord clothed Adam and Eve in tunics made of animal skin with the contemporary craze for the unnatural plumage of birds. Turning to dyes, he is willing to accept natural colors, but expresses concern that human vanity has corrupted them into bright red, rose, green, saffron, and violet and violated their natural purity so that they exceed the flowers of the fields that the Gospels (Matthew 6:29; Luke 12:27) say are greater than Solomon's glory. He is in part reacting to the lavish garments and elaborate jewelry worn by local aristocracy and described in contemporary romance literature.*

In the following section from the same Verbum abbreviatum, *Peter takes issue with the superfluity of grandiose buildings, a theme already voiced by Bernard of Clairvaux a generation earlier (see Doc. 66). In his day the Cathedral of Notre Dame was in full expansion, as were many buildings both sacred and secular in and around Paris. Peter contrasts the loftiness of contemporary edifices with the simplicity of human dwellings in the Bible. In typical scholastic fashion, he provides citations of passages from authorities (Scripture, Christian writers, classical authors) and other exempla to discourage vice and promote virtue.*

Source: trans. G.G. Coulton, *Life in the Middle Ages* (New York: The Macmillan Company, 1930), 25–28. Latin.

Even as, in the superfluity and curiousness of raiment and food, the labor of nature is perverted and the matter falls into wrong if it be without art, so also is it in the superfluity, curiousness and sumptuousness of buildings. For behold how far we have departed from the simplicity of the ancients in this matter of buildings. We read that Abraham, in the first days of faith, dwelt in tabernacles, possessing on this earth not even whereon the sole of his foot might rest: for he pitched his tent between Bethel and Ai, not as a citizen, but like unto a stranger and pilgrim that has no abiding habitation; and under this roof-tree—that is, under his thatched hut—he had the angels for guests. So likewise Lot and Noah lived in tents; as some of the ancients dwelt in rocky caverns, others under the bark of hollow trees, so that, being seen to issue thence, they were fabulously believed by some to be born of stones and trees. Elisha had no dwelling of his own, but (by the charity of a widow) a little chamber under another's roof, where he had this little chamber, his little table, his little bed and his candlestick. . . . Moreover, seeing that not only in stature but even in length of life we [moderns] are abridged by reason of our manifold superfluities and our sins; seeing that the end of the world and the consummation of all things are come upon us, what madness and excess it is that we should be so solicitous concerning the bigness and curiousness and costliness of the buildings that we make, as though such works would never perish! More especially seeing that the ancients—to whom God granted longer lives, and who, born at the very birth of the world, were far removed from its end—cared for no such things, believing rather that at the end of the world all the foundations of the earth shall be moved; to wit, that she shall be purged even to her inmost bowels, so far as the works of sinful men have gone downwards, and so far as their works have risen upwards into the air.

Wherefore said a certain clerk of Rheims, "If these builders believed that the world would ever come to an end, no such lofty masses would be reared up to the very sky, nor would such foundations be laid even in the abysses of the earth. Wherein they resemble those giants who built the tower of Babel, rearing themselves up against the Lord: wherefore let them fear lest they themselves also be scattered abroad from the face of the earth (that is, God's Church), and be then confounded in the fires of hell." Moreover, this superfluity and costliness of buildings and stone wall is a cause why we have in these days less pity and alms for the poor; since we are not rich enough to feed them while we spend also upon such superfluous expenses. Let us remember also what Esaias said: "Heaven is my throne, and the earth my footstool; what is this house that you will build to me? And what is my place of rest?" Moreover, Jerome said, "I know that there is a people, to wit the men of Megara, who build as though they would live for ever, eating meanwhile and drinking as though they must die on the morrow; for they say, 'Let us eat and drink, for tomorrow we die.'" Moreover, Paul the first hermit dwelt in a crypt, that is in a cave under the earth; and an angel fed him with half a loaf [daily]: wherefore Saint Anthony, archimandrite and father of the hermits, hearing of his sanctity, came to visit him and knocked at his door: whom Paul supposed to be a wild beast or a wolf. . . . Moreover he asked very many questions of Anthony, among which he enquired whether the idolatry [of the heathen] and the obstinacy of the Jews were yet removed, and whether the Christian religion imitated the Gentile worship in the costliness of its edifices, saying: "Do the towers and bulwarks still rise to heaven, with the palaces, and all those so lofty and costly buildings of Rome?" "Yes," said Anthony: whereat the other bewailed this superfluity even with tears, moaning that men were given up to such vanities, whereas Christians ought rather to exhort each other saying: "We have not here a lasting city, but we seek one that is to come." . . .

But monastic or ecclesiastical edifices are raised from the usury and breed of barren metal among covetous men, from the lying deceits and deceitful lies of hireling preachers; and whatsoever is built from ill-gotten gains is in much peril of ruin: for, as Ovid said, "A sordid prey has no good issue" [*Elegy* I]. For example, Saint Bernard wept to see the shepherds' huts thatched with straw, like unto the first huts of the Cistercians, who were then beginning to live in palaces of stone, set with all the stars of heaven. But oftentimes to the religious themselves, as to other men, their own offence becomes an instrument to punish them for this disease of building: for the construction of comely and ample houses is

Figure 14: By the late twelfth century one finds increasing portrayals of daily life both in buildings (as in the sculptures and stained glass of Chartres) and in illuminated manuscripts. This facsimile of a miniature of a Psalter from the thirteenth century represents warlike, scientific, commercial, and agricultural activities.

Source: Paul Lacroix, *The Arts in the Middle Ages and at the Period of the Renaissance* (London: Chapman and Hall, 1870), 455.

an invitation to proud guests. Even the granges of the monks are oftentimes castellated in self-defense; and Religious oftentimes conceal the truth and leave God's righteousness, lest they should lose such granges, not daring to murmur against princes, since they have lost their old freedom whereof the poet spoke: "The traveler that has no money in his purse will sing in the robber's presence" [Juvenal, *Satires*, 10]. This (I say) they have lost for the sake of rich granges and lands, suffering robbers and usurers to build them dormitories and refectories, for a sign and an eternal memorial of their covetousness; though they should not have suffered this even had the money pertained to good men, but should rather have bid them apply such moneys to the feeding of the poor and the redemption of captives. Men sin even in building churches; for, seeing that their heads should be more lowly than their bodies for the mystery's sake (since our head, which is Christ, is more lowly than his Church), yet they are now built higher.

69. ALEXANDER NECKAM DESCRIBES CONTEMPORARY ARTS AND CRAFTS

Alexander Neckam (1157–1217) was an English scholar, teacher, theologian, and the abbot of the Augustinian abbey of Cirencester in Gloucestershire. His interests ranged across many fields of inquiry, from theology and Aristotelianism to classical poetry, medicine, and natural history. His On the Nature of Things *provides a minor manual on scientific knowledge, even though it was intended as part of a broader program of biblical commentary. In addition to showing a keen interest in medical science, he also provides some very precise observations of the arts and crafts of his day, from the utensils of professional scribes and weavers to a description of the interior of a country house and what the appropriate furnishings of a church should be. Elsewhere in the work, Neckham provides the first known European description of the magnetized compass used by seamen.*

Source: trans. Urban Tigner Holmes Jr., *Daily Living in the Twelfth Century: Based on the Observations of Alexander Neckam in London and Paris* (Madison: The University of Wisconsin Press, 1952), 69–70, 99, 147, 209–10. Latin.

Let him have a razor or knife for scraping pages of parchment or skin; let him have a "biting" pumice for cleaning the sheets, and a little scraper for making equal the surface of the skin. He should have a piece of lead and a ruler with which he may rule the margins on both sides—on the back and on the side from which the flesh has been removed.

There should be a fold of four sheets (a quaternion). I do not use the word *quarternio* because that means "a squad in the army." Let these leaves be held together at the top and bottom by a strip [of parchment threaded through]. The scribe should have a bookmark cord and a pointed tool about which he can say, "I have pricked [*punxi*] not pinked [*pupigi*] my quaternion." Let him sit in a chair with both arms high, reinforcing the back rest, and with a stool at the feet. Let the writer have a heating basin covered with a cap; he should have a knife with which he can shape a quill pen; let this be prepared for writing with the inside fuzzy scale scraped out, and let there be a boar's or goat's tooth for polishing the parchment, so that the ink of a letter may not run (I do not say a whole alphabet); he should have something with which letters can be canceled. Let him have an indicator [*speculum*] or line marker [*cavalla*] in order that he may not make a costly delay from error. There should be hot coals in the heating container so that the ink may dry more quickly on the parchment in foggy or wet weather. Let there be a small window through which light can enter; if perchance the blowing of the north wind attacks the principal window, let this be supplied with a screen of linen or of parchment, distinct in color; green and black to offer more comfort to the eyes. Whiteness, when too intense, disturbs the sight and throws it into disorder. There should be red lead for forming red Phoenician or Punic letters or capitals. Let there be dark powder and blue that was discovered by Solomon [that is, ultramarine].

The notary or scribe should know when he is about to write Ψ, when an aspirate, when ω, when o, when ζ, when η, when δ, when small ϝ, when τ, when υ, when ι, when σ, when antisigma (ↄ), in order that he may not make a barbarism

in writing or a slip in speaking; a wrong letter is frequent among barbarians. . . .
Furthermore, let a style of writing be acquired for seals, manuscripts, and documents, transactions, other manner for a text, another kind for glosses. But a gloss,
for brevity, should be written by titles [abbreviations]. . . .

Let the main hall [of a country house] be furnished with a vestibule near
which the portico may be properly set up. There should be also an outer
court that is named from *ater* because kitchens used to be constructed near
open spaces in order that the passers-by might smell the odor and vapor of the
kitchen. In the hall let there be posts set apart with proper distances. There is
need for nails, poles, siding, beams, and crosspieces extending to the roof. Raf-
ters are required, reaching across the house. Walls should not be strictly parallel;
the higher they rise, the farther apart they should be, otherwise all the stricter
will be threatened by ruin and there will be a hazard. Let windows be suitably
placed in the house, looking toward the east, in which gourds or "twisted pots"
should be placed, not on the outside, in which may be kept storax from Aleppo,
but not Trojan storax, . . . Serapian balsam, balm of Mecca, euphorbia, Persian
gum, mastic, black poplar ointment, laurel oil, juice of green grapes, elder oil,
and castoreum. [These are to bring the proper odors in through the window.]
Let some basket weave be added to the roof and let the whole be covered or
thatched with marsh reed, or, if planking is laid up there, this can be covered
with tiles or slates. . . .

The weaver has a [breast] roller to which the cloth to be rolled up is fastened.
Let there be beamlike strips marked with holes and facing each other from
opposing sides, with wires shaped like a shepherd's crook and the strips going
in the same way as the warp threads, also [let there be] linen threads as slender
as those that are properly associated with fringes [tied to] rods in the heddles,
these threads set at intervals; let the weaver draw the warp threads [with such
a heddle], the upper series of threads and then the lower. When the weft has
been passed through by means of a shuttle, let him beat down the work accomplished, and let the shuttle have an iron or wooden bobbin between open spaces.
The bobbin should be filled from a spool, and this spool should be covered in
the manner of a clew of yarn with a weight. Let the material of the weft thread
be pulled from this weighted spool, so that the one hand of the weaver tosses the
shuttle to the other, to be returned vice versa.

But in vain does one weave a cloth unless previously iron combs, working
upon the wool, to be softened by flame, have carded the strands in long and
reciprocal endeavor. Thus the better and finer parts of the combed wool may
be reserved for the thread, with the woolly dregs like coarse tow being left over.
Afterwards let the wool thread be aided by the application of madder or woad
such as is done in Beauvais, or let the material to be dyed be saturated with
frequent dipping in *graine*. Then let the weaver reclaim it; but before it makes

its appearance in the form of clothing, it should be subjected to the care of the fuller, demanding frequent washing. . . .

The furnishings [of a church] are these: a baptismal font, a crucifix, a Little Mary, and other images; a lectern of some kind, a ewer, a small ewer, basins, a chair, the chancel, an elevated seat, a stool, candlesticks, the piscine or lavabo, the altar stone, a case for images, cruets, and pyxides. Let there be a bier for the dead, a hand towel, a face towel, and a fine cloth [on the altar]. There should be gilded vessels, a thurible, gilded columns and bronze veneering with silver and marble bases. . . . There should be books: Missal, Breviary, Antiphonal, Gradual, Processional, Manual, Hymnal, Psalter, Troper, and Ordinal. The priest's vestments are surplice, silk cap, cincture, headband, baldric, stole, maniple, and chasuble. [In the ceiling] there should be beams of maplewood or oak, crosspieces where the roof adheres to the beams or to the leads. Wooden pegs and iron nails are required where the tiles and roof siding are suspended. Small bells, immense bells, and little bells must be hung in the tower. A cupola, tower, and bell tower are the same thing. A weathercock can be placed on top. Bent bars, bolts, hinges, and locks should be there [on the doors]. There should be an entry vestibule for temple, or church, or monastery, or oratory, or chapel. . . . Let there be a tabernacle in which the Eucharist may be kept most worthily, the salvation of faithful souls, for he who does not believe cannot be saved.

CHAPTER EIGHT

HISTORICAL WRITING AND ROMANCE

The resurgence in historical writing has long been considered one of the main-stays of an intellectual renaissance in the twelfth century. Chronicles, annals, biographies (including saints' lives), and records of recent events abound, often producing works of great length and considerable style. Owing to the growth and expansion of the Norman and Angevin Empires, the twelfth century was a particularly outstanding period for historical writing in England and Normandy, although a rise in a historical awareness can also be observed in many corners of Europe. The role of the past and the way it was treated varied considerably from one author to the next, of course, not least because "history" was not a defined academic discipline. For most writers (and readers) of this period, history was treated more as a branch of ethics, offering moral and ethical guidelines that were applicable to the present.

This chapter illustrates the range of this new historical awareness with selec-tions from works that are purely historical (for instance chronicles of past and current events) as well as from works that today we would perhaps label as fic-tion or romance, since much of the material amounts to historical legend. Here it is important to recall that for twelfth-century writers, *historia* ("a story") did not have to be "historical" in modern terms. The contrast lay not between true and false histories, but between *historia* and *fabula*, tales that did or did not merit belief. Finally, a notable feature of the historical writing of the twelfth century is that it reached back to the distant past, especially to Greece, with a revival of interest in Alexander the Great and the Trojan War. This former concern is nowhere better reflected than in the verse *Alexandreis* of Walter of Châtillon (Doc. 78), a best-seller from its time of composition onward.

70. GEOFFREY OF MONMOUTH, *HISTORY OF THE KINGS OF BRITAIN*

Geoffrey of Monmouth (c. 1100–c. 1155) is often called the father of Arthurian romance. His History of the Kings of Britain *(completed before 1139) survives in over 200 manuscripts and has inspired numerous translations and paraphrases. In addition to raising Arthur to the status of an imperial monarch and introducing us to the mysterious enchanter Merlin, Geoffrey also relates the adventures of many other heroes both clas-sical and early medieval: Brutus, the great-grandson of Virgil's Aeneas and the alleged founder of Britain; Corineus, the slayer of the giant Geomagog; Locrine; Cymbaline;*

and the immortal King Lear. While Geoffrey's account might be regarded today as something closer to a historical novel (perhaps the very first), until the sixteenth century the History *was generally accepted as an accurate account of pre-Saxon Britain. Nor is the work entirely fanciful: Geoffrey's historical sources include Gildas (sixth century), Bede (seventh–eighth centuries), Nennius's* History of the Britons *(ninth century), and the contemporary chronicler William of Malmesbury (d. 1143). Geoffrey's* History *is divided into 11 books and is accompanied by a dedicatory epistle to Earl Robert of Gloucester, explaining his authorial intentions. Some manuscript versions of the work include a second dedication to Count Waleran of Meulun (1104–66), which is also included here.*

Source: trans. Justin Lake, from *Geoffrey of Monmouth: The History of the Kings of Britain*, ed. Michael D. Reeve (Woodbridge, UK: The Boydell Press, 2007), 4; with supplements from Aaron Thompson, trans., with revisions by J.A. Giles, *The British History of Geoffrey of Monmouth* (London: J. Bohn, 1842), 131–32, 176–78; slightly revised. Latin.

Book 1

CHAPTER 1: THE DEDICATORY EPISTLE TO ROBERT, EARL OF GLOUCESTER

As I was deeply pondering a number of things, my thoughts turned to the history of the kings of Britain and I marveled that in the account that Gildas and Bede had given of them in their elegant works I found nothing about the kings who lived here before the Incarnation of Christ, and also nothing about Arthur or the many others who succeeded to the throne after the Incarnation, although their actions are worthy of immortal fame and many people recite them from memory for entertainment, as though they had been written down. As I frequently meditated upon these and similar thoughts, Walter, archdeacon of Oxford, a man learned in the art of eloquence and in foreign histories, presented me a very ancient book in the British tongue that set forth in an elegant style a continuous account of all of their deeds from Brutus, the first king of the Britons, down to Cadwallader, son of Cadwallo. At his request, therefore, I undertook to translate this book into the Latin tongue, although I had not gathered richly attired words from the gardens of others and had to content myself with the rustic style of my own pipes. For if I had bedaubed the pages with grandiloquent turns of phrases, I would have tired out my readers by forcing them to spend more time teasing out the meaning of my words than understanding the narrative itself. Therefore, Robert, earl of Gloucester, may you bestow your favor on this modest work, so that it may be corrected by your instruction and advice in such a way that it will not be said to have arisen from the meager spring of Geoffrey of Monmouth, and so that instead, having been seasoned with the salt of your wisdom, it may be called the product of the illustrious King Henry of England's son, whom Philosophy has instructed in the liberal arts and whose native courage has set him over knights in wartime, so that now in our own day Britain inwardly rejoices as though it had obtained another Henry.

[Most manuscripts of Geoffrey's history contain only the dedication to Robert of Gloucester. Ten manuscripts, however, append to it an additional dedication to Count Waleran of Meulun.] May you, too, Count Waleran of Meulun, the second pillar of our kingdom, apply yourself so that through your joint efforts this work may shine more beautifully when made public. For mother Philosophy took you, who are descended from the stock of that most illustrious king Charles [Charlemagne], into her lap and instructed you in the subtleties of her doctrines, and afterwards she sent you to the royal castle so that you might distinguish yourself in knightly training. There, having surpassed your fellow warriors in bravery, you learned under the auspices of your forebears to be a terror to your enemies and a source of protection to your own people. As the faithful shield of your people, therefore, take me your poet and this book, which was written for your enjoyment, under your protection, so that reclining under the covering of your outspread branches, I can play on the pipe of my muse a melody safe from the envious and the perverse.

CHAPTER 2: THE FIRST INHABITANTS OF BRITAIN

Britain, the best of islands, is situated in the Western Ocean, between France and Ireland, being eight hundred miles long, and two hundred broad. It produces everything that is useful to man, with a plenty that never fails. It abounds with all kinds of metal, and has plains of large extent, and hills fit for the finest tillage, the richness of whose soil affords variety of fruits in their proper seasons. It has also forests well stored with all kinds of wild beasts; in its lawns cattle find good change of pasture, and bees variety of flowers for honey. Under its lofty mountains lie green meadows pleasantly situated, in which the gentle murmurs of crystal springs gliding along clear channels, give those that pass an agreeable invitation to lie down on their banks and slumber. It is likewise well watered with lakes and rivers abounding with fish; and besides the narrow sea which is on the Southern coast towards France, there are three noble rivers, stretching out like three arms, namely, the Thames, the Severn, and the Humber; by which foreign commodities from all countries are brought into it. It was formerly adorned with eight and twenty cities, of which some are in ruins and desolate, others are still standing, beautified with lofty church towers, wherein religious worship is performed according to the Christian institution. It is lastly inhabited by five different nations, the Britons, Romans, Saxons, Picts, and Scots; among whom the Britons before the rest did formerly possess the whole island from sea to sea, till divine vengeance, punishing them for their pride, made them give way to the Picts and Saxons. But in what manner, and from whence, they first arrived here, remains now to be related in what follows.

Book 7

CHAPTER 1: GEOFFREY OF MONMOUTH'S PREFACE TO MERLIN'S PROPHECY

I had not got thus far in my history, when the subject of public discourse happening to be concerning Merlin, I was obliged to publish his prophecies at the request of my acquaintance, but especially of Alexander, bishop of Lincoln, a prelate of the greatest piety and wisdom. There was not any person, either among the clergy or laity, who was attended with such a train of knights and noblemen, whom his settled piety and great munificence engaged in his service. Out of a desire, therefore, to gratify him, I translated these prophecies, and sent them to him with the following letter.

CHAPTER 2: GEOFFREY'S LETTER TO ALEXANDER, BISHOP OF LINCOLN

"The regard which I owe to your great worth, most noble prelate, has obliged me to undertake the translation of Merlin's prophecies out of British into Latin, before I had made an end of the history which I had begun concerning the acts of the British kings. For my design was to have finished that first, and afterwards to have taken this work in hand, lest by being engaged on both at once I should be less capable of attending with any exactness to either. Notwithstanding, since the deference that is paid to your penetrating judgment will screen me from censure, I have employed my rude pen, and in a coarse style I present you with a translation out of a language with which you are unacquainted. At the same time, I cannot but wonder at your recommending this matter to one of my low genius, when you might have caused so many men of greater learning, and a richer vein of intellect, to undertake it; men who, with their sublime strains, would much more agreeably have entertained you. Besides, without any disparagement to all the philosophers in Britain, I must take the liberty to say that you yourself, if the business of your high station would give you leisure, are capable of furnishing us with loftier productions of this kind than any man living. However, since it was your pleasure that Geoffrey of Monmouth should be employed in this prophecy, he hopes you will favorably accept his performance, and vouchsafe to give a finer turn to whatever you shall find unpolished, or otherwise faulty in it.

Book 9

CHAPTER 1: ARTHUR SUCCEEDS HIS FATHER UTHER IN THE KINGDOM OF BRITAIN

Uther Pendragon being dead, the nobility from several provinces assembled together at Silchester, and proposed to Dubricius, archbishop of Legions, that he should consecrate Arthur, Uther's son, to be their king. For they were now in great straits, because, upon hearing of the king's death, the Saxons had invited over their countrymen from Germany, and, under the command of Colgrin, were attempting to exterminate the whole British race. They had also entirely subdued all that part of the island that extends from the Humber to the sea of Caithness. Dubricius, therefore, grieving for the calamities of his country, in conjunction with the other bishops set the crown upon Arthur's head. Arthur was then fifteen years old, but a youth of such unparalleled courage and generosity, joined with that sweetness of temper and innate goodness, has gained him universal love. When his coronation was over, he, according to usual custom, showed his bounty and munificence to the people. And such a number of soldiers flocked to him upon it, that his treasury was not able to answer that vast expense. But such a spirit of generosity, joined with valor, can never long be in need to support itself. Arthur, therefore, the better to keep up his munificence, resolved to make use of his courage, and to fall upon the Saxons, that he might enrich his followers with their wealth. To this he was also moved by the justice of the cause, since the entire monarchy of Britain belonged to him by hereditary right. Hereupon, assembling the youth under his command, he marched to York, of which, when Colgrin had intelligence, he met him with a very great army, composed of Saxons, Scots, and Picts, by the river Duglas; where a battle happened, with the loss of the greater part of both armies. Not withstanding, the victory fell to Arthur, who pursued Colgrin to York, and there besieged him. Baldulph, upon the news of his brother's flight, went towards the siege with a body of six thousand men, to his relief, for at the time of the battle he was upon the seacoast, waiting the arrival of Duke Cheldric with succors from Germany. And being now no more than ten miles distant from the city, his purpose was to make a speedy march in the nighttime, and attack the enemy by way of surprise. But Arthur, having intelligence of his design, sent a detachment of six hundred horses, and three thousand foot soldiers, under the command of Cador, duke of Cornwall, to meet him the same night. Cador, therefore, falling into the same road along which the enemy was passing, made a sudden assault upon them, and entirely defeated the Saxons, and put them to flight. Baldulph was excessively grieved at this disappointment in the relief that he intended for his brother, and began to think of some other stratagem to gain access to him, in which if he could but succeed, he thought they might together suggest measures for their safety. And since he had no other way for it, he shaved his head and beard, and put on the habit of a jester with a harp, and in this disguise walked up and down in the camp, playing upon his instrument as if he had been a harper. He thus passed unsuspected, and little by little went up to the walls of the city, where he was at last discovered by the besieged, who thereupon drew him up with cords, and conducted him to his brother. At this unexpected though much desired meeting, they spent some time joyfully embracing each other, and then began to consider various stratagems for their delivery. At last, just as they were considering their desperate case, the ambassadors returned from Germany, and brought with them to Albania a fleet of six hundred sails, laden with brave soldiers, under the command of Cheldric. Upon this news, Arthur was dissuaded by his council from continuing the siege any longer, for fear of hazarding a battle with so powerful and numerous an army.

71. WACE, *THE ROMAN DE BRUT*

*The Norman poet Wace (c. 1110–c. 1175) is the author of two important vernacular verse chronicles, one a history of Britain (*Roman de Brut*) and the other a history of Normandy (*Roman de Rou*). The* Roman de Brut *(1155) recounts the fanciful deeds of the kings of Britain and includes the timeless tales of Brutus, Lear, Belin and Brennes, Vortigern, Uther Pendragon, Arthur, and others. It is in many ways a microcosm of the medieval imagination—a world filled with kings, battles, castles, famine, love, sin, salvation and more. Wace reworked his Latin sources (including Geoffrey of Monmouth) into Norman French verse—the* Roman *is written in rhymed octosyllabic couplets—for the royals and nobles at the court of Henry II, which at that time spoke French. Because he was writing to a lay public, Wace told his tale in a language and in terms that were familiar to them. Through his poetry, we learn something about the cultural values held by Wace and his audience, and this included a sense of lineage to the heroes of the classical past. In addition to recounting the deeds of Brutus and Arthur, Wace also offers important commentary on the linguistic differences among Celtic-, English-, and French-speaking populations.*

Source: trans. A.W. Glowka, Wace, *Le Roman de Brut: The French Book of Brutus* (Temple: Arizona Center for Medieval and Renaissance Studies, 2005), 3–5, 273–74, 365–66, 393–97. Old French.

1. Brutus

And so the book relates the story
That when the Greeks had conquered Troy

And had then ravaged the whole land
In vengeance for the acts of Paris,
Who stole Helen from the Greeks,   5
Duke Eneas, at some cost,
Made an escape from the great slaughter.
He led away a son he had
Who bore the name Ascanius;
He had no other boy or girl.   10
With relatives, chattels, and slaves,
He loaded up a score of ships.
He wandered on the sea at length—
Many and great the dangers, storms,
And labors that he was to pass.   15
Later, he came to Italy,
The land where Rome was later founded.
But there was nothing then at Rome,
Though later it was a great place.
Eneas labored hard and long: 20
Much did he sail, much did he row;
He sailed across a lot of oceans
And wandered through a lot of lands.
At last, he came to Italian shores,
In a rich place of good and plenty,   25
There where the Tiber joins the sea,
A place not far from future Rome.
Latinus, the king who ruled that land,
Who held the reign entirely in peace,
A man both rich and powerful,   30
Was old and past his prime, however.
He greatly honored Duke Eneas;
He granted him a portion of
His land that lay beside the sea.
Despite the wishes of the queen,   35
He promised him his daughter's hand
With which he'd also get the kingdom.
Since he'd no heir beside the girl,
She'd get it all when he was gone.
The girl was very beautiful,   40
And she was called Lavine, by name.
But Turnus had a prior claim,
The lord and duke of Tuscany.

Turnus, who lived nearby by chance,
This man of power, learned Latinus   45
Had given his daughter to Eneas.
He was in pain; he suffered envy—
He'd loved the woman for a while,
And she'd been guaranteed to him.
He launched a war against Eneas;   50
Man against man set into battle.
Turnus the knight was strong and hardy,
But he was vanquished, killed at last.
Eneas wed the beauty then;
King he was as she was queen.   55
He found no other to defy him
Or even dare to be against him.
After Eneas took Lavine
And conquered all that land entirely,
He lived and reigned for some four years,   60
And to a castle that he built,
He gave the name of his dear wife,
And it was called Lavinium.
Four years he held the crown and woman;
The fourth year, when his end arrived,   65
Had not yet brought the child to term;
But come to term it did on time,
And then Lavine produced a son.
Silvius was his proper name;
Postumus was his second name.   70
In great love was Silvius raised
By the first-born Ascanius,
Who with his father came from Troy;
Creusa was his mother's name,
The daughter of Priam the king;   75
But in the tumult and confusion,
When leaving from the falling Troy,
Eneas lost her in the crowd.
Ascanius then held the throne
For many days after his father   80
And had a great city constructed
That had the name of Albalona;
And to his father's wife he left
The land and also quit his claim

To the castle that Eneas made, 85
Both of which were gotten by force.
He kept the gods of Troy, however,
Which had been taken by Eneas;
He wanted them to stay in Alba,
But they could not remain there ever: 90
He never knew just how to move them
So that he could keep them on hand;
They always went back to the temple,
But I don't know at all just how.
He held the land for four and thirty 95
Years and never fought a war. . . .

11. Arthur at the Height of Power

When he had peace in all the land
And there was no war anywhere,
To the old men and married men
Who had been with him a long time
He tendered gifts and cash awards 5
And sent them back into their lands.
The bachelors and the young men,
Who were intent on making conquest,
Who did not have a wife or children,
Remained nine years in France with him. 10
The nine years that he spent in France
Produced a plethora of marvels.
He brought down many prideful men
And brought in line a lot of felons.
In Paris during Eastertide, 15
He held a massive feast for friends.
He gave his men their property
And gave them well-deserved rewards.
He rendered service to each one
According to the way he'd served. 20
To Kay, his master seneschal,
A knight who was both brave and true,
He gave Anjou and all Angers,
And he received them willingly.
To Bedevere, his butler knight, 25
One of the counselors in his household,

He gave all Normandy in fief,
Whose name was Neüstria.
These two indeed were very loyal,
And they were privy to his thoughts.   30
And he gave Flanders to Holdin,
Le Mans to Borel, a relative.
He gave Boulogne to Ligier
And gave Puntif to Richier.
To many according with their rank,   35
To many according with their service,
He gave out honors with largesse
And gave out lands to feudal vassals.
When he'd endowed his lords with fiefs
And made his household company rich,   40
In April when the summer starts,
He went across the sea to England.
You would have seen at his return
Many men and women happy.
The ladies kissed their husbands then,   45
And mothers gave their sons some kisses.
Sons and daughters kissed their fathers,
And mothers cried a lot from joy.
Cousins gave each other kisses,
And neighbors kissed each other too.   50
Friends gave kisses to their friends
And took more pleasure at their leisure.
Aunts gave kisses to their nephews.
Great joy was had by one and all.
Upon the roads and at the crossroads,   55
You would have seen a lot appear
To find out how it was for them
And what they did out on their conquests:
What they did and what they found
And why they'd been away so long.   60
These men recounted their adventures,
Both the battles strong and hard
And the hard work they had done
And the dangers that they had observed. . . .
        Gurmund destroyed a lot of towns   65
And lots of castles of great age,
Lots of churches, lots of clergy,

Lots of bishoprics, lots of abbeys,
Which were not afterwards restored
And were not lived in afterwards. 70
Still there one can see the ruins,
The deserted and the wasted things,
That Gurmund left in many places
To take the Britons fiefs away.
When he had laid their land to waste, 75
Burned the towns and taken booty,
He gave the kingdom to the Saxons
As he had sworn that he would do
If he succeeded in its conquest.
He did so and did right by them. 80
The Saxons then received the land
That they had coveted so long.
For the tribal group to which the first
Ones who received the land belonged,
They called themselves *the English* then 85
To keep their origins in mind.
And *England* was the word they used
To name the land that they were given.
In French one calls it *Angleterre*;
In English one says *Engleland*: 90
"Land of the Angles" is what it means,
and that's the explanation for it.
After Brutus came from Troy,
Britain always bore his name
Until the time that I have told you 95
In which it lost its name through Gurmund
And got some new inhabitants
And some new kings and some new lords
These men desired to keep their customs
And not to learn another language. 100
They changed the names of all the towns
And gave them names in their own language . . .

England was impoverished then.
The wheat crop failed; the people died.
Most of the land was left deserted, 105
For there was no one there to work it.
Eleven years and more it lay

In waste devoid of laborers.
Whatever Britons that there were
Stayed in the mountains and the forests. 110
The Englishmen who were still there,
The ones who had escaped the famine
And many who were born much later,
Survived the best way that they knew.
Both to fix the cities up 115
And to do labor on the land,
They sent off word to Saxony,
There where their ancestors were born,
That with their wives and with their children,
That with their households and their servants 120
They should all come as an armed force.
They would have land as they desired.
They would have good arable land.
They needed nothing more than men.
These men came in massive numbers, 125
In massive hordes, at many times.
They set up camps throughout the land.
They grew and multiplied a lot.
They found no one who would disturb them
Or who'd refuse the land to them. 130
They often came in massive groups.
They held the customs and the laws
Their forefathers had held before
There in the land from which they'd come.
The names, the language, and the laws 135
They wished to keep as they received them.
They said *chester* instead of *kaer;*
And they said *shire* instead of *suiz;*
And they said *town* instead of *tref.*
Map is Welsh; English is *son.* 140
In French the Welsh *kaer* is "city,"
Map, "fiz"; *tref,* "vile" *suiz* "cunté."
But some say French *cuntrée*
Means just what *suiz* does in Welsh;
And some folks say a *shire* in English 145
Can mean what *suiz* does in Welsh.
Among the Welsh there still endures
The language coming straight from British.

The counties and the baronies,
The countries and the earldoms—   150
They keep them there in their divisions
Just as the Britons drew them out.
Athelstan was then the king.
He was the first one of the English
Who had all England in his power   155
Except for just Cornwall and Wales.
He was anointed first and blessed,
And he was crowned the very first.
Many say he was a bastard.
His father was Edward the king,   160
Who went to Rome to say his prayers
And granted at St. Peter's there
And made his offering at the altar
Of a silver penny every year
From every man who had a house   165
And lived within his royal sway.
The first to ever make this gift
Was his forebear, a man called Yng.
The later heirs maintained the gift;
They rendered it unto the pope.   170
        Chadwalader wished to return
And wanted to maintain his land.
When he learned it was populated
And the plague now had gone away,
He wished to go back to his land.   175
He made his travel preparations;
He then asked God with all his heart
To make it very clear to him
If his return might give him pleasure,
For he desired to do his pleasure.   180
A voice that was divine told him
To leave this trip and take another.
He should not go to England then;
He should go to the pope of Rome.
With sins of his forgiven there,   185
He would then go among the blessed.
The English should own Britain now;
Britain would never be recovered
Until the time of prophecy

That Merlin said would come to pass.   190
These things could never happen, though
Until that certain time would come
When relics of his very corpse,
Drawn outside of his sepulcher,
Would be transported out of Rome   195
And be presented there in Britain.
Chadwalader was quite amazed,
And in amazement he was troubled
By this divine announcement that
He heard so openly like this.   200
To King Alain, who was his friend,
He told what he had heard just then.
Alain then had the closets opened
And had the learned clerks appear.
He had the histories brought out   205
And had men search and find the proof
That what Chadwalader had said
About the vision that he had
Accorded with the dicts of Merlin
And of Aquilus the good divine   210
And with what Sybil had recorded.
Chadwalader did nothing then;
He left his navy and his men.
He called to Yvor and to Yni.
Yvor was his legal son;   215
Yni, his nephew, his sister's son.
"To Wales," he said, "you will now go,
and you will be the lords of the Britons
so that through lack of noble lords
the Britons don't become dishonored."   220
They did what he commanded them,
And he made travel preparations.
He went to Saint Sergius, the pope,
Who cherished him and honored him.
He made confession of his sins   225
And did his penance afterwards.
He hardly had arrived in Rome
When he fell into sickness there.
He was quite sick; he had to die.
Eleven days before May came,   230

He died on the nineteenth day of April,
Freed from his earthly exile here,
One less than seven hundred years
Since Christ took flesh in Holy Mary.
The corpse was laid out very nicely   235
And put among the bodies of saints.
His soul flew up to Paradise,
Where we with him may someday sit.
    Yvor and Yni crossed the sea
With great numbers of ships and people.   240
The remnants of the British people,
Whom we refer to as the Welsh,
Who are a way off in the west,
Became the subjects of these men.
They never later had the strength   245
It took to hold the realm of Logres.
All had moved; all was changed.
All was different and lacked
The honor, customs, nobleness
And life of those who'd lived before.   250
Wales had come to be its name
From Duke Gualon, who ruled in Wales,
Or from Galaes, who was queen
To whom the land was once subjected.
    So ends the book of British deeds   255
And ends the line of noble lords
Who as descendants of King Brutus
Ruled over England a long time.
Master Wace wrote this book
One thousand one hundred fifty-five   260
Years after God assumed our flesh
To gain our souls' redemption.

72. GALBERT OF BRUGES ON HISTORICAL METHOD

The County of Flanders was plunged into a political crisis when, on 2 March 1127, its leader Count Charles "the Good" (b. 1084) was assassinated as he prayed in the church of St-Donatian in Bruges. The murder shocked contemporaries, not so much because of the violence of the act as because the count was slain by his own vassals in church during the holy time of Lent. The event and its ensuing crisis prompted a notary in the local administration to keep a detailed record of the events following the murder. The result was the extraordinary history of Galbert of Bruges, who first took notes on waxed tablets and later worked them up into a complete account of the murder and its aftermath. Galbert writes not so much as a conscious historian or even as a biographer, but rather as a day-by-day reporter of events that seemed to be plunging his fatherland into chaos. In this sense Galbert is most unusual, since his intended audience is his fellow townsmen rather than the more typical ecclesiastical or royal audience for whom chronicles and saints' lives were usually written. Nevertheless, his historical acumen and attention to detail are vividly on display in the prologue to his history.

Source: trans. Justin Lake, from *Histoire du meurtre de Charles le Bon*, ed. Henri Pirenne (Paris: A. Picard, 1891), 1–3; in Lake, ed. *Prologues to Ancient and Medieval History*, Readings in Civilizations and Cultures: XVII (Toronto: University of Toronto Press, 2013), 196–97. Latin.

At a time when an ardent zeal to win fame and glory through knightly exploits and a shared intention to rule well were conspicuous among the rulers of the kingdoms that we see around us, Henry, who ruled as emperor of the Romans and died without heirs after sitting on the throne for many years, was a man of lesser fame and power, and the king of England, who occupied his realm without children, was likewise inferior in fame and power to Charles, marquis of Flanders, our natural lord and prince, a man ennobled by his exploits in war and the royal blood of his family, who, in the seventh year of his countship, while he presided over the churches of God as a father and advocate, being a man generous to the poor, courteous and honorable among the magnates, cruel and cunning toward his enemies, and also without heir, was betrayed and killed by his own men, or rather by his most debased serfs [vassals], laying down his life for justice. As I set out to recount the death of so great a prince, I did not strive to adorn my narrative with the ornaments of eloquence or the various figures of rhetoric, but simply pursue the truth, and though the style is barren, I have nonetheless commended the remarkable series of events that followed his murder to the memory of the faithful in writing. For my own part, when I wanted to apply myself to this task, I had neither a location nor a suitable occasion to write, since at that time our place [the castle of Bruges] was beset by fear and hardship, to the point that without exception the clergy and the people were constantly threatened with the destruction of the possessions and their lives. Amid so many obstacles, therefore, and in the most cramped conditions, I undertook to calm my seething mind, which was tossed about as if it were in Euripus, and focus it on the task of writing. In the midst of these mental demands, one tiny spark of love sustained and nourished by its own flame ignited all of the spiritual powers of my heart and endowed my person, which had been possessed by fear of what was happening outside, with the freedom to write. Thus, if anyone is keen to belittle and disparage this work to which I have devoted myself, and which I have commended to your hearing and that of all the faithful in common, despite being placed in such difficult straits, I do not much care. What gives me assurance is the fact that I am speaking the truth, as it is known to everyone who endured the same perils that I did, and that I am commending it to be remembered by those who come after us. I ask and advise, therefore, that if this little work, with its arid style and limited scope, comes into anyone's hands, that he not scorn and deride it, but rather marvel with fresh wonderment at the things written here, which have come to pass only in our time by the ordinance of God, and that he learn not to despise or betray to their death those earthly powers that have been set over us—as we are obliged to believe—by divine ordinance, whence the apostle says, "Let every soul be subject to every power, whether it be to the kings as [*tamquam*] supreme or to governors as [*tamquam*] sent by him" [1 Peter 2:13–14]. *Tamquam* here is not comparative, but affirmative. For in the sacred scriptures *tamquam* is used to mean that which is true, so that "as a betrothed" [*tamquam sponsus*] means "truly betrothed" [*vere sponsus*]. These murderers, drunkards, fornicators, and slaves to all the vices of our earth did not deserve to be ruled over by a prince who was good, pious, and powerful, catholic, a sustainer of the poor after God, an advocate of the churches of God, a defender of his country, and one in whom the remaining power of earthly rule assumed the form and matter of a virtuous ruler and servant of God. When the devil, therefore (as you will see in what follows), saw the progress of the Church and the Christian faith, he shook the foundations of the earth (that is, of the Church of God) and threw it into confusion with treachery, betrayals, and the shedding of innocent blood.

73. CHRONICLES OF THE DEEDS OF THE COUNTS OF THE ANGEVINS

The Chronicles of the Deeds of the Counts of the Angevins *is a narrative of the history of the princely dynasty that ruled the county of Anjou in northwestern France from its legendary origins in the ninth century through the end of the twelfth century. The* Chronicles *is an excellent example of what has been called a "living text," a work that was continuously copied, revised, and continued by various authors and communities over the course of the twelfth century. Although the earliest surviving manuscripts date from the mid-twelfth century, and carry the narrative of the Anjou comital dynasty until 1151, it is clear that the work was begun earlier, probably around 1106, by a learned author bearing all the hallmarks of an education in the schools of the Loire valley. The author shows no preference for any religious house and never refers to scriptural or patristic writings, suggesting that he may have been a household cleric rather than a monk. In these opening chapters of the work, he draws heavily upon the works of the Roman historian Sallust (c. 86–c. 35 BCE), in particular his histories of the Catiline conspiracy (63 BCE) and the war with Jugurtha (112–106 BCE). While Sallust was a very popular stylistic source for twelfth-century Latin writers, our author distinguishes himself by his artful interweaving of borrowed passages and turns of phrase to argue that true nobility comes not only from noble birth but from noble deeds. He sometimes draws on the original context of his source to strengthen his argument, and at other times he creates an image that is entirely opposed to the one intended by Sallust. Further resonance between the Roman past and the medieval present is created through the author's repeated use of the term* consul, *the highest office of the Roman Republic occupied by the heroes of Sallust's works, to mean "count," a usage that the counts of Anjou themselves frequently adopted.*

Source: trans. Nicholas Paul, from *Chroniques des comtes d'Anjou et des seigneurs d'Amboise*, ed. Louis Halphen and René Poupardin (Paris: A. Picard, 1913), 25–27. Latin.

Prologue

Since I have already explained in the foregoing exposition of the kings of the Franks that which I judge to be necessary to understand both the preceding work and especially the one that follows, I will now make clear briefly and skillfully what I found in writings relating to the counts of the Angevins, writings that were very confused and unpolished but which I will set forth "as truthfully and in as few words as I am able" [Sallust, *Catiline* 4.3]. For since our "life is short" [1.3], we ought "to make the memory" of them "last as long as possible" [1.4], the ones "whose virtue is regarded as splendid and lasting" [1.5]. Since truly knighthood proceeds to the highest summit by the fortitude of the soul and of the body [5.1], it was the custom that the judicious lordship of ancient cities "should pass from the less good to some of the very best men" [2.6]. Therefore at the time of Charles the Bald [king of the Franks, r. 840–877] "several new and non-noble men, better" than the nobles with regard to "goodness and honesty," were made great and outstanding [Sallust, *Jugurtha* 8.1]. Indeed, the king did not doubt that those men, "who he saw to be thirsting for military glory, would place themselves in danger and so put fortune to the test" [8.1]. There were in those days "men of ancient lineage with many ancestral images" who boasted not of their own deeds, but of the deeds of their ancestors [85.10]. Those men, when they were elected to any weighty office, would select "someone from among the common people as an adviser in the affairs of their office," so that when the king "ordered them to rule" over others, they sought "someone else to command them in turn" [85.11]. Therefore King Charles had few from that "noble clique" with him; instead he freely offered to the new men the spoils of war and inheritances won through many labors and dangers. From among that generation was Tertullus, from whom the lineage of the counts of the Angevins took its beginning, a man who had "learned to strike down the foe, to keep watch and ward, to fear nothing save ill repute, to endure heat and cold alike, to sleep on the ground, to bear privation and fatigue at the same time" [85.33]. By doing these things and others he was said to have brought forth nobility for himself and his lineage. Regarding his father, we will say what is necessary. I beseech, however, those who are reading to hold faithfully to what is said here, and not judge me to have written falsehoods.

On Tertullus

There was a certain man from Armorica Gallia [Roman Brittany] named Torquatius, who was descended from those who had once been expelled from Armorica by the Bretons under the orders of emperor Maximian. This man was known as "Tortulfus" in the vulgar language of the Bretons, who were ignorant of his own ancient and Roman name. In the same year when Charles the Bald expelled the Normans from Anjou and from his entire kingdom, he established Torquatius as the forester of Limelle. Indeed, as many others recount, his people had lived for a long time in the forests against the wishes of the Bretons. He was born a peasant in the region of Redon, subsisting off the exercise of hunting and the abundance of the forest. Such men, some say, are called *bigrios* by the Bretons but we Franks say *byrsarios* or *pedicarios*. There are those who would rather that he had lived in the common places with the peasants of Redon. Which of these two might be more true does not matter greatly, because the tellers of these stories themselves do not disagree strongly, and no wonder, for indeed we read that senators once worked in the fields, and were snatched from the plow to become emperors. In this man, when he had attained the fullness of years, "the armaments of old age" [Cicero, *De senectute* 3.9], that is to say "the knowledge of a life well spent and the memory of many deeds worthily performed" were, to him, most delightful.

This man however begat Tertullus, who is reckoned by the ancient storytellers in their genealogies to be the first of the lineage of the counts of the Angevins. They hold that assuredly Tertullus, overcoming his own circumstances and unstable affairs, boldly set out once he had reached his majority. At around that time Charles the Bald, son of Louis, grandson of Charlemagne, had been made a king among the trio of rulers [with his half-brothers Lothar and Louis the German] (he did not reign for long). The aforesaid Tertullus, leaving the poverty of his father's holdings and having confidence in his strength, hoped and wished that he would be lifted up, went out from the western frontier and made his way into Francia and undertook to go soldiering under the patronage of the king. Others of that time, made aware of their bravery in arms and eager for fame and honor, wanting to become greater through virtue, came together from different regions of the world, especially allured by the benevolence of the generous king and incited by the opportunities of the age.

74. HISTORY AND LEGEND OF RICHARD THE LIONHEART

King Richard I "the Lionheart" of England (r. 1189–99) is one of the most famous kings of the Middle Ages. He was the third son of Henry II (r. 1154–89) and Eleanor of Aquitaine, and, although he was born in England, he spent most of his adult life in Aquitaine or on crusade. In his lifetime he spoke the langue d'oïl, *a northern French dialect, and Occitan, a southern French dialect. His participation in the Third Crusade and his epic (though unsuccessful) showdown with the Muslim leader Saladin in 1191 helped to solidify his reputation for bravery and leadership, and his heroic deeds in the Latin East became the basis of many tales of high adventure.*

The three selections below highlight the fine line between history and romance in the twelfth century. The first is from a chronicle by Richard of Devizes, who was a monk at St Swithin's house in Winchester. The chronicle covers only the first three years of Richard's reign and is, therefore, devoted largely to Richard's exploits during the Third Crusade. His account of the preparations for crusade, of the battles themselves, and of England's domestic affairs during the king's absence is insightful and possibly satiric, but not historically reliable. His chronicle is notable as well for being the first work to use the word "holocaust" for the riots against the Jews in London during Richard's coronation in 1189. The song of Richard I, the second text, is a fine example of a trouvère *composition. It used to be thought that the king wrote it himself during his imprisonment at the castle of Duke Leopold of Austria; more likely it was written by one of the king's court minstrels and reflects an evolving legend about his life. The third selection offers something of a blend of both the chronicle and poetic genres. Ambroise was a Norman poet of some education who accompanied Richard on his crusade to the Holy Land. His* History of the Holy War *describes in rhyming Old French verse the crusade adventures of the king. Although Ambroise is often disparaging about the French, he is usually accurate in his chronology, no doubt on account of having witnessed many of the events firsthand.*

a. Richard of Devizes's Chronicle of the Third Crusade

Source: trans. J.A. Giles, *Chronicles of the Crusades, Being Contemporary Narratives. . .*, ed. H.G. Bohn (London: Henry G. Bohn, 1848), 55–56, 60–64; revised. Latin.

Richard, the king of the English, had already spent two years in conquering the region around Jerusalem, and during all that time no aid had been sent to him from any of his realms. Nor yet were his only and uterine brother, John, count of Mortain, nor his justiciars, nor his other nobles, observed to take any care to send him any part of his revenues, and they did not even think of his return. The church, however, prayed to God for him without ceasing. The king's army shrank daily in the Promised Land, and besides those who were slain by the sword, many thousands of people perished every month by the too sudden extremities of the nightly cold and daily heat. When it appeared that they would all have to die there, every one had to choose whether he would die as a coward or in battle.

On the other side, the strength of the infidels greatly increased, and their confidence was strengthened by the misfortunes of the Christians; their army was relieved at certain times by fresh troops; the weather was natural to them; the place was their native country; their labor, health; their frugality, medicine. Among us, on the contrary, that which brought gain to our adversaries became a disadvantage. For if our people had too little to eat even once in a week, they were rendered less effective for seven weeks after. The mingled nation of French and English fared sumptuously every day, at whatever cost, while their treasure lasted; and (no offense to the French) they ate until they were sick. The well-known custom of the English was continually kept up even under the clarions and the clangor of the trumpet or horn: with due devotion they drained their wine-cups to the dregs. The merchants of the country, who brought the victuals to the camp, were astonished at their wonderful and extraordinary habits, and could scarcely believe even what they saw to be true, that one people, and that small in number, consumed three times more bread and a hundred times more wine than that on which many nations of the infidels had been sustained, and some of those nations innumerable. And the hand of the Lord was deservedly laid upon them according to their merits. Such great lack of food followed their great gluttony, that their teeth scarcely spared their fingers, as their hands presented to their mouths less than their usual allowance. To these and other calamities, which were severe and many, a much greater one was added by the sickness of the king.

The king was extremely sick, and confined to his bed; his fever continued without intermission; the physicians whispered that it was an acute semitertian fever. And as they despaired of his recovery even from the beginning, terrible dismay was spread from the king's abode through the camp. There were few among the many thousands who did not consider fleeing, and the utmost confusion of dispersion or surrender would have followed, had not Hubert Walter, bishop of Salisbury, immediately assembled the council. By strenuous argument he won this concession: that the army should not break up until a truce was requested from Saladin. All the armed men stood in array more steadily than usual, and with a threatening look concealing the reluctance of their mind, they feigned a desire for battle. No one spoke of the king's illness, lest the secret of their intense sorrow should be disclosed to the enemy; for it was well known that

Saladin feared the charge of the whole army less than that of the king alone; and if he should know that he was sick in bed, he would instantly pelt the French with cow-dung, and intoxicate the best of the English drunkards with a dose which should make them tremble. . . .

[The Saracens eventually proposed a truce in these terms:] If it pleased King Richard, for the space of three years, three months, three weeks, three days, and three hours, such a truce would be observed between the Christians and the infidels, that whatever either one party or the other in any possessed, he would possess without molestation to the end. During the interval the Christians would be permitted at their pleasure to fortify Acre only, and the infidels Jerusalem. All contracts, all commerce, every act and every thing would be mutually carried on by all in peace. [Saladin's brother] Saffadin himself was dispatched to the English as the bearer of this offer. . . .

While King Richard was sick at Jaffa, word was brought to him that the duke of Burgundy was taken dangerously ill at Acre. It was the day for the king's fever to take its turn, and through his delight at this report, it left him. The king immediately with uplifted hands imprecated a curse upon the duke, saying, "May God destroy him, for he would not destroy the enemies of our faith with me, although he had long served in my pay." . . . [Eventually,] having resumed his strength of body more by the greatness of his mind than by repose or nourishment, he issued a command for the whole coast from Tyre to Ascalon, that all who were able to serve in the wars should come to fight at the king's expense. A countless multitude assembled before him, the greater part of whom were on foot. Having rejected them as useless, he mustered the cavalry, and found scarcely five hundred knights and two thousand shield-bearers whose lords had perished. And not discouraged by their small number, he, being a most excellent orator, strengthened the minds of the fearful with a timely speech. He commanded that it be proclaimed through the companies that on the third day they must follow the king to battle, either to die as martyrs or to take Jerusalem by storm. This was the sum of his project, because as yet he knew nothing of the truce. For there was no one who dared even hint to him, when he had so unexpectedly recovered, that which they had undertaken without his knowledge, through fear of his death. Hubert Walter, bishop of Salisbury, however, took counsel with Count Henry concerning the truce, and obtained his ready concurrence in his wishes. So having deliberated together how they might safely hinder such a hazardous engagement, they conceived of the one stratagem out of a thousand, namely, to try to dissuade the people from the enterprise. And the matter turned out most favorably; the spirit of those who were going to fight had so greatly failed even without dissuasion, that on the appointed day, when the king, according to his custom leading the van, marshaled his army, of all the knights and shield-bearers not more than 900 were found. On account of which defection, the king, greatly enraged, even raving, and gnawing the pine rod which he held in his hand, at length opened his indignant lips as follows: "O God!" said he, "O God, my God, why has thou forsaken me? For whom have we foolish Christians, for whom have we English come hither from the furthest parts of the earth to bear our arms? Is it not for the God of the Christians? O fie! How good art thou to us thy people, who now are for thy name given up to the sword; we shall become a portion for foxes. O how unwilling should I be to forsake thee in so forlorn and dreadful a position, were I thy lord and advocate as thou art mine! In sooth, my standards will in future be despised, not through my fault but through thine; in sooth, not through any cowardice of my warfare, art thou thyself, my King and my God, conquered this day, and not Richard thy vassal."

He spoke, and returned to the camp extremely dejected; and as a fit occasion now offered, Bishop Hubert and Henry, count of Champagne, approaching him with unwonted familiarity, as if nothing had yet been arranged, begged under diverse pretexts the king's consent for making such overtures to the infidels as were necessary. And thus the king answered them: "Since a troubled mind is usually more likely to thwart than to afford sound judgment—I, who am greatly troubled in mind, authorize you, whom I see to be calm of mind, to arrange what you shall think most proper for the good of peace." Having gained their desires, they chose messengers to send to Saffadin upon these matters; Saffadin, who had returned from Jerusalem, was suddenly announced to be at hand. The count and the bishop went to meet him, and being assured by him of the truce, they instructed him how he must speak with the lord, their king. Being admitted to an interview with the king as one who previously had been his friend, Saffadin could scarcely prevail upon the king not to destroy himself but to consent to the truce. For so great were the man's strength of body, mental courage, and entire trust in Christ, that he could hardly be prevailed upon not to undertake in his own person a single combat with a thousand of the choicest infidels, as he was destitute of soldiers. And as he was not permitted to attack, he chose this evasion, that, after a truce of seven weeks, the stipulations of the compact being preserved, it should remain for him to choose whether it were better to fight or to forbear. The two parties put their right hands to the final agreement, that they would faithfully observe it; and Saffadin, more honored than burdened with the king's present, went back again to his brother, to return at the expiration of the term for the final conclusion or breaking of the above truce.

b. A Song of Richard I

Source: trans. J.J. Wilhelm, *Medieval Song: An Anthology of Hymns and Lyrics* (New York: E.P. Dutton & Co, Inc., 1971), 263–64. Old French.

A man imprisoned can never speak his mind
As cleverly as those who do not suffer,
But through his song he can some comfort find.
I have a host of friends, poor the gifts they offer.
Shame on them if this ransoming should trail   5
       Into a second year in jail!

This they know well, my barons and my men,
English, Norman, Gascon, and Poitevin,
What I'd leave of my property in prison!
O I'm not saying this to cast derision,   10
       But I'm still here in jail!

Here is a truth that I know can be told:
Dead men and prisoners have neither parents nor friends,
No one to offer up his silver and gold.
It matters to me, but much more to my men,   15
For after my death, they'll be bitterly assailed
       Because I'm so long in jail!

No wonder if I have a grieving heart
When I see my land torn by its lord asunder:
If he'll recall the pact in which we took part   20
And remember the pledges we vowed we'd both live under,
Truly within the year, without a fail,
       I'd be out of jail!

This they know, the Angevins and Tourains,
Those bachelors there who are strong and own a lot,   25
While I'm encumbered here in another's hands;
They loved me lots, but now they don't love a jot;
Over the plains I don't see a piece of mail
       Although I'm still in jail!

I've loved and I love still my companions true,   30
The men of Cahiu and the men of Porcherain,
But tell me, song, if they still love me too,
For never to them was I double-faced or vain:
They're villains if my lands they now assail—
       Since I am here in jail!   35

c. Ambroise's *History of the Holy War*

Source: trans. Marianne Ailes, *The History of the Holy War: Ambroise's Estoire de la Guerre Sainte* (Woodbridge, UK: The Boydell Press, 2003), 29–31, 105–6. Old French.

[The Crusade Begins]

He who would deal with a long story must take great care that he does not burden himself by beginning a work he cannot finish. Rather, if he undertakes such a task, he should do it in such a way that he is able to complete what he has undertaken. For this reason I have begun briefly, so that the subject will not be too burdensome. I want to get right to my subject for it is a story that should be told, a story which tells of the misadventure that happened to us, and justly so, a few years ago in the land of Syria, because of our excessive folly. For God did not wish us to continue without feeling the consequences. And he certainly did cause us to feel them, in Normandy and in France, and throughout Christendom. Whether the folly was great or whether it was little, the consequences were felt directly; all this because of the Cross which the world worships and which at that time was taken away and moved by the pagans from the land where it was to be found, the land God deigned to be born and to die . . . [the land] of the Hospital and of the Holy Temple, causing much pulling of the temple, [the land] of the Sepulcher, where God was placed, lost to us through sin. This is not how it should be said—it was through God, who wished to bring to himself his people whom he had redeemed and who at that time served him not at all.

Through this great disaster all people, throughout the world, of high or low estate, were afflicted and could scarcely be comforted. The dances, the sounds, the songs, the words and all earthly joys of Christian people were abandoned, until the pope in Rome, Gregory the Eighth, as is written in the accounts, through whom God saved many men, issued a pardon that brought relief; for God's sake and in contempt of the devil he declared that any man who went against the infidels who had disinherited the worthy king of truth, will be acquitted of all his sins. Because of this many kings and counts and other men beyond number took the Cross to seek God in the distant land of Syria. All the most esteemed men took the Cross together.

Richard, the valiant count of Poitiers, did not wish to fail God at the time of His need and His call. So he took the Cross for love of Him. He was the first of the great men of the lands from which we came [to do so]. Then the king entered His service, expending great effort and expense. No-one put off the taking up of the Cross, even if it meant selling his inheritance. No knight, whether old or young, sought to hide what was in his heart; all wanted to show how heavy upon them was the need to take vengeance for the shame committed against God, who had not deserved it, because of his land that had been devastated, where His people were so pressed that they did not know what to do. But no-one should be surprised that they were then defeated. They were a good people, a chosen race, but it was the will of God that they should die and that others should come to their aid. They died in body but live on in heaven. This is what happens to those who die there but who abide in the service of God. . . .

There was a long-standing war between France and Normandy, a war at once cruel, terrible and mighty, full of wickedness and danger. The war was between King Philip and King Henry of England, Henry head of a fine family, noble, wise and prudent, the good father of the young king, who jousted with such vigor, the father of Richard [who is] shrewd, wise and full of talent, the father of Geoffrey of Brittany, who also did great deeds, and the father of John Lackland, because of whom he suffered such trouble and war.

The king who had such a family and who knew himself to be rich could easily sustain a war if anyone wished to wage war on him and had he done what they wanted, to people such as they were. The two kings were in disagreement, so that no-one could make them agree until God brought them together, at a meeting that was of such great importance; it was held between Gisors and Trie in the great and lovely meadow. Much was said there, words of wisdom and of foolishness. One was concerned for peace; the other had no such concern. There were many people there, of all sorts, who could not see how peace was to be sought, but, it seems to me, God willed that they should take the Cross together. At that meeting many quarrels were raised, old and new, many quarrels which were troublesome, arousing pride and haughtiness; these were followed up without rest. . . .

King Richard, who remained in Syria in the service of our Lord God, made a request of the king of France, whom he distrusted, for their fathers had distrusted one another and often harmed one another. Richard wished that Philip would reassure him and swear on the relics of the saints that he would do no harm to his land, nor harm him at all while he was on God's journey and on his pilgrimage, and that when he had returned to his land, that he would cause no disturbance or war nor do him any harm, without warning him by his French [messengers] forty days before. The king made this oath, giving as pledges great men, of whom we still remember the duke of Burgundy and Count Henry, and other pledges, five or more in number, but I cannot name the others.

The king of France took his leave but I tell you one thing, on leaving he received more curses than blessings. The marquis and he went by sea to Tyre, taking with them Karakush and their share of the Saracens, who had been shared out, for whom the kings thought to receive one hundred thousand besants of their treasury, with which they hoped to support and retain their people until Easter. However, all the hostages were abandoned [by their own side], many of them dying in sorrow, so that not a farthing was received for them, nor anything of any worth at that time, nor any beast, except for half the equipment that the French found at Acre. They often reproved him for having no other payment and it was a subject of much dispute. In the end the king of England, from whom the duke of Burgundy asked for help, lent five thousand silver marks of his own to the duke, against the surety of the hostages, with which they could pay their men greatly to their advantage. But this was much later. . . .

The king of France went home and King Richard, who did not wish to be neglectful of God, made his preparations. Then he had summoned and called together the army, which remained for another two weeks, beyond the term set, then another week, for Saladin did not wish to fulfill his obligations to our people—or God did not wish it—whichever. So the armies waited and the king immediately had his mangonels and catapults loaded, so that he was prepared [to depart]. Now the summer passed and he got everything prepared. He had the walls of Acre rebuilt as high, indeed higher, than when they had been destroyed. He himself liked to go and see the workers working, for he was very keen to return God's heritage to him. The waiting wearied him. He would have recovered God's heritage had it not been for the workings of envy.

75. OTTO OF FREISING, *HISTORY OF THE TWO CITIES*

Otto of Freising (c. 1115–58) was the most important German historian of the twelfth century and one of the most incisive and detail-oriented historical thinkers of the central Middle Ages. He was born into the highest ranks of the nobility. His father was Margrave Leopold III of Austria (r. 1095–1136) and his mother, Agnes, was the daughter of Holy Roman Emperor Henry IV (r. 1084–1105). Otto studied in Paris and then joined a Cistercian monastery in Champagne, becoming its abbot in 1136/37. In 1138 he was elected bishop of the Bavarian city of Freising and worked diligently to rebuild the diocese, which had suffered badly during the political turmoil of the previous decades. In 1152 Otto's nephew Frederick Barbarossa succeeded to the throne as emperor, uniting the feuding Welf and Staufen factions and inaugurating a period of renewed strength for the empire.

Otto's scholastic education and privileged position as bishop and court insider make him one of the most valuable sources of historical information about the German empire in the mid-twelfth century, even if his perspective is understandably one-sided. He wrote two major works, the History of the Two Cities, *a universal chronicle from Creation to 1146, and the* Deeds of Emperor Frederick I, *a panegyric on the emperor that was left incomplete at his death in 1158. As the title suggests, the* History of the Two Cities *is grounded in the Augustinian belief that human history is characterized by the ceaseless opposition between the heavenly City of God and the earthly City of Man. In the prologue Otto also invokes the biblical theory of the four world empires, which was ultimately derived from Daniel's interpretation of King Nebuchadnezzar's dream, but circulated most influentially by the early Church Fathers Jerome and Orosius. The Roman Empire was understood to be the last of the four empires, but according to Otto its strength had been compromised by its transference first to Byzantium, then to the Franks, and now to the German emperors. Otto's philosophy of history reflects on the one hand a strong belief in the* translatio imperii *that brought the German emperors to power, and on the other a deep pessimism about the state of church–state relations in the twelfth century. These conflicting elements are illustrated by his dedicatory epistles to the emperor and to the emperor's chancellor, Rainald of Dassel, in which he additionally explains the value of history as a subject of study.*

Source: trans. Justin Lake, from *Ottonis episcopi Frisingensis Chronica sive Historia de Duabus Civi-tatibus*, ed. A. Hofmeister, Monumenta Germanica Historica: Scriptores Rerum Germanicarum in Usum Scholarum (Hanover and Leipzig: Hahn, 1912), 1–11; in Justin Lake, ed., *Prologues to Ancient and Medieval History: A Reader* (Toronto: University of Toronto Press, 2013), 221–27. Latin.

[Dedicatory Epistle to Emperor Frederick I]

To his lord, the victorious, celebrated, and triumphant Frederick, ever venerable emperor of the Romans, Otto, by the grace of God what he is in the church of Freising, wishing prosperity in him who gives salvation to kings [Psalm 143:10].

Your imperial majesty requested of our insignificance that the book on the mutability of history that we were prompted to write several years ago by the troubled state of affairs should be conveyed to your serenity. I submitted to your command gladly and willingly, and I did so all the more eagerly because I thought it most befitting of your royal excellency that you should wish to acquaint yourself with the deeds of the kings and emperors of the past in order to better keep the realm safe through force of arms and mold it through laws and judgments. In the same way, the great king of the Persians Ahasuerus, or Artaxerxes, although he had not obtained the knowledge of the true light through the worship of one God, nonetheless believing through the nobility of his soul that it would benefit the royal majesty, decreed that the annals that had been compiled during his reign and those of his predecessors should be read out to him. And in this way he won renown because an innocent man was not punished as though he were guilty, and the guilty party did not escape punishment as though he were innocent [Esther 6:1ff].

No one can be found on earth who is not subject to earthly laws and constrained to obey them. It is only kings, who have been set above the law and reserved for divine judgment, who are not confined by the laws of this world. Whence comes the testimony of the man who was both king and prophet: "To thee only I have sinned" [Psalm 50:6]. It therefore befits a king who is not only ennobled by the greatness of his soul, but has also been illuminated by divine grace in order to know his creator, to keep God, the king of kings and the lord of lords, foremost in his mind, and to take care in every way possible not to fall into his hands. For since, according to the apostle, "it is a fearful thing to fall into the hands of the living God" [Hebrews 10:31], it will be all the more terrible for kings, who have no one above them to fear apart from God, because they have more freedom to sin than others, according to the wise man who says: "Listen, therefore, kings, and understand; learn, you who are judges over the ends of the earth; give ear, you who rule the people and please your-selves in multitudes of nations. For power has been given to you by the Lord, and strength by the Most High, who will examine your works and search out your thoughts. Because, though you are ministers of his kingdom, you have not judged rightly, nor kept the law of justice, nor walked according to the will of God, horribly and speedily will he appear to you. For a most severe judgment shall await those who rule" [Wisdom 6:2–6]. But you, most renowned prince, who in fact and in name are justly called "peacemaker" because you have brought back the joyous sights of a tranquil morning after a dismal and rainy night, and restored the blessings of peace to the world while preserving each person's possessions, with God, who is the origin, granting you perseverance, through the favor of divine mercy you will not incur the penalty of so bitter a pronouncement.

An understanding of history, therefore, will be both honorable and useful for your excellency. For by contemplating the deeds of valiant men and the power and might of God, who takes away and bestows earthly rule upon whomever he wishes and permits temporal change, you will always conduct yourself in fear of him and reign for many years with continuing good fortune. Accordingly we ask that your nobility recognize that we were prompted by the turmoil of the times to write this history of the troubled era that preceded you in bitterness of spirit, and for this reason we did not so much commit to writing the course of events, but—in the manner of a tragedy—the misery that attended them. Thus, we have ended each of the books down to the seventh and eighth (through which are signified the repose of souls and the twofold garment of resurrection) in sorrow.

And so if it pleases your majesty to commend an account of your most noble deeds to the memory of posterity in writing, and if your highness's clerks will arrange it by chapter and send it to me, I shall not hesitate—God willing and as long as I am still living—to carry out this joyous task with a joyful spirit, expect-ing nothing as a reward other than the aid that your imperial mercy may wish to render to the church that I serve in the hour of its need.

For the sake of the honor of the empire and the glory of your own person I was glad to hear of the expedition that you have organized against the arrogance of the Milanese, and I was honored to receive the instructions on this matter that you directed to my lowliness. We have sent as bearers of the present work the venerable abbot Raboto of Saint-Stephen and our chaplain Rahewin, who took down this history from our lips, so that with your permission they may offer a suitable response in this matter on our behalf.

[Dedication to Rainald of Dassel]

To his cherished friend Rainald, noble chancellor of the ruler who stands supreme among all the rulers of the world, Otto, by the grace of God bishop of the church of Freising, sends greetings and obedience.

Because I share with Boethius the belief that life's greatest solace lies in learning and practicing all the branches of philosophy, I embrace your noble personage all the more familiarly and joyfully for knowing that hitherto you have toiled in the pursuit of philosophy and become supremely accomplished in it. For this reason, I write to you as a philosopher rather than a neophyte concerning the book that I sent to the lord emperor, trusting in your diligence and hoping to find in you one who will give a favorable, rather than a hostile, interpretation of certain of its contents. For you know that every branch of learning consists of two things: avoidance and selection. To begin with grammar, therefore, which comes first for those embarking upon the study of philosophy, by its own precepts grammar instructs us to choose what is appropriate to our purpose and to avoid what is contrary to it. For example, it instructs us by a hard and fast rule to join words together on the basis of similar qualities, while avoiding and eliminating constructions that do not follow this rule, such as barbarisms and solecisms. Likewise, logic, which deals chiefly with the principles of syllogisms, purging and instructing our judgment, avoids and eliminates any series of premises that results in an invalid syllogism, while selecting only the valid ones for use. For while sixteen combinations of premises can be devised, only four, according to Aristotle, are valid in the first figure, while twelve are invalid. Likewise, in the second figure four are valid and twelve are invalid, and in the third six are valid and twelve are invalid. The geometrician, too, by taking part of an incorrect diagram and demonstrating its impossibility, shows that it is to be avoided, while proving with incontrovertible arguments that his own proof must be accepted. In the same way the writing of history has certain things that it avoids and eliminates, and others that it chooses and employs for its subject matter. Specifically, it shuns falsehood and chooses truth. And so may your judgment not take offense, or, as I have said, interpret it in an unfavorable way to the ears of the emperor, if, for the sake of preserving the truth, certain statements in our history are critical of his predecessors or ancestors, since it is better to fall into the hands of men than to abandon the duty of a writer by painting over an unpleasant exterior with deceptive hues. . . .

Prologue

As I meditate often and deeply on the instability and uncertainty of temporal affairs, and their random and unpredictable course, I find, after rational reflection, that as it ill befits a wise man to cling to such things, he should pass over and turn away from them. For it is the duty of a wise man not to turn like a spinning wheel, but to stand fast in the stability of the virtues like a squared block. Because the mutability of time can never stand still, therefore, who of sound mind will deny that a wise man, as I have said, ought to turn away from what is temporal toward the eternal city that stands firm and endures? This is the City of God, the heavenly Jerusalem, to which the sons of God who have been set upon this pilgrimage aspire, though they are weighted down by the confusion of temporal affairs like the Babylonian captivity. For because there are two cities—one temporal and the other eternal, one worldly and the other heavenly, one belonging to the Devil and the other to Christ—catholic authors have declared the former to be Babylon and the latter Jerusalem.

Because a great many pagan authors wrote at length about one of these cities in order to commend the deeds of their ancestors to posterity, they have left us (as they believed) with numerous examples of their virtues, although in our opinion they constitute rather a procession of miseries. In this regard there are extant the celebrated histories of Pompeius Trogus, Justin, Cornelius, Varro, Eusebius, Jerome, Orosius, Jordanes, and countless others, both Christian and pagan, whom it would be tedious to enumerate. The thoughtful reader will discover in these works not so much the history of mankind as the wretched tragedy of the calamities that have befallen him. Of course, we believe that these things happened in accordance with the sound and provident dispensation of our Creator, so that man, who in his vanity clings longingly to earthly and transitory things, might be frightened by the uncertainty of his condition and prompted by the wretchedness of his fleeting life to turn from the world and recognize his creator. We, however, who have been appointed to live, as it were, at the end of time, do not so much read about the tribulations of mankind in these books as discover them in our midst from the experiences of our own day. For to say nothing of other examples, the Roman Empire, which in the book of Daniel is compared to iron because it has conquered the entire earth and exercises uncontested authority over it (what the Greeks call "monarchy"), has, after so many vicissitudes, particularly in our own day, declined from the height of nobility to become almost contemptible, so that according to the poet, scarcely "the shadow of a great name remains" [Lucan, *Civil War* 1.135]. Transferred from Rome to the Greeks, from the Greeks to the Franks, from the Franks to the Lombards, and from the Lombards back to the Teutonic Franks, not only has the empire grown decrepit with old age, but through its own mutable nature it has acquired numerous stains and various defects, like a smooth pebble tossed this way and that by the waves. Thus the sorrows of the world are revealed at its very head, and its fall threatens to destroy the whole body.

Yet it is hardly surprising that human power is transitory, when even the wisdom of mortals is fleeting. For we read that the Egyptians once possessed such wisdom that according to Plato they called the Greek philosophers childish and immature. Moses the lawgiver, moreover, with whom God spoke like one neighbor to another, and whom he filled with divine wisdom, did not blush to be instructed in all the wisdom of Egypt. And was it not the case that the great patriarch Abraham, whom God appointed to be father of the gentiles and who was instructed in the teachings of the Chaldaeans and endowed with knowledge, abandoned his ways at the call of the Lord but did not lose his wisdom? And yet according to the prophecy of Isaiah Babylon the great, the famous pride of the Chaldaeans, which was not only famed for its wisdom but also glorious among kingdoms, was made the temple of sirens, the house of serpents and ostriches, and the lair of snakes, without any hope of restoration. Egypt, too, is said for the most part to be uninhabitable and trackless. The careful investigator of history will discover that from Egypt wisdom was transferred to the Greeks, and from there to the Romans, and finally to the Gauls and the Spaniards. And it should be observed that all human power and wisdom have begun in the East and will come to an end in the West, so that in this way the mutability and imperfection of the world is revealed. God willing, we shall demonstrate this in greater detail in what follows.

Because examples such as these demonstrate the instability of the world, dearest brother Isingrim, I deemed it necessary to respond to your request to write a history in which, through God's generosity, I could display the wretchedness of the citizens of Babylon and the glory of the kingdom of Christ, which the citizens of Jerusalem hope to experience when this life is finished, but which they must now wait for and experience a foretaste of. It was my intention, insofar as God granted me the ability, to give an account of the conflicts and sorrows of this life down to our own day, and to the degree that I could, glean information about it from the scriptures, not to remain silent about the hope of the life to come, but to leave a record of its citizens as they make their pilgrimage in this life. In this work I am following the lead of Augustine and Orosius, those most distinguished lights of the church, and I have decided to draw from these sources whatever is relevant to my subject matter and my purpose. One of the two discoursed subtly and learnedly about the origin and progress of the glorious city of God and its destined limits, about how it has always made headway among the citizens of the world, and about which of its citizens and rulers were contemporary with the rulers and citizens of the worldly city. The other, arguing against those who babbled senselessly about how they preferred the time before the Christian era, composed a most useful history about the various catastrophes suffered by mankind in the past, about wars and the hazards of warfare, and about the rise and fall of kingdoms from the creation of the world down to his own time. Following in their footsteps, we intend to speak about both cities in such a way as not to lose sight of the course of history, so that the pious hearer will be able to recognize what to avoid in his worldly dealings on account of the countless miseries of their transitory nature, while the studious and diligent investigator will find an orderly account of past history.

I do not think that I can be fairly criticized for having presumed to write in my unskillful way after eminent men of such great wisdom and eloquence, since I abbreviated what they wrote about extensively and in detail, and recounted in an uncultivated style those things done after their time by the citizens of the world to the benefit or detriment of the Church of God. Nor do I think that I deserve to be cudgeled with the verse of the satiric poet in which he says that "learned and unlearned alike, we all write poems" [Horace, *Epistles* 2.1.117], since it was not out of rashness or frivolity that I dared to undertake so difficult a task, despite my lack of learning, but out of love, which can always compensate for inability. Nor will anyone have ground to accuse me of falsehood concerning those things that may seem incredible by the standards of our own day, since down to recent times I have included nothing save what I found in the writings of trustworthy authors, and only a small portion of that. For I do not think that they should be condemned if some of them maintained an apostolic simplicity in their writing, for just as cleverness is sometimes revealed to be the source of error, pious sincerity is always the friend of truth.

76. WALTER MAP DESCRIBES THE TRIFLES OF COURTIERS

Walter Map (c. 1130–1210) was a Welshman by birth, a secular cleric in the service of the bishop of Hereford and London, who eventually rose to become the archdeacon of Oxford. The sole work that can be confidently attributed to him is a volume of anecdotes that we know simply as De nugis curialium *(On the Trifles of Courtiers). John of Salisbury (c. 1120–80) had dedicated his work of political theory, the* Policraticus, *to the leading courtier of the day, Archbishop Thomas Becket (1118–70), and bestowed upon it the subtitle "on the trifles of courtiers and the footprints of philosophers." But while John had meant the term in the sense of stories or examples drawn from the past, Walter seems to be amassing trifles for the courtiers' spare time in the sense of idle tales to amuse them. Like other historians and writers of romance in the twelfth century, Map professes to be telling the truth, but in fact much of his history makes no claim to be more than legend. In telling stories of the contemporary world, Map therefore takes a certain license and indulges in a degree of falsification that is often mild, but sometimes grotesque, such as in his description of the obscene rites of the Cathar heretics. In doing this he was imitating the poets who lay midway between history and romance, men like Wace (see Doc. 71), who embellished without altering the basic frame of the story they told. Map also possessed a scholastic education that he likely acquired at Paris. He is fond of drawing on both scriptural and classical references, and like Master Gratian (Doc. 44) and Peter Lombard (Doc. 10) he divides his work into five "distinctions," the prologues and epilogues of which offer some of his most acute historical insights, particularly regarding his patronage and audience at court.*

Source: trans. Frederick Tupper and Marbury Bladen Ogle, *Master Walter Map's Book De Nugis Curialium (Courtiers' Trifles)* (London: Chatto and Windus, 1924), 1–3, 130–31, 177–78, 180–82; slightly revised. Latin.

First Distinction

"I am in time, and I speak of time," said Augustine, and straightaway added, "I know not what time is." With like wonderment can I say that I am in the court, and speak of the court, and know not—God alone knows—what the court is. This I know withal that the court is not time; it partakes, indeed, of time's temper, a thing of flux and change, of a place, and yet of subtle shifts, "never persisting in the same substance." At my withdrawal from it, I know it through and through; on my return to it, I find little or nothing that I have left there; having become a stranger I view it as a thing altogether strange. The court is the same, but the members are changed. If I shall describe the court as Porphyry defines "genus," perchance I shall not lie in saying that it is a multitude which stands in some relation or other to one chief principle. Certainly we are an unnumbered multitude, striving to please only one man, and today we are one multitude, tomorrow we shall be another. The court indeed is not changed, it is always the same. It is a hundred-handed giant, utterly maimed yet quite unaltered, and it is a hundred-handed hydra of many heads which renders futile and despises the labors of Hercules, and feels not the taming hand of that most masterful champion, and, more fortunate than Antaeus, has for its mother earth, sea, and air; it will not be crushed to the breast of Hercules; to it the whole universe furnishes increased strength. Whenever Hercules the omnipotent wills, his will be done. If what Boethius asserts truthfully of fortune, we shall say of the court, our saying, indeed, will be right in this too, "that it alone is constant in its change." The court pleases only those who attain its favor, for it gives favor arbitrarily; it does not, indeed, love the loveable or those deserving to be loved, but presents those unworthy of life with its favor. For this is the favor which comes without reason, which abides without desert, and which aides the ignoble, for reasons that do not appear. As "the mystical fan" of God, by true judgment, by just winnowing, separates for its own purpose the wheat from the chaff, so this fan of the court, with no less care, separates for its purpose the chaff from the wheat: what the first wisely chooses, the second unwisely casts out, and conversely, as very often happens. So many are the goads with which Avarice, sovereign mistress of court, drives us on that laughter is cast out to make way for annoying care. He who laughs is laughed at; he who sits glum is deemed wise. Wherefore it comes to pass that even our judges punish joys and reward sorrow, although the good, from their good conscience, have just reasons for joy, and from their evil conscience the bad are deservedly glum. Hence the hypocrites are sad, and the worshippers of God are ever joyous. The judge who without distinction calls good evil and evil good is, according to his very nature, thoroughly kind to the evil and evil to the kind. The prime reason, however, for the continual joy of the good is the indwelling of the Holy Spirit, and the main reason for the sadness of the evil is their inflation by the filthy spirit, who, in his wanderings over the breast of the evil thinker, plucks the garlic harmful to him, and this, though delightful in the eating, makes when eaten a foul stench. That garlic is offered to us in court chiefly by him who has envied us from the beginning of things—the devil. He who is delighted by the trap of the devil is displeased by the training of God.

Third Distinction: Prologue

When our counselors leave the business of counseling, wearied by the greatness of a king's tasks, they take pleasure in unbending to join conversation with the lowly, and in lightening with jests the weight of serious affairs. In this way may it please you, after you have rested from the counsel of a book of philosophy, or, it may be, of the divine book, to hear or read for the sake of pastime or pleasure the savorless and sapless trifles of this book. For it is not of contests of the courts or of the magnitude of a philosopher's maxims that I am going to treat; the stage and the arena I now occupy, a naked boxer and unarmed, whom in such wise you have, actually of your own motion, sent to face the well-armed tiers of hissing spectators. And yet if this stage or this arena should be visited by Cato or by Scipio or by both, I hope for their pardon, provided they do not judge me too critically. You bid me to record *exempla* for posterity, which will either provoke a laugh or point a moral. Although it is impossible for me to carry out your bidding, because "the poor poet knows not the cave of the muses," it is not difficult to collect or to write that which a good man's goodness will make useful for him, since "all things work together for good to the good" [cf. Romans 8:28], or to entrust to a rich soil seeds which shall bring forth good fruit. But who can cultivate a worthless and ill-conditioned mind, since, according to Scripture, "Vinegar upon nitre is he that sings songs to an evil heart" [Proverbs 25:20]? Here are songs sung by Sadius; it is your pleasure to hear them.

Fourth Distinction: Prologue

The gain of us all in knowledge is enhanced if no man among us lives with closed eyes or ears, or indeed with any of the senses inactive; and it is, moreover, meet and right for us to build up ourselves within by means of things without. Amid these things, to be sure, because we are blind to the future, we see face to face certain happenings of the past which we have not seen. Nor let us despise the things that have not come to our ears, but, leaving the future in the hands of God, let us lose no time in informing ourselves from those things which the Lord has set for us to imitate or to avoid. Let us ever ask of him, who is our present help, to promote in us the pursuit of the free choice of good and to offer a refuge to us when fugitives from evil.

I see younger men either despising or disparaging whatever they see and hear, and many men biding sluggishly at home in an old age which is either base or else does not rise above the level of the crowd. I once knew a lad, whom I am proud to count among my kinsmen and who was educated among us and by us, always "hanging on the lips of the speaker," clinging to his elders, seeking the society of good men, assaying brave deeds, never idle but indefatigably busy, ever so keen in his quest of all honorable things that though, to my regret, he was not a scholar, he could at least transcribe any written page whatever. Before he was twenty, he left our mother and his, England, and attached himself, a solitary foreigner, to Philip, Count of Flanders, in order to gain from him instruction in arms, and chose him as his lord; nor was the choice unwise, for all of the princes of this age, with the sole exception of our own, this nobleman is the most valiant in war and the strongest in government since the passing of the young king, Henry, the son of Henry, who has—God be thanked—no peer among living men. . . .

Epilogue

At the court of King Henry [II] I penned the pages of this little book by snatches and divorced it with all force from my heart, in the endeavor to obey the bidding of my lord. I shrank from my task, I strove to conquer the unconquerable. For, although the muses are exiles from all courts, they have foresworn ours above all the rest, because it has persistently turned its back on them and has turned its face far more on others, in that its fret and fury did not furnish sufficient respites of repose for sleep, far less for study. I tried to compel them, and they were disdainful. When, however, the news of the death of my lord, the aforesaid king, was brought, I myself died daily with the tears attendant upon two years of mourning. But now I rise up for the business of life with a newborn sense of my inestimable gain in being free from the court. Now that I am delivered from its bonds, I perceive, in my freshly found quiet, my full wretchedness when in bondage there. "In quiet," I say correctly, if it be quiet to recognize, by certain proofs, one's escape from the prince of darkness and to rule, in every wise, the kingdom of one's own soul, with the consent of the Lord, who has driven the devil forth to bondage. . . . And now, for the first time, I can be content with the business of life, because the muses are changed with the world's changes, and it no longer behooves one to speak from the caves, nor to be bound in the rules of arts. We do whatever we please, drawing no distinction between virtue and vice. If Cato shall return, Numa be restored, the Fabii revive, the Curii be recalled, the Rusones be resurrected, things will go on just the same, for where there is no vestige of culture, Cato will not use his wisdom, Numa his justice, Fabius his innocence, Curius his courtesy, Ruso his piety. Whenever none of those virtues, from which is derived worth, is held in high esteem, such men forsooth are dull. . . .

May my book now find such readers! They will deem me a poet; but indeed "the impious read not so, surely not so" [cf. Psalm 1:4], and hence will cast this poor little book as dust to the winds, for they hate it before they have heard it, they discount it before they count its worth, they grudge it before they greet it. Assault itself, if one may say so, assails it.

77. AN ANONYMOUS CHRONICLE OF THE DUKES AND PRINCES OF THE POLES

Gallus Anonymus ("the anonymous from Gaul") is the name conventionally assigned to a monastic chronicler who wrote a history of the dukes of Poland between 1112 and 1118. As his name suggests, he was probably of French origin, and one theory is that he was a monk of St-Gilles in Provence who spent time at his abbey's daughter-house at Somogyvár in Hungary before traveling to Poland in the early twelfth century. In Poland he came into contact with the members of the chapel of Duke Bolesław III Wrymouth (1102–38). The author began work on his chronicle probably around 1112, at a time of rising opposition to the duke's rule. The chief purpose of the Chronicle *was therefore to glorify Bolesław and legitimize the rule of the Piast dynasty to which he belonged. Each of the three books of the* Chronicle *begins with an introductory epistle. In the first of these the author addresses five Polish bishops—Martin of Gniezno, Simeon of Plock, Paul of Poznań, Maur of Kraków, and Żyrosław of Wrocław—as well as the chancellor Michael, who may have commissioned the work.*

Source: trans. Justin Lake, from *Galli Anonymi Cronica et Gesta ducum sive principum Polonorum*, ed. Karol Maleczynski, Monumenta Poloniae Historica: Nova series, vol. 2 (Kraków: Nakl. Polskiej Akademii Umiejętności, 1952), 1–4, 6–9; in Justin Lake, ed., *Prologues to Ancient and Medieval History: A Reader* (Toronto: University of Toronto Press, 2013), 184–86. Latin.

[Introductory Epistle to Book 1]

To Lord Martin, archbishop by the grace of God, to Simeon, Paul, Maur, and Zyrosław, men worthy of God and venerable bishops of the territory of Poland, and to his collaborator, the venerable chancellor Michael, artisan of the work that has been undertaken, the writer of the following modest work wishes that you might see the flock that has been entrusted to your vigilant care standing upon Mount Zion, which is holy to God, and that, progressing from virtue to virtue you might behold the God of gods face to face.

If I were not supported by your authority, aforementioned fathers, and if I could not rely upon your help, in vain would I venture upon so difficult a task and launch my rickety boat upon the boundless depths of the perilous sea. Yet a sailor can sit in his ship and travel securely through the waves of the raging sea, if he has an experienced helmsman who knows how to use the winds and stars to steer his craft unerringly. Had it not pleased your charity to assist my little craft with the guidance of your oars, I would not have been able to avoid a disastrous shipwreck. Nor would I have been able to find my way out of such a dense forest, being unfamiliar with the path, had it not pleased your benevolence to reveal to me the boundary-markers within to guide me. Because I have been honored by the assistance of such worthy helmsmen, therefore, I will escape the howling winds and put into port safely. Nor will I hesitate to feel my way along an unknown path with bleary vision, since I know that the eyes of the guides who have gone before me gleam more brightly than light. Because I have sent advocates such as these out in advance to plead on my behalf, I will pay no heed to the muttering and grumbling of spiteful critics. Because fortune has gratified my wish and won you as my supporters in this worthy endeavor, I thought it fitting that men of your eminence should be inserted, as it were, into the events of this chronicle. For in your day, and through your valuable prayers, God glorified Poland through the memorable and celebrated deeds of Bolesław the Third. And although I shall pass over many outstanding deeds performed during your lifetimes, I shall not fail in what follows to commend some of these things to the memory of posterity. But for now let us speak of you and extol you together as one, and let us join together in our praise those who are linked by the indissoluble bond of charity. For it is fitting that as priests your deeds should also be recorded, since divine grace, by endowing you with spiritual gifts, makes you to rule over the rulers themselves. And just as through your stewardship heavenly nourishment is given in response to the faithful prayers of your subjects, let your patronage watch over and protect this meager product of our feeble abilities. For it is fitting that those whom God has ordained to be pre-eminent over others by virtue of the privilege of their office should be especially vigilant in looking out for the welfare and needs of individual men. Therefore, lest we seem to be humble men trying to make the fringes of our vanity long [Matthew 23:5], we have decided to designate this little book not with our own name, but with yours. Let us therefore impute whatever praise and honor is accorded to this work to the rulers of this land, and let us confidently entrust our labor and the reward for our labor to the discernment of your judgment. May the grace of the Holy Spirit, which ordained you as shepherds of the Lord's flock, imbue your minds with wise counsel so that the duke will grant worthy gifts to the one who deserves them, so that honor will redound to you and glory to the one who makes you this offering. Rejoice always, and grant your favor to this work and its author.

[Proem to Book 1]

Throughout the whole expanse of the world many things worthy of memory that have been accomplished by numerous kings and dukes are covered up in silence because of the contemptuous neglect of philosophers, or perhaps because there is a dearth of them. For this reason, we thought it worthwhile for the sake of a certain most glorious and triumphant duke named Bolesław to set down in writing certain deeds of the Polish princes, preferring to do so in an immature style rather than forgo preserving anything noteworthy for the memory of posterity, especially since he was born through the dispensation of God and the prayers of Saint Giles, through whom we believe that he enjoyed good fortune and was always victorious. Because the territory of the Poles is remote from the paths taken by travelers and is known to few apart from traders passing through on their way to Russia, a brief examination of the topic ought not to seem out of place to anyone, and no one should consider it irksome if we give an account of the whole region instead of a partial description.

On the north, then, Poland comprises the northern part of Slavonia, and it borders Russia on the east, Hungary on the south, Moravia and Bohemia on the southeast, and Dacia and Saxony in the west. On the northern, or Amphitry-onic, sea it counts as neighbors three savage tribes of pagan barbarians, namely Selencia, Pomerania and Prussia. The duke of the Poles is constantly waging war against these territories in order to convert them to the faith, but it has proven impossible either to turn their hearts from faithlessness with the sword of preaching or to exterminate this brood of vipers with the sword of destruc-tion. On many occasions their leaders have sought refuge in baptism after being defeated in battle by the duke of the Poles, but after recovering their strength they have renounced the Christian faith and renewed their wars against the Christians. Beyond these people and within the arms of the Amphitryonic Sea there are still more barbarous tribes of pagans and uninhabitable islands where there is perpetual snow and ice.

In the north, then, the land of Slavonia consists of these regions, into which it is divided and which comprise its parts. It extends from the Sarmatians, who are also called Getae, to Dacia and Saxony, and from Thrace through Hungary, which was formerly occupied by the Huns (who are also called the Hungarians), and passing through Carinthia it ends in Bavaria. On the south, starting with Epirus near the Mediterranean Sea and going up through Dalmatia, Croatia, and Istria, it comes to an end on the Adriatic Sea, which separates it from Italy, where Venice and Aquileia are located. Although this area is heavily forested, it abounds in gold and silver, bread and meat, fish, and honey, and it is greatly preferable to other regions in that, while it is surrounded by the many aforementioned peoples, both Christian and pagan, and it has been attacked by all of them together and separately on numerous occasions, it has never been completely subjugated by any of them. It is a land where the air is healthful, the fields are fertile, the woods are dripping with honey, the water is full of fish, the soldiers are warlike, the peasants are hardworking, the horses are hardy, the oxen are suited to the plow, and the cows abound with milk and the sheep with wool. But lest we appear to be making too lengthy of a digression, let us return to our chosen topic. For it is our aim to give an account of Poland and especially of Duke Bolesław, and to recount for his sake certain deeds of his predecessors that are worthy of memory. Now, therefore, let us commence to address our theme in such a way that we may climb from the roots of the tree to its branches. The section of narrative that follows will reveal how the office of duke passed into the hands of the family that holds it now.

78. WALTER OF CHÂTILLON, *THE ALEXANDREIS*

Walter of Châtillon was considered by at least one thirteenth-century author to be comparable to the ancient poets Homer and Lucan (39–65 CE). Born in Lille around 1135, he studied at Paris and Rheims before directing the school of Laon and then heading a school in one of the towns of Châtillon. Sometime later, perhaps after studying law at Bologna, he entered the service of William of the White Hands (1135–1202), the great-grandson of William the Conqueror (r. 1066–87) and archbishop of Sens and then Rheims. It is to him that Walter dedicated his epic poem, The Alexandreis, *thus providing a sort of historical-poetic adaptation of the mirror of princes genre. Written during a five-year period, probably sometime between 1171 and 1181, the poem chronicles the life of Alexander the Great from his quest to defeat his rival Darius to his death, a task that, as Walter himself states in his prologue, had never been attempted by the classical poets. An immensely popular work in its own time, the poem in ten books survives in more than 200 manuscripts, many of which include copious glosses to the text, suggesting that the work was a part of the literary curriculum of the schools. Although Walter also penned satirical poems (some of which poke fun at schoolroom studies) and a prose refutation of the Jews in dialogue form,* The Alexandreis *was by far his most influential work. It became, as Walter hoped it would, an integral part of the literary canon, known to scholars and kings across Christendom.*

Source: trans. David Townsend, *The Alexandreis: A Twelfth-Century Epic* (Peterborough, ON: Broadview Press, 2007), 32–33, 71, 74–75, 119–20, 208–11. Latin.

Book 1

How generously the duke of Macedon
dispensed his wealth, with what a splendid host
he conquered Darius's and Porus's lands,
tell us, Muse; how Greece laughed in her triumph,
and once again to Corinth tribute came   5
home from the Persians—these are deeds well known
through all the earth. Had sufferance of the Fates
allowed this man to live till our own day,
unbroken by the ravages of age,
Fame never would have sung the victory-song   10
for Caesar, and all glory of Rome's race
would lie abject, the great blaze of his worth
engulfing that scant flame. The Wain's slow stars
would grow more languid still, and Lucifer
would turn pale at the rising of his sun.   15
        But you [William], whose royal forebears Britain vaunts,
be with me now, you who as bishop brought
to Sens no less praise than when Brennius
broke Rome with arms of Sens, and would have made
Tarpeius' citadel his own, had not   20
the silver goose roused those who should have watched.
When you at last gained the see of Rheims,
the warlike land lost any earlier name
for harshness. From the moment of your birth,
Philosophy took you as foster child: 25
she gave you milk of Helicon to drink,
laid bare the holy teaching of her breast,
and granted, scattering the veiling clouds,
that you who were long purged by study's fire
should penetrate the hidden causes of things.   30
Stay with me as I steer for open sea;

pour out the holy waters, and upon
your head set laurel—grant I may ascribe
to you the inspiration of my song. . . .

Book 3

Now din of arms and war's fierce slaughter conquered
the blare of trumpets. Arrows veiled the stars,
and thickened clouds of javelins obscured
the upper air. Foremost against the Persians,
more swiftly than a catapulted stone,   5
the Macedonian thrust his spear point forward.
He turned his mount where gold flashed from the shields
of kings set side by side, where plenteous gems
shone proudly upon helmets: there the shape
of Darius' flaming dragon burned with terror   10
and sucked the winds into its golden jaws. . . .
         . . . The sodden turf lay hidden by the corpses
that now concealed the earth; fields were awash
in swamps of gore; valleys were filled with blood.
Each side sustained great carnage, but the slaughter   15
of Medes made drunker still the fields. Though countless,
the barbarous foe was thinned and failed in spirit,
nor did the smaller Macedonian band
cease striking—fervent zeal made up their numbers.
Like lightning Alexander pressed upon them   20
amidst their flight, and through the trackless spaces,
through swords and throngs of knights, he picked his way
toward Darius. But Oxatreus, closest
in birth to Darius, pulled in the column.
Here grief and moans arose. Youths of keen spirit   25
perished on either side, and death enfolded
the leaders of both parties in a whirlwind.
Bellona scattered from her gory hands
death's every guise upon the Persians: here
one groans through his slashed throat, another lies   30
pierced through the bowels with iron. Here a stake
has brained one man, the sling or bow slays others.
One vomits bloody slime—his neck is broken;
Another's guts fall out, swords claim a third.
Some tremble, dying; some lie still and dead.   35

Book 5

    . . . Adversity left faint the wise man's spirit;
scant counsel could he offer to himself,
while hope languished defenseless, and remorse
for earlier undertakings now consumed him.
Which way should Darius turn? Amidst his madness   5
how should he rule himself, when flight's not safe,
nor may he find his companions, if he tarries?
Of many thousands whom he'd earlier trusted,
scarcely a thousand had survived the battle
to shield their country. Shame and reputation   10
forbade his flight, yet trepidation urged it.
But while his wavering breast still trembled, dumbstruck,
while yet he half resolved to take his flight,
or else, in hatred of his life, to welcome
his captor's chains, the Persians turned their backs   15
almost as one, as though still in formation,
and rushed across the fields, leaving their king.
Unwillingly, at last he loosed the reins
upon the horse he's seized, and so retreated
through lands bedewed with slaughter of his men.   20
Doomed king, where will your aimless flight direct you?
You know not, lost man, whom you flee, you know not,
But run to meet your foe while foe you flee.
You fall to Scylla while you shun Charybdis.
Bessus, Narbanzanes, your wealth's great sharers,   25
feel no dread breaking fealty, though you raised
them both to princely rank from lowly station;
but spurning all the governance of law,
in their lord's death—great shame!—these slaves conspire.
They'll slay your reverend head for all its whiteness. . . .   30

Book 10

    . . . But now had come that fatal hour, in which
that master great of heart would be cast down.
The Fates would brook no further hesitation
but sped that crime of universal ruin.
Redolent with the perfumes of the East,   5
the hall shone brightly where the people and

the princes' sacred order had assembled.
A great part of the day had been consumed
in speeches, and the duke had doled out treasure,
enriching all, when brimming cups of wine   10
were borne at his command unto the ministers.
And thus, as lord and father among friends
he perished, who so often had laid waste
the foe's prowess and yet emerged unscathed.
      His body stiffened with a sudden torpor.   15
His knees grew slack; his limbs he scarce could master,
and so upon a bed they laid him. All
the palace shook at once with mortal tumult,
though still none dared to show the grief he felt,
in hope that Fortune's remedy might yet   20
be near at hand—for she had stood beside him
on all occasions when he chanced to fall.
But when the poison had imbued his veins,
and when his pulse gave signs of coming death,
he ordered that his bed be laid in hall.   25
There, once the frantic army had assembled,
the noble band of dukes, commingled with
the common rank and file, he gazed upon them
scoring their faces, eyes awash with tears.
"Where shall such men attain a worthy king,"   30
he said, "when I depart the earth? Enough
it is for me, that I have ruled the world.
All favorable chance beneath the stars
has come to me compliantly in warfare.
No longer am I pleased to be confined   35
by mortal frame. I've spent my allotted season
consumed by human cares, and long enough
I've tarried thus till now among mere mortals.
Henceforth to greater matters am I summoned.
High heaven itself calls me to rule Olympus;   40
there, having gained my seat and royal throne
among the stars, with Jove I shall dispose
the secrets of all things and give my judgments
of men's brief outcomes and the gods' affairs.
Perhaps presumption arms once more those brothers   45
buried at Etna, and Pelorus's ridge
has loosed Typhoeus's savage limbs against

the gods' host and their lofty citadels.
They think the gods and stars can easily
be taken from a senile Jove; again   50
they mount their challenge, and since Mars himself
without me flees the danger of the fray,
I'm summoned, though resistant and unwilling,
by counsel of great Jove and of the gods,
to a new realm." When he had spoken thus,   55
with lamentation and with flowing tears
they pressed forward, to ask whom he desired
to leave as heir and ruler of the world.
"The best," he said, "and worthiest of power
shall be your king." But afterward no voice   60
remained to him. Then, drawing from his finger
a golden ring, to Perdicas he gave it,
and so the dukes supposed the king desired
that Perdicas succeed him in the realm.
Immediately, the warmth of life departed   65
the corpse, now slack with cold; and, breaking forth
from its prison of clay, the spirit passed
into thin air. Then from their grief was loosed
the bitterest of mourning; lamentation
broke in all its strength, nor did the crowd   70
further suppress its fearful tumult. Such
a crashing does not press against the stars,
when, hurling thunder, the four brother winds
strike at the pole of heaven and its lights.
　　　O happy race of mortals, if at all times   75
we might consider the eternal Good,
might fear the end which, though unseen, approaches
for noblemen and commoner alike.
We search out wealth in peril of our souls;
around our mortal eyes deceitful glory   80
of action flies on wings of vanity.
In grasping at those honors now for sale,
we scour the sea's billows and, in hatred
of our own lives, unto the tumid surge
commit our persons and our goods. Perhaps   85
through Alpine winters and a horde of thieves
we strive to reach the walls of greedy Rome
and Romulus' citadels: if by some chance

we come again to our ancestral land
and native soil, the onset of a slight   90
and sudden fever scatters all we've gathered
in all our years. Thus will the Great One serve
as an example. Five feet of carved stone
sufficed for his abode in tunneled earth,
for whom the world held insufficient space.   95
The noble corpse there rested in scant soil,
until that remnant of dread Fate, honored
by all the world, was moved by Ptolemy—
to whom you read that Egypt fell as lot—
into that town which he named for the prince.   100
  But now the sun's about to plunge his gaze
in headlong night; he steers his breathless chariot
towards the sea. Now is it all played out,
now comes the time to end the game. O Muses,
hereafter other souls may be enticed   105
by your sweet strains. I seek another fount:
once drunk, it remedies a second thirst.
  But you, whose full-horned bounty has poured out
your wealth upon me, that I might despise
the tongues of enemies, receive, O great   110
prelate, the zealous labor of your Walter.
Do not disdain to join around your brow
the poet's ivy to the sacred mitre.
For though this song may be unworthy of
so great a bishop, yet when spirit passes   115
from mortal limbs, together we shall live.
Surviving with his poet, William's glory
Shall live undying through all time to come.

CHAPTER NINE

MEDICINE, SCIENCE, AND TRANSLATION

The three topics grouped together in this final chapter reflect the sustained engagement with ancient and Islamic learning in a new Christian, and therefore Latin, context. To the medical practitioners, scientists, and writers who were introduced to this learning beginning in the second half of the eleventh century, almost all of which required able (if frustratingly elusive) translators to render it accessible, the encounter with this vast and untapped body of knowledge marked a momentous discovery. It would dramatically affect their approach to the non-Christian world and usher in a new era in both medicine and natural science. It led scientists like the Englishman Adelard of Bath (c. 1080–c. 1152) to travel to distant lands in search of exotic knowledge and texts, and it led converts like the Spaniard Petrus Alfonsi to praise the medical and scientific achievements of the Arabs above those of his new Christian brethren. Medicine, mathematics, cosmology, and philosophy were all subjects that were reinvigorated by the encounter with these new texts. Salerno and Toledo emerged as two of the cities most active in the heady business of translating these foreign works (see Docs. 79, 82, and 83), but some modern scholars have seen a school of Platonists among the teachers at Chartres, a trend perhaps best exemplified in the literary masterpiece by Bernard Silvestris (Doc. 84). Muslims, Christians, and Jews all participated in this translation movement, in processes of intellectual exchange that are now just beginning to be understood. The study of Greek and Arabic slowly but surely became serious topics of study, and by the end of the twelfth century medicine had achieved a prominent place in the emerging university curriculum alongside theology and law.

79. MEDICINE AT SALERNO: AN OVERVIEW

One outcome of western European society's deepening intellectual sophistication in the twelfth century was a concerted effort to locate and appropriate ancient "scientific" knowledge. The search for medical knowledge was especially attractive to men (and women) of learning and this involved translating texts into Latin, either directly from Greek or via Arabic translations. The Arabic translations of medicine, much like the Arabic translations of science and philosophy, were often accompanied by commentaries, encyclopedias, and specialized treatises that enlarged Europe's library of medical learning. The end result of this translation project was a significant shift in how medicine was defined and conceptualized. An important locus for this new activity in medicine and translation was the southern Italian port city of Salerno, which in the late eleventh century came under Norman rule but was conveniently situated at the meeting point among Christians, Muslims, and Jews.

The first of the texts excerpted below describes an elusive figure from North Africa known as Constantine the African, whose translations and adaptations of Arabic medical writings helped to lay the foundations for the expansion of European medical learning. He arrived in Salerno before 1077 and died as a monk in Monte Casino sometime between 1085 and 1098. Under the patronage of Archbishop Alfanus of Salerno and Abbot Desiderius of Monte Casino, Constantine translated a range of texts from Arabic, some of which are referred to in the notice by Master Matthaeus, who later in the twelfth century wrote a gloss on Constantine's translation of Isaac Judaeus's Universal Diets. The second text is from Constantine's translation of the Isagoge (Introduction) by a ninth-century Nestorian Christian named Hunayn ibn Ishaq. The catalogue-like structure of the Isagoge was of great pedagogical value because it helped facilitate memorization. Though Constantine confuses or even misunderstands some of the technical and philosophical terms used by Hunayn, the work paved the way for a renewed interest in medicine and natural philosophy. The third text is possibly, though by no means certainly, from Master Bartholomew, who corresponded with Peter the Venerable regarding Peter's illness. The Demonstration provides a generous introduction that distills the important elements of Galenic physiology, as summarized in the Isagoge and in the medieval adaption of Galen's On the Usefulness of Parts, translated by Bartholomew's collaborator Burgundio of Pisa (see also Doc. 82b–c). The author narrates what he is doing as he moves along, even interjecting questions from students, all of which suggests a new interest in teaching physiology through demonstration.

a. Master Matthaeus's Description of Constantine the African

Source: trans. Faith Wallis, from R. Creutz, ed., "Die Ehrenrettung Konstantins vons Afrika," *Studien und Mitteilungen des Benediktiner Ordens* 49 (1931): 40–41; in Faith Wallis, ed., *Medieval Medicine: A Reader*, Readings in Medieval Civilizations and Cultures, vol. XV (Toronto: University of Toronto Press, 2010), 138–39. Latin.

This work is not by Constantine, but by Isaac, as we said; however, Constantine translated it. But because Constantine never said how he came here and translated the books, we have obtained this information from Johannes [Afflacius]. Constantine was a Saracen. He was a merchant, and he came here in the course of business, and brought much merchandise with him which he peddled on the street. He went to the court of St Peter [in Rome], in which there was a very distinguished *medicus*, the brother of a prince, and who was called "the abbot" by the curia. Constantine, watching him judge urines and not knowing our language, paid some Saracen servants to translate the judgments for him. Learning through the interpreters that [the *medicus*] was quite competent in medicine, [Constantine] asked him, through the interpreters, whether there were many books in Latin concerning *physica*. [The *medicus*] answered that he had none, but that he had learned through much diligence and drill. So Constantine, returning to Africa, devoted himself to the study of *physica* for three continuous years; then he came back, bringing with him many books. When he approached Palermo, he met with a storm which swamped the ship and caused him to lose part of the *Practice of the Pantegni*. But when he came here, he learned the Roman and Latin tongue, and became a Christian and a monk at the monastery of Saint Benedict at Monte Cassino. And he translated those books into our language. But of the practical part of the *Pantegni* he only translated three books, because it was damaged by the water. A certain Stephen of Pisa went to [Arab lands] and learned the language and translated them, so that the *Practice of the Pantegni* is now ascribed to Stephen. But in [Monte Cassino] Constantine composed the *Book of Simple Medicines* dedicated to Archbishop Alfanus, who had done him great service. Archbishop Alfanus wished to cover his expenses for the completion of the *Pantegni*.

b. From Joannitius, *Isagoge*

Source: trans. Faith Wallis, from the edition by Gregor Maurach, "Johannicius. Isagoge ad Techne Galieni," *Sudhoffs Archiv* 62.2 (1978): 148–74; in *Medieval Medicine: A Reader*, 142–50.

[The Naturals]

The powers. The powers are divided into three. There is the natural power, the spiritual power, and the animal power. One natural power ministers, and another is ministered to. Sometimes it generates, at another time it nourishes, and at another time it feeds. But the power that ministers sometimes seeks out, retains, digests, and expels the things that minister to the feeding power, just as the feeding power ministers to the nourishing power. The other two serve the generating power, one by altering food, the other by re-fashioning it. These differ from one another in that the first power alters, and it serves the generating power through the activity of refashioning. But the operation of the re-fashioning power are five: assimilation, hollowing out, perforating, roughening, and smoothing.

Spiritual power. From the spiritual power, two others proceed: one is operative and the other is operated upon. The operative power is that which dilates the heart and arteries and then contracts them. From the one which is operated upon come anger, indignation, triumph, domination, astuteness, and anxiety.

Animal power [the power of *animus* or mind]. Animal power encompasses three things. One animal power arranges, discriminates, and assembles; a second one moves with voluntary motions; the third is called "sensing." From the ordering, discriminating, and assembling power come these things: imagination in the front part of the head, cognition or reasoning in the brain, and memory in the occipital region. The [second animal] power moves with voluntary motion. And the sensing power consists in sight, hearing, taste, smell, and touch.

Faculties. Faculties are of two kinds. There are faculties of which each accomplishes on its own what pertains to it, such as appetite for food [which works] by means of heat and dryness; digestion [which works] by means of heat and dryness; digestion [which works] by means of heat and moisture; retention [which works] by means of cold and dryness; expulsion [which works] by cold and moisture. There are also composite faculties which are composed of two [faculties]; such are desire and expulsion. For desire is compounded of two powers; one longs for something and the other senses, for the stomach senses its emptiness. Expulsion is composed of two or more powers, one which expels and the other which senses.

Spirit. The spirits are three. First, the natural spirit takes its origin from the liver; second, the vital spirit, [originating] from the heart; third, the animal spirit, from the brain. Of these three the first is diffused throughout the whole body in the veins which have no pulse; the second is transmitted by the arteries; and the third by the nerves. These are considered in the seventh division of the seven natural things, that is, the spirit.

The ages [of life]. There are four ages; namely, youth, prime of life, maturity, and old age. Adolescence is of a hot and moist complexion; in adolescence the body increases and grows up to the twenty-fifth or thirtieth year. The prime of life follows, which is hot and dry, preserving the body in a perfect state, with no diminution of its powers, and it ends at age thirty-five or forty. After this comes maturity, which is cold and dry, in which the body begins to decline and decrease, although its power is not abated, and it lasts to the fiftieth or sixtieth year. After this comes old age, abounding in phlegmatic humor, cold and wet, in which it is apparent that there is a decline of power, and it ends with the end of life.

Skin color. The colors of the skin are two kinds: those due to internal causes and those due to external. The internal causes again are two in number; namely excess or equality of humors. From equality comes that tint which is composed of white and red; from inequality proceed black, yellow, red, greyish (*glaucus*), and white. Red, black, and yellow signify that heat dominates in the body: yellow alone signifies reddish bile; black alone, black bile; red alone, an abundance of blood. White and greyish signify abundant cold; but greyish shows that the cause is black bile, white shows it is phlegm. Colors also arise from external circumstances: for example, from cold among the Irish; from heat among the Ethiopians; and from many other incidental factors. There are also spiritual colors, originating in fear, or anger, or other disturbances of the mind. . . .

The quality of the body. The qualities of the body are three in number: namely, health, sickness, and the neutral state. Health is a balanced condition [*temperamentum*] that composes the natural things according to the course of nature. Sickness is an imbalanced condition outside the course of nature from which harm results. The neutral state is that which is neither healthy nor diseased. But there are three kinds of neutral state: when health and disease co-exist in different parts of the same body; [a state] such as obtains in the body of an elderly person, where not a single member remains that is not causing trouble or suffering; and [a state] such as obtains in the body of a man who is sometimes healthy and sometimes sick— for instance those who are sick in the winter and healthy in the summer; those who are of a moist nature are sick in childhood, but well in youth and old age, while those of a dry nature are healthy in childhood, but sick in youth and old age. Health, sickness, and the neutral state are found in three things: in the body in which any one of the three qualities occurs; or in the cause which produces and establishes these [qualities]; or in the signs which signify them.

Types of causes. There are two kinds of causes: either what is natural or what is outside the course of nature. Natural causes either produce health or preserve it. The causes that preserve, pertain to health; and the causes which produce, pertain to illness. Some of the causes that transgress nature pertain to illness, and others to the neutral state. But sickly causes produce sickness and also the things that maintain sickness. Those that pertain neither to health nor to sickness, preserve or constitute the neutral state. There are six types of causes that are associated with health and sickness. The first is the air which surrounds the human body, [then] food and drink, exercise and rest, sleep and waking, fasting and fullness, and incidental conditions of the mind. All these preserve health from accidents, if used with appropriate moderation as to quantity, quality, time, function, and order. But if anything is done contrary to this, diseases occur and persist.

c. Bartholomew of Salerno, Second Salernitan Demonstration

Source: trans. George W. Corner, *Anatomical Texts of the Earlier Middle Ages* (Washington, DC: Carnegie Institute, 1929), 54–66. Latin.

[The Testicles]

The testicles, which are the instruments of the sperm, are formed of glandular, white, soft, and spongy flesh, in order that sperm may be generated in them. Each is covered by a membrane, which is derived from the *siphac*. The substance of the sperm before it comes to the testicle is received in a certain follicle, in which it is altered and whitened, and this membrane is below the kidneys and above the testicles; in some animals there is found in the said membrane a great quantity of that moisture which is the material of the sperm; in other animals little is found, and in others none; and as we have shown you, there are two passages, one on each side of the membrane, through which this material descends to the testicles. Proceeding from the inferior part of the testicles are two vessels called [seminal], through which the sperm passes from the testicles to the penis, and these vessels are long, white, and hard like muscular flesh; they are long, so that the testicular excretion may better undergo concoction as it passes along, and broad, that the sperm may pass quickly from these vessels into the penis and from the penis into the female pudenda. In your presence I have incised one of these ducts and have shown you the sperm. . . .

[The Process of Conception]

Acting upon the mass composed of male and female sperm, the natural force and heat cause solidification in the liquid and more subtle parts as well as in the superabundant and more consumable grosser elements and alters them into a kind of membrane, just as a crust forms on dough when a hot iron is brought near it. Then when the rest of the mass is coagulated throughout by similar action of force and heat and becomes transmuted into the essence of the organs, its swelling bursts in the middle of the crust. Veins and arteries emerge and are united with the veins and arteries of the uterus to form the *secundines* [*placenta*], or membranes of the fetus; and through these veins the four humors, the natural spirit, and the vital spirit are borne for the nourishment and vivification of the fetus. The sources of the veins and arteries of the uterus, to which the veins and arteries are joined, are called cotyledons. By these veins and arteries, as if by ligaments, the fetus is suspended and is restrained in the uterus, but they are broken when the fetus departs at birth, and after the waters have been discharged the midwife ties them with a thread at a distance of three or four fingers' breadth from the umbilicus. It often happens that due to pain from the ligature humors are drawn thither and cause suppuration of the umbilicus.

[The Ovaries]

After considering this, note the two testicles situated at the summit of the *collum matricis*, one right and the other left. You will find them by a long straight incision above the *collum matricis*. The testicles are smaller than in men, round, superficially somewhat flattened, glandular, and harder than in men. To each of them comes a single vein from the kidneys, and they lie under the trumpet-like extremities of the uterus. From each testicle there goes a stem-like cord, through which the testicle ejects sperm into the spermatic vessel. Observe, moreover, that the female organ, which as we have said is called *collum matricis*, is different in women according to varying times, ages, and natures; for in pregnant women it is greater than in the non-pregnant because of the enlargement caused by conception; it is never so large in those who have never been pregnant as in those who have borne children; and moreover it increases in size during the course of pregnancy. In girls and elderly women this organ is smaller than in adults, and in ardent women it is larger than in those who are not passionate.

80. THE *TROTULA*: THE SALERNITAN TRADITION OF GYNECOLOGY

The Trotula *is the title of a text assembled at the close of the twelfth century by the amalgamation of three Salernitan tracts on health care for women:* On the Conditions of Women, Treatments for Women, *and* Women's Cosmetics. *The second of these tracts is by Trota or Trocta, a female physician of Salerno about whom nothing more is known, but it is from her name that the ensemble of texts came to be known. The* Trotula *("Little Trota") achieved a level of authority in the emerging world of academic medicine because it offered a perspective on Galenic gynecology previously unknown in the medieval West. Galen himself (c. 130–c. 210 CE) wrote very little on gynecology, but his Arab commentators, who were more informed and more systematic than their medieval Western counterparts, successfully integrated non-Galenic accounts of women's disorders within a physiological framework understandable to readers of Galen. Salerno's location within a Norman kingdom that included a substantial Muslim population explains the numerous references to "Saracens" and "Saracen women" as sources of medical practices.*

As Monica Green has stressed, "the Trotula *texts attest not simply to how the diseases of women were formally theorized by medical writers eager to assimilate the new Arabic texts, but also of how local Salernitan practitioners, with or without formal training, conceptualized and treated the medical conditions of women." Whatever relationship these texts have to Trota or the other women of Salerno, the* Trotula *constituted a foundation for all of later medieval medicine: versions of the text have been found in the libraries of physicians and surgeons, monks and philosophers, theologians and princes from Italy to Ireland, from Spain to Poland.*

Source: trans. Monica Green, *The Trotula: A Medical Compendium of Women's Medicine* (Philadelphia: University of Pennsylvania Press, 2001), 71, 83, 85, 125, 127, 187. Latin.

On Female Physiology

When God, the creator of the universe in the first establishment of the world differentiated the individual natures of things each according to its kind, he endowed human nature above all things with a singular dignity, giving to it above the condition of all other animals the freedom of reason and intellect. And wishing to sustain its generation in perpetuity, he created the male and the female with provident, dispensing deliberation, laying out in the separate sexes the foundation for the propagation of future offspring. And so that from them there might emerge fertile offspring, he endowed their complexions with a certain pleasing commixtion, constituting the nature of the male hot and dry. But lest the male overflow with either of these qualities, he wished by the opposing frigidity and humidity of the woman to rein him in from too much excess, so that the stronger qualities, that is the heat and the dryness, should rule the man, who is the stronger and more worthy person, while the weaker ones, that is to say the coldness and humidity, should rule the weaker [person], that is the woman. And [God did this] so that by his stronger quality the male might pour out his duty in the woman just as seed is sown in its designated field, and so that the woman by her weaker quality, as if made subject to the function of man, might receive the seed poured in the lap of Nature.

On the Suffocation of the Womb

Sometimes the womb is suffocated, that is to say, when it is drawn upward, whence there occurs [stomach] upset and loss of appetite from an overwhelming frigidity of the heart. Sometimes they suffer syncope, and the pulse vanishes so that from the same cause it is barely perceptible. Sometimes the woman is contracted so that the head is joined to the knees, and she lacks vision, and she loses the function of the voice, the nose is distorted, the lips are contracted and she grits her teeth, and the chest is elevated upward beyond what is normal.

Galen tells of a certain woman who suffered thus and she lost her pulse and her voice and it was as if she had expired, because no exterior sign of life was apparent, though around her heart Nature still retained a little bit of heat. Whence certain people judged her to be dead. But Galen put some well-carded wool to her nose and mouth, and by its motion he knew that she was still alive.

This [disease] happens to women because corrupt semen abounds in them excessively, and it is converted into a poisonous nature.

This happens to those who do not [have sexual relations with] men, especially to widows who were accustomed to carnal commerce. It regularly comes upon virgins, too, when they reach the age of marriage and are not able to use men and when the semen abounds in them a lot, which Nature wishes to draw out by means of the male. From this superabundant and corrupt semen, a certain cold fumosity is released and it ascends to the organs which are called by the common people the "collaterals," because they are near to the heart and lungs and the rest of the principal instruments of the voice. Whence an impediment of the voice generally occurs. This kind of illness is accustomed to originate principally from a defect of the menses. And if both the menses are lacking and the semen is abundant, the illness will be so much the more menacing and wide-ranging, especially when it seizes the higher organs.

The best remedy is that the hands and feet of the woman be rubbed moderately with laurel oil and that there be applied to the nose of the patient those things which have a foul odor, such as galbanum [a bitter gum resin], opoponax [sweet myrrh], castoreum [scent oil from beavers], pitch, burnt wool, burnt linen cloth, and burnt leather. On the other hand, their vaginas ought to be anointed with those oils and hot ointments which have a sweet odor, such as iris oil, chamomile oil, musk oil, and nard oil. For these things attract and provoke the menses. Let cupping glasses be applied to the inguinal area and the pubic area. The women ought also to be anointed inside and out with oils and ointments of good smell. Likewise, in the evening let her take *diaciminum* with the juice of wild celery or with a syrup of calamint or catmint, or with the juice of henbane or juice of catmint. Or take one dram each of castoreum, white pepper, costmary, mint, and wild celery; let them be ground, and let them be mixed with white or sweet wine. And give one dram of it in the evening.

On the Dangerous Things Happening to Women Giving Birth

There are some women for whom things go wrong in giving birth, and this is because of the failure of those assisting them: that is to say, this is kept hidden by the women. For there are some women in whom the vagina and the anus become one opening and the same pathway. Whence in these women the womb comes out and hardens. We give aid to such women by repositioning [the womb]. We put on the womb warm wine in which butter had been boiled, and diligently we foment it until the womb has been rendered soft, and then we gently replace it. Afterwards we sew the rupture between the anus and the vagina in three or four places with a silk thread. Then we place a linen cloth unto the vagina to fill the vagina completely. Then let us smear it with liquid pitch. This makes the womb withdraw because of its stench. And we heal the rupture with a powder made of comfrey, that is, of bruisewort, and daisy and cumin. The powder ought to be sprinkled [on the wound], and the woman should be placed in bed so that her feet are higher [than the rest of her body], and there let her do all her business for eight or nine days. And as much as necessary let her eat; there let her relieve herself and do all customary things. It is necessary that she abstain from baths until she seems to be able to tolerate them. Also, it is fitting that she abstain from all things that cause coughing and from all things that are hard to digest, and this especially ought to be done. In [subsequent] birth we should aid them thus. Let a cloth be prepared in the shape of an oblong ball and place it in the anus, so that in each effort of pushing out the child, it is pressed into the anus firmly so that there not be [another] solution of continuity of this kind.

On the Exit of the Womb and Its Treatment

There are also some women to whom it happens that the womb comes out from another cause, such as those who are not able to tolerate the virile member because of its magnitude or length; having been forced all the same, they endure it. But when [the womb] comes out, it hardens. For such women we offer aid in the above-mentioned manner. And if we do not have pitch, we take a cloth and anoint it with warm pennyroyal oil or musk oil, and then we squeeze it and we smear it on or put it in the vagina, and we tie it on until the womb recedes by itself and becomes warm. For this condition, we suggest that whatever causes coughing not be eaten.

On Whitening Teeth

The teeth are whitened thus. Take burnt white marble and burnt date pits, and white natron, and red tile, salt, and pumice. From all of these make a powder in which damp wool has been wrapped in a fine linen cloth. Rub the teeth inside and out.

The same thing cleans the teeth and renders them very white. The woman should wash her mouth after dinner with very good wine. Then she ought to dry [her teeth] well and wipe [them] with a new white cloth. Finally, let her chew each day fennel or lovage or parsley, which is better to chew because it gives off a good smell and cleans good gums and makes teeth very white.

81. PETRUS ALFONSI URGES THE STUDY OF ARABIC SCIENCE

In his polemical Dialogue against the Jews *(Doc. 29), the Spanish convert Petrus Alfonsi makes extensive recourse to science and astronomy in justifying his choice to turn to Christianity. The sources of his scientific knowledge were scholars in Muslim Spain, and this at least partly explains why he devotes an entire chapter to explaining his decision to convert to Christianity rather than to Islam. In his later* Epistle to the Peripatetics of France *(c. 1116), he attempts to persuade French scholars of the importance of astronomy in general and of the superiority of the astronomical doctrines of the Arabs in particular. In it, he incorporates sections taken directly from the introduction to the astronomical tables of al-Kwarizmi, which he had translated. He also introduces a radically different ordering of the liberal arts, devaluing grammar and raising dialectic (the science of which leads to logical conclusions) to the pinnacle of the arts. He omits rhetoric altogether. In addition to the importance he gives to astronomy, he also gives far more attention to medicine than do his Latin contemporaries. Alfonsi had at this point spent considerable time in England and in France and was keenly aware of the Latin West's deficiencies in the realm of scientific learning. What little understanding Christians had, Alfonsi believed, was still dependent on the errors, myths, and fables found in ancient authorities such as Macrobius's fifth-century commentary on Cicero's* Dream of Scipio.

Source: trans. John Tolan, *Petrus Alfonsi and His Medieval Readers* (Gainesville, FL: University Press of Florida, 1993), 173–75. Latin.

. . . We have found that many of you study the science of grammar. This cannot be counted among the seven liberal arts, since it is neither knowledge subject to proof nor is it in every language the same, but in each one different. Still, it is valid, and it is necessary for studying the arts. Through grammar vernacular words are controlled as if by law and rule, and without it the intention of the mind cannot manifest itself plainly. If there were no grammar, we would sometimes understand plural or singular or vice versa, the future for the present, and would frequently have doubts in many other things.

Many are also studying dialectic, which is first in order of all the arts. Indeed, it is a sublime art and a valid one. As far as I know, you, through subtlety, have surpassed the peoples of all nations and all languages in this art at this time. The art of dialectic, I say, is sublime and valid; it is not useful in and of itself, but it is useful and necessary to the other arts. It is indeed like that instrument in which gold and silver are examined. For, just as through that instrument counterfeit and genuine gold or silver are distinguished, or as through a file one can distinguish which body resists cutting more weakly and which more strongly, likewise through dialectic right is discerned from wrong, and true from false. Just as a scale or a file is useless when there is nothing for it to examine, even though they themselves have force and vigor; just so dialectic, since it is similar to these things in all ways, confers no gain if one does not strive to cherish the other arts which should be prepared through dialectic and learned in addition to it.

We can show that each of the other arts is useful for itself and for the remaining arts. For instance, arithmetic, second of the arts in order, is valid and is necessary to the other arts. It is useful to geometry in numbering points, lines, angles, measures, etc. To music it is useful in numbering chords and their movements, voices, tones and consonances. To medicine indeed it is necessary in numbering elements, complexions, species and their grades, the weights of medicines, diseases, days, weeks, dates of termination for fevers, and many other necessary things. To astronomy it is necessary in numbering circles, zodiacal signs, degrees, minutes and seconds, planets and the rest of the stars and many other things which would take long to enumerate. Indeed arithmetic is also valuable in itself to one who is skilled in it (even if he does not understand the other arts), for through it he will greatly prosper in worldly business. Similarly, if one diligently inspects the other arts, he will see that each one except dialectic is both valid in itself and very useful to the remaining arts.

Medicine is very useful and very necessary to humans and to the other animals in this world. It is an art through which health is preserved and through which a long life can be known in this world. Medicine can only be fully known through astronomy since through astronomy the permutations of the four seasons of the year are predicted before they arrive. According to these changes in the season, the imminent diseases of men and animals are known; when these are predicted, treatment can be sought, through which diseases can either be avoided or at least more easily cured. Through astronomy, also, are obtained the proper times for cauterizing, making incisions, puncturing abscesses, bloodletting or applying suction cups where that is necessary, giving or taking potions, the days and also the hours in which fevers are to end; and many other things useful and pertinent to medicine can be known only through astronomy as Constantine [the African] testified in the book which he translated from Arabic into Latin. Through astronomy, also, fair or cloudy weather is predicted, which is very useful for sea crossings, and should be closely observed. Many other things will be found in the following letter, along with pleasures through which indeed the soul delights from knowledge of celestial things.

Since, as I say, astronomy is necessary to medicine and indeed to other things, it is obvious that astronomy itself is more useful, more pleasant, and more worthy than the remaining arts. Since I have discovered that all Latins are devoid of knowledge of this art of astronomy, though I have practiced it for a long time and I have learned a small part of it, I have decided, if it pleases you, to share it with you and to present it—with diligence and kindness—as something rare, sweet, and delicious.

It has come to our ears that some of those men who investigate wisdom according to what can be comprehended through similitudes prepare to traverse distant provinces and exile themselves in remote regions in order to acquire a fuller knowledge of astronomy. To them I reply without hesitation that since the truth is what they desire to see, they will soon have what they wish, and that which they prepare to seek in remote places is close at hand, unless they have some doubt that we are somewhat gifted in this art. I am not aware that it is another custom of learned men to pass judgment concerning that of which you are ignorant and to accuse that which you have not tested. This art may only be understood firstly through practice, and similarly no one can master the art without practice. Others, indeed, after they have read Macrobius and others who seem to have labored in this art, suppose that they might be satisfied with themselves and that they have obtained a full knowledge of this art. Furthermore, when their reasoning is examined by those who claim to know themselves, they fail in arguing and they fling back to their authorities all their force of proof. . . .

82. THE TOPOGRAPHY OF TRANSLATIONS

One of the most remarkable developments of the twelfth century is the upsurge in Latin translations that resulted from enhanced encounters with Greek and Arabic learning. A notable center for this translation activity was the Spanish city of Toledo, especially after Christian forces under King Alfonso VI of Castile (r. 1072–1109) conquered it in 1085, but translations took place wherever a sufficient number of multilingual scholars could devote themselves to the business of translating the meaning of the texts from one language to another. The short selections below offer glimpses into the activities of translators in places such as Toledo, where a sizeable community of Jewish scholars often served as cultural and linguistic intermediaries, as well as in more eastern locations such as Constantinople and Antioch. In many cases we know the names of the translators themselves, as well as the works that they set down to translate. These selections offer a sampling of the persons, places, and topics of study involved in translations, often across confessional boundaries. As the translators frequently make quite clear in their prologues, the interpretative act of "carrying over" (trans + latio = translatio) the meaning of a text from one language to another is itself embedded in the broader context of intellectual and intercultural exchange.

The figures represented in these selections include Hugo of Santalla, a Spanish ecclesiatic working in Tarazona who produced Latin translations of alchemy, astronomy, astrology, and geomancy; Burgundio of Pisa, an Italian jurist knowledgeable in Greek who translated, among other works, the commentaries of the famous early Church Father John Chrysostom (c. 349–407); The Jewish scholar Avendeuth (or Abraham ibn Daud), who came to Toledo as a refugee from the Almohad persecutions in Cordoba; Daniel Morley, an English scientist and philosopher who studied in Paris and Toledo before returning to England; Gerard of Cremona, the most accomplished translator of scientific texts active in late-twelfth-century Toledo; Paschalis Romanus, about whom almost nothing is known except that he translated a book of magic entitled Kyranides *in*

Constantinople around 1169 and also wrote a Dialogue against the Jews; *and Stephen of Antioch (or Pisa), who seems to have studied medicine in Salerno and translated Islamic scientific texts in both Antioch and southern Italy.*

a. Hugo of Santalla, *Art of Geomancy*

Source: trans. Charles Burnett, from Charles Homer Haskins, *Studies in the History of Medieval Science*, 2nd ed. (Cambridge, MA: Harvard University Press, 1927), 78. Latin.

Here begins the prologue to the *Art of Geomancy* according to the interpreter, Master Hugo of Santalla, who translated it from Arabic into Latin. God the creator of things, who founded everything as a new creation without an exemplar, deciding in his mind about the future state of these things before they come into being, distributes as he wishes to each man what he thinks right to bestow upon the rational creature from the treasury of his whole being. Hence all created beings, whether rational, irrational or inanimate, show the same obedience to him and, although in a life that has descended to the level of the secular world, nevertheless venerate him from unity alone. Having all things in the form of images before they come to be, he pours a kind of intuited and intellectual notion of them into the secret place of hearts. This arrangement of created beings is established so that he may deliberately unite the leaders and venerable teachers of writing and computation as if by a certain bond, so that when all disputes arising from difference have been abolished, he may make them allies by an equable, reasonable bond, or "positive justice."

b. Preface to Burgundio's Translation of Chrysostom's *Commentary on St John's Gospel*

Source: trans. Charles Burnett, from Peter Classen, *Burgundio von Pisa*, Sitzungsberichte der Heidelberger Akademie der Wissenschaften, phil.-hist. Klasse, Jahrgang 1974, 4 Abhandlung (Heidelberg: Carl Winter Universitaetsverlag, 1974), 8, 87–95 (for the inscription in c, below). Latin.

Fearing lest, if I Burgundio were to take the sense of the commentary of this holy Father and pronounce it in my own manner, I would change in any way the deep meaning in the opinions of these two most wise men [that is, John the Evangelist and John Chrysostom], and I would incur the danger of falling into some deviation in such an important matter (since we are dealing with the words of the Christian Faith), I took up the more difficult path and decided to keep in my translation both (a) words with the same meaning, and (b) the same style and order that is among the Greeks. But the ancient interpreters among both the Greeks and the Latins are said to have done the same thing all the time. For the 72

Jewish interpreters, chosen by the chief priest as the six men from each tribe who knew the Hebrew and Greek languages best, and sent from Jerusalem to Alexandria, translated the whole Old Testament *de verbo ad verbum* [word for word] from Hebrew into Greek for Ptolemy, king of Egypt. But Aquila, Theodosion, Symmachus and many other Christian Greeks, because they suspected that the 72 interpreters, in that they were writing for this king as an idol-worshipper, substituted some things for others, afterwards learnt the Hebrew language in order to correct their translation. But after a long and most careful investigation of the translation, they found that the 72 interpreters had hardly erred in anything.

. . . If [equivalent] words can be found, and the idiom of each language does not prevent it, and if one does not wish to establish one's own glory and to pretend that what belongs to others is one's own, the translation *de verbo ad verbum* should not be rejected by a diligent and completely faithful translator. If you wish foreign material to be thought your own and under your control, "you will not care to render word for word like a *fidus interpres*," as Horace says [*Ars Poetica* 132–33]; rather, taking the sense of that matter, you will explain it by the combination of your own words, and so you will not be an interpreter but you will seem to have composed your own words from yourself, which is what both Cicero and Terence attest that they do. . . . But even Saint Jerome, who attacks the *de verbo ad verbum* translation excessively, says that he, "in the interpretation of the Greeks, will not explain them word for word, but *sensum de sensu* [sense from sense], except in the case of holy scriptures where even the order of words is a mystery" [*Letter* 57]. . . . Since, then, this translation of mine is holy script and in my work I seek not glory but the pardon of the Lord for my sins and those of my son, I have decided with good reason that, preserving among the Latins too the glory of his own work for our Father, John Chrysostom, the *verbum ex verbo* method of translation should be followed.

c. The Inscription on Burgundio's Grave

Source: see b above.

> Who, what kind of man, and how great a man lies enclosed in
>   this marble,
> The following words reveal as a great man.
> Burgundio died as an old man in his own city,
> To whom scarcely anyone was, is, or will be similar.
> Everything which is born on earth, or located under the Sun,
> He knew fully, whatever was knowable.
> As a consummate translator he brought many things
> from Greek sources into Roman eloquence.

d. Avendeuth to the Bishop of Toledo

Source: trans. Charles Burnett, from *Avicenna Latinus, Liber de anima seu sextus de naturalibus, I-II-III*, ed. S. Van Riet (Louvain and Leiden: E. Peeters and E.J. Brill, 1972), 4. Latin.

To John, the most reverend archbishop of Toledo and primate of Spain, Avendauth, the Israelite philosopher, gives homage, recognizing the debt that is due to him. . . . Therefore, Sir, I have attempted to put into effect your order to translate the book of Avicenna the philosopher concerning the soul, so that by your support and our labor the Latins may be certain about what hitherto has been unknown, namely, whether the soul exists, what and how it is, according to essence and effect, proved by the truest arguments. Thus, you have the book, translated from Arabic, with me taking the lead and rendering each word in the vernacular language, and Archdeacon Dominicus turning the words into Latin.

e. Daniel of Morley, *Philosophia*

Source: trans. Charles Burnett, from *Philosophia*, ed. Gregor Maurach, *Mittellateinisches Jahrbuch* 14 (1979): 204–55, paragraphs 192–95. Latin.

When Gerard of Toledo was affirming to his audience that these and similar things necessarily happen in this way in the *Introduction* of Japhar [Abu Ma'shar]—[Gerard] who Latinized the *Almagest*, when Ghalib the Mozarab was interpreting—I was amazed, along with the others who were present, and I took objection and, as if angry with him, I countered with the homily of the Blessed Gregory [Gregory the Great, *Hom. in Evang.* 1.10.5], in which he attacks astrologers. . . . I admired the subtlety of his intelligence, but nevertheless pretending not to, I said: "You will not escape in this way, because we often see the son of a king and the son of a peasant having the same configuration of stars; nevertheless one remains in his peasant condition, the other is raised to kingship." He heard me out patiently and at last replied: "Have you ever read Julius Firmicus?" When I said that I had, he said, "From what he writes when he deals with nativities, we know that two things have to be asked concerning a nativity: the stellar configuration and the nature. If the nature does not agree with the stellar configuration, or *vice versa*, the stellar configuration will not always achieve its effect. So if, as you say, the son of a king and the son of a peasant are born under the same constellation, both will be kings, but not in the same way. For, the son of the king by nature has to succeed his father in the kingship. But, although the nature of the son of the peasant might detract from the stellar configuration, nevertheless he will reign among peasants and be more powerful than all those who belong to his kind. Why are you surprised? I too, who am speaking, am a king, in that

I was born under a royal sign, with the Sun ruling and the other circumstances conspiring." When I asked him ironically where he ruled, he replied: "In the mind/soul, because I serve no mortal man."

f. Gerard of Cremona, *Vita*

Source: trans. Charles Burnett, from the *Vita* of Gerard of Cremona, in Burnett, "The Coherence of the Arabic-Latin Translation Program in Toledo in the Twelfth Century," *Science in Context* 14 (2001): 254–56. Latin.

Just as a candle should not be put in a hidden place or under a bushel [cf. Luke 8:16], but must be raised up on a candlestick, so the glowing deeds of good men should not be left unspoken of, as if buried under silence and neglect, but should be presented to the ears of the people of today [*moderni*], since they open the door of virtue to those coming afterwards, and the examples of the ancients, worthily commemorated, as it were instill an ideal image of life into the eyes of those now living. Lest, then, Master Gerard of Cremona lie hidden under the darkness of silence, lest he lose the favor of the renown that he has merited, lest through presumptuous theft an alien heading be affixed to the books translated by him—especially since he himself inscribed none of them with his name—all the works translated by him, as much those on dialectic as those on geometry, as much those on astronomy as those on philosophy, as much also those on medicine as those on other sciences, have been listed very carefully by his students at the end of this *Tegni*, translated by him last (or most recently)—imitating Galen in commemorating his own books at the end of the same work—so that if anyone who is an admirer of their aims is looking for one of his works, through this list he might find it more quickly and become more confident about it. For, although Gerard spurned the glory of fame, although he fled fawning praises and the empty pomp of this world, although he refused to allow his name to be spread around by clutching at clouds and vanities, nevertheless the aroma of the fruit of his works, diffused through the centuries, announces and declares his goodness.

Although he flourished also with temporal goods, his mind was not elated or depressed by the abundance or absence of those goods, but in a manly way faced good and bad turns of fortune alike, and always remained in the same state of constancy. An enemy to the desires of the flesh, he adhered to spiritual values only; he labored to benefit all present and future generations, not unmindful of those words of Ptolemy: "Do even better when you approach the end of life."

Although from his very cradle he had been educated in the lap of philosophy and had arrived at the knowledge of each part of it according to the study of the Latins, nevertheless, because of his love for the *Almagest*, which he did not find at all among the Latins, he made his way to Toledo, where, seeing an abundance of books in Arabic on every subject [*facultas*] and, pitying the poverty he had experienced among the Latins concerning these subjects, out of his desire to translate, he thoroughly learnt the Arabic language, and in this way, trustworthy in each—that is, the subject-matter [*scientia*] and the language (as Ahmad [ibn Yusuf al-Daya] in his letter *On Ratio and Proportion* says, "It is necessary that the translator, in addition to the excellence which he has acquired from the knowledge of the languages from which and into which he translates, should also have knowledge of the subject [*ars*] which he translates"), in the manner of a prudent man who, walking through green meadows, weaves a crown from flowers—not from all of them, but from the more beautiful—he read through the writings of the Arabs, from which he did not cease until the end of his life to transmit to Latinity, as if to a beloved heir, in as plain and intelligible way as was possible for him, books of many subjects—whatever he esteemed as the most choice. He went the way of all flesh in the seventy-third year of his life, in the year of our lord Jesus Christ 1187.

g. Paschalis Romanus, *Kyranides*

Source: trans. Charles Burnett, from Charles Homer Haskins, *Studies in the History of Medieval Science*, 2nd ed. (Cambridge, MA: Harvard University Press, 1927), 219. Latin.

You have asked me to translate this medical book from Greek eloquence into Latin speech: an easy thing to ask, but difficult to fulfill. But I have not refused to obey, moved by your charitable love and your kindness. Since there are various translations from the Saracen language into Greek, as you know, I have copied the Greek book which you have given me carefully and faithfully; I have refused to pass over those two prologues, however rough they are in being deprived of their ancient titles, but I have not reproduced the words, which are of barbaric sterility, but rather the sense, which is productive. If you find anything out of place, it should be attributed not to unfaithfulness or malevolence, but simply to error. For no one is so wise that he cannot be labeled with ignorance. I wish, however, you to know that among the Greeks there is a certain book of Alexander the Great about the seven herbs of the seven planets, and another one which is called "the mystery of Thessalus" addressed to Hermes, that is, Mercury, about the 12 herbs attributed to the 12 signs of the zodiac and another seven herbs [distributed among] the other seven stars, which, if they happen to come into my hands or yours, because they imitate the worthiness of the heavens, rightly should be prefixed to this work. This book is translated at Constantinople, during the reign of Manuel, in the year of the world 6,677, the year of Christ 1169.

h. Stephen of Antioch, Preface to the *Theorica* of the *Liber regalis dispositionis*

Source: trans. Charles Burnett, "Antioch as a Link between Arabic and Latin Culture in the Twelfth and Thirteenth Centuries," in *Occident et Proche-Orient: contacts scientifiques au temps des croisades*, ed. Isabelle Draelants, Anne Tihon, and Baudouin van den Abeele (Turnhout: Brepols, 2000), 26–30, 35–36. Latin.

Therefore, following the command of Solomon, I strove for the sake of wisdom to search through not only the Latin, but also the Arabic language, so that the more I should have the knowledge of different languages, the more expressly I should understand the substance, the dimensions and the quality of what I had once learnt as a mere beginner in the cradle of philosophy. . . . We have, then, proposed to devote the effort of our labor first to these books, although the Arabic language has, hidden within it, other things more noble than these: namely, all the secrets of philosophy, to the translating of which, afterwards, if divine kindness permits, we shall devote our skill once it has become practiced. . . . If we should seem to them to have made a mistake in these things, they should consult the Arabic Truth and, if they can, prove us wrong. . . . For we do not take pains for the invidious or the lazy, but for those who desire to learn, and who do not blush to support their reasonings on the labor of others. . . .

. . . But since we are translating this work from the Arabic language, and almost all the names of the medicaments placed here are put forward in the language of the Arabs, and we hardly have common Latin words for them, we put them forward as they are in Arabic, sometimes even those which are known to us, in all cases where they are unknown, but we have declined them according to the form of Latin declensions. . . . I preferred, then, to seem a little infirm than not to transmit knowledge, since it is less of a task for someone to ask about a few things than about everything, when Latinity has the first part incomplete, and the second part not at all, or at least some disordered piece of work which rather gets in the way of knowledge.

83. A TOLEDAN TRANSLATOR OF ARABIC PHILOSOPHY

Dominicus Gundissalinus (d. c. 1190) was archdeacon of Segovia and later of Toledo. He was a key figure in the transmission of Arabic and Hebrew philosophical works into Latin intellectual culture and is believed to have been at the center of a circle of translators active in Toledo in the twelfth century. Gundissalinus translated many Arabic philosophical texts, including al-Farabi's (d. 850) De scientiis, al-Kindi's (d. 873) On the Intellect, and

THE TWELFTH–CENTURY RENAISSANCE: A READER

Avicenna's (d. 1037) On the Soul. *He also wrote a number of independent treatises in which he drew upon the works he translated, undertaking to harmonize them with the sources of the Latin intellectual tradition.*

Gundissalinus's On the Division of Philosophy *draws heavily from texts in the Arabic philosophical and scientific tradition, especially al-Farabi's* De scientiis, *but he also relies upon older and contemporary Latin writings, including works by Augustine, Boethius, Isidore of Seville, Bede, and even Thierry of Chartres's commentary on Cicero's* De inventione. *In typical scholastic fashion, he attempts to juxtapose and reconcile Arabic and Latin sources in his treatment of individual arts. This is notably the case in his discussion of grammar as a preparatory instrument of philosophy, but it can also be observed in his general treatment of scientific categories. He adopts the Arabic practice of dividing the parts of logic according to the books of Aristotle's* Organon, *which in the Islamic tradition had been extended to include the* Rhetoric *and the* Poetics *(works that would not be translated into Latin until the thirteenth century). On the Division of Philosophy is both an important resource for understanding the Latin reception of Arabic scientific thought and a witness to a rapidly expanding interest in the nature and purpose of the arts of philosophy.*

Source: trans. Rita Copeland and Ineke Sluiter, *Medieval Grammar and Rhetoric: Language Arts and Literary Theory, AD 300–1475* (Oxford: Oxford University Press, 2009), 463–65, 482. Latin.

The Division of Philosophy

Here begins the book about the division of philosophy into its parts and the subdivisions of those parts, according to the philosophers.

Prologue

Happy was the former age that brought forth so many wise men who, like the stars, illuminated the world's darkness. For with as many sciences as those wise men brought forth they bequeathed to us many torches to illuminate the ignorance of our minds. But because now people are dedicated to worldly concerns, some are busy with the study of eloquence, others burn with ambition for temporal honor. Thus, nearly all grow listless in the pursuit of wisdom, and like blind men they pay no attention to the light that is there. Thus, for their sake we thought it worthwhile to give a brief account of what wisdom is and what parts it has, and to offer them a taste of what use and pleasure it contains in each of its parts, so that at least they might taste a concise summary of wisdom (which is abhorred by those who are miserably drunk on worldly vanity); and so that, attracted by a taste of a part, they might strive to claim the whole for themselves, knowing from tasting part of it that its sweetness is great.

We say, then, that since there is no one who does not desire one particular thing rather than another, and man does not want anything by nature except what he knows contributes to the advantage of flesh or spirit, from which he is directly composed, therefore man's desire is more forceful either for things of the flesh or of the spirit. . . .

Things that are the spirit are either harmful or vain or useful. Vices such as pride, avarice, vainglory, and the like are harmful. Secular honors and magical arts are vain. Useful things are virtues and legitimate sciences, and from these two the whole perfection of man is comprised. Neither virtue alone, without knowledge, nor knowledge alone, without virtue, produces the perfected man. Some legitimate sciences are divine; others are human.

Divine science [*divina scientia*] is called because it is known to have been transmitted to men by God's authority, namely in the Old Testament and New Testament. Whence the words "God said" are found throughout the Old Testament, and in the New Testament, "Jesus said to his disciples."

Human science [*humana scientia*] is so called because it is proven that it was discovered through human reasoning, such as all the arts that are called liberal. Some of these clearly pertain to eloquence, others to wisdom. The arts that pertain to eloquence, that is, grammar, poetic, rhetoric, and human law, are all the ones that teach us to speak correctly or in embellished style. The arts that pertain to wisdom are all those that either illumine the soul of man to bring about knowledge of the truth or kindle it so that it loves the good. All of these are philosophical sciences. For this reason, since there is no science which is not some part of philosophy, at the outset these points must be considered: what is philosophy and why is it so called; then, what is the intention and its goal [*finis*]; then, what are its parts and the parts of those parts; and finally, what is to be observed about each one of these parts. . . .

It is clear that everything that exists either comes from our actions and our will or not from our actions, but from those of God or nature. But because there is no science which does not have a subject that it treats, and there is nothing which does not derive from one of these two categories, therefore philosophy is primarily divided into two kinds: the first, by which we know the disposition of our actions; the second, by which we know everything else that exists. The first of these is the part of philosophy which has us know what ought to be done, and this is called "practical"; the other part has us know what ought to be understood, and this is called "theoretical." The latter is in the intellect, the former in effect; one consists only in mental cognition, the other in the performance of actions. Because philosophy was invented so that the soul might be perfected through it, and there are two ways by which the soul is perfected, knowledge and action, therefore philosophy, which is the ordering of the soul, is necessarily divided into knowledge and action, just as the soul is divided into the senses and reason. Action belongs to the sensible part of the soul, and speculation belongs to the rational part of the soul. But because the rational part of the soul is divided into cognition and divine things (which do not derive from our action) and cognition of human things (which result from our action), therefore the goal of philosophy is the perfection of the soul, not only that one may know what one should understand, but so that one may know what one should do, and do it. Now, the goal of speculation is to grasp the meaning of what is to be understood; the goal of practice is to grasp the meaning of what is to be done.

Thus the parts into which philosophy is first divided are theoretical and practical. Now it remains to consider what and how many are the parts of each of these main divisions of philosophy. . . .

On Logic

. . . According to al-Farabi there are eight parts of logic: *Categories, Peri hermeneias* [*On Interpretation*], *Prior Analytics, Posterior Analytics, Topics, Sophistical Refutations, Rhetoric, Poetics.* The names of books are given for the names of sciences which are contained in them. Each of these parts has a property which is its purpose and means of proof, and a manner in which it works, and a use which comes from it. . . .

From the aforesaid eight parts there are five by which knowledge is verified: demonstration, topics, sophistic, rhetoric, poetics.

The property of demonstration is to give the most determined knowledge—of which the contrary is impossible, and in which there exists no fallacy—about a question proposed either by oneself or by another.

The property of *Topics* is to produce belief about a doubtful issue using probable arguments that are either true or plausible.

The property of sophistic is to feign and dissimulate and to make what is not true appear to be true, and the reverse. Sophistic is the name of a certain power through which a man knows how to deceive someone else and lead him into error even though he may be of good character. The name "sophist" is from Greek *sophos*, which is wisdom, and "estos," which is deception. Thus sophistic is called deceptive wisdom, and the sophist is action that proceeds from his particular power is the work of a sophist.

The property of rhetoric is to move the mind of the hearer through persuasive speech, and to incline the hearer to the purpose that the speaker wants, so that what he says is believed, and he produces in the hearer reasoning that is proximate to certitude.

84. BERNARD SILVESTRIS, THE *COSMOGRAPHIA*

There is much that is uncertain about the life of Bernard Silvestris, but he is indisputably one of the finest Platonist poets of the twelfth century. He has often been associated with the circle of teacher-scholars in and around Chartres who turned their gaze to the study of Platonist philosophy. The dedication of his poetic masterpiece, after all, is to Thierry of Chartres (see Doc. 14), and the work was most likely completed sometime in the middle decade of the twelfth century, since he seems to have presented it to Pope Eugenius III (r. 1145–53) in 1147. Philosophically, the Cosmographia *endeavors to expand the limits of rational speculation and to affirm both the dignity of man and the dignity of the natural order. Its cosmology and the pattern of analogy between the larger universe (*megacosmos*) and the smaller human universe (*microcosmos*) are modeled on Plato's* Timaeus, *the only work of Plato to survive (albeit partially) in medieval Latin. The* Cosmographia *is unusual in that it is both poetry and philosophy. It is a brilliant distillation of the tradition of Neoplatonist encyclopedism on the one hand, and of epic poetry and the quest for self-knowledge reaching back to Virgil's* Aeneid *on the other. Finally, the work is deeply concerned with the discovery of Nature, a power identified precisely with the preservation of life and order, and the obedience of all creation to cosmic law. The* Cosmographia *thus crystallizes in poetic form some of the main themes of twelfth-century humanism.*

Source: trans. Winthrop Wetherbee, *The Cosmographia of Bernardus Silvestris* (New York: Columbia University Press, 1973), 65–66, 69–71, 123–24. Latin.

[Dedication to Thierry of Chartres]

To Thierry, doctor most renowned for true eminence in learning, Bernardus Silvestris offers his work.

For some time, I confess, I have been debating with my innermost self, whether to submit my little work for a friendly hearing or destroy it utterly without waiting for judgment. For since a treatise on the totality of the universe is difficult by its very nature, and this the composition of a dull wit as well, it fears to be heard and perused by a perceptive judge.

To be sure, your kindly willingness to inspect a piece of writing lacking in art, but dedicated to you, has aroused my boldness, quickened my spirits, and strengthened my confidence. Yet I have decided that a work so imperfect should not declare the name of its author until such a time as it shall have received from your judgment the verdict of publication or suppression. Your discernment, then, will decide whether it ought to appear openly and come into the hands of all. If meanwhile it is presented for your consideration, it is submitted for judgment and correction, not for approval.

May your life be long and flourishing.

[Summary]

In the first book of this work, which is called *Megacosmos*, or "the Greater Universe," Nature, as if in tears, makes complaint to Noys, or Divine Providence, about the confused state of the primal matter, or Hyle, and pleads that the universe be more beautifully wrought. Noys, moved by her prayers, assents willingly to her appeal, and straightaway separates the four elements from one another. She sets the nine hierarchies of angels in the heavens; fixes the stars in the firmament; arranges the signs of the Zodiac and sets the seven planetary orbs in motion beneath them; sets the four cardinal winds in mutual opposition. Then follow the creation of living creatures and an account of the position of earth at the center of things. Then famous mountains are described, followed by the characteristics of animal life. Next are the famous rivers, followed by the characteristics of trees. Then the varieties of scents and spices are described. Next the kinds of vegetables, the characteristics of grains, and then the powers of herbs. Then the kinds of swimming creatures, followed by the race of birds. Then the source of life in animate creatures is discussed. Thus in the first book is described the ordered disposition of the elements.

In the second book, which is called *Microcosmos*, or the "Lesser Universe," Noys speaks to Nature, glories in the refinement of the universe, and promises to create man as the completion of her work. Accordingly she orders nature to search carefully for Urania, who is queen of the stars, and Physis, who is deeply versed in the nature of earthly life. Nature obeys her instructress at once, and after searching for Urania through all the celestial spheres, finds her at last, gazing in wonder at the stars. Since the cause of Nature's journey is already known to her, Urania promises to join her, in her task and in her journey. Then the two set out, and after having passed through the circles of the planets and forewarned themselves of their several influences, they at last discover Physis, dwelling in the very bosom of the flourishing earth amid the odors of spices, attended by her two daughters, Theory and Practice. They explain why they have come. Suddenly Noys is present there, and having made her will known to them she assigns to the three powers three kinds of speculative knowledge, and urges them to the creation of man. Physis then forms man out of the remainder of the four elements and, beginning with the head and working limb by limb, completes her work with the feet. . . .

Chapter Two

Here Nature made an end. Then Noys, her countenance brightening, raised her eyes to the speaker, and, as if summoned forth to discourse from the inner chambers of her mind, replied, "Truly, O Nature, blessed fruitfulness of my womb, you have neither dishonored nor fallen away from your high origin; daughter of Providence as you are, you do not fail to provide for the universe and its creatures.

"And I am Noys, the consummate and profound reason of God, whom his prime substance brought forth of itself, a second self, not in time, but out of that eternal state in which it abides unmoved. I, Noys, am the knowledge and judgment of the divine will in the disposition of things. I conduct the operations over which I preside accordingly as I am bidden by the harmonious action of that will. For unless the will of God be sought, and until his judgment concerning created existence is pronounced, your haste to bring created life into substantial existence is vain. The nativity of creatures is celebrated first in the divine mind; the effect which ensues is secondary. Thus the plan of a cosmogony, which you had conceived by sacred and blessed instincts and in accordance with a higher plan, could not be brought to present realization until the term established by higher laws. Unbending and invincible necessity and indissoluble bonds had been imposed, so that the cultivation and adornment which you desire for the universe might take place no earlier. Now at last, because you appeal at the proper time, and appeal in behalf of causes which concur in the impulse to order, your desires are served.

"Now Hyle exists in an ambiguous state, suspended between good and evil, but because her evil tendency preponderates, she is more readily inclined to acquiesce in its impulses. I recognize that this wild and perverse quality cannot be perfectly refined away or transformed; being present in such abundance, and sustained by the native properties of the matter in which it has been established itself, it will not readily give way. However, so that the evil of Silva may not disrupt my work or the order I impose, I will refine away the greater part of her coarseness. Moreover, the teeming mass, now violently assailed by a restless movement born of confusion, will be reduced to carefully established confines by that peace which is my special concern. I will produce a form for Silva, through union with which she may come to flower, and no longer cause displeasure by her ill-ordered appearance. I have ordained that her substance be refashioned in a better condition. I will instill amity in the universe and regularity in the elements. I am indeed troubled that the initial state of creation should be so deprived. But the emergence of shape will remove this privation from material existence.

"Accordingly I will now begin the work which I have promised, for he who acts too slowly torments those who await the issue. And since you, Nature, are well endowed with intelligence, and seek to realize this object through your prayers, I will not scorn to accept you as ally and companion in this task."

Nature stood alert, her mind intent upon the voice; for this speech wrought out of things she had hoped for was delightful to her ears. And when she understood that what she had desired was granted, she bowed low before Providence, grateful in mind and countenance alike, and threw herself at her feet.

Hyle was Nature's most ancient manifestation, the inexhaustible womb of generation, the primary basis of formal existence, the matter of all bodies, the foundation of substance. Her capaciousness, confined by no boundaries or limitations, extended itself from the beginning to such vast recesses and such scope for growth as the totality of creatures would demand. And since diverse and intricate qualities pervaded her, the matter and foundation of their perpetuity, she could not but be thrown into confusion, for she was assailed in such manifold ways by all natural existence. The numerous and uninterrupted concourse of natures dispelled stability and peaceful repose, and departing multitudes only afforded space for more to enter. Hyle existed without rest and could not remember a time when she might have been less continually engaged in the formation of new creatures or the reassimilation of those deceased. Vacillating, and ever liable to change from one state of quality and form to another, no material nature might hope to be assigned an identity proper to itself, and so each went forth unnamed, putting on a borrowed appearance. And since it was liable to assume any shape, it was not specially stamped with the seal of a single form of its own.

Yet this freedom to move at random was restrained by a certain agreement, in that the restless material was sustained by the more stable substantiality of the elements, and clung, as it were, to these four roots. Because of this Silva might more safely suffer herself to be drawn out and enlarged by an infinite range of essences, qualities, and quantities. Yet to the very extent that her nature proved fertile and prolific in conceiving and giving birth to all creatures in common, it was equally impartial with respect to evil. For there was infused in her seed-bed from old the taint of a certain malign tendency which would not readily abandon the basis of its existence. The seeds of things, too, warring with one another in the chaotic mass—fiery particles with icy, the sluggish with the volatile—dissipated the material or substantial qualities of their common subject matter by the clash of their contradictory tendencies.

Accordingly divine Providence, to remedy this condition by the promised transformation, reviewed the resources of her mind, mustered her faculties, and summoned up her imaginative powers. Since the reconciliation of discords, the aggregation of incongruities, and the yoking of mutually repellent forces seemed to be the only principles of arrangement, she resolved to separate mixed natures, to give order to their confusion and to refine their unformed condition. She imposed law and restrained their freedom of motion. Rude though they were, she effected a balance of properties among her undisciplined and recalcitrant material, joined them with means, and so bound them together in arithmetical proportion. As the bonds of a reconciling concord, sprung from the inner deliberations of Providence, were thus interposed, the rough and, as it were, the uncivilized strain in matter changed its obstinacy to cooperation, and submitted its innate conflict to a general reconciliation. Once this rigidity of ancient, even primordial lineage had been overcome, an adaptability took its place capable of being drawn into such channels as Providence decreed. . . .

Chapter Fourteen

Man was formed with masterly and prudent skill, the masterwork of powerful Nature. Belief holds that wisdom chose the head as its seat, and divided into it three chambers. In these three is placed the threefold power of the soul; each part fulfills its function in an unalterable sequence. The recollective faculty is placed at the rear, the speculative power is foremost, and reason exercises its power at the center. All share in the work when the five attendant senses inform them of the external events which they perceive. A messenger of sense enters and arouses the tranquil mind to confirm the matter by sure judgment.

That nerve which illuminates the eyes with its light draws from the brain the power which it radiates. An inner light, a daylight of the soul, responds to the rays of the sun's fire and the brilliance of the ether. From this cooperation the power and the organ of sight derive the principle and the material means of their existence. A beam of this inner light applies itself to the forms of things, and makes a careful record of them. However, it does not perceive all things with the same clarity; its power is feeble at one moment, ample at another. It fixes most clearly upon things which are bright and most like itself, but applies only vaguely and dully to things unlike. As splendor is at home with splendor, so is light with light; in shadow and darkness sight falls idle. The smooth surface of a rounded and polished body: this was the form best suited to the eyes. The images of things adhere most clearly to a smooth surface, and it will possess a capacity for livelier motion. Because the eye is endowed with both motion and brightness both are reflected in the creation of its form. That it may not suffer injury its light lies well covered, contained by a sevenfold jacket. The forest of the brow protects it from any hazard which so delicate and unstable an organ might fear. It is not for nothing that there are two, since if one fails the other may perform the work of its partner. The lids are a bed of rest, at the time when peaceful sleep soothes the laboring orbs. Just as the sun, the world's eye, excels its companion stars and claims as its own below the firmament, even so the sight overshadows the other senses in glory; the whole man is expressed in this sole light. To one who asked why he is alive, Empedocles replied, "That I may behold the stars; take away the firmament, I will be nothing." The unseeing hand spoils its work, the foot strays drunkenly, when they perform their tasks in darkness, without light.

The hearing holds an inferior place, is inferior in power, more sluggish in perception, and of less usefulness. Sound merges from the windpipe and stirs the still air. Once aroused, the agitation spreads, until the last wave of motion slackens, having attained its limit and been drawn out to its full extent. Air provides the substance, and the instrument of speech and form; from these two sound derives the shape and essence of speech. For the tongue forges sounds to the form and image of speech and serves as the hammer in the process. Shaped by its efforts, the articulated substance of speech travels to the open ears. Having first been admitted to the ear as though to the outer vestibule, the voice calls out and is admitted to the inner rooms. The ear keeps outside the rhythm and the resonance of the words, but the thought signified gains admittance. The ear interprets what comes from without, the tongue reveals what is within; and each requires the aid of the other. The channel of the ear is tortuous, lest cold air should pass by too open a path to the brain. Nature feared for its frail condition, and so a winding path leads inward from the curving shore. All that Rome learned, all that you studied, O Athenians, whatever the east possessed of Chaldean wisdom, whatever Aristotle perceived in his inspired breast, or the Pythagorean band, or the Platonists, whatever Gaul debates in syllogism with subtle speech, or Italy pronounces in the art of medicine, all this is the result of hearing. The wise and learned letter would perish if man existed with deaf ears.

Though the tongue promotes and assists the needy arts, it is well known for doing harm in countless evil ways. Whenever it whispers indiscreetly in the jealous ear backbiting and poisonous words, it separates loving brothers, destroys friendships, breaks bonds of trust, divides marriages, makes the land teem with thieves, the form with quarrels, the city with war; it discovers secrets, and opposes all established institutions.

85. WILLIAM OF CONCHES, *A DIALOGUE ON NATURAL PHILOSOPHY*

William of Conches's Dragmaticon Philosophiae *(c. 1147–49) is an exhaustive work on natural philosophy dedicated to Geoffrey Plantagenet, the duke of Normandy (1113–51). William (c. 1090–1154) served as a tutor to Geoffrey's son, the future Henry II of England (r. 1154–89). Even prior to the completion of the* Dragmaticon, *William was a renowned scholar and philosopher. He was one of the most famed products of the school of Bernard of Chartres (see Doc. 13), where he received the finest education in grammar, rhetoric, and the liberal arts. William is credited with a number of glosses and commentaries on earlier works, as well as the* Philosophia *(written c. 1125–30), which sets out many elements of the later* Dragmaticon *and has been seen by some as a sort of first edition. Like many of the thinkers associated with Chartres, he treats cosmological*

questions at great length, seeking to explain the Genesis account of creation and to har-
monize it with the cosmological myth of Plato's Timaeus.

The title Dragmaticon *is a medieval transliteration of a Greek word meaning "dramatic." Appropriately, the work takes the form of a dialogue between the Philosopher (presumably William) and the Duke (presumably Geoffrey) and together they explore a wide variety of subjects ranging from theology to physics to biology. It displays significant influences from Greek and Arabic medical writings, recently translated for the first time into Latin (see Docs. 79 and 82), and there are repeated allusions to the teachings of Plato, mediated through Calcidius's fourth-century commentary on the* Timaeus. *The selections below touch on created substance, the moon, the earth, and the substance of the soul. William concludes with an elegant summary of the qualities necessary to be a good teacher and the order in which the seven liberal arts are to be approached.*

Source: trans. Italo Ronca and Matthew Curr, from William of Conches, *A Dialogue on Natural Philosophy* (*Dragmaticon Philosophiae*), Notre Dame Texts in Medieval Culture, 2 (Notre Dame, IN: University of Notre Dame Press, 1997), 8–10, 86, 120–21, 172–75. Latin.

Book 1.4: The Created Substance [The Five Classes of Rational Beings]

Philosopher: Created substance is divided in two, for it is either invisible or visible. But in order to dwell a little longer on the subject of visible substance, which needs much more discussion, concerning the invisible we will not adduce our own opinion, but Plato's.

Duke: If the opinion of a pagan is to be cited, I prefer you to quote Plato than any other, for he accords better with our faith.

Philosopher: Plato, the most learned of philosophers, divided the world into five regions: heaven, ether, air, the moist region, and earth. He calls heaven the region in which the fixed stars are found; ether, the region stretching from there as far as the lunar circle; air, the upper half of the atmosphere; the moist region, the lower part of the atmosphere. He wanted none of these regions to be without rational living beings. Therefore, he said there existed in heaven a visible, rational, immortal, and impassible living being, namely, the stars; that on earth there was a visible, rational, passible [i.e., capable of feeling], and mortal being, namely, man; in the three middle regions, he said, there were creatures that shared some of the qualities of the outermost regions but differed in others.

We shall give a definition common to these three groups of intermediate creatures; the intelligent reader may work out, from the definition, which characteristics they share with the outermost ones and which they lack. So, the middle creature, which is located in the three regions, is defined by Plato as rational, immortal, invisible, passible. The three groups differ, however, with regard to their passions. For owing to their natural goodness, the two higher ones love human beings, rejoice with them in prosperity and mourn at their adversity. In this way they are passible, for joy and sorrow are counted among the passions.

The creature of the ether, however, has greater knowledge and dignity, so that it sometimes rules over the creature of the air. But the creature of the air runs to and fro between God and man almost as a mediator and reveals the will of God to men through a voice, a dream, imagination, or visible signs. He reports the prayers of man to God, who is not ignorant of his needs yet wishes to be asked. For this reason he is called an angel, that is, a messenger.

The creature of the moist region is passible in a different way: he is full of wickedness, hatred, and envy; it tortures him to see men do well, but it delights him to see them in distress, because he fell through his pride from the very place to which man ascends through humility. This creature suggests base thoughts, makes man sharp-tongued and quarrelsome, causes backbiting and false testimony, incites men to dishonest actions: in short, he rushes about to prevent all good. Sometimes he takes on some bodily form and has intercourse with a woman; from that union a human being is often produced.

Duke: That seems to be abhorrent to our faith.

Philosopher: If you do not believe me, believe Augustine, who affirms that the Huns were born like this in the marshes of the Maeotis.

Duke: Let it be, then, as we are not allowed to contradict such an authority. But go on to the next point.

Book 4.14: The Moon

Duke: I would be pleased if you could tell me why the moon waxes and wanes.

Philosopher: Certain philosophers have said that the moon has her own light; when, however, it is in the same sign as the sun, it is obscured by the far greater brightness of the sun. But when it moves away from the sun, its brightness becomes partly visible, and the farther it moves away, the more its brilliance is seen; the nearer it is to the sun, the less. If this were true, the moon would never rise in the west but only in the east, which is farther from the sun. But the moon always rises on the side of the earth turned toward the sun.

Therefore, some philosophers reasoned more sensibly that the moon has a denser body than the other planets from its proximity to the earth and the [celestial] water. So it has no heat or brightness of its own. For if it had its own heat, since it is nearer to the earth and every month ascends to Cancer and descends to Capricorn, the moon would cause every month the alteration of summer heat and winter cold on earth, and with such continual change of seasons nothing could survive on our planet.

Therefore, the moon has always lacked its own heat and brightness, but it is illuminated—not always equally for us—by the sun placed over it. For when it is directly below the sun, the sun lights up the upper part of the moon and throws its shadow against the earth, which explains why we do not see it. But when it moves away from the sun, a little brightness appears gradually visible in the shape of a slender horn, and it is called crescent-shaped [*menoeides*], and the farther it moves sideways from the sun, the more its brightness descends, so that on the seventh day it appears to be *dichotomos*, that is, cut in half.

Book 6.2: The Form of the Earth

Philosopher: As we mentioned earlier, earth is the element placed in the middle of the world and for that reason at the lowest point. For in every spherical object, whatever is at the middle is the lowest. But since earth occupies the lowest place, it cannot descend anywhere. Therefore, it is not necessary for it to be supported by anything. But since we have said enough about this before, we should not say anymore now. What, however, Thales has to say about the earth being supported by water like a ship, or what some have said about it plummeting downward, although we do not sense it because it is falling into infinity: these ideas are not worth refuting, for they are blatantly false.

Duke: I do not care about disproving these, but I do have some doubts about the shape of the earth. Please, therefore, explain your standpoint.

Philosopher: Some people, like animals trusting their feelings ahead of their reason, have said that the earth is flat: for wherever they move, they do not sense its roundness. I will set myself to destroy their opinion with probable arguments. If the earth were flat, rainwater falling on its surface would not run off but collect in one place to form a lake.

Again, if it were flat, a city situated in the east would have morning and mid-day at the same time: for no sooner had the sun risen there than it would be high above the city; but a city located in the west would have midday and evening at the same time. And the closer the cities were to the east, the smaller would be the space between morning and midday, the greater between midday and evening; but the closer they were to the west, the other way round [that is, the greater would be the space, and so forth] . . . .

Since for all people the time interval from morning till midday and from midday till sunset is equally long, it is clear that the earth is not flat but round. For this reason people in the east experience sunrise, midday, and sunset earlier than those in the west.

Book 6.26: The Faculties of the Soul

Philosopher: It is one thing to know the literal meanings [*proprietates*] of the words, another their usages and figurative meanings [*translationes*]. You have heard about the proper meaning of the noun *reason*. Now hear about its usage. Sometimes every true and certain judgment about a particular thing is called reason, and in this sense it is said that in God there is reason. Sometimes [we call reason] whatever is reasonable, as when we say, "It stands to reason that we should love God." Sometimes [reason means] computation or account, as in the [Gospel] passage, "Account for your administration of my estate" [Luke 16:2]. Sometimes it means the order of doing things, by which we know what should be done or said in what place. It is in these and many other accepted meanings that one and the same word *reason* occurs.

Duke: Since reason and intelligence are faculties of the soul, why is it that infancy and childhood lack these faculties, although infants and children have a soul?

Philosopher: If the body, which is corruptible, did not oppress the human soul of man, then from the moment it comes into existence, the soul would have full and perfect knowledge of those things that can be known in this life by humans. This can be concluded by examining the soul of the first parent, which had full knowledge from the first moment of its existence.

But now that mankind has been corrupted, the soul is oppressed from the moment it is joined to the corrupt body: so while retaining the power and faculty to discern and understand, it neither discerns nor understands until, by the experience acquired from long exercise and awakened by someone's teaching, it begins to discern and understand—just as someone with keen eyesight who is dragged down into a dark prison cannot see unless he grows used to the darkness or a light is lit.

That the soul is weakened by the body like that is attested by Solomon who says, "The body, which falls into corruption, weighs down the soul, and its earthly seat oppresses the mind so full of thoughts," and Virgil, "As far as burdensome bodies do not restrain [the souls]." The first age [of infancy] neither has any previous practical experience nor can be suitable for learning. For since infancy is warm and moist, the child digests food at once and seeks more, so that it stands in need of frequent intake and excretion, and a thick and continuous vapor is produced that, making for the brain, in which the soul exercises its faculty of discerning and understanding, upsets the soul.

Philosopher: But when one has reached the stage of youth, which is warm and dry—for the moisture one collected from the womb of one's mother has dried up—so thick a vapor does not arise, nor is there such an inner turmoil, and one is then ready for discernment. This is attained perfectly if the lamp of adequate teaching is lit. Youth is followed by old age, which is cold and dry, for the natural heat is dead. It is for this reason that memory flourishes in this age, but the strength of the body fails. For memory comes from coldness and dryness, whose properties are to hold together; the strength of the body from heat, whose property is to provide impetus. The final stage is decrepitude, cold and damp. As a result, at that age memory becomes sodden [*madida*] and people delirious. Once the natural heat has failed altogether, one ceases to live.

Book 6.27: Teaching and Learning

Philosopher: And because we have said enough about man, whose prerogative is to teach and be taught, let us say what qualities teachers and pupils should possess, what complexion is suitable for learning, at what age teaching should begin and when it should be concluded, and what should be the order of learning. The man eligible for the office of teaching should be such as will teach neither in order to be praised nor in the hope of temporal emolument but for the sole love of wisdom. For if he desires his own praise he would never wish his pupil to reach his own degree of perfection. Indeed, he will withhold some teaching lest he be equaled or surpassed in his favorite field.

However, if he is hired to teach in the hope of material remuneration, he will not care what he says, provided that he can squeeze out money. For often trifles please more than useful knowledge. But if he has embraced the teaching profession through love of knowledge, he will not secretly withhold teaching out of jealousy or flee from acknowledged truth just to squeeze out some money, or become unfaithful [to his calling] even if a great number of his fellow teachers should do so. But he will be vigilant and diligent for his own instruction and that of the others.

The type of person eligible for being taught should be someone who neither resists learning nor is proud nor considers himself to be something when he is nothing, someone who loves his teacher as his own father or even more than his father. For we ought to love him more, from who we received greater and more worthy gifts. From our father we have received our being unformed, from our teacher our being erudite: a greater and more worthy gift. Good teachers are, therefore, more to be loved than parents. It is not only right that teachers should be loved, but [also] useful, that their thoughts and words may find our favor. For if we do not love a person, we often dislike even what is good about that person and tend to shun it, while we endeavor not to imitate those we do not love.

Although the sanguine complexion is suitable for learning since it is temperate in everything, one can attain perfection in any complexion through hard work, because *obstinate labor conquers all* [Virgil, *Georgics*]. Adolescence is the right age to start with learning because, as Plato says, that age in a person's life is similar to wax, which, if it becomes too soft, neither receives nor retains shapes; similarly, if it is too hard. Therefore, the right age to learn is neither too hard nor too soft. The end of learning is nothing but death. So, when a certain learned man was asked at what point in life learning should end, he replied, "When life itself ends." Another one, a philosopher, while he was dying in his nineties, asked by a pupil whether he regretted death, answered, "Yes, I regret it." As the other asked, "Why?" he replied, "Because now I was just beginning to learn."

The order of learning is such that, because all learning takes place through eloquence, we are first to be instructed in eloquence. Eloquence consists of three parts: to write correctly and to pronounce correctly what is written, which is imparted by grammar; to prove that which needs to be proven, which is imparted by dialectics; to embellish words and thoughts, which is acquired through rhetoric. We should, therefore, start the curriculum with grammar, then go on with dialectics and afterward with rhetoric. Once instructed in these and equipped, as it were, with the [necessary] tools, we ought to proceed to the study of philosophy.

This should proceed in the following order: first [we should be taught] the *quadrivium*, that is, arithmetic first, music second, geometry third, and astronomy fourth, then the divine writings: because it is through the knowledge of the creatures that we arrive at the knowledge of the Creator.

86. HENRY OF HUNTINGDON'S VERSE HERBAL

Archdeacon Henry of Huntingdon (c. 1088–c. 1154) is best known as the author of the History of England, *one of the most important historical works produced in the first half of the twelfth century. His* Anglicanus Ortus *is a recent discovery and opens a new window onto the uses of poetry and the knowledge of medicine in twelfth-century England. Written in Latin verse, the herbal is a monumental work, treating 160 different medicinal herbs and spices in the context of 169 separate poems arranged into six books. An additional two books (which survive only incompletely) treat gems and stones. The compendium is a rich storehouse of information and is illustrated with classical allusions, Christian symbolism, and occasional historical or autobiographical digressions. Henry drew on centuries of learned medicine to compose this work, employing the medical knowledge of the ancient authors Pliny the Elder and Dioscorides and of medieval scholars like Walahfrid Strabo and Constantine the African (see Doc. 79). It is, therefore, a key work in the spread north of the Alps of Salernitan medicine based on Greek and Arabic sources. His rambling but highly learned discussion of generation, reproduction, and the elements in the passage devoted to dill, for instance, is indebted variously to Claudian, Boethius's* Consolation of Philosophy, *and perhaps William of Conches (see Doc. 85). Both Henry and William of Conches were in substantial agreement that the study of the natural causes of things is a noble and worthy pursuit, and not (as some maintained) an irreligious endeavor.*

The literary form of the work is particularly intriguing. It is staged first as a discussion between a master and a student walking around a garden, inspecting the plants in their separate beds, and then as a performance by the same master before Apollo and a critical audience, seated in a theater at the garden's center. As the prose prologue makes clear, the entire work is framed as a prayer to God's generative capacity and the rational order of nature.

Source: trans. Winston Black, *Henry of Huntingdon: Anglicanus Ortus: A Verse Herbal of the Twelfth Century* (Toronto: Pontifical Institute of Mediaeval Studies, 2012), 75, 103, 105, 179, 181, 261, 263. Latin.

Prose Prologue

> May Generation, the beginning of things and their end,
> Inspire this work, and bring it to a close, I pray.

I have set forth a single work suitable for both the religious and the secular, although they are very different, and . . . in which they differ, nor is it without use. It is fitting to place it before the religious, for there are three effective things: prayer, service, giving. The wicked use these things, but in a different way: the religious in order to gather up treasure, the wicked in order to deceive. In order to clarify this, let [each one] plead in the evening for his acts during the day in this manner: the argument of the just man with himself: "Seven times today I have praised the Lord. After this I did a great work in the Lord. After this, out of those things given by God I gave a part to his people. Now, as his useful servant, I seek the silence of the night, yet with praises to him." Likewise, the argument of the other: "In the early morning I prayed that I might prosper, and it was done. I have heaped up gold and silver for myself, and what is more precious, a property glittering with groves and streams, which I have given in perpetual inheritance to my heirs for the praise and honor of my name. Therefore, let us recall the joys of this day in the splendors of wine and feasting."

I shall speak first to the first one: "Today, brother, you have conducted business very shrewdly. Each word that you have spoken in praise of the Lord has been laid up in an eternal treasury. The least of these praises will never fail. The daily service which you have directed to good uses has also been placed in a heavenly storehouse. The least part will survive through the ages; that which you have paid out to the Lord from your just acquisitions is kept and heaped up with interest many times over. The least farthing bestows on you a talent of gold that will never fail. All these things you will find on the day of need, which cannot be perceived by this world."

I will also speak to the other: "While you gained gold, silver, and a property for yourself today, you have been occupied with nothing and to no purpose; I would rather you had slept. The act is done, the joy will pass, the memory will fade. Where is that which you have done? You are doing nothing; you will find nothing on the day of need, on the day of misery and disaster! O fool, you have treasured up for yourself as a young man those things which seemed fairest to you, but in the time of old age what will you find when you are about to receive your treasure?"

[*Wall Germander,* Teucrium chamaedrys L.]

Germander, you're called *germandreia* in Latin and *camedreos*
in Greek, an herb ever green, low-lying, bitter, aromatic,
both dry and hot: your degree is third in each.
France was wont to blend you with the twice-born god,
for while I was drinking the honeyed rivers
flowing from the fonts of Anselm, I was often apt
(and you, citizens of Laon, were often apt) to mix you so.
If you are drunk, when mixed with water, you expel a foetus,
and you heal bruises. If mixed with vinegar and drunk,
you thus assist the dropsical and purge the menstrual courses,
thus you dry the spleen and counteract savage bites,
and when ground and applied you're good for all these things.
They grind you with honey and apply you ground with honey
to purge an unclean wound, albeit very old.
They anoint the eyes with honey and your juice,
and render them clear after the cloudiness is removed.
They mix you ground with oil and anoint a body
so you thus force out the cold and recall the warmth.
The antidote *dyacamedreos* is prepared from it like this:
take two parts of Germander and ten parts Juniper,
but one each of Pepper, Ivy, and Myrrh. And finally
mix all these things together and add a dram of honey-water.
This is just as good for sciatica, a thing by no means surprising.

[*Dill,* Peucedanum graveolens *Benth*]

Cheerful Dill makes sport while sitting in his father's seat,
a progeny now born from father's seed and ready to produce
a fatherly seed to be made anew by progeny renewed
(and someone would in vain plant figs for dill root!).

446

Perhaps if, in the following year, a wind blows from the balmy south,
fennel will hang while dill is preparing to hang;
a similar nature created these similar in appearance,
and a dissimilar seed will reveal them to be dissimilar.
Examples will make you a believer, if you don't believe.
In such a way do streams turn into mists, and mists to clouds,
and in this manner clouds turn into snow and snow to hail.
From primal matter elements are made, but from the elements come
the "elemented." Granted, you may turn these things back again:
you'll see genus transform into species, species into lower classes,
and then pass right back again. A power known even
to the half-blind grows clear: man was a seed, a bird was an egg,
afterwards they will be dust. Thus, all things change their essence.
Scatter powdered deer's horn as if it were seed:
from this Celery grows; Basil, growing more thickly than proper,
breeds on the ground and shudders at the specks produced.
The farmers lament that wheat seed turned into Cockle
but they do not lament that Cockle has turned back again.
Enough of this. Dill is proven to be hot and dry;
its degree is said to be second in either of these.
It both benefits and harms the eyes, for the root,
first ground and applied, takes away their heat.
If drunk too often it harms the eyes and destroys the genital path,
drying the moisture of semen from within.
The flower cooked in oil makes Dill into a medicine
both for a head disease and for problems borne from cold;
it soothes pulled tendons, removes your chills,
and if swollen uvula is burdened by a bloody humor,
the powder of the burnt seed lifts the uvula,
as do ashes of the root, which is believed to be more powerful.
Taken as a decoction, it's been apt to give milk in abundance
and, if a sick man drinks three teaspoons of it warm,
it thus could conquer various diseases of the stomach.

[Epilogue 2 of Book 4]

Apollo brought these poems to me on the praise of herbs,
and the poet was not ashamed; nor does Normandy
hold you in wars, King Henry, nor indeed does envy,
which gnaws the best, leave your prowess unaccompanied,
but those who bite you blunt their teeth and molars,

and while they freely oppress, they're oppressed (you scarcely notice).
But lest you think that we have brought here falsehoods,
if you wish to learn their authors, I have written
what was sung by Phoebus, Phoebus's son, by Olympius the author,
by Themison, by Apollodorus, by the Sisters,
or what was sung by eminent Hippocrates, divinely sick,
by Prodymus, Chrysippus too, and by the mighty Pliny,
what Justus mentions, what Galen has foretold,
and what Xenocrates, whom philosophy adores,
what Cato, Pythagoras, and Palladius asserted,
what Stephen, what Mellitius of the honeyed mouth,
and Asclepius, father of medicine, a splendid author,
what Dioscorides, what Philo, what Menemachus,
what polished Macer, and Macer's follower Strabo,
what Oribasius orders, matching the known to the unknown,
or what others teach, whom fame, green with a flowering crown,
has girt with shining hand around their hollow temples.

SOURCES

Ailes, Marianne, trans. *The History of the Holy War: Ambroise's Estoire de la Guerre Sainte*. Woodbridge, UK: The Boydell Press, 2003. 29–31. Reprinted by permission of Boydell & Brewer Ltd.

Berger, David, trans. From *The Jewish-Christian Debate in the High Middle Ages: A Critical Edition of the Nizzahon Vetus*. Philadelphia: The Jewish Publication Society of America, 1979. Reprinted by permission of David Berger.

Black, Winston, trans. Henry of Huntingdon, *Anglicanus Ortus: A Verse Herbal of the Twelfth Century*. Toronto: Pontifical Institute of Mediaeval Studies, 2012. Reproduced by permission of the Pontifical Institute of Mediaeval Studies.

Copeland, Rita, and Ineke Sluiter, ed. and trans. From *Medieval Grammar and Rhetoric: Language Arts and Literary Theory, AD 300–1475*. Oxford: Oxford University Press, 2009. Copyright © 2009. Reprinted by permission of Oxford University Press.

Corner, George W., trans. From *Anatomical Texts of the Earlier Middle Ages*. Washington, DC: Carnegie Institute, 1929. Reprinted with permission.

Coulton, G.G., trans. From *Life in the Middle Ages*, Vol. 1. Cambridge: Cambridge University Press, 1928. Copyright © 1928, 1967 Cambridge University Press. Reprinted with the permission of Cambridge University Press.

Criste, Ambrose, O.P., and Carol Neel, trans. From *Anselm of Havelberg: Anticimenon, On the Unity of the Faith and the Controversies with the Greeks*. Collegeville, MN: Liturgical Press, 2010. Copyright © 2010 by Cistercian Publications, Inc., copyright © 2008 by Order of Saint Benedict, Collegeville, Minnesota. Reprinted with permission.

Doss-Quimby, Eglal, trans. "*Dame & Rolant de Riems: Jeu-parti.*" *Songs of the Women Trouvères*, ed. Joan Tasker Grimbert, Wendy Pfeffer, and Elizabeth Aubrey. New Haven, CT: Yale University Press, 2001. Copyright © 2001 by Yale University Press. Reproduced by permission.

Dove, Mary, trans. From *The* Glossa Ordinaria *on the Song of Songs*. Kalamazoo, MI: Medieval Institute Publications, 2004. Reprinted with permission.

Fassler, Margot E., trans. *Gothic Song: Victorine Sequences and Augustinian Reform in Twelfth-Century Paris*, 2nd ed. Notre Dame: University of Notre Dame Press, 2011.

Feiss, Hugh, trans. From *Interpretation of Scripture: Theory*, ed. Franklin T. Harkins and Frans van Liere. Hyde Park, NY: New City Press, 2013. Reproduced by permission of Brepols.

Fox, Matthew, and Ronald Miller, trans. From *Hildegard of Bingen's Book of Divine Works, with Letters and Songs*, by Matthew Fox. Copyright © 1987. Reprinted by permission of Inner Traditions International and Bear & Company. www.innertraditions.com.

McLaughlin, Mary Martin, and Bonnie Wheeler, ed. and trans. From *The Letters of Heloise and Abelard*. Hounds Mills, UK: Palgrave MacMillan, 2010. Reproduced with permission of Palgrave Macmillan.

Mierow, C.C., trans. From Otto of Freising, *The Deeds of Frederick Barbarossa*. New York: Columbia University Press, 1966. Copyright © 1966. Republished with permission of Columbia University Press; permission conveyed through Copyright Clearance Center, Inc.

Monroe, James T., trans. From *Hispano-Arabic Poetry*. Gorgias Press, 1974. Copyright © 1974. Reprinted by permission of Gorgias Press.

Novikoff, Alex J., trans. From Jean-Claude Schmitt, *The Conversion of Herman the Jew: Autobiography, History, and Fiction in the Twelfth Century*. Philadelphia: University of Pennsylvania Press, 2010. Reprinted with permission of the University of Pennsylvania Press.

Paden, William D., trans. From *An Introduction to Old Occitan*, pages 520–21, 523–25, 534–36. Reprinted by permission of copyright owner, the Modern Language Association of America.

Panofsky, Erwin, trans. From Abbot Suger, *On the Abbey Church of St. Denis and Its Art Treasures*, 2nd ed. Princeton, NJ: Princeton University Press, 1979. Copyright © 1979. Republished with permission of Princeton University Press; permission conveyed through Copyright Clearance Center, Inc.

Parry, John Jay. From Andreas Capellanus, *The Art of Courtly Love*. New York: Columbia University Press, 1941. Copyright © 1941. Reproduced by permission of Columbia University Press.

Radding, Charles M., and Francis Newton, trans. From *Theology, Rhetoric, and Politics in the Eucharistic Controversy, 1078–1079: Alberic of Monte Cassino Against Berengar of Tours*. New York: Columbia University Press, 2003. Copyright © 2003. Reproduced by permission of Columbia University Press.

Ronca, Italo, and Matthew Curr, trans. From William of Conches, *A Dialogue on Natural Philosophy (Dragmaticon Philosophiae): Translation of the New Latin Critical Text with a Short Introduction and Explanatory Notes*, Notre Dame Texts in Medieval Culture Vol. 2. Copyright © 1997.

Silano, Giulio. From Peter Lombard, *The Sentences: Book 4: On the Doctrine of Signs*. Toronto: Pontifical Institute of Mediaeval Studies, 2010. Reproduced by permission of the Pontifical Institute of Mediaeval Studies.

Somerville, Robert, and Bruce C. Brasington, ed. and trans. From *Prefaces to Canon Law Books in Latin Christianity: Selected Translations, 500–1245*. New Haven, CT: Yale University Press, 1998. Copyright © 1998 by Yale University Press. Reproduced by permission.

Talbot, C.H., trans. From Aelred of Rievaulx, *Dialogue on the Soul*. Kalamazoo, MI: Cistercian Publications, 1981. Copyright © 1981 by Cistercian

INDEX OF TOPICS

The references in this index are to the document numbers and their introductory paragraphs. Classical and medieval names are listed alphabetically by first name.